The

AMERICAN HERITAGE®

dictionary

of
Indo-
European
Roots

Revised and Edited by
CALVERT WATKINS

THIRD
EDITION

Houghton Mifflin Harcourt
BOSTON   NEW YORK

Visit our websites: www.ahdictionary.com or www.hmhco.com

Library of Congress Cataloging-in-Publication

The American heritage dictionary of Indo-European roots / revised and edited by Calvert Watkins. -- 3rd ed.
    p. cm.
  Includes index.
  ISBN 978-0-547-54944-6
1. Indo-European languages--Roots--Dictionaries. 2. English language--Etymology--Dictionaries. I. Watkins, Calvert.
  P615.A43 2011
  412.03--dc23   2011018794

PICTURE CREDITS: **Zoroastrian manuscript** British Library, 1323 CE Mihraban Kaikhusraw Vendidad in Avestan and Pahlavi, MS Avestan 4, folios 265v-266r, chapter 19, verses 6-89 **map of Indo-European peoples** Mapping Specialists, Ltd., Madison, Wisconsin **Germanic drinking vessel** Imagestate/Heritage Images/CM Dixon **cave fresco** Beta_m_common **Greek ostracon** Corbis/Gianni Dagli Orti **Cernunnos** Alamy/David Levenson **Chariot of the Sun** Getty Images/DEA/A. Dagli Orti **raised stone** SuperStock/Exactostock **Celtic ringfort** Alamy/David Lyons **racing chariot** Getty Images/Danita Delimont **war chariot** Art Resource, New York/Erich Lessing **funerary mask** SuperStock/Joe Vogan **stele** The Bridgeman Art Library **limestone relief** Dick Osseman at www.pbase.com

Manufactured in the United States of America

5 6 7 8 9 10 - EB - 18 17 16 15
4500554166

Contents

Preface

In my original article "The Indo-European Origin of English" in the First Edition of *The American Heritage Dictionary of the English Language* (1969), I wrote that "a reconstructed grammar and dictionary cannot claim any sort of completeness, to be sure, and the reconstruction may be changed because of new data or better analysis." Fifteen years later, when I revised the article for the First Edition of *The American Heritage Dictionary of Indo-European Roots* (1985), I wrote that the revised edition "stands as eloquent testimony to the accuracy of that statement. Indo-European studies have not stood still between the 1960s and the 1980s, and both advances in theory and an increase in the database have made a thoroughgoing revision not only possible but necessary."

Scholarship, fortunately, never stands still and never rests. The Third Edition of *The American Heritage Dictionary of the English Language* (1992) saw fresh revisions to the Appendix of Indo-European Roots, and the Fourth Edition (2000) reflected the stocktaking of the advances in scholarship during the 1990s. These developments, collectively, made obligatory and appropriate the fundamental revisions in content, format, and material of the Second Edition of *The American Heritage Dictionary of Indo-European Roots*. This Third Edition of *The American Heritage Dictionary of Indo-European Roots* (2011) has been prepared in order to incorporate the fruits of research in Indo-European studies that have appeared since the turn of the millennium. Over two hundred new words have been added to the English vocabulary treated in *The American Heritage Dictionary of Indo-European Roots*, as well as several newly discovered Indo-European roots. The goal of these revisions has been, quite simply, to enhance the material from the previous editions, and to convey more accurate, up-to-date, and interesting information about the history of words in our language.

This dictionary is designed and written for the general English-speaking public and not for specialists in the field of Indo-European linguistics. As in the Appendix of Indo-European Roots in the Fifth Edition of *The American Heritage Dictionary,* we have revised and brought into line with current thinking older etymologies, and we have not hesitated to propose new etymologies or adopt those proposed by others where it seemed proper to do so. We are grateful to those colleagues for their proposals, which they may recognize in these pages. The introductory essay and the attendant charts have also been revised and brought up to date, and new illustrations and visual aids provided.

Several staff members in the Trade and Reference Division of Houghton Mifflin Harcourt were instrumental in the technical aspects of the production of this dictionary and deserve special acknowledgement. Christopher Granniss supervised the conversion of the manuscript to type and compiled the index. Margaret Anne Miles oversaw the selection of the art, and Christopher Leonesio, Vice President and Managing Editor, provided the crucial support for the book's development and publication.

In the preparation of the revisions I have been fortunate to have the assistance and collaboration of two of my former students in linguistics at Harvard. Dr. Benjamin Fortson, formerly Senior Lexicographer in the Houghton Mifflin Trade and Reference Division and now Associate Professor in the Department of Classical Studies at the University of Michigan, Ann Arbor, helped bring the Second Edition of this work to press. He is responsible for many improvements and innovations in presentation, notably the Language and Culture notes scattered through the dictionary entries, and he has saved me from error on a number of occasions. The contribution of Dr. Patrick Taylor, Senior Lexicographer at Houghton Mifflin Harcourt, has over the past decade been of inestimable value in helping me prepare the present Third Edition and bring it to press. Together we have tried to put more order into the presentation of a vast amount of linguistic information. We have also tried to introduce only as much technical background explanation as is required without burdening the reader with unnecessary detail. The amount introduced may seem overmuch to some, but human language is not simple, and a part of the fascination of the study of human language lies in the recognition of its complexity.

Calvert Watkins

Indo-European and the Indo-Europeans

Indo-European is the name given for geographic reasons to the large and well-defined linguistic family that includes most of the languages of Europe, past and present, as well as those found in a vast area extending across Iran and Afghanistan to the northern half of the Indian subcontinent. In modern times the family has spread by colonization throughout the Western Hemisphere.

A curious byproduct of the age of colonialism and mercantilism was the introduction of Sanskrit in the 18th century to European intellectuals and scholars long familiar with Latin and Greek and with the European languages of culture—Romance, Germanic, and Slavic. The comparison of the classical language of India with the two classical languages of Europe revolutionized the perception of linguistic relationships.

Speaking to the Asiatick Society in Calcutta on February 2, 1786, the English Orientalist and jurist Sir William Jones (1746–1794) uttered his now famous pronouncement:

> The Sanskrit language, whatever be its antiquity, is of a wonderful structure; more perfect than the Greek, more copious than the Latin, and more exquisitely refined than either, yet bearing to both of them a stronger affinity, both in the roots of verbs and in the forms of grammar, than could possibly have been produced by accident; so strong, indeed, that no philologer could examine them all three, without believing them to have sprung from some common source, which, perhaps, no longer exists.

Jones was content with the assertion of a common original language, without exploring the details. Others took up the cause, but it remained for the German philologist Franz Bopp (1791–1867) to found the new science of comparative grammar, with the publication in 1816 of his work *On the Conjugational System of the Sanskrit Language, in Comparison with that of the Greek, Latin, Persian, and Germanic Languages*. He was 25 years old when it appeared.

It has been rightly said that the comparatist has one fact and one hypothesis. The one fact is that certain languages present similarities among themselves which are so numerous and so precise that they cannot be attributed to chance and which are such that they cannot be explained as borrowings or as universal features. The one hypothesis is that these languages must then be the result of descent from a common original. Certain similarities may be accidental: the Greek verb "to breathe," "blow," has a root *pneu-*, and in the language of the Klamath of Oregon the verb "to blow" is *pniw-*, but these languages are not remotely related. Other similarities may reflect universal or near-universal features of human language: in the languages of most countries where the bird is known, the *cuckoo* has a name derived from the noise it makes. A vast number of languages around the globe have "baby talk" words like *mama* and *papa*. Finally, languages commonly borrow words

Zoroastrian manuscript with text in Avestan and Middle Persian (AD 1323). After noting the similarities of Sanskrit and the ancient Iranian languages to Greek, Latin, and other languages of Europe, scholars in the 1700s began to formulate the idea of the Indo-European language family.

and other features from one another, in a whole gamut of ways ranging from casual or chance contact to learned coinages of the kind that English systematically makes from Latin and Greek.

But where all of these possibilities must be excluded, the comparatist assumes genetic filiation: descent from a common ancestor. In the case of Indo-European, as Sir William Jones surmised over two centuries ago, that ancestor no longer exists.

In the early part of the 19th century scholars set about systematically exploring the similarities observable among the principal languages spoken now or formerly in the regions from Iceland and Ireland in the west to India in the east and from Scandinavia in the north to Italy and Greece in the south. They were able to group these languages into a family that they called *Indo-European* (the term first occurs in English in 1813, though in a sense slightly different from today's). The similarities among the different Indo-European languages require us to assume that they are the continuation of a single prehistoric language, a language we call *Indo-European* or *Proto-Indo-European*. In the words of the greatest Indo-Europeanist of his age, the French scholar Antoine Meillet (1866–1936), "We will term *Indo-European language* every language which at any time whatever, in any place whatever, and however altered, is a form taken by this ancestor language, and which thus continues by an uninterrupted tradition the use of Indo-European."

The dialects or branches of Indo-European still represented today by one or more languages are Indo-Iranian, Greek, Armenian, Balto-Slavic, Albanian, Celtic, Italic, and Germanic. The present century has seen the addition of two branches to the family, both of which are extinct: Hittite and other Anatolian languages, the earliest attested in the Indo-European family, spoken in what is now Turkey in the second and first millennia BC; and the two Tocharian languages, the easternmost of Indo-European dialects, spoken in Chinese Turkestan (modern Xinjiang Uygur) in the first millennium AD. (An outline of all the branches is provided further below in the text.)

It should be pointed out that the Indo-European family is only one of many language families that have been identified around the world, comprising several thousand different languages. We have good reason, however, to be especially interested in the history of the Indo-European family. Our own language, English, is its most prevalent member, the native language of nearly 350 million people and the most important second language in the world. The total number of speakers of all Indo-European languages amounts to approximately half the population of the earth.

English is thus one of many direct descendants of Indo-European: one of the dialects of the parent language became prehistoric Common Germanic, which subdivided into dialects of which one was West Germanic; this in turn broke up into further dialects, one of which emerged into documentary attestation as Old English. From Old English we can follow the development of the language directly, in texts, down to the present day.

This history is our linguistic heritage; our ancestors, in a real cultural sense, are our linguistic ancestors. But it must be stressed that linguistic heritage, while it may tend to correspond with cultural continuity, does not imply genetic or biological descent. The transmission of language by conquest, assimilation, migration, or any other ethnic movement is a complex and enigmatic process that this discussion does not propose to examine—beyond the general proposition that in the case of Indo-European no genetic conclusions can or should be drawn.

Although English is a member of the Germanic branch of Indo-European and retains much of the basic structure of its origin, it has an exceptionally mixed lexicon. During the 1400 years of its documented history, it has borrowed extensively and systematically from its Germanic and Romance neighbors and from Latin and Greek, as well as more sporadically from other languages. At the same time, it has lost the great bulk of its original Old English vocabulary. However, the inherited vocabulary, though now numerically a small proportion of the total, remains the genuine core of the language; all of the 100 words shown to be the most frequent in the Corpus of Present-Day American English, also known as the Brown Corpus, are native words; and of the second 100, 83 are native. A children's tale like *The Little Red Hen,* for example, contains virtually no loanwords.

Yet precisely because of its propensity to borrow from ancient and modern Indo-European languages, especially those mentioned above but including nearly every other member of the family, English has in a way replaced much of the Indo-European lexicon it lost. Thus, while the distinction between native and borrowed vocabulary remains fundamentally important, more than 50 percent of the basic roots of Indo-European as represented in Julius Pokorny's *Indogermanisches Etymologisches Wörterbuch* [*Indo-European Etymological Dictionary*] (Bern, 1959) are represented in modern English by one means or the other. Indo-European therefore looms doubly large in the background of our language.

After the initial identification of a prehistoric language underlying the modern Indo-European family and the foundation of the science of comparative linguistics, the detailed reconstruction of Proto-Indo-European proceeded by stages still fascinating to observe. The main outlines of the reconstructed language were already seen by the end of the 1870s, but it was only during the course of the 20th century that certain of these features received general acceptance. The last decades of the 20th century and the first decade of the 21st have happily witnessed a resurgence of Indo-European studies, catalyzed by advances in linguistic theory and an increase in the available data that have resulted in a picture of the reconstructed protolanguage that is, in a word, tighter. The grammar of Indo-European today is more thoroughly organized and more sharply focused, at all levels. There are fewer loose ends, fewer hazy areas, and those that remain are more clearly identified as such. New etymologies continue to be made, new roots are recognized, and older etymologies undergo revision to incorporate new evidence or better analyses. Research continues to uncover previously unknown items of the most basic vocabulary of the Indo-Europeans. The German scholar Eva Tichy has recently proposed the new root **oit-**, "to take along, fetch," with reflexes in Greek *oisomai,* "I will carry, fetch" (OESOPHAGUS) and Latin *ūtī,* "to use" (USE); the American scholar Craig Melchert has added Cuneiform Luwian *ḫizza(i)-,* "to fetch," to the evidence supporting this new root. The attention to detail in reconstruction in this newly revised *Dictionary of Indo-European Roots* reflects these ongoing developments in the field: Indo-European studies are alive with excitement, growth, and change.

The comparative method—what we have called the comparatist's "one fact and one hypothesis"—remains today the most powerful device for elucidating linguistic history. When it is carried to a successful conclusion, the comparative method leads not merely to the assumption of the previous existence of an antecedent common language but to a reconstruction of all the salient features of that language. In the best circumstances, as with Indo-European, we can reconstruct the sounds, forms, words, even the structure of sentences—in short, both grammar and lexicon—of a language spoken before the human race had invented the art of writing. It is worth reflecting on this accomplishment. A reconstructed grammar and dictionary cannot claim any sort of completeness, to be sure, and the reconstruction may always be changed because of new data or better analysis. But it remains true, as one distinguished scholar has put it, that a reconstructed protolanguage is "a glorious artifact, one which is far more precious than anything an archaeologist can ever hope to unearth."

The Branches of Indo-European

According to the most widely accepted model, the Indo-European family contains ten principal branches. Some of the branches likely belong together in larger subgroupings, but the details are controversial and need not detain us. A general outline of the historical settings of the branches is given below in the order of their earliest attestation, with an emphasis on the geographical and temporal locations of the relevant peoples. This outline is meant to complement the chart of the family on pages 150–151, to which the reader is referred for a comprehensive listing of the individual languages.

Anatolian. Discovered only in the 20th century, the extinct Anatolian branch contains the oldest preserved Indo-European languages, spoken in what is now Turkey and Syria. Best known is Hittite, attested in over 10,000 clay tablet fragments in Babylonian cuneiform script found in Boğazköy (central Turkey) and dating from ca. 1700–ca. 1200 BC. Cuneiform Luvian and the closely related Hi-

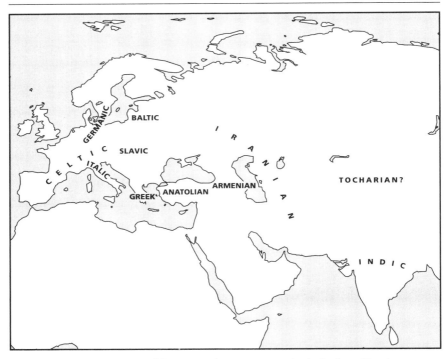

Geographical distribution of the major Indo-European peoples in the first millennium BC.

eroglyphic Luvian were spoken in southern and western Anatolia. A form of Luvian was probably the language of Troy and the Trojans. Hieroglyphic Luvian continued to be attested in monumental and other inscriptions in southeast Turkey and northern Syria until ca. 750 BC. Inscriptions in other Anatolian languages, in a variety of scripts, date to as late as the fourth century BC.

Indo-Iranian. The Indo-Iranian branch includes various ancient and modern languages of a large part of central and southern Asia. The original homeland of the Indo-Iranians is not certain, but by the early second millennium BC, Indic and Iranian peoples had migrated southward into Afghanistan and the eastern Iranian plateau. The Iranian tribes remained or moved westward and would later spread out over vast stretches of western and central Asia. An Indo-Aryan group apparently established itself as a ruling class among speakers of Hurrian (a non-Indo-European language of the ancient Near East), perhaps in Iran, who later migrated into eastern Anatolia where they established the kingdom of Mittanni (the details are conjectural). The Mittanni in Anatolia would eventually die out, but not before leaving us (via Hittite) the first remains in an Indic language—a number of words and names preserved in Anatolian inscriptions from ca. 1500 BC. The oldest preserved literature in both Indic and Iranian is in the form of orally-composed hymns: the Rig-Veda in the Indic language Sanskrit, probably dating from the latter half of the second millennium BC; and the songs traditionally attributed to Zarathustra (Zoroaster) in the Iranian language Avestan, more or less contemporary with the Rig-Veda. These texts were not written down until long after they were composed. The oldest written Indic texts are in Middle Indic (Pali) from about the fifth century BC, and the oldest Iranian texts are in Old Persian, found in monumental inscriptions from the Achaemenid dynasty (sixth to fourth centuries BC), notably those of Darius and his son Xerxes. Iranian is continued by the modern languages of Iran and Afghanistan and by languages spoken by minorities in Iraq and Turkey; Indic is continued by Hindi-Urdu and the other Indo-Aryan languages of southern Asia.

Greek (Hellenic). The sole member of the Hellenic branch is Greek, the European language with the longest recorded history (over 3000 years down to the present). It has at various times been spoken not only in Greece but also in colonies in Asia, Africa, and Italy. The oldest Greek inscriptions, in the Mycenaean dialect, are written in a non-alphabetic script called Linear B that was not deciphered until 1952; they date from about the 13th century BC. The oldest alphabetic Greek is the poetry of Homer, originally oral compositions that reached something like their present form by the eighth century BC.

Italic. The Italic branch is inscriptionally attested in central and southern Italy from the sixth or seventh century BC. At that time it consisted of many languages and dialects of limited geographic distribution (such as Oscan, Umbrian, and Faliscan), most of them known only from meager remains. One of these local languages, however, would eventually eclipse all the rest and spread throughout the Mediterranean basin: Latin, the language of Rome. The other Italic languages died out, at least in written form, by the dawn of the Christian era. The descendants of Latin are the modern Romance languages.

Celtic. The Celtic branch and most of its speakers are now restricted geographically to parts of the British Isles and northern France but the Celts once were the most powerful and widespread people of western Europe. By the latter half of the first millennium BC, Celtic territory stretched from the Iberian peninsula north through France and east through southern Germany, Switzerland, northern Italy, Austria, the former Czechoslovakia, and the Danube plain, with some groups as far east as Galatia in central Anatolia. The extinct Celtic languages of continental Europe, forming the Continental Celtic branch, are attested inscriptionally from the sixth or seventh century BC to the third century AD; best known of these is Gaulish. The Celtic languages of the British Isles (Insular Celtic) first appear inscriptionally around 400 AD with the earliest Irish stone carvings in the ogham alphabet. The surviving Insular Celtic languages of culture, Irish, Welsh, and Breton (brought to Brittany by migration from Britain), are now the only branch of Indo-European threatened with extinction.

Germanic. Germanic dialects were spoken prehistorically by tribes occupying an area of northern Europe east of the Rhine and stretching north through Denmark into parts of Norway and Sweden. Successive waves of migration in the first millennium AD resulted in a great expansion of Germanic-speaking territory. The earliest Germanic inscriptions, in a language called Runic, are from Scandinavia and are written in runes; they date from the early third century AD. The oldest extensive text in a Germanic language is a translation of the New Testament written in Gothic (now extinct) in the fourth century AD. Of the living Germanic languages, English has the longest recorded history, with inscriptions dating to the fifth century AD and literature to the eighth.

Armenian. The oldest Armenian text dates from the fifth century AD, a Bible translation in Classical Armenian; but Armenians are present in the historical record from much earlier, having probably already settled in eastern Turkey by the mid-second millennium BC. Today Armenian is spoken in diverse dialects in Armenia and surrounding areas of Turkey, the Caucasus, and the Near East, and, following the 20th-century diaspora, in Europe and the Americas.

Tocharian. Like Anatolian, Tocharian was

Replica of a Germanic horn-shaped drinking vessel or musical instrument. The lost original (made circa AD 400) was found near Gallehus, Denmark, and bore one of the oldest inscriptions in Old Norse, *ek Hlewagastiz Holtijaz horna tawidō*, "I Hlewagastiz [having famous guests] Holtijaz made this horn."

not discovered until the 20th century and is an extinct branch of the family. The two Tocharian languages, termed A and B, are preserved in Buddhist writings from ca. 600–800 and were unearthed in Chinese Turkestan (now Xinjiang in western China).

Cave fresco in northwestern China showing Buddhist monks (ninth century AD). The East Asian features of the monk on the right and the red hair, blue eyes, and large nose of the monk on the left, perhaps a Tocharian, show the ethnic variety of peoples living in medieval Central Asia.

Balto-Slavic. Slavic languages have been spoken since prehistoric times in areas of eastern Europe that were bordered on the west by territories inhabited by Germanic peoples. Christian missionaries from Byzantium converted the Slavs in the ninth century and introduced writing; the earliest surviving text is an Old Church Slavonic translation of the Bible, also from the ninth century. The closely related Baltic languages, spoken (also apparently since ancient times) to the north, first appear in writing with words and phrases in the extinct Old Prussian from the 14th and 16th centuries. The two living Baltic languages, Lithuanian and Latvian, were written down starting in the 16th century.

Albanian. Albanian, spoken now in Albania and parts of Italy in two dialects, northern (Gheg) and southern (Tosk), is not attested until the 15th century. The prehistory of Albanian is controversial; the language is considered by some to be the descendant of a very poorly known ancient Balkan language, Daco-Mysian.

Other Branches. Besides these ten branches, a number of scantily attested (and not well understood) ancient languages are known that are clearly Indo-European but of uncertain filiation within the family: Phrygian in Anatolia, Thracian in the Balkans, Venetic and Messapic in Italy. They are preserved in short inscriptions mostly from the first millennium BC.

An Example of Reconstruction

Before proceeding with a survey of the lexicon and culture of the Indo-Europeans, it may be helpful to give a concrete illustration of the method used to reconstruct the Proto-Indo-European vocabulary and a brief description of some of the main features of the Proto-Indo-European language. The example will serve as an introduction to the comparative method and indicate as well the high degree of precision that the techniques of reconstruction permit. [Here and in the rest of this essay, certain typological conventions will be observed to differentiate the variety of linguistic forms under discussion. Terms in **boldface** are Indo-European roots and words that appear as entries in the dictionary. Words in SMALL CAPITALS are Modern English derivatives of Indo-European roots. All other linguistic forms under discussion are rendered in *italics*. Finally, an asterisk (*) is used to signal a word or form that is not preserved in any written documents but that can be reconstructed on the basis of other evidence.]

A number of Indo-European languages show a similar word for the kinship term "daughter-in-law": Sanskrit *snuṣā́,* Old English *snoru,* Old Church Slavonic *snūkha* (Russian *snokhá*), Latin *nurus,* Greek *nuós,* and Armenian *nu.* Albanian has a word *nuse* in the meaning "bride," a meaning shared by the Armenian form. In a patrilocal and patriarchal society (such as most, if not all, early Indo-European societies), where the bride went to live in her husband's father's house, "daughter-in-law" and "bride" were equivalents.

All of these forms, called *cognates,* provide evidence for the phonetic shape of the prehistoric Indo-European word for "daughter-in-law" that is their common ancestor. Sanskrit, Germanic, and Slavic agree in showing an Indo-European word that began with *sn-.* We know that an Indo-European *s* was lost before *n* in other words in Latin, Greek, Armenian, and Albanian, so we can confidently assume that Latin *nurus,* Greek *nuós,* Armenian *nu,* and Albanian *nuse* also go back to an Indo-European **sn-.* (Compare Latin *nix* [stem *niv-*], "snow," with English SNOW, which preserves the *s.*) This principle is spoken of as the *regularity of sound correspondences*; it is basic to the sciences of etymology and comparative linguistics.

Sanskrit, Latin, Greek, Armenian, and Albanian agree in showing the first vowel as *-u-.* We know from other examples that Slavic *ŭ* regularly corresponds to Sanskrit *u* and that in this position Germanic *o* (of Old English *snoru*) has been changed from an earlier *u.* It is thus justifiable to reconstruct an Indo-European word beginning **snu-.*

For the consonant originally following **snu-,* closer analysis is required. The key is furnished first by the Sanskrit form, for we know there is a rule in

Sanskrit that *s* always changes to *ṣ* (a *sh*-like sound) after the vowel *u*. Therefore a Sanskrit *snuṣ*- must go back to an earlier **snus*-. In the same position,
after *u,* an old *s* changes to *kh* (like the *ch* in Scottish *loch* or German *ach*) in
Slavic; hence the Slavic word, too, reflects **snus*-. In Latin always, and in Germanic under certain conditions, an old *-s*- between vowels changed to *-r*-. For
this reason Latin *nurus* and Old English *snoru* may go back to older **snus*- (followed by a vowel) as well. In Greek and Armenian, on the other hand, an old
-s- between vowels disappeared entirely, as we know from numerous instances.
Greek *nuós* and Armenian *nu* (stem *nuo*-) thus regularly presuppose the same
earlier form, **snus*- (followed by a vowel). Finally, that *-s*- between vowels is still
preserved—almost accidentally, one might say—in Albanian *nuse*. All the comparative evidence agrees, then, on the Indo-European root form **snus*-.

For the ending, the final vowels of Sanskrit *snuṣá*, Old English *snoru*, and Slavic
snŭkha all presuppose earlier *-ā* (**snus-ā*), which is the ordinary feminine ending
of these languages. On the other hand, Latin *nurus*, Greek *nuós*, and Armenian *nu*
(stem *nuo*-) all regularly presuppose the earlier ending **-os* (**snus-os*). We have
an apparent impasse; but the way out is given by the gender of the forms in Greek
and Latin. They are feminine, even though most nouns in Latin *-us* and Greek *-os*
are masculine.

Feminine nouns in Latin *-us* and Greek *-os,* since they are an abnormal type,
cannot have been created afresh; they must have been inherited. This suggests that
the original Indo-European form was **snusos*, of feminine gender. On the other
hand, the commonplace freely formed ending for feminine nouns was **-ā*. It is
reasonable to suggest that the three languages Sanskrit, Germanic, and Slavic replaced the peculiar feminine ending **-os* (because that ending was normally masculine) with the ordinary feminine ending **-ā*, and thus that the oldest form of the
word was **snusos* (feminine).

One point remains to be ascertained: the accent. Languages from five groups—
Anatolian, Indo-Iranian, Greek, Balto-Slavic, and Germanic—offer us information on the accent of Indo-European. Anatolian lacks a cognate, but Indo-Iranian,
Greek, and Balto-Slavic agree in showing a form accented on the last syllable: Sanskrit *snuṣá*, Russian *snokhá*, Greek *nuós*. The Germanic form is equally precise,
however, since the rule is that old *-s*- became *-r*- (Old English *snoru*) only if the
accented syllable came after the *-s*-.

On this basis we may add the finishing touch to our reconstruction: the full
form of the word for "daughter-in-law" in Indo-European is **snusós*.

It is noteworthy that no single language in the family preserves this word intact.
In every language, in every tradition in the Indo-European family, the word has
been somehow altered from its original shape. It is the comparative method that
permits us to explain the different forms in this variety of languages by the reconstruction of a unitary common prototype, a common ancestor.

Proto-Indo-European Grammar: Sounds and Forms

A large part of the success of the comparative method with the Indo-European
family is due to the number and the precision of the agreements among the lan-

guages, not only in the regular sound correspondences of the roots but even more strikingly in the particulars of morphology, the forms of language in their grammatical function. Consider the partial paradigms of the words for "dog" (*kwon-) and "to kill" (*gʷhen-):

	Hittite	Greek	Vedic Sanskrit
nominative	kuwas	kúōn	ś(u)vā́
accusative	kuwanan	kúna	śvā́nam
genitive	kūnas	kunós	śúnas

	Lithuanian	Old Irish	Proto-Indo-European
nominative	šuõ	cú	*k(u)wō̄(n)
accusative	šùni	coin	*kwónṃ
genitive	šuñs	con	*kunés

	Hittite	Vedic Sanskrit	Proto-Indo-European
third singular present indicative	kuenzi	hánti	*gʷhén-ti
third plural present indicative	kunanzi	ghnánti	*gʷhn-énti

The agreement of detail in sound correspondences (see the table on pages 148–149), in vowel alternations and their distribution, in the accent, in the grammatical forms (endings), and in the syntactic functions is little short of astounding.

Speech Sounds and their Alternations. The system of *sounds* in Proto-Indo-European was rich in stop consonants. There was an unvoiced series, *p, t, k̂* (like the *ky* sound at the beginning of *cute*), *k* (like the *c* of *cup*), *kʷ* (like the *qu* of *quick*); a voiced series, *b, d, ĝ, g, gʷ*; and a voiced aspirate or "murmured" series, *bh, dh, ĝh, gh, gʷh*, pronounced like the voiced series but followed by a puff of breath. (Some scholars would reinterpret the traditional voiced series as an unvoiced ejective, or glottalized, one. While this new glottalic theory accounts for some typological difficulties, it introduces more problems than it solves. In this work, as in most current handbooks, Indo-European forms appear in their traditional shape.)

The three series of k-like sounds, or velars, seen above—termed palatal (*k̂, ĝ, ĝh*), plain (*k, g, gh*), and labiovelar (*kʷ, gʷ, gʷh*)—were reduced to two in most of the daughter languages. In the so-called "centum" languages (comprising Greek, Italic, Germanic, and Celtic), the palatal velars became plain velars and the labiovelars at first remained, while in the "satem" languages (Indo-Iranian, Balto-Slavic, and Armenian), the labiovelars became plain velars and the palatals became sibilants. (The terms "centum" and "satem" come respectively from the Latin and Avestan words for "hundred," illustrating the two developments.) The notation of the different velars has been partially simplified in the dictionary; see page xxxvi of the Guide.

If Proto-Indo-European was rich in stop consonants, it was correspondingly poor in continuants, or fricatives, such as English *f, v, th, s,* and *z,* having only *s,* which was voiced to *z* before voiced stop consonants. For a number of reconstructed Proto-Indo-European roots, the evidence provided by the daughter languages suggests the reconstruction of two forms of the same root: one beginning with a consonant or consonant cluster and another beginning with *s* plus that consant or consonants, as for example **(s)mer-[1],** "to remember," with *s*-less forms in Latin *memor,* "mindful" (MEMORY) and Germanic (MOURN), but with *s-* in Sanskrit *smṛtiḥ,* "remembrance, tradition, body of sacred texts," for example. The technical term for such an *s-* is the Latin expression *s mobile,* "movable s, shifting s."

Proto-Indo-European had as well three *laryngeals* or *h*-like sounds, h_1, h_2, h_3, of disputed phonetic value (equivalent notations are H_1, H_2, H_3 and $ə_1$, $ə_2$, $ə_3$). The sounds are preserved as such (at least in part) only in Hittite and the other Anatolian languages in cuneiform documents from the second millennium BC. Compare Hittite *paḫs-,* "to protect," coming directly from Indo-European *pah_2-s-* (PASTOR, see **pā-**), or Hittite *ḫarb-,* "to change allegiance or status," from Indo-European *$h_3$orbh-*, probably originally "to turn" (ORPHAN, see **orbh-**). In all the other languages of the family, the laryngeals are lost, and their former presence in a word can only be deduced from indirect evidence such as the vowel "coloring" and the contractions discussed below. Elucidation of the details of these laryngeals remains one of the most interesting problems confronting Indo-Europeanists today.

Proto-Indo-European had two nasals, *m* and *n,* two liquids, *r* and *l,* and the glides *w* and *y.* A salient characteristic of Indo-European was that these sounds could function both as consonants and as vowels. Their consonantal value was as in English. As vowels, symbolized $ṃ$, $ṇ$, $ḷ$, and $ṛ$, the liquids and nasals sounded much like the final syllables of English *bottom, button, bottle,* and *butter.* The vocalic counterparts of *w* and *y* were the vowels *u* and *i.* The laryngeals too could function both as consonants and as vowels: their consonantal value was that of *h*-like sounds, while as vowels they were varieties of schwa (*ə*), much like the final syllable of English *sofa;* hence the choice of schwa to represent laryngeals in the main text of this dictionary.

The other vowels of Indo-European were *e, o,* and *a.* These, as well as *i* and *u,* occurred both long and short, as did the diphthongs *ei, oi, ai, eu, ou, au.* (All vowels are pronounced as in Latin or Italian.) Since we can distinguish chronological layers in Proto-Indo-European, it can be said that a number of the long vowels of later Indo-European resulted from the contraction of early Indo-European short vowels with a following laryngeal, a process consisting of the loss of the laryngeal with compensatory lengthening of the preceding vowel. Already in Proto-Indo-European itself, two of the three laryngeals had the property of "coloring" an adjacent fundamental vowel *e* to *a* and *o,* respectively, before the contractions took place. Thus the root **pā-,** "to protect," is contracted from older *pah_2-*, with "a-coloring" from *pah_2-*; the root **dō-,** "to give," is contracted from older *doh_3-*, with "o-coloring" from *deh_3-*; and the root **dhē-,** "to set, put," is contracted from older *$dheh_1$-*, without coloring. The fundamental vowel in each of these roots, as in most Indo-European roots, was originally *e.* In scholarly usage it is now customary to write the noncoloring laryngeal as h_1, the a-coloring laryngeal as h_2, and the o-coloring laryngeal as h_3.

Laryngeals also colored a following vowel e (but not o) before their loss. Thus **ant-,** "front, forehead," is from earlier $*h_2ent$-, colored to $*h_2ant$- (Hittite ḫant-, "front, forehead"); **op-[1],** "to work, produce in abundance," is from earlier $*h_3ep$-, colored to $*h_3op$- (Hittite ḫapp-in-ant-, "rich"); and **ed-,** "to eat," is from earlier $*h_1ed$- (Hittite ed-, "to eat"), without coloring. Note that only the vowel e could be colored by a laryngeal; **owi-,** "sheep," is from $*h_2owi$-, while **ap-[1],** "to take," is from $*h_2ep$- with coloring. Occasionally, the evidence provided by the daughter languages allows us to exclude the reconstruction of one of the laryngeals but does not permit a choice between the remaining two. For example, the available evidence may preclude the possibility that a laryngeal was h_a but not further allow us to chose between h_2 or h_3. Current scholarly usage notates such a laryngeal as $h_{2/3}$. Furthermore, when the evidence indicates the presence of a laryngeal in a root but does not permit us to specify its identity any further, such a laryngeal is given the notation h_x or $H.$ in current scholarly usage.

The notation of the laryngeals is somewhat simplified in this dictionary for convenience's sake. For details, see page xxxvi of the Guide.

A characteristic feature of Indo-European was the system of vocalic *alternations* termed *apophony* or *ablaut*. This was a set of internal vowel changes expressing different morphological functions. A clear reflex of this feature is preserved in the English strong verbs, where, for example, the vocalic alternations between *write* and *wrote, give* and *gave,* express the present and past tenses. Ablaut in Indo-European usually affected the vowels e and o. The fundamental form was e; this e could appear as o under certain conditions, and in other conditions both e and o could disappear entirely. On this basis we speak of given forms in Indo-European as exhibiting, respectively, the *e-grade* (or *full grade*), the *o-grade,* or the zero *grade.* The e and the o might furthermore occur as long $ē$ or $ō$, termed the *lengthened grade.*

To illustrate: the Indo-European root **ped-,** "foot," appears in the e-grade in Latin ped- (PEDAL), but in the o-grade in Greek pod- (PODIATRIST). Germanic **fōtuz* (FOOT) reflects the lengthened o-grade **pōd-*. The zero grade of the same root shows no vowel at all: **pd-*, **bd-*, a form attested in Sanskrit.

When the zero grade involved a root with one of the sounds $m, n, r, l, w,$ or y (collectively termed *resonants*), the resonant would regularly appear in its vocalic function, forming a syllable. We have the e-grade root **seng^w-** in English SINK, the o-grade form **song^w-* in SANK, and the zero-grade form **sng̠^w-* in SUNK.

In the paradigms cited earlier, the word for "dog," **kwon-,** appears in the o-grade in the accusative case **kwón-(m̥)*, in the zero grade in the genitive case **kun-(és)*, and in the lengthened o-grade in the nominative case **kwō(n)*. Note that the nonsyllabic resonant w appears as the vowel u when it becomes syllabic. The verb "to kill," **g^when-,** appears in the e-grade in the third singular **g^whén-(ti)*, and in the zero grade in the third plural **g^whn-(énti)*. It appears in the o-grade **g^whon-* in Germanic **ban-ōn-* (BANE). The n of the zero grade **g^whn-* becomes syllabic ($n̥$) before a consonant: **g^whn̥-(tyā́-)* becoming Germanic **gundjō* (GUN).

In the case of roots with long vowels arising from contraction with a laryngeal, the ablaut can be most clearly understood by referring to the older, uncolored and uncontracted forms. Thus **pā-,** "to protect," had as its earliest form **peh₂-* which was later colored to **pah₂-*, and its zero grade was **ph₂-* (given as **pə-* in the simpli-

fied notation of this dictionary); **dō-,** "to give," from *$*deh_3$-* colored to *$*doh_3$-,* has a
zero grade *$*dh_3$-* (given as *$*də$-* in the simplified notation of this dictionary); **dhē-,**
"to place," contracted from *$*dhh_1$-,* has a zero grade *$*dhh_1$-* (given as *$*də$-* in the
simplified notation of this dictionary). The fundamental vowel of the full grade dis-
appears in the zero grade, and only the ə remains. Long $\bar{u}$ and long $\bar{\imath}$ could also arise
from contraction: full grade **peuə-,** "to purify," has a zero grade *$*puh_x$-* contracted
to *$*pū$-* (PURE); full grade **peiə-,** "to be fat, swell," has a zero grade *$*piə_3$-* contracted
to *$*pī$-* (IRISH). In roots of the structure of **pō(i)-;** "to drink," from earlier *$*peə_3(i)$-,*
the variant with *i* formed a zero-grade *$*piə$-,* contracted to *$*pī$-* (PIROGI).

It may finally be noted that a small number of roots had *a* as the basic vowel
and not *e*. These roots could also occasionally exhibit o-grade, zero-grade, and
lengthened-grade forms: the root **ag-1** (*$*h_1aĝ$-*), "to drive," had an o-grade derivative *$*og$-mo-* (*$*h_1oĝ$-mo-*) that is the source of the word OGHAM and the word for
"salt," **sal-,** had a zero-grade (*$*s\mathring{l}$-*) and lengthened-grade (*$*sāl$-*), forms found in
German and Irish respectively.

Grammatical Forms and Syntax. Proto-Indo-European was a highly inflected
language. Grammatical relationships and the syntactic function of words in the
sentence were indicated primarily by variations in the endings of the words. Nouns
had different endings for different cases, such as the subject and the direct object
of the verb, the possessive, and many other functions, and for the different numbers, namely the singular, plural, and a special dual number for objects occurring
in pairs. Verbs had different endings for the different persons (first, second, third)
and numbers (singular, plural, dual), for the voices active, passive, and middle (a
sort of reflexive), as well as special affixes for a rich variety of tenses, moods, and
categories such as causative-transitive (*$*-éyo$-*) and stative-intransitive (*$*-ē$-*) verbs.
Practically none of this rich inflection is preserved in Modern English, but it has
left its trace in many formations in Germanic and in other languages such as Latin
and Greek. These are noted in the appendix where they are relevant.

With the exception of the numbers five to ten and a group of particles including
certain conjunctions and quasi-adverbial forms, all Indo-European words under-
went inflection. The structure of all inflected words, regardless of part of speech, was
the same: *root* plus one or more *suffixes* plus *ending.* Thus the word *$*ker$-wo-s,* "a stag,"
is composed of the root **ker-1,** "horn," plus the noun suffix *$*-u$-,* plus the possessive
adjective suffix *$*-o$-,* plus the nominative singular ending *$*-s$:* "the horned one." The
root contained the basic semantic kernel, the underlying notion, which the suffix
could modify in various ways. It was primarily the suffix that determined the part of
speech of the word. Thus a single root like **prek-,** "to ask," could, depending on the
suffix, form a verb *$*p\mathring{r}k$-sko-,* "to ask" (Latin *poscere*), a noun *$*prek$-,* "prayer" (Latin
precēs), and an adjective *$*prok$-o-,* "asking" (underlying Latin *procus,* "suitor"). Note
that *$*prek$-,* *$*prok$-,* and *$*p\mathring{r}k$-* have, respectively, e-grade, o-grade, and zero grade.

The root could undergo certain modifications. *Extensions* or *enlargements* did
not affect the basic meaning and simply reflect formal variations between languages. Suffixes had more specific values. As represented in this dictionary, there
were verbal suffixes that made nouns into verbs (**-yo-2**) and others that marked
different types of action, like transitive (*$*-éyo$-,* **-eyo-**) and stative-intransitive
(**-ē-**). There were nominal suffixes that made agent nouns (**-ter-**), abstract nouns

(**-ti-**), verbal nouns (**-wer/-wen-**) and verbal adjectives (**-to-, -nt-**), and nouns of instrument (**-tro-**) and other functions.

The root plus the suffix or suffixes constituted the *stem*. The stems represented the basic lexical stock of Indo-European, the separate words of its dictionary. Yet a single root would commonly furnish a large number of derivative stems with different suffixes, both nominal and verbal, much as English *love* is both noun and verb as well as the base of such derivatives as *lovely, lover,* and *beloved*. For this reason it is customary to group such collections of derivatives, in a variety of Indo-European languages, under the root on which they are built. The root entries of the dictionary are arranged in this way, with derivatives that exhibit similar suffixes forming subgroups consisting of Indo-European stems or words.

Indo-European made extensive use of suffixation in the formation of words but had very few prefixes. The use of such prefixes ("preverbs") as Latin *ad-, con-, de-, ex-* (ADVENT, CONVENE, DERIVE, EXPRESS) or Germanic *be-* (BECOME, BEGET) can be shown to be a development of the individual languages after the breakup of the common language. In Indo-European such *compounds* represented two independent words, a situation still reflected in Hittite and the older Sanskrit of the Vedas (the sacred books of the ancient Hindus) and surviving in isolated remnants in Greek and Latin.

An important technique of word formation in Indo-European was *composition,* the combining of two separate words or notions into a single word. Such forms were and continue to be built on underlying simple sentences an example in English would be "he is someone who *cuts wood,*" whence "he is a *woodcutter.*" It is in the area of composition that English has most faithfully preserved the ancient Indo-European patterns of word formation, by continuously forming them anew, re-creating them. Thus *housewife* is immediately analyzable into *house + wife,* a so-called descriptive compound in which the first member modifies the second; the same elements compounded in Old English, *hūs + wīf,* have been preserved as an indivisible unit in *hussy*. Modern English has many different types of compounds, such as *catfish, housewife, woodcutter, pickpocket,* or *blue-eyed*; exactly similar types may be found in the other Germanic languages and in Sanskrit, Greek, Latin, Celtic, and Slavic.

The comparative study of Indo-European poetics has shown that such compounds were considered particularly apt for elevated, formal styles of discourse; they are a salient characteristic especially of Indo-European poetic language. In addition, it is amply clear that in Indo-European society the names of individual persons—at least in the priestly and ruling (or warrior) classes—were formed by such two-member compounds. Greek names like *Sophocles,* "famed for wisdom," Celtic names like *Vercingetorix,* "warrior-king," Slavic names like *Mstislav,* "famed for vengeance," Old Persian names like *Xerxes,* "ruling men," and Germanic names like *Bertram,* "bright raven," are all com-

Greek ostracon inscribed *Themistokles Phreareios,* "Themistocles of the Phrearian deme" (fifth century BC). The name *Themistokles* means "having righteous fame."

pounds. The type goes as far back as Proto-Indo-European, even if the individual names do not. English family names continue the same tradition with such types as *Cartwright* and *Shakespeare,* as do those of other languages, like Irish *(O')Toole,* "having the people's valor."

Semantics. A word of caution should be entered about the semantics of the roots. It is perhaps more hazardous to attempt to reconstruct meaning than to reconstruct linguistic form, and the meaning of a root can only be extrapolated from the meanings of its descendants. Often these diverge sharply from one another, and the scholar is reduced in practice to inferring only what seems a reasonable, or even merely possible, semantic common denominator. The result is that reconstructed words and particularly roots are often assigned hazy, vague, or unspecific meanings. This is doubtless quite illusory; a portmanteau meaning for a root should not be confused with the specific meaning of a derivative of that root at a particular time and place. The apparent haziness in meaning of a given Indo-European root often simply reflects the fact that with the passage of several thousand years the different words derived from this root in divergent languages have undergone semantic changes that are no longer recoverable in detail. Nevertheless, some roots can be given specific semantic values, such as **nes-1,** "to return safely home" (NOSTALGIA).

Lexicon and Culture

The reconstruction of a *protolanguage*—the common ancestor of a family of spoken or attested languages—has a further implication. Language is a social fact; languages are not spoken in a vacuum but by human beings living in a society. When we have reconstructed a protolanguage, we have also necessarily established the existence of a prehistoric society, a speech community that used that protolanguage. The existence of Proto-Indo-European presupposes the existence, in some fashion, of a society of Indo-Europeans and an Indo-European culture.

Language is intimately linked to culture in a complex fashion; it is at once the expression of culture and a part of it. Especially the lexicon of a language—its dictionary—is a face turned toward culture. Though by no means a perfect mirror, the lexicon of a language remains the single most effective way of approaching and understanding the culture of its speakers. As such, the contents of the Indo-European lexicon provide a remarkably clear view of the whole culture of an otherwise unknown prehistoric society.

The evidence that archaeology can provide is limited to material remains. But human culture is not confined to material artifacts. The reconstruction of vocabulary can offer a fuller, more interesting view of the culture of a prehistoric people than archaeology because it includes nonmaterial culture.

Consider the case of religion. To form an idea of the religion of a people, archaeologists proceed by inference, examining temples, sanctuaries, idols, votive objects, funerary offerings, and other material remains. But these may not be forthcoming; archaeology is, for example, of little or no utility in understanding the religion of the ancient Hebrews. Yet, for the Indo-European-speaking society, we can reconstruct with certainty the word for "god," **deiw-os,* and the two-word name of the chief deity of the pantheon, **dyeu-pəter-* (Latin *Iūpiter,* Greek *Zeus* *patēr*, Sanskrit *Dyauṣ pitar-*, and Luvian *Tatis Tiwaz*). The forms **dyeu-* and **deiw-os* are both derivatives of a root **dyeu-,** meaning "to shine," which appears in the word for "day" in numerous languages (Latin *diēs*; but English DAY is not related). The notion of deity was therefore linked to the notion of the bright sky.

The second element of the name of the chief god, **dyeu-pəter-*, is the general Indo-European word for FATHER, used not in the sense of father

Silver relief figure of Cernunnos, the Celtic stag god, holding a torque and a serpent. Detail of a panel from the Gundestrup cauldron, dating from the first century BC and unearthed in Denmark.

as parent but with the meaning of the adult male who is head of the household, the sense of Latin *pater familias*. For the Indo-Europeans the society of the gods was conceived in the image of their own society as patriarchal. The reconstructed words **deiw-os* and **dyeu-pəter-* alone tell us more about the conceptual world of the Indo-Europeans than a roomful of graven images.

The comparative method enables us to construct a basic vocabulary for the society of speakers of Proto-Indo-European that extends to virtually all aspects of their culture. This basic vocabulary is, to be sure, not uniform in its attestation. Most Indo-European words are found only in some of the attested languages, not in all, which suggests that they may have been formed at a period later than the oldest common Indo-European we can reconstruct. There are also dialectal words that are limited in the area of their extension, as in the case of an important sociological term such as the word for "people," **teutā-,** which is confined to the western branches: Italic, Celtic, and Germanic. (It is the base of German *Deutsch* and of DUTCH and TEUTONIC.) In cases such as these, where a word is attested in several traditions, it is still customary to call it Indo-European, even though it may not date from the remotest reconstructible time. It is in this sense, universally accepted by scholars, that the term *Indo-European* has been used in this dictionary.

We may examine the contents of this Indo-European lexicon, which aside from its inherent interest permits us to ascertain many characteristics of Indo-European society. It is remarkable that by far the greater part of this reconstructed vocabulary is preserved in native or borrowed derivatives in Modern English.

General Terms. It is appropriate to begin with a sampling of basic terms that have no special cultural value but attest to the richness of the tradition. All are widespread in the family. There are two verbs expressing existence, **es-** and **bheuə-,** found in English IS, Latin *esse*, and English BE, Latin *futūrus* (FUTURE), respectively. There are verbs meaning "to sit" (**sed-[1], ēs-**), "to lie" (**legh-, kei-[1]**), and "to stand" (**stā-**). There are a number of verbs of motion, like **gʷā-,** "to come," **ei-[1],** "to go," **terə-[2],** "to cross over," **sekʷ-[1],** "to follow," **keiə-,** "to set in motion," and the variants of "rolling or turning motion" in **wel-[3], wer-[3],** and **kʷel-[1].**

The notion of carrying is represented by the widespread root **bher-¹** (BEAR¹), found in every branch except Anatolian. This root is noteworthy in that it formed a phrase **nŏ-men- bher-**, "to bear a name," which is reconstructible from several traditions, including English. This phrase formed a counterpart to **nŏ-men-dhē-**, "to give a name," with the verb **dhē-**, "to set, put," in Sanskrit, Greek, and Slavic tradition. The persistence of these expressions attests the importance of the name-giving ritual in Indo-European society.

For the notions of eating and drinking, the roots **ed-** and **pō(i)-** are most widespread. The metaphor in "drunk, intoxicated," seems to have been created independently a number of times in the history of the Indo-European languages; Latin *ēbrius*, "drunk" (INEBRIATED), was without etymology until a cognate turned up in the Hittite verb meaning "to drink;" both are derived from the root **egʷh-**.

The verb "to live" was **gʷeiə-¹**; it formed an adjective **gʷī-wos*, "alive," which survives in English QUICK, whose original sense is seen in the biblical phrase *the quick and the dead*. For the notion of begetting or giving birth there are two roots, **tek-** and the extremely widely represented **genə-**, which appears not only as a verb but also in various nominal forms like **genə-os*, "race," and the prototypes of English KIN and KIND.

A number of qualitative adjectives are attested that go back to the protolanguage. Some come in semantic pairs: **sen-**, "old," and **newo-**, "new;" also **sen-**, "old," and **yeu-**, "youthful vigor;" **tenu-*, "thin" (under **ten-**), and **tegu-**, "thick;" **gʷerə-²**, "heavy," and **legʷh-**, "light." There are also the two prefixes **(e)su-**, "good, well-," and **dus-**, "bad, ill-," in the Greek forms borrowed as EU- and DYS-. But normally adjectives denoting value judgments like "good" and "bad" are not widespread in the family and are subject to replacement; English *good*, Latin *bonus*, and Greek *agathos* have nothing to do with one another, and each is confined to its own branch of the family.

The personal pronouns belong to the very earliest layer of Indo-European that can be reached by reconstruction. Their forms are unlike those of any other paradigms in the language; they have been called the "Devonian rocks" of Indo-European. The lack of any formal resemblance in English between the subject case (nominative) I and the object case (accusative) ME is a direct and faithful reflection of the same disparity in Proto-Indo-European, respectively **eg** (**egō*) and **me-¹**. The other pronouns are **tu-** (**te-*), "thou," **nes-²** or **we-**, "we," and **yu-**, "you." No pronouns for the third person were in use.

The cognate languages give evidence for demonstrative and interrogative pronouns. Both have also developed into relative pronouns in different languages. The most persistent and widespread pronominal stems are **to-** and **kʷo-**, which are preserved in the English demonstrative and interrogative-relative pronouns and adverbs beginning with *th-* (THIS, THEN) and *wh-* (WHO, WHICH, WHEN).

All the languages of the family show some or all of the Indo-European numerals. The language had a decimal system. There is complete agreement on the numerals from two to ten: **dwo-** (**duwō*), **trei-** (**treyes*), **kʷetwer-** (**kʷetwores*), **penkʷe**, **s(w)eks, septm̥, oktō(u), newn̥, dekm̥**. For the numeral "one" the dialects vary. We have a root **sem-¹** in some derivatives, while the western Indo-European languages Germanic, Celtic, and Latin share the form **oi-no-**. The word for "hundred," formed from **dekm̦,** "ten," was *(d)km̦tom. No common form for "thousand" or any other higher number can be reconstructed for the protolanguage. The deeper origins of the names of the numbers are purely speculative. They were occasionally subject to renewal: "four" in the most ancient branch, Anatolian, is a derivative of **mei-²,** "small," extended to *meiu-: the meaning was "little (hand)," minus the thumb.

Nature and the Physical Environment. A large number of terms relating to time, weather, seasons, and natural surroundings can be reconstructed from the daughter languages, some of which permit certain inferences about the homeland of the Indo-European-speaking people before the period of migrations took them to the different localities where they historically appear.

There are several words for "year," words that relate to differing conceptions of the passage of time. Such are **yēr-** (YEAR), related to words denoting activity; **wet-²,** the year as a measure of the growth of a domestic animal (WETHER, basically "yearling"); and **at-** in Latin annus (ANNUAL), from a verb meaning "to go," referring to the year as passage or change. The seasons were distinguished in Indo-European: **ghei-²,** "winter," **wes-r̦,** "spring," **sem-²,** "summer," and **es-en-,** "fall, harvest," the latter plausibly reflected in Germanic *aznōn, "to earn," referring to harvest labor in an agricultural society.

The lunar month was a unit of time. The word for "month" (*mēns-) is in some languages identical with the word for "moon," in others a derivative of it, as in Germanic *mēnōth- remade from *mēnōs-. "Moon/month" in Indo-European is a derivative of the verb "to measure," **mē-².** The adjective **sen-** (*seno-), "old," was also used for the waning of the moon, on the evidence of several languages.

The other celestial bodies recognized were the sun, **saəwel-,** and the stars, **ster-².** There is evidence from several traditions for similar designations of the constellation Ursa Major, though these may not go back to the earliest Indo-European times. The movement of the sun dictated the names for the points of the compass. The word EAST is derived from the verbal root **aus-¹,** "to shine," as is the word for "dawn" (Latin Aurōra), deified since Indo-European times on the evidence of Greek, Lithuanian, and Sanskrit. The setting sun furnished the word for "evening" and "west," **wespero-,** related in a complex fashion to an older word for "night," kʷsep-. The Indo-Europeans oriented themselves by facing east. Therefore the root **deks-,** "right," could also denote "south." "Right" was considered lucky; the terms for "left" vary from language to language (one Indo-European term is **laiwo-**) and were evidently subject to taboo.

The most widespread of the words for "night" was **nekʷ-t-,** although an earlier meaning "morning or evening twilight" can still be discerned for this

Chariot of the Sun. Bronze and gold-leaf statue from the Trundholm region of Denmark showing a horse pulling the sun on a chariot (14th century BC).

word. Words for "day" include **āmer-** and **agh-²** and such dialectal creations as Latin *diēs*; **ayer-** refers to the morning. The old word for "darkness," **regʷ-es-,** shows up in Greek as a term for the underworld.

The Indo-Europeans knew snow in their homeland; the word **sneigʷh-** is nearly ubiquitous. Curiously enough, however, the word for "rain" varies among the different branches; we have words of differing distribution such as **seuə-², ombh-ro-,** and **reg-².**

Conceptions of the sky, or heaven, are varied in the different descendant languages. Although, as we have seen, the root **dyeu-** occurs widely as the divine bright sky, certain languages viewed the heavens as basically cloudy; **nebh-** is "sky" in Balto-Slavic and Iranian, but "cloud" elsewhere. Another divine natural phenomenon is illustrated by the root **(s)tenə-,** "thunder," and the name of the Germanic god THOR.

A word for the earth can be reconstructed as **dhghem-** (**dheghom*). Other terms of lesser distribution, like **kaito-** and **welt-** (WILD), designated forest or uncultivated land. Swampy or boggy terrain was apparently also familiar, judging from the evidence of the roots **sel-es-** and **pelə-¹.** But since none of these runs through the whole family, it would not be justifiable to infer anything from them regarding the terrain of a hypothetical original homeland of the Indo-Europeans.

On the other hand, from the absence of a general word for "sea" we may deduce that the Indo-Europeans were originally an inland people. The root **mori-** is attested dialectally (MERE), but it may well have referred to a lake or other smaller body of water. Transportation by or across water was, however, known to the Indo-Europeans, since most of the languages attest an old word for "boat" or "ship," **nāu-²,** probably propelled by oars or a pole (**erə-¹,** "to row").

The names for a number of different trees are widely enough attested to be viewed as Proto-Indo-European in date. The general term for "tree" and "wood" was **deru-.** The original meaning of the root was doubtless "to be firm, solid," and from it is derived not only the family of English TREE but also that of English TRUE. Note that the semantic evolution has here been from the general to the particular, from "solid" to "tree" (and even "oak" in some dialects), and not the other way around.

There are very widely represented words for the beech tree, **bhāgo-,** and the birch, **bherəg-.** These formerly played a significant role in attempts to locate the original homeland of the Indo-Europeans, since their distribution is geographically distinct. But their ranges may have changed over several millennia, and, more important, the same word may have been applied to entirely different species of tree. Thus the Greek and Latin cognates of BEECH designate a kind of oak found in the Mediterranean lands. Of fruit trees in the usual sense, only the apple (**abel-**) and the cherry (**ker-⁵**) were known.

Indo-European had a generic term for "wild animal," **ghwer-** (FERAL). The wolf was known and evidently feared its name is subject to taboo deformation (the conscious alteration of the form of a tabooed word, as in English *gol-derned, dad-burned*). The variant forms **wḷkʷo-,** **lupo-,* and **wḷp-ē-** (also "fox") are all found. The name of the bear was likewise subject to a hunter's taboo: the animal could not be mentioned by its real name on the hunt. The southern Indo-European languages have the original form, **r̥tko-** (Latin *ursus,* Greek *arktos*), but all the northern languages have a substitute term. In Slavic the bear is the "honey-eater," in Germanic the "brown one" (BEAR², and note also BRUIN).

The BEAVER was evidently known (*bhi-bhru-, from **bher-²**), at least in Europe, and the MOUSE (**mūs-**)—then as now—was ubiquitous. The HARE, probably named from its color (**kas-,** "gray"), is also widespread. Domesticated animals are discussed below.

A generic term for "fish" existed, **dhghū-** (also **peisk-** in Europe). The salmon (**laks-**) and the eel (**angʷhi-**) were known, the latter also in the meaning "snake." Several birds were known, including the crane (**gerə-²**) and the eagle (**or-**), the THRUSH (**trozdo-**), the STARLING (**storo-**), and, at least in some dialects, the SPARROW (**sper-³**), FINCH (**(s)ping-**), and woodpecker (**(s)peik-**). The generic term for "bird" was **awi-** (Latin *avis*), and from this was derived the well-represented word for "egg," *ōwyo-*.

The names for a number of insects can be reconstructed in the protolanguage, including the WASP (**wopsā-**), the hornet (*kr̥s-ro-, a derivative of **ker-¹,** "head," from the shape of the insect), and the fly (**mu-**). A root **sker-¹** is the base of a word *kori-, attested in different languages as either "bedbug" or "moth." English NIT faithfully continues Indo-European **knid-,** "louse, louse egg," attested in many branches of the family. And **lūs-,** "louse," has rhymed with **mūs-,** "mouse," since Indo-European times.

The BEE (**bhei-**) was particularly important as the producer of honey, for which we have the common Indo-European name **melit-** (MILDEW). Honey was the only source of sugar and sweetness (**swād-,** "sweet," is ancient), and notably was the base of the only certain Indo-European alcoholic beverage, **medhu-,** which in different dialects meant both MEAD ("wine" in Greece and Anatolia) and "honey." The Germanic languages have innovated, perhaps from a taboo on speaking the name while gathering wild honey; the common Germanic English word HONEY is from an old word for "yellow," **k(e)nəko-.**

People and Society. For human beings themselves, a number of terms were employed, with different nuances of meaning. The usual terms for "man" and "woman" are **wĭ-ro-** (VIRILE) and *gʷenā-; from **gʷen-** (GYNECOLOGY). For "person" in general, the oldest word was apparently *manu- (**man-¹**), as preserved in English MAN (nominative plural *manw-es, becoming Germanic *mann-iz, becoming Old English *menn,* MEN) and in Slavic and Sanskrit. A word for "woman" recently identified in Anatolian Luvian, **esōr,** combining form *-s(o)r-, formed the feminine of the numbers "three" and "four," as well as appearing in **swesor-,** sister, and the Latin word for "wife." The Germanic word for "woman" (WIFE) was completely isolated until a cognate was recently identified in Tocharian. For its curious semantic history, see **ghwībh-.** In other dialects we find interesting metaphorical expressions that attest a set of religious concepts opposing the gods as immortal and celestial to humankind as mortal and terrestrial. Humans are either *mr̥tos, "mortal" (**mer-²,** "to die"), or *dhghomyo-, "earthling" (**dhghem-,** "earth").

The parts of the body belong to the basic layer of vocabulary and are for the most part faithfully preserved in Indo-European languages. Such are **ker-¹,** "head" (also **kaput-** in dialects, doubtless a more colloquial word), **genu-²,** "chin, jaw," **dent-,** "tooth," **okʷ-,** "to see," whence "eye," **ous-,** "ear," **nas-,** "nose," **leb-,** "lip," **bhrū-,** "brow," **ōs-,** "mouth," **dn̥ghū-,** "tongue," and **mon-,** "neck." The word for "foot" is attested everywhere (**ped-**), while that for "hand" differs according to dialect; the most widespread is **ghes-ōr* (**ghes-,** CHIRO-).

Internal organs were also named in Indo-European times, including the heart (**kerd-¹**), womb (**gʷelbh-**), gall (**ghel-²**), and liver (**yěkʷr̥**). The male sexual organs, **pes-** and **ergh-,** are common patrimony, as is **ors-,** "backside."

A large number of kinship terms have been reconstructed. They are agreed in pointing to a society that was patriarchal, patrilocal (the bride leaving her household to join that of her husband's family), and patrilineal (descent reckoned by the male line). "Father" and "head of the household" are one: **pəter-,** with his spouse, the **māter-.** These terms are ultimately derived from the baby-talk syllables *pa(pa)* and *ma(ma),* but the kinship-term suffix *-ter-* shows that they had a sociological significance over and above this in

Raised stone, Lovön Island in Lake Mälaren, Sweden (11th century AD). The runic inscription reads *Thorkisl auk Sikniutr thiz raistu stain at uik fathur sin,* "Thorgísl and Signjótr, they raised the stone in memory of Vígr, their father."

the Indo-European family. Related terms are found for the grandfather (**awo-**) and the maternal uncle *(*awon-),* and correspondingly the term **nepōt-** (feminine **neptī-*) applied to both grandson (perhaps originally "daughter's son") and nephew ("sister's son"). English SON and DAUGHTER clearly reflect Indo-European **sūnu-* (from **seuə-¹**) and **dhugəter-.**

Male blood relations were designated as **bhrāter-** (BROTHER), which doubtless extended beyond those with a common father or mother; the Greek cognate means "fellow member of a clan-like group." The female counterpart was **swesor-** (SISTER), probably literally "female member of the kin group," with a word for woman (**esōr**) and the root **s(w)e-,** designating the self, one's own group.

The Celtic ringfort Dún Aonghasa on the island of Inishmore, Ireland, occupied from the late second millennium BC into the first millennium AD. The Irish word *dún,* "ringfort," derives from Celtic **dū-no-.*

While there exist many special terms for relatives by marriage on the husband's side, like **daiwer-,** "husband's brother," fewer corresponding terms on the wife's side can be reconstructed for the protolanguage. The terms vary from dialect to dialect, providing good evidence for the patrilocal character of marriage.

The root **dem-** denoted both the house (Latin *domus*) and the household as a social unit. The father of the family (Latin *pater familiās*) was the "master of the house" (Greek *despotēs*) or simply "he of the house" (Latin *dominus*). A larger unit was the village, designated by the word **weik-¹**. The community may have been grouped into divisions by location; this seems to be the basic meaning of the **dā-mo-* (from **dā-**) in Greek *dēmos,* people (DEMOCRACY).

Human settlements were frequently built on the top of high places fortified for defense, a practice taken by Indo-European migrants into central and western Europe and into Italy and Greece, as confirmed by archaeological finds. Words for such fortified high places vary; there are **pelə-³** (ACROPOLIS), the Celtic word for "ringfort," **dhū-no-* (**dheuə-,** TOWN), and **bhergh-²** (*-burg* in place names).

Economic Life and Technology. A characteristic of Indo-European and other archaic societies was the principle of exchange and reciprocal gift-giving. The presentation of a gift entailed the obligation of a countergift, and the acts of giving and receiving were equivalent. They were simply facets of a single process of generalized exchange, which assured the circulation of wealth throughout the society.

This principle has left clear traces in the Indo-European vocabulary. The root **dō-** of Latin *dōnāre* means "to give" in most dialects but in Hittite means "to take." The root **nem-** is "to distribute" in Greek (NEMESIS), but in German it means "to take," and the cognate of English GIVE (**ghabh-**) has the meaning "to take" in Irish. The notion of exchange predominates in the roots **mei-¹** and **gher-⁵**. The root **dap-** means "to apportion in exchange," which may also carry a bad sense; Latin *damnum* is "damage entailing liability." The GUEST (**ghos-ti-**) in Indo-European times was the person with whom one had mutual obligations of hospitality. But he was also the stranger, and the stranger in an uncertain and warring tribal society may well be hostile: the Latin cognate *hostis* means "enemy." The Indo-Europeans evidently practiced both ransom and enslavement of enemy captives: **kemb-,** "to exchange," furnishes the Irish for "captive," and the roots **algʷh-,** "to fetch a price," and **wes-¹,** "to buy or sell," refer in the oldest texts to traffic in people, as does the root **des-** of Greek *doulos,* "slave" (HIERODULE).

The Indo-Europeans practiced agriculture and the cultivation of cereals. We have several terms of Indo-European antiquity for grain: **gr̥ə-no-** (CORN), **yewo-,** and **pūro-,** which may have designated wheat or spelt. Of more restricted distribution are **wrughyo-,** "rye," and **bhars-²,** "barley." Such terms for cereals could originally have designated the wild rather than cultivated varieties. A root for grinding is attested, **melə-** (MEAL², MILL). Another Indo-European term is **sē-¹,** "to sow," not found in Greek, Armenian, or Indo-Iranian. The verb "to plow" is **arə-²,** again a common European term, with the name of the plow, **arə-trom.* Other related roots are **yeug-,** "to yoke," and **kerp-,** "to gather, pluck" (HARVEST). The root **gʷerə-¹,** "heavy," is the probable base of **gʷerə-nā-,* "hand mill" (QUERN). The term is found throughout the Indo-European-speaking world, including India.

Stockbreeding and animal husbandry were an important part of Indo-European economic life. Names for all the familiar domesticated animals are present throughout the family: **gʷou-,** "cow" and "bull," **owi-,** "sheep," **agʷh-no-,** "lamb," **aig-** and **ghaido-,** "goat," **sū-,** "swine," and **porko-,** "farrow." The domestic dog

Greek vase depicting a racing chariot (sixth century BC). Chariot racing for sport and ritual purposes was prominent in the culture of many early Indo-European peoples, such as the Indo-Iranians, Greeks, and Irish.

was ancient (**kwon-**). The common Indo-European name of the horse, **ekwo-,** is probably derived from the adjective **ōku-,** "swift." The expansion and migration of the Indo-European-speaking peoples in the later third and early second millennia BC is intimately bound up with the diffusion of the horse. The verbal root **demə-,** "to force," acquired the special sense of "to tame horses," whence English TAME. Stock was a source and measure of wealth; the original sense of **peku-** was probably "wealth, riches," as in Latin *pecūnia,* which came to mean "wealth in cattle" and finally "cattle" proper.

The verbal roots **pā-,** "to protect," and **kʷel-1,** "to revolve, move around," are widely used for the notion of herding or watching over stock, and it is interesting to note that the metaphor of the god or priest watching over humankind like a shepherd (Latin *pāstor*) over his flock occurs in many Indo-European dialects as well as outside Indo-European.

Roots indicating a number of technical operations are attested in most of the languages of the family. One such is **teks-,** which in some dialects means "to fabricate, especially by working with an ax," but in others means "to weave" (TEXTILE). The root **dheigh-,** meaning "to mold, shape," is applied both to bread (DOUGH) and to mud or clay, whence words for both pottery and mud walls (Iranian **pari-daiza-,* "walled around," borrowed into Greek as the word that became English PARADISE).

The house (**dem-**) included a **dhwer-** (DOOR), which probably referred originally to the gateway into the enclosure of the household. The house would have had a central hearth, denoted in some languages by **as-** (properly a verb, "to burn"). Fire itself was known by two words, one of animate gender (**egni-,** Latin *ignis*) and one neuter (**paəwr̥,** Greek *pūr* and English FIRE).

Indo-European had a verb "to cook" (**pekʷ-,** also having the notion "to ripen") and an adjective "raw" (**om-**). Another operation is denoted by **peis-1,** "to crush." Meat (**mēms-**) was an established item of diet, and some sort of sauce or broth is indicated by the term **yeuə-** (**yū-s-,* JUICE, from Latin). Other household activities included spinning (**(s)nē-**), weaving (**webh-**), and sewing (**syū-**). The verb **wes-4** (WEAR) is ancient and everywhere attested.

The Indo-Europeans knew metal and metallurgy, to judge from the presence of the word **ayes-* in Sanskrit, Germanic, and Latin. The term designated copper and perhaps bronze. Iron is a latecomer, technologically, and the terms for it vary from dialect to dialect. Latin has *ferrum,* while the Germanic and Celtic term was **isar-no-,* properly "holy (metal)," from **eis-1,** perhaps so called because the first iron was derived from small meteorites. Gold, **ghel-2,** also dialectally **aus-o-,* probably "yellow (metal)" or "shining," was known from ancient times, though the names for it vary. Silver was **arg-,** with various suffixes, doubtless meaning "white (metal)."

It was probably not long before the dispersal of the Proto-Indo-European community that the use of the wheel and wheeled transport was adopted. Despite the existence of widespread word families, most terms relating to wheeled vehicles seem to be metaphors formed from already existing words, rather than original, unanalyzable ones. So NAVE, or hub of the wheel (**nobh-**), is the same word as NAVEL. This is clearly the case with WHEEL itself, where the widespread *$k^w(e)$-$k^w l$-

Achaemenid gold model of a war chariot found in Tajikistan (fifth to fourth century BC). The warrior stands to the side, ready to do battle, while a charioteer holds the reins. Early Indo-European literature features famous warrior-and-charioteer pairs, such as Achilles and Automedon in Greece.

o- is an expressive derivative of a verb (**k^wel-1**) meaning "to revolve or go around." Other words for "wheel" are dialectal and again derivative, such as Latin *rota* from a verbal root **ret-,** "to run." The root **wegh-,** "to go, transport in a vehicle" (WAGON), is attested throughout the family, including now Hieroglyphic Luvian. This evidence for the late appearance of the wheel agrees with archaeological findings that date the distribution of the wheel in Europe to the latter part of the fifth millennium BC, the latest possible date for the community of Proto-Indo-European proper. The word *ansiyo-*, "rein," represented in Old Irish *éisi* and Greek *ēniai*, "reins," designated the reins that guided the oxen that drew the heavy carts of the Proto-Indo-Europeans. However, the introduction of the lighter chariot, drawn by horses and intimately associated with the warrior elite of later societies speaking Indo-European languages, postdates the early dispersal of the individual branches of Indo-European and is a phenomenon of the Bronze Age.

Ideology. We pointed out earlier that the great advantage of the lexicon as an approach to culture and history is that it is not confined to material remains. Words exist for natural phenomena, objects, and things that can be found in nature or identified from their material remains. But there are also words for ideas, abstractions, and relations. The reconstructed protolanguage of the Indo-Europeans is particularly rich in such vocabulary items.

A number of verbs denoting mental activity are found. The most widespread is **men-1,** preserved in English MIND. Other derivatives refer to remembering, warning (putting in mind), and thinking in general. A root notable for the diversity of its derivatives is **med-,** which may be defined as "to take the appropriate measures." Reflexes of this verb range in meaning from "rule," through "measure" (MODICUM, from Latin), to "physician" (Latin *medicus*).

The notions of government and sovereignty were well represented. The presence of the old word for tribal king, *reg-* (**reg-1**), only in the extreme east (RAJAH) and the extreme west (Latin *rēx*, Celtic *-rīx*) virtually guarantees its presence in the earliest

Indo-European society. (Here is an example of the phenomenon of marginal or peripheral conservation of a form lost in the central innovating area.) Roman tradition well attests the sacral character of kingship among the Indo-Europeans. The functions of king and priest were different aspects of a single function of sovereignty. It is this that is symbolized by the divine name *dyeu-pətər- (**dyeu-**), the chief of the gods.

Mycenean gold funerary mask (16th century BC).

Another aspect of the function of sovereignty is the sphere of the law. There is an old word, **yewes-,** probably for "religious law," in Latin *iūs.* Latin *lēx* is also ancient (**leg-¹** or **legh-**), though the details of its etymology are uncertain. In a society that emphasized the principle of exchange and reciprocity, it is scarcely surprising that the notion of contractual obligation should be well represented. Several roots specify the notion of "bond": **bhendh-, ned-, leig-¹,** and **sai-²,** all of which have derivatives with technical legal meanings in various languages, including Hittite *išḫiul,* "contract," the oldest attested Indo-European word, borrowed into the Semitic language of Assyrian merchant colonies in Anatolia in the 19th century BC. The root **dlegh-** furnishes Germanic words meaning "to engage oneself" (PLEDGE), as well as the Irish word for "law." The Greek word for "justice," *dikē,* is derived metaphorically from the notion of "boundary marker" (**deik-**). The verb **kʷei-¹** meant "to pay compensation for an injury."

A nominal derivative of **kʷei-¹**, **kʷoinā-,* became *poinā,* "punishment," in the Doric dialect of Greek and and was into the most ancient Roman legal terminology as Latin *poena,* with associated verb *pūnīre,* whence English PENAL, PUNISH, and a host of other legal terms. The root **kʷei-¹** forms a deverbative nasal-suffixed form **kʷi-nu-* attested in Greek, Celtic, and Indo-Iranian. The root **kʷei-³**, a verb of perception, is regarded by some as the same as **kʷei-¹**, but the special legal semantics of the latter dictates the separation of the two. With a laryngeal root suffix, it appears as **kʷei-ə-,* with zero-grade **kʷi-ə-,* becoming **kʷī-* in the prehistory of Greek and seen in Greek *tiein,* "to honor, value" with its derived noun *tīmē,* "honor, worth" (TIMOCRACY). Enlarged by *–s-,* **kʷei-³** furnished the verb "to see," (stem **kʷis-yo-*), in both Continental Celtic (Gaulish) and Insular Celtic (Welsh, Cornish, and Breton). In Indo-Iranian **kʷei-s-* appears in other verbs of perception and mental activity, such as Old Iranian *kaēš-,* "to determine." A suffixed o-grade form of **kʷei-s-,* **kʷoi-s-o-,* has been identified in the Latin noun *cūra,* "care," with derived verb *cūrāre* (earlier *coerāre*), "to take care of." Previously of unknown etymology, *cūra* is the source of English CURE and numerous other derivatives (CURATE, SINECURE, etc.).

As the examples above show, homophonous roots are common in Proto-Indo-European, with ambiguity avoided through the addition of root enlargements ("extended forms") and stem-forming suffixes to the roots and also as by the addition of grammatical suffixes to roots and their derived stems. For example, yet another Proto-Indo-European root can be restructed as *kʷei-*, namely **kʷei-²**, "to build up, make." This root is well represented in Greek in the form of the suffix *-poi(w)o-* (from earlier *-kʷoiwo-*), found as the second member of nominal compounds meaning "making (a certain thing)" such as *pharmakopoios,* "making drugs" (PHARMACOPIA). Within the prehistory of Greek, *-kʷoiwo-* served as the base from which was formed a denominative verb *kʷoiw-eyo-,* the source of Greek *poiein,* "to make, create" (POEM, POESY, PEOT, etc.).

Indo-European is particularly rich in religious vocabulary. An important form, which is also found only in the peripheral languages Sanskrit, Latin, and Celtic, is the two-word metaphoric phrase **kred-dhē-,* literally "to put (**dhē-**) heart (**kerd-¹**)." The two words have been joined together in the western languages, as in Latin *crēdō,* "I believe." Here a term of the most ancient pagan religion has been taken over by Christianity. A common word for religious "formulation," **bhreghmen-,* may be preserved in *Brahmin,* a member of the priestly class, from Sanskrit, although the etymology is controversial.

Oral prayers, requests of the deity, and other ritual utterances must have played a significant role in Indo-European religion. We have already seen **prek-** (PRAY), and note also the roots **wegʷh-** (VOW), **sengʷh-** (SING), and **gʷerə-²,** which in Latin *grātia* (GRACE) has had a new life in Christianity.

Several words apparently denoted specific ritual actions, like **ghow-ē-,** "to honor, worship," and **sep-el-yo-* (**sep-²**), with the specific notion "to perform ritual manual operations on or about a corpse," found in the Latin verb *sepelīre,* "to bury," also "to embalm." The root **spend-** has the basic meaning of "to make an offering or perform a rite," whence "to engage oneself by a ritual act." Its Latin derivative *spondēre* means "to promise" (SPOUSE).

A hint of Indo-European metaphysics appears in the word **aiw-,** "vital force," whence "life everlasting, the eternal recreation of life, eternity" (EON). It is noteworthy that the idea of "holy" is intimately bound up with that of "whole, healthy," in a number of forms: **kailo-** (WHOLE and HOLY), **solə-,** whence Latin *salvus* (SALVATION), and **swen-to-** (SOUND²), a rhymeform to **kwento-* which underlies the Avestan word for "holy" and the Baltic and Slavic word for "saint." An ancient root relating solely to religion is **sak-** (SACRED).

Finally we may add that poetry and a tradition of poetics are also common patrimony in most of the Indo-European tradi-

Inscription on a fragment of a stele from the Lapis Niger, a shrine in the Roman Forum (circa 570–550 BC). One of the earliest Latin inscriptions, it relates to the kingship of Rome and the sanctity of the shrine and contains the phrase *sakros esed,* "let it be sacred."

tions. The hymns of the Rig-Veda are composed in meters related to those used by the Greek poets, and the earliest verse forms found among the Celts and the Slavs go back to the same Indo-European source. Many, perhaps most, of the stylistic figures and embellishments of poetic language that we associate with "classical" poetics and rhetoric can be shown, by the comparative method, to have their roots in Indo-European poetics itself.

A number of metaphorical expressions appear to be creations of ancient, even Indo-European date. Thus the verb **gʷher-,** "to burn, warm," forms derivatives in Latin and Celtic which mean "to keep warm, cherish," and refer especially to the duties of the pious son toward his aged parent. Latin *terra,* "earth" (TERRAIN), is historically a transferred epithet, "dry (land)," from **ters-,** "to dry," whose English descendant is THIRST. One securely reconstructible Indo-European place name rests squarely on a metaphor: **Pīwer-iā* in Greek *Pīeriā* (PIERIAN SPRING) and **Īwer-ion-,* the prehistoric Celtic name for Ireland (Gaelic *Éire, Érin*), both continue an Indo-European feminine adjective **pīwer-iə,* "fat," metaphorically "fertile," from **peiə-,** the same root that gives English FAT.

Most interesting are the cases where it is possible to reconstruct from two or more traditions (usually including Homer and the Rig-Veda) a poetic phrase or formula consisting of two members. Such are the expressions "imperishable fame," **klewos n̥dhgʷhitom* (**kleu-, dhgʷhei-**); "holy (mental) force," **isərom menos* (**eis-¹, men-¹**); and the "weaver (or crafter) of words," the Indo-European poet himself, **wekʷōm teks-ōn* (**wekʷ-, teks-**). The immortality of the gods (**n̥-mr̥to-,* from **mer-²**) is emphasized anew by the vivid verb phrase **nek-¹ terə-²,** "to overcome death," appearing in the Greek word *nektar,* the drink of the gods. And at least one three-member formula (in the sense of the word in traditional oral poetry) can be reconstructed for the poetic language of prayer, on the combined evidence of four languages, Latin, Umbrian, Avestan, and Sanskrit: "Protect, keep safe, man and cattle!" (**pā- wǐ-ro- peku**).

The comparative method when applied to the poetry and mythology of the speakers of Proto-Indo-European also reveals the same Indo-European origins of the formulaic language used by those speakers to convey those myths and narratives: in short, the "Indo-European touch." This is what distinguishes the Indo-European tale from all the other versions, common across many cultures, in which a god or hero kills a dragon, serpent, or monstrous adversary who symbolizes the forces of stagnation, dormancy, and death. In the oldest branch of Indo-European, Anatolian, this adversary is called *Illuyankas,* to be interpreted perhaps as "eel-snake" and compared with English *eel* (see **el-³**) and Latin *anguis,* "eel" (see **angʷh-**), and the god who slays him is the Anatolian storm god. In Luwian, the storm god's name is *Tarḫunza,* and although his Hittite name is always written with Sumerian signs that hide its exact form, it was probably pronounced *Tarḫunnas.* The narration of the storm god's heroic deed, his victory of over the monster, also features a form the Hittite verb *tarḫ-* "to overcome": *Illuyankan taraḫḫūwan dāis,* "he began to overcome Illuyankas." Both the god's name and the verb are derived from the verbal root **terə-²** and thus form a so-called "etymological figure": *The Overcomer overcame (his adversary).*

In this Anatolian formulaic pairing, recurrence or repetition marks both verb and grammatical subject. What is repeated are forms derived from a single root that share meaning as well as outward phonetic form: *slay/ slayer, slay/slew, slay/slays.* But the minimal token of repetition in formulaic language can lack meaning or semantics altogether and be just a single speech sound—in the case of the Indo-European dragon-slaying tale, *g^wh-*. The "basic formula" of the dragon-slaying myth in Vedic is *áhann áhim*

Limestone relief of the Anatolian storm god killing a dragon, originally located in Arslantepe, Turkey (850–800 BC).

"(he) slew (the) serpent." Both sequences of *áh-* in this sentence are phonetically identical, and have been since Indo-European times. The formula is built from inherited material: Proto-Indo-European **g^{w}hen-** and **og^{w}hi-,** the latter doubtless influenced by semantically allied words **eghi-** as well as **ang^{w}hi-** seen above in the name of the serpent *Illuyankas.*

While a Greek or Vedic poet would have known nothing of the cognate verb phrases of the Indo-European family, he would certainly have been sensitive to the figure of repetition of speech sounds like alliteration, and in the best of circumstances (involving phonetic, metrical, and other clues) to recurrent and marked variations in syntactic patterns like VERB OBJECT word order, in contrast to the ordinary OBJECT VERB word order that is characteristic of most older Indo-European languages.

Conclusion

This survey has touched on only a representative sample of the available reconstructed Indo-European lexicon and has made no attempt to cite the mass of evidence in all the languages of the family, ancient and modern, for these reconstructions.

For this essay, we have given only the information about Indo-European culture that could be derived from language and lexicon alone. Other disciplines serve to fill out and complete the picture to be gathered from the study of vocabulary: archaeology, prehistory, comparative religion, and the history of institutions.

Archaeologists have not in fact succeeded in locating the Indo-Europeans. An artifact other than a written record is silent on the language of its user, and prehistoric Eurasia offers an abundant choice of culture areas. Archaeologists are generally agreed that the so-called Kurgan peoples, named after the Russian word for their characteristic "barrow" or "tumulus" grave structure, spoke an Indo-European language. The correlation between the Kurgan cultural features described by archaeologists and the Indo-European lexicon is striking: for example, small tribal units (**teutā-**) ruled by powerful chieftains (**reg-¹**), a predominantly pastoral (**pā-**) economy including horse (**ekwo-**) breeding (**demə-**) and plant cultivation (**yewo-**), and architectural features such as a small subterranean or aboveground rectangular hut (**dom-*, **dem-**) of timber uprights (**kli-t-*, **klei-,** and **stu-t-*, **stā-,** still with us in English STUD).

Some time around the middle of the fifth millennium BC, these people expanded from the steppe zone north of the Black Sea and beyond the Volga into the Balkans and adjacent areas. These Kurgan peoples bore a new mobile and aggressive culture into Neolithic Europe, and it is not unreasonable to associate them with the coming of the Indo-Europeans. But the Kurgan peoples' movement into Europe took place in distinct waves from the fifth to the third millennium BC. The earliest so far discovered might be compatible with a reasonable date for Proto-Indo-European, that is, a date sufficiently long ago for a single language to develop into forms as divergent as Mycenaean Greek and Hittite as they are historically attested by the middle of the second millennium BC. But the subsequent Kurgan immigrations, after 4000 BC, are too late to be regarded as incursions of speakers of undifferentiated Proto-Indo-European. The archaeological evidence for the later waves of Kurgan migrations points to their having had an Indo-European culture, but the languages spoken by the later Kurgan peoples must have been already differentiated Indo-European dialects, some of which would doubtless evolve into some of the historical branches of the family tree. We must be content to recognize the Kurgan peoples as speakers of certain Indo-European languages and as sharing a common Indo-European cultural patrimony. The ultimate "cradle" of the Indo-Europeans may well never be known, and language remains the best and fullest evidence for prehistoric Indo-European society. It is the comparative method in historical linguistics that can illumine not only ancient ways of life but also ancient modes of thought.

Guide to the Dictionary

This dictionary supplies the prehistoric component of the etymologies given in *The American Heritage Dictionary of the English Language,* Fifth Edition, by tracing the ultimate Indo-European derivations of those English words that are descended from Indo-European roots. All relevant steps between an Indo-European form and the earliest attested ancestor of a modern English word are given; the intermediate steps between that attested ancestor and the English word, however, are not given except occasionally, as this information is readily found in the etymologies of *The American Heritage Dictionary of the English Language.*

The form given in **boldface** type at the head of each entry is, unless otherwise identified, an Indo-European root in its basic form. The basic root form is followed in some cases by one or more variants, also in boldface type. Then the basic reconstructed meaning or meanings of the root are given (but see the cautionary note under "Semantics" in the preceding essay, page xx). Meanings that are different parts of speech are separated by a semicolon:

> **kei-¹** To lie; bed, couch; beloved, dear.
>
> **pelə-²** Flat; to spread.
>
> **leg-¹** To collect with derivatives meaning "to speak."
>
> **yĕkwr̥** Liver.
>
> **-mno-** Suffix forming passive participles to verbs.

Most roots as given in their citation forms were not independent words in Indo-European, but existed only in combination with suffixes or endings; this fact is indicated by the final hyphens. An exception is **yĕkwr̥;** above. Over thirty common suffixes are included in the dictionary, indicated by initial and final hyphens, like **-mno-.**

After the basic meaning there may appear further information about the phonological shape or nature of the root:

> **skei-** To cut, split. Extension of **sek-.**
>
> **kʷr̥mi-** Worm. Rhyme word to *wr̥mi-, worm (see **wer-²**).

The boldface forms **sek-** and **wer-²** are cross-references to those roots, which are main entries in this dictionary. Every boldface form appearing in the text of an entry is such a cross-reference.

The dictionary includes a number of entries that are not, strictly speaking, Indo-European, because they are found in only one branch or are known to have been borrowed into the family from an outside source. These are included because of their importance for English etymology, and are enclosed in brackets:

> **[līk-** Body, form; like, same. Germanic root. ... **]**
>
> **[wīn-o-** Wine. Italic noun, related to words for wine in Greek, Armenian, Hittite, and non-Indo-European Georgian and West Semitic. ... **]**

For ease of use and reference, the boldface entry words (and cross-references) do not distinguish between the plain velars *k, g, gh* and the palatal velars *k̂, ĝ, ĝh*, notating both sets as **k, g, gh.** (See page xv for a discussion of these sounds.) Velars should be assumed to be plain unless indicated otherwise in parentheses following the English gloss of the root:

> **kleu-** To hear. (Oldest form **k̂leu-*.)
>
> **segh-** To hold. (Oldest form **seĝh-*.)
>
> **sak-** To sanctify.

The first two examples show that the velar **k** and **gh** contained in the roots **kleu-** and **segh-** was a palatal velar in the root's oldest (pre-Germanic) form, but the velar in **sak-** was a plain velar. This information is given for the interested or more specialized reader only, and is not taken note of anywhere else in an entry.

A similar simplification has been adopted in the notation of laryngeals (see pages xvi-xvii for an explanation of these sounds). The cover symbol ə is used for any of the three laryngeals in entry words, cross-references, and generally throughout an entry; however, for the interested reader, more specific information is given parenthetically when it is known:

> **gʷelə-³** To swallow. (Oldest form **gwelh₁-*.)
>
> **pā-** To protect, feed. (Oldest form **peh₂-*, colored to **pah₂-*, contracted to **pā.*)
>
> **bheuə-** Also **bheu-.** To be, exist, grow.

The parenthetical information in the first two examples specifies which laryngeal was contained in the root's oldest (pre-Germanic) form. No such information is provided in the case of **bheuə-,** indicating that there is not enough evidence to determine precisely which laryngeal it contained. In the case of **pā-,** following the oldest root form are given the steps of coloring and contraction that led from the oldest form to the citation form; these changes are described on page xvi. In some instances, the information needed to understand the relationship among variant forms of a root is more complex and must be given in greater detail. An example is **terə-²;** below:

> **terə-²** To cross over, pass through, overcome. (Oldest form **terh₂-*, with variant [metathesized] form **treh₂-*, colored to **trah₂-*, contracted to **trā-.*)

The parenthetical information here not only specifies which laryngeal was contained in the root, but also the origin of the variant root form *trā-; it goes back to a form of the root that was metathesized, that is, where two adjacent sounds were reversed.

The text of each entry describes in detail the development of Modern English words from the root. Each numbered section of an entry begins with a list, in SMALL CAPITALS, of the Modern English words derived from a particular form of the root. (This list may be preceded by an intermediate step; see further below.) The simple (uncompounded) derivatives are given first; the compounds follow, after a semicolon. In some cases no further semantic or morphological development needs to be explained, and the *lemma*, the historically attested representative of the root, follows, as *avis* at the entry **awi-:**

> **awi-** Bird. **I. 1.** AVIAN, AVIARY, AVIATION; AVICULTURE, AVIFAUNA, BUSTARD, OCARINA, OSPREY, OSTRICH, from Latin *avis,* bird.

Much more commonly, however, intermediate developments require explanation. These intermediate stages are reconstructions representing a word stem in Indo-European that is necessary to explain the lemma following it (see the section "Grammatical Forms and Syntax" in the preceding essay, pages xviii–xx). The reconstructed forms are not historically attested; they are preceded by an asterisk (*) to note this fact. Sometimes earlier or later developments of the intermediate forms are given in parentheses, as in the example of **stā-,** below. In these cases the symbol < is used to mean "derived from" and the symbol > is used to mean "developed into." Intermediate stages that are in fact attested (such as the stages between Latin *avis* and English BUSTARD in the example above) are usually not given in the dictionary. The following terms are used to describe typical morphological processes of Indo-European:

Full-grade form. A form with e-vocalism (the basic form); so identified for descriptive contrast. It is usually the same as the citation form of the root.

O-grade form. A form with o-vocalism:

> **dhers-** O-grade form *dhors-* . . .

Zero-grade form. A form with zero-vocalism:

> **men-¹ I.** Zero-grade form *mṇ-*.

Lengthened-grade form. A form with lengthened vocalism:

> **ked- 1.** Lengthened-grade form *kēd-*.

Secondary full-grade form. A new full-grade form created by inserting the fundamental vowel *e* in the zero-grade form of an extended root:

> **stā-** . . . **V.** Zero-grade extended root *stū-* (< *stuə-*). . . . **VI.** Secondary full-grade form *steu-*.

Basic form. The unchanged root; so identified for descriptive contrast.

Suffixed form. A form with one or more suffixes, written with an internal hyphen:

> **laks-** Suffixed form **laks-o-*.
>
> **maghu-** Suffixed form **magho-ti-*.
>
> **mel-² 1.** Suffixed (comparative) form **mel-yos-*.

Prefixed form. A form with a prefix, written with an internal hyphen:

> **op-¹** . . . **6.** . . . from prefixed form **co-op-*.

Extended form. A form with an extension or enlargement, written without internal hyphens:

> **pel-⁶** . . . **II.** Extended form **pelh₂-*.

Nasalized form. A form with a nasal infix, written with internal hyphens:

> **tag- 1.** Nasalized form **ta-n-g-*.

Reduplicated form. A form prefixed by its own initial consonant followed by a vowel:

> **segh-** . . . **5.** Reduplicated form **si-sgh-*.

Compound form. A form compounded with a form of another root, written with internal hyphens:

> **dem-** . . . **3.** Compound form **dems-pot-*.

Expressive form. A form with "expressive gemination" (doubling of the final consonant), written without internal hyphens:

> **gal-²** . . . **3.** Expressive form **gall-*.

Shortened form. A form with shortened vocalism:

> **syū-** . . . **III.** Suffixed shortened form **syu-men-*.

Reduced form. A form with loss of one or more sounds:

> **ambhi** Reduced form **bhi*.

Variant form. A form altered in any way other than those described in the above categories:

> **deru-** . . . **2.** Variant form **dreu-*.

These terms can be combined freely to describe in as much detail as necessary the development from the root to the lemma.

> **dhē(i)- 1.** Suffixed reduced form *dhē-mnā-*. FEMALE, FEMININE; EF-FEMINATE, from Latin *fēmina,* woman (< "she who suckles").
>
> **gerə-¹ 1.** Suffixed lengthened-grade form *gērə-s-*. AGERATUM, GERIAT-RICS, from Greek *gēras,* old age.
>
> **petə-** . . . **2.** Suffixed (stative) variant zero-grade form *pat-ē-*. PATENT, PATULOUS, from Latin *patēre,* to be open.

In order to emphasize the fact that English belongs to the Germanic branch of Indo-European and give precedence to directly inherited words in contrast to words borrowed from other branches, the intermediate stages in Germanic etymologies are covered in fuller detail. The Common or Proto-Germanic (here called simply Germanic) forms underlying English words are always given. Where no other considerations intervene, Germanic is given first of the Indo-European groups, and Old English is given first within Germanic, although this order of precedence is not rigidly applied.

The final item in most entries is an abbreviated reference, in brackets, to Julius Pokorny's *Indogermanisches Etymologisches Wörterbuch* (*Indo-European Etymological Dictionary*; Bern, 1959). This, the standard work of reference and synthesis in the Indo-European field, carries a full range of the actual comparative material on which the roots are reconstructed. Our dictionary presents only those aspects of the material that are directly relevant to English. For example, the English word MANY is found at the root **menegh-,** "copious." This entry describes the transition of the Indo-European form through Germanic *managa-* to Old English *manig, mænig,* "many." It does not cite the comparative evidence from outside English and Germanic on which this assertion is based, but it refers to "Pokorny *men(e)gh-* 730." The entry *men(e)gh-* on page 730 in Pokorny's dictionary cites, in addition to the Old English word, the forms attested in Sanskrit, Celtic, Gothic, Old High German, Old Norse, Slavic, and Lithuanian, from which the reconstruction of the root was made. These references should serve as a reminder that the information given in this appendix is assertive rather than expository and that the evidence and evaluation upon which its assertions are based are not presented here.

A few roots are not in Pokorny's dictionary; this is also indicated in brackets at the end of an entry, and brief comparative information is supplied on which the reconstruction has been based.

Twenty-six entries conclude with a Language and Culture Note, set off from the rest of the entry and including additional cultural and linguistic information that was deemed of interest to the general reader.

Symbols: * unattested
   < derived from
   > developed into

Parentheses within a form enclose sound(s) or letter(s) sometimes or optionally present, such as *s mobile* (see page xvi).

Indo-European Roots

-ā- (Oldest form *-eh₂-, colored to *-ah₂-, contracted to *-ā-. Also appears as *-a, from zero-grade *-h₂, especially in composite forms *-ya and *-wa.) Suffix forming abstract or collective nouns, and marking the feminine gender in most adjectives ending in *-o-. It ultimately appears in the following English suffixes: **a.** -CY, from Latin -tia, abstract suffix (< *-ti-ā; *-ti-, abstract suffix, see **-ti-**); **b.** *(i)* -ERY, -Y², from Latin -ia, abstract suffix; *(ii)* -IA¹, from Greek -iā, abstract suffix. Both *(i)* and *(ii)* from Indo-European compound abstract suffix *-iā-; **c.** -ESS, from Greek -issa, feminine suffix (not productive until Late Greek), from composite suffix *-ikya. [Not in Pokorny.]

ab(e)l- Apple. **1.** APPLE, from Old English æppel. **2.** DAPPLE-GRAY, from Old Norse *apall, apple (in apalgrár, dapple-gray). Both **1** and **2** from Germanic *ap(a)laz. [Pokorny ǎbel- 1.]

ad- To, near, at. **1a.** AT¹; ATONE, TWIT, from Old English æt, near, by, at; **b.** ADO, from Old Norse at. Both **a** and **b** from Germanic *at. **2.** AD-, -AD; ADJUVANT, AID, AMOUNT, PARAMOUNT, from Latin ad, ad-, to, toward. **3.** Celtic *ad-, to, at, in compounds (see **bher-¹**, **sed-¹**). **4.** Suffixed zero-grade form *əd-ilo-. **a.** TILL²; UNTIL, from Old Norse til, to, toward, from Germanic noun *tilam, end, limit, goal (compare Old High German noun zil, end, goal). **b.** TILL¹, from Old English tilian, to strive, work, from denominative Germanic verb *tilōjan, *tilējan, from *tilam (see above). [Pokorny 1. ad- 3.]

adheso- Adze, possibly a culture word circulating in late Proto-Indo-European dialectal times. ADZE, from Old English adesa. [Not in Pokorny; compare Hittite ateš-, a kind of ax.]

ag-¹ To drive, draw, move. (Oldest form *h₁aǵ-.) **1a.** ACT, ACTIVE, ACTOR, ACTUAL, ACTUARY, ACTUATE, AGENDUM, AGENT, AGILE, AGITATE, ALLEGE, AMBAGE, AMBIGUOUS, ASSAY, CACHE, COAGULUM, COGENT, ESSAY, EXACT, EXACTA, EXAMINE, EXIGENT, EXIGUOUS, INTRANSIGENT, REDACT, RETROACTIVE, SQUAT, TRANSACT, from Latin agere, to do, act, drive, conduct, lead, weigh. **b.** also from this root, when used as the second member of compound nouns, is Latin denominative and deadjectival suffix -igāre, abstracted and generalized from such denominative verbs as rēmigāre, to row, derived from rēmex, rēmig-, oarsman, compound of rēmus, oar + *-ag-s, noun suffix: FUMIGATE, FUSTIGATE, LEVIGATE, LITIGATE, NAVIGATE, OBJURGATE, PRODIGAL, VARIEGATE; **c.** formed in the same manner as the foregoing, although the details are obscure, is the Latin denominative and deadjectival suffix -īgāre, with lengthening of -i-: CASTIGATE, FATIGABLE, FATIGUE, INDEFATIGABLE, INVESTIGATE. **2.** -AGOGUE, AGONY; ANAGOGE, ANTAGONIZE, CHORAGUS, DEMAGOGUE, EPACT, GLUCAGON, HYPNAGOGIC, MYSTAGOGUE, PEDAGOGUE, PROTAGONIST, STRATAGEM, SYNAGOGUE, from Greek agein, to drive, lead, weigh. **3.** Suffixed form *ag-to-. AMBASSADOR, EMBASSAGE, EMBASSY, from Latin ambactus, servant, from Celtic *amb(i)-ag-to-, "one who goes around" (*ambi, around; see **ambhi**). **4.** Suffixed form *ag-ti-, whence adjective *ag-ty-o-, "weighty." AXIOM; AXIOLOGY, CHRONAXIE, from Greek axios, worth, worthy, of like value, weighing as much.

5. Possibly suffixed form *ag-ro-, driving, pursuing, grabbing. PELLAGRA, PODAGRA, from Greek agrā, a seizing. **6.** O-grade suffixed form *og-mo-, furrow, track, metaphorically "incised line." OGHAM, from Old Irish Ogma (from Celtic *Ogmios), name of a Celtic god and traditional inventor of the ogham alphabet. [Pokorny aǵ- 4.] See also derivative **agro-**.

ag-² To speak. (Oldest form *h₂eǵ-, colored to *h₂aǵ-.) Suffixed zero-grade form *əg-yo-. **1.** ADAGE, from Latin adagium, saying, proverb, "a speaking to" (ad-, to; see **ad-**). **2.** PRODIGY, from Latin prōdigium, a portent, "a foretelling" (prōd-, variant of prō-, before; see **per¹**). [Pokorny ēǵ- 290.]

ag-es- Fault, guilt. ACHE, from Old English acan, to ache (perhaps < "to cause mental pain"). [Pokorny agos- 8.]

agh-¹ To be depressed, be afraid. **1.** Suffixed form *agh-lo-. AIL, from Old English eglan, eglian, to trouble, afflict. **2.** Suffixed form *agh-es-. AWE, from Old Norse agi, fright, ultimately from Germanic *agiz-. [Pokorny agh- 7.]

agh-² A day (considered as a span of time). (Oldest form *aǵh-.) **1.** DAY, DAISY, TODAY, from Old English dæg, day. **2.** LANDTAG, from Old High German tag, day. **3.** DAWN, from Old English denominative dagian, to dawn. **1–3** all from Germanic *dagaz (with initial d- of obscure origin), day. [Pokorny ǎǵher- 7.]

agro- Field. (Oldest form *h₁aǵro-; probably originally a derivative of *h₁aǵ-, to drive ["place where cattle are driven"]; see **ag-¹**.) **1.** ACRE, from Old English æcer, field, acre, from Germanic *akraz. **2.** AGRARIAN; AGRICULTURE, PEREGRINE, PILGRIM, from Latin ager (genitive agrī), earlier *agros, district, property, field. **3.** AGRIA, AGRO-; AGROSTOLOGY, ONAGER, STAVESACRE, from Greek agros, field, and agrios, wild. [In Pokorny aǵ- 4.]

agw(e)sī- Ax. AX¹, from Old English æx, ax, from Germanic *akusjō-. [Pokorny agu(e)sī 9.]

agʷh-no- Lamb. **1.** YEAN, from Old English ēanian, to bring forth young, from Germanic *aunôn, denominative from *aunaz, lamb. **2.** AGNUS DEI, from Latin agnus, lamb. [Pokorny agʷh-no-s 9.]

ai-¹ To give, allot. **1.** Suffixed extended form *ai-t-yā-. ETIOLOGY, from Greek aitiā, cause, responsibility. **2.** Suffixed form *ai-tā-. DIET¹, DIET², from Greek diaitān, to treat. [Pokorny 3. ai- 10.]

ai-² To burn. (Oldest form *h₂ei-, colored to *h₂ai-.)

I. Basic form *ai-. **1.** Suffixed form *ai-mo-. EMBER, from Old English æmerge, ember, from Germanic compound *aim-uzjōn-, ashes, from *aima-, ashes (*uzjō, to burn; see **eus-**). **2.** Probably suffixed form *ai-lo-. ANNEAL, from Old English āl, fire, from Germanic *ail- (though this has also been taken from *aidh-lo- with irregular loss of dental, from extended form *aidh- in **II** below).

II. Extended form *ai-dh-. **1.** Suffixed form *aidh-sto-. OAST, from Old English āst, kiln, from Germanic *aistaz. **2.** Suffixed form *aidh-t-. **a.** Further suffixed form *aidh-t-o-. ESTIVAL, ESTIVATE, from Latin aestās (syncopated from *aestotās), heat, summer; **b.** further suffixed form *aidh-t-u-. ESTUARY, from Latin aestus, heat, swell, surge, tide. **3.** Suffixed form *aidh-i-*. AE-DILE; EDIFICE, EDIFY, from Latin *aedēs*, building, house (< "hearth"). **4.** Suffixed form *aidh-er-*. AETHER, ETHER, from Greek *aithēr*, air. **5.** Suffixed form *aidh-nā-*. ETNA, from Latin *Aetna*, borrowed from a form *aith-nā* ("the fiery one") in an indigenous language of Sicily. [Pokorny *ai-dh-* 11.]

aig- Goat. (Oldest form *aig̑-*.) AEGIS, from Greek *aigis*, goatskin (emblem of Athena), from *aix*, goat. [Pokorny *aig̑-*, 3. *aig-* 13.]

aik-¹ To be master of, possess. (Oldest form *h₂eik̑-*, colored to *h₂aik̑-*.) **1.** OUGHT¹, OWE, from Old English *āgan*, to possess, from Germanic *aigan*, to possess. **2a.** OWN, from Old English *āgen*, one's own. **a.** EIGENSTATE, EIGENVALUE, EIGENVECTOR, from Old High German *eigan*, one's own. Both **a** and **b** from Germanic participial form *aigana-*, possessed, owned. **3.** FRAUGHT, FREIGHT, from Middle Low German and Middle Dutch *vrecht*, *vracht*, "earnings," hire for a ship, freight, from Germanic prefixed form *fra-aihtiz*, absolute possession, property (*fra-*, intensive prefix; see **per¹**). **4.** Reduplicated zero-grade (perfect) form *əe-aik-*, remade to *əi-aik-* (> *ī-k-*). GANESH, from Sanskrit *īṣṭe*, he rules over. [Pokorny *ēik-* 298.]

aik-² To strike. (Oldest form *h₂eik-*, colored to *h₂aik-* (see in Greek *aikhmē*, spear), with reduplicated zero stem *h₂i-h₂ik-*, becomin *īk-*). ICTUS, from Latin *īcere*, to strike. [Pokorny *ăik̑-* 15.]

aim- Copy. (Oldest form *h₂eim-*, colored to *h₂aim-*.) **1.** Suffixed full-grade form *aim-olo-*. EMULATE, EMU-LOUS, from Latin *aemulus*, emulous. **2.** Zero-grade form *əim-*. **a.** IMITATE; INIMITABLE, from Latin *imitāre*, to imitate, from suffixed form *im-eto-*; **b.** IMAGE, IMAGINE, IMAGO, from Latin *imāgō*, image. [Not in Pokorny; compare Hittite *ḫimma-*, ritual substitute.]

ais- To wish, desire. (Oldest form *h₂eis-*, colored to *h₂ais-*.) Suffixed form *ais-sk-*. ASK, from Old English *āscian*, *ācsian*, to ask, seek, from Germanic *aiskōn*. [Pokorny 1. *ais-* 16.]

aiw- Also **ayu-**. Vital force, life, long life, eternity; also "endowed with the acme of vital force, young." (Oldest forms *h₂eiw-*, *h₂eyu-*, colored to *h₂aiw-*, *h₂ayu-*.) **1a.** NO¹, from Old English *ā*, ever; **b.** AUGHT¹, from Old English *āwiht*, *āuht*, anything, "ever a creature"; **c.** EVER; EVERY, NEVER, from Old English *ǣfre* (second element obscure), ever; **d.** AYE²; NAY, from Old Norse *ei*, ever. **a**, **c**, and **d** all from extended Germanic form *aiwi*; **b** from Germanic *aiwi* + *wihti*, "ever a thing, anything" (*wihti-*, thing; see **wekti-**). **2.** Suffixed form *aiw-ā-*. ECHT, from Middle Low German *echte*, true, legitimate, akin to Old High German *ēohaft*, according to custom, from *ēohaft*, from *ēwa*, custom, right (< "what is eternal, what endures") + *-haft*, having, possessing (see **kap-**). **3a.** Suffixed form *aiw-o-*. COEVAL, LONGEVITY, MEDIEVAL, PRIMEVAL, from Latin *aevum*, age, eternity; **b.** further suffixed form *aiwo-tā(ti)-*. AGE; COETANEOUS, from Latin *aetās* (stem *aetāti-*), age; **c.** further suffixed form *aiwo-t-erno-*. ETERNAL, ETERNE, ETERNITY; SEMPITERNAL, from Latin *aeternus*, eternal. **4.** Suffixed form *aiw-en-*. EON, from Greek *aiōn*, age, vital force. **5.** Zero-grade form *yu-* (earlier *əyu-*) in compound *əyu-gʷⁱə-es-*, "having a vigorous life" (*gʷⁱə-es-*, life; see **gʷeiə-¹**). HYGIENE, from Greek *hugiēs*, healthy. **6.** O-grade form *oyu-* (earlier *h₂oyu-*). **a.** UTOPIA, from Greek *ou*, not, variant of *ouk*, probably from a pre-Greek phrase *(ne) oyu (kʷid)*, "(not on your) life" (*ne*, not, and *kʷid*, indefinite pronoun used as emphasizing particle; see **ne** and **kʷo-**); **b.** AYURVEDA, from Sanskrit *āyuḥ*, life, health, from suffixed form *oyu-s-*. [Pokorny *aiu̯* 17.] See also derivative **yeu-**.

---

for example Sanskrit has a noun, *āyu*, with exactly that meaning, which goes back to an Indo-European noun *oyu*, "life everlasting"; and the zero-grade of this noun, *yu-*, could form an adjective, *yu-əon-*, "having life force, youthful," that is the source of Latin *iuvenis* and English *young* (see **yeu-**). However, the direct Greek descendant of *oyu* is very unexpected—the conjunction *ouk(i)* or *ou*, "not" (a word ultimately showing up in English *utopia*). To understand how a word for "life everlasting" came to mean "not," one must imagine a pre-Greek colloquial phrase *ne oyu kʷid*, meaning roughly "not on your life, not ever" (with *ne*, "not," and *kʷid*, an intensifying particle). Essentially, *oyu kʷid* just strengthened the force of the negative *ne*. In the histories of many languages, words that are used to strengthen negative expressions often come to be understood as having negative force themselves; and when this happens, the original negative word may be dropped as superfluous. This is precisely what happened with *ne oyu kʷid*: the literal meaning of the phrase *oyu kʷid* was lost and it was reinterpreted as simply meaning "not." The *ne* was then dropped, and after various sound changes had run their course in the prehistory of Greek, *oyu kʷid* became *ouk(i)* or *ou*. ● In modern French, the word *pas* "not" has a very similar history: it originated in the phrase *ne. . .pas*, which once meant "not a step," that is, "not at all," with *pas* strengthening the negative word *ne*. Eventually *pas* became interpreted as a negative itself, as in the phrase *pas mal*, "not bad."

---

ak- Sharp. (Oldest form *h₂ek̑-*, colored to *h₂ak̑-*.) **1.** Suffixed form *ak-yā-*. **a.** EDGE; SELVAGE, from Old English *ecg*, sharp side, from Germanic *agjō*; **b.** EGG², from Old Norse *eggja*, to incite, goad, from Germanic *agjan*. **2.** Suffixed form *ak-u-*. **a.** EAR², from Old English *æhher*, *ēar*, spike, ear of grain, from Germanic *ahuz-*; **b.** ACICULA, ACUITY, ACULEATE, ACUMEN, ACUPUNCTURE, ACUTE, AGLET, AGUE, EGLANTINE, from Latin *acus*, needle; **c.** ACEROSE, from Latin *acus*, chaff. **3.** Suffixed form *ak-i-*. ACIDANTHERA, from Greek *akis*, needle. **4.** Suffixed form *ak-men-*, stone, sharp stone used as a tool, with metathetic variant *ka-men-*, with variants: **a.** *ka-mer-*. (i) HAMMER, from Old English *hamor*, hammer; (ii) HAMERKOP, from Middle Dutch *hamer*, hammer. Both (i) and (ii) from Germanic *hamaraz*, hammer. **b.** *ke-men-* (probable variant). HEAVEN, from Old English *heofon*, *hefn*, heaven, from Germanic *hibin-*, "the stony vault of heaven," dissimilated form of *himin-*. **5.** Suffixed form *ak-onā-*, independently created in: **a.** AWN, from Old Norse *ögn*, ear of grain, and Old English *agen*, ear of grain, from Germanic *aganō*; and **b.** PARAGON, from Greek *akonē*, whetstone. **6.** Perhaps suffixed form *ak-en-i-* (although the details of the formation remain obscure). ANACONDA, from Sanskrit *aśaniḥ*, missile, thunderbolt. **7.** Suffixed lengthened form *āk-ri-*. ACERATE, ACRID, ACRIMONY, EAGER¹; CARVACROL, VINEGAR, from Latin *ācer*, sharp, bitter. **8.** Suffixed form *ak-ri-* (in further suffixed Proto-Italic form *akritho-*, although the details of the formation are obscure): ACERBIC, EXACERBATE, from Latin *acerbus*, bitter, sharp, tart. **9.** Suffixed (stative) form *ak-ē-*. ACID, from Latin *acēre*, to be sharp. **10.** Suffixed form *ak-ēto-*. ACETABULUM, ACETIC, ACETUM; ESTER, from Latin *acētum*, vinegar. **11.** Suffixed form *ak-mā-*. ACME, ACNE, from Greek *akmē*, point. **12.** Suffixed form *ak-ro-*. ACRO-; ACROBAT, ACROMION, from Greek *akros*, topmost. **13.** Perhaps suffixed form *ak-t-* in Greek *aktis* (stem *aktīn-*), ray; see **nekʷ-t-**. **14.** Suffixed o-grade form *ok-su-*. AMPHIOXUS, OXA-LIS, OXYGEN, OXYTONE, OXYURIASIS, PAROXYSM, from Greek *oxus*, sharp, sour. [Pokorny 2. *ak̑-* 18, 3. *k̑em-* 556.]

aks- Axis. (Oldest form *ak̑s-*.) **1.** Suffixed form *aks-lo-*. AXLE, from Old Norse *öxull*, axle, from Germanic *ahsulaz. **2.** Suffixed form *aks-i-. **a.** AXIS; ROTAXANE, from Latin *axis,* axle, pivot; **b.** AXILLA, from Latin *axilla,* armpit (< "axis point of the arm and shoulder"). **3.** Suffixed form *aks-lā. AILERON, AISLE, ALA, ALAR, ALARY, ALATE, ALULA; ALIFORM, from Latin *āla* (< *axla*), wing, upper arm (see *axilla* in **2. b.** for semantic transition). **4.** Suffixed form *aks-on-. AXON, AXONEME; AXOPLASM, from Greek *axōn,* axis. [In Pokorny *aĝ-* 4.]

akʷ-ā- Water. **1a.** AIT; ISLAND, from Old English *īg, īeg,* island; **b.** ORKNEY ISLANDS, from Old Norse *Orkney-jar,* "seal islands" (*orkn,* seal), from Old Norse *ey,* island (also in other place names in *-ey* such as GUERNSEY, JERSEY); **c.** SCANDINAVIA, from Latin *Scandināvia,* name of a large island in northern Europe, earlier *Scatināvia* (as recorded by Pliny the Elder), perhaps from Germanic compound *Skathinaujō,* perhaps to be interpreted as "danger island" (*skathi-,* harm; see **skét-**), since the Germanic peoples living to the south may have considered the Scandinavian peninsula, bounded on the Atlantic to the west and the Baltic to the east, to be an island. **a–c** all from Germanic *aujō,* "thing on the water," from *agwjō.* **2.** ETON, from Old English *Éatūn* (> early Middle English *Eitun*), "town on the river (Thames)," from *ēa,* water, river, from Germanic *ahwō.* **3.** AQUA, AQUARELLE, AQUARIUM, AQUATIC, AQUI-, EWER, GOUACHE; AGUA FRESCA, AGUARDIENTE, AQUAMARINE, AQUATINT, AQUAVIT, AQUEDUCT, SEWER¹, from Latin *aqua,* water. [Pokorny *akʷā-* 23.]

al-¹ Beyond. (Oldest form probably *h₂el-, colored to *h₂al-.) **1.** O-grade form *ol- (earlier *h₂ol-), "beyond." **a.** Compound forms *ol-se-, *ol-so- (*so-, pronominal stem; see **so-**). ALARM, ALERT, ALFRESCO, ALLIGATOR, EL NIÑO, HOOPLA, LAGNIAPPE, LANGUE D'OÏL, LARIAT, VOILÀ, from Latin *ille* (feminine *illa,* neuter *illud*), "yonder," that from Archaic Latin *ollus;* **b.** suffixed forms *ol-s, *ol-tero-. OUTRÉ, ULTERIOR, ULTIMATE, ULTRA-, UTTERANCE², from Latin *uls, *ulter, ultrā,* beyond. **2.** Suffixed form *al-tero-, "other of two." **a.** ALTER, ALTERCATE, ALTERITY, ALTERNATE, ALTRUISM; SUBALTERN, from Latin *alter,* other, other of two; **b.** ADULTERATE, ADULTERINE, ADULTERY, from Latin *adulterāre,* to commit adultery with, pollute, probably from the phrase *ad alterum,* "(approaching) another (unlawfully)" (*ad,* to; see **ad-**); **c.** variant suffixed form *an-tero-, "other (of two)." OTHER, from Old English *ōther,* from Germanic *anthara-.* **3.** Suffixed form *al-eno-. ARANYAKA, from Sanskrit *araṇa,* foreign. **4.** Extended form *alyo-, "other of more than two." **a.** (i) ELSE; ELDRITCH, from Old English *el-, elles,* else, otherwise, from Germanic *aljaz* (with adverbial suffix); (ii) ALSACE, ALSATIA, from Old High German *Ali-sāzzo, Eli-sāzzo,* "inhabitant of the other (bank of the Rhine)" (> Medieval Latin *Alisātia, Alsātia* > French *Alsace*), from Germanic *alja-, *ali-, other (Old High German *-sāzzo,* "one who sits," inhabitant; see **sed-¹**); **b.** ALIAS, ALIEN; ALIBI, ALIQUOT, HIDALGO, from Latin *alius,* other of more than two; **c.** ALLO-; ALLEGORY, ALLELOMORPH, ALLELOPATHY, MORPHALLAXIS, PARALLAX, PARALLEL, TROPHALLAXIS, from Greek *allos,* other. [Pokorny 1. *al-* 24, 2. *an* 37.]

al-² To wander. **1.** Compound *ambh(i)-al-ā- (see **ambhi-**). **2.** EXILE, from Latin *exsul, exul,* wanderer, exile (*ex-,* out; see **eghs-**). [Pokorny 3. *ǎl-* 27.]

al-³ To grow, nourish.
I. Suffixed (participial) form *al-to-, "grown." **1a.** ALDERMAN, OLD, from Old English *eald, ald,* old; **b.** ELDRED (personal name), from Old English *Ealdrēd,* "old in counsel" (*-rēd,* from *rēd,* counsel; see **rē-**); **c.** ELDER¹, from Old English (comparative) *ieldra, eldra,* older, elder; **d.** ELDEST, from Old English (superlative) *ieldesta, eldesta,* eldest; **e.** Germanic compound *wer-ald-,* "age of man" (see **wǐ-ro-**). **a–e** all from Germanic *alda-.* **2.** ALT, ALTO, HAUGHTY, HAWSER; ALTIMETER, ALTIPLANO, ALTITUDE, ALTOCUMULUS, ALTOSTRATUS,

ENHANCE, EXALT, HAUTBOY, from Latin *altus,* high ("grown tall"), deep.
II. Suffixed form *al-mo-. ALMA MATER, from Latin *almus,* nurturing, nourishing.
III. Suffixed form *al-o-. ADOLESCENT, ADULT, ALIBLE, ALIMENT, ALIMONY, ALTRICIAL, ALUMNUS; COALESCE, from Latin *alere,* to nourish, and *alumnus,* fostering, step-child, originally a participle of *alere* ("being nourished," < *al-o-mno-).
IV. Suffixed (causative) form *ol-eye-. ABOLISH, from Latin *abolēre,* to retard the growth of, abolish (*ab-,* from; see **apo-**).
V. Compound form *pro-al- (*pro-, forth; see **per¹**). PROLETARIAN, PROLIFEROUS, PROLIFIC, from Latin *prōlēs,* offspring.
VI. Extended form *aldh-. ALTHEA, from Greek *althein, althainein,* to get well. [Pokorny 2. *al-* 26.]

al-⁴ To grind, mill. Suffixed form *al-euro-. ALEURONE, from Greek *aleuron,* meal, flour. [Pokorny 5. *al-* 28.]

al-⁵ All. Germanic and Celtic root. **1.** Suffixed form *al-na-. **a.** ALL; ALBEIT, ALREADY, ALSO, ALTHOUGH, ALWAYS, AS, from Old English *all, eall, eal-, al-,* all; **b.** ALTHING, from Old Norse *allr,* all. Both **a** and **b** from Germanic *allaz.* **2.** Germanic *ala-,* all, in compound *Ala-manniz (see **man-¹**). [In Pokorny 1. *al-* 24.]

albho- White. **1.** Possibly Germanic *albiz, *albaz, elf, if meaning "white ghostly apparition." **a.** ELF, from Old English *ælf,* elf, also in such personal names as: (i) ALFRED, from Old English *Ælfrǣd,* "elf counsel" (*rǣd,* counsel; see **rē-**); (ii) OLIVER, from Old English *Ælfhere,* "elf army" (*here,* army; see **koro-**); **b.** OAF from Old Norse *alfr,* elf; **c.** ERL-KING, from Danish *elv,* elf; **d.** (i) AUBREY (personal name), from Old High German *Alberich* (> French *Auberi*), "ruler of elves" (*-rīh, -rich,* ruler; see **reg-¹**); (ii) OBERON, from Old French *Auberon,* from a source akin to Old High German *Alberich.* Both (i) and (ii) from Old High German *alb,* elf. **2.** ELFIN, from Old English *-elfen,* elf, possibly from Germanic *albinjō.* **3.** ABELE, ALB, ALBEDO, ALBESCENT, ALBINO, ALBITE, ALBUM, ALBUMEN, AUBADE, AUBURN; DAUB, from Latin *albus,* white. [Pokorny *albho-* 30.]

algʷh- To earn, be worth. Greek, Indo-Iranian, and Hittite root. (Oldest form *h₂elgʷh-, colored to *h₂al-gʷh-.) **1.** ARHAT, from Sanskrit *arhati,* he is worthy. **2.** ALPHEUS (river name), from Greek *Alpheus,* from *alphanein,* to yield a return. [Pokorny *algʷh-* 32.]

alu- In words related to sorcery, magic, possession, and intoxication. Perhaps related to **al-².** Suffixed form *alu-t-. ALE, from Old English *ealu,* from Germanic *aluth-.* [Pokorny *alu-* 33.]

am- Various nursery words. Latin and Celtic root. **1.** AMAH, from Medieval Latin *amma,* mother. **2.** Suffixed form *am-os-. AMORETTO, AMOUR; ENAMOR, PARAMOUR, from Latin *amor,* love. **3.** Suffixed form *am-ā-. AMATEUR, AMATIVE, AMATORY; INAMORATA, from Latin *amāre,* to love. **4.** AMICABLE, AMIGO, AMITY; ENEMY, INIMICAL, from Latin *amīcus,* friend. **5.** AUNT, from Latin *amita,* aunt. [In Pokorny *am(m)a* 36.]

ambhi- Also ṃbhi. Around. Probably derived from *ant-bhi, "from both sides" (see **ant-**). **1.** Reduced form *bhi. **a.** BY¹; ABAFT, BUT, from Old English *bi, bī, be,* by; **b.** BE-, from Old English *be-,* on all sides, be-, also intensive prefix; **c.** BELEAGUER, from Middle Dutch *bie,* by; **d.** BIVOUAC, from Old High German *bi,* by, at. **a–d** all from Germanic *bi, *bi- (intensive prefix). **2a.** EMBER DAY, from Old English *ymbe,* around; **b.** OMBUDSMAN, from Old Norse *um(b),* about, around; **c.** UMLAUT, from Old High German *umbi,* around. **a–c** all from Germanic *umbi.* **3a.** AMBI-, from Latin *ambi-,* around, about; **b.** ALLEY¹, ALLEY-OOP, AMBULANCE, AMBULATE, ANDANTE; FUNAMBULIST, PERAMBULATE, PREAMBLE, from Latin *ambulāre,* to go about, walk (*ambh(i)-al-ā-; *-al-, to wander, go; see **al-²**). **4.** AMPHI-, from Greek *amphi*, around, about. **5.** Celtic *ambi*, around, in compound *amb(i)-ag-to-* (see **ag-¹**). [Pokorny *ambhi* 34.]

ambhō Both. **1.** Reduced form *bhō. BOTH, from Old Norse *bādhir*, both (< *bai thaiz*, "both the"; *thaiz*, plural third person pronoun; see **to-**), from Germanic *bā. **2.** Full form *ambhō. **a.** AMBSACE, from Latin *ambō*, both; **b.** AMPHOTERIC, from Greek *amphō*, both. [In Pokorny *ambhi* 34.]

āmer- Day. Suffixed form *āmer-ā-. EPHEMERAL, HEMERALOPIA, HEMEROCALLIS, from Greek *hēmerā*, day. [Pokorny *āmer-* 35.]

ams- Black; blackbird (original color meaning found only in Hittite). (Oldest form *h₂ems-, colored to *h₂ams-, with variant [metathesized] form *h₂mes-.) **1.** Suffixed form *ams-ol-. OUZEL, from Old English *ōsle*, blackbird, from West Germanic *amslōn-. **2.** Form *(ə)mes-. Suffixed forms *mes-olā-, *mes-olo-. MERLE, MERLON, MERLOT, from Latin *merula, merulus*, merle, blackbird. [Pokorny *ames-* 35.]

an-¹ On.
  I. Extended form *ana. **1a.** ON; ACKNOWLEDGE, ALIKE, from Old English *an, on, a*, on, and prefixed *on-*; **b.** ALOFT, AMISS, from Old Norse *ā*, in, on; **c.** ANLAGE, ANSCHLUSS, from Old High German *ana-*, on; **d.** ONSLAUGHT, from Middle Dutch *aen*, on. **a–d** all from Germanic *ana, *anō. **2.** ANA², ANA-, from Greek *ana*, on, up, at the rate of.
  II. Variant form *no. NAPRAPATHY, from Old Church Slavonic *na*, in, on, to, from Slavic *na. [Pokorny 4. *an* 39.]

an-² Old woman, ancestor (nursery word). ANILE, from Latin *anus*, old woman. [Pokorny 1. *an-* 36.]

an-³ To pour, draw water. (Oldest form *h₂en-, colored to *h₂an-.) Suffixed form *an-tlo-. ANTLIA, from Greek *antlos*, bilge water, bucket. [In Pokorny 1. *sem-* 901.]

andh- Bloom. Suffixed form *andh-es-. ANTHEMION, ANTHER, ANTHESIS, ANTHO-; ACIDANTHERA, AGAPANTHUS, CHRYSANTHEMUM, DIANTHUS, EXANTHEMA, HYDRANTH, MONANTHOUS, STROPHANTHIN, from Greek *anthos*, flower. [Pokorny *andh-* 40.]

andho- Blind, dark. Perhaps suffixed o-grade form *ondh-ro-. UMBEL, UMBRA, UMBRELLA; ADUMBRATE, SOMBER, SOMBRERO, from Latin *umbra*, shadow. [Pokorny *andho-* 41.]

anə- To breathe. (Oldest form *h₂enh₁-, colored to *h₂anh₁-.) **1.** Suffixed form *anə-mo-. **a.** ANIMA, ANIMADVERT, ANIMAL, ANIMATE, ANIMATO, ANIMISM, ANIMOSITY, ANIMUS; EQUANIMITY, LONGANIMITY, MAGNANIMOUS, PUSILLANIMOUS, UNANIMOUS, from Latin *animus*, reason, mind, spirit, and *anima*, soul, spirit, life, breath; **b.** ANEMO-, ANEMONE, from Greek *anemos*, wind. **2.** Suffixed form *anə-tyo-. ENID (personal name), from Middle Welsh *eneit*, soul. [Pokorny 3. *an(ə)-* 38.]

anət- Duck. (Oldest form *h₂enə₂t-, colored to *h₂anh₂t-.) **1.** SOLAN, from Old Norse *önd*, duck, from Germanic *anud-. **2.** GOOSANDER, perhaps a compound of *goose* (see **ghans-**) + *–ander*, an element of uncertain origin but possibly akin to Old Norse *önd* and Old High German *anut*, duck. [Pokorny *anət-* 41.]

anətā- Doorjamb. ANTA, from Latin *antae* (plural), a pair of pillars on the opposite sides of a door. [Pokorny *anətā* 42.]

[angelos Messenger. Greek noun, possibly akin to Greek *angaros*, mounted courier, both from an unknown Oriental source. Sanskrit *ajira-*, swift, traditional epithet of *dūtah*, messenger, may be relevant. **1.** ANGEL, ANGELICA, ANGELUS; ARCHANGEL, EVANGEL, from Greek *angelos*, messenger. **2.** ANGARIA, ANGARY, from Greek *angaros*, mounted courier.**]**

angh- Tight, painfully constricted, painful. (Oldest form *angh-.) **1.** AGNAIL, HANGNAIL, from Old English *ang-nægl*, "painful spike (in the flesh)," corn, excrescence (*nægl*, spike; see **nogh-**), from Germanic *ang-*, compressed, hard, painful. **2.** Suffixed form *angh- os-. ANGER, from Old Norse *angr*, sorrow, grief, from Germanic *angaz. **3.** Suffixed form *angh-os-ti-. ANGST¹, from Old High German *angust*, anxiety, from Germanic *angusti-. **4.** ANXIOUS, from Latin *angere*, to strangle, torment. **5.** Suffixed form *angh-os-to-. ANGUISH, from Latin *angustus*, narrow. **6.** QUINSY, from Greek *ankhein*, to squeeze, embrace. **7.** ANGINA, from Greek *ankhonē*, a strangling. [Pokorny *anĝh-* 42.]

angʷhi- See **ogʷhi-**. [Pokorny *angʷ(h)i-* 43.]

ank- Also **ang-**. To bend. (Oldest forms *h₂enk-, *h₂eng-, colored to *h₂ank-, *h₂ang-.) **1.** Suffixed form *ank-ulo-. **a.** (i) ANGLE¹, from Old English *angel*, fishhook; (ii) ENGLAND, from Old English *Englaland*, "land of the Angles," from *Engle*, the Angles (< the shape of their original homeland, the Angul district of Schleswig; (iii) ANGLE, from Latin *Anglī*, the Angles. (i) and probably (ii) and (iii) from Germanic *ang-ul-; **b.** ANKYLOSIS; ANCYLOSTOMIASIS, from Greek *ankulos*, crooked, bent. **2.** ANCHOR, from Greek *ankurā*, anchor. **3.** ANCON, from Greek *ankōn*, elbow. **4.** Suffixed o-grade form *onk-o-. **a.** UNCINARIA, UNCINATE, UNCUS; UNCIFORM, from Latin *uncus*, hooked, bent; **b.** ONCIDIUM; ONCHOCERCIASIS, from Greek *onkos*, barb, hook. **5.** Variant form *ang-. **a.** ANKLE, from Old English *ancleow* and Old Norse *ankula*, ankle, both from Germanic *ankulaz; **b.** suffixed form *ang-olo-. ANGLE², from Latin *angulus*, angle, corner. [Pokorny 2. *ank-* 45.]

āno- Ring. **1.** ANUS; ANILINGUS, ANOSCOPE, from Latin *ānus*, ring, anus. **2.** ANNULAR, ANNULET, ANNULUS, from Latin diminutive *annulus*, ring, signet ring. **3.** AGNOLOTTI, from Latin diminutive *ānellus*, little ring, finger ring. [Pokorny *āno-* 47.]

ans- Loop, handle. ANSATE, from Latin *ānsa*, handle. [Pokorny *ansa* 48.]

ansu- Spirit. (Oldest form *h₂ensu- [colored to *h₂ansu-] or *h₂onsu-; probably a derivative of the verbal root *h₂ens-, to give birth.) **1a.** Old English *ōs*, god, in personal names: (i) OSCAR, from Old English *Ōsgār*, "god's spear" (*gār*, spear; see **ghaiso-**); (ii) OSWALD, from Old English *Ōsweald*, "god's power" (*weald*, power; see **wal-**); **b.** AESIR; ASGARD, from Old Norse *āss*, god; **c.** Old High German *ans-*, god, in personal name *Ansehelm* (see **kel-²**). **a–c** all from Germanic *ansu-. **2.** Suffixed zero-grade form *ṇsu-ro-. AHURA MAZDA, ORMAZD, from Avestan *ahura-*, spirit, lord, from Indo-Iranian *asuras. [Pokorny *ansu-* 48.]

ant- Front, forehead. (Oldest form *h₂ent-, colored to *h₂ant-.)
  I. Inflected form (locative singular) *anti, "against," with derivatives meaning "in front of," "before"; also "end." **1.** UN-²; ALONG, from Old English and-, indicating opposition, from Germanic *andi-* and *anda-*. **2.** END, from Old English *ende*, end, from Germanic *andjaz. **3.** ANCIENT¹, ANTE, ANTE-, ANTERIOR; ADVANCE, ADVANTAGE, VANGUARD, from Latin *ante*, before, in front of, against. **4.** ANTI-; ENANTIOMER, ENANTIOMORPH, from Greek *anti*, against, and *enantios*, opposite. **5.** Compound form *anti-əkʷo-, "appearing before, having prior aspect" (*əkʷ-, "appearing before, having prior aspect" (*əkʷ-; see **okʷ-**). ANTIC, ANTIQUE, from Latin *antīquus*, former, antique. **6.** Reduced form *ṇti-. **a.** UNTIL, from Old Norse *und*, until, unto; **b.** ELOPE, from Middle Dutch *ont-*, away from. Both **a** and **b** from Germanic *und-*. **7.** Variant form *anto-. VEDANTA, from Sanskrit *antah*, end.
  II. Probable inflected form (ablative plural) *ant-bhi, "from both sides," whence *ambhi, around. See **ambhi-**. [Pokorny *ant-s* 48.]

ap-¹ To take, reach. (Oldest form *h₂ep-, colored to *h₂ap-.) **1.** APT, APTITUDE, ARTILLERY, ATTITUDE; INEPT, from Latin *apere*, to attach, join, tie to. **2.** ADEPT, from Latin *apīscī*, to attain. **3.** APEX, from Latin *apex*, top, summit (< "something reached"). **4.** Prefixed form **ko-ap-* (**ko-*, together; see **kom**). CABALETTA, COPULA, COPULATE, COUPLE, from Latin *cōpula*, bond, tie, link. **5.** AMENT, from Latin *ammentum, āmentum*, thong, strap, perhaps < **ap-mentum*, "something tied." [Pokorny 1. *ap-* 50.]

ap-² Water. (Oldest form **h₂ep-*, colored to **h₂ap-*.) **1a.** JULEP, from Persian *āb*, water. **b.** PUNJAB, from Persian *Panjāb*, "five waters, (land of) five rivers" (*panj*, five; see **penkʷe**). Both **a** and **b** from Iranian **ap-*, water. **2.** Zero-grade **ap-*. DHIVEHI, from Sanskrit *dvípaḥ*, island, from earlier **dvi-ap-o-*, "having water on two sides" (**dvi-*, two; see **dwo-**). [Pokorny 2. *ắp-* 51.]

Language and Culture Note Proto-Indo-European sometimes had two words for the same thing, one of animate gender, and one of inanimate gender. For example, it had two words for "water," **ap-²** (animate) and **wod-ṛ* (inanimate; see **wed-¹**). The former is reflected for example in Sanskrit *āpaḥ*, "waters," and the latter in Hittite *wātar*, Greek *hudōr*, and English *water*. Proto-Indo-European also had two words for "fire," **egni-** (animate) and **paəwṛ** (inanimate). The former underlies Sanskrit *agníḥ* and Latin *ignis*, and the latter Hittite *paḥḥur*, Greek *pūr*, and English *fire*. It is believed that the neuter-gender terms referred to water or fire as a substance, while the animate (gendered) terms were used when water or fire was conceived of as an active, living force.

āpero- Shore. Perhaps a derivative of **ap-²**. Suffixed form **āper-yo-*. EPEIRIC SEA, EPEIROGENY, from Greek *ēpeiros*, land, mainland, continent. [Pokorny *āpero-* 53.]

apo- Also **ap-**. Off, away. **1a.** OF, OFF, OFFAL, from Old English *of, æf*, off; **b.** EBB, from Old English *ebba*, low tide; **c.** ABLAUT, from Old High German *aba*, off, away from; **d.** AFT; ABAFT, from Old English *æftan*, behind, from Germanic **aftan-*. **a–d** all from Germanic **af*. **2.** AB-¹, from Latin *ab-, ab-*, away from. **3.** APO-, from Greek *apo*, away from, from. **4.** Suffixed (comparative) form **ap(o)-tero-*. AFTER, from Old English *æfter*, after, behind, from Germanic **aftar-*. **5.** Suffixed form **ap-t-is-*. EFTSOONS, from English *eft*, again, from Germanic **aftiz*. **6.** Suffixed form **apu-ko-*. AWKWARD, from Old Norse *ǫfugr*, turned backward, from Germanic **afuga-*. **7.** Basic form **apo*. Iranian **apa*, back, away, after, in (comparative) **apara-*, back farther (see **dānu-**). **8.** Possible variant root form **po(s)*, on, in. **a.** POGROM, from Russian *po*, at, by, next to; **b.** POST, POSTERIOR; POSTMORTEM, PREPOSTEROUS, PUISNE, PUNY, from Latin *post*, behind, back, afterward; **c.** APPOSITE, APPOSITION, APROPOS, COMPONENT, COMPOSE, COMPOSITE, COMPOSITION, COMPOST, COMPOTE, COMPOUND¹, CONTRAPPOSTO, DEPONE, DEPOSIT, DISPOSE, EXPONENT, EXPOSE, EXPOUND, IMPONE, IMPOST¹, IMPOST², INTERPOSE, JUXTAPOSE, OPPOSE, POSITION, POSITIVE, POST², POST³, POSTICHE, POSTURE, PREPOSITION¹, PROPOSE, PROVOST, PUNT¹, REPOSIT, SUPPOSE, TRANSPOSE, from Latin *pōnere*, to put, place, from **po-s(i)nere* (*sinere*, to leave, let; of obscure origin). [Pokorny *apo-* 53.]

apsā- Aspen. ASPEN, from Old English *æspe*, aspen, from Germanic **aspōn-*. [Pokorny *apsā* 55.]

ar- To fit together. (Oldest form **h₁ar-*.) **1.** Suffixed form **ar-mo-*. **a.** ARM¹, from Old English *earm*, arm, from Germanic **armaz*; **b.** AMBRY, ARM², ARMADA, ARMADILLO, ARMATURE, ARMOIRE, ARMY; ALARM, DISARM, GENDARME, from Latin *arma*, tools, arms; **c.** ARMILLARY SPHERE, from Latin *armus*, upper arm. **2.** Suffixed form **ar-smo-*. HARMONY, from Greek *harmos*, joint, shoulder. **3.** Suffixed form **ar-ti-*. **a.** ART¹, ARTISAN, ARTIST; INERT, INERTIA, from Latin *ars* (stem *art-*), art, skill, craft; **b.** further suffixed form **ar-ti-o-*.

ARTIODACTYL, from Greek *artios*, fitting, even. **4.** Suffixed form **ar-tu-*. ARTICLE, from Latin *artus*, joint. **5.** Suffixed form **ar-to-*. COARCTATE, from Latin *artus*, tight. **6.** Suffixed form **ar-dhro-*. ARTHRO-; ANARTHROUS, DIARTHROSIS, DYSARTHRIA, ENARTHROSIS, SYN- ARTHROSIS, from Greek *arthron*, joint. **7.** Suffixed (superlative) form **ar-isto-*. ARISTOCRACY, from Greek *aristos*, best (< "most fitting"). [Pokorny 1. *ar-* 55.]

arə- To plow. (Oldest form **h₂erh₃-*, colored to **h₂arh₃-*.) ARABLE, from Latin *arāre*, to plow. [Pokorny *ar(ə)-* 62.]

arg- To shine; white; the shining or white metal, silver. (Oldest form **h₂(e)rǵ-*, colored to **h₂(a)rǵ-*.) **1.** Suffixed form **arg-ent-*. ARGENT, ARGENTINE, SELEGILINE, from Latin *argentum*, silver. **2.** Suffixed form **arg-i-l(l)-*. ARGIL, from Greek *argillos*, white clay. **3.** Suffixed form **arg-u-ro-*. LITHARGE, PYRARGYRITE, from Greek *arguros*, silver. **4.** Suffixed form **arg-i-n-*. ARGININE, from Greek *arginoeis*, brilliant, bright-shining. **5.** Suffixed form **arg-u-*, brilliant, clear. ARGUE, from Latin denominative *arguere*, to make clear, demonstrate (< **argu-yo-*). **6.** Further suffixed form **argu-no-*. ARJUNA, from Sanskrit *Arjunaḥ*, Arjuna, from *arjuna-*, white, silvery. **7.** Suffixed zero-grade form **ṛg-ro-*, becoming **arg-ro-*. AGRIMONY, possibly from Greek *argos*, white (< **argros*). [Pokorny *ar(e)-ǵ-* 64.]

ark- To hold, contain, guard. (Oldest form **h₂erk-*, colored to **h₂ark-*.) **1.** ARCANE, ARK, from Latin *arca*, chest, box. **2.** COERCE, EXERCISE, from Latin *arcēre*, to enclose, confine, contain, ward off. **3.** AUTARKY, from Greek *arkein*, to ward off, suffice. [Pokorny *areq-* 65.]

[arkhein To begin, rule, command. Greek verb of unknown origin, but showing archaic Indo-European features like alternation arkh- : o-grade orkh-, with derivatives *arkhē*, rule, beginning, and *arkhos*, ruler. ARCH-, -ARCH, ARCHAEO-, ARCHAIC, ARCHI-, ARCHIVE, ARCHON, -ARCHY; AUTARCHY, EXARCH, MENARCHE.]

arku- Bow and arrow (uncertain which, perhaps both as a unit). **1.** ARROW, from Old English *ar(e)we, earh*, and Old Norse **arw-*, arrow, from Germanic **arhwō*. **2.** ARC, ARCADE, ARCH¹, ARCHER; ARBALEST, ARCHIVOLT, ARCIFORM, ARCUATE, from Latin *arcus*, bow. [Pokorny *arqu-* 67.]

[aryo- Self-designation of the Indo-Iranians. Perhaps a derivative of **ar-**. **1.** ARYAN, from Sanskrit *ārya-*, compatriot. **2.** IRAN, from Middle Persian *Ērān (Šahr)*, (land) of the Iranians, genitive plural of *Ēr*, an Iranian, from Old Persian *āriya-*, compatriot. [Pokorny *arjo-* 67.]]

as- To burn, glow. (Oldest form **h₂es-*, colored to **h₂as-*.) **1.** Extended form **asg-*. **a.** ASH¹, from Old English *æsce, asce*, ash. **b.** POTASSIUM, from Old English *æsce, asce*, ash, from Middle Dutch *asche*, ash. Both **a** and **b** from Germanic **askōn-*, ash. **2.** Suffixed form **ās-ā-*. ARA, from Latin *āra*, altar, hearth. **3.** Suffixed (stative) form **ās-ē-*. **a.** ARID, from Latin *āridus*, dry, parched, from *ārēre*, to be dry; **b.** ARDENT, ARDOR, ARSON, from Latin *ārdēre*, to burn, be on fire, from *āridus*, parched. **c.** CARNE ASADA, from Latin *assus*, roasted, from **ārs(s)us*, a secondary past participle formation (as if **ārd-to-*) from *ārdēre*, to burn. **4.** Extended form **asd-*. **a.** ZAMIA, from Greek *azein*, to dry; **b.** AZALEA, from Greek *azaleos*, dry. [Pokorny *ās-* 68.]

[asinus Ass. Latin noun, akin to Greek *onos*, ass, probably ultimately from the same source as Sumerian *anše*, ass. **1.** ASININE, ASS¹, EASEL, from Latin *asinus*, ass. **2.** ONAGER, from Greek *onos*, ass.]

asp- To cut. (Oldest form **h₂esp-*, colored to **h₂asp-*.) **1.** Suffixed form **asp-ro-* or **asp-ero-*. ASPERATE, ASPERITY, DIAPER, EXASPERATE, from Latin *asper*, jagged, rough, harsh. **2.** Possibly suffixed form **aspid-* in Greek *aspis, aspid-*, shield (< "a cutting, a hide," shields originally being made of hide stretched over a frame), Egyptian cobra (< "snake with a shield-like hood"): ASP, ASPIDISTRA. [Not in Pokorny; compare Hittite *ḫasp-*, to cut.]

at- To go; with Germanic and Latin derivatives meaning a year (conceived as "the period gone through, the revolving year"). Suffixed form **at-no-*. ANNALS, ANNUAL, ANNUITY; ANNIVERSARY, BIENNIUM, DECENNIUM, MILLENNIUM, PERENNIAL, QUADRENNIUM, QUINCEAÑERA, QUINDECENNIAL, QUINQUENNIUM, SEPTENNIAL, SEXENNIAL, SUPERANNUATED, TRIENNIUM, VICENNIAL, from Latin *annus*, year. [Pokorny *at-* 69.]

at-al- Race, family. Compound root, probably related to Greek *atallein*, to foster, and to Tocharian A *ātāl*, man. Compounded from **at(i)-*, over, beyond, super-, and **al-³**, to nourish, but a separate word in Indo-European, perhaps "noble fosterling." **1.** ATHELING, from Old English *ætheling*, prince. **2a.** AUDREY (personal name); TAWDRY, from Old English *æthelthrȳth*, "noble might" (*thrȳth*, might); **b.** ETHELRED (personal name), from Old English *æthelrēd*, "noble counsel" (*rēd*, counsel; see **rē-**). Both **a** and **b** from Old English *æthele*, noble. **3.** EDELWEISS, from Old High German *edili*, noble, from Germanic suffixed form **ath(a)l-ja-*. **4.** Old High German *adal*, (noble) lineage, in personal names: **a.** ADELAIDE, ALICE, from Old High German *Adalhaid* (> Old French *Aliz*) "nobility" (*-heit, -haid, -hood*; see **(s)kai-¹**); **b.** ADOLPH, from Old High German *Athalwolf, Adulf*, "noble wolf" (*wolf*, wolf; see **wḷkʷo-**). **1–4** all from Germanic **athala-*. [In Pokorny *ātos* 71.]

āter- Fire. **1.** Suffixed zero-grade form **ātr-o-*. ATRABILIOUS, from Latin *āter* (feminine *ātra*), black (< "blackened by fire"). **2.** Suffixed zero-grade form **ātr-yo-*. ATRIUM, from Latin *ātrium*, forecourt, hall, atrium (perhaps originally the place where the smoke from the hearth escaped through a hole in the roof). **3.** Compound *shortened* zero-grade form **atro-əkʷ-*, "black-looking" (**əkʷ-*, "looking"; see **okʷ-**). ATROCIOUS, from Latin *ātrōx*, frightful. **4.** Basic form **āter*. ZIRCON, from Old Persian **ātar*, fire (stem *āç-* attested in month name *Āçiyādiya*, "(month) of fire-worship"), from Indo-Iranian **ātar*. **5.** Possibly, but obscurely related to this root is Sanskrit *atharvā, atharvan-*, priest (*-van-*, possessive suffix): ATHARVA-VEDA. [Pokorny *āt(e)r-* 69.]

atto- Father (nursery word). Possibly Latin *atta*, father: ATAVISM. [In Pokorny *ātos* 71.]

au-¹ Pronominal base appearing in particles and adverbs. **1.** Suffixed form **au-ge* possibly in Germanic **auke* (but this is perhaps better referred to as **aug-¹**). EKE², from Old English *ēac, ēc*, also. **2.** Suffixed form **au-ti*. OSSIA, from Latin *aut*, or. [Pokorny 4. *au-* 73.]

au-² Off, away. **1.** UKASE, from Russian *ukazat'*, to indicate, give orders, from Old Russian *u-*, away. **2.** AVATAR, from Sanskrit *ava*, off, down. **3.** Suffixed form **au-tyo-*. **a.** OTIOSE, from Latin *ōtium*, spare time, leisure (< "absence of work, being off"), from earlier **autium*, with *ō-* for *au-* influenced by *negōtium*, business (see below). **b.** NEGOTIATE, from Latin *negōtium*, business, from earlier **neg-autium* ("no absence of work"; *neg-*, not; see **ne**), from **autium* (see above). **4.** Perhaps Latin *autumnus*, autumn (see **temə-**). [Pokorny 3. *au-* 72.]

au-³ To weave. (Oldest form **h₂eu-*, colored to **h₂au-*.) Extended form **wedh-* (< earlier **h₂wedh-*). **1.** WEED², from Old English *wēd*, *wēde*, garment, cloth, from Germanic **wēdō*. **2.** WATTLE, from Old English *watel, watul*, wattle, from Germanic **wadlaz*. [Pokorny 5. *au-* 75.]

au-⁴ To perceive. (Oldest form **h₂au-*.) Compound forms **au-dh-*, **awis-dh-*, "to place perception" (**dh-*, to place; see **dhē-**). **1.** Suffixed form **awisdh-yo-* or **audh-yo-*. AUDIBLE, AUDIENCE, AUDILE, AUDIO-, AU-

DIT, AUDITION, AUDITOR, AUDITORIUM, AUDITORY, OYEZ; OBEY, SUBAUDITION, from Latin *audīre*, to hear. **2.** AESTHETIC; ANESTHESIA, from Greek *aisthanesthai*, to feel. [Pokorny 8. *au-* 78.]

aug-¹ To increase. (Oldest form **h₂eug-*, colored to **h₂aug-*, with variant [metathesized] form **h₂weg-*.) **1.** EKE¹, from Old English *ēacan, ēcan*, to increase; **b.** NICKNAME, from Old English *ēaca*, an addition. Both **a** and **b** from Germanic **aukan*; **c.** possibly Germanic imperative **auke*, "increase, add," perhaps the source of the particle **auke*, also (but this is usually referred to **au-¹**). **2.** Variant form **(ə)weg-*, extended to **wegs-* (o-grade **wogs-*). **a.** WAX²; WOODWAXEN, from Old English *weaxan*, to grow, from Germanic **wahsan*; **b.** WAIST, from Old English *wæst*, growth, hence perhaps waist, size, from Germanic **wahs-tu-*. **3.** Form **aug-ē-*. AUCTION, AUGEND, AUGMENT, AUTHOR, AUTHORIZE, from Latin *augēre*, to increase. **4.** AUGUR; INAUGURATE, from Latin *augur*, diviner (< "he who obtains favorable presage" < "divine favor, increase"). **5.** AUGUST, from Latin *augustus*, majestic, august. **6.** Suffixed form **aug-s-*. **a.** AUXILIARY, from Latin *auxilium*, aid, support, assistance; **b.** AUXIN, AUXESIS, from Greek *auxein, auxanein*, to increase. [Pokorny *aueg-* 84.]

aug-² To shine. Suffixed form **aug-ā-*. AUGITE, from Greek *augē*, light, ray. [Pokorny *aug-* 87.]

aukʷ- Cooking pot. **1.** OVEN, from Old English *ofen*, furnace, oven, from Germanic **ufna-*, from Germanic suffixed form **uhw-na-*. **2.** Suffixed form **aukʷ-slā-*. OLLA, from Latin *aulla, olla*, olla, pot, jar. [Pokorny *auqʷ(h)-* 88.]

aulo- Hole, cavity. **1.** Variant (metathesized) form **alwo-*. ALVEOLUS, from Latin *alvus*, belly, stomach. **2.** Basic form **aulo-*. CAROL, HYDRAULIC, from Greek *aulos*, pipe, flute, hollow tube. [Pokorny *au-lo-s* 88.]

aus-¹ To shine (said especially of the dawn). (Oldest form **h₁aus-* or [less likely] **h₂eus-* [colored to **h₂aus-*]; perhaps an extension of **au-⁴**.) **1a.** EAST, from Old English *ēast*, east (< "the direction of the sunrise"); **b.** OSTMARK, from Old High German *ōstan*, east. Both **a** and **b** from Germanic **aust-*. **2a.** EASTERN, from Old English *ēasterne*, eastern; **b.** AUSTRIA, from German *Österreich* (> New Latin *Austria*), "eastern kingdom," from Old High German *ōstar*, eastern; **c.** OSTROGOTH, from Late Latin *ostro-*, eastern. **a–c** all from Germanic **austra-*. **3.** EASTER, from Old English *ēastre*, Easter, from Germanic **austrōn-*, dawn. **4.** Possibly in Latin *auster*, the south wind, formally identical to the Germanic forms in **2** and **3**, but the semantics are unclear: AUSTRAL, AUSTRO-¹. **5.** Probably suffixed form **ausōs-*, dawn, also Indo-European goddess of the dawn. **a.** AURORA, from Latin *aurōra*, dawn; **b.** EO-, EOS; EOSIN, from Greek *ēōs* (< **āwōs* < **ausōs*), dawn. [Pokorny *aues-* 86.]

aus-² Gold. Root found in Latin, Baltic, Tocharian, and possibly Armenian. Connection with **aus-¹** likely. Suffixed form **aus-o-*. AUREATE, AUREOLE, AURIC; AURIFEROUS, DARIOLE, DORY², EYRIR, MOIDORE, OR³, ÖRE, ORIFLAMME, ORIOLE, ORMOLU, OROIDE, ORPHREY, ORPIMENT, from Latin *aurum*, gold. [In Pokorny *aues-* 86.]

aus-³ To draw water. (Oldest form **h₂eus-*, colored to **h₂aus-*.) Suffixed form **aus-yo-*. HAUSTELLUM, HAUSTORIUM; EXHAUST, from Latin *haurīre*, to draw up. [Pokorny *aus-* 90.]

aus-⁴ Ear. (Oldest forms **h₂eus-*, colored to **h₂aus-*, and o-grade **h₂ous-*.) **1.** Suffixed o-grade form **ous-en-*. EAR¹, from Old English *ēare*, ear, from Germanic **auzōn-*. **2.** Suffixed form **aus-i-*. AURAL¹, AURICLE, AURIFORM, ORCHIL, ORMER, from Latin *auris*, ear. **3.** AUSCULTATION, SCOUT¹, from Latin *auscultāre*, to listen to (< **aus-klit-ā-*; **aus-* + **kli-to-*, inclined; see **okʷ-**). **4.** Oldest form **h₂us-* developing in Greek as **aus-*, altered to **ous-*, after **okʷ-*, eye. **a.** Suffixed form *ous-os (appearing as Greek nominative and accusative singular form ous, ear), with further suffixed form *ous-s-ṇt (with zero-grade of the suffix *-os-), simplified to *ous-ṇt, becoming *ōat-, contracted in Greek to ōt-, stem of ous. OTIC, OTO-; MYOSOTIS, PAROTID GLAND, from Greek ous (stem ōt-), ear. **5.** Basic form *ous- in Greek compound *lag-ous- (see **slēg-**), whence, with accented possessive suffix -o-, *lag-ō-o-, "having floppy ears," becoming Greek lagōs, lagos, hare. [Pokorny 2. ōus- 785.]

awi- Bird. (Oldest form *h₂ewi-, colored to *h₂awi-.)
I. 1. AVIAN, AVIARY, AVIATION; AVICULTURE, AVIFAUNA, BUSTARD, OCARINA, OSPREY, OSTRICH, from Latin avis, bird. **2.** Compound *awi-spek-, "observer of birds" (*spek-, to see; see **spek-**). AUSPICE, from Latin auspex, augur.
II. A possible derivative is the Indo-European word for egg, *ōwyo-, *ōyyo- (< suffixed lengthened o-grade form *h₂ōw-yo-). **1a.** COCKNEY, from Old English æg, egg; **b.** EGG¹, from Old Norse egg, egg. Both **a** and **b** from Germanic *ajja(m). **2.** OVAL, OVARY, OVATE, OVI-, OVOLO, OVULE, OVUM, from Latin ōvum, egg. **3.** OO-; AVGOLEMONO, from Greek ōion, egg. **4.** CAVIAR, from a source akin to Middle Persian khāyak, egg, from Old Iranian *āvyaka-, diminutive of *āvya-, egg. [Pokorny aṷei- 86, ō(ṷ)i̯-om 783.]

awo- An adult male relative other than one's father. **1.** ATAVISM, from Latin avus, grandfather. **2.** AVUNCULAR, UNCLE, from Latin avunculus, maternal uncle. **3.** AYAH, from Latin avia, grandmother. [Pokorny aṷo-s 89.]

ayer- Day, morning. **1a.** EARLY, ERE, OR², from Old English ær, before; **b.** OR², from Old Norse ār, before. Both **a** and **b** from Germanic *airiz. **2.** ERST, from Old English ǣrest, earliest, from Germanic (superlative) *airista-. [Pokorny ā̆i̯er- 12.]

ayes- A metal, copper or bronze. **1.** AENEOUS, ERA, from Latin aes, bronze, money. **2.** ESTIMATE, from Latin aestimāre, to estimate, perhaps from a denominative verb from a pre-Latin compound *ais-tomos, "one who cuts the bronze," in reference to the pieces cut from metal ingots used as payment (*tomos, a cutting; see **tem-**). [Pokorny ai̯os- 15.]

badyo- Yellow, brown. A western Indo-European word. BAY³, from Latin badius, chestnut-brown (used only of horses). [Pokorny badi̯os 92.]

bak- Staff used for support. **1.** Probably Middle Dutch pegge (> Middle English pegge), pin, peg: PEG. **2.** BACILLUS, BACULUM, BAGUETTE, BAIL⁴, BAILEY, BACULIFORM, DEBACLE, IMBECILE, from Latin baculum, rod, walking stick. **3.** BACTERIUM; CORYNEBACTERIUM, from Greek baktron, staff. [Pokorny bak- 93.]

band- A drop. Possibly Irish bainne, milk: BONNYCLABBER. [Pokorny band- 95.]

[bassus Low. Late Latin adjective (> Medieval Latin bassus, Old French bas, and Middle English bas), possibly from Oscan. BASE², BASS², BASSO; ABASE, BAS-RELIEF, BASSET HORN, BASSET HOUND, DEBASE.**]**

[bat- Yawning. Latin root of unknown origin; probably imitative. **1a.** BAY², BEVEL; ABASH, ABEYANCE, from Old French ba(y)er, to yawn, gape; **b.** BADINAGE, from Provençal badar, to yawn. Both **a** and **b** from Latin *batāre, to yawn, gape. **2.** BAY⁴, from Old French (a)baiier, to bay, from Vulgar Latin *abbaiāre, possibly from Latin *batāre.**]**

bel- Strong. **1.** Suffixed o-grade form *bol-iyo-. BOLSHEVIK, from Russian bol'shoĭ, large. **2.** Prefixed form *dē-bel-i-, "without strength" (dē-, privative prefix; see **de-**). DEBILITATE, DEBILITY, from Latin dēbilis, weak. [Pokorny 2. bel- 96.]

bend- Protruding point. Possible root, found only Celtic and Germanic. **1.** PEN², from Old English penn, pen for cattle, from Germanic *pannja-, "structure of stakes." **2.** POND, POUND³; IMPOUND, PINFOLD, from Old English pund- (> Middle English pound) in pund-

fald, enclosure for stray animals, possibly from Germanic *pund-. **3.** PINTLE, from Old English pintel, penis, from Germanic *pin-. [Pokorny bend- 96.]

beu- Also **bheu-.** Probably imitative root, appearing in words loosely associated with the notion "to swell."
I. Basic form *beu-. **1a.** POCK, from Old English pocc, pustule; **b.** POACH¹, POCKET, POKE³, POUCH, PUCKER, from Old French po(u)che and Old North French poke, bag. Both **a** and **b** from Germanic *puk-. **2.** PUFF, from Old English pyffan, to blow out. **3.** POUT², from Old English -pūte, "fish with large head" (in æle-pūte, eelpout). **4a.** BILL¹, BILLET¹, BOLA, BOULE², BOWL², BULL², BULLA, BULLATE, BULLET, BULLETIN; BOULEVERSEMENT, from Latin bulla, bubble, round object, amulet (> Old French boule and Spanish bola, ball); **b.** BOIL¹, BOUILLON, BUDGE¹, BULLION, BULLY²; BOUILLABAISSE, EBULLIENCE, GARBOIL, PARBOIL, from Latin denominative verb bullīre, to bubble, boil (> French bouiller). **5.** Possibly Latin bucca, cheek (> Old French boucle, buckle, curl, and Spanish boca, mouth): BOCACCIO, BOUCLÉ, BUCCAL, BUCKLE¹, BUCKLE²; AMUSE-BOUCHE, DEBOUCH, DISEMBOGUE, EMBOUCHURE. **6.** BUBO, from Greek boubōn, groin, swollen gland.
II. Variant form *bheu- with various Germanic derivatives. **1.** BUCKBOARD, from Old English būc, belly, pitcher, from Germanic *būkaz, belly. **2.** TREBUCHET, from Frankish *būk (> Old French buc), trunk of the body. **3.** BOIL², from Old English bȳl(e), pustule, from West Germanic *būljō(n-). **4.** BOAST¹, from Middle English bost, a bragging, from a source akin to German dialectal baustern, to swell. [Pokorny 2. b(e)u- 98.]

bhā-¹ To shine. (Oldest form *bheh₂-, colored to *bhah₂-, contracted to *bhā-.) **1.** Suffixed zero-grade form *bhǝ-w-. **a.** BEACON, from Old English bēac(e)n, beacon; **b.** BECKON, from Old English bēcnan, biecnan, to make a sign, beckon, from Germanic denominative *bauknjan; **c.** BUOY, from Old French boue, buoy. **a–c** all from Germanic *baukna-, beacon, signal. **2.** Perhaps Germanic *basjam, *bazjam, berry (< "bright-colored fruit"). **a.** BERRY, MULBERRY, from Old English berie, berige, berry, and Old High German beri, berry, from Germanic *bazjōn-, remade from *baz- jam; **b.** FRAMBESIA, from Old French framboise, raspberry, alteration of Frankish *brām-besi, "bramble berry," from Germanic *basjam. **3a.** BANDOLEER, from Spanish banda, sash; **b.** BANDERILLA, BANDEROLE, BANNER, BANNERET¹, BANNERET², from Late Latin bandum, banner, standard. Both **a** and **b** from Germanic *bandwa-, "identifying sign," banner, standard, sash, also "company united under a (particular) banner." **4.** Suffixed zero-grade form *bhǝ-w-es-. PHOS-, PHOT, PHOTO-; PHOSPHORUS, from Greek phōs (stem phōt-), light. **5.** Suffixed zero-grade form *bhǝ-w-. PHAËTHON, from Greek phaeithein, to shine, burn. **6.** Extended and suffixed zero-grade form *bhǝn-yo-. FANTASY, PANT, -PHANE, PHANTASM, PHANTOM, PHASE, PHENO-, PHENOMENON; DIAPHANOUS, EMPHASIS, EPIPHANY, HIEROPHANT, PHANERITIC, PHANEROGAM, PHANEROZOIC, PHANTASMAGORIA, PHOSPHENE, SYCOPHANT, THEOPHANY, TIFFANY, from Greek phainein, "to bring to light," cause to appear, show, and phainesthai (passive), "to be brought to light," appear, with zero-grade noun phasis (*bhǝ-ti-), an appearance. [Pokorny 1. bhā- 104.]

bhā-² To speak. (Oldest form *bheh₂-, colored to *bhah₂-, contracted to *bhā-.) **1.** FABLE, FABLIAU, FABULOUS, FADO, FAIRY, FANDANGO, FATE, FAY²; AFFABLE, FANTOCCINI, INEFFABLE, INFANT, INFANTRY, PREFACE, from Latin fārī, to speak. **2.** -PHASIA; APOPHASIS, PROPHET, from Greek phanai, to speak. **3a.** BAN¹, from Old English bannan, to summon, proclaim, and Old Norse banna, to prohibit, curse; **b.** BANAL, BANNS; ABANDON, from Old French ban, feudal jurisdiction, summons to military service, proclamation, Old French bandon, power, and Old English gebann, proclamation; **c.** BANISH, from Old French *banir*, to banish; **d.** CONTRABAND, from Late Latin *bannus*, *bannum*, proclamation; **e.** BANDIT, from Italian *bandire*, to muster, band together (< "to have been summoned"). **a–e** all from Germanic suffixed form **banwan*, **bannan*, to speak publicly (used of particular kinds of proclamation in feudal or prefeudal custom; "to proclaim under penalty, summon to the levy, declare outlaw"). **4.** Suffixed form **bhā-ni-*. **a.** BOON[1], from Old Norse *bōn*, prayer, request; **b.** BEE[1], perhaps from Old English *bēn*, prayer, from a Scandinavian source akin to Old Norse *bōn*, prayer. Both **a** and **b** from Germanic **bōni-*. **5.** Suffixed form **bhā-mā-*. **a.** FAME, FAMOUS; DEFAME, INFAMOUS, from Latin *fāma*, talk, reputation, fame; **b.** EUPHEMISM, POLYPHEMUS, from Greek *phēmē*, saying, speech. **6.** Suffixed o-grade form **bhō-nā-*. PHONE[2], -PHONE, PHONEME, PHONETIC, PHONO-, -PHONY; ANTHEM, ANTIPHON, APHONIA, CACOPHONOUS, EUPHONY, SYMPHONY, from Greek *phōnē*, voice, sound, and (denominative) *phōnein*, to speak. **7.** Suffixed zero-grade form **bha-to-*. CONFESS, PROFESS, from Latin *fatērī*, to acknowledge, admit. **8.** BLAME, BLASPHEME, from Greek *blasphēmos*, blasphemous, perhaps from **mḷs-bhā-mo-*, "speaking evil" (**mḷs-*, evil; see **mel-⁵**). [Pokorny 2. *bhā-* 105.]

bha-bhā- Broad bean. **1.** FAVA BEAN, FAVELA, from Latin *faba*, broad bean. **2.** Variant form **bha-un-*. BEAN, from Old English *bēan*, broad bean, bean of any kind, from Germanic **baunō*. **3.** Possible suffixed form **bha-ko-*. PHACOEMULSIFICATION, from Greek *phakos*, lentil. **4.** Variant form **bha-bho-*. BUPKIS, from a Slavic source such as Polish *bób*; akin to Russian *bob*, bean, both from Slavic **bobŭ*. [Pokorny *bhabhā* 106.]

bhad- Good. **1.** BETTER, from Old English *betera*, better, from Germanic (comparative) **batizō*. **2.** BEST, from Old English *bet(e)st*, best, from Germanic (superlative) **batista-*. **3.** BOOT[2], from Old English *bōt*, remedy, aid, from Germanic **bōtō*. **4.** BATTEN[1], ultimately from Old Norse *batna*, to improve, from Germanic **batnan*, to become better. [Pokorny *bhăd-* 106.]

bhag- To share out, apportion, also to get a share. **1.** -PHAGE, -PHAGIA, PHAGO-, -PHAGOUS; ESOPHAGUS, from Greek *phagein*, to eat (< "to have a share of food"). **2.** PORGY, from Greek *phagros*, whetstone ("eater, that eats metal"), also a name for the sea bream, from Greek suffixed form **phag-ro-*. **3a.** Slavic **bogŭ*, god, in Czech *boh*, god, in personal name *Bohuslav* (see **kleu-**); **b.** NEBBISH, from a Slavic source akin to Czech *neboh*, poor, unfortunate, from Common Slavic **ne-bogŭ*, poor ("un-endowed"). **4.** PAGODA; BHAGAVAD-GITA, from Sanskrit *bhagaḥ*, good fortune. **5.** BHAKTI, from Sanskrit *bhajati*, he apportions. **6.** Extended form **bhags-*. BAKSHEESH, BUCKSHEE, from Persian *bakhshīdan*, to give, from Old Iranian **bakhsh* (Avestan *bakhsh-*). [Pokorny 1. *bhag-* 107.]

bhāghu- Arm. (Oldest form **bhāĝhu-*.) BOUGH, from Old English *bōg*, *bōh*, bough, from Germanic **bōguz*. [Pokorny *bhāghú-s* (misprint for *bhāĝhú-s*) 108.]

bhāgo- Beech tree. **1a.** BOOK, from Old English *bōc*, written document, composition; **b.** BUCKWHEAT, from Middle Dutch *boek*, beech; **c.** BOKMÅL, from Norwegian *bok*, book. **a–c** all from Germanic **bōkō*, beech, also "beech staff for carving runes on" (an early Germanic writing device). **2.** BEECH, from Old English *bēce*, beech, from Germanic **bōkjōn-*. [Pokorny *bhāgó-s* 107.]

bhardh-ā- Beard. **1.** BEARD, from Old English *beard*, beard, from Germanic **bardaz*. **2.** HALBERD, from Old High German *barta*, beard, ax, from Germanic **bardō*, beard, also hatchet, broadax. **3.** BARB[1], BARBEL[1], BARBELLATE, BARBER, BARBETTE, BARBICEL, BARBULE, BARBUT, BICHON; REBARBATIVE, from Latin *barba*, beard. [Pokorny *bhardhā* 110.]

bhars-¹ Also **bhors-**. Projection, bristle, point. **I.** Suffixed o-grade form **bhors-o-*. BASS[1], from Old English *bærs*, perch, bass (a fish that has a spiny dorsal fin), from Germanic **barsaz*. **II.** Zero-grade form **bhṛs-*. **1.** BUR[1], from Middle English *burre*, bur, from a Scandinavian source akin to Swedish *borre*, bur, from Germanic **burz-*. **2.** Suffixed from **bhṛs-dh-*. BRAD, from Old Norse *broddr*, spike, from Germanic **bruzdaz*, point, needle. **3.** Suffixed zero-grade form **bhṛs-ti-*. **a.** BRISTLE, from Old English *byrst* (> Middle English *bristel*), bristle, from Germanic **bursti-*; **b.** FASTIGIATE, FASTIGIUM, from Latin *fastīgium*, summit, top, extremity. **4.** Possibly suffixed form **bhṛs-tu-*. FASTIDIOUS, from Latin *fastus*, *fastidium*, disdain (from the notion of prickliness). **5.** Suffixed form **bhṛs-tio-*. BORSCHT, from Russian *borshch*, cow parsnip (from its sharp leaves). [Pokorny *bhar-* 108.]

bhars-² Barley. Probably from **bhars-¹**, from its appearance. **1a.** BARN, from Old English *bere*, barley, from Germanic **bariz-*; **b.** BARLEY, from Old English *bærlic*, barley-like, of barley, from Germanic **barz-*. **2.** FARINA, FARINACEOUS, FARRAGINOUS, FARRAGO, FARRO, from Latin *far* (stem *farr-*), emmer. [Pokorny *bhares-* 111.]

bhasko- Band, bundle. **1.** FASCES, FASCICLE, FASCINE, FASCISM, from Latin *fascis*, bundle (as of rods, twigs, or straw), also crowd of people. **2.** FAJITA, FASCIA, FESS[1], from Latin *fascia*, band, bandage. **3.** Possibly Latin *fascinum*, *fascinus*, an amulet in the shape of a phallus, hence a bewitching: FASCINATE. [Pokorny *bhasko-* 111.]

bhau- To strike. (Oldest form **bheh₂u-*, colored to **bhah₂u-*, contracted to **bhau-*, with variant [me- tathesized] form **bheuh₂-*, whence zero-grade **bhuh₂-*, contracted to **bhū-*.) **I.** Germanic extended form **baut-*. **1.** BEAT, from Old English *bēatan*, to beat, from Germanic **bautan*. **2.** BEETLE[3]; BATTLEDORE, from Old English *bȳtl*, hammer, mallet, from Germanic **bautilaz*, hammer. **3.** BASTE[3], probably from a Scandinavian source akin to Old Norse *beysta*, to beat, denominative from Germanic **baut-sti-*. **4.** BUTTOCK, from Old English diminutive *buttuc*, end, strip of land, from Germanic **būtaz*. **5a.** HALIBUT, from Middle Dutch *butte*, flatfish; **b.** TURBOT, from a Scandinavian source akin to Old Swedish *but*, flatfish. Both **a** and **b** from Germanic **butt-*, name for a flatfish. **6.** BOUTON, BUTT[1], BUTTON, BUTTRESS; ABUT, REBUT, SACKBUT, from Old French *bo(u)ter*, to strike, push, from Germanic **buttan*. **II.** Zero-grade variant form **bhū-*. **1.** Suffixed form **bhū-t-ā-*. **a.** CONFUTE, from Latin *cōnfūtāre*, to check, suppress, restrain (*com-*, intensive prefix; see **kom**); **b.** REFUTE, from Latin *refūtāre*, to drive back, rebut (*re-*, back; see **re-**). **2.** Possibly reduced suffixed form **bhu-tu-* (**bhəu-*). FOOTLE; CLAFOUTI, from Latin *futuere*, to have intercourse with (a woman). [Pokorny 1. *bhău-* 112.]

bhē- To warm. (Contracted from earlier **bheh₁-*.) **1.** Suffixed zero-grade form **bha-to-*. BATH[1], BATHE, from Old English *bæth*, bath, and its denominative *bathian*, to bathe. **2.** Extended zero-grade form **bhəg-*. **a.** BAKE, from Old English *bacan*, to bake; **b.** ZWIEBACK, from Old High German *bakan*, *bakkan*, to bake. Both **a** and **b** from Germanic **bakan*, to bake. [Pokorny *bhē-* 113.]

bhedh- To dig. O-grade form **bhodh-*. **1.** BED, from Old English *bed(d)*, bed, from Germanic **badjam*, garden plot, also sleeping place. **2.** FOSSA, FOSSE, FOSSIL, FOSSORIAL, from Latin *fodere*, to dig. [Pokorny 1. *bhedh-* 113.]

bheg- To break. Possibly in various Germanic forms. Akin to **bhreg-**. **1a.** BANG[1], probably from a Scandinavian source akin to Old Norse *banga*, to hammer;

b. BUNGLE, possibly from a Scandinavian source akin to Swedish dialectal *bangla*, to work inefficiently. Both **a** and **b** from Germanic nasalized form **bang-*. **2a.** BENCH, from Old English *benc*, bench; **b.** BANK¹, from a Scandinavian source akin to Old Danish *banke*, sandbank; **c.** BANK², BANTLING, BUNCO; BANKRUPT, from Old High German *banc*, *bank*, bench, money-changer's table (> Italian *banca*); **d.** BANK³, from Old French *banc*, bench; **e.** BANQUETTE, from Provençal *banca*, bench; **f.** BANQUET, from Old Italian *banco*, bench. **a–f** all from Germanic nasalized forms **bankiz* and **bankōn-*, bank of earth (possibly < "feature where the contour of the ground is broken," escarpment, riverbank, possibly also associated with "manmade earthwork"), later also bench, table. **3.** BHANG, from Sanskrit *bhaṅgaḥ*, ("pounded") hemp, seen by some as the same word as *bhaṅga-*, breaking, pounding, from nasalized form **bheng-*. [Pokorny *bheg* 114.]

bheg^w- To run. **1.** O-grade form **bhog^w-*. BECK², from Old Norse *bekkr*, a stream, from Germanic **bak-jaz*, a stream. **2.** -PHOBE, -PHOBIA, from Greek *phebesthai*, to fear, and derived o-grade noun *phobos*, fear. [Pokorny *bhegu-* 116.]

bhei- A bee. From Old English *bēo*, a bee, from Germanic suffixed form **bīōn-*. [Pokorny *bhei-* 116.]

bheid- To split; with Germanic derivatives referring to biting (hence also to eating and to hunting) and woodworking. **1a.** BEETLE¹, BITE, from Old English *bītan*, to bite; **b.** TSIMMES, from Old High German *bizan*, *bizzan*, to bite. Both **a** and **b** from Germanic **bītan*. **2.** Zero-grade form **bhid-*. **a.** BIT², from Old English *bite*, a bite, sting, from Germanic **bitiz*; **b.** *(i)* BIT¹, from Old English *bita*, a piece bitten off, morsel; *(ii)* BITT, from a Germanic source akin to Old Norse *biti*, bit, crossbeam; *(iii)* PIZZA, from Italian *pizza*, pizza, from a Germanic source akin to Old High German *bizzo*, *pizzo*, bite, morsel. *(i)-(iii)* all from Germanic **bitōn-*; **c.** suffixed form **bhid-ro-*. BITTER, from Old English *bit(t)er*, "biting," sharp, bitter. **3.** O-grade form **bhoid-*. **a.** BAIT¹, from Old Norse *beita* (verb), to hunt with dogs, and *beita* (noun), pasture, food; **b.** ABET, from Old French *beter*, to harass with dogs. Both **a** and **b** from Germanic **baitjan*. **4.** BATEAU, BOAT; BOATSWAIN, from Old English *bāt*, boat, from Germanic **bait-*, a boat (< "dugout canoe" or "split planking"). **5.** GIBLETS, from Old French *gibiez*, hunting, game, from Germanic **ga-baiti-* (**ga-*, collective prefix; see **kom**). **6.** Nasalized zero-grade form **bhi-n-d-*. -FID, FISSI-, FISSILE, FISSION, FISSURE, VENT², from Latin *findere*, to split (past participle *fissus* < suffixed zero-grade form **bhid-to-*). [Pokorny *bheid-* 116.]

bheidh- To trust. **1.** Probably Germanic **bīdan*, to await (< "to await trustingly, expect, trust"). ABIDE, ABODE, from Old English *bīdan*, to wait, stay. **2.** FIANCÉ, FIDUCIAL, FIDUCIARY; AFFIANCE, AFFIANT, AFFIDAVIT, CONFIDANT, CONFIDE, CONFIDENT, DEFIANCE, DEFY, DIFFIDENT, from Latin *fīdere*, to trust, confide, and *fīdus*, faithful. **3.** Suffixed o-grade form **bhoidh-es-*. FEDERAL, FEDERATE; CONFEDERATE, from Latin *foedus* (stem *foeder-*), treaty, league. **4.** Zero-grade form **bhidh-*. FAITH, FAY³, FEALTY, FIDEISM, FIDELITY; INFIDEL, PERFIDY, from Latin *fidēs*, faith, trust. [Pokorny 1. *bheidh-* 117.]

Language and Culture Note The root **bheidh-**, "to trust," whose English derivatives include *faith*, *fidelity*, and *confererate*, is noteworthy in that its descendants in several of the Indo-European daughter languages refer specifically to the mutual trust on which covenants and social contracts must stand in order to be binding. Latin, for example, gets the general word for "trust," *fidēs*, as well as the word for "treaty," *foedus*, from this root. In Greek, various derivatives of the root appear together with the noun *(pro)xeniā*, "guest-friendship, hospitality," and related words, as in phrases translating "I trust in hospitality": the guest-

host relationship was a covenant of central importance between strangers in ancient Indo-European societies (see the note at **ghos-ti-**). Finally, and perhaps most interestingly, is an obscure word from Northern Albanian customary law referring to a pledge given by the family of a murdered man to the family of the murderer that they would refrain for a time from blood-feud. This pledge or truce, called *besë*, is a fundamental expression of the social contract, and comes from **bhidh-tyā-*, a suffixed zero-grade form of **bheidh-**.

bheiə- To strike. (Oldest form **bheih₂-*.) **1.** BILL², from Old English *bile*, bird's beak, possibly from Germanic suffixed form **bili-*. **2.** BILL³, from Old English *bil(l)*, sharp weapon, from Germanic suffixed form **bilja-*. **3.** BOHEMIA, BOHEMIAN, from Latin *Boihaemum*, "home of the Boii," from *Boiī*, "fighters," Celtic tribe that originally inhabited the region (*-haemum*, home, from Germanic; see **tkei-**). [Pokorny *bhei(ə)-* 117.]

bheig^w- To shine. An uncertain but plausible root. O-grade form **bhoig^w-*. PHOEBE, PHOEBUS, from Greek *phoibos*, shining. [Pokorny *bheigu-* 118.]

bhel-¹ To shine, flash, burn; shining white and various bright colors.

I. Suffixed full-grade form **bhel-o-*. **1a.** BELUGA, from Russian *belyĭ*, white; **b.** Old Church Slavonic *belŭ*, white, ultimately in Serbo-Croatian compound *Beograd* (see **gher-¹**). Both **a** and **b** from Slavic **belŭ*; **c.** BELTANE, from Scottish Gaelic *bealltainn*, from Old Irish *beltaine*, "fire of Bel" (*ten*, *tene*, fire; see **tep-**), from *Bel*, name of a pagan Irish deity akin to the Gaulish divine name *Belenos*, from Celtic **bel-o-*, bright. **2.** PHALAROPE, from Greek *phalaros*, having a white spot. **2.** PHALAENOPSIS, from Greek *phallaina*, moth (< ***"white creature").

II. Extended root **bhleh₁-*, contracted to **bhlē-*. **1.** Suffixed full-grade form **bhlē-wo-*. BLUE, from Old French *bleu*, blue, from Germanic **blēwaz*, blue. **2.** Suffixed zero-grade form **bhḷ-wo-*. FLAVESCENT, FLAVO-; FLAVIN, FLAVONE, FLAVOPROTEIN, from Latin *flāvus*, golden or reddish yellow.

III. Various extended Germanic forms. **1.** BLEACH, from Old English *blǣcan*, to bleach, from Germanic **blaikjan*, to make white. **2.** BLEAK¹, from Old Norse *bleikr*, shining, white, from Germanic **blaika-*, shining, white. **3.** BLITZKRIEG, from Old High German *blĕcchazzen*, to flash, lighten, from Germanic **blikkatjan*. **4a.** BLAZE¹, from Old English *blæse*, torch, bright fire; **b.** BLESBOK, from Middle Dutch *bles*, white spot; **c.** BLEMISH, from Old French *ble(s)mir*, to make pale. **a–c** all from Germanic **blas-*, shining, white. **5a.** BLIND; BLINDFOLD, PURBLIND, from Old English *blind*, blind, from Germanic **blinda-*, blind (< "cloudy"); **b.** BLENDE, from Old High German *blentan*, to blind, deceive, from Germanic **blandjan*, to blind (perhaps < "to make cloudy, deceive"); **c.** BLEND, from Old Norse *blanda*, to mix, from Germanic **blandan*, to mix (< "to make cloudy"); **d.** BLOND, from Old French *blond*, blond, from Frankish **blund-*, from Germanic **blunda-*. **6a.** BLENCH¹, from Old English *blencan*, to deceive; **b.** BLANCH, BLANK, BLANKET; BLANCMANGE, PINOT BLANC from Old French *blanc*, white. Both **a** and **b** from Germanic **blenk-*, **blank-*, to shine, dazzle, blind. **7.** BLUSH, from Old English *blyscan*, to glow red, from Germanic **blisk-*, to shine, burn.

IV. Extended root **bhleg-*, to shine, flash, burn. **1.** O-grade form *bhlog-*. BLACK, from Old English *blæc*, black, from Germanic **blakaz*, burned. **2.** Zero-grade form **bhḷg-*. **a.** FULGENT, FULGURATE; EFFULGENT, FOUDROYANT, REFULGENT, from Latin *fulgēre*, to flash, shine, and *fulgur*, lightning; **b.** FULMINATE, from Latin *fulmen* (< **fulg-men*), lightning, thunderbolt. **3a.** FLAGRANT; CONFLAGRANT, CONFLAGRATION, DEFLAGRATE, from Latin *flagrāre*, to blaze; **b.** CHAMISE, FLAMBÉ, FLAMBEAU, FLAMBOYANT, FLAME, FLAMINGO, FLAMMABLE; INFLAME, from Latin *flamma* (<

flag-ma), a flame. **4.** PHLEGM, PHLEGMATIC, PHLEGE-
THON, from Greek *phlegein*, to burn. **5.** O-grade form
bhlog-. PHLOGISTON, PHLOX; PHLOGOPITE, from
Greek *phlox*, a flame, also a wallflower. [Pokorny 1.
bhel- 118, *bheleg-* 124, *bhleu-(k)-* 159.]

bhel-² To blow, swell; with derivatives referring to
various round objects and to the notion of tumescent
masculinity. **1.** Zero-grade form *bhl̥-*. **a.** BOWL¹, from
Old English *bolla*, pot, bowl; **b.** BOLE, from Old Norse
bolr, tree trunk; **c.** BULK, from Old Norse *bulki*, cargo
(< "rolled-up load"); **d.** BOULEVARD, BULWARK, from
Middle High German *bole*, beam, plank; **e.** BOLL,
from Middle Dutch *bolle*, round object; **f.** BILTONG,
from Middle Dutch *bille*, buttock; **g.** BOULDER, from
a Scandinavian source akin to Swedish *bullersten*,
"rounded stone," boulder, from *buller-*, "round object." **a–g** all from Germanic *bul-*. **2.** Suffixed zero-
grade form *bhl̥-n-*. **a.** BULL¹, from Old Norse *boli*,
bull, from Germanic *bullōn-*; **b.** BULLOCK, from
Old English *bulluc*, bull, from Germanic *bulluka-*;
c. PHALLUS; ITHYPHALLIC, from Greek *phallos*, phallus; **d.** possibly Latin *fullō*, a fuller: FULL²; REFOULE-
MENT. **3.** O-grade form *bhol-*. **a.** BOLLIX, BOLLOCK,
from Old English *beallucas*, testicles; **b.** BALL¹, from
Old English **beall*, ball; **c.** BILBERRY, probably from
a Scandinavian source akin to Danish *bolle*, round
roll; **d.** BALLOON, BALLOT, BALLOTTEMENT, from Italian dialectal *balla*, ball; **e.** PALL-MALL, from Italian
palla, ball; **f.** BALE¹, from Old French *bale*, rolled-up
bundle; **g.** FOOSBALL, from Old High German *ball*.
a–g all from Germanic *ball-*. **4.** Possibly suffixed
o-grade form *bhol-to-*. **a.** BOLD, from Old English
bald, beald, bold; **b.** BAWD, from Old Saxon *bald*, bold;
c. Old High German *bald*, bold, in personal names:
(i) ARCHIBALD, from Old High German *Erchanbald*,
"genuine bold" (*erchan*, genuine; see **arg-**); *(ii)* LEO-
POLD, from Old High German *Leutpald, Liutbald*,
"bold among the people" (*liut*, people; see **leudh-²**);
d. BALDER, from Old Norse *ballr, baldr*, brave. **a–d**
all from Germanic *baltha-*, bold. **5.** Suffixed o-grade
form *bhol-n-*. FILS², FOLLICLE, FOLLY, FOOL, from Latin *follis*, bellows, inflated ball. **6.** Possibly Greek *phal(l)
aina*, whale: BALEEN. **7.** Conceivably from this root
(but more likely unrelated) is Greek *phellos*, cork, cork
oak: PHELLEM; PHELLODERM, PHELLOGEN. [Pokorny
3. *bhel-* 120.] See also derivatives **bhel-³**, **bhelgh-**,
bhlei-, and **bhleu-**.

bhel-³ To thrive, bloom. Possibly from **bhel-²**.
    I. Suffixed o-grade form *bhol-yo-*, leaf. **1.** FOIL²,
FOLIAGE, FOLIO, FOLIUM; CINQUEFOIL, DEFOLIATE,
EXFOLIATE, FEUILLETON, MILFOIL, PERFOLIATE, PORT-
FOLIO, TREFOIL, from Latin *folium*, leaf. **2a.** -PHYLL,
PHYLLO-, -PHYLLOUS; CHERVIL, GILLYFLOWER, PODO-
PHYLLIN, from Greek *phullon*, leaf; **b.** PHYLLIS (per-
sonal name), from Greek *phullis*, leaf.
    II. Extended form *bhlē-* (contracted from earlier
bhleh₁-). **1.** O-grade form *bhlō-*. **a.** Suffixed form
bhlō-w-. BLOW³, from Old English *blōwan*, to flower,
from Germanic *blō-w-*; **b.** *(i)* BLOOM¹, from Old
Norse *blōm, blōmi*, flower, blossom; *(ii)* BLOOM², from
Old English *blōma*, a hammered ingot of iron (se-
mantic development obscure). Both *(i)* and *(ii)* from
Germanic suffixed form *blō-mōn-*; **c.** BLOSSOM, from
Old English *blōstm, blōstma*, flower, blossom, from
Germanic suffixed form *blō-s-*; **d.** FERRET², FLORA,
FLORA, FLORAL, FLORET, FLORIATED, FLORID, FLORIN,
FLORIST, -FLOROUS, FLOUR, FLOURISH, FLOWER; CAU-
LIFLOWER, DEFLOWER, EFFLORESCE, ENFLEURAGE,
FLORIGEN, MILLEFIORI GLASS, MILLEFLEUR, from
Latin *flōs* (stem *flōr-*), flower, from Italic suffixed form
flō-s-; **e.** suffixed form *bhlō-to-*, possibly in the
meaning "swell, gush, spurt" in Germanic *blōdam*,
blood. *(i)* BLOOD, from Old English *blōd*, blood; *(ii)*
BLEED, from Old English *blēdan*, to bleed, from
Germanic denominative *blōdjan*; *(iii)* BLESS, from
Old English *bloedsian, blētsian*, to consecrate, from

Germanic *blōdisōn*, to treat or hallow with blood. **2.**
EMBLEMENTS, from Medieval Latin *blādum, bladium*,
produce of the land, grain, from Germanic suffixed
form *blē-da-*. **3.** Suffixed zero-grade form *bhlǝ-to-*.
BLADE, from Old English *blæd*, leaf, blade, from Germanic *bladaz*. [Pokorny 4. *bhel-* 122.]

bhel-⁴ To cry out, yell. **1a.** BELL², from Old English
bellan, to bellow, bark, roar, from Germanic **bellan*; **b.**
BELL¹, from Old English *belle*, a bell; **c.** BELLOW, perhaps from Old English *belgan*, to be enraged, and *byl-
gan*, to bellow; **d.** BAWL, from Middle English *baulen*,
to howl, from a Scandinavian source akin to Icelandic
baula, to low. **a–d** all from Germanic *bell-*. **2.** BELCH,
from Old English *bealcan, *bealcian*, to utter, belch
forth, perhaps from Germanic *bell-*. [Pokorny 6. *bhel-*
123.] See also extended root **bhlē-¹**.

bheld- To knock, strike. Zero-grade form *bhl̥d-*.
BOLT¹, from Old English *bolt*, heavy arrow, bolt, from
Germanic *bulta-*, missile. [Pokorny *bheld-* 124.]

bhelg- Also **bhelk-**. A plank, beam. **1.** O-grade form
bholg-. **a.** BALK, from Old English *balc(a)*, ridge; **b.**
DEBAUCH, from Old French *bauch*, beam; **c.** BALCONY,
from Old Italian *balcone*, scaffold. **a–c** all from Germanic *balkōn-*. **2.** Suffixed zero-grade variant form
bhl̥k-yo-. FULCRUM, from Latin *fulcīre*, to prop up,
support. **3.** Possibly Greek *phalanx*, beam, finger
bone, line of battle: PHALANGE, PHALANX. [Pokorny
5. *bhel-* 122.]

bhelgh- To swell. (Oldest form *bhelĝh-*; extension
of **bhel-²**.) **1.** O-grade form *bholgh-*. BELLOWS,
BELLY, from Old English *bel(i)g, bælig*, bag, bellows,
from Germanic *balgiz*. **2.** Zero-grade form *bhl̥gh-*.
a. BILLOW, from Old Norse *bylgja*, a wave, from Germanic *bulgjan*; **b.** BOLSTER, from Old English *bolster*,
cushion, from Germanic *bulgstraz*. **3.** O-grade form
bholgh-. **a.** FIR BOLG, IMBOLC, from Old Irish *bolc,
bolg*, bag; **b.** BUDGET, BULGE, from Latin *bulga*, leather
sack, of Gaulish origin. Both **a** and **b** from Celtic
bolg-. [Pokorny *bhelĝh-* 125.]

bhel-u- To harm. O-grade form *bhol-u-*. BALE², from
Old English *bealo, b(e)alu*, harm, ruin, bale, from Germanic *balwaz*. [Pokorny *bheleu-* 125.]

bhendh- To bind. **1a.** BIND; WOODBINE, from Old
English *bindan*, to bind; **b.** BINDLESTIFF, from Old
High German *binten*, to bind. Both **a** and **b** from Germanic *bindan*. **2.** BANDANNA, from Sanskrit *band-
hati*, he ties. **3.** O-grade form *bhondh-*. **a.** BEND²,
from Old English *bend*, band, and Old French *bende*,
band, from Germanic *bandjō*; **b.** BEND¹, from Old
English *bendan*, to bend, from Germanic *bandjan*; **c.**
(i) BAND¹, BOND, from Old Norse *band*, band, fetter;
(ii) GUM BAND, from Old High German *band*, band;
(iii) BAND¹, from Old French *bande*, bond, tie, link.
(i)–*(iii)* all from Germanic *bandam*; *(iv)* RIBBON,
from Old French *ruban*, ribbon, perhaps from Germanic *bandam* (first element unclear). **a–c** all from
Germanic *band-*. **4.** Suffixed form *bhond-o-*. BUND¹;
CUMMERBUND, from Avestan *banda-*, bond, fetter. **5.**
Zero-grade form *bhn̥dh-*. **a.** BUND², from Middle
High German *bunt*, league; **b.** BUNDLE, from Middle
Dutch *bondel*, sheaf of papers, bundle. Both **a** and **b**
from Germanic *bund-*. [Pokorny *bhendh-* 127.]

bhengh- Thick, fat. (Oldest form *bhengh-*.) Suffixed
zero-grade form *bhn̥gh-u-*. **1.** PACHYCEPHALOSAUR,
PACHYDERM, PACHYSANDRA, PACHYTENE, from Greek
pakhus, thick, fat. **2.** BAHUVRIHI, from Sanskrit *bahu-*,
much. [Pokorny *bhenĝh-* 127.]

bher-¹ To carry; also to bear children. **1a.** *(i)* BEAR¹,
from Old English *beran*, to carry; *(ii)* FORBEAR¹, from
Old English *forberan*, to bear, endure (*for-*, for-; see
per¹). Both *(i)* and *(ii)* from Germanic *beran*; **b.**
BIER, from Old English *bēr, bǣr*, bier, and Old French
biere, bier, both from Germanic *bērō*; **c.** BORE³, from
Old Norse *bāra*, wave, billow, from Germanic *bēr-*.
2a. BAIRN, from Old English *bearn*, child, from Ger-

manic *barnam; **b.** BARROW¹, from Old English *bear-we*, basket, wheelbarrow, from Germanic *barwōn-. **3.** Zero-grade form *bhr̥-, becoming Germanic *bur-. **a.** BURLY, from Old English *borlic*, excellent, exalted (< "borne up"); **b.** BURDEN¹, from Old English *byr- then*, burden, from Germanic *burthinja-; **c.** BIRTH, from a source akin to Old Norse *burdhr*, birth, from Germanic *burthiz; **d.** BIRR¹, from Old Norse *byrr*, favorable wind, perhaps from Germanic *burja-. **4.** Compound root *bhrenk-, to bring (< *bher- + *enk-, to bring; see **nek-³**). BRING, from Old English *bringan*, to bring, from Germanic *brengan. **5.** -FER, FERTILE; AFFERENT, CIRCUMFERENCE, CONFER, DEFER¹, DEFER², DIFFER, EFFERENT, INFER, OFFER, PREFER, PROFFER, REFER, SUFFER, TRANSFER, VOCIFERATE, from Latin *ferre*, to carry. **6.** Celtic *ber-. **a.** INVERNESS, *after Inverness*, from Scottish Gaelic *Ionarnis, Inbhirnis*, "mouth of the river Ness," from Old Irish *in(d)ber*, "a carrying in," estuary, from Celtic *endo-ber-o- (*endo-, in; see **en**); **b.** ABERDEEN, from Scottish Gaelic, "mouth of the Don river," from *aber*, mouth (of a river), from Celtic *ad-ber-o- (*ad-, to; see **ad-**). **7.** Prefixed and suffixed zero-grade form *pro-bhr-o-, "something brought before one" (*pro-, before; see **per¹**). OPPROBRIUM, from Latin *probrum*, a reproach. **8.** Possibly suffixed zero-grade form *bhr̥-tu- in Latin words having to do with chance (? < "a bringing, that which is brought"). **a.** FORTUITOUS, from Latin *fortuītus*, happening by chance; **b.** FORTUNA, FORTUNE, from Latin *fortūna*, chance, good luck, fortune, and *Fortūna*, goddess of good fortune. **9.** Probably lengthened o-grade form *bhōr-. FERRET¹, FURTIVE, FURUNCLE; FURUNCULOSIS, from Latin *fūr*, thief. **10.** FERETORY, -PHORE, -PHORESIS, -PHOROUS; AMPHORA, ANAPH- ORA, DIAPHORESIS, EUPHORIA, METAPHOR, PERIPHERY, PHEROMONE, TELPHER, TOCOPHEROL, from Greek *phe- rein*, to carry, with o-grade noun *phoros*, a carrying. **11.** PARAPHERNALIA, from Greek *phernē*, dowry ("something brought by a bride"). **12.** SAMBAL, from Sanskrit *bharati*, he carries, brings. [Pokorny 1. *bher*- 128.]

bher-² Also **bherə-**. To cut, pierce, bore. **1.** BORE¹, from Old English *borian*, to bore, from Germanic *burōn. **2.** BARROW³, from Old English *bearg, barg*, castrated pig, from Germanic suffixed form *barugaz. **3.** BURIN, from French *burin*, perhaps from Germanic *bor-. **4.** Suffixed o-grade form *bhor-ā-. FORAMEN; PERFORATE, from Latin *forāre*, to pierce, bore. **5.** Perhaps Greek *pharunx*, throat (< "a cutting, cleft, passage"): PHARYNX. **6.** DUKHOBOR, from Russian *borot'*, to overcome, from Slavic *bor-, to fight, overcome (also in Russian personal name BORIS). [Pokorny 3. *bher*- 133.] See also extension **bhreu-**.

bher-³ Bright, brown. **1.** Suffixed variant form *bhrū-no-. **a.** BROWN, from Old English *brūn*, brown; **b.** BRUIN, from Middle Dutch *bruun*; **c.** BRUNO (personal name), from Old High German *Bruno*, from *brun*, brown; **d.** BRUNET, BURNET, BURNISH, from Old French *brun*, shining, brown. **a–d** all from Germanic *brūna-, brown. **2.** Reduplicated form *bhibhru-, *bhebhru-, "the brown animal," beaver. BEAVER¹, from Old English *be(o)for*, beaver, from Germanic *bebruz. **3a.** BEAR², from Old English *bera*, bear; **b.** BERNARD (personal name), from German *Bernhard*, "bold bear," from Old High German *bero*, bear (*hart, hard*, stern, bold; see **kar-¹**). Both **a** and **b** from Germanic *berō, "the brown animal," bear. **4.** Perhaps Old Norse *ber-serkr*, berserker, if originally meaning "he who wears a bear skin" and akin to Old Norse *björn*, bear, from Germanic *bernuz, bear (*serkr*, shirt): BERSERK, BERSERKER. Alternatively, the first part of Old Norse *berserkr* has been derived from Old Norse *berr*, bare (see **bhoso-**). [Pokorny 5. *bher*- 136.]

bher-⁴ To cook, bake. **1.** Extended root form *bhrīg-. FRICANDEAU, FRICASSEE, FRISÉ, FRIT, FRITTATA, FRITTER², FRIZZ¹, FRY¹; CUCHIFRITO, SOFRITO, SOFFRITTO, from Latin *frīgere*, to roast, fry. **2.** Perhaps variant root

form *bhreig (oldest form *bhreiǵ-). BIRYANI, from Persian *biryān*, roasted, akin to *birištan, birēz-*, to roast, from Middle Persian *brištan, brēz-*. [Pokorny 6. *bher*- 137.]

bherdh- To cut. **1.** Zero-grade form *bhr̥dh-. **a.** BOARD; STARBOARD, from Old English *bord*, board; **b.** SMORGASBORD, from Old Norse *bordh*, board, table; **c.** BORDELLO, BORDER, from Old French *borde*, hut, and *bort*, border. **a–c** all from Germanic *burdam, plank, board, table. **2.** Possibly Latin *forfex*, a pair of scissors: FORFICATE. [Pokorny *bheredh*- 138.]

bherəg- To shine; bright, white. (Oldest form *bherh₃ǵ-.) **1a.** BRIGHT, from Old English *beorht*, bright; **b.** Old High German *beraht*, bright, in personal names (where it is often reduced to *ber(h)t*): *(i)* ALBERT, from Old High German *Adalbert*, "noble bright" (*adal*, noble; see **at-al-**); *(ii)* BERTHA, from Old High German *Beratha*, "the bright one"; *(iii)* GILBERT, from Old High German *Gīselberht*, "bright hostage" (*gīsel*, pledge, hostage); *(iv)* HERBERT, from Old High German *Heriberht*, "bright army" (*heri*, army; see **koro-**); *(v)* Old High German *Hrōdebert* (see **kar-²**); **c.** CAMEMBERT, *after Camembert* (French village), from Medieval Latin *Campus Maimberti*, "field of Maimbert" (personal name), from West Germanic *Magin-berht-, "bright with strength" (**magin-*, strength, from Germanic *maginam; see **magh-¹**). **a–c** from Germanic *berhta-, bright. **2.** "The white tree," the birch (also the ash). **a.** BIRCH, BIRK, from Old English *birc(e)*, birch, from Germanic *birkjōn-; **b.** probably suffixed zero-grade form *bhrag-s-. FRAXINELLA, from Latin *fraxinus*, ash tree. [Pokorny *bherəĝ*- 139.]

bherək- To shine, glitter. A by-form of **bherəg-**. (Oldest form *bherh₃k̑-.) Variant form *bhrek-, possible root of various Germanic forms. **1.** BRAID; UPBRAID, from Old English *bregdan*, to move quickly, weave, throw, braid, from Germanic *bregdan, to move jerkily (< "to shimmer"). **2.** BRIDLE, from Old English *brīdel*, bridle, from derivative West Germanic *brigdila-, bridle (referring to the movements of a horse's head). **3.** BRAE, from Old Norse *brā*, eyelash, from Germanic *brēhwō, eyelid, eyelash. **4.** BREAM¹, from Old French *bre(s)me*, from West Germanic *bresmo, a bream, from Germanic *breh(w)an, to shine. [Pokorny *bherək*- 141.]

[bherg- To make noise. Hypothetical base of Germanic strong verb *berkan. BARK¹, BIRKIE, from Old English *beorcan*, to bark, from Germanic *berkan. [Pokorny *bhereg*- 138.]]

bhergh-¹ To hide, protect. (Oldest form *bherĝh-.) **1a.** Germanic compound *h(w)als-berg- (see **kʷel-¹**); **b.** Germanic compound *skēr-berg- (see **(s)ker-¹**). Both **a** and **b** from Germanic *bergan, to protect. **2.** Zero-grade form *bhr̥gh-. **a.** BURY, from Old English *byrgan*, to bury, from Germanic *burgjan; **b.** BURIAL, from Old English *byrgels*, burial, from Germanic derivative *burgisli-. **3a.** BORROW, from Old English *borgian*, to borrow, from Germanic *borgēn, to pledge, lend, borrow; **b.** BARGAIN, from Old French *bargaignier*, to haggle, from Germanic derivative *borganjan. [Pokorny *bherĝh*- 145.]

bhergh-² High; with derivatives referring to hills and hill-forts. (Oldest form *bherĝh-.) **1a.** BARROW², from Old English *beorg*, hill; **b.** ICEBERG, from Middle Dutch *bergh*, mountain; **c.** INSELBERG, from Old High German *berg*, mountain; **d.** Germanic compound *harja-bergaz (see **koro-**). **a–d** all from Germanic *bergaz, hill, mountain. **2.** BELFRY, from Old French *berfroi*, tower, from Germanic compound *berg-frithu-, "high place of safety," tower (*frithu-, peace, safety; see **prī-**). **3.** Zero-grade form *bhr̥gh-. **a.** BOROUGH, BURG, from Old English *burg, burh, byrig*, (fortified) town, also becoming the Modern English suffix *-bury* in place names such as CANTERBURY; **b.** BURGOMASTER, from Middle Dutch *burch*, town; **c.**

BOURG, BOURGEOIS, BURGESS, BURGLAR; FAUBOURG, from Late Latin *burgus*, fortified place, and Old French *burg*, borough; **d.** BURGHER, from Old High German *burgāri*, townsman, from Germanic compound **burg-warōn-*, "city protector" (**warōn-*, protector; see **wer-**[5]). **a–d** all from Germanic **burgs*, hill-fort. **4.** Suffixed zero-grade form **bhr̥gh-n̥t-*, high, mighty. **a.** BURGUNDY, from Medieval Latin *Burgundia*, akin to Late Latin *Burgundiōnēs*, "highlanders" or "mighty ones" (Germanic tribal name), from Germanic **burgund-*; **b.** BRIDGET (personal name), from Old Irish *Brigit*, name of a goddess, from Celtic **Brigantī*. **5.** Possibly suffixed zero-grade form **bhr̥gh-to-*. FORCE, FORT, FORTALICE, FORTE[1], FORTE[2], FORTIS, FORTISSIMO, FORTITUDE, FORTRESS; COMFORT, DEFORCE, EFFORT, ENFORCE, FORTIFY, PANFORTE, PIANOFORTE, REINFORCE, from Latin *fortis*, strong (but this is also possibly from **dher-**[2]). [Pokorny *bhereĝh-* 140.]

bhers- Quick. FESTINATE, from Latin *festināre*, to hasten, probably from *festīnus* (< **fers-tī-*), quick, in a hurry. [Pokorny *bheres-* 143.]

bhes-[1] To rub. **1.** Zero-grade form **bhs-amadho-* (in Greek *psamathos*, sand), with unclear suffix, reduced to **samadho-* (in Greek *amathos*, sand, and in Germanic). SAND, from Old English *sand*, from Germanic **sam(a)dam*, **sandam*. **2.** Suffixed extended zero-grade form **(bh)sa-dhlo-*. SABULOUS, from Latin *sabulum*, coarse sand. **3.** Perhaps suffixed zero-grade form **bhs-ā-*. **a.** PALIMPSEST, from Greek *psēn*, to rub, scrape (but more likely of uncertain origin); **b.** PSEPHOLOGY, from Greek *psēphos*, ballot, pebble (but more likely of uncertain origin). **4.** Perhaps suffixed zero-grade form **bhs-īlo-*. EPSILON, PSILOMELANE, UPSILON, from Greek *psīlos*, smooth, simple (but more likely of uncertain origin). [Pokorny 1. *bhes-* 145.]

bhes-[2] To breathe. Probably imitative. Zero-grade form **bhs-*. PSYCHE[1], PSYCHIC, PSYCHO-; METEMPSYCHOSIS, from Greek *psūkhē*, spirit, soul, from *psūkhein* (< **bhs-ū-kh-*), to breathe. [Pokorny 2. *bhes-* 146.]

bheudh- To be aware, to make aware. **1a.** BID, from Old English *bēodan*, to proclaim; **b.** FORBID, from Old English *forbēodan*, to forbid; **c.** VERBOTEN, from Old High German *farbiotan*, to forbid. **a–c** all from Germanic **(for)beudan* (**for*, before; see **per**[1]). **2.** BODE[1], from Old English *bodian*, to announce, from *boda*, messenger, from Germanic **budōn-*. **3.** BEADLE, from Old English *bydel*, herald, messenger, and Old High German *butil*, herald, both from Germanic **budilaz*, herald. **4.** OMBUDSMAN, from Old Norse *bodh*, command, from Germanic **budam*. **5.** BUDDHA[2]; BODHISATTVA, BODHI TREE, BO TREE, from Sanskrit *bodhati*, he awakes, is enlightened, becomes aware, and *bodhiḥ*, perfect knowledge. [Pokorny *bheudh-* 150.]

bheua- Also **bheu-**. To be, exist, grow. **I.** Extended forms **bhwiy(o)-*, **bhwī-*. **1.** BE; FOREBEAR, from Old English *bēon*, to be, from Germanic **biju*, I am, will be. **2.** FIAT, from Latin *fierī*, to become. **3.** Possibly suffixed form **bhwī-lyo-*, seen by some as the source of Latin *filius*, son, but this is more likely from **dhē(i)-**.
II. Lengthened o-grade form **bhōw-*. **1.** BONDAGE, BOUND[4]; BUSTLE[1], HUSBAND, from Old Norse *būa*, to live, prepare, and *būask*, to make oneself ready (*-sk*, reflexive suffix; see **s(w)e-**). **2.** BAUHAUS, from Old High German *būan*, to dwell. **3.** BOOTH, from Middle English *bothe*, market stall, from a Scandinavian source akin to Old Danish *bōth*, dwelling, stall. **1–3** all from Germanic **bōwan*.
III. Zero-grade form **bhu-*. **1a.** BUILD, from Old English *byldan*, to build, from *bold*, dwelling, house, from Germanic **buthlam*; **b.** BOODLE, from Middle Dutch *bōdel*, riches, property, from alternate Germanic form **bōthlam*. **2.** PHYSIC, PHYSICS, PHYSIO-, PHYSIQUE, -PHYTE, PHYTO-, PHYTON; APOPHYSIS, DIAPHYSIS, DIPHYODONT, EPIPHYSIS, EUPHUISM, HYPO-

PHYSIS, IMP, MONOPHYSITE, NEOPHYTE, PERIPHYTON, SYMPHYSIS, TRACHEOPHYTE, from Greek *phuein*, to bring forth, make grow, *phutos*, *phuton*, a plant, and *phusis*, growth, nature. **3.** Suffixed form **bhu-tā-*. **a.** EISTEDDFOD, from Welsh *bod*, to be; **b.** BOTHY, from Old Irish *both*, a hut. **4.** Suffixed form **bhu-tu-*. FUTURE, from Latin *futū- rus*, "that is to be," future.
IV. Zero-grade form **bhū-* (< **bhua-*). **1a.** BOWER[1], from Old English *būr*, "dwelling space," bower, room; **b.** NEIGHBOR, from Old English *gebūr*, dweller (*ge-*, collective prefix; see **kom**); **c.** BOER, BOOR, from Middle Dutch *gheboer*, *ghebuer*, peasant. **a–c** all from Germanic **būram*, dweller, especially farmer. **2.** BYRE, from Old English *bȳre*, stall, hut, from Germanic **būrjam*, dwelling. **3.** BYLAW, from a Scandinavian source akin to Old Norse *bȳr*, settlement, from Germanic **būwi-*. **4.** Suffixed form **bhū-lo-*. PHYLE, PHYLETIC, PHYLUM; PHYLOGENY, from Greek *phūlon*, tribe, class, race, and *phūlē*, tribe, clan.
V. Zero-grade reduced suffixal form **-bhw-*, in Latin compounds. **1.** Latin *dubius*, doubtful, and *dubitāre*, to doubt, from **du-bhw-io-* (see **dwo-**). **2.** Latin *probus*, upright, from **pro-bhw-o-*, "growing well or straightforward" (see **per**[1]). **3.** Latin *superbus*, superior, proud, from **super-bhw-o-*, "being above" (see **uper**).
VI. Possibly Germanic **baumaz* (and **bagmaz*), tree (? < "growing thing"). **1.** BEAM, from Old English *bēam*, tree, beam. **2.** BOOM[2], from Middle Dutch *boom*, tree. **3.** BUMPKIN[1], BUMPKIN[2], from Flemish *boom*, tree. [Pokorny *bheu-* 146.]

bheug-[1] To flee. **1.** Zero-grade form **bhug-*. FUGACIOUS, FUGITIVE; CENTRIFUGAL, FEVERFEW, REFUGE, RE- FUGIUM, SUBTERFUGE, from Latin *fugere*, to flee. **2.** Suffixed zero-grade form **bhug-ā-*. **a.** -FUGE, FUGUE; FEBRIFUGE, from Latin *fuga*, flight, and derived verb *fugāre*, to drive away; **b.** APOPHYGE, from Greek *phugē*, flight. [Pokorny 1. *bheug-* 152.]

bheug-[2] To enjoy. Nasalized zero-grade form **bhu-n-g-*. FUNCTION, FUNGIBLE, DEFUNCT, PERFUNCTORY, from Latin *fungī*, to discharge, perform. [Pokorny 4. *bheug-* 153.]

bheug-[3] To bend; with derivatives referring to bent, pliable, or curved objects. **I.** Variant form **bheugh-* in Germanic **beug-*. **1a.** BEE[2], from Old English *bēag*, a ring; **b.** BAGEL, from Old High German *boug*, a ring. Both **a** and **b** from Germanic **baugaz*. **2a.** BOW[3]; AKIMBO, from Old English *boga*, a bow, arch; **b.** Germanic compound **elino-bugōn-* (see **el-**[1]); **c.** BOW[1], from a source akin to Middle Low German *boog*, bow of a boat; **d.** BOWLINE, BOWSPRIT, from Middle Low German *bōch*, bow of a boat. **a–d** all from Germanic **bugōn-*. **3.** BOW[2], BUXOM, from Old English *būgan*, to bend, from Germanic **būgan*. **4.** BAIL[3], from Middle English *beil*, a handle, perhaps from Old English **bēgel* or from a Scandinavian source akin to Old Swedish **bøghil*, both from Germanic **baugil-*. **5.** BIGHT, from Old English *byht*, a bend, angle, from Germanic **buhtiz*.
II. BOG, from Scottish and Irish Gaelic *bog*, soft, from Celtic **buggo-*, "flexible." [Pokorny 3. *bheug-* 152.]

bhlād- To worship. Suffixed form **bhlād-(s)men-*. FLAMEN, from Latin *flāmen*, priest (of a particular deity). [In Pokorny *bhlag-men-* 154.]

bhlāg- To strike. (Oldest form **bhleh₂g-*, colored to **bhlah₂g-*; zero-grade **bhlag-* from **bhlh₂g-*.) **1.** BAT[2], from Middle English *bakke*, probably from a Scandinavian source akin to Old Swedish (*natt-)backa*, (night) bat, perhaps from a form **blacka* continued in Icelandic (*ledhr-)blaka*, "(leather-)flutterer," bat, from Germanic **blak-*. **2.** FLAGELLATE, FLAGELLUM, FLAIL, FLOG, from Latin *flagrum*, a whip (diminutive *flagellum*, little whip). **3.** FLAGITIOUS, from Latin *flāgitāre*, to demand importunately. [Pokorny *bhlaĝ-* 154.]

bhlē-¹ To howl. (Probably contracted from earlier *bhleh₁-, extended from **bhel-⁴**.) **1a.** BLEAT, from Old English *blǣtan*, to bleat; **b.** BLARE, from Middle English *bleren*, to roar. Both **a** and **b** from Germanic *blē-. **2.** FEEBLE, from Latin *flēre*, to weep. [Pokorny *bhlē-* 154.]

bhlē-² To blow. (Contracted from earlier *bhleh₁-, or possibly lengthened grade *bhlēh₁- from alternative root *bhleh₂-. Possibly identical to **bhel-³** II *bhlē- above.) **1.** BLOW¹, from Old English *blāwan*, to blow, from Germanic suffixed form *blē-w-. **2a.** BLADDER, from Old English *blǣdre*, blister, bladder; **b.** BLATHER, from Old Norse *bladhra* (noun), bladder, and *bladhra* (verb), to prattle. Both **a** and **b** from Germanic suffixed form *blēdram, "something blown up." **3a.** BLAST, from Old English *blǣst*, a blowing, blast; **b.** ISINGLASS, from Middle Dutch *blas(e)*, a bladder; **c.** BLASÉ, BLAZE³, from Middle Dutch *blāsen*, to blow up, swell. **a–c** all from Germanic extended form *blēs-. **4.** Zero-grade form *bhl̥ə- (> *bhlā-). FLABELLUM, FLAGEOLET, FLATULENT, FLATUS, FLAVOR; AFFLATUS, CONFLATE, DEFLATE, INFLATE, INSUFFLATE, SOUFFLÉ, from Latin *flāre*, to blow. [In Pokorny 3. *bhel-* 120.]

bhlei- To blow, swell. Extension of **bhel-²**. **1.** BLAIN, from Old English *blegen*, a boil, blister, from Germanic *blajjinōn-, a swelling. **2.** Perhaps in the Germanic source of Old French *blestre*, a blister (akin to Old Norse *blāstr*, blister, and Middle Dutch *blyster*, blister): BLISTER. [Pokorny 2. *bhlei-* 156.]

bhleu- To swell, well up, overflow. Extension of **bhel-²**. **1.** Possibly Germanic *blaut-. BLOAT, from Old Norse *blautr*, soft, wet. **2.** Extended form *bhleug^w-. FLUCTUATE, FLUENT, FLUID, FLUME, FLUOR, FLUORO-, FLUSH², FLUVIAL, FLUX; AFFLUENT, CONFLUENT, EFFLUENT, EFFLUVIUM, EFFLUX, FLUORIDE, FLUVIOMARINE, INFLUENCE, INFLUENZA, INFLUX, MELLIFLUOUS, REFLUX, SOLIFLUCTION, SUPERFLUOUS, from Latin *fluere*, to flow, and *-fluus*, flowing. **3.** Zero-grade form *bhlu-. PHLYCTENA, from Greek *phlūein*, *phlūzein*, to boil over. **4.** Possibly Greek *phloos*, *phloios*, tree bark (< "swelling with growth"): PHLOEM. [Pokorny *bhleu-* 158.]

bhlīg- To strike. AFFLICT, CONFLICT, INFLICT, PROFLIGATE, from Latin *flīgere*, to strike. [Pokorny *bhlīĝ-* 160.]

bhoso- Naked. **1.** BARE¹, from Old English *bær*, bare. **2.** BALLAST, from Old Swedish and Old Danish *bar*, bare. Both **1** and **2** from Germanic *baza-. **3.** Perhaps Old Norse *berserkr*, berserker, if originally meaning "he who fights nude" (that is, "he who has nakedness for his shirt" and making reference to the fact that ancient European warriors often fought nude), from *berr*, bare (*serkr*, shirt): BERSERK, BERSERKER. Alternatively, the first part of Old Norse *berserkr* has been derived from the Germanic word for "bear" (see **bher-**). [Pokorny *bhoso-s* 163.]

bhrag- To smell. **1.** BRACH, from Old High German *bracc(h)o*, dog that hunts game by scent, from Germanic *brak-. **2.** Suffixed form *bhrag-ro-. FLAIR, FRAGRANT, from Latin *fragrāre*, to smell. [Pokorny *bhrag-* 163.]

bhragh-men- Form, ritual form. (Oldest form *bhraĝh-men-.) BRAHMA¹, BRAHMAN, BRAHMIN, from Sanskrit *brahma* (stem *brahman-*), prayer, ritual formulation, and derivative *brahmā* (stem *brahmān-*), priest ("the one of the prayer"). [Pokorny *bhlagh-men-* 154.]

bhrāter- Brother, male agnate. **1a.** BROTHER, from Old English *brōthor*, brother; **b.** BULLY¹, from Middle Dutch *broeder*, brother. Both **a** and **b** from Germanic *brōthar. **2.** FRA, FRATERNAL, FRATERNITY, FRATERNIZE, FRIAR; CONFRERE, CONFRATERNITY, from Latin *frāter*, brother. **3.** PHRATRY, from Greek *phrātēr*, fellow member of a clan. **4.** PAL, from Sanskrit *bhrātā* (stem *bhrātar-*), brother. [Pokorny *bhrā´ter-* 163.]

bhreg- To break. **1a.** BREAK, from Old English *brecan*, to break; **b.** BREACH, from Old English *brēc*, a breaking; **c.** BRASH², BRECCIA, from Italian *breccia*, breccia, rubble, breach in a wall, from Old High German *brehha*, from *brehhan*, to break; **d.** BRAY², from Old French *breier*, to break; **e.** BRIOCHE, from Old French *brier*, dialectal variant of *broyer*, to knead. **a–e** all from Germanic *brekan. **2.** BRACKEN, BRAKE⁴, from Middle English *brake(n)*, bracken, probably from a Scandinavian source akin to Old Norse *brakni*, undergrowth; **b.** BRAKE⁵, from Middle Low German *brake*, thicket. Both **a** and **b** from Germanic *brak-, bushes (< "that which impedes motion"). **3.** BRAKE², from Middle Low German *brake*, flax brake, from Germanic *brāk-, crushing instruments. **4.** Nasalized zero-grade form *bhr̥-n-g-. FRACTAL, FRACTED, FRACTION, FRACTIOUS, FRACTURE, FRAGILE, FRAGMENT, FRAIL¹, FRANGIBLE; ANFRACTUOUS, CHAMFER, DEFRAY, DIFFRACTION, INFRACT, INFRANGIBLE, INFRINGE, IRREFRANGIBLE, OSSIFRAGE, REFRACT, REFRAIN², REFRINGENT, SASSAFRAS, SAXIFRAGE, SEPTIFRAGAL, from Latin *frangere*, to break. **5a.** SUFFRAGAN, SUFFRAGE, from Latin *suffrāgium*, the right to vote, from *suffrāgārī*, to vote for (? < "to use a broken piece of tile as a ballot"); **b.** IRREFRAGABLE, from Latin *refrāgārī*, to vote against. [Pokorny 1. *bhreĝ-* 165 (but ĝ not on good evidence).]

bhreiə- To cut, break. Zero-grade *bhrī- (< *bhrih_x-). **1.** Possibly Latin *fricāre* (> French *frotter*), to rub: FRAY², FRICATIVE, FRICTION, FROTTAGE; AFFRICATE, DENTIFRICE. **2.** Possibly Latin *friāre*, to crumble: FRIABLE. **3.** BRISANCE; DEBRIS, from Vulgar Latin *brīsāre* (> Old French *brisier*, to break), of Celtic origin. [Pokorny *bhrēi-* 166.]

bhrek^w- To cram together. **1.** Probably Latin *frequēns*, frequent, crowded: FREQUENT. **2.** Suffixed zero-grade form *bhr̥k^w-yo-. **a.** FARCE, FARCI, FARCY; INFARCT, from Latin *farcīre*, to cram, stuff; **b.** DIAPHRAGM, PHRAGMITES, from Greek *phrassein*, to fence in, enclose, block up. [Pokorny *bharek^u-* 110.]

bhrem-¹ To growl. **1.** FREMITUS, from Latin *fremere*, to growl, roar. **2.** Perhaps o-grade variant form *brom-. BRONTOSAUR, from Greek *brontē*, thunder. [Pokorny 2. *bherem-* 142.]

bhrem-² To project; a point, spike; an edge. **1a.** BROOM, from Old English *brōm*, broom; **b.** BRAMBLE, from Old English diminutive *bremel*, *brǣmbel*, bramble. Both **a** and **b** from Germanic *brēma-, name of prickly shrubs. **2a.** BRIM, from Middle English *brimme*, edge; **b.** BERM, from Middle Dutch *berme*, *barm*, edge of a dike. Both **a** and **b** from Germanic *berm-, *brem-. [Pokorny 1. *bherem-* 142.]

bhres- To burst. BURST, from Old English *berstan*, to burst, from Germanic *brest-. [Pokorny *bhres-* 169.]

bhreu- Also **bhreuə-**. To cut, break up. Extension of **bher-²**.

I. Basic form *bhreu-. **1.** Suffixed form *bhreu-d-. BRITTLE, from Middle English *britel*, brittle, from Germanic *brutila-, brittle, from *breutan, to break up. **2.** Suffixed zero-grade form *bhreu-t-. BROTHEL, from Old English *brēothan*, to deteriorate, from Germanic *breuthan, to be broken up.

II. Extended zero-grade form *bhrūs- (< *bhruəs-). **1.** BRUISE, partly from Old English *brȳsan*, to crush, pound (from Germanic *brūsjan) and partly from Old North French *bruisier*, to crush (from Gaulish *brūs-). **2.** Suffixed zero-grade form *bhrus-to-. FRUSTULE, FRUSTUM, from Latin *frustum*, piece. [Pokorny 1. *bhrĕu-* 169, 2. *bhreu-s-*171.]

bhreuə- Also **bhreu-**. To boil, bubble, effervesce, burn; with derivatives referring to cooking and brewing. (Oldest form *bhreuh₁-; variant [metathesized] form *bhreh₁u-.)

I. 1. BREW, from Old English *brēowan*, to brew, from Germanic *breuwan, to brew. **2.** BREAD, from Old English *brēad*, piece of food, bread, from Ger-

manic *braudam, (cooked) food, (leavened) bread. **3a.** BROTH, from Old English *broth,* broth; **b.** BREWIS, BROIL[2]; EMBROIL, IMBROGLIO, from Vulgar Latin *brodum,* broth. Both **a** and **b** from Germanic *brudam,* broth.
    II. Variant form *bhrē- (contracted from earlier *bhreh₁-). Germanic extended form *brēd- in verb *brēdan, to warm. **1a.** BROOD, from Old English *brōd,* offspring, brood; **b.** BREED, from Old English *brēdan,* to beget or cherish offspring, breed, from Germanic denominative *brōdjan, to rear young. Both **a** and **b** from Germanic derivative *brōd-ō, "a warming," hatching, rearing of young. **2a.** BRATWURST, SAUERBRATEN, from Old High German *brāt, brāto,* roast meat; **b.** BRAWN, from Old English *braon,* meat. Both **a** and **b** from Germanic derivative *brēd-ōn-, roast flesh.
    III. Variant form *bhres-. **1.** BRAISE, BRAZE[2], BRAZIER[2], BREEZE[2], BRESAOLA, from Old French *brese,* burning coal, ember. **2.** BRACIOLA, from Italian dialectal *brasa,* burning coal. Both **1** and **2** from Germanic *bres-.
    IV. Reduced form *bher-, especially in derivatives referring to fermentation. **1a.** Suffixed form *bhermen-, yeast. BARM, BARMY, from Old English *beorma,* yeast, from Germanic *bermōn-; **b.** further suffixed form *bhermen-to-. FERMENT, from Latin *fermentum,* yeast. **2.** Extended form *bherw-. FERVENT, FERVID, FERVOR; DEFERVESCENCE, EFFERVESCE, from Latin *fervēre,* to be boiling or fermenting.
    V. As a very archaic word for a spring. **1.** Suffixed zero-grade form *bhru-n(e)n-. BOURN[1], BURN[2], from Old English *burn, burna,* spring, stream, from Germanic *brunnōn-. **2.** Suffixed form *bhrēw-r̥. PHREATIC, from Greek *phrear,* spring. [Pokorny *bh(e)reu-* 143, 2. *bher-* 132.]

bhreus- To swell. **1.** Suffixed form *bhreus-t-. BREAST, from Old English *brēost,* breast, from Germanic *breustam, "swelling," breast. **2.** Suffixed zero-grade form *bhrus-t-. BROWSE, from Old French *broust, brost,* shoot, twig, from Germanic *brust-, bud, shoot. **3.** Suffixed zero-grade form *bhrus-k-. BRISKET, from Middle English *brusket,* breast of an animal, probably from a Scandinavian source akin to Danish *brusk,* cartilage (since the brisket of livestock includes or lies over masses of cartilage). [Pokorny 1. *bhreu-s-* 170.]

bhrū- Eyebrow. (Contracted from *bhruhₓ-.) **1.** BROW, from Old English *brū-,* eyebrow, eyelid, eyelash, from Germanic *brūs. **2.** Possibly in the sense of a beam of wood, and perhaps a log bridge. BRIDGE[1], from Old English *brycg(e),* bridge, from Germanic *brugjō (with cognates in Celtic and Slavic). [Pokorny 1. *bhrū-* 172, 2. *bhrū-* 173.]

bhrūg- Agricultural produce; also to enjoy (results, produce). Italic and Germanic root. **1a.** BROOK[2], from Old English *brūcan,* to enjoy, use. **b.** GEBRAUCHSMUSIK, from Old High German *brūhhan, brūhhen,* to enjoy. Both **a** and **b** from Germanic *brūkan, to enjoy **2.** FRUGAL, FRUGIVOROUS, from Latin *frūx* (stem *frūg-),* fruit. **3.** Suffixed form *bhrūg-wo-. FRUIT, FRUITION, FRUMENTACEOUS, FRUMENTY; FRUCTIFY, INFRUCTESCENCE, from Latin *fruī,* to enjoy, with derivatives *frūmentum (< *frūg-smentom),* grain, produce, and *frūctus,* enjoyment, produce, results. [Pokorny *bhrūg-* 173.]

bhudh- Also **budh-.** Bottom, base. (The precise preforms of the words listed below are obscure.) **1.** BOTTOM, from Old English *botm,* bottom, from Germanic *butmaz. **2.** BUMBOAT, from Middle Dutch *bodem,* (ship's) bottom, from Germanic *buthmaz. **3.** FOND[2], FOUND[1], FOUNDER, FUND, FUNDAMENT, FUNDUS; LATIFUNDIUM, PROFOUND, from Latin *fundus,* bottom, base. **4.** Suffixed variant form *budh-o-. ABYSS, from Greek *buthos, bussos,* bottom of the sea. [Pokorny *bhudh-m(e)n* 174.] Compare **dheub-.**

bhugo- Male animal of various kinds; stag, ram, he-goat. (Oldest form *bhug̑o-.) **1a.** BUCK[1], from Old English *buc, bucca,* stag, he-goat; **b.** BLESBOK, BONTEBOK, SPRINGBOK, STEENBOK, from Middle Dutch *boc, bok,* buck; **c.** GEMSBOK, from Old High German *boc,* buck. **a–c** all from Germanic *bukkaz (possibly borrowed from the Celtic form in **2** below). **2.** BUTCHER, from Old French *boc,* buck, from Celtic *bukkos, he-goat. [Pokorny *bhug̑o-s* 174.]

[brāk- Trousers. A northern European word, found only in Celtic and Germanic. **1.** BREECH, BREEKS, BROGUE[1], from Old English *brōc* (plural *brēc)* from Germanic *brōk-. **2.** BRACKET, BRAIL, from Latin *brāca,* trousers (plural *brācae),* from Gaulish *brāka.]

[bursa Skin, hide. Greek noun of unknown origin. BOLSON, BOURSE, BURSA, BURSAR, BURSE, PURSE; DISBURSE, REIMBURSE, SPORRAN.]

[busk- A bush. Germanic root, possibly connected with **bheua-.** **1.** ROOIBOS, from Middle Dutch *bosch,* woods, forest. **2.** BOSCAGE, BOUQUET, from Old French *bosc,* forest. **3.** BUSH[1]; HAUTBOY, OBOE, from Old French *bois,* wood. **4.** BUSK[1], from Italian *busco,* splinter. **5.** BOSQUET, from Old Italian *bosco,* wood. **6.** AMBUSCADE, AMBUSH, from Late Latin *buscus,* forest.]

[carcer Enclosure, prison, barrier. Latin noun, probably borrowed from an unidentified source. **1.** INCARCERATE, from Latin *carcer* (representing reduplicated form *kar-kr-o-). **2.** CANCEL, CHANCEL, CHANCELLOR, from Latin *cancer,* lattice (representing a dissimilated form *kankro-).]

[caupō Small trader. Latin noun of unknown origin, borrowed early into Germanic. CHEAP; CHAP[2], CHAPMAN, from Old English *cēap,* trade, from Germanic *kaupōn-.]

dā- To divide. (Oldest form *deh₂-, colored to *dah₂-, contracted to *dā-.)
    I. Suffixed form *dā-mo-, perhaps "division of society." DEME, DEMOS, DEMOTIC; DEMAGOGUE, DEMIURGE, DEMOCRACY, DEMOGRAPHY, ENDEMIC, EPIDEMIC, PANDEMIC, from Greek *dēmos,* people, land.
    II. Extended form *dai- (contracted from earlier *dah₂i-, colored from oldest form *deh₂i-), with zero-grade *dī- (< *diə-, metathesized from *dəi-). **1.** Root form *dai-. GEODESY, from Greek *daiesthai,* to divide. **2.** Suffixed form *dai-mon-, divider, provider. DAIMON, DEMON, from Greek *daimōn,* divinity. **3.** Suffixed zero-grade form *di-ti-. **a.** TIDE[1]; EVENTIDE, from Old English *tīd,* time, season; **b.** TIDE[2], from Old English denominative *tīdan,* to happen (< "to occur in time"); **c.** TIDING, from Old Norse *tīdhr,* occurring; **d.** YAHRZEIT, ZEITGEBER, ZEITGEIST, from Old High German *zīt,* time. **a–d** all from Germanic *tīdiz, division of time. **4.** Suffixed zero-grade form *dī-mon-. TIME, from Old English *tīma,* time, period, from Germanic *tīmōn-. [Pokorny *dā : də-* 175.] See also extension **dail-.**

dail- To divide. Northern Indo-European root extended from *da(ə)i- (see **dā-).** **1.** DEAL[1], from Old English *dǣlan,* to share, from Germanic *dailjan. **2a.** DOLE[1], from Old English *dāl,* portion, lot, from Germanic *dailaz. **3.** ORDEAL, from Old English *ordāl,* trial by ordeal, from Germanic prefixed form *uz-dailjam, "a portioning out," judgment (*uz-, out; see **ud-).** **4.** FIRKIN, from Middle Dutch *deel,* part, from Germanic *dailiz. [In Pokorny *dā : də-* 175.]

daiwer- Husband's brother. LEVIRATE, from Latin *lēvir,* husband's brother (probably a dialect borrowing). [Pokorny *dāiu̯ēr* 179.]

dakru- Tear. (Oldest form *daḱru-.) **1a.** TEAR[2], from Old English *tēar, tehher,* tear; **b.** TRAIN OIL, from Middle Dutch *trane,* tear, drop. Both **a** and **b** from Germanic *tahr-, *tagr-. **2.** Suffixed form *dakru-mā-. LACHRYMAL, from Latin *lacrima* (Archaic Latin *dacruma),* tear. [Pokorny *daḱru-* 179.]

[dan- Low ground. Germanic root. **1.** DEN, from Old English *denn*, lair of a wild beast, from suffixed form **dan-jam*. **2.** Possibly Old English *Dene*, the Danes, and Old Norse *Danr*, Dane: DANE, DANISH; DANELAW. [In Pokorny 2. *dhen-* 249.]]

dānu- River. **1.** DON (river in Scotland), from Old English *Don*, from Celtic. **2.** DANUBE, from Latin *Dānuvius*, from Celtic suffixed form **dānu(w)-yo-*. **3a.** DON (river in Russia), from Russian *Don*, from an Iranian source akin to Ossetic *don*, river; **b.** DNIEPER, from Russian *Dnepr*, from Scythian **dānu apara*, "river in the rear, farther river" (**apara*, farther; see **apo-**); **c.** DNIESTER, from Russian *Dnestr*, from Scythian **dānu nazdya* "nearer river, river in front" (**nazdya-*, nearer). **a–c** all from Iranian **dānu-*, river. [Pokorny *dā-* 175.]

dap- To apportion (in exchange). Suffixed form **dap-no-*. DAMAGE, DAMN; CONDEMN, INDEMNIFY, INDEMNITY, from Latin *damnum*, damage entailing liability (for reparation), harm. [In Pokorny *dā : də-* 175.]

Language and Culture Note   Derivatives of the root **dap-** (which yields such English words as *damage* and *damn*) furnish a useful window on the nature of reciprocal exchange relationships, which were central to the ancient Indo-European peoples. In their societies, and in Proto-Indo-European society itself, a gift entailed a countergift, and an act causing damage entailed the payment of recompense. The root **dap-** embodies the notion of apportionment in a reciprocal exchange relationship of either sort. In Latin, the word *damnum*, from a suffixed form **dap-no-*, meant "damage entailing liability." Its Old Irish cognate, *dúan* (also from **dap-no-*), however, meant "poem." How the same Indo-European form can come to mean "damage entailing liability" in one language and "poem" in another makes perfect sense in light of the relationship obtaining between the Indo-European poet and his patron (typically a king): the poet sang the patron's fame, and in return the patron bestowed largesse on the poet. The relationship was vital to both parties: the king's livelihood depended on the poet's singing his praises (in Ireland, for example, a "king without poets" was proverbial for "nothing"), and the poet lived off the largesse bestowed by the king. The poem therefore was a vehicle of this reciprocal exchange relationship; it was a gift entailing a countergift just as surely as damages entail reparation.

---

de- Demonstrative stem, base of prepositions and adverbs. **1.** Form **dō* (possibly instrumental). **a.** *(i)* TO, TOO, from Old English *tō*, to; *(ii)* TSIMMES, from Old High German *zuo, ze*, to; *(iii)* TATTOO¹, from Middle Dutch *toe*, to, shut. *(i)–(iii)* all from Germanic **tō*; **b.** Italic *dō* in compound **kʷām-dō* (see **kʷo-**). **2.** Form **dē* (possibly instrumental), perhaps source of forms meaning "from, out of." **a.** DE-, from Latin *dē, dē-*, from; **b.** DETERIORATE, from Latin *dēterior*, worse, from suffixed form **dē-tero-*; **c.** compound **dē-bel-i-* (see **bel-**); **d.** Celtic **dī*, from, in compound **eks-dī-sedo-* (see **sed-¹**). [Pokorny *de-* 181.]

dē- To bind. (Contracted from earlier **deh₁-*.) DESMID; ANADEM, ASYNDETON, DIADEM, PLASMODESMA, SYNDESMOSIS, SYNDETIC, from Greek *dein*, to bind. [Pokorny *dē-* 183.]

deigh- Insect. (Oldest form **deiĝh-*.) Possibly Germanic **tīk-ō, *tikk-ō*. TICK², from Middle English *teke*, tick. [Pokorny *deiĝh-* 187.]

deik- Also **deig-**. To show, pronounce solemnly; also in derivatives referring to the directing of words or objects. (Oldest forms **deiĝ-*, **deiĝ-*.)

    I. Variant **deiĝ-*. O-grade form **doiĝ-*. **a.** TEACH, from Old English *tǣcan*, to show, instruct, from Germanic **taikjan*, to show; **b.** *(i)* TOKEN, from Old English *tācen, tācn*, sign, mark; *(ii)* BETOKEN, from Old English *tācnian*, to signify; *(iii)* TETCHY, from Gothic *taikns*, sign; *(iv)* TACHISME, from Old French *tache, teche*, mark, stain. *(i)–(iv)* all from Germanic **taiknam*. **2.** Zero-grade form **dig-*. DIGIT, from Latin *digitus*, finger (< "pointer," "indicator").

    II. Basic form **deik-*. **1.** Possibly o-grade form **doik-*. TOE, from Old English *tā, tahe*, toe, from Germanic **taihwō*. **2.** Basic form **deik-*. DICTATE, DICTION, DICTUM, DITTO, DITTY; ADDICT, BENEDICTION, CONDITION, CONTRADICT, EDICT, FATIDIC, HERB BENNET, INDICT, INDICTION, INDITE, INTERDICT, JURIDICAL, JURISDICTION, MALEDICT, MALISON, PREDICT, VALEDICTION, VERDICT, VERIDICAL, VOIR DIRE, from Latin *dīcere*, to say, tell. **3.** Suffixed zero-grade form **dik-ā-*. ABDICATE, DEDICATE, PREACH, PREDICAMENT, PREDICATE, from Latin *dicāre*, to proclaim. **4.** Agential suffix **-dik-*. **a.** INDEX, INDICATE, from Latin *index*, indicator, forefinger (*in-*, toward; see **en-**); **b.** JUDICIAL; PREJUDICE, from Latin *iūdex* (< **yewes-dik-*), judge, "one who shows or pronounces the law" (*iūs*, law; see **yewes-**); **c.** VENDETTA, VINDICATE; AVENGE, REVENGE, from Latin *vindex* (first element obscure), surety, claimant, avenger. **5.** DEICTIC, DEIXIS; APODICTIC, PARADIGM, POLICY², from Greek *deiknunai*, to show, and noun *deigma* (**deik-mn̥*), sample, pattern. **6.** Zero-grade form **dik-*. DISK; DICTYOSOME, from suffixed form **dik-skos*, from Greek *dikein*, to throw (< "to direct an object"). **7.** Form **dikā-*. DICAST; SYNDIC, THEODICY, from Greek *dikē*, justice, right, court case. [Pokorny *deik-* 188.]

dek-¹ To take, accept. (Oldest form **deḱ-*.) **1.** Suffixed (stative) form **dek-ē-*. DECENT, from Latin *decēre*, to be fitting (< "to be acceptable"). **2.** Suffixed (causative) o-grade form **dok-eye-*. **a.** DOCENT, DOCILE, DOCTOR, DOCTRINE, DOCUMENT, from Latin *docēre*, to teach (< "to cause to accept"); **b.** DOGMA, DOGMATIC; CHIONODOXA, DOCETISM, DOXOLOGY, HETERODOX, ORTHODOX, PARADOX, from Greek *dokein*, to appear, seem, think (< "to cause to accept or be accepted"). **3.** Suffixed form **dek-es-*. **a.** DÉCOR, DECORATE, from Latin *decus*, grace, ornament; **b.** DECOROUS, from Latin *decor*, seemliness, elegance, beauty. **4.** Suffixed form **dek-no-*. DAINTY, DEIGN, DIGNITY; CONDIGN, DIGNIFY, DISDAIN, INDIGN, INDIGNANT, INDIGNATION, from Latin *dignus*, worthy, deserving, fitting. **5.** Reduplicated form **di-dk-ske-*. DISCIPLE, DISCIPLINE, from Latin *discere*, to learn. **6.** DOWEL, PANDECT, SYNECDOCHE, from Greek *dekhesthai*, to accept. **7.** Suffixed o-grade form **dok-o-*. DIPLODOCUS, from Greek *dokos*, beam, support. [Pokorny 1. *dek̑-* 189.]

dek-² Referring to such things as a fringe, lock of hair, horsetail. (Oldest form **deḱ-*.) **1.** Suffixed o-grade form **dok-lo-*. TAIL¹, from Old English *tægl)l*, tail, from Germanic **taglaz*. **2.** Perhaps Germanic **tag-*. **a.** TAG¹, from Middle English *tagge*, pendent piece, from a Scandinavian source akin to Swedish *tagg*, prickle; **b.** SHAKO, from Middle High German *zacke*, nail (> German *Zacken*, point); **c.** TACHE, TACK¹, from Old French *tache*, fastening, nail. [Pokorny 2. *dek̑-* 191.]

dekm̥ Ten. (Oldest form **deḱm̥*.)

    I. Basic form **dekm̥*. **1a.** TEN, from Old English *tīen*, ten; **b.** Old Norse *tjan*, ten, in compound *āttjan* (see **oktō(u)**). Both **a** and **b** from Germanic **tehun*. **2.** EIGHTEEN, FIFTEEN, FOURTEEN, NINETEEN, SEVENTEEN, SIXTEEN, THIRTEEN, from Old English suffix *-tēne, -tīne, -tȳne*, ten, -teen, from Germanic **tehan*. **3.** DECI-, DECIMAL, DECIMATE, DECUPLE, DECURION, DICKER, DIME; December, DECEMVIR, DECENNARY, DECENNIUM, DECUSSATE, DOZEN, DUODECIMAL, OCTODECIMO, SEXTODECIMO, from Latin *decem*, ten. **4.** DENARIUS, DENARY, DENIER², DINAR, from irregular Latin distributive *dēnī*, by tens, ten each (formed by analogy with *nōnī*, nine each). **5.** DEAN, DECA-, DECADE, DOYEN; DECAGON, Dec- ALOGUE, DODECAGON, from Greek *deka*, ten.

II. Germanic *tigu-, ten, decad (of uncertain formation, as though < *deku-), in compound *twēgentig (see **dwo-**).

III. Ordinal number *dekm̥to-. TENTH, TITHE, from Old English teogotha, tēotha, tenth, from Germanic *teguntha-.

IV. Suffixed zero-grade form *-dkm̥-tā, reduced to *-km̥tā, and lengthened o-grade form *-dkōm-tā, reduced to *-kontā. **1.** NONAGENARIAN, OCTOGENARIAN, SEPTUAGINT, SEXAGENARY, from Latin -gintā, ten times. **2.** PENTECOST, from Greek *-konta, ten times.

V. Suffixed zero-grade form *dkm̥-tom, hundred, reduced to *km̥tom. **1.** HUNDRED, from Old English hundred, from dialectal North and West Germanic *hund(a)-rada- (*-rada-, from Germanic *radam, number; see **ar-**), from Germanic *hundam, hundred. **2.** Germanic compound *thūs-hundi, "swollen hundred," thousand (see **teuə-²**). **3.** CENT, CENTAL, CENTAVO, CENTENARIAN, CENTENARY, CENTESIMAL, CENTI-, CENTIME, CENTNER, CENTUM, QUINDARKA; CENTENNIAL, CINQUECENTO, PERCENT, QUATTROCENTO, SEICENTO, SEN², SENITI, SEXCENTENARY, TRECENTO, from Latin centum, hundred. **4.** HECATOMB, HECTO-, from Greek hekaton, a hundred (? dissimilated from *hem-katon, one hundred; *hem-, one; see **sem-¹**). **5.** SATEM, from Avestan satəm, hundred. [Pokorny dekm̥ 191.] See also **wīkm̥tī**.

deks- Right (opposite left); hence, south (from the viewpoint of one facing east). (Oldest form *deks-.) Suffixed form *deks(i)-tero-. DESTRIER, DEXTER, DEXTERITY, DEXTRO-; AMBIDEXTROUS, from Latin dexter, right, on the right side. [In Pokorny 1. dek̑- 189.] Compare **ner-¹**.

del-¹ Long.

I. Probably extended and suffixed zero-grade form *dlon-gho-. **1a.** LONG¹; ALONG, LONGSHORE, from Old English lang, long, long; **b.** LANGLAUF, from Old High German lang, long; **c.** BELONG, from Old English gelang, along; **d.** LONG², from Old English denominative langian, to grow longer, yearn for, from Germanic *langōn; **e.** LINGER, from Old English lengan, to prolong (possibly influenced by Old Norse lengja, to lengthen), from Germanic *langjan, to make long; **f.** LOMBARD, from Latin compound Longobardus, Langobardus (with Germanic ethnic name *Bardi). **a–f** all from Germanic *langaz, long. **2a.** LENGTH, from Old English lengthu, length; **b.** LENT, from Old English lengten, lencten, spring, Lent, from West Germanic *langitinaz, lengthening of day. Both **a** and **b** from Germanic abstract noun *langithō. **3.** LING¹, from Middle English lenge, ling, ling, from a Low German source akin to Dutch lenghe, linghe, "long one," from Germanic *langīn-. **4.** LONGERON, LONGITUDE, LOUNGE; ELOIGN, ELONGATE, LONGEVITY, LUNGE, OBLONG, PROLONG, PURLOIN, from Latin longus, long.

II. Possibly suffixed variant form *dl̥ə-gho-. DOLICHOCEPHALIC, DOLICHOCRANIAL, from Greek dolikhos, long. [Pokorny 5. del- 196.]

del-² To recount, count. O-grade form *dol-. **1.** TELL¹, from Old English tellan, to count, recount, from Germanic *taljan. **2.** TALL, from Old English getæl, quick, ready, from West Germanic *(ge-)tala-. **3a.** TALE, from Old English talu, story; **b.** TAAL², from Middle Dutch tāle, speech, language. Both **a** and **b** from Germanic *talō. **4.** TALK, from Middle English talken, to talk, from a source probably akin to Old English denominative talian, to tell, relate. **5.** Perhaps Greek dolos, ruse, snare: DOLERITE, SEDULOUS. [Pokorny 1. del- 193.]

del(ə)- To split, carve, cut. **1.** Suffixed form *del-to-. TILT², from Old English teld, awning, tent, from Germanic *teldam, "thing spread out." **2.** TILLER³, from Old English telgor, telgra, twig, branch, from Germanic extended form *telg-. **3.** Perhaps suffixed o-grade form *dol-ē-. DOLE², DOLOR; CONDOLE, INDOLENT, from Latin dolēre, to suffer (? < "to be beaten"). **4.**

Suffixed o-grade form *dol-ā-. DOLABRIFORM, from Latin dolāre, to chisel, hew (derivative dolābra, a heavy chopping tool). [Pokorny 3. del- 194.]

dem- House, household. **1.** Suffixed o-grade form *dom-o-, *dom-u-, house. **a.** DOME, DOMESTIC, DOMICILE; MAJOR-DOMO, from Latin domus, house; **b.** suffixed form *dom-o-no-. DAME, DAN²; DANGER, DOM, DOMAIN, DOMAINE, DOMINATE, DOMINICAL, DOMINIE, DOMINION, DOMINO¹, DOMINO², DON¹, DONNA, DUNGEON; BELLADONNA, DUENDE, MADAM, MADAME, MADEMOISELLE, MADONNA, PREDOMINATE, from Latin dominus, master of a household (feminine domina). **2.** Possibly suffixed lengthened-grade form *dōm-n̥. DOME, from Greek dōma, house. **3.** Compound *dems-pot-, "house-master" (*-pot-, powerful; see **poti-**). DESPOT, from Greek despotēs, master, lord. **4.** Root form *dem(h₂)-, to build (possibly a separate root). **a.** TIMBER, from Old English timber, building material, lumber, from Germanic *timram; **b.** TOFT, from Old Norse topt, homestead, from Germanic *tumftō. [Pokorny dem- 198.]

demə- To constrain, force, especially to break in (horses). (Oldest form *demh₂-.) **1.** Suffixed o-grade form *dom(ə)-o-. TAME, from Old English tam, domesticated, from Germanic *tama-. **2.** O-grade form *domā-. DAUNT; INDOMITABLE, from Latin domāre, to tame, subdue. **3.** Zero-grade form *dmə-. ADAMANT, DIAMOND, from Greek damān, to tame (> adamās, unconquerable, from *n̥-dmə-nt-). [Pokorny (demə-) 199.]

denk- To bite. (Oldest form *denk̑-.) **1.** TOUGH, from Old English tōh, tenacious, sticky (< "holding fast"), from Germanic *tanhu-. **2.** TONGS, from Old English tang(e), tong(e), pincers, tongs, from Germanic *tangō. **3.** TANG¹, from Middle English tonge, tange, point, tang, from a Scandinavian source akin to Old Norse tangi, a point, sting, from Germanic *tang-. **4.** ZINC, from Old High German zinko, spike, prong, from Germanic *teng-. [Pokorny denk̑- 201.]

dens-¹ To use mental force. Reduplicated and suffixed zero-grade form *di-dn̥s-sko-. DIDACTIC; AUTODIDACT, from Greek didaskein, to teach. [Pokorny 1. dens- 201.]

dens-² Dense, thick. **1.** Suffixed form *dens-o- or *dn̥s-o-. DENSE; CONDENSE, from Latin dēnsus, thick. **2.** Suffixed zero-grade form *dn̥s-u-. DASYURE, from Greek dasus, hairy, shaggy. [Pokorny 2. dens- 202.]

dent- Tooth. (Originally *h₁d-ent-, "biting," present participle of *h₁ed-, to eat, in the earlier meaning "to bite"; see **ed-**.) **1.** O-grade form *(ə)dont-. **a.** TOOTH, from Old English tōth, tooth, from Germanic *tanthuz; **b.** -ODON, -ODONT, ODONTO-; CERATODUS, MASTODON, from Greek odōn, odous, tooth. **2.** Zero-grade form *dn̥t-. TUSK¹, from Old English tūsc, tūx, canine tooth, from Germanic *tunth-sk-. **3.** Full-grade form *dent-. DENTAL, DENTATE, DENTI-, DENTICLE, DENTIST; DANDELION, EDENTATE, EDENTULOUS, INDENT¹, INDENTURE, TRIDENT, from Latin dēns (stem dent-), tooth. [In Pokorny ed- 287.]

deph- To stamp. Uncertain root form. **1.** Suffixed form *deph-s-ter-. DIPHTHERIA, from Greek diphtherā, prepared hide, leather (used to write on). **2.** LETTER, LITERAL, LITERARY, LITERATIM; ALLITERATE, ALLITERATION, ILLITERATE, OBLITERATE, TRANSLITERATE, from Latin littera, litera, letter (possibly borrowed from Greek diphtherā in the sense of "tablet" via Etruscan). [Pokorny deph- 203.]

der-¹ Assumed base of roots meaning "to run, walk, step." **1.** Zero-grade form *dr- in extended Germanic form *tred-. **a.** TREAD, TREADLE, from Old English tredan, to step; **b.** TRADE, from Middle Low German trade, course, track. **2.** Extended form *dreb-. **a.** TRAP¹, from Old English træppe, treppe, snare; **b.** TRAP³, from from Middle Low German trappe, stair; **c.** WENTLETRAP, from Middle Dutch trappe, stair; **d.**

ENTRAP, from Old French *trap(p)e*, snare; **e.** TRIP, from Middle Dutch *trippen*, to stamp, trample. **a–e** all from Germanic **trep-*, "something on or into which one steps." **3a.** TRAMP, from Middle Low German *trampen*, to stamp, tread; **b.** TRAMPOLINE, from Italian *trampoli*, stilts. **a** and **b** from nasalized Germanic root **tremp-*. **4.** TROT, from Old French *troter*, to trot, from Germanic **trott-*, expressive derivative of **tred-*. **5.** Extended zero-grade form **drā-* possibly in reduplicated Germanic form **ti-trā-*. TEETER, from Old Norse *titra*, to tremble. **6.** Root form **drem-* in suffixed o-grade form **drom-o-*. **a.** -DROME, DROMOND, -DROMOUS; ANADROMOUS, LOXODROME, PALINDROME, PRODROME, from Greek *dromos*, a running, race, racecourse; **b.** DROMEDARY, from Greek *dromas*, running. [Pokorny 3. *(der-)* 204.]

der-² To split, peel, flay; with derivatives referring to skin and leather. **1.** TEAR¹, from Old English *teran*, to tear, from Germanic **teran*. **2.** TART¹, from Old English *teart*, sharp, severe, from Germanic **ter-t-*. **3.** Suffixed zero-grade form **dr̥-tom*, "something separated or discarded." TURD, from Old English *tord*, turd, from Germanic **turdam*, turd. **4.** Reduplicated form **de-dr-u-*. TETTER, from Old English *tet(e)r*, eruption, skin disease. **5.** Suffixed form **der-mn̥*. -DERM, DERMA¹, -DERMA, DERMATO-; EPIDERMIS, from Greek *derma*, skin. **6.** DAHL, DALIT, DHURRIE, from Sanskrit *darati*, he splits. [Pokorny 4. *der-* 206.]

derbh- To wind, compress. Zero-grade form **dr̥bh-*. **1.** TURF, from Old English *turf*, slab of sod or peat. **2.** TURBARY, from Medieval Latin *turba*, turf. Both **1** and **2** from Germanic **turb-*. [Pokorny *derbh-* 211.]

derə- To work. (Oldest form **derh₂-*, with variant [metathesized] root form **dreh₂-*, colored to **drah₂-*, contracted to **drā-*.) Variant form **drā-*. DRAMA, DRASTIC, from Greek *drān*, to do. [Pokorny *derə-* 212.]

dergh- To grasp. **1.** Perhaps Germanic **targ-* in Old French *targe*, shield: TARGE, TARGET. **2.** Perhaps zero-grade **dr̥gh-*. DIRHAM, DRACHMA, from Greek *drassesthai*, to grab (> *drakhmē*, "handful," drachma). [Pokorny *dergh-* 212.]

derk- To see. (Oldest form **derk-*.) Suffixed zero-grade form **dr̥k-on(t)-*. Suffixed zero-grade form **dr̥k-on(t)-*. DRAGON, DRAGOON, DRAKE²; RANKLE, TARRAGON, from Greek *drakōn*, serpent, dragon (< "monster with the evil eye"). [Pokorny *derk-* 213.]

deru- Also **dreu-**. To be firm, solid, steadfast; hence specialized senses "wood," "tree," and derivatives referring to objects made of wood. **1.** Suffixed variant form **drew-o-*. **a.** TREE, from Old English *trēow*, tree, from Germanic **trewam*; **b.** TRUCE, from Old English *trēow*, pledge, from Germanic **treuwō*. **2.** Variant form *dreu-*. **a.** TRUE, from Old English *trēowe*, firm, true; **b.** TROW, from Old English *trēowian*, *trūwian*, to trust; **c.** TRIG¹, from Old Norse *tryggr*, firm, true; **d.** TROTH, TRUTH; BETROTH, from Old English *trēowth*, faith, loyalty, truth, from Germanic abstract noun **treuwithō*; **e.** TRUST, from Old Norse *traust*, confidence, firmness, from Germanic abstract noun **traustam*; **f.** TRYST, from Old French *triste*, waiting place (< "place where one waits trustingly"), probably from a source akin to Old Norse denominative *treysta*, to trust, make firm. **a–f** all from Germanic **treuwaz*. **3.** Variant form **drou-*. TRAY, from Old English *trēg*, *trīg*, wooden board, from Germanic **traujam*. **4.** Suffixed zero-grade form **dru-ko-*. **a.** TROUGH, from Old English *trog*, wooden vessel, tray; **b.** TRUG, from Old Norse *trog*, trough. Both **a** and **b** from Germanic **trugaz*. **5.** Suffixed zero-grade form **dru-mo-*. **a.** TRIM, from Old English *trum*, firm, strong; **b.** SHELTER, from Old English *truma*, troop. Both **a** and **b** from Germanic **trum-*. **6.** Variant form **derw-*. TAR¹, from Old English *te(o)ru*, resin, pitch (obtained from the pine tree), from Germanic **terw-*. **7.** Lengthened zero-grade form **drū-*. DRUPE, DRYAD; DRYOPITHECUS,

GERMANDER, HAMADRYAD, from Greek *drūs*, oak. **8.** Reduplicated form **der-drew-*, dissimilated with suffix in **der-drew-on*. DENDRO-, DENDRON; PHILODENDRON, RHODODENDRON, from Greek *dendron*, tree. **9.** DRUID, from Latin *druides*, druids, probably from Celtic compound **dru-wid-*, "strong seer" (**wid-*, seeing; see **weid-**), member of the Celtic priestly caste (compare Old Irish *druí*, druid). **10.** O-grade form **doru-*. DEODAR, from Sanskrit *dāru*, wood, timber. [Pokorny *deru-* 214.]

des- Enemy, foreigner, slave. Possible root, found only in Indo-Iranian and Greek. Suffixed o-grade form **dos-elo-* (feminine **dos-elā-*). DOULA, DULOSIS; HIERODULE, from Greek *doulos* (feminine *doulē*), slave (oldest Mycenaean Greek form *doelos*, *doela*). [Not in Pokorny; compare Sanskrit *dāsaḥ*, enemy (< **dos-o-*).]

deu-¹ To lack, be wanting. **1.** Possibly suffixed form **deu-s-*. **a.** TIRE¹, from Old English *tēorian*, tyrian, to fail, tire (< "to fall behind"), from Germanic **teuzōn*; **b.** DEONTOLOGY, from Greek *dein*, to lack, want. **2.** Suffixed form **deu-tero-*. DEUTERO-; DEUTERAGONIST, DEUTERIUM, DEUTERONOMY, from Greek *deuteros*, "missing," next, second. **3.** Suffixed zero-grade form **du-s-*, combining form of **dew-es-*, "a lack", treated separately under **dus-**. [Pokorny 3. *deu-* 219.]

deu-² To do, perform, show favor, revere. **1.** Suffixed zero-grade form **dw-eno-*. **a.** BONBON, BONITO, BONNY, BONUS, BOON²; BONANZA, BONHOMIE, DEBONAIR, from Latin *bonus*, good (< "useful, efficient, working"); **b.** adverbial form **dw-enē*. BENEDICTION, BENEFACTION, BENEFACTOR, BENEFIC, BENEFICENCE, BENEFIT, BENEVOLENT, BENIGN, BEN TROVATO, HERB BENNET, from Latin *bene*, well; **c.** diminutive form **dw-en-elo-*. BEAU, BEAUTY, BELLE; BELDAM, BELLADONNA, BELVEDERE, EMBELLISH, from Latin *bellus*, handsome, pretty, fine. **2.** Possibly suffixed zero-grade form **dw-eye-*. BEATITUDE; BEATIFIC, BEATIFY, from Latin *beāre*, to make blessed. **3.** Possible (but unlikely for formal and semantic reasons) suffixed zero-grade form **du-nə-*. DYNAMIC, DYNAMITE, DYNAST, DYNASTY; AERODYNE, from Greek *dunasthai*, to be able. [Pokorny 2. *(deu-)* 218.]

deuə- Long (in duration). (Oldest form **deuh₂-*, with metathesized variant form **dweh₂-*, colored to **dwah₂-*, contracted to **dwā-*.) Suffixed zero-grade form **dū-ro-* (< **duə-ro-*). DOUR, DURABLE, DURAMEN, DURANCE, DURATION, DURESS, DURUM; DURAIN, DURA MATER, ENDURE, INDURATE, OBDURATE, PERDURABLE, THERMODURIC, from Latin *dūrus*, hard (< "long-lasting, enduring") with derived verb *dūrāre*, to last.

deuk- To lead. **1a.** TUG; WANTON, from Old English *tēon*, to pull, draw, lead; **b.** ZUGUNRUHE, ZUGZWANG, from Old High German *ziohan*, to pull. Both **a** and **b** from Germanic **teuhan*. **2.** Suffixed zero-grade form **duk-ā-*. TOW¹, TAUT, from Old English *togian*, to draw, drag, from Germanic **tugōn*. **3.** Suffixed o-grade form **douk-eyo-*. TIE, from Old English *tīegan*, *tigan*, to bind. **4.** Suffixed o-grade form **douk-mo-*. TEAM, from Old English *tēam*, descendant, family, race, brood, team, from Germanic **tau(h)maz*. **5.** TEEM¹, from Old English *tēman*, *tīeman*, to beget, from Germanic denominative **tau(h)mjan*. **6.** Basic form **deuk-*. DOGE, DOUCHE, DUCAL, DUCAT, DUCE, DUCHESS, DUCHY, DUCT, DUCTILE, DUKE; ABDUCENS, ABDUCT, ADDUCE, AQUEDUCT, CIRCUMDUCTION, CON³, CONDOTTIERE, CONDUCE, CONDUCT, DEDUCE, DEDUCT, EDUCE, ENDUE, INDUCE, INTRODUCE, PRODUCE, REDOUBT, REDUCE, SEDUCTION, SUBDUCTION, SUBDUE, TRADUCE, TRANSDUCER, from Latin *dūcere*, to lead (past participle *ductus* < suffixed zero-grade form **duk-to-*). **7.** Suffixed zero-grade form **duk-ā-*. EDUCATE, from Latin *ēducāre*, to lead out, bring up (*ē-* < *ex-*, out; see **eghs**). [Pokorny *deuk-* 220.]

dhabh- To fit together. **1.** DAFT, DEFT, from Old English *gedæfte*, mild, gentle, from Germanic **dab-*, to be fitting, in participial adjective **gadafta-*, fitting, becoming (**ga-*, collective prefix; see **kom**). **2.** Probably suffixed form **dhabh-ro-*. FABRIC, FABRICATE, FORGE[1], from Latin *faber*, artisan (< "he who fits together"). [Pokorny 2. *dhabh-* 233.]

dhal- To bloom. **1.** Suffixed form **dhal-yo-*. THALIA, THALLUS; PROTHALLUS, from Greek *thallein*, to flourish (> *thallos*, a shoot). **2.** Suffixed o-grade form **dhol-isko-*, from Old Irish *duilesc*, a type of alga, dulse. [Pokorny *dhāl-* 234.]

dhē- To set, put. (Contracted from earlier **dheh₁-*.)
I. Basic form **dhē-*. **1.** Suffixed form **dhē-ti-*, "thing laid down or done, law, deed." DEED; INDEED, from Old English *dǣd*, doing, deed, from Germanic **dēdiz*. **2.** Suffixed form **dhē-k-*. THECA, TICK[3]; AMPHITHECIUM, APOTHECARY, APOTHECIUM, BIBLIOTHECA, BODEGA, BOUTIQUE, CLEISTOTHECIUM, ENDOTHECIUM, PERITHECIUM, from Greek *thēkē*, receptacle. **3.** Basic form **dhē-*. BARD[2], PURDAH, from Old Persian *dā-*, to place. **4.** Suffixed form **dhē-to-*, set down, created, in Old Iranian compound **khvatō-dāta-* (see **s(w)e-**). **5.** Reduplicated form **dhe-dhē-*. SAMHITA, SANDHI, from Sanskrit *dadhāti*, he places (past participle *-hita-*, from suffixed zero-grade **dhə-to-*).
II. O-grade form **dhō-*. **1.** DO[1]; FORDO, from Old English *dōn*, to do, from Germanic **dōn*. **2.** Suffixed o-grade form **dhō-men-*. ABDOMEN, from Latin *abdōmen*, belly, abdomen, perhaps "part placed away, concealed part" (*ab-*, away; see **apo**). **3.** Suffixed o-grade form **dhō-mo-*. **a.** DOOM, from Old English *dōm*, judgment (< "thing set or put down"); **b.** -DOM, from Old English *-dōm*, abstract suffix indicating state, condition, or power; **c.** Old Norse *-dōmr*, condition, in compound *hōrdōmr* (see **kā-**); **d.** (*i*) DUMA, from Russian *duma*, thought, council, Duma; (*ii*) DUMKA, from Ukranian *duma*, thought, narrative poem. Both (*i*) and (*ii*) from a Germanic source akin to Gothic *dōms*, judgment; **e.** DEEM, from Old English *dēman*, to judge, from Germanic denominative *dōmjan*. **a–e** all from Germanic *dōmaz*.
III. Zero-grade form **dhə-*. **1a.** Prefixed form **kom-dhə-*. ABSCOND, INCONDITE, RECONDITE, SCONCE[2], from Latin *condere*, to put together, establish, preserve (**kom*, together; see **kom**); **b.** prefixed and suffixed form **kom-dh(ə)-yo-*. CONDIMENT, SALMAGUNDI, from Latin *condīre*, to season, flavor; **c.** compound **kred-dhə-* (see **kerd-**[1]); **d.** compound suffixed form **gʷṛə-dh(ə)-o-* (see **gʷerə-**[3]); **e.** compound suffixed forms **werə-dh(ə)-o-* and **wṛə-dh(ə)-o-* (see **werə-**[3]). **2.** Suffixed zero-grade form **dhə-k-* (perhaps zero-grade of **dhē-k-* in **I. 2.** above). **a.** -FACIENT, FACT, FACTION[1], -FACTION, FACTITIOUS, FACTITIVE, FACTOR, FACTORY, FAENA, FASHION, FEASIBLE, FEAT[1], FEATURE, FETISH, -FIC, -FY, HACIENDA; AFFAIR, AFFECT[1], AFFECT[2], AFFECTION, AMPLIFY, ARTIFACT, ARTIFICE, BEATIFIC, BENEFACTION, BENEFIC, BENEFICE, BENEFICENCE, BENEFIT, CHAFE, COMFIT, CONFECT, CONFETTI, COUNTERFEIT, DEFEASANCE, DEFEAT, DEFECT, DEFICIENT, DISCOMFIT, EDIFICE, EDIFY, EFFECT, EFFICACIOUS, EFFICIENT, FACSIMILE, FACTOTUM, FECKLESS, FORFEIT, INFECT, JUSTIFY, MALEFACTOR, MALFEASANCE, MANUFACTURE, MISFEASANCE, MODIFY, MOLLIFY, NIDIFY, NOTIFY, NULLIFY, OFFICINAL, ORIFICE, PERFECT, PETRIFY, PLUPERFECT, PONTIFEX, PREFECT, PROFICIENT, PROFIT, PUTREFY, QUALIFY, RAREFY, RECTIFY, REFECT, REFECTORY, RUBEFACIENT, SACRIFICE, SATISFY, SPINIFEX, SUFFICE, SUFFICIENT, SURFEIT, TUBIFEX, TUMEFACIENT, VIVIFY, from Latin *facere* (< **fak-yo-*), to do, make, and Latin combining form *-fex* (< **-fak-s*), "maker"; **b.** FAÇADE, FACE, FACET, FACIAL, FACIES; DEFACE, EFFACE, SURFACE, from Latin derivative *faciēs*, shape, face (< "form imposed on something"); **c.** OFFICE, from Latin compound *officium* (< **opi-fici-om*), service, duty, business, performance of

work (**opi-*, work; see **op-**[1]); **d.** further suffixed form **dhə-k-li-*. FACILE, FACILITATE, FACULTY, DIFFICULTY, from Latin *facilis* (< Archaic Latin *facul*), feasible, easy. **3.** Suffixed zero-grade form **dhə-s-* (probably identical with zero-grade of **dhēs-**). NEFARIOUS, from Latin *fās*, divine law, right. **4.** MULTIFARIOUS, OMNIFARIOUS, from Latin *-fāriam*, adverbial suffix, as in *bifāriam*, in two places, parts, double, from **dwi-dh(ə)-*, "making two" (**dwi-*, two; see **dwo-**). **5.** Reduplicated form **dhi-dhə-*. THESIS, THETIC; ANATHEMA, ANTITHESIS, DIATHESIS, EPENTHESIS, EPITHET, HYPOTHECATE, HYPOTHESIS, METATHESIS, PARENTHESIS, PROSTHESIS, PROTHESIS, SYNTHESIS, from Greek *tithenai*, to put, with zero-grade noun *thesis* (**dhə-ti-*), a placing, and verbal adjective *thetos* (**dhə-to-*), placed. **6.** Suffixed zero-grade form **dhə-mṇ*. THEMATIC, THEME; SPELEOTHEM, from Greek *thema*, that which is placed or laid down, proposition, pile. **7.** Reduced form **dh-* in compound **au-dh-* (see **au-**[4]). [Pokorny 2. *dhē-* 235.]

dheb- Dense, firm, compressed. DAPPER, from Middle Dutch and Middle Low German *dapper*, heavy, strong; later quick, nimble, from Germanic suffixed form **dap-ra-*. [Pokorny *dheb-* 239.]

dhegʷʰ- To burn, warm. **1.** Suffixed o-grade (causative) form **dhogʷʰ-eyo-*. FOMENT, FOMITE, from Latin *fovēre*, to warm, cherish, foment. **2.** Suffixed basic form **dhegʷʰ-rā-*. TEPHRA, from Greek *tephrā*, ash. [Pokorny *dheguh-* 240.]

dhē(i)- To suck. (Contracted from earlier **dheh₁(i)-*.)
I. Unextended form **dhē-*. **1.** Suffixed form **dhē-mnā-*. FEMALE, FEME, FEMININE; EFFEMINATE, from Latin *fēmina*, woman (< "she who suckles"). **2.** Suffixed form **dhē-to-*. FAWN[2], FETAL, FETUS; EFFETE, FETICIDE, SUPERFETATE, from Latin *fētus*, pregnancy, childbearing, offspring, with adjective *fētus*, *fēta*, pregnant. **3.** Suffixed form **dhē-kwondo-*. FECUND, from Latin *fēcundus*, fruitful. **4.** Suffixed form **dhē-no-*. FENNEL, FINOCHIO; FENUGREEK, SAINFOIN, from Latin *fēnum*, *faenum*, hay (< "produce"). **5.** Suffixed form **dhē-lo-*. FELLATIO, from Latin *fēlāre*, *fellāre*, to suck. **6.** Suffixed form **dhē-l-īk-*. FELICITATE, FELICITY; FELICIFIC, INFELICITY, from Latin *fēlīx*, fruitful, fertile, lucky, happy. **7.** Suffixed form **dhē-lā-*. ENDOTHELIUM, EPITHELIUM, MESOTHELIUM, from Greek *thēlē*, nipple. **8.** Suffixed form **dhē-l-u-*. THEELIN from Greek *thēlus*, female.
II. Extended form **dhēi-*, with zero-grade **dhī-* (< **dhiə-*, metathesized from **dhəi-*). Probably suffixed form **dhī-lyo-* (< **dhiə-lyo-*). FILIAL, FILIATION, FILS[1]; AFFILIATE, HIDALGO, from Latin *fīlius*, son, and *fīlia*, daughter (but these are conceivably from the root **bheuə-**). [Pokorny *dhē(i)-* 241.]

dheiə- To see, look. (Oldest form **dheih₂-*, with variant [metathesized] form **dhyeh₂-*, colored to **dhyah₂-*, contracted to **dhyā-*.) **1.** Suffixed variant form **dhyā-mṇ*. SEMANTIC, SEMATIC; POLYSEMOUS, SEMAPHORE, SEMASIOLOGY, SEMEME, SEMIOCHEMICAL, SEMIOLOGY, SEMIOTIC, from Greek *sēma* (stem *sēmat-*) and *sēmeion*, sign. **2.** ZEN; ZAZEN, from Sanskrit *dhyāti*, he meditates (< "observes mentally"). [Pokorny *dheiə-* 243.]

dheigh- To form, build. (Oldest form **dheiĝh-*.) **1.** DAIRY, from Old English *dǣge*, bread kneader, from Germanic **daigjōn-*. **2.** Zero-grade form **dhigh-*. LADY, from Old English compound *hlǣfdige*, mistress of a household (< "bread kneader"; *hlāf*, bread, loaf), from Germanic **dig-*. **3.** Suffixed o-grade form **dhoigh-o-*. **a.** DOUGH, from Old English *dāg*, dough; **b.** TEIGLACH, from Old High German *teic*, dough. Both **a** and **b** from Germanic **daigaz*; **c.** PARADISE, from Avestan *daēza-*, wall (originally made of clay or mud bricks). **4.** Suffixed zero-grade form **dhigh-ūrā-*. FIGURE, FIGURINE; CONFIGURE, DISFIGURE, PREFIGURE, TRANSFIGURE, from Latin *figūra*, form, shape. **5.** Nasalized zero-grade form **dhi-n-gh-*. FAINÉANT,

FAINT, FEIGN, FEINT, FICTILE, FICTION, FIGMENT; EFFI-
GY, from Latin *fingere*, to shape. **6.** Probable nasalized
zero-grade form **dhi-n-g(h)-*. THIGMOTAXIS, THIX-
OTROPY, from Greek *thinganein*, to touch. [Pokorny
dheigh- 244.]

dhel- A hollow. **1.** DELL, from Old English *dell*, valley,
from Germanic **daljō*. **2a.** DALE, from Old English
dæl, valley; **b.** NEANDERTHAL, THALWEG, from Old
High German *tal*, valley (also in Modern German
Neandert(h)al, valley of the Neander River). Both **a**
and **b** from Germanic **dalam*, valley. **3.** DALLES, from
Old Norse *dæla*, wooden gutter on a ship, from Germanic **del-*. [Pokorny 1. *dhel-* 245.]

dhelbh- To dig, excavate. DELVE, from Old English *delfan*, to dig, from Germanic *delban*. [Pokorny
dhelbh- 246.]

dhembh- To bury. Suffixed zero-grade forms
*dhṃbh-o- and **dhṃbh-ā-*. **1.** CENOTAPH, EPITAPH,
TAPHONOMY, from Greek *taphos* (< **thaphos*) and
taphē, tomb. **2.** DAKHMA, from Avestan *daxma-* (<
*dafma-), dakhma (< ***"tomb"). [Pokorny *(dhembh-)*
248.]

dhen-¹ To run, flow. Suffixed o-grade form **dhon-ti-*.
FONT¹, FONTANEL, FOUNTAIN, from Latin *fōns* (stem
font-), spring, fountain. [Pokorny 1. *dhen-* 249.]

dhen-² Palm of the hand. Suffixed form **dhen-r̥*. THE-
NAR, from Greek *thenar*, palm of the hand. [Pokorny
2. *dhen-* 249.]

dher-¹ To make muddy; darkness. Assumed base of
various suffixed and extended root forms. **1.** Suffixed
form **dher-g-*. DARK, from Old English *deorc*, dark,
from Germanic **derka-*. **2.** Suffixed zero-grade form
*dhr-egh-. **a.** DROSS, from Old English *drōs*, dregs,
from Germanic suffixed form **drah-sta-*; **b.** DREG,
from Old Norse *dregg*, dregs, from Germanic **dragjō*.
3. Suffixed extended zero-grade form **dhrə-bh-*. **a.**
DRIVEL, from Old English *dreflian*, to drivel; **b.** DRAB²,
from a Celtic source probably akin to Middle Irish
drab, dregs; **c.** DRABBLE, from Middle English *drabel-
en*, to draggle, from a Low German source akin to Low
German *drabbelen*, to paddle in water or mire, drag-
gle. **a** and **b** and probably **c** from Germanic **drab-*. **4.**
Suffixed extended zero-grade form **dhr̥ə-gh-* (oldest
form **dhr̥h₂-gh-*). **a.** ATARACTIC, from Greek *taras-
sein* (Attic *tarattein*), to confuse, disturb; **b.** TRACHEA,
TRACHOMA, TRACHYTE, from Greek *trakhus*, rough.
[Pokorny 1. *dher-* 251.]

dher-² To hold firmly, support. **1.** Suffixed form
*dher-mo-. FARM, FERMATA, FIRM¹, FIRM², FIRMA-
MENT; AFFIRM, CONFIRM, FURL, INFIRM, INFIRMARY,
from Latin *firmus*, firm, strong. **2.** Perhaps extended
form **dhergh-*, seen by some as the source of Latin
fortis, strong, but this is more likely from **bhergh-²**.
3. Suffixed zero-grade form **dhr-ono-*. THRONE, from
Greek *thronos*, seat, throne (< "support"). **4.** Suffixed
form **dher-mn̥*. DHARMA, from Sanskrit *dharma*,
statute, law (< "that which is established firmly").
5. Suffixed form **dher-eno-*. DHARNA, from Prakrit
dharaṇa, a holding firm. **6.** Suffixed o-grade form
*dhor-o-. CHURIDAR, SIRDAR, TAHSILDAR, ZAMINDAR,
from Iranian *dāra-*, holding, whence Persian *-dār*. **7.**
Suffixed o-grade form **dhor-eyo-*. DARIUS, from Old
Persian *dāra-yava(h)uš*, "holding the firm good," from
dāraya-, to hold firm, uphold (*va(h)uš*, good; see
wesu-). [Pokorny 2. *dher-* 252.]

dher-³ To drone, murmur, buzz. Assumed base of extended zero-grade form **dhrēn-*. **1.** DRONE¹, from Old
English *drān, drǣn*, male honeybee, from Germanic
*drēn-. **2.** THRENODY, from Greek *thrēnos*, dirge, lament. [Pokorny 3. *dher-* 255.]

dhers- To venture, be bold. O-grade form **dhors-* and
zero-grade form **dhr̥s-*. DARE, DURST, from Old English *dearr* and *durst*, first and third person singular
present and past indicative of *durran*, to venture, re-

spectively from Germanic **dars-* and **durz-*. [Pokorny
dhers- 259.]

dhēs- Root of words in religious concepts. (Contracted from earlier **dheh₁s-*; possibly an extension of
*dheh₁-, to put, set; see **dhē-**.) **1.** Suffixed form **dhēs-
yā-*. FAIR², FERIA, from Latin *fēriae* (< Archaic Latin
fēsiae), holidays. **2.** Suffixed form **dhēs-to-*. FEAST,
FEST, FESTAL, FESTIVAL, FESTIVE, FESTOON, FETE, FI-
ESTA; OKTOBERFEST, from Latin *fēstus*, festive. **3.** Suffixed zero-grade form **dhas-no-*. FANATIC; PROFANE,
from Latin *fānum*, temple. **4.** Suffixed zero-grade form
*dhas-o-. THEO-; APOTHEOSIS, ATHEISM, ENTHUSIASM,
HENOTHEISM, PANTHEON, POLYTHEISM, TIFFANY, from
Greek *theos* (< **thes-os*), god, also in personal names:
a. DOROTHY, THEODORE, from Greek *Dōrothea* and
Theodōros, both meaning "gift of god" (*dōron*, gift; see
dō-); **b.** TIMOTHY, from Greek *Tīmotheos*, "honoring
god" (*tīmē*, honor; see **kʷeiə-¹**). [Pokorny *dhēs-* 259.]

dheu-¹ Also **dheuə-**. The base of a wide variety of
derivatives meaning "to rise in a cloud," as dust, vapor,
or smoke, and related to semantic notions of breath,
various color adjectives, and forms denoting defective
perception or wits.
 I. Zero-grade form **dhū-* (< **dhuə-*). **1.** Suffixed
form **dhū-mo-*, smoke. **a.** FUMAROLE, FUMATORIUM,
FUMATORY, FUME; FUMARIC ACID, FUMIGATE, FUMI-
TORY, FUNKY¹, PERFUME, SFUMATO, from Latin *fūmus*,
smoke; **b.** -THYMIA; ENTHYMEME, from Greek *thūmos*,
soul, spirit; **c.** THYME, from Greek *thumon, thumos*,
thyme (< "plant having a strong smell"). **2.** Suffixed
form **dhū-li-*. FULIGINOUS, from Latin *fūlīgō*, soot.
 II. Extended form **dheus-*. **1.** Possibly Germanic
*dus-. **a.** DIZZY, from Old English *dysig*, foolish (<
"stupefied," "confused"); **b.** DOZE, probably from a
Scandinavian source akin to Danish *døra*, to make
drowsy. **2.** Suffixed form **dheus-o-*. **a.** DEER; WILDER-
NESS, from Old English *dēor*, animal; **b.** REINDEER,
from Old Norse *dȳr*, animal, deer. Both **a** and **b** from
Germanic **deuzam*, breathing creature, animal (for
the semantics compare Latin *animal* from *anima*,
breath, spirit). **3.** Suffixed o-grade form **dhous-o-*.
DUKHOBOR, from Russian *dukh*, breath, spirit, from
Slavic **dukhŭ*. **4.** Variant form **dhwes-* in nasalized
form **dhwens-*, zero-grade **dhuns-*. **a.** (i) DUST, from
Old English *dūst*, dust, from Germanic suffixed form
*duns-taz; (ii) DOWN², DUVET, DUVETYN; EIDERDOWN,
from Old Norse *dūnn*, bird's down (< "fine like dust").
Both (i) and (ii) from Germanic **duns-*, dust, meal;
b. suffixed form **dh(w)es-es-* in Greek further suffixed
form **th(w)es-es-yon*. THIO-, THION-, from Greek
theion, brimstone, sulfur. **5.** Zero-grade form **dhus-*.
THUJA, THURIBLE; THURIFER, from Greek *thuos*, burnt
sacrifice, incense (> Latin *thūs*, incense), and *thuiā*,
sandarac. **6.** Suffixed zero-grade form **dhus-ko-*. **a.**
DUSK, from Old English *dox*, twilight, from Germanic
*duskaz; **b.** FUSCOUS; OBFUSCATE, SUBFUSC, from
Latin *fuscus*, dark, dusky. **7.** Suffixed zero-grade form
*dhus-no-. **a.** DUN², from Old English *dun(n)*, dark-
brown, from Welsh *dwn*, dull brown color; **b.** DUN-
CAN (personal name), from Irish Gaelic *Donnceann*,
"brown head" (*ceann*, head, from Old Irish *cenn*),
from Middle Irish *donn*, brown (also appearing in
other personal names beginning *Dun-*).
 III. Extended form **dheubh-*. **1.** Zero-grade form
*dhubh-. TYPHUS; ÉTOUFFÉE, STEW, STOVE¹, TYPHLO-
SOLE, from Greek *tūphein* (< **thūphein*), to make
smoke, and *tuphlos*, blind. **2.** Basic form **dheubh-*,
"beclouded in the senses" (but perhaps a separate
root), in suffixed o-grade form **dhoubh-o-*. **a.** DEAF,
from Old English *dēaf*, deaf, from Germanic **daube-*;
b. (i) DUMB, from Old English *dumb*, dumb; (ii) DUM-
MKOPF, from Old High German *tumm, tumb*, dumb.
Both (i) and (ii) from Germanic **dumba-*, from nasalized form **dhu-m-bho-*; **c.** DOVE¹, from Old English
dūfe, dove (< "dark-colored bird"), built on Germanic
*dūbōn-.

IV. Extended zero-grade forms. **1.** Form **dhwel-*.
a. DWELL, from Old English *dwellan*, to deceive (but
influenced in sense by cognate Old Norse *dvelja*, to
tarry), from Germanic **dwelan*, to go or lead astray;
b. *(i)* DOLDRUMS, from Old English *dol*, dull; *(ii)* DOLT,
DULL, from Middle Low German *dul*, dull. Both *(i)*
and *(ii)* from Germanic **dula-*. **2.** Perhaps Old English *docce*, dock (< "dark-colored plant"): DOCK⁴. **3.**
Perhaps Irish *dúd*, pipe: DUDEEN. [Pokorny 4. *dheu-*
261.]

dheu-² To flow. **1.** DEW, from Old English *dēaw*, dew.
2. SUNDEW, from Middle Dutch *dau*, dew. **3.** Germanic
compound **melith-dauwaz* (see **melit-**). **1–3** all from
Germanic **dauwaz*, dew. [Pokorny 1. *dheu-* 259.]

dheu-³ Also **dheuə-** (oldest form **dheuh₂-*). To die.
1. Suffixed o-grade form **dhou-to-*. DEAD, from Old
English *dēad*, dead, from Germanic **dauda-*. **2.** Suffixed o-grade form **dhou-tu-*. DEATH, from Old English *dēath*, death, from Germanic **dauthuz*. **3.** Suffixed o-grade form **dhow-yo-*. DIE¹, from Old Norse
deyja, to die. **4.** Extended zero-grade form **dhuəi-*,
metathesized to **dhwiə-*, contracted to **dhwī-*, whence
suffixed form **dhwī-no-*. DWINDLE, from Old English *dwīnan*, to diminish, languish, from Germanic
*dwīnan. [Pokorny 2. *dheu-* 260.] Compare **dheuə-**.

dheub- Also **dheubh-**. Deep, hollow. **1.** DEEP,
DEPTH, from Old English *dēop*, deep, from Germanic
*deupa-. **2.** DIP, from Old English *dyppan*, to immerse, dip, from Germanic expressive denominative
*duppjan. **3.** Parallel root form **dheubh-*. DIVE¹, from
Old English *dȳfan*, to dip, and *dūfan*, to sink, dive,
from Germanic verb **dūbjan*, from **deub-*, **dub-*.
4. Suffixed parallel root form **dhūbh-(o)n-*, with expressive variants. PYTHON, PYTHON, TYPHON, from
Greek *Pūthōn* and *Tuphōn*, mythical monsters, from
*dhub(h)-n- and **b(h)ud(h)-n-*, which already in Indo-European were doublets by inversion, referring to
"bottom," "foundation," "depths," and the mythological
monsters that inhabited them. **5.** Suffixed zero-grade
form **dhub(h)-no-* in Celtic **dubno-*, world (< "earth,
ground" < "bottom"). DONALD (personal name), from
Old Irish *Domnall*, from Celtic **dubno-walos*, "ruler of
the world" (**walos*, ruler; see **wal-**). [Pokorny *dheu-b-*
267.] Compare **bhudh-**.

dheubh- Wedge, peg, plug. **1.** DUB¹, from Old English
dubbian, to tap, strike (with a sword). **2.** DUB², from
Low German *dubben*, to hit. **3.** DOWEL, from Middle
Low German *dövel*, peg, from Germanic diminutive
*dub-ila-. **1–3** all from Germanic **dub-*. [Pokorny
dheubh- 268.]

dheuə- To close, finish, come full circle. (Oldest
form **dheuh₂-*; perhaps related to or identical with
dheu-³, to die.) **1.** Suffixed zero-grade form **dhū-
no-* (< **dhuə-no-*), enclosed, fortified place; *hill-fort*.
a. *(i)* DOWN¹, DOWN³, from Old English *dūn*, hill (also
becoming Modern English *-don* in such place-names
as WIMBLEDON); *(ii)* DUNE, from Middle Dutch *dūne*,
sandy hill. Both *(i)* and *(ii)* from Germanic **dūnaz*,
possibly from **dhū-no-*; **b.** Celtic **dūnon*, hill, hill-
fort. *(i)* LYON, from Gallo-Latin *Lugudūnum*, "fort of
Lug" (*Lug*, Celtic deity); *(ii)* VERDUN, from Gallo-Latin *Virodūnum*, "fort of men" (*viro-*, man, from Celtic
wiros; see **wī-ro-**); *(iii)* TOWN, from Old English *tūn*,
enclosed place, homestead, village, from Germanic
*tūnaz, fortified place, borrowed from Celtic **dūnon*.
2. Suffixed form **dhū-nes-* (< **dhuə-nes-*). FUNERAL,
from Latin *fūnus*, funeral. [In Pokorny 4. *dheu-* 261.]

dheugh- To produce something of utility. **1.** DOUGH-
TY, from Old English *dyhtig*, *dohtig*, strong (< "productive"), from Germanic extended form **duht-*. **2.** Suffixed form **dheugh-os-*. HEPTATEUCH, HEXATEUCH,
PENTATEUCH, from Greek *teukhos* (< **theukhos*), gear,
anything produced, tool, container, scroll. [Pokorny
dheugh- 271.]

dhghem- Earth. (Oldest form **dhg̑hem-*.) **1.** Suffixed
zero-grade form **(dh)g̑hm̥-on-*, "earthling." BRIDE-
GROOM, from Old English *guma*, man, from Germanic
*gumōn-. **2.** O-grade form **dh(e)ghom-*. CHTHONIC,
ALLOCHTHON, AUTOCHTHON, from Greek *khthōn*,
earth. **3.** Zero-grade form **(dh)g̑hm̥-*. CHAMAEPHYTE,
CHAMELEON, CHAMOMILE, GERMANDER, from Greek
khamai, on the ground. **4.** Suffixed o-grade form **(dh)
g̑hom-o-*. HUMBLE, HUMILIATE, HUMILITY, HUMUS¹;
EXHUME, INHUME, TRANSHUMANCE, from Latin *hu-
mus*, earth. **5.** Suffixed o-grade form **(dh)g̑hom- on-*,
"earthling." **a.** HOMAGE, HOMBRE¹, HOMINID, HOMI-
NIN, HOMO¹, HOMUNCULUS, OMBRE, OMERTA; BONHO-
MIE, HOMICIDE, from Latin *homō*, human being, man;
b. HUMAN, HUMANE, from Latin *hūmānus*, human,
kind, humane (in part from **dhghem-**). **6.** Suffixed
form **(dh)g̑hem-yā-*. CHERNOZEM, SIEROZEM, ZEMST-
VO, from Old Russian *zemĭ*, land, earth. **7.** Full-grade
form **(dh)g̑hem-*. ZAMINDAR, from Persian *zamīn*,
earth, land. [Pokorny *g̑hdem-* 414.]

Language and Culture Note We normally
think of *earthling* as a word useful for distinguish-
ing humans from invading Martians or other extra-
terrestrials. Words meaning "earthling" have been
around for millennia, however, and in Indo-European
distinguish humans from gods—celestial beings of a
different sort. The root **dhghem-** "earth" furnished
the base for a number of words meaning "human being" in the daughter languages. The locative case form,
*dhg̑h(e)mon, "on the earth," could be made into a
noun, **dhg̑h(e)mōn*, "one that is on the earth, earthling, human being." In Latin this became *homo* (stem
homin-, Archaic Latin *hemon-*), "man, human being,"
where the consonant cluster **dhg̑h* was simplified to
h. A related form, **dhg̑hm̥-ōn*, **(dh)g̑hm̥-on-*, became
Old English *guma*, "man," a word that survives today
(in rather hidden form) as the second element of
bridegroom, literally "man of the bride," altered from
Middle English *bridegome* by folk-etymology. • The
contrast inherent in **dhg̑h(e)mōn* between earthlings
and gods is preserved quite clearly in a newly-discov-
ered Gaulish inscription which contains a compound
word *teuoxtonion*, "belonging to gods (and) humans," where *teuo-* (phonetically *dēwo-*) means "god"
(see **dyeu-**) and *-khtonion* (phonetically *ghdonion*)
means "humans."

---

dhghū- Fish. (Oldest form **dhg̑hū-*.) ICHTHYO-, from
Greek *ikhthūs*, fish. [Pokorny *g̑hdū-* 416.]

dhgh(y)es- Yesterday. (Oldest form **dhg̑h(y)es-*.
Originally an archaic compound *dhg̑h(y)es*, "on this
day," of a deictic particle *g̑h(i)* derived from the pronominal stem **gho-** and a noun *dyes*, day, derived
from the root **dyeu-**.) Suffixed (comparative) form
*(dh)ghes-ter-. YESTER-, YESTERDAY, from Old English
geostran, *giestran*, "yester-," from Germanic **ges-ter-*.
[Pokorny *g̑hdiés* 416.]

dhgʷhei- To perish, die away. Zero-grade form
*dhgʷhi-. **1.** Suffixed form **dhgʷhi-n-wo-*. PHTHISIS,
from Greek *phthīnein*, to die away. **2.** Suffixed form
*dhgʷhi-yo-. KHAPRA BEETLE, from Sanskrit *kṣiyate*,
he perishes, and causative *kṣāpayati*, he destroys.
[Pokorny *g̑hdei(ə)-* 487.]

dhgʷher- To flow, move forcefully, with derivatives
referring to ruin and destruction. Perhaps Greek
phtheir, louse (if from *phtheirein*, to scatter, sweep
off course, destroy, from suffixed form **dhgʷher-*):
PHTHIRIASIS. [Pokorny *gʷhder-* 487.]

dhīgʷ- To stick, fix. **1a.** DIKE¹, DITCH, from Old
English *dīc*, trench, moat; **b.** DIG, from Middle Eng-
lish *diggen*, to dig, from a source perhaps akin to Old
French *digue*, trench. Both **a** and **b** from Germanic
*dīk-. **2.** FIBULA, FICHU, FINCA, FISHGIG, FIX, FIXATE,
FIXITY, FIXTURE; AFFIX, ANTEFIX, CRUCIFY, INFIBU-

LATE, INFIX, MICROFICHE, PREFIX, SUFFIX, TRANSFIX, from Latin *fīgere*, to fasten, fix, and from *fībula*, clasp (shortened from **fīvibula*, from *fīvere*, archaic variant of *fīgere*). [Pokorny *dhēigʷ-* 243.]

-dhlo- See **-tro-**.

dhragh- To draw, drag on the ground. Rhyming variant of **tragh-**. **1a.** DRAW, from Old English *dragan*, to draw, pull; **b.** DRAG, from Old Norse *draga*, to draw, pull (or Old English *dragan*); **c.** DRAY, from Old English *dræge*, dragnet; **d.** DRAFT, from Middle English *draught*, a pull, from a Scandinavian source akin to Old Norse **drāhtr*, *drāttr*, act of drawing. **a–d** all from Germanic **dragan*, to draw, pull. **2.** DROSHKY, from Russian *drogi*, a wagon. [Pokorny *dherāgh-* 257.] See also variant form **dhreg-**.

dhreg- To draw, glide. Variant form of **dhragh-**. (Oldest form **dhreǵ-*.) **1.** DRINK, from Old English *drincan*, to drink, from nasalized Germanic form **drenkan*, to draw into the mouth, drink. **2.** DRENCH, from Old English *drencan*, to soak, from nasalized o-grade Germanic causative form **drankjan*, "to cause to drink." **3.** DROWN, from a Scandinavian or late Old English source similar to Old Norse *drukkna*, to drown, from Germanic zero-grade suffixed form **drunk-nōn*. [Pokorny *dhreǵ-* 273.]

dhregh- To run. **1.** TROCHANTER, TROCHE, TROCHEE; TROCHOPHORE, from Greek *trekhein* (< **threkhein*), to run, and o-grade derivative *trokhos*, wheel. **2.** O-grade form **dhrogh-*. TROCHLEA, TRUCK¹, TRUCKLE, from Greek *trokhileia*, *trokhilia*, system of pulleys, roller of a windlass. [Pokorny 1. *dhregh-* 273.]

dhreibh- To drive, push; snow. **1.** DRIVE, DROVE², from Old English *drīfan*, to drive, rush, from Germanic **drīban*. **2.** DRIFT, from Middle English *drift*, drove, herd, akin to Old Norse *drift*, snowdrift, and Middle Dutch *drift*, herd, from Germanic zero-grade suffixed form **driftiz*. [Pokorny *dhreibh-* 274.]

dhreu- To fall, flow, drip, droop. **1.** Extended form **dhreus-*. DRIZZLE, from Old English *-drysnian* (in *gedrysnian*, to pass away, vanish), from zero-grade Germanic derived verb **drus-inōn*. **2.** Extended o-grade form **dhrous-*. **a.** DREARY, from Old English *drēor*, flowing blood, from Germanic **drauzaz*; **b.** DROWSE, from Old English *drūsian*, to be sluggish, from Germanic **drūsjan*. **3.** Extended zero-grade form **dhrub-*. **a.** DROP, from Old English *dropa*, drop, from Germanic **drupan*; **b.** DROOP, from Old Norse *drūpa*, to hang down, from Germanic **drūpōn*, to let fall; **c.** DRIP, from Middle English *drippen*, to drip, drop, from an unattested Old English **dryppan* or another source akin to Old English *droppa*, drop, from Germanic geminated **drupp-*; **d.** Germanic **drup-*, to drip, in compound **obisdrup-* (see **upo-**). **4.** Suffixed zero-grade form **dhrubh-yo-*. LITHOTRIPTER, LITHOTRITY, from Greek *thruptein*, to crumble. [Pokorny *dhreu-* 274.]

dhreugh- To deceive. DREAM, from Old English *drēam*, joy, music (modern senses from Old Norse *draumr*, vision, dream), from Germanic suffixed form **drau(g)maz*. [Pokorny 2. *dhreugh-* 276.]

-dhro- See **-tro-**.

dhugǝter- Daughter. (Oldest form **dhugh₂ter-*.) DAUGHTER, from Old English *dohtor*, daughter, from Germanic **dohtar*. [Pokorny *dhug(h)ǝter* 277.]

dhwen- To make noise. DIN, from Old English *dyne*, noise, from Germanic **duniz*. [Pokorny *dhu̯en-* 277.]

dhwenǝ- To disappear, die. (Oldest form **dhwenh₂-*.) Suffixed zero-grade form **dhwṇǝ-tos*. THANATOS; EUTHANASIA, TANSY, THANATOLOGY, from Greek *thanatos*, death. [In Pokorny 4. *dheu-* 261.]

dhwer- Door, doorway (usually in plural). Originally an ablauting noun **dhwor*, **dhur-*, in the plural, designating the entrance to the enclosure (**dhwor-o-*) surrounding the house proper. **1.** Zero-grade form **dhur-* in suffixed forms **dhur-ṇs* (accusative plural) and **dhur-o-* (neuter). DOOR, from Old English *duru*, door (feminine, originally plural), and *dor*, door (neuter), respectively from Germanic **durunz* and **duram*. **2.** Suffixed o-grade form **dhwor-āns* (accusative plural). FAROUCHE, FOREIGN, VICAR FORANE, from Latin *forās*, (toward) out of doors, outside. **3.** Suffixed o-grade form **dhwor-ois* (locative plural). FOREST; AFFOREST, FAUBOURG, FORECLOSE, FORFEIT, from Latin *forīs*, (being) out of doors. **4.** Suffixed o-grade form **dhwor-o-*. FORENSIC, FORUM, from Latin *forum*, marketplace (originally the enclosed space around a home). **5.** DARI; DURBAR, from Old Persian *duvara-*, door, gate. **6.** Zero-grade form **dhur-*. THYROID; THYREOPHORAN, from Greek *thurā*, door. [Pokorny *dhu̯ĕr-* 278.]

digh- A goat. Possibly related (by metathesis) to **gh(a)id-o-**. TYKE, from Old Norse *tīk*, bitch, from Germanic **tikk-* (with expressive consonantism), from **tig-*. [Pokorny *digh-* 222.]

dlegh- To engage oneself. European root found in Celtic, Germanic, Slavic, and possibly Latin. **1a.** PLAY, from Old English *plegian*, to exercise oneself, play; **b.** PLEDGE; FRANKPLEDGE, REPLEVIN, from Late Latin *plevium* (> Old French *plevir*, to pledge), pledge, guarantee; **c.** PLIGHT², from Old English *pliht*, danger, peril, from Germanic derivative noun **plehtiz*. **a–c** from Germanic **plegan*, probably altered (by dissimilation) from **tlegan*. **2.** Zero-grade form **dlgh-*. INDULGE, from Latin *indulgēre*, to indulge, explained by some as from prefixed and suffixed stative form **en-dlgh-ē-* (**en-*, in; see **en**). [Pokorny *dhlgh-* 271.]

dlk̑-u- Sweet. **1.** Suffixed form **dlk̑-wi-*. DOLCE, DOLCETTO, DOUCEUR, DULCET; BILLET-DOUX, DULCE DE LECHE, DULCIFY, from Latin *dulcis*, sweet (> French *doux*). **2.** Basic form **dlk̑u-*, dissimilated to **glk̑u-* in Greek. **a.** GLUCO-, GLUCOSE; LICORICE, from Greek *glukus*, sweet; **b.** suffixed form **gluk-ero-*. GLYCERIN, from Greek *glukeros*, sweet. [Pokorny *dlk̑ú-* 222.]

dṇghū- Tongue. (Oldest form **dṇĝhū-*.) **1a.** TONGUE, from Old English *tunge*, tongue; **b.** BILTONG, from Middle Dutch *tonghe*, tongue. Both **a** and **b** from Germanic **tungōn-*. **2.** LANGUAGE, LANGUET, LIGULA, LIGULE, LINGO, LINGUA, LINGUINE, LINGUIST; BILINGUAL, from Latin *lingua* (< Archaic Latin *dingua*), tongue, language. [Pokorny *dṇghū* 223.]

dō- To give. (Oldest form **deh₃-*, colored to **doh₃-*, contracted to **dō-*.) **1.** Zero-grade form **də-*. DADO, DATE¹, DATIVE, DATUM, DIE²; ADD, BETRAY, EDITION, PERDITION, RENDER, RENT¹; SURRENDER, TRADITION, TRAITOR, TREASON, VEND, from Latin *dare*, to give. **2.** Suffixed form **dō-no-*. DONATION, DONATIVE, DONOR; CONDONE, PARDON, from Latin *dōnum*, gift. **3.** Suffixed form **dō-t(i)-*. **a.** DOT², DOWAGER, DOWER, DOWRY; ENDOW, from Latin *dōs* (genitive *dōtis*), dowry; **b.** DACHA, from Russian *dacha*, gift, dacha, from Slavic **datja*; **c.** SAMIZDAT, from Russian *samizdat*, samizdat, from *dat'*, to give. **4.** Suffixed form **dō-ro-*. LOBSTER THERMIDOR, PANDORA, from Greek *dōron*, gift. **5.** Reduplicated form **di-dō-*. DOSE; ANECDOTE, ANTIDOTE, APODOSIS, EPIDOTE, from Greek *didonai*, to give, with zero-grade noun *dosis* (< **də-ti-*), something given. **6.** Suffixed compounding form **-dō-t-* in compound **sakro-dōt-* (see **sak-**). [Pokorny *dō-* 223.]

Language and Culture Note Most of the derivatives of the root **dō-** refer to "giving": Sanskrit *dadāti*, Greek *didonai*, Latin *dare*, Old Church Slavonic *dati*, Lithuanian *duoti*, and Armenian *tam* are all verbs meaning "give." However, the picture seems skewed somewhat by the Hittite cognate of these forms, the verb *dā-*, which means "take"— seemingly the opposite of "give." In fact, "taking" is not so much the opposite as the flip-side of "giving": it depends on whose point of view one takes when one views the whole transaction, which involves one party giving and one party receiving or taking. From the point of view of the giver, the action is "giving"; from the point of view of the receiver, the action is "receiving." Thus the descendant of **dō-** in Hittite refers to the same action as its cognates in the other Indo-European languages, just from the point of view of the receiver. It is in fact quite common for roots that refer to types of exchange to have some descendants referring to the one half, and some referring to the other half, of the exchange relationship. Thus the English reflex of **ghabh-** is *give*, while the Irish cognate *gaibid* means "takes"; German *nehmen* "take" is cognate with Greek *nemein* "to apportion out, distribute" (see **nem-**); and compare also English *to loan*, meaning either "to lend" (as in *I loaned her the money*) or, regionally, "to borrow" (as in *I loaned the book from the library*).

drem- To sleep. Suffixed zero-grade form **dṛm-yo-*. DORMANT, DORMER, DORMITORY, from Latin *dormīre*, to sleep. [Pokorny *drē-* 226.]

[dreug- Dry. Germanic root. **1.** DROUGHT, from Old English *drūgoth, drūgath*, dryness, drought. **2.** DRY, from Old English *drȳge*, dry, from Germanic suffixed form **drūg-i-*. **3.** DRAIN, from Old English *drēahnian*, to strain, drain, from Germanic variant form **draug-.*]

dus- Bad, evil; mis- (used as a prefix). Derivative of **deu-¹. 1.** DYS-, from Greek *dus-*, bad. **2.** DURGA, from Sanskrit *Durgā*, Durga, (short for *Durgā Devī*, "goddess who is difficult to approach"), from *durgā*, feminine of *durgaḥ*, difficult to approach, from *dus-* (becoming *dur-* before voiced consonants), bad, difficult (**-ga-*, going, coming; see **gʷā-**). [Pokorny *dus-* 227.]

dwei- To fear. Original meaning "to be in doubt, be of two minds"; related to **dwo-**. **1.** Suffixed form **dwei-ro-*. DIRE, from Latin *dīrus*, fearful, horrible (originally a dialect form). **2.** Suffixed form **dwey-eno-*. DEINON-YCHUS, DINOSAUR, DINOTHERE, from Greek *deinos*, fearful, monstrous. **3.** Suffixed form **dwei-mo-*. DEIMOS, from Greek *deimos*, fear. [Pokorny *dṷei-* 227.]

dwo- Two.
  I. Variant form **duwo*. **1a.** TWO, from Old English *twā*, two (nominative feminine and neuter); **b.** TWAIN, TWAYBLADE, from Old English *twēgen*, two (nominative and accusative masculine). Both **a** and **b** from Germanic **twa*, two. **2.** TWELFTH, TWELVE, from Old English *twelf*, twelve, and *twelfta*, twelfth, from Germanic compound **twa-lif-*, "two left (over from ten)," twelve (**-lif-*, left; see **leikʷ-**).
  II. Adverbial form **dwis* and combining form **dwi-*. **1a.** TWILIGHT, from Old English *twi-*, two; **b.** ZWIEBACK, ZWITTERION, from Old High German *zwi-*, twice; **c.** TWILL, from Old English *twilic*, double, woven of double thread, partial translation of Latin *bilīx*, woven of double thread, **a–c** all from Germanic **twi-*. **2.** BI-¹, BIS, BIS-; BALANCE, BAROUCHE, BEZEL, BISCUIT, BISTORT, from Latin *bis* (combining form *bi-*), twice. **3.** DI-¹, from Greek *dis* (combining form *di-*), twice. **4.** TWIST, from Old English *-twist*, divided object, fork, rope, from Germanic **twis*. **5.** TWICE, from Old English *twige, twiga*, twice, from Germanic **twiyes*. **6.** TWENTY, from Old English *twēntig*, twenty, from Germanic compound **twēgentig*, "twice ten" (**-tig*, ten; see **dekm̥**). **7.** TWINE, from Old English *twīn*, double thread, from Germanic **twiznaz*, double thread, twisted thread. **8.** BETWEEN, BETWIXT, TWIXT, from Old English *betwēonum* and *betweox, betwix*, between, from Germanic compounds **bi-twīhna* and **bi-twisk*, "at the middle point of two" (*bi*, at, by; see **ambhi**). **9.** Suffixed form **dwis-no-*. **a.** TWIN, from Old English *twinn, getwinn*, two by two, twin, from Germanic **twisnaz*, double; **b.** BI-¹, BINAL, BINARY; COMBINE, PINOCHLE, from Latin *bīnī*, two by two, two each. **10.** Suffixed form **dwi-ko-*. TWIG¹, from Old English *twigge*, a branch, from Germanic **twig(g)a*, a

fork. **11.** Compound **dwi-plo-*, twofold (**-plo-*, -fold; see **pel-³**). DIPLO-, DIPLOE, DIPLOID, DIPLOMA; ANA-DIPLOSIS, DIPLODOCUS, from Greek *diploos, diplous*, twofold. **12.** Suffixed reduplicated form **dwi-du-mo-*. DIDYMIUM, DIDYMOUS; EPIDIDYMIS, from Greek *didumos*, double, twin. **13.** Suffixed form **dwi-gha*. DICHA-SIUM, DICHO-, from Greek *dikha*, in two. **2.** DHIVEHI, from Sanskrit *dvīpaḥ*, island (see **ap-²**).
  III. Inflected form **duwō*. **1.** DEUCE¹, DOZEN, DUAL, DUET, DUO, DUO-; DUODECIMAL, DUUMVIR, from Latin *duo*, two. **2.** DUAD, DYAD; DODECAGON, HENDIADYS, from Greek *duo, duō*, two.
  IV. Variant form **du-*. **1.** Compound **du-plo-*, twofold (**-plo-*, -fold; see **pel-³**). DOUBLE, DOUBLET, DOUBLOON, DUPLE, from Latin *duplus*, double. **2.** Compound **du-plek-*, twofold (**-plek-*, -fold; see **plek-**). DUPLEX, DUPLICATE, DUPLICITY; CONDUPLICATE, from Latin *duplex*, double. **3.** Suffixed form **du-bhwio-*. DOUBT, DUBIOUS; REDOUBTABLE, from Latin *dubius*, doubtful (< "hesitating between two alternatives"), and *dubitāre*, to be in doubt. [Pokorny *dṷō(u)* 228.]

dyeu- To shine (and in many derivatives, "sky, heaven, god"). Zero-grades **dyu-* (before consonants) and **diw-* (before vowels).
  I. Basic form **dyeu-*, Jove, the name of the god of the bright sky, head of the Indo-European pantheon. **1.** JOVE, JOVIAL; APOJOVE, SANGIOVESE, from Latin *Iovis*, Jupiter, or *Iov-*, stem of *Iuppiter*, Jupiter. **2.** JULY, from Latin *Iūlius*, "descended from Jupiter" (name of a Roman gens), from derivative **iou-il-*. **3.** Vocative compound **dyeu-pəter*, "O father Jove" (**pəter-*, father; see **pəter-**). JUPITER, from Latin *Iuppiter, Iūpiter*, head of the Roman pantheon. **4.** DIONE, ZEUS; DIAN-THUS, DIOSCURI, from Greek *Zeus* (genitive *Dios* < *Diwos*), Zeus.
  II. Noun **deiwos*, god, formed by *e*-insertion to the zero-grade **diw-* and suffixation of (accented) *-o-*. **1a.** TIU, TUESDAY, from Old English *Tīw* (genitive *Tīwes*), god of war and sky; **b.** TYR, from Old Norse *Týr*, sky god. Both **a** and **b** from Germanic **Tīwaz*. **2.** DEISM, DEITY, JOSS; ADIEU, ADIOS, DEIFIC; DEUS EX MACHINA from Latin *deus*, god. **3.** DIVA, DIVINE, from Latin *dīvus*, divine, god. **4.** DIS, DIVES, from Latin *dīves*, rich (< "fortunate, blessed, divine"). **5.** Suffixed zero-grade form **diw-yo-*, heavenly. DIANA, from Latin *Diāna*, moon goddess. **6.** DEVA, DEVI; DEODAR, DEVANAGARI, from Sanskrit *devaḥ*, god, and *deva-*, divine. **7.** ASMODEUS, from Avestan *daēuua-*, spirit, demon.
  III. Variant form **dyē-* (< earlier **dyeh₁-*). DIAL, DI-ARY, DISMAL; DIURNAL, JOURNAL, JOURNEY; ADJOURN, AJOURÉ, CIRCADIAN, MERIDIAN, POSTMERIDIAN, QUO-TIDIAN, SOJOURN, from Latin *diēs*, day.
  IV. Variant form **deia-* (earlier **deih₂-*). PSYCHE-DELIC, ADELGID, from Greek *dēlos* (< *deyalos*), clear.
  V. Suffixed variant form **dye-s-* in **gh-dyes*, "on this day." See **dhgh(y)es-**. [Pokorny 1. *dei-* 183.]

ē- Adverbial particle. **1a.** OAKUM, from Old English *ā-, ǣ-*, away, off; **b.** Germanic compound **ē-mait-jōn-* (see **mai-¹**). Both **a** and **b** from Germanic **ē*. **2a.** ANANDAMIDE, ASHRAM, KALANCHOE, SATYAGRAHA, from Sanskrit *ā-*, to; **b.** KALA-AZAR, from Old Persian *ā-*, to. Both **a** and **b** from Indo-Iranian **ā, *ā-*, to. [Pokorny *ē* 280.]

-ē- (Contracted from earlier **-eh₁-*.) Verbal suffix forming stative denominative verbs from adjectives, such as **rudh-ē-*, to be red (see **reudh-¹**). [Not in Pokorny.]

ed- To eat; original meaning "to bite." (Oldest form **h₁ed-*.) **1a.** EAT, from Old English *etan*, to eat; **b.** ETCH, from Old High German *ezzen*, to feed on, eat; **c.** ORT, from Middle Dutch *eten*, to eat; **d.** (i) FRET¹, from Old English *fretan*, to devour; (ii) FRASS, from Old High German *frezzan*, to devour. Both (i) and (ii) from Germanic compound **fra-etan*, to eat up (**fra-*, completely; see **per¹**). **a–d** all from Germanic **etan*. **2.** EDACIOUS, EDIBLE, ESCAROLE, ESCULENT, ESURI-

ENT; COMEDO, COMESTIBLE, OBESE, from Latin *edere*, to eat. **3.** PRANDIAL, from Latin compound *prandium*, lunch, probably from **prām-(e)d-yo-*, "first meal" (**prām-*, first; see **per¹**). **4.** Suffixed form **ed-un-o-*. JOTUN, from Old Norse *jötunn*, giant, Jotun, from Germanic **idunaz* (perhaps *"man-eating giant" or "immense eater"). **5.** Suffixed form **ed-un-ā-*. ANODYNE, PLEURODYNIA, from Greek *odunē*, pain (< "gnawing care"). **6.** Suffixed zero-grade form **əd-ti-*. ALFALFA from Old Iranian compound **aspa-sti-*, clover, alfalfa (< "horse fodder"), from **-sti-*, fodder, food (**aspa-*, horse; see **ekwo-**). **7.** SAMOYED, from Russian *-ed*, eater. [Pokorny *ed-* 287.] See also derivative **dent-**.

eg I. Nominative form of the personal pronoun of the first person singular. (Oldest form **eĝ*; for oblique forms see **me-¹**.) **1.** I¹, from Old English *ic*, I, from Germanic **ek*. **2.** Extended form **egō*. EGO, EGOIST, EGOTISM, from Latin *ego*, I. [Pokorny *eĝ-* 291.]

eg- To lack. Suffixed (stative) form **eg-ē-*. INDIGENT, from Latin *egēre*, to lack, be in want. [Pokorny *eg-* 290.]

eghero- Lake. (Oldest form **eĝhero-*.) Possible suffixed variant form **agher-ont-* in Greek *Akherōn*, a river in Hades: ACHERON. [Pokorny *eĝhero-* 291.]

eghi- Snake, eel. (Perhaps originally a taboo deformation of **ogʷhi-**.) **1.** ECHINO-, ECHINUS, from Greek *ekhīnos*, hedgehog (< "snake-eater"); **2.** ECHIDNA, from Greek *ekhidna*, snake, viper. Both **1** and **2** from Greek *ekhis*, snake. See **ogʷhi-**. [Pokorny *angʷ(h)i-* 43.]

eghs Out. (Oldest form **eĝhs*.) **1.** Variant **eks*. **a.** EX¹, EX-; DEUS EX MACHINA, from Latin *ex*, *ex-*, out of, away from; **b.** ECTO-, EX-, EXO-, EXOTERIC, EXOTIC; EKPYROTIC, ELECTUARY, LEKVAR, SYNECDOCHE, from Greek *ex*, *ek*, out of, from. **2.** Suffixed (comparative) variant form **eks-tero-*. **a.** ESTRANGE, EXTERIOR, EXTERNAL, EXTRA-, STRANGE, from Latin *exter*, outward (feminine ablative *exterā*, *extrā*, on the outside); **b.** further suffixed (superlative) form **eks-t(e)r-ēmo-*. EXTREME, EXTREMUM, from Latin *extrēmus*, outermost (**-mo-*, superlative suffix). **3.** Suffixed form **eghs-ko-*. ESCHATOLOGY, from Greek *eskhatos*, outermost, last. **4.** Celtic **eks-*, out (of), in compound **eks-dī-sedo-* (see **sed-¹**). **5.** SAMIZDAT, from Russian *iz*, from, out of, from Balto-Slavic **iz*. [Pokorny *eĝhs* 292.]

egni- Also **ogni-**. Fire. **1.** IGNEOUS, IGNITE; GELIGNITE, IGNITRON, from Latin *ignis*, fire. **2.** AGNI, from Sanskrit *agniḥ*, fire. [Pokorny *egnis* 293.]

egʷh- To drink. Suffixed lengthened-grade form **ēgʷh-r-yo-*. **1.** INEBRIATE, RYEGRASS, from Latin *ēbrius*, drunk. **2.** Latin compound *sōbrius* (see **s(w)e-**). [Not in Pokorny; compare Hittite *ekuzi*, he drinks, and Greek *nēphein*, to be sober (< "to not drink," **ne-ēgʷh-*).]

ei-¹ To go. (Oldest form **h₁ei-*.) **1.** Full-grade form **ei-*. **a.** ADIT, AMBIENT, AMBITION, CIRCUIT, COITUS, COMITIA, EXIT, INTROIT, ISSUE, OBITUARY, PERISH, PRAETOR, PRETERIT, SEDITION, SUBITO, SUDDEN, TRANCE, TRANSIENT, TRANSIT, TRANSITIVE, from Latin *īre*, to go (past participle *itus* < suffixed zero-grade form **i-to-*); **b.** ION; ANION, CATION, DYSPROSIUM, from Greek *ienai*, to go; **c.** RAMAYANA, from Sanskrit *eti*, he goes (< Indo-Iranian **ai-ti*), and abstract noun *ayanam*, a going, way. **2.** Suffixed zero-grade form **i-t-*. **a.** Further suffixed form **i-t-yo-*. COMMENCE, INITIAL, INITIATE, from Latin *initium*, entrance, beginning (*in-*, in; see **en**); **b.** COUNT², COUNTY; CONCOMITANT, CONSTABLE, VISCOUNT, from Latin *comes* (stem *comit-*), companion (< "one who goes with another"; *com-*, with; see **kom**). **3.** Suffixed form **i-ti-* (see **orbh-**). **4.** Suffixed form **i-ter*. ERRANT, EYRE, ITINERANT, ITINERARY, from Latin *iter*, journey. **5.** Extended form **yā-* (contracted from earlier **h₁yah₂-*, colored from oldest form **h₁yeh₂-*). Suffixed forms **yā-no-*, **yā-nu-*. **a.** JANITOR, JANUARY, JANUS, from Latin *iānus*, archway,

and *Iānus*, god of doors and of the beginning of a year; **b.** HINAYANA, MAHAYANA, from Sanskrit *yānam*, way (in Buddhism, "mode of knowledge," "vehicle"). [Pokorny 1. *ei-* 293.]

ei-² Reddish, motley; yellow. Suffixed form **ei-wo-*. YEW, from Old English *īw*, yew, from Germanic **īwaz*, yew. [Pokorny 3. *ei-* 297.]

eis-¹ In words denoting passion. **1.** Suffixed form **eis-ā-*. IRASCIBLE, IRATE, IRE, from Latin *īra*, anger. **2.** Suffixed zero-grade form **is-(ə)ro-*, powerful, holy. HIERATIC, HIERO-; HIERARCH, HIERARCHY, HIERODULE, HIEROGLYPHIC, HIEROPHANT, from Greek *hieros*, "filled with the divine," holy. **3a.** IRON, from Old English *īse(r)n*, *īren*, iron; **b.** GISARME, SPIEGELEISEN, from Old High German *īsarn*, *īsan*, iron. Both **a** and **b** from Germanic **īsarno-*, "holy metal" (possibly from Celtic). **4.** Suffixed o-grade form **ois-tro-*, madness. ESTRUS; ESTROGEN, ESTRONE, from Greek *oistros*, gadfly, goad, anything causing madness. **5.** Suffixed form **eis-mo-*. ASMODEUS, from Avestan *aēšma-*, anger. [Pokorny 1. *eis-* 299.]

eis-² Ice, frost. **1.** ICE, from Old English *īs*, ice. **2.** ICEBERG, from Middle Dutch *ijs*, ice. Both **1** and **2** from Germanic **īs*, ice. [Pokorny 2. *ei-s-* 301.]

ekwo- Horse. (Oldest form **ek̑wo-*. Probably to be segmented **ek̑w-o-*, a suffixed form akin to the lengthened o-grade adjective **ôk̑u-*, swift; see **ōku-**.) **1.** EQUESTRIAN, EQUID, EQUINE, EQUITANT, EQUITATION, EQUULEUS; EQUISETUM, from Latin *equus*, horse. **2.** EOHIPPUS, HIPPOCAMPUS, HIPPOCRENE, HIPPODROME, HIPPOGRIFF, HIPPOPOTAMUS, from Greek *hippos*, horse, also in personal names: **a.** HIPPOCRATES, from Greek *Hippokratēs*, "having the power of a horse" (*-kratēs*, power; see **kar-¹**); **b.** PHILIP, from Greek *Philippos*, "lover of horses" (*philein*, to love). **3.** ALFALFA, from Old Iranian compound **aspa-sti-*, clover, alfalfa (< "horse fodder"), from **aspa-*, horse (**-sti-*, fodder, food; see **ed-**). [Pokorny *ek̑uo-s* 301.]

el-¹ Elbow, forearm. **1.** Extended form **el-inā-*, elbow. **a.** ELL², from Old English *eln*, forearm, cubit, from Germanic **elinō*; **b.** ELBOW, from Old English *elnboga*, elbow, from Germanic compound **elino-bugōn-*, "bend of the forearm," elbow (**bugōn-*, bend, bow; see **bheug-³**); **c.** ULNA, from Latin *ulna*, forearm. **2.** Extended o-grade form **ol-enā-*. UILLEANN PIPE, from Old Irish *uilenn*, elbow. **3.** Extended lengthened o-grade form **ōl-enā-*. OLECRANON, from Greek *ōlenē*, elbow. **4.** Extended basic form **el-in-*. ARSHIN, from Old Persian *arash-*, ell, from Indo-Iranian **aratn(i)-*, probably from a variant **el-etn-* of **el-in-*. [Pokorny 8. *el-* 307.]

el-² Red, brown (forming animal and tree names). **1.** Extended form **elmo-*. ELM, from Old English *elm*, elm, from Germanic **elmaz*. **2.** Suffixed o-grade form **ol-is-*. ALDER, from Old English *alor*, alder, from Germanic **aluz-* (probably remade from **aliz-*), alder. **3.** Possibly Old English *ellen*, *ellærn*, the elder: ELDER². **4.** Extended o-grade form **olki-*. ELK, from Old Norse *elgr*, elk (akin to Old English *eolh*, elk), from Germanic **algiz*, elk. **5.** Perhaps extended Germanic form **alk-*. ALCID, AUK, from Old Norse *ālka*, auk. **6.** Extended form **elno-*. HELLEBORE, from Greek *ellos*, *hellos*, fawn. **7.** Extended form **eləni-*. ELAND, from a Baltic source akin to Lithuanian *elnias*, deer. [Pokorny 1. *el-* 302.]

el-³ Eel, worm, snakelike creature. Lengthened grade form in **ēl-o-*. EEL, from Old English *ǣl*, from Germanic **ēlaz*. [Not in Pokorny; compare Latin (attested in a gloss) *illa*, worm and the second part of Greek *enkhelos*.]

[elaiā Olive. Greek noun (oldest form *elaiwā*) of Mediterranean origin. LATKE, OIL, -OLE, OLEAGINOUS, OLEASTER, OLEO-, OLIVE; AIOLI, OLICOOK, PETROLEUM.]

elə- To go. (Oldest form *elh₂-.) Suffixed extended form *ela-un-yo-. ELASTIC, ELATER, ELATERITE; ELASMOBRANCH, from Greek *elaunein*, to drive (< "to cause to go"). [Pokorny 6. *el-* 306.]

elk-es- Wound. (Oldest form *elk̂-es-.) ULCER, from Latin *ulcus* (stem *ulcer-*), a sore. [Pokorny *elkos-* (misprint for *elk̂os-*) 310.]

em- To take, distribute. **1.** ADEMPTION, EXAMPLE, EXEMPLARY, EXEMPLIFY, EXEMPLUM, EXEMPT, IMPROMPTU, PEREMPTORY, PREEMPTION, PREMIUM, PROMPT, PRONTO, RANSOM, REDEEM, REDEMPTION, SAMPLE, VINTAGE, from Latin *emere*, to obtain, buy. **2.** SUMPTUARY, SUMPTUOUS; ASSUME, CONSUME, PRESUME, RESUME, SUBSUME, from Latin *sūmere* (< *sus(e)m-*), to take, obtain, buy (*sus-*, variant of *sub-*, up from under; see **upo**). [Pokorny *em-* 310.]

en In. **1a.** IN¹ (preposition), from Old English *in*, in; **b.** IN¹ (adverb), from Old English *inn*, into, *inne*, inside; **c.** INN, from Old English *inn*, habitation, inn; **d.** TSIMMES, from Old High German *in*, in; **e.** INNER, from Old English *innera*, farther in, inner, from Germanic (comparative) *inn(e)ra*; **f.** (*i*) BEN, from Old English *binnan*, within; (*ii*) BILANDER, from Middle Dutch *binnen*, within. Both (*i*) and (*ii*) contracted from *be innan*, (*be*, at; see **ambhi**), from Germanic *innan*. **a–f** all from Germanic *in*. **2.** EN-¹, IN-², from Latin *in*, *in-*, in, into. **3.** EN-²; ENKEPHALIN, PARENCHYMA, PARENTHESIS, from Greek *en*, *en-*, in. **4.** Suffixed form *en-t(e)ro-*. **a.** INTRO-; INTRODUCE, INTROIT, INTROMIT, INTRORSE, INTROSPECT, from Latin *intrō*, inward, within; **b.** ENTER, INTRA-; INTRADOS, from Latin *intrā*, inside, within; **c.** INTERIM, INTRINSIC, from Latin *interim*, meanwhile, with ablative suffix *-im*, and *intrīnsecus*, on the inside, from *int(e)rim* + *secus*, alongside (see **sekʷ-¹**). **5.** Suffixed form *en-ter*. ENTRAILS, INTER-, INTERIOR, INTERN, INTERNAL, from Latin *inter*, *inter-*, between, among. **6.** INTIMA, INTIMATE², from Latin (superlative) *intimus*, innermost (*-mo-*, superlative suffix). **7.** Extended form *en-do*. **a.** INDUSTRY, from Latin *industrius*, diligent (Archaic Latin *indostruus*; *stru-*, to construct; see **sterə-**); **b.** INDIGENT, from Latin *indigēre*, to be in need (*egēre*, to be in need). Both **a** and **b** from Latin *indu-*, within, from Archaic Latin *endo*; **c.** ENDO-, from Greek *endon*, *endo-*, within; **d.** Celtic *endo*, in, in compound *endo-ber-o-* (see **bher-¹**). **8.** Suffixed form *en-tos*. **a.** DEDANS, INTESTINE, INTINE, INTUSSUSCEPTION, from Latin *intus*, within, inside; **b.** ENTO-, from Greek *entos*, within. **9.** Suffixed form *en-tero-*. **a.** ENTERIC, ENTERO-, ENTERON; DYSENTERY, EXENTERATE, MESENTERY, from Greek *enteron*, intestine; **b.** ATOLL, perhaps ultimately from Sanskrit *antara-*, interior. **10.** Extended form *ens*. **a.** EPISODE, from Greek *eis*, into; **b.** suffixed form *ens-ō*. ESOTERIC, ESOTROPIA, from Greek *esō*, within. **11.** Possibly suffixed zero-grade form *ṇ-dha*. AND, from Old English *and*, and, from Germanic *anda*, *unda*. [Pokorny 1. *en* 311.]

-en- (With many variants.) Suffix forming nouns and adjectives. Basis of very common Germanic "weak" nouns in *-ōn-*, such as *hazōn-*, hare (see **kas-**). [Not in Pokorny.]

en-es- Burden. ONEROUS, ONUS; EXONERATE, from Latin *onus* (stem *oner-*), burden. [Pokorny *enos-* 321.]

engʷ- Groin, internal organ. Suffixed zero-grade form *ṇgʷ-en-*. **1.** INGUINAL, from Latin *inguen*, groin. **2.** ADENO-; LYMPHADENITIS, SIALADENITIS, from Greek *adēn*, gland, gut. [Pokorny *engʷ-* 319.]

-eno- See **-no-**.

-ent- See **-nt-**.

epi Also **opi**. Near, at, against. **1.** OB-, from Latin *ob*, *ob-*, before, to, against. **2.** EPI-, from Greek *epi*, on, over, at. **3.** OPISTHOBRANCH, OPISTHOGNATHOUS, from Greek *opisthen*, behind, at the back. **4.** Zero-grade form *pi*, on, in Greek *piezein* (see **sed-¹**). **5.** OBLAST, from Russian *oblast'*, oblast, from Old Church

Slavonic *ob*, on. **6.** Reduced prefixal form *op-* in *opwer-yo-* (see **wer-⁵**). **7.** DUOPSONY, OPSONIN, from Greek *ops*, extra on the side, with, in noun *opson*, condiment, cooked food. [Pokorny *epi* 323.]

er-¹ To move, set in motion. (Oldest form *h₁er-.) **I.** Basic form *er-*. **1.** Probably Germanic *ar-*, *or-*, to be, exist. ARE¹, ART², from Old English *eart* and *aron*, second person singular and plural present of *bēon*, to be. **2.** Perhaps Germanic suffixed form *er-n-os-ti-*. **a.** EARNEST¹, from Old English *eornoste*, zealous, serious; **b.** ERNEST (personal name), from Old High German *ernust*, battle, vigor. **3.** Uncertain o-grade suffixed form *ori-yo-*. ORIENT, ORIGIN, ORIGINAL; ABORT, from Latin *orīrī*, to arise, appear, be born. **4.** Suffixed o-grade form *or-smā-*. HORMESIS, HORMONE, from Greek *hormē*, impulse, onrush. **II.** Enlarged extended form *arei-s-*. **1.** RISE; ARISE, from Old English *rīsan*, from Germanic *rīsan*; **2.** Suffixed o-grade (causative) form *rois-ye-*. **a.** REAR², from Old English *rǣran*, to rear, raise, lift up; **b.** RAISE, from Old Norse *reisa*, to raise. Both **a** and **b** from Germanic *raizjan*. [Pokorny 3. *er-* 326; *ergh-* 339.]

er-² Earth, ground. Extended form *ert-*. **1.** EARTH, from Old English *eorthe*, earth. **2.** AARDVARK, AARDWOLF, from Middle Dutch *aerde*, *eerde*, earth. Both **1** and **2** from Germanic *erthō*. [Pokorny 4. *er-* 332.]

erə-¹ To row. (Oldest form *h₁reh₁-, with variant [metathesized] form *h₁reh₁-, contracted to *h₁rē-.) **1.** Variant form *rē-*. **a.** ROW², from Old English *rōwan*, to row, from Germanic *rō-*; **b.** suffixed form *rō-tro-*. RUDDER, RUS, RUSSIAN, RUSSKY, from Old English *rōther* and Old Norse *rōdhr*, steering oar, both from Germanic *rōthra*, rudder; **c.** suffixed form *rē-smo-*. BIREME, REMEX, TRIREME, from Latin *rēmus*, oar. **2.** Greek form *erē-* (< *ərē-*). TRIERARCH, from Greek *triērēs*, trireme. [Pokorny 1. *erə-* 338.]

erə-² To separate. (Earlier *h₁erh₁-, metathesized from oldest form *h₁reh₁-, contracted to *h₁rē-.) **1.** Suffixed zero-grade form *rə-ti-*. RATITE, from Latin *ratis*, raft (< "grating," "latticework"). **2.** Suffixed form *rē-ti-*. RESEAU, RETE, RETIARY, RETICLE, RETICULE, RETINA; RETIFORM, from Latin *rēte*, *rētis*, a net. **3.** Full-grade form *ərē-*. EREMITE, HERMIT; EREMURUS, from Greek *erēmos*, empty, desolate, bereft. [Pokorny 5. *er-* 332.]

erə-³ To separate, adjoin. (Oldest form *h₁erh₂-.) **1.** Suffixed zero-grade form *rā-ro-* (< *rə-ro-*). RARE¹, from Latin *rārus*, "having intervals between," "full of empty spaces," rare. **2.** Probably Greek *erasthai*, to love (< "be separated from"), with derivatives *erasmios*, lovely, pleasant (> Latin *Erasmus*), and *erōs*, sexual love: ERASMUS (personal name), ERATO, EROS, EROTIC; EROGENOUS, EROTOMANIA, PEDERAST. **3.** Probably Greek *eris*, strife, discord: ERIS, ERISTIC. [Not in Pokorny; compare Old Hittite *arḫāš*, border ("thing that separates"), Old Irish *or*, border, and Lithuanian *irti*, to be dissolved ("separated").]

erədh- High. (Oldest form possibly *h₁(e)rh₃dh-, but the details are obscure.) **1.** Suffixed zero-grade form *ərədh-wo-*. ARDUOUS, from Latin *arduus*, high, steep. **2.** ORTHO-, ORTHOTIC; ANORTHITE, from Greek *orthos*, upright, straight, correct. [Pokorny *er(ə)d-* 339, *u̯erdh-* 1167.]

ergh- To mount. (Oldest form *h₁erĝh-.) **1.** Suffixed o-grade form *orgh-i-*. ORCHID, ORCHIS, ORCHITIS; ORCHIECTOMY, from Greek *orkhis*, testicle; **b.** perhaps Latin *orbis*, disc, sphere, and *orbita*, track made by a wheel (probably from *orbis*): ORB, ORBICULAR, ORBICULATE, ORBIT. **2.** Suffixed o-grade form *orgheyo-*. ORCHESTRA, from Greek *orkheisthai*, to dance. [Pokorny *orĝhi-* 782, *ergh-* 339.]

erkʷ- To radiate, beam, praise. RIG-VEDA, from Sanskrit *ṛk* (stem *ṛc-*, *ṛk-*), "brightness," praise, poem. [Pokorny *erkʷ-* 340.]

ers-¹ To be in motion. **1.** Variant form *rēs-*. RACE², from Old Norse *rās*, rushing, from Germanic *rēs-*.

2. Suffixed form *ers-ā-. ERR, ERRATIC, ERRATUM, ERRONEOUS, ERROR; ABERRATION, from Latin errāre, to wander. **3.** Possible zero-grade form *ṛs-i-. RISHI, from Sanskrit ṛṣiḥ, poet, seer. [Pokorny 2. ere-s- 336.] Compare **wers-¹**.

ers-² To be wet. Derived form *ros-, dew. **1.** ROSEMARY, from Latin rōs, dew. **2.** Perhaps (but doubtfully) Greek drosos, dew: DROSERA; DROSOPHILA. **3.** Suffixed zero-grade form *ṛs-en-, man, male (< "that sprinkles or ejects semen"). Old Persian arshan-, man, in compound khshayārshan- (see **tkē-**). [Pokorny 2. ere-s- 336.] Compare **wers-²**.

es- To be. (Oldest form *h₁es-.) **1.** Athematic first person singular form *es-mi. AM, from Old English eam, eom, am, from Germanic *izm(i). **2.** Athematic third person singular form *es-ti. IS, from Old English is, is, from Germanic *ist(i). **3.** Optative stem *sī- (< *əs-iə-). YES, from Old English gēse, yes, from sīe, may it be (so) (gēa, yea; see **i-**), from Germanic *sijai-. **4.** Suffixed zero-grade (participial) form *əs-ont-, becoming *sont-, being, existing, hence real, true. **a.** SOOTH, SOOTHE, from Old English sōth, true, from Germanic *santhaz; **b.** suffixed (collective) zero-grade form *sṇt-yā-, "that which is." SIN¹, from Old English synn, sin, from Germanic *sun(d)jō, sin (< "it is true," "the sin is real"); **c.** SUTTEE; BODHI- SATTVA, SATYAGRAHA, from Sanskrit sat-, sant-, existing, true, virtuous. **5.** Basic form *es-. ENTITY, ESSENCE; ABESSIVE, ABSENT, ADESSIVE, ESSIVE, IMPROVE, INESSIVE, INTEREST, OSSIA, PRESENT¹, PRESENT², PROUD, QUINTESSENCE, REPRESENT, STOVER, from Latin esse, to be. **6.** Basic form *es-. -ONT, ONTO-; -BIONT, HOMOIOUSIAN, PAROUSIA, SCHIZONT, from Greek einai (present participle ont-, being), to be. **7.** Suffixed form *es-ti-. SWASTIKA, from Sanskrit svasti, well-being (su-, good; see **(e)su-**). [Pokorny es- 340.] See also derivatives **ēs-, (e)su-**.

Language and Culture Note
A glance at the derivatives of **es-** above will reveal one derivative, English sin, whose connection to the root's basic meaning of "to be" may seem unclear. The connection makes more sense in light of the way ancient Indo-European peoples confessed to crimes and misdeeds. Hittite texts preserve a phrase used in the Hittite confessional formula, "It is; it (is) being," followed by a verb form meaning "I did (it)." (Compare English "It's true; I did it.") The Hittite word referring to the existence of the transgression or sin ("it (is) being, it (is) true") continues the Indo-European present participle of **es-**, *əs-ont-, "being, really existing." This same form also became the Latin word for "guilty": the guilty one is the one who says "It is true; I did it." English sin, from Germanic *sunt-jō, is simply the abstract or collective noun from this utterance: "(the fact of saying) it is so."

ēs- To sit. Found only in Greek, Indo-Iranian, and Anatolian. (Oldest form *h₁ēs-, originally lengthened-grade form of *h₁es-, to be [see **es-**], but a separate verb in Indo-European.) **1.** ASANA, from Sanskrit āsanam, "a sitting," sitting position, from āste, he sits. **2.** Suffixed form *ēs-eno-. KHAN²; BARBICAN, GYMKHANA, from Middle Persian khān, house, from Iranian *āhanam, "seat." [Pokorny ēs- 342.]

-es- Also **-os-**. Suffix forming abstract nouns from verbs, as in *od-es-, smell (see **od-¹**). [Not in Pokorny.]

es-en- Harvest, fall. O-grade form *osn-. EARN¹, from Old English earnian, to serve, gain as wages, from Germanic *aznōn, to do harvest work, serve, denominative verb from *aznō, harvest (work). [Pokorny es-en- 343.]

esōr Woman. Zero-grade combining form *-sōr, *-sṛ-. **1.** Compound *swe-sor-, "woman of one's own (kin group), sister" (see **swesor-**). **2.** Compound *uk-sor-, "woman who gets accustomed to (her husband's kin

group), wife" (see **euk-**). [Not in Pokorny; compare Hittite -(š)šaraš, feminine suffix, and Sanskrit ti-sraḥ, cata-sraḥ, feminine of the numerals for "three" and "four" (with cognate forms in Celtic).]

(e)su- Good. (Oldest form *h₁(e)su-; originally suffixed form of *h₁es-, to be [< "being true, being good"]; see **es-**.) **1.** EU-, from Greek eu-, well, combining form of eus, good. **2a.** (i) SWASTIKA, from Sanskrit svasti, well-being, good luck (-asti, being; see **es-**); (ii) NAINSOOK, from Sanskrit sukha-, running easily (said of a chariot), pleasant ("having good axle-holes"; kham, axle-hole). Both (i) and (ii) from Sanskrit su-, good; **b.** Avestan hu-, good, in compound hupərathuua- (see **per-²**). **c.** Perhaps Persian xuš (Modern Iranian Persian xoš), good (see **okʷ-**). **a-c** from Indo-Iranian *su-. [Pokorny esu-s 342.]

eti Above, beyond. **1.** EDDY, from Old Norse idha, countercurrent, whirlpool, from Germanic *ith-, a second time, again. **2.** ET CETERA, from Latin et, and (< "furthermore"). [Pokorny eti 344.]

ētī- Eider duck. A probable root. EIDER, from Old Norse ædhr, eider, from North Germanic *āthī, from Germanic *ēthī. [Pokorny ētī- 345.]

ētmen- Breath. (Contracted from earlier *eh₁tmen-.) ATMAN, from Sanskrit ātmā (stem ātmǎn-), breath, soul. [Pokorny ēt-mén- 345.]

-eto- See **-to-**.

eu- To dress. **1.** ENDUE, INDUMENT, from Latin induere, to don (ind-, variant of in-, in, on; see **en**). **2.** EXUVIAE, from Latin exuere, to doff (ex-, off; see **eghs**). **3.** REDUVIID, from Latin reduvia, fragment (red-, back, in reverse; see **re-**). [Pokorny 2. eu- 346.] See also extended root **wes-⁴**.

euə- To leave, abandon, give out, whence nominal derivatives meaning abandoned, lacking, empty. (Oldest form *h₁euh₂-, with zero-grade form *h₁uh₂- becoming *ū-; variant [metathesized] full-grade form *h₁weh₂-, colored to *h₁wah₂-, contracted to *h₁wā-.) **1.** Suffixed zero-grade form *wə-no-. **a.** WANE; WANTON, from Old English wanian, to lessen (from Germanic *wanēn) and wan-, without; **b.** WANT, from Old Norse vanta, to lack, from North Germanic *wanatōn. **2.** Suffixed form *wā-no-. VAIN, VANITY, VAUNT; EVANESCE, VANISH, from Latin vānus, empty. **3.** Extended form *wak-. VACANT, VACATE, VACATION, VACUITY, VACUUM, VOID; AVOID, DEVOID, EVACUATE, from Latin vacāre (variant vocāre), to be empty. **4.** Extended and suffixed form *wās-to-. WASTE; DEVASTATE, from Latin vāstus, empty, waste. [Pokorny 1. eu- 345.]

euə-dh-ṛ Udder. Related to **wē-r-**. **1.** Suffixed zero-grade form *ūdh-ṛ (< *uə-dh-ṛ). UDDER, from Old English ūder, udder, from Germanic *ūdr-. **2.** Suffixed o-grade form *oudh-ṛ. EXUBERANT, EXUBERATE, from Latin adjective ūber, fertile, derived from ūber, "breast." [Pokorny ēudh- 347.]

euk- To become accustomed. Zero-grade form uk-. **1.** Suffixed (feminine) form *uk-sor-, "she who gets accustomed (to the new household)" after patrilocal marriage (*-sor-, woman; see **esōr**). UXORIAL, UXORIOUS; UXORICIDE, from Latin uxor, wife. **2.** Nasalized form *u-n-k-. TWIG², from Old Irish tuicim, I understand, "get accustomed to" (< *to-ucc-; to-, to; see **to-**). [Pokorny euk- 347.]

eus- To burn. **1.** UREDINIUM; ADUST, COMBUSTION, from Latin ūrere, to burn. **2.** Zero-grade form *us-. EMBER, from Old English ǣmerge, ember, from Germanic compound *aim-uzjōn, ashes (*aim-, ashes, ember; see **ai-²**), from *uzjōn, to burn. **3.** Possibly in the non-Greek source of Greek Euros, the east wind: EURUS. [Pokorny eus- 347.]

-eyo- Verbal suffix forming causatives (transitive) and iteratives (intransitive) from verbal roots, as in *mon-eyo-, "to cause to think," warn (see **men-¹**). Usually entails o-grade of the root; becomes *-jan- in Germanic. [Not in Pokorny.]

[ferrum Iron. Latin noun, possibly borrowed (via Etruscan) from the same obscure source as Old English *bræs*, brass. **1.** FARRIER, FERRI-, FERRO-, FERROUS, FERRUGINOUS; FER-DE-LANCE, from Latin *ferrum*, iron. **2.** BRASS, BRAZEN, BRAZIER[1], from Old English *bræs*, brass.]

[Frankon- Frank (member of a Germanic tribe, "javelin"). Germanic root. **1.** FRANC, FRANCHISE, FRANCO-, FRANK[1], FRANK, FRANKINCENSE, FRANKLIN; FRANKPLEDGE, from Frankish *Frank-*, Frank, borrowed into Late Latin as *Francus*, Frank. **2.** FRENCH, from Old English *frencisc*, French, from derivative adjective *frankiska-*, of the Franks. **3.** FRANCE, from Medieval Latin *Francia*, land of the Franks.]

[gagina Also **gagana**. Against. Germanic root. **1.** GAINSAY, from Old English *gegn-*, against. **2.** AGAIN, AGAINST, from Old English *ongeagn, ongēan*, against, back, again, from Germanic *ana-gagina* (*ana-*, toward; see **an-**[1]), *in the opposite direction*. **3.** UNGAINLY, from Old Norse *gegn*, straight, direct, helpful. **4.** GEGENSCHEIN, from Old High German *gegin, gagan*, against.]

gal-[1] Bald, naked. **1.** Suffixed form *gal-wo-*. CALLOW, from Old English *calu*, bare, bald, from Germanic *kalwa-*. **2.** GALYAK, from Russian *golyĭ*, smooth, bald, from Slavic *golŭ*. [Pokorny 1. *gal-* 349.]

gal-[2] To call, shout. **1.** CALL, from Old Norse *kalla*, to call, from Germanic expressive form *kall-*. **2.** CLATTER, from Old English *clatrian*, to clatter, from Germanic *klat-*. **3.** Expressive form *gall-*. GALLINACEOUS, GALLINULE; PICO DE GALLO, from Latin *gallus*, cock (< "the calling bird"; but probably also associated with *Gallus*, Gallic, as if to mean "the bird of Gaul," the cock being archaeologically attested as an important symbol in the iconography of Roman and pre-Roman Gaul). **4.** Suffixed form *gal-so-*. GLASNOST, from Old Church Slavonic *glasŭ*, voice. **5.** Reduplicated form *gal-gal-*. GLAGOLITIC, from Old Church Slavonic *glagolŭ*, word. [Pokorny 2. *gal-* 350.]

gal-[3] To be able, have power. GALLIARD, from Old French *galliart*, lively, from Gallo-Roman *galia*, strength, power. [Pokorny 3. *gal-* 351.]

gar- To call, cry. Expressive root. **1a.** CARE, from Old English *cearu*, care; **b.** CHARY, from Old English *cearig*, sorrowful, from Germanic adjective *karaga-*, sorrowful. Both **a** and **b** from Germanic *karō*, lament, hence grief, care. **2.** SLOGAN, from Irish Gaelic *gairm*, shout, cry, call, from Celtic suffixed form *gar-(s)mn̥*. **3.** Suffixed form (with expressive gemination) *garr-iyo-*. GARRULOUS, from Latin *garrīre*, to chatter. [Pokorny *ĝār-* 352.]

[garwian To make, prepare, equip. Germanic verb. **1.** GAR[2], from Old Norse *gera*, to make, do. **2.** Noun form *garwi-*, equipment, adornment. GARB, from Italian *garbo*, grace, elegance of dress, from Germanic. **3.** Adjective form *garwa-*, prepared. YARE, from Old English *gearu, gearo*, ready. **4.** Noun form *garwīn-*. GEAR, from Old Norse *gervi*, equipment, gear.]

gāu- To rejoice; also to have religious fear or awe. (Oldest form *geh₂u-*, colored to *gah₂u-*, contracted to *gau-* [before consonants] and *gāw-* [before vowels].) **1.** Suffixed extended form *gāw-idh-ē-*. GAUD, GAUDY[1], GAUDY[2], JOY; ENJOY, REJOICE, from Latin *gau- dēre*, to rejoice. **2.** Form (with nasal infix) *ga-n-u-*. GANOID, from Greek *ganusthai*, to rejoice. [Pokorny *gāu-* 353.]

[gē Also **gaia**. The earth. Greek noun of unknown origin. GAEA, GEO-; APOGEE, EPIGEAL, GEANTICLINE, GEODE, GEORGIC, HYPOGEAL, NEOGAEA, PERIGEE. Also in proper name *Geōrgios*, from *geōrgos*, "worker of the earth," farmer (*-orgos*, worker; see **werg-**): GEORGE.]

gēi- To sing. (Contracted from earlier *geh₁i-*, with variant [metathesized] form *geih₁-*, whence zero-grade *gih₁-*, contracted to *gī-*.) Suffixed zero-grade form *gī-tā-*. BHAGAVAD-GITA, from Sanskrit *gītā*, song. [Pokorny *gē(i)-* 355.]

geiə- To sprout, split, open. (Oldest form *ĝeih₂-*.) Zero-grade form *gī-* (< *giə-*). **1.** CHINK[1], from Old English *cine, cinu*, cleft, ravine cut by a stream, from Germanic *kīnan*. **2.** SCION, from Old French *cion*, shoot, from Frankish *kid-*, from Germanic *ki-dōn-*. **3.** Perhaps Germanic *kidia-*. KID, from Old Norse *kidh*. [Pokorny *ĝēi-* 355.]

gel-[1] Bright. **1.** Extended form *glei-*. **a.** CLEAN, from Old English *clǣne*, pure, clean; **b.** CLEANSE, from Old English *clǣnsian*, to purify, cleanse. Both **a** and **b** from Germanic *klai-ni-*, bright, pure. **2.** Extended zero-grade form *glə-* (oldest form *glh₁-*). Suffixed form *glə-nā-*. EUGLENA, from Greek *glēnē*, eyeball. **3.** Old Irish *gel*, bright, in Irish Gaelic compound *Muirgheal* (see **mori-**). [Pokorny *ĝel-* 366.]

gel-[2] Cold; to freeze. **1.** CHILL, from Old English *c(i)ele*, chill, from Germanic *kaliz*, coldness. **2.** COLD, from Old English *ceald*, cold, from Germanic *kalda-*, cold. **3a.** COOL, from Old English *cōl*, cold, cool; **b.** KEEL[3], from Old English *cēlan*, to cool, from Germanic *kōljan*, to cool. Both **a** and **b** from Germanic *kōl-*, cool. **4.** Suffixed form *gel-ā-*. GELATIN, GELATION, JELLY; CONGEAL, from Latin *gelāre*, to freeze. **5.** Suffixed form *gel-u-*. GELID, from Latin *gelū*, frost, cold. **6.** Probably suffixed zero-grade form *gl-k-*. GLACÉ, GLACIAL, GLACIATE, GLACIER, GLACIS; DEMI-GLACE, VERGLAS, from Latin *glaciēs*, ice. [Pokorny 3. *gel(ə)-* 365.]

gembh- Tooth, nail. (Oldest form *ĝembh-*.) **1.** Suffixed o-grade form *gombh-o-*. **a.** *(i)* COMB, KAME, from Old English *comb, camb*, comb; *(ii)* CAM, from Dutch *kam*, cog, comb; *(iii)* UNKEMPT, from Old English *cemban*, to comb, from Germanic denominative *kambjan*, to comb. *(i)–(iii)* all from Germanic *kambaz*, comb; **b.** GOMPHOSIS, from Greek *gomphos*, tooth, peg, bolt. **2.** Suffixed zero-grade form *gm̥bh-ōn-*. OAKUM, from Old English *ā-cumba*, part of flax separated in hackling, combed out ("stuff combed off"; *ā-*, away, off). **3.** Perhaps Germanic *kimb-*. CHIME[2], from Old English *cim-, cimb-*, rim (only in compounds). **4.** Possibly suffixed form *gembh-mā-*. GEM, GEMMA, GEMMATE, GEMMULE, from Latin *gemma*, bud, hence gem. [Pokorny *ĝembh-* 369.]

gemə- To marry. (Oldest form *ĝemh₁-*.) Suffixed zero-grade form *gm̥ə-o-*. GAMETE, GAMO-, -GAMOUS, -GAMY, from Greek *gamos*, marriage. [Pokorny *ĝem(e)-* 369.]

[g(e)n- To compress into a ball. Hypothetical Indo-European base of a range of Germanic words with initial *kn-* referring to compact, knobby bodies and projections and sharp blows. **1a.** KNAP, from Middle English *knappen*, to strike sharply, snap, hence "to have a bite"; **b.** KNAPSACK, from Low German *knappen*, to bite; **c.** KNOP; KNAPWEED, from Old English *cnop*, knob. **a–c** all from Germanic *kn-a-pp-*. **2.** KNACKWURST, from Middle High German *knacken*, to crack, from Germanic *kn-a-k-*. **3a.** GNARLED, KNAR, from Middle English *knarre*, knob, from a source akin to Norwegian *knart*, knot in wood; **b.** KNUR, KNURL, from Middle English *knor*, a swelling. Both **a** and **b** from Germanic *kn-a-r-*. **4.** KNOB, NUB, from Middle Low German *knobbe, knubbe*, knot in wood, knob, from Germanic *kn-u-b-*. **5a.** KNOCK, from Old English *cnocian*, to knock; **b.** GNOCCHI, from Italian *gnocco, nocchio*, knot in wood; **c.** KNUCKLE, from Middle English *knakel*, knuckle, from a source akin to Middle Low German *knökel*, knuckle. **a–c** all from Germanic *kn-u-k-*. **6a.** KNELL, KNOLL[2], from Old English *cnyllan*, to strike; **b.** KNOLL[1], from Old English *cnoll*, a knoll. Both **a** and **b** from Germanic *kn-u-l-*. **7.** KNOBKERRIE, from Middle Dutch *cnoppe*, knob, from Germanic *kn-u-p-*. **8a.** KNIT, from Old English *cnyt- ten*, to tie in a knot; **b.** KNOT[1], from Old English *cnotta*, knot in a cord; **c.** KNOUT, from Old Norse *knútr*, knot in cord. **a–c** all from Germanic *kn-u-t-*. **9.** QUENELLE, from Old High German *knodo*, knob, knot (> French *quenelle*), from Germanic **kn-u-th-*. **10.** KNIFE, from Old English *cnīf*, knife, from Germanic **kn-ī-b-*. **11.** KNEAD, from Old English *cnedan*, to knead, ferment, from Germanic **kn-e-d-*. [Pokorny gen- 370.]]

genə- Also **gen-**. To give birth, beget; with derivatives referring to aspects and results of procreation and to familial and tribal groups. (Oldest form **ĝenh₁-*.)
   I. Basic form **genə-*. **1.** Suffixed form **genə-es-*. **a.** GENDER, GENERAL, GENERATE, GENERATION, GENERIC, GENEROUS, GENRE, GENUS; CONGENER, DEGENERATE, ENGENDER, MISCEGENATION, from Latin *genus*, race, kind; **b.** GENE; ALLOGENEIC, GENEALOGY, GENOCIDE, GENOTYPE, HETEROGENEOUS, SYNGENEIC, from Greek *genos* and *geneā*, race, family; **c.** -GEN, -GENY; EPI-GENE, from Greek suffix *-genēs*, "-born." **2.** Suffixed form **gen(ə)-yo-*. **a.** GENIAL¹; GENIUS; CONGENIAL, from Latin *genius*, procreative divinity, inborn tutelary spirit, innate quality; **b.** ENGINE, INGENIOUS, from Latin *ingenium*, inborn character (*in-*, in; see **en**). **3.** Suffixed form **genə-ā-*. INDIGEN, INDIGENOUS, from Latin *indigena*, born in (a place), indigenous (*indu-*, within; see **en**). **4.** Suffixed form **genə-wo-*. GENUINE, INGENUOUS, from Latin *ingenuus*, born in (a place), native, natural, freeborn (*in-*, in; see **en**). **5.** Suffixed form **gen(ə)-men-*. GERM, GERMAN², GERMANE, GERMINAL, GERMINATE, from dissimilated Latin *germen*, shoot, bud, embryo, germ.
   II. O-grade form **gonə-*, reduced to **gon-* in suffixed form **gon-o-*. **1.** GONAD, GONO-, -GONY; ARCHEGONIUM, CARPOGONIUM, EPIGONE, from Greek *gonos*, child, procreation, seed. **2.** HARIJAN, from Sanskrit *janaḥ*, offspring, child, person.
   III. Zero-grade form **gṇə-*. **1.** Suffixed form **gṇə-yo-*. **a.** KIN; KINDRED, from Old English *cyn(n)*, race, family, kin; **b.** KING, from Old English *cyning*, king, from Germanic **kuningaz*, king. Both **a** and **b** from Germanic **kunjam*, family. **2.** Suffixed form **gṇə-t-*. **a.** KIND², from Old English *cynd*, *gecynd(e)*, origin, birth, race, family, kind, from Germanic **kundjaz*, family, race; **b.** KIND¹, from Old English *gecynde*, natural, native, fitting (*ge-*, collective prefix; see **kom**), from Germanic **kundi-*, natural, native; **c.** suffixed form **gṇə-ti-*. *(i)* GENS, GENTEEL, GENTILE, GENTLE, GENTRY, JAUNTY; GENDARME, from Latin *gēns* (stem *genti-*), race, clan; *(ii)* GENESIS, -GENESIS, from Greek *genesis*, birth, beginning; **d.** KINDERGARTEN, KRISS KRINGLE, WUNDERKIND, from Old High German *kind*, child, from Germanic secondary full-grade variant **kentham*; **e.** suffixed form **gṇə-to-*. JATAKA, from Sanskrit *jāta-*, born (verbal adjective of *janate*, he is born). **3.** Reduplicated form **gi-gn(ə)-*. GENITAL, GENITIVE, GENITOR, GENITURE, GINGERLY; CONGENITAL, PRIMOGENITOR, PRIMOGENITURE, PROGENITOR, PROGENY, from Latin *gignere* (past participle *genitus*), to beget. **4.** Reduced form **gn-* in suffixed form **-gn-o-*. BENIGN, MALIGN, from Latin *benignus*, good-natured, kindly (*bene*, well; see **deu-²**), and *malignus*, evil-natured, malevolent (*male*, ill; see **mel-⁵**). **5.** Zero-grade form **gṇə-* becoming **gnā-*. PREGNANT¹; IMPREGNATE, from Latin *praegnās*, pregnant (*prae-*, before; see **per¹**). **6.** Suffixed form **gṇə-sko-* becoming **gnā-sko-*. NADA, NAIVE, NASCENT, NATAL, NATION, NATIVE, NATURE, NÉE, NOËL; ADNATE, AGNATE, COGNATE, CONNATE, ENATE, INNATE, NEONATE, PUISNE, PUNY, RENAISSANCE, from Latin *gnāscī*, *nāscī* (past participle *gnātus*, *nātus*), to be born. **7.** Reduced form **gṇ-* in Sanskrit compound *kṛmi-ja-* (see **kʷṛmi-**). [Pokorny 1. ĝen- 373.]

genu-¹ Knee; also angle. (Oldest form **ĝenu-*.) **1.** Variant form **gneu-*. **a.** KNEE, from Old English *cnēo*, knee, from Germanic **knewam*; **b.** KNEEL, from Old English *cnēowlian*, to kneel, from Germanic **knewljan*. **2.** Basic form **genu-*. GENICULATE, GENUFLECT, from Latin *genū*, knee. **3.** O-grade form **gonu*. POLYGONUM, PYCNOGONID, from Greek *gonu*, knee. **4.**

Suffixed variant form **gōnw-yā-*. -GON, AMBLYGONITE, DIAGONAL, GONIOMETER, ORTHOGONAL, from Greek *gōniā*, angle, corner. [Pokorny 1. ĝenu- 380.]

genu-² Jawbone, chin. (Oldest form **ĝenu-*.) **1.** Prevocalic form **genw-*. CHIN, from Old English *cin(n)*, chin, from Germanic **kinnuz*. **2.** Basic form **genu-*. GENIAL²; GENIOGLOSSUS, from Greek *genus*, jaw, chin. **3.** Suffixed variant form **gnə-dho-*. GANACHE, GNA-THAL, GNATHIC, -GNATHOUS; AGNATHAN, COMPSOGNATHUS, CHAETOGNATH, GNATHOSTOME, from Greek *gnathos*, jaw. **4.** Variant form **g(h)enu-*. HANUMAN, from Sanskrit *hanuḥ*, jaw. [Pokorny 2. ĝenu- 381.]

gep(h)- Also **gebh-**. Jaw, mouth. (Oldest forms **ĝep(h)-*, **ĝebh-*.) **1.** Probably Germanic **kaf-*, to gnaw, chew. CHAFF¹, from Old English *ceaf*, husks, chaff. **2.** CHAFER; COCKCHAFER, from Old English *ceafor*, *ceafer*, beetle, from Germanic **kabraz*, "gnawer." **3.** JOWL¹, from Old English *cēafl*, jaw, cheek, from Germanic **kēfalaz*. [Pokorny ĝep(h)- 382.]

ger-¹ To gather. (Oldest form **h₂ger-*.) **1.** Extended form **grem-*. CRAM, from Old English *crammian*, to stuff, cram, from Germanic **kramm-*. **2.** Reduplicated form **gre-g-*. GREGARIOUS, GREIGE; AGGREGATE, CON-GREGATE, EGREGIOUS, SEGREGATE, from Latin *grex* (stem *greg-*), herd, flock. **3.** Basic form **əger-*, with suffixed o-grade form **əgor-ā-*. AGORA¹, AGORAPHO-BIA, ALLEGORY, CATEGORY, PANEGYRIC, from Greek *ageirein*, to assemble, and *aguris*, *agorā*, marketplace. [Pokorny 1. ger- 382.]

[g(e)r-² Curving, crooked; hypothetical Indo-European base for a variety of Germanic words with initial *kr-*.
   I. Words meaning to bend, curl; bent, crooked, hooked; something bent or hooked. **1a.** AGRAFFE, KREPLACH, from Old High German *krāpfo*, a hook; **b.** GRAPE, from Old French *grape*, vine, grape, backformation from *graper*, to harvest grapes; **c.** GRAPNEL, from Old French *grapan*, grapnel; **d.** GRAPPLE, from Old French *grape*, a hook; **e.** GRAPPA, from Italian dialectal *grappa*, vine stem, brandy. **a–e** all from Germanic **krappōn-*, a hook, especially one used in harvesting grapes. **2a.** CRUMMIE, CRUMPET, CRUMPLE, from Old English *crump*, *crumb*, crooked, bent, stooping; **b.** KRUMKAKE, KRUMMHOLZ, KRUMMHORN, from Old High German *krump*, curved. Both **a** and **b** from Germanic **krumpa-*, **krumba-*. **3.** CRIMP¹, from Low German *krimpen*, to wrinkle. **4.** CRAMP², from Middle Dutch *crampe*, hook, and Frankish **kramp*, hook. **5.** CRAMP¹, from Old French *crampe*, cramp, from a Germanic source akin to Old High German *krampfo*, a cramp. **6.** CRIPPLE, from Old English *crypel*, a cripple, from Germanic **krupila-*, crippled. **7.** CREEP, from Old English *crēopan*, to creep, from Germanic **kreupan*. **8.** CRINGLE, from Middle Low German *krink*, a ring. **9.** CRINGE, from Old English *cringan*, to yield, from Germanic **krengan*. **10.** CRINKLE, from Middle English *crinkelen*, to make kinks in, akin to Middle Dutch *crinkelen*. **11.** CREEK, from Old Norse *kriki*, a bend, nook. **12.** CROOK¹, CROOK², from Old Norse *krōkr*, a hook. **13.** CROCHET, CROCKET, CROQUET, CROTCH, CROTCHET, CROUCH; ENCROACH, from Old French *croc*, a hook, from Frankish **krōk-*. **14.** CRUTCH, from Old English *crycc*, (bent) staff, crutch, from Germanic **krukjō*. **15.** CROSIER; LACROSSE, from Old French *crosse*, crook. **16.** CRULLER, CURL, from Middle Dutch *crulle*, curly. **17.** CRANK¹, from Old English *cranc- (stæf)*, a weaving implement. **18.** CROCK³, from Middle English *crok*, an old ewe, from a source akin to Norwegian *krake*, a sickly beast. **19.** CARP¹, from Old Norse *karpa*, to boast. **20.** GROSSULARITE, GOOSEBERRY, from Old French *grosele*, gooseberry, from a source akin to Middle Dutch *kroes*, curled.
   II. Words meaning "a rounded mass, collection; a round object, vessel, container." **1.** CRUMB, from Old English *cruma*, a fragment, from West Germanic **krumōn-*. **2.** CROUP², CROUPIER, CRUPPER, from Old

French *croup*, rump, from a source akin to Frankish **kruppa*, rump. **3.** CROP, from Old English *cropp*, cluster, bunch, ear of corn. **4.** GROUP, from Italian *gruppo*, an assemblage. **5.** CROCK[1], from Old English *crocc*, pot. **6.** CRUSE, from Middle Dutch *cruyse*, pot. **7a.** CRIB, from Old English *cribb*, manger, from West Germanic **kribjōn-*; **b.** CRÈCHE, from Old French *cre(s)che*, crib, from a source akin to Frankish **kripja*, cradle, from Germanic **kripja-*. **8.** CRADLE, from Old English *cradel*, cradle. **9.** CART, from Old English *cræt* and Old Norse *kartr*, wagon. **10.** CROFT, from Old English *croft*, small enclosed field. [Pokorny 3. *ger-* 385.]]

gerbh- To scratch. **1.** CARVE, from Old English *ceorfan*, to cut, from Germanic **kerban*. **2.** KERF, from Old English *cyrf*, a cutting (off), from zero-grade Germanic form **kurbiz*. **3.** Variant form **grebh-*. **a.** CRAB[1], from Old English *crabba*, a crab, from Germanic **krab(b)-*; **b.** CRAYFISH, from Old High German *kerbiz*, edible crustacean, from Germanic **krabiz-*; **c.** perhaps Germanic **krab-*. CRAWL[1], from Old Norse *krafla*, to crawl. **4.** Zero-grade form **grbh-*. **a.** GLAMOUR, GRAFFITO, GRAFT[1], GRAM[1], -GRAM, GRAMMAR, -GRAPH, -GRAPHER, GRAPHIC, -GRAPHY; AGRAPHA, AGRAPHIA, ANAGRAM, DIAGRAM, EPIGRAM, EPIGRAPH, GRAPHITE, ICONOGRAPHY, LIPOGRAM, PARAGRAPH, PARALLELOGRAM, PROGRAM, PSEUDEPIGRAPHA, TETRAGRAMMATON, TOPOGRAPHY, from Greek *graphein*, to scratch, draw, write, *gramma* (< **grbh-mn̥*), a picture, written letter, piece of writing, and *grammē*, a line; **b.** LANDGRAVE, MARGRAVE, PALSGRAVE, from Middle Dutch *grāve* and Middle Low German *grave*, count, from West Germanic **grafa*, a designation of rank, possibly borrowed from Greek *grapheus*, scribe. [Pokorny *gerebh-* 392.]

[gerere To carry, carry on, act, do. Latin verb of unknown origin. Oldest form *ges-*, past participle *gestus*. GERENT, GERUND, GEST, GESTATION, GESTICULATE, GESTURE, JEST; ARMIGER, BELLIGERENT, CONGERIES, CONGEST, DIGEST, EGEST, INGEST, REGISTER, SUGGEST, VELIGER.]

gerə-1 To grow old. (Oldest form **ĝerh₂-*.) **1.** Suffixed lengthened-grade form **gērə-s-*. AGERATUM, GERIATRICS, from Greek *gēras*, old age. **2.** Suffixed form **gerə-ont-*. GERONTO-, from Greek *gerōn* (stem *geront-*), old man. [Pokorny *ĝer-* 390.]

gerə-2 To cry hoarsely; also the name of the crane. (Oldest form **gerə₂-*.)

I. Words meaning "to cry hoarsely"; also words denoting the crow. **1a.** CROW[1], from Old English *crāwe*, a crow; **b.** CROW[2], from Old English *crāwan*, to crow; **c.** CRACK, from Old English *cracian*, to resound; **d.** CRACKNEL, from Middle Dutch *krāken*, to crack; **e.** CRAKE, from Old Norse *krāka*, a crow; **f.** CROON, from Middle Dutch *krōnen*, to groan, lament. **a–f** all from Germanic **krē-*. **2.** Possibly from this root (but more likely imitative) is Germanic **kur(r)-*. CUR, from Middle English *curre*, cur, akin to Old Norse *kurra*, to growl.

II. Words denoting a crane. **1a.** CRANE, from Old English *cran*, crane; **b.** CRANBERRY, from Middle Low German *kran*, crane. Both **a** and **b** from Germanic **kran-*, crane. **2.** Extended form **grū-*. GRUS; PEDIGREE, from Latin *grūs*, crane. **3.** Suffixed zero-grade form **grə-k-*, becoming **grā-k-*. GRACKLE, from Latin *grāculus*, jackdaw. **4.** Suffixed extended form **gerə-no-*. GERANIUM, from Greek *geranos*, crane. [Pokorny 2. *ger-* 383.]

geuə- To hasten. (Oldest forms **ĝeuh₄-*, **geuh₄-*.) Possibly Germanic **kaurjan*. SKIJORING, from Old Norse *keyra*, to drive. [Pokorny *ĝeu* 399.]

g(e)u-lo- A glowing coal. **1.** COAL, COLLIE, COLLIER, from Old English *col*, a glowing coal, from Germanic **kulam*. **2.** CHOLLA, from dialectal Old French *cholle*, round lump, head, probably from Germanic **kulam*, **kolam*. [Pokorny *g(e)u-lo-* 399.]

geus- To taste, choose. (Oldest form **ĝeus-*.) **1a.** CHOOSE, from Old English *cēosan*, *ceōsan*, to choose, from Germanic **keusan*; **b.** CHOICE, from a Germanic source akin to Gothic *kausjan*, to test, taste, from Germanic causative **kausjan*. **2.** Zero-grade form **gus-*. VALKYRIE, from Old Norse *Valkyrja*, "chooser of the slain," Valkyrie (*valr*, the slain; see **welə-2**), from Germanic **kuz-*. **3.** AGEUSIA, from Greek *geuesthai*, to taste. **4.** Suffixed zero-grade form **gus-tu-*. **a.** GUST[2], GUSTO; RAGOUT, from Latin *gustus*, taste; **b.** Celtic **gustu-*, "strength," in personal names: *(i)* ANGUS, from Old Irish *Oengus*, "having solitary strength" (*oen*, one; see **oi-no-**); *(ii)* FERGUS, from Old Irish *Fergus*, "having the strength of men" (*fer*, man; see **wī-ro-**). Both *(i)* and *(ii)* from Old Irish *gus(s)*, strength. **5.** Suffixed zero-grade form **gus-to-*, whence further suffixed (frequentative) form **gus-t-ā-*. GUSTATION; DEGUST, DISGUST, from Latin *gustāre*, to taste. [Pokorny *ĝeus-* 399.]

ghabh- Also **ghebh-**. To give or receive. **1.** Form **ghebh-*. **a.** GIVE, from Old English *giefan*, to give, and Old Norse *gefa*, to give; **b.** FORGIVE, from Old English *forgi(e)fan*, to give, give up, leave off (anger), remit, forgive, from Germanic compound **far-geban*, to give away (**far-*, away; see **per1**). **c.** ZEITGEBER, from Old High German *geban*, to give. **a-c** all from Germanic **geban*, to give. **2.** Suffixed form **ghebh-ti-*, something given (or received). GIFT, from Old Norse *gipt, gift*, a gift, from Germanic **giftiz*. **3.** O-grade form **ghobh-*. GAVEL[2], from Old English *gafol*, tribute, tax, debt, from Germanic **gab-ulam*, something paid (or received). **4.** Form **ghabh-ē-*. **a.** ABLE, BINNACLE, HAB- ILE, HABIT, HABITABLE, HABITANT, HABITAT; AVOIRDUPOIS, COHABIT, EXHIBIT, INHABIT, INHIBIT, MALADY, PREBEND, PROHIBIT, PROVENDER, from Latin *habēre*, to hold, possess, have, handle (> *habitāre*, to dwell); **b.** DEBENTURE, DEBIT, DEBT, DEVOIR, DUE, DUTY; ENDEAVOR, from Latin *dēbēre*, to owe (*dē-*, away from; see **de-**). [Pokorny *ghabh-* 407.] Compare **kap-**.

ghabholo- A fork, branch of a tree. JAVELIN, from Old French *javelot*, a throwing spear, probably from Celtic **gablakko-*. [Pokorny *ghabh(o)lo-* 409.]

ghāi- To yawn, gape. (Oldest form **ĝheh₂i-*, colored to **ĝhah₂i-*, contracted to **ĝhai-* [before consonants] and **ĝhāy-* [before vowels].) **1.** Variant form **ghyā-* (< **ghyaa-*). **a.** Nasalized form **ghi-n-ā-*. YAWN, from Old English *ginan, ginian, geonian*, to yawn, from Germanic **ginōn*; **b.** HIATUS; DEHISCE, from Latin *hiāre*, to gape, be open. **2.** Suffixed variant form **ghə-smn̥-*. CHASM; CHASMOGAMOUS, from Greek *khasma*, yawning gulf, chasm. **3.** Suffixed variant form **ghə-n-yo-*. ACHENE, from Greek *khainein*, to gape. **4.** Labial extensions: **a.** GAP, from Old Norse *gap*, chasm; **b.** GAPE, from Old Norse *gapa*, to open the mouth; **c.** GASP, from Old Norse *geispa*, to yawn. **5.** GILL[3], from Old Norse *gil*, ravine, chasm, from Germanic **gil-*. **6.** GYRFALCON, LAMMERGEIER, from Old High German *gīr*, vulture, from Germanic **gīr-*, vulture (< "voracious or yawning bird"). [Pokorny 2. *ĝhē-* 419.] Compare **ghēu-**.

gh(a)id-o- A goat. Possibly related (by metathesis) to **digh-**. GOAT, from Old English *gāt*, she-goat, from Germanic **gaitō*. [Pokorny *ghaido-* 409.]

ghais- To adhere, hesitate. Suffixed form **ghais-ē-*. HESITATE; ADHERE, COHERE, INHERE, from Latin *haerēre*, to stick, cling. [Pokorny *ghais-* 410.]

ghaiso- A stick, spear. **1a.** GORE[1]; GARFISH, GARLIC, from Old English *gār*, spear, also in personal names: *(i)* EDGAR, from Old English *Ēadgār*, "happy spear, rich spear" (*ēad*, happiness, riches); *(ii)* Old English *Ōsgār* (see **ansu-**); **b.** Old High German *gēr*, spear, in personal names: *(i)* GERALD, from Old High German *Gērwald, Gērald*, "spear rule" (*-wald*, power; see **wal-**); *(ii)* GERARD, from Old High German *Gērhart*, "strong with the spear" (*hart*, stern, strong; see **kar-1**);

(iii) GERTRUDE, from Old High German *Gĕrdrūd*, "spear strength" (*drūd*, strength); *(iv)* Old High German *Hrōdgēr* (see **kar-²**); **c.** Germanic compound *nabō-gaizaz* (see **nobh-**); **a–c** all from Germanic *gaizaz*, spear. **2.** GORE², from Old English *gāra*, corner, point of land, from Germanic *gaizōn-*. [Pokorny *ĝhaiso-* 410 (but palatal *ĝh* not on good evidence).]

ghalgh- Branch, rod. (Oldest form *ĝhalgh-*.) **1.** GALLOWS, from Old English *g(e)alga*, cross, gallows. **2.** GAUGE, from Old North French *gauge*, gauge. Both **a** and **b** from Germanic *galgōn-*. [Pokorny *ĝhalg(h)-* 411.]

ghans- Goose. (Oldest form *ĝhans-*.) **1a.** GOOSE¹, GOSHAWK, from Old English *gōs* (nominative plural *gēs*), goose; **b.** GOSLING, from Old Norse *gās*, goose; **c.** GUNSEL, from Old High German *gans*, goose; **d.** GONZO, from Spanish *ganso*, goose, from a Germanic source akin to Old High German *gans*, goose; **e.** SMORGASBORD, from Old Norse *gās*, goose. **a–e** all from Germanic *gans-* (nominative plural *gansiz*). **2.** GANDER, from Old English *ganra*, *gandra*, gander, from Germanic *gan(d)rōn-*. **3.** GANNET, from Old English *ganot*, gannet, from Germanic *ganotōn-*. **4.** Suffixed form *ghans-er-*. ANSERINE; MERGANSER, from Latin *ānser* (< *hanser*), goose. **5.** Basic form *ghans-*. CHENOPOD, from Greek *khēn*, goose. [Pokorny *ĝhan-s-* 412.]

ghazdh-o- Rod, staff. (Oldest form *ĝhazdh-o-*.) **a.** YARD¹, from Old English *gierd*, *geard*, staff, twig, measuring rod, from Germanic *gazdjō*; **b.** GAD², from Old Norse *gaddr*, rod, goad, spike. Both **a** and **b** from Germanic *gazdaz*. **2.** Form *ghazdh-ā-*. HASLET, HASTATE, from Latin *hasta*, spear. [Pokorny 1. *ĝhasto-* 412.]

ghē- To release, let go; (in the middle voice) to be released, go. (Contracted from earlier *ĝheh₁-*.) **1.** GO¹; AGO, FOREGO¹, FORGO, from Old English *gān*, to go, from Germanic variant form *gaian*. **2.** Suffixed form *ghē-ro-*. HEIR, HEREDITAMENT, HEREDITY, HERITAGE; INHERIT, from Latin *hērēs*, heir (? < "orphan" < "bereft"). **3.** Possibly suffixed o-grade form *ghō-ro-*, "empty space." **a.** –CHORE, HORIATIKI; ANCHORITE, CHOROGRAPHY, from Greek *khōros*, place, country, particular spot; **b.** CHORIPETALOUS, from Greek *khōris*, *khōri*, apart, asunder. **4.** Possible suffixed zero-grade form *ghǝ-t(w)ā-*. **a.** GAIT, GATE², from Old Norse *gata*, path, street; **b.** GANTLET¹, GAUNTLET², from Old Swedish *gata*, lane. Both **a** and **b** from Germanic *gatwōn-*, a going. **5.** Suffixed zero-grade form *ghǝ-no-*. HINAYANA, from Sanskrit *hīna-*, inferior, verbal adjective of *jahāti*, he leaves, lets go (< reduplicated *ghe-ghē-ti* < *ghe-gheǝ-ti*). [Pokorny 1. *ĝhē-* 418.]

ghebh-el- Head. **1.** GABLE, from Old Norse *gafl*, gable, from Germanic *gablaz*, top of a pitched roof. **2.** Form *kephal-*, dissimilated from *khephal-*. CEPHALIC, CEPHALO-, -CEPHALOUS; AUTOCEPHALOUS, ENCEPHALO-, ENKEPHALIN, HYDROCEPHALUS, PACHYCEPHALOSAUR, from Greek *kephalē*, head. [Pokorny *ghebh-el-* 423.]

ghedh- To unite, join, fit. **1.** Lengthened o-grade form *ghōdh-*. GOOD, from Old English *gōd*, good, from Germanic *gōdaz*, "fitting, suitable." **2.** TOGETHER, from Old English *tōgædere*, together (*tō*, to; see **de-**), from Germanic *gadurī*, "in a body." **3.** GATHER, from Old English *gad(e)rian*, to gather, from Germanic *gadurōn*, "to come or bring together." [Pokorny *ghedh-* 423.]

ghei-¹ To propel, prick. (Oldest form *ĝhei-*.) **1.** Suffixed and extended o-grade form *ĝhoidh-ā-*. GOAD, from Old English *gād*, goad, from Germanic *gaidō*, goad, spear. **2.** Suffixed form *ghei-s-* perhaps in nasalized zero-grade form *ghi-n-s-*. AHIMSA, from Sanskrit *hiṁsati*, he injures. [Pokorny 1. *ĝhei-* 424.]

ghei-² Theoretical base (oldest form *ĝhei-*) of *ghyem-*, *ghiem-*, winter (oldest forms *ghyem-*, *ĝhiem-*). **1.** Form *ghiem-*. HIEMAL, from Latin *hiems*, winter. **2.** Suffixed variant form *gheim-ri-no-*. HIBERNACULUM, HIBERNATE, from Latin *hībernus*, pertaining to winter. **3.** O-grade form *ghiom-*. CHIONODOXA, from Greek *khiōn* (stem *khion-*), winter, from earlier *khiōn*, *khiom-*, with *-n* (< *-m*) generalized to the oblique stem from the nominative singular *khiōn* (< *khiōm* with lengthened o-grade). **4.** Suffixed zero-grade form *ghim-r-yo*, "female animal one year (winter) old." CHIMERA, from Greek *khimaira*, she-goat. **5.** Suffixed zero-grade form *ghi-mo-*. HIMALAYA MOUNTAINS, from Sanskrit *himālayaḥ*, "abode of snow," from *himaḥ*, snow (*ālayaḥ*, abode; see **(s)lei-**). [Pokorny 2. *ĝhei-* 425.]

gheis- Used of the emotion of fear or amazement (original part of speech uncertain). Suffixed o-grade form *ghois-do-*. **1.** GHOST; AGHAST, BARGHEST, from Old English *gāst*, ghost. **2.** POLTERGEIST, SNOLLYGOSTER, ZEITGEIST, from Old High German *geist*, ghost. **3.** GAST, from Old English *gǣstan*, to scare, from Germanic denominative *gaistjan*. **1–3** all from Germanic *gaistaz*, a ghost. [Pokorny *gheis-* (misprint for *ĝheis-*) 427.]

ghel-¹ To call. **1a.** YELL, from Old English *gellan*, *giellan*, to sound, shout; **b.** YELP, from Old English *gielpan*, to boast, exult; **c.** NIGHTINGALE, from Old English *galan*, to sing. **a–c** all from Germanic *gel-*, *gal-*. **2.** Reduplicated form *ghi-ghl-*. CICHLID, from Greek *kikhlē*, thrush, later also the name for a kind of wrasse (a sea fish that has bright colors and jagged waving fins, reminiscent of the plumage of a bird). **3.** CELANDINE, from Greek *khelidwōn*, *khelidōn*, the swallow. [Pokorny *ghel-* 428.]

ghel-² To shine; with derivatives referring to colors, bright materials, gold (probably "yellow metal"), and bile or gall. (Oldest form *ĝhel-*.)

I. Words denoting colors. **1.** Suffixed form *ghel-wo-*. YELLOW, from Old English *geolu*, yellow, from Germanic *gelwa-*. **2.** Suffixed variant form *ghlō-ro-*. CHLORO-; CHLORITE¹, from Greek *khlōros*, green, greenish yellow. **3.** Suffixed variant form *ghlo-wo-*. CHLOASMA, from Greek *khloos* (< *khlo-wo-s*), greenish color. **4.** O-grade form *ghol-*. PODZOL, from Russian *zola*, ashes (from their color). **5.** Suffixed form *ghel-i-*. HARE KRISHNA, HARIJAN, from Sanskrit *hari-*, tawny yellow. **6.** Possibly suffixed zero-grade form *ghl̥-wo-* in Latin *fulvus*, tawny (with dialectal *f-* as in *fel*, gall; see **III.** 3. below): FULVOUS; GRISEOFULVIN.

II. Words denoting gold. **1.** Suffixed zero-grade form *ghl̥-to-*. GOLD, from Old English *gold*; **b.** GILD¹, from Old English *gyldan*, to gild, from Germanic denominative verb *gulthjan*; **c.** GUILDER, GULDEN, from Middle Dutch *gulden*, golden; **d.** GOWAN, from Middle English *gollan*, yellow flower, possibly from a source akin to Old Norse *gullinn*, golden. **a–d** all from Germanic *gultham*, gold. **2.** Suffixed o- grade form *ghol-to-*. ZLOTY, from Polish *złoto*, gold. **3.** Suffixed full-grade form *ghel-no-*. ARSENIC, from Syriac *zarnīkā*, orpiment, from Middle Iranian *zarnīk-*, from Old Iranian *zarna-*, golden.

III. Words denoting bile. **1.** Suffixed o-grade form *ghol-no-*. GALL¹, from Old English *gealla*, gall, from Germanic *gallōn-*, gall. **2.** Suffixed o-grade form *ghol-ā-*. CHOLE-, CHOLER, CHOLERA; ACHOLIA, MELANCHOLY, from Greek *kholē*, bile. **3.** Suffixed full-grade form *ghel-n-*. FELON², from Latin *fel*, bile (with dialectal *f-*).

IV. A range of Germanic words with initial *gl-* (where no preforms are given, the words are late creations). **1.** GLEAM, from Old English *glǣm*, bright light, gleam, from Germanic *glaimiz*. **2.** GLIMPSE, from Middle English *glimsen*, to glimpse, from a source akin to Middle High German *glimsen*, to gleam. **3.**

GLINT, from Middle English *glent*, a glint, and *glenten*, to shine, from a source akin to Swedish dialectal *glinta*, to shine. **4.** GLIMMER, from Middle English *glimeren*, to glimmer, from a source akin to Swedish *glimra*, glimmer. **5.** GLITTER, from Old Norse *glitra*, to shine. **6.** GLITZ, from Old High German *glīzan*, to sparkle. **7.** GLISTEN, from Old English *glisnian*, to shine. **8.** GLISTER, from Middle Dutch *glinsteren* or Middle Low German *glisteren*, to glisten. **9.** GLASS, GLAZE, GLAZIER, from Old English *glæs*, glass, from Germanic **glasam*, glass. **10.** GLARE¹, from Middle English *glaren*, to glitter, stare, from a source akin to Middle Low German *glaren*, to glisten, from Germanic **glaz-*. **11.** GLOSS¹, from a source perhaps akin to Icelandic *glossi*, a spark. **12.** GLANCE², from Old High German *glanz*, bright. **13.** GLEG, from Old Norse *glöggr*, clear-sighted. **14.** GLAD¹, from Old English *glæd*, shining, joyful, from Germanic **glada-*. **15.** GLEE; GLEEMAN, from Old English *glēo*, sport, merriment, from Germanic **gleu-jam*. **16a.** GLEED, from Old English *glēd*, ember; **b.** GLOGG, from Old Norse *glodh*, ember. Both **a** and **b** from Germanic **glō-di-*. **17a.** GLOW, from Old English *glōwan*, to glow; **b.** GLOWER, from Middle English *gloren*, to gleam, stare, probably from a source akin to Norwegian dialectal *glora*, to gleam, stare; **c.** GLOAT, from a source perhaps akin to Old Norse *glotta*, to smile (scornfully). **a–c** all from Germanic **glō-*. **18.** GLOAMING, from Old English *glōm*, twilight, from Germanic **glō-m-*. **19.** Possibly distantly related to this root is Germanic **glīdan*, to glide. **a.** GLIDE, from Old English *glīdan*, to slip, glide; **b.** GLISSADE, from Old French *glier*, to glide; **c.** GLITCH, from High German *glītan*, to glide; **d.** GLEDE, from Old English *glida*, kite (< "gliding, hovering bird"), from derivative Germanic **glidōn-*. **20.** GLIB, from a source possibly akin to Middle Low German *glibberich*, slippery. [Pokorny 1. *ĝhel-* 429.]

ghel-³ To cut. (Oldest form **ĝhel-*.) **1.** GELD¹, GELDING, from Old Norse *gelda*, to castrate, and *geldingr*, a castrated animal, from Germanic **galdjan*, to castrate. **2.** GILT², from Old Norse *gyltr*, a sow (< "castrated pig"), from Germanic zero-grade **gulti-*. [Pokorny 2. *ĝhel-* 434.]

gheldh- To pay. Root found only in Germanic and Slavic. **1a.** GELD²; DANEGELD, WERGELD, from Old English *geld, gield*, payment, service; **b.** GELT¹, from Old High German *gelt*, payment, reward. **a** and **b** from Germanic **geldam*, payment. **2.** YIELD, from Old English *gieldan*, to pay, yield, from Germanic **geldan*, to pay. **3.** GUILD, from Old Norse *gildi*, guild, from Germanic **geldjam*, payment, contribution, hence an association founded on contributions, a craftsmen's guild. [Pokorny *ghel-tō* 436.]

ghelegh- A metal. (Oldest form **ĝheleĝh-*.) Possible root of Greek *khalkos*, copper, which, however, is more likely borrowed from an unknown source. CHALCID, CHALCOCITE; CHALCOLITHIC, CHALCOPYRITE. [Pokorny *ghel(ĕ)ĝh-* 435.]

gheləd- Hail. (Oldest form **ghelh₂d-*.) Zero-grade form **ghḷəd-*. CHALAZA, CHALAZION, from Greek *khalaza* (< **khalad-ya*), a hailstone, hard lump, also a small cyst. [Pokorny *gheləd-* 435.]

ghelū- Tortoise. Suffixed form **ghel-ōnā-*. CHELONIAN, from Greek *khelōnē*, tortoise. [Pokorny *ghel-ōu-* 435.]

ghel-unā- Jaw. **1.** GILL¹, from Middle English *gile*, gill, from a Scandinavian source akin to Old Norse **gil*, gill of a fish, from Germanic **geliz*. **2.** Suffixed variant form **ghel-wo-*. CHEILOSIS, CHILOPOD, from Greek *kheilos*, lip. [Pokorny *ghelunā* 436.]

[gh(e)n]- To gnaw. Hypothetical base of various Germanic forms beginning with *gn-*. **1a.** GNAW, from Old English *gnagan*, to gnaw; **b.** NAG¹, possibly from a Scandinavian source akin to Old Norse *gnaga*, to bite. **a** and **b** from Germanic **gnagan*. **2.** NOSH, from Old High German *nascon*, to nibble, from Germanic

*(g)naskōn, from suffixed form **gnag-sk-*. **3.** Perhaps related is Germanic **gnatt-*, "biting insect." GNAT, from Old English *gnæt*, gnat. **4.** NATTER, from dialectal English *gnatter*, to nibble, natter (preform uncertain). [Pokorny *ghen-* 436.]]

ghend- Also **ghed-**. To seize, take. **1a.** GET, from Old Norse *geta*, to get; **b.** BEGET, from Old English *beg(i)etan*, to get, beget, from Germanic compound **bigetan*, to acquire (**bi-*, intensive prefix; see **ambhi**); **c.** FORGET, from Old English *forg(i)etan*, to forget, from Germanic compound **fer-getan*, "to lose one's hold," forget (**fer-*, prefix denoting rejection; see **per¹**). **a–c** all from Germanic **getan*. **2.** GUESS, from Middle English *gessen*, to guess, from a Scandinavian source akin to Old Swedish *gissa*, to guess, from Germanic **getisōn*, "to try to get," aim at. **3.** Basic form **ghend-*. PREHENSILE, PREHENSION, PRISON, PRIZE², PRIZE³, PRY²; APPREHEND, APPRENTICE, APPRISE, COMPREHEND, COMPRISE, EMPRISE, ENTERPRISE, ENTREPRENEUR, IMPRESARIO, MISPRISION¹, PREGNABLE, REPREHEND, REPRIEVE, REPRISAL, REPRISE, SURPRISE, from Latin *prehendere, prēndere*, to get hold of, seize, grasp (*pre-, prae-*, before; see **per¹**). **4.** Form **ghed-*. PREDATORY, PREY, SPREE; DEPREDATE, OSPREY, from Latin *praeda*, booty (< **prai-hedā*, "something seized before"; *prai-, prae-*, before; see **per¹**). [Pokorny *ghend-* 437.]

ghengh- To go, walk. (Oldest form **ĝhengh-*.) **1a.** GANG¹, from Old English *gang*, a going; **b.** GANGUE, from Old High German *gang*, a going. Both **a** and **b** from Germanic **gangaz*, a going. **2.** GANGLING, from Old English *gangan*, to go, from Germanic **gangan*. [Pokorny *ĝhengh-* 438.]

gher-¹ To grasp, enclose; with derivatives meaning "enclosure." (Oldest form **ĝher-*.) Suffixed zero-grade form **ghṛ-dh-*. **a.** GIRD¹, GIRT¹, from Old English *gyrdan*, to gird, from Germanic **gurdjan*; **b.** GIRDLE, from Old English *gyrdel*, girdle; **c.** GIRTH, from Old Norse *gjördh*, girdle. **2.** Suffixed o-grade forms **ghor-to-*, **ghor-dho-*, an enclosure. **a.** Form **ghor-to-*. HORTICULTURE, ORTOLAN, from Latin *hortus*, garden; **b.** form **ghor-to-* or **ghor-dho-*. *(i)* YARD²; ORCHARD, from Old English *geard*, enclosure, garden, yard; *(ii)* GARTH; ASGARD, from Old Norse *gardhr*, enclosure, garden, yard; *(iii)* KINDERGARTEN, from Old High German *garto*, garden; *(iv)* GARDEN, JARDINIÈRE, from Old North French *gart*, garden; *(v)* HANGAR, from Old French *hangard*, shelter, possibly from Germanic **haimgardaz* (**haimaz*, home; see **tkei-**); *(vi)* Germanic compound **midja-gardaz* (see **medhyo-**). *(i)–(vi)* all from Germanic **gardaz*; **c.** form **ghor-dho-* in Slavic **gordŭ*, citadel, town. *(i)* Russian *gorod*, town, city, in names of cities ending in *-gorod* like NOVGOROD, "new city" (*novyj*, new, from Slavic **novŭ*; see **newo-**); *(ii)* Russian *-grad*, city, in names of cities ending in *-grad* like LENINGRAD, PETROGRAD; *(iii)* BELGRADE, from Serbo-Croatian *Beograd* (earlier *Belgrad*), "white town" (*bel-, beo-*, from Old Church Slavonic *belŭ*, white; see **bhel-¹**). Both *(ii)* and *(iii)* from Old Church Slavonic *gradŭ*, town, city. **3.** Suffixed zero-grade form **ghṛ-dho-*. GADJO, from Romani *gadjo*, gadjo, perhaps from Prakrit **gajjha-*, domestic (as opposed to itinerant), ultimately from Sanskrit *grhah*, house. **4.** Prefixed and suffixed zero-grade form **ko(m)-ghṛ-ti-* (**ko(m)-*, collective prefix, "together"; see **kom**). COHORT, CORTEGE, COURT, COURTEOUS, COURTESAN, COURTESY, COURTIER, CURTILAGE, CURTSY, from Latin *cohors* (stem *cohort-*), enclosed yard, company of soldiers, multitude. **5.** Perhaps suffixed o-grade form **ghor-o-*. CAROL, CHOIR, CHORAL, CHORALE, CHORE, CHORISTER, CHORUS, HORA; CHORAGUS, TERPSICHORE, from Greek *khoros*, dancing ground (? perhaps originally a special enclosure for dancing), dance, dramatic chorus. [Pokorny 4. *ĝher-* 442, *ĝherdh-* 444.]

gher-² To call out. Extended root *ghrēd-. GREET, from Old English grētan, to speak to, greet, from Germanic *grōtjan. [Pokorny 1. gher- 439.]

[gh(e)r-³ To shine, glow; gray. Hypothetical base of various Germanic forms beginning with gr-. **1a.** GRAY, from Old English græg, gray, from Germanic *grēwa-, gray; **b.** GREYHOUND, from Old English grīg-hund, greyhound, probably from Germanic *grēwa-. **2a.** GRISAILLE, GRISETTE, GRISON, GRIZZLE; AMBERGRIS, PINOT GRIS, from Old French gris, gray, from Frankish *grīs; **c.** PINOT GRIGIO, from Italian grigio, gray, of Germanic origin; **c.** GRISEOUS; GRISEOFULVIN, from Medieval Latin grīseus, gray, grayish. **a-c** all from Germanic *grisja-, gray. [Pokorny 3. ǵher- 441.]]

gher-⁴ To scrape, scratch. Extended zero-grade form *ghṛ(ə)-k-. **1.** CHARACIN, from Greek kharax, a pointed stake, also a kind of sea bream. **2.** CHARACTER, GASH, from Greek kharassein, to sharpen, notch, carve, cut. [Pokorny 2. gher- 439, 2. ǵher- 441.] See also extended root **ghrēu-**.

gher-⁵ To like, want. (Oldest form *ǵher-.) **1.** Suffixed form *gher-n-. YEARN, from Old English giernan, gyrnan, to strive, desire, yearn, from Germanic *gernjan. **2.** Possibly extended form *ghrē-. **a.** GREEDY, from Old English grǣdig, hungry, covetous, greedy, from Germanic *grēdiga-, hungry, formed from *grēduz, hunger; **b.** CATACHRESIS, CHRESTOMATHY, from Greek khrēsthai, to lack, want, use, from khrē, it is necessary. **3.** Suffixed zero-grade form *ghṛ-to-. HORTATIVE; EXHORT, from Latin hortārī, to urge on, encourage (< "to cause to strive or desire"). **4.** Suffixed zero-grade form *ghṛ-i-. CHARISMA; EUCHARIST, from Greek kharis, grace, favor. **5.** Suffixed zero-grade form *ghṛ-yo-. CHERVIL, from Greek khai- rein, to rejoice, delight in. [Pokorny 1. ǵher- 440.]

gherə- Gut, entrail. (Oldest form *ǵherh₂-.) **1.** Suffixed form *gherə-no-. YARN, from Old English gearn, yarn, from Germanic *garnō, string. **2.** Suffixed form *gherə-n-. HERNIA, from Latin hernia, "protruded viscus," rupture, hernia. **3.** Suffixed o-grade form *ghorə-d-. CHORD²; CORD, CORDON; HARPSICHORD, HEX- ACHORD, TETRACHORD, from Greek khordē, gut, string. **4.** O-grade form *ghorə-. CHORION, from Greek khorion, intestinal membrane, afterbirth. **5.** Possible suffixed zero-grade form *ghṛə-u-. HARUSPEX, from Latin haruspex, "he who inspects entrails," diviner (-spex, "he who sees"; see **spek-**), but perhaps borrowed from Etruscan. [Pokorny 5. ǵher- 443.]

ghers- To bristle. (Oldest form *ǵhers-.) **1.** Extended zero-grade form *ghṛzd-, prickly plant. **a.** GORSE, from Old English gorst, furze, gorse, from Germanic *gorst-; **b.** ORGEAT, ORZO, HORCHATA, from Latin hordeum, barley. **2.** Lengthened-grade form *ghēr(s)-. URCHIN, from Latin hēr, ēr, hedgehog. **3.** Suffixed lengthened-grade form *ghēr(s)-ūkā-. ARUGULA, ROCKET²; ERUCIC ACID, from Latin ērūca, cabbage, rocket. **4.** Suffixed full-grade form *ghers-tu-, remade to *hirsu- in Latin. HIRSUTE, from Latin hirsūtus, bristly, shaggy, hairy. **5.** Suffixed full-grade form *ghers-kʷo-. HISPID, from Latin hispidus, bristly, shaggy, prickly (probably a dialect borrowing). **6.** Suffixed o-grade form *ghors- eyo-. HORRIBLE, HORRID, HORROR; ABHOR, HORRIPILATION, ORDURE, from Latin horrēre, to bristle, shudder, be terrified, look frightful. **7.** Suffixed full-grade form *ghers-o-. CHERSONESE, from Greek khersos, dry land. [Pokorny ǵhers- 445.]

ghes- Hand. (Oldest form *ǵhes-.) **1.** Suffixed form *ǵhes-ōr, stem *ghes-(e)r-. CHIRO-; CHIRONOMID, CHIRURGEON, ENCHIRIDION, SURGEON, SURGERY, from Greek kheir, hand. **2.** Suffixed form *ghes-to-. PRESS², PRESTO; IMPREST, from Latin praestō, at hand, perhaps from prefixed form *prai-ghes-to- (*prai-, before; see **per¹**). [Pokorny 1. ǵhesor- 447.]

gheslo- Seen by some as a base for words meaning "thousand." (Oldest form *ǵheslo-.) **1.** Suffixed form *ghesl-yo-. CHILIAD, KILO-, from Greek khílioi, thousand. **2.** Compound *sm̥-gheslo-. HAZARA, from Old Iranian *hazahram, thousand (Avestan hazaŋrəm). **3.** MIL¹, MILE, MILLENARY, MILLESIMAL, MILLI-, MILLIARY, MILLIME, MILLION; MILFOIL, MILLEFIORE GLASS, MILLEFLEUR, MILLENNIUM, MILLEPORE, MILLIPEDE, PER MIL, from Latin mīlle, thousand, which has been analyzed as *smī-, "one" + a form *ghslī-, but is of obscure origin. [Pokorny ǵhéslo- 446.]

gheu- To pour, pour a libation. (Oldest form *ǵheu-.)
I. Extended form *gheud-. **1.** Zero-grade form *ghud-. **a.** GUT, from Old English guttas, intestines, from Germanic *gut-. **b.** GYTTJA, from Swedish gyttja, mud, ooze, perhaps from Germanic *gutjōn. **2.** Nasalized zero-grade form *ghu-n-d-. FOISON, FONDANT, FONDUE, FONT², FOUND², FUNNEL, FUSE², FUSILE, FUSION; AFFUSION, CIRCUMFUSE, CONFOUND, CONFUSE, DIFFUSE, EFFUSE, INFUSE, PERFUSE, PROFUSE, REFUND, REFUSE¹, REFUSE², SUFFUSE, TRANSFUSE, from Latin fundere, to melt, pour out.
II. Extended form *gheus-. **1a.** GUST¹, from Old Norse gustr, a cold blast of wind, from Germanic suffixed form *gustiz; **b.** GUSH, from Middle English gushen, to gush, perhaps akin to Icelandic gusa, to gush. Both **a** and **b** from Germanic zero-grade form *gus-. **2.** GEYSER, from Old Norse geysa, to gush, from Germanic suffixed o-grade form *gausjan. **3a.** Suffixed zero-grade form *ghus-mo-. CHYME, ECCHYMOSIS, from Greek khūmos, juice; **b.** suffixed zero-grade form *ghus-lo-. CHYLE, from Greek khūlos, juice.
IV. Basic form *gheu-. **1.** ALCHEMY, PARENCHYMA, from Greek khein (stem khu-), to pour. **2.** Suffixed form *gheu-ti-. FUTILE, from Latin fūtilis, "(of a vessel) easily emptied, leaky," hence untrustworthy, useless. **3.** O-grade form *ghou-. **a.** CHOANOCYTE, from Greek khoanē, funnel. **b.** OINOCHOE, from Greek oinokhoē, oinochoe, from khoē (< *khowā), a pouring (oinos, wine; see **wĭn-o-**). **4.** Suffixed zero-grade form *ghu-trā. CHYTRID, from Greek khutrā, pot. **5.** Suffixed zero-grade form *ghu-to-, "poured," perhaps in Germanic *gudam, god (but this is traditionally referred to **gheu(ə)-**; see note below.) [Pokorny ǵheu- 447.]

Language and Culture Note The etymologies of basic religious terms are not always straightforwardly ascertainable. Such is the case with that most fundamental one in English, god. The English word has exact cognates in all the other Germanic languages that allow one to reconstruct a Germanic ancestral form *gudam. Traditionally, this is derived from the root **gheu(ə)-**, "to invoke." But there is an alternative view that derives it instead from the root **gheu-**, "to pour," a root that also occupied a rather prominent role in religious terminology. It was used to refer to making a libation, or pouring a liquid sacrifice, as well as to the action of "pouring" or heaping earth to form a burial mound. Thus, Greek has the phrase khutē gaia, "poured earth," to refer to a burial mound. Greek khutē continues the Indo-European verbal adjective *ghu-to-, "poured." If we take the neuter of this, *ghu-tom, and imagine what it would have become in prehistoric Germanic (applying the sound changes that we know occurred from Proto-Indo-European to Germanic), we would in fact get a form *gudam, none other than our reconstructed word for "god." Given the Greek facts, the Germanic form may have referred in the first instance to the spirit immanent in a burial mound. Deriving *gudam from **gheu-** rather than from **gheu(ə)-** would help to explain two odd facts: Germanic *gudam had neuter gender, not masculine (so it may not have referred to a god in the first instance), and for technical reasons, we would really expect *gūdam with a long vowel (rather than *gudam) if the word came from the root **gheu(ə)-**.

ghēu- To yawn, gape. (Oldest form *g̑hēu-.) **1.** GUM[2], from Old English *gōma*, palate, jaw, from Germanic suffixed form *gō-ma-. **2.** Variant form *ghau-. CHAOS, GAS, from Greek *khaos*, chasm, empty space, chaos. [Pokorny g̑hēu- 449.] Compare **ghāi-**.

gheu(ə)- To call, invoke. (Oldest form *g̑heu(ə)-.) Suffixed zero-grade form *ghu-to-, "the invoked," god. **1.** GOD, from Old English *god*, god. **2.** GIDDY, from Old English *gydig, gidig*, possessed, insane, from Germanic *gud-iga-, possessed by a god. **3.** GÖTTERDÄMMERUNG, from Old High German *got*, god, also in personal name GODFREY, from *Godafrid*, "peace of god" (*fridu*, peace; see **prī-**). **1–3** all from Germanic *gudam, god (but this is perhaps better referred to under **gheu-**, see note there). [Pokorny g̑hau- 413.]

gho- Base of demonstrative pronouns and deictic pronouns. **1.** Suffixed form *ghi-ke, neuter *ghod-ke, with *i* alternating with *o* as in other pronouns (-ke, here, deictic particle; see **ko-**). ENCORE, HOCUS POCUS, LANGUE D'OC, LANGUE D'OÏL, OCCITAN, from Latin *hic, haec, hoc*, this. **2.** Deictic particle *gh(i) in compound form *gh-dyes, "on this day, yesterday." See **dhgh(y)es-**. [Pokorny ghe- 417.]

ghō- Behind, after. (Oldest form *g̑hō-.) SASTRUGA, from Russian *za*, by, to, from Slavic *za. [Pokorny g̑hō 451.]

ghos-ti- Stranger, guest, host; properly "someone with whom one has reciprocal duties of hospitality." **1.** Basic form *ghos-ti-. **a.** (i) GUEST, from Old Norse *gestr*, guest; (ii) GASTARBEITER, from Old High German *gast*, guest. Both (i) and (ii) from Germanic *gastiz; **b.** HOST[2], HOSTILE, from Latin *hostis*, enemy (< "stranger"). **2.** Compound *ghos-pot-, *ghos-po(d)-, "guest-master," one who symbolizes the relationship of reciprocal obligation (*pot-, master; see **poti-**). HOSPICE, HOSPITABLE, HOSPITAL, HOSPITALITY, HOST[1], HOSTAGE, HOSTEL, HOSTLER, from Latin *hospes* (stem *hospit-*), host, guest, stranger. **3.** Suffixed zero-grade form *ghs-en-wo-. XENIA, XENO-, XENON; AXENIC, EUXENITE, PYROXENE, from Greek *xenos*, guest, host, stranger. [Pokorny ghosti-s 453.]

Language and Culture Note The basic meaning of the Indo-European word **ghos-ti-** was "someone with whom one has reciprocal duties of hospitality." In practical terms it referred to strangers in general, as well as to both *guests* and *hosts* (both of which words are descended from it). The word **ghos-ti-** was thus the central expression of the guest-host relationship, a mutual exchange relationship highly important to ancient Indo-European society. A guest-friendship was a bond of trust between two people that was accompanied by ritualized gift-giving and created an obligation of mutual hospitality and friendship that, once established, could continue in perpetuity and be renewed years later by the same parties or their descendants. The bond created by guest-friendship resembled kinship. A famous example is the story of the Trojan warrior Glaucus and the Greek warrior Diomedes in the *Iliad*, who agree not to fight one another when they realize that Glaucus's grandfather Bellerophon had been a guest at the home of Diomedes's grandfather Oeneus many years before. The two warriors instead embrace and exchange armor as a testimony to the guest-friendship still binding their families two generations later. The importance of hospitality is also seen in various Indo-European personal names, like Runic (ancient Germanic) *Hlewagastiz*, "having famous guests," and Lepontic Gaulish *Uvamo-kotsis*, "having supreme guests": the elements comprising names usually reflect culturally important concepts. • Strangers are potential guest-friends but also potential enemies; note that the Latin cognate of English *guest*, namely *hostis*, means "enemy."

ghow-ē- To honor, revere, worship. **1.** GAWK, from Old Norse *gā*, to heed, from Germanic *gawōn. **2.** FAVOR, FAVORITE, from Latin *favēre*, to favor, be favorable. [Pokorny ghou(ē)- 453.]

ghrē- To grow, become green. (Contracted from *ghreh₁-.) **1.** O-grade form *ghrō-. GROW, from Old English *grōwan*, to grow, from Germanic *grō(w)an. **2.** Suffixed o-grade form *ghrō-n-yo-. GREEN, from Old English *grēne*, green, from Germanic *grōnja-, green. **3.** Suffixed zero-grade form *ghra-so-. GRASS, GRAZE[1], from Old English *græs*, grass, from Germanic *grasam, grass. [Pokorny (ghrē-) 454.]

ghrebh-[1] To seize, reach. **1.** Zero-grade form *ghr̥bh-. SATYAGRAHA, from Sanskrit *gr̥bhṇāti, gr̥hṇāti*, he seizes. **2a.** GRASP, from Middle English *graspen*, to grasp; **b.** GRAB[1], from Middle Dutch or Middle Low German *grabben*, to seize. Both **a** and **b** from parallel (imitative) Germanic creations with base *grab-, *grap-. [Pokorny 1. ghrebh- 455.]

ghrebh-[2] To dig, bury, scratch. **1.** O-grade form *ghrobh-. **a.** (i) ENGRAVE, from Old English *grafan*, to dig, engrave, scratch, carve; (ii) GRABEN, from Old High German *graban*, to dig; (iii) GRAVLAX, from Swedish *grava*, to bury; (iv) GRAVURE, from Old French *graver*, to engrave. (i)–(iv) all from Germanic *graban; **b.** GRAVE[1], from Old English *græf*, trench, grave, from Germanic *grabam. **2.** GRUB, from Old English *grybban*, to dig, from Germanic *grub(b)jan (with secondary ablaut). **3.** GROOVE, from Middle Dutch *groeve*, ditch, from Germanic *grōbō. [Pokorny 2. ghrebh- 455.]

ghredh- To walk, go. Suffixed zero-grade form *ghr̥dh-yo-. **1.** GRESSORIAL; AGGRESS, CONGRESS, DEGRESSION, DIGRESS, EGRESS, INGREDIENT, INGRESS, INTROGRESSION, PLANTIGRADE, PROGRESS, REGRESS, RETROGRADE, RETROGRESS, TARDIGRADE, TRANSGRESS, from Latin *gradī* (past participle *gressus*), to walk, go. **2.** GRADE, GRADUAL, GRADUATE, GREE; CENTIGRADE, DEGRADE, DEGREE, from Latin *gradus* (< deverbative *grad-u-*), step, stage, degree, rank. [Pokorny ghredh- 456.]

ghrēi- To rub. (Oldest form *g̑hreh₁i-, with variant [metathesized] form *g̑hreih₁-, whence zero-grade *g̑hrih₁-, contracted to *g̑hrī-.) **1.** GRISLY, from Old English *grislīc*, terrifying, from Germanic *gris-, to frighten (< "to grate on the mind"). **2.** GRIME, from Middle English *grime*, grime, from a source akin to Middle Dutch *grīme*, grime, from Germanic *grīm-, smear. **3.** Extended form *ghrīs-. CHRISM, CHRIST[2], CHRISTEN, CHRISTIAN; CHRISTMAS, CREAM, KRISS KRINGLE, from Greek *khrīein*, to anoint. [Pokorny ghrēi- 457.]

ghreib- To grip. **1.** GRIP[1], from Old English *gripe*, grasp, and *gripa*, handful, from Germanic *grip-. **2a.** GRIPE, from Old English *grīpan*, to grasp; **b.** GRIPPE, from Old French *gripper*, to seize. Both **a** and **b** from Germanic *grīpan. **3.** O-grade form *ghroib-. GROPE, from Old English *grāpian*, to feel for, grope, from Germanic *graip-. [Pokorny ghreib- 457.]

ghrem- Angry. **1a.** GRIM, from Old English *grim(m)*, fierce, severe; **b.** GRIMACE, from Old French *grimace*, a grimace. Both **a** and **b** from Germanic *grimma-. **2.** GRUMBLE, from Middle English *grummen*, to grumble, probably akin to Middle Dutch *grommen*, to mutter angrily, from Germanic *grum-. **3.** Suffixed o-grade form *ghrom-o-. POGROM, from Russian *grom*, thunder. [Pokorny 2. ghrem- 458.]

ghrendh- To grind. **1.** GRIND, from Old English *grindan*, to grind, from Germanic *grindan. **2.** GRIST, from Old English *grist*, the action of grinding, from Germanic *grinst-, a grinding. **3.** FRAISE, FRENULUM, FRENUM; REFRAIN[1], from Latin *frendere*, to grind. **4.** Sometimes but improbably regarded as from this root (in variant form *ghrend-) is Greek *khondros*, granule, groats, hence cartilage: CHONDRO-; HYPOCHONDRIA, MITOCHONDRION. [Pokorny *ghren-* 459.]

ghrēu- To rub, grind. (Oldest form *ghreə₁u-*; extension of **gher-⁴**.) **1.** GRIT, from Old English *grēot*, sand, gravel, from Germanic **greut-*. **2.** GROATS, from Old English *grotan*, pieces of hulled grain, groats, from Germanic **grut-*. **3a.** GROUT, from Old English *grūt*, coarse meal; **b.** GRUEL, from Old French *gruel*, porridge. Both **a** and **b** from Germanic **grūt-*. **4a.** GREAT, from Old English *grēat*, coarse, thick, bulky, large; **b.** GROAT, from Middle Dutch *groot*, thick. Both **a** and **b** from Germanic **grauta-*, coarse, thick (< "coarsely ground"). **5.** GRUESOME, from Middle English *grue*, horrible, akin to Middle Dutch *grūwen*, to abhor, from Germanic **grūw-*, to recoil from (< "to be offended, be grated on by"). **6.** O-grade form *ghrō(u)-*. **a.** RHODOCHROSITE, from Greek *khrōs*, skin (< "rough surface"?), hence flesh, complexion, color; **b.** suffixed form *ghrō-mn̥*. CHROMA, CHROMATIC, CHROMATO-, CHROME, -CHROME, CHROMIUM, CHROMO-; ACHROMATIC, from Greek *khrōma*, skin, complexion, color (semantic development as in **6a** *above*). **7.** Probably Celtic **graw-*. GRAVEL, from Old French *grave*, *greve*, coarse sand, gravel. **8.** Probably Latin **grau-* in *congruere*, to agree (*con-*, together; see **kom**): CONGRUENT. [Pokorny *ghrēu-* 460.]

ghwer- Wild beast. (Oldest form **ĝhwer-*.) **1.** Suffixed form **ghwer-o-*. FERAL, FERINE, FIERCE, from Latin *ferus*, wild. **2.** Compound **ghwero-ək^w-*, "of wild aspect" (**-ək^w-*, "-looking"; see **ok^w-**). FEROCIOUS, from Latin *ferōx* (stem *ferōc-*), fierce. **3.** Lengthened-grade form **ghwēr-*. TREACLE; BALUCHITHERE, DINOTHERE, EUTHERIAN, INDRICOTHERE, MEGATHERE, THEROPOD, from Greek *thēr*, wild beast. [Pokorny *ĝhu̯ēr-* 493.]

gladh- Smooth. Suffixed form **gladh-ro-*. GLABELLA, GLABROUS, from Latin *glaber*, smooth, bald. [In Pokorny 1. *ĝhel-* 429.]

glei- Clay. **1a.** CLAY, from Old English *clǣg*, clay, from Germanic **klajjaz*, clay; **b.** probably Medieval Greek *glia*, *gloia*, glue: GLIADIN; MESOGLEA, NEUROGLIA, ZOOGLOEA; **c.** GLEY, from Russian dialectal *gleĭ*, clay. **2.** Variant root form **gleu-*. GLUE, GLUTEN, GLUTINOUS; AGGLUTINATE, CONGLUTINATE, DEGLUTINATE, from Latin *glūten*, glue. [In Pokorny 1. *gel-* 357.]

gleibh- To stay stuck. Possible root found only in Germanic and Balto-Slavic (compare Old Church Slavonic *u-glĭbǫ*, I got stuck), perhaps ultimately a derivative of **glei-** above. **1.** Zero-grade form **glibh-*. CLEAVE², from Old English *cleofian*, from Germanic **klibōjan*. **2.** Nasalized zero-grade form **gli-n-bh-*. CLIMB, from Old English *climban*, from Germanic **klimban* (< "to raise oneself by holding on fast"). **3.** Probably secondarily derived within Germanic from **klimban* (see above) is **klemman*, to bind, grip (compare Old English *climman*, to bind, enclose). FARKLEMPT, from Middle High German *verklemmen*, to grip, clamp, choke up (*ver-*, intensive prefix, from Germanic **fer-*; see **per¹**). [Pokorny *gleibh-* 363.]

gleubh- To tear apart, cleave.
I. Basic form **gleubh-*. **1.** CLEAVE¹, from Old English *clēofan*, to split, cleave, from Germanic **kleuban*. **2.** Probably o-grade form **gloubh-*. CLEVER, from Middle English *cliver*, nimble, skillful, perhaps akin to East Frisian *klüfer*, *klifer*, skillful, and Old Norse *kleyfr*, easy to split, from Germanic **klaubri-*.
II. Zero-grade form **glubh-*. **1a.** CLOVE², from Old English *clufu*, clove (of garlic); **b.** KLOOF, from Middle Dutch *clove*, a cleft; **c.** CLEVIS, from a Scandinavian source akin to Old Norse *klofi*, a cleft. **a–c** all from Germanic **klub-*, a splitting. **2.** CLEFT, from Old English *geclyft*, fissure, from Germanic **klufti-* (**klub-ti-*). **3.** GLYPH, GLYPTIC; ANAGLYPH, HIEROGLYPHIC, from Greek *gluphein*, to carve. **4.** Suffixed zero-grade form **glubh-mā-*. GLUME, from Latin *glūma*, husk of grain. [Pokorny *gleubh-* 401.]

glōgh- Thorn, point. (Oldest form **gleh₃gh-*, colored to **gloh₃gh-*, contracted to **glōgh-*.) **1.** Suffixed form **glōgh-i-*. GLOCHIDIUM, from Greek *glōkhis*, barb of an arrow. **2.** Suffixed form **glōgh-ya*. GLOSS², GLOSSA, GLOSSARY, GLOSSATOR, GLOTTIS; BUGLOSS, DIGLOSSIA, GENIOGLOSSUS, GLOSSOLALIA, HETEROGLOSSIA, HYOGLOSSUS, ISOGLOSS, MACROGLOSSIA, MICROGLOSSIA, POLYGLOT, PROGLOTTID, from Greek *glōssa*, *glōtta*, tongue. [Pokorny *glōgh-* 402.]

gnō- To know. (Oldest form **ĝneh₃-*, colored to **ĝnoh₃-*, contracted to **ĝnō-*.) **1.** Lengthened-grade form **gnē-* (contracted from **gnēə-*). KNOW; KNOWLEDGE, ACKNOWLEDGE, from Old English *cnāwan*, to know, from Germanic **knē(w)-*. **2.** Zero-grade form **gnə-*. **a.** CAN¹, CON², CUNNING, from Old English *cunnan*, to know, know how to, be able to, from Germanic **kunnan* (Old English first and third singular *can* from Germanic **kann*, from o-grade **gonə-*); **b.** KEN, KENNING, from Old English *cennan*, to declare, and Old Norse *kenna*, to know, name (in a formal poetic metaphor), from Germanic causative verb **kannjan*, to make known; **c.** (*i*) COUTH; UNCOUTH, from Old English *cūth*, known, well-known, usual, excellent, familiar; (*ii*) CUTHBERT (personal name), from Old English *Cūthbeorht*, "famous (and) bright" (*beorht*, bright; see **bherəg-**). Both (*i*) and (*ii*) from Germanic **kuntha-*; **d.** KITH AND KIN, from Old English *cȳth(the)*, *cȳththu*, knowledge, acquaintance, friendship, kinfolk, from Germanic **kunthithō*. **3.** Suffixed form **gnō-sko-*. NOTICE, NOTIFY, NOTION, NOTORIOUS; ACQUAINT, COGNITION, COGNIZANCE, CONNOISSEUR, INCOGNITO, QUAINT, RECOGNIZE, RECONNAISSANCE, RECONNOITER, from Latin *(g)nōscere*, *cognōscere*, to get to know, get acquainted with. **4.** Suffixed form **gnō-ro-*. IGNORANT, IGNORE, from Latin *ignōrāre*, not to know, to disregard (*i-* for *in-*, not; see **ne**). **5.** Suffixed form **gnō-dhli-*. NOBLE, from Latin *nōbilis*, knowable, known, famous, noble. **6.** Reduplicated and suffixed form **gi-gnō-sko-*. GNOME², GNOMON, GNOSIS, GNOSTIC; AGNOSIA, DIAGNOSIS, PATHOGNOMONIC, PHYSIOGNOMY, PROGNOSIS, from Greek *gignōskein*, to know, think, judge (verbal adjective *gnōtos*, known), with *gnōsis* (< **gnō-ti-*), knowledge, inquiry, and *gnōmōn*, judge, interpreter. **7.** Suffixed zero-grade form **gnə-ro-*. NARRATE, from Latin *narrāre* (< **gnarrāre*), to tell, relate, from *gnārus*, knowing, expert. **8.** Suffixed zero-grade form **gnə-ti-*. ZEND-AVESTA, from Avestan *zainti-*, knowledge (remade from earlier **zāti-* after *zan-*, to know). **9.** Traditionally but improbably referred here are: **a.** NOTE; ANNOTATE, CONNOTE, PROTHONOTARY, from Latin *nota*, a mark, note, sign, cipher, shorthand character; **b.** NORM, NORMA, NORMAL; ABNORMAL, ENORMOUS, from Latin *norma*, carpenter's square, rule, pattern, precept, possibly from an Etruscan borrowing of Greek *gnōmōn*, carpenter's square, rule. [Pokorny 2. *ĝen-* 376.]

gras- To devour. **1.** CRESS, from Old English *cresse*, *cærse*, cress, from Germanic **krasjō*, **krasjōn-*, fodder. **2.** Suffixed form **gras-men-*. GRAMA, GRAMINEOUS, from Latin *grāmen*, "fodder," grass. **3.** Suffixed form **gras-ter-*, "the devourer." GASTRIC, GASTRO-, GASTRULA; EPIGASTRIUM, from Greek *gastēr*, stomach, belly (dissimilated from **gras-ter-*). **4.** Reduplicated form **gar-gro-*. GANGRENE, from Greek *gangraina*, gangrene (dissimilated from **gar-gr-*). [Pokorny *gras-* 404.]

[grat- Also **krat-**. To scratch. Germanic root. **1.** SCRATCH, from Middle Dutch *cratsen*, to scrape, from Germanic *krattōn*. **2.** GRATE¹, from Old French *grater*, to scrape, from Germanic **grat-*. [In Pokorny *gred-* 405.]]

greut- To compress, push. **1.** CROWD¹, from Old English *crūdan*, to press, hasten, from Germanic **krūdan*. **2.** CRUD, CURD, from Old English *crod*, a squeezing. [Pokorny *greut-* 406.]

grə-no- Grain. (Oldest form *ǵrə-no-.) **1a.** CORN¹, from Old English *corn*, grain; **b.** KERNEL, from Old English derivative noun *cyrnel*, seed, pip; **c.** EINKORN, from Old High German *korn*, grain. **a–c** all from Germanic *kornam. **2.** GARNER, GARNET¹, GRAIN, GRAM², GRANADILLA, GRANARY, GRANGE, GRANI-, GRANITA, GRANITE, GRANULE, GRENADE, GRENADINE; FILIGREE, GROSGRAIN, POMEGRANATE, from Latin *grānum*, grain. [In Pokorny ǵer- 390.]

gru- To grunt. Imitative. **1.** GRUNT, from Old English *grunettan*, to grunt, probably akin to *grunnian*, to grunt, from Germanic *grun-. **2.** GRUDGE, from Old High German *grunnizōn*, from Germanic intensive form *grunnatjan. **3.** GRUNION, from Latin *grunnīre*, *grundīre*, to grunt. [Pokorny gru- 406.]

gʷā- Also **gʷem-** (in **1–4** below). To go, come. (Oldest form *gʷeh₂-, colored to *gʷah₂-, contracted to *gʷā-.) **1a.** COME, from Old English *cuman*, to come; **b.** WELCOME, from Old English *wilcuma*, a welcome guest, and *wilcume*, the greeting of welcome, from Germanic compound *wil-kumōn-, a desirable guest (*wil-, desirable; see **wel-²**), from *kumōn-, he who comes, a guest; **c.** BECOME, from Old English *becuman*, to become, from Germanic compound *bikuman*, to arrive, come to be (*bi-, intensive prefix; see **ambhi**). **a–c** all from Germanic *kuman. **2.** Suffixed variant form *gʷ(e)m-yo-. VENIRE, VENUE; ADVENT, ADVENTITIOUS, ADVENTURE, AVENUE, CIRCUMVENT, CONTRAVENE, CONVENE, CONVENIENT, CONVENT, CONVENTICLE, CONVENTION, COVEN, COVENANT, EVENT, EVENTUAL, INTERVENE, INVENT, INVENTORY, MISADVENTURE, PARVENU, PREVENIENT, PREVENT, PROVENANCE, PROVENIENCE, REVENANT, REVENUE, SOUVENIR, SUBVENTION, SUPERVENE, from Latin *venīre*, to come. **3.** Suffixed zero-grade variant form *gʷṃ-yo-. BASE¹, BASIS; ABASIA, ACROBAT, ADIABATIC, AMPHISBAENA, ANABAENA, ANABASIS, BATOPHOBIA, DIABASE, DIABETES, HYPERBATON, KATABATIC, STEREOBATE, STYLOBATE, from Greek *bainein*, to go, walk, step, with *basis* (< *gʷṃ-ti-, suffixed zero-grade form of *gʷā-), a stepping, tread, base, *-batos* (< *gʷə-to-), going, and *-batēs* (< *gʷə-tā-), agential suffix, "one that goes or treads, one that is based." **4.** Suffixed lengthened-grade form *gʷēm-yo-. QUIM, from Old English *gecwēme*, fitting, pleasant (< "becoming," compare German *bequem*, easy, convenient from the same Germanic form with a different prefix), from Germanic *-kwēmja- (ge-, intensive prefix; see **kom**). **5.** Suffixed zero-grade form *gʷ(ə)-u- in compound *pres-gʷu- (see **per¹**). **6.** Basic form *gʷā-. BEMA, from Greek *bēma*, step, seat, raised platform. **7.** Basic form *gʷā- or zero-grade from *gʷṃ- in Sanskrit compound *durgaḥ*, difficult to approach. DURGA, from Sanskrit *Durgā*, Durga (short for *Durgā Devī*, "goddess who is difficult to approach"), from *durgā*, feminine of *durgaḥ*, difficult to approach, from *dus-, dur-, bad, difficult (see **dus-**) + -ga-, going. **8.** Reduplicated form *gʷe-gʷā-. JUGGERNAUT, from Sanskrit *jagat*, moving, the world, originally present participle of *jagāti (remade as *jigāti), he goes. [Pokorny gʷā- 463.]

gʷābh-¹ To dip, sink. (Oldest form *gʷeh₂bh-, colored to *gʷah₂bh-, contracted to *gʷābh-.) Suffixed zero-grade form *gʷəbh-yo-. BAPTIST, BAPTIZE; ANABAPTIST, from Greek *baptein*, to dip. [Pokorny 1. gʷēbh- 465.]

gʷādh- To sink. (Oldest form *gʷeh₂dh-, colored to *gʷah₂dh-, contracted to *gʷādh-.) **1.** Suffixed zero-grade form *gʷədh-u-. BATHOS, BATHY-, from Greek *bathus*, deep (> *bathos*, depth). **2.** BENTHOS, from Greek *benthos*, depth, formed to *bathos* on analogy with *penthos*, grief, and *pathos*, passion, suffering, or it may be from an unrelated root *gʷ(e)ndh-. [Pokorny gʷādh- 465.]

[gʷebh- Hypothetical base of some Germanic words associated with the notion of sliminess, and related to

the Latin and Slavic words for frog. (Contracted from *gʷeh₁bh-.) **1.** QUACKSALVER, from Middle Dutch *quac-, unguent, liquid. **2.** QUAVER, from Middle English *quaven*, to tremble, akin to Low German *quabbeln*, to shake like jelly, tremble. **3.** Suffixed o-grade form *gʷōbh-on-. BUFOTENINE, from Latin *būfō*, toad (a dialect borrowing). [Pokorny 2. gʷēbh- 466.]]

gʷeiə-¹ Also **gʷei-.** To live. (Oldest form *gʷeih₃-, with variant [metathesized] form *gʷyeh₃-, colored to *gʷyoh₃-, contracted to *gʷyō-.)
I. Suffixed zero-grade form *gʷi-wo-, *gʷī-wo- (< *gʷi(ə)-wo-), living. **1a.** QUICK; QUICKSILVER, from Old English *cwic, cwicu*, living, alive; **b.** COUCH GRASS, QUITCH GRASS, from Old English *cwice*, couch grass (so named from its rapid growth). Both **a** and **b** from Germanic *kwi(k)waz. **2a.** (i) SEMPERVIVUM, VIVIFY, VIVIPAROUS, from Latin *vīvus*, living, alive; (ii) VIPER, WEEVER, WYVERN, from Latin *vīpera*, viper, contracted from *vīvipera, "bearing live young" (since many viper species bear live young, the eggs hatching inside the mother's body), from feminine of earlier *vīvo-paros (-paros), bearing; see **perə-¹**); **b.** VIAND, VICTUAL, VIVA, VIVACIOUS, VIVID; CONVIVIAL, REVIVE, SURVIVE, from Latin denominative *vīvere*, to live. **3.** AZOTH, from Middle Persian *zhīwak*, alive, from Old Persian *jīvaka-, extension of *jīva-, alive. **4.** Further suffixed form *gʷī-wo-tā-. VIABLE, VITAL; VITAMIN, from Latin *vīta*, life. **5.** Further suffixed form *gʷi-wo-tūt-. USQUEBAUGH, WHISKEY, from Old Irish *bethu*, life.
II. Suffixed zero-grade form *gʷiə-o-. BIO-, BIOTA, BIOTIC; AEROBE, AMPHIBIAN, ANABIOSIS, CENOBITE, DENDROBIUM, MICROBE, RHIZOBIUM, SAPROBE, SYMBIOSIS, from Greek *bios*, life (> *biotē*, way of life).
III. Variant form *gʷyō-. **1.** AZO-; DIAZO, HYLOZOISM, ZOETROPE, from Greek *zoē*, life. **2.** Suffixed form *gʷyō-yo-. ZODIAC, -ZOIC, ZOO-, ZOON¹, -ZOON, from Greek *zōon, zōion*, living being, animal.
IV. Compound suffixed zero-grade form *yu-gʷiəes- (see **aiw-**).
V. Possibly Old English *cwifer-, nimble: QUIVER¹. [Pokorny 3. gʷei- 467.]

gʷeiə-² To press down, conquer. JAIN, from Sanskrit *jayati*, he conquers. [Pokorny gʷeiə- 469.]

gʷel- To fly; a wing. **1.** Possibly Latin *volāre*, to fly: VOLANT, VOLATILE, VOLE², VOLITANT, VOLLEY. **2.** Possibly Sanskrit *Garuḍaḥ*, Garuda, a winged creature of Hindu myth (compare Sanskrit *garut-* (< *gʷel-ut-), wing): GARUDA. [Not in Pokorny.]

gʷelbh- Womb. **1.** Suffixed form *gʷelbh-u-. DELPHINIUM, DOLPHIN, from Greek *delphus*, womb, whence *delphís*, dolphin (referring to its shape). **2.** Prefixed and suffixed form *sṃ-gʷelbh-(e)yo-, "of one womb" (*sṃ-, one; see **sem-¹**). DIADELPHOUS, MONADELPHOUS, from Greek *adelph(e)os*, brother, originally adjective meaning "of the same womb" in the reconstructed syntagma *phrātēr adelpheos*, uterine brother. [Pokorny gʷelbh- 473.]

gʷelə-¹ Also **gʷel-.** To throw, reach, with further meaning to pierce. (Oldest form *gʷelh₁-, with variant [metathesized] form *gʷleh₁-, contracted to *gʷlē-.)
I. Words denoting to throw, reach. Variant form *gʷlē-, contracted from *gʷlea-. **1.** Nasalized zero-grade form *gʷḷ-n-ə-. **a.** BALLISTA; AMPHIBOLE, ARBALEST, ASTROBLEME, BOLIDE, DEVIL, DIABOLICAL, EMBOLISM, EMBOLY, EPIBOLY, HYPERBOLA, HYPERBOLE, METABOLISM, PALAVER, PARABLE, PARABOLA, PARLEY, PARLIAMENT, PARLOR, PAROL, PAROLE, POLARI, PROBLEM, SYMBOL, from Greek *ballein*, to throw (with o-grade *bol- and variant *blē-); **b.** BALL², BALLAD, BALLET, BAYADERE, from Greek *ballizein*, to dance. **2.** Suffixed o-grade form *gʷol(ə)-ā-. BOLOMETER, from Greek *bolē*, beam, ray. **3.** Possible suffixed o-grade form *gʷol(ə)-sā-. BOULE¹, ABULIA, from Greek *boulē*, determination, will (< "throwing

forward of the mind"), council. **4.** Suffixed full-grade form *gʷelə-mno-. BELEMNITE, from Greek *belemnon*, dart, javelin. **II.** Words denoting to pierce. **1.** Suffixed o-grade form *gʷol-eyo-. **a.** QUELL, from Old English *cwellan*, to kill, destroy; **b.** QUAIL², from Middle Dutch *quelen*, to be ill, suffer. Both **a** and **b** from Germanic *kwaljan. **2.** Suffixed zero-grade form *gʷl̥-yo-. KILL¹, from Middle English *killen*, to kill, perhaps from Old English *cyllan, to kill, from Germanic *kuljan. **3.** Suffixed full-grade form *gʷel-onā-. BELONEPHOBIA, from Greek *belonē*, needle. [Pokorny 2. gʷel- 471, 1. gʷel- 470.]

gʷelə-² An acorn. (Oldest form *gʷelh₂-.) **1.** Suffixed zero-grade form *gʷl̥ə-nd-. GLAND¹, GLANDERS, GLANDULAR, GLANS, from Latin *glāns* (stem *gland-*), an acorn. **2.** Suffixed zero-grade form *gʷl̥ə-no-. VALONIA; MYROBALAN, from Greek *balanos*, acorn, date. [Pokorny 3. gʷel- 472.]

gʷelə-³ To swallow. (Oldest form *gʷelə₁-.) Reduced form *gel-. **1.** JOWL², from Middle English *cholle*, throat, perhaps akin to Old English *ceolu*, throat, dewlap, from Germanic *kel-. **2.** KEEL¹, from Old Norse *kjölr*, keel, from Germanic *keluz. **3.** Suffixed zero-grade form *gul-ā-. GOLIARD, GULAR, GULES, GULLET, from Latin *gula*, gullet, throat. **4.** Extended (*expressive*) form *glutt-. **a.** GLUT; DEGLUTITION, from Latin *gluttīre, glūtīre*, to swallow; **b.** GLUTTON, from Latin *gluttō*, a glutton. [In Pokorny 2. gel- 365.] Compare **gʷerə-⁴**.

gʷen- Woman. **1.** Suffixed form *gʷen-ā-. **a.** QUEAN, from Old English *cwene*, woman, prostitute, wife, from Germanic *kwenōn-; **b.** BANSHEE, from Old Irish *ben*, woman; **c.** ZENANA, from Persian *zan*, woman. **2.** Suffixed lengthened-grade form *gʷēn-i-. QUEEN, from Old English *cwēn*, woman, wife, queen, from Germanic *kwēniz. **3.** Suffixed zero-grade form *gʷn̥-ā-. GYNE, -GYNE, GYNO-, -GYNOUS, -GYNY; GYNECOCRACY, GYNECOLOGY, GYNOECIUM, from Greek *gunē*, woman. [Pokorny gʷēnā 473.]

gʷerə-¹ Mountain. (Oldest form *gʷerh₃-.) **a.** BOREAS, from Greek *boreios*, "coming from the north" (? < "coming from the mountains of Thrace, north of Greece"), whence *Boreas*, the north wind. **b.** HYPERBOREAN, from Greek *Huperboreioi, Huperboreoi*, name of a people living in the far north, variously explained as "they who live beyond the north wind" and "they who live beyond the mountains" (*huper-*, beyond; see **uper**). Both **a** and **b** possibly from o-grade form *gʷorə-. [Pokorny 3. gʷer- 477.]

gʷerə-² Heavy. (Oldest form *gʷerh₂-.)
I. Zero-grade form *gʷr̥ə-. **1.** Suffixed form *gʷr̥ə-wi-. GRAVE², GRAVID, GRAVIMETER, GRAVITY, GRIEF, GRIEVE; AGGRAVATE, AGGRIEVE, from Latin *gravis*, heavy, weighty. **2.** Suffixed form *gʷr̥ə-u-. **a.** BARITE, BARIUM, BARYON, BARYTA; BARITONE, BARYCENTER, BARYSPHERE, CHARIVARI, from Greek *barus*, heavy; **b.** GURU, from Sanskrit *guru-*, heavy, venerable. **3.** Suffixed form *gʷr̥ə-es-. BAR², BARO-; CENTROBARIC, ISALLOBAR, ISOBAR, from Greek *baros*, weight. **4.** Possibly *gʷr̥ī- in Greek compound *u(d)-bri- (see **ud-**).
II. Suffixed extended form *gʷrū-to-. BRUT, BRUTE, from Latin *brūtus*, heavy, dull, stupid, brutish.
III. Suffixed extended form *gʷrī-g-. **1.** BRIO, from Spanish *brio* or Provençal *briu*, vigor, from Celtic *brīg-o-, strength. **2.** BRIG, BRIGADE, BRIGAND, BRIGANTINE, from Old Italian *briga*, strife, from Celtic *brīg-ā-, strife. **3.** BLITZKRIEG, SITZKRIEG, from Old High German *krēg, chrēg*, stubbornness, from Germanic *krīg-.
IV. Suffixed full-grade form *gʷerə-nā-, millstone. QUERN, from Old English *cweorn*, quern. [Pokorny 2. gʷer- 476.]

gʷerə-³ To favor. (Oldest form *gʷerh₂-.) **1.** Suffixed zero-grade form *gʷr̥ə-to-. GRACE, GRATEFUL, GRATIFY, GRATIS, GRATITUDE, GRATUITOUS, GRATUITY; AGREE, CONGRATULATE, DISGRACE, INGRATE, INGRATIATE, MAU- GRE, from Latin *grātus*, pleasing, beloved, agreeable, favorable, thankful, with related suffixed forms *gʷr̥ə-ti-, *gʷr̥ə-t-ā-, *gʷr̥ə-t-olo-. **2.** Compounded zero-grade form *gʷr̥ə-dh(ə)-o- in Celtic *bardo-, praise poet, who produces and bestows praise poetry as gratification to his patron (*-dh(ə)-, to place, put; see **dhē-**). BARD¹, from Welsh *bardd* and Scottish and Irish Gaelic *bard*, bard, from Celtic *bardo-. [Pokorny 4. gʷer(ə)- 478.]

gʷerə-⁴ To swallow. (Oldest form *gʷerh₃-.) **1.** Possibly suffixed extended form *gʷ⁽ʷ⁾ro-gh-. **a.** CRAW, from Middle English *crawe*, craw, possibly from Old English *craga, throat; **b.** SCRAG, from Middle Dutch *crāghe*, throat. Both **a** and **b** from Germanic *krag-, throat. **2.** Suffixed o-grade form *gʷor-ā-. VORACIOUS, -VOROUS; DEVOUR, from Latin *vorāre*, to swallow up. **3.** Expressive reduplicated form *gʷr̥-g-. GARGET, GORGE, GORGET, GURGITATION, INGURGITATE, REGURGITATE, from Latin *gurges*, throat, also gulf, whirlpool. **4.** Zero-grade form *gʷr̥ə-, becoming brō- (< *gʷrō-) in Greek. **a.** Suffixed reduplicated form *gʷi-gʷrō- sko-. HELLEBORE, from Greek *bibrōskein*, to eat; **b.** nasalized variant form *gʷro-n-kh-. BRONCHO-, BRONCHUS, from Greek *bronkhos*, windpipe, throat; **c.** suffixed form *gʷrō-mn̥. THEOBROMINE, from Greek *brōma*, food; **d.** suffixed form *gʷrō-ti-. AMBROSIA, from Greek *brōsis*, eating. **5.** Perhaps extended zero-grade form *gʷrə-i-, metathesized to *gʷria-, contracted to *gʷrī- in suffixed form *gʷrī-wā-, back of the neck; see **gʷrīwā-**. [Pokorny 1. gʷer- 474.] Compare **gʷelə-³**.

gʷes- To be extinguished. (This root is attested as such, with no initial *s-, in Indo-Iranian, Tocharian, Balto-Slavic, and Germanic. Greek alone shows some forms indicating a root *sgʷes-, but the *s- is a Greek innovation and not even found in all dialects of Greek. It is lacking, for example, in the form *zeinamen*, we extinguish, cited by the 5th century Greek lexicographer Hesychius, from *gʷes-nā-; compare standard Attic Greek *sbennumen*, we extinguish, from pre-Greek *sgʷes-nā-. The American scholar Jay Jasanoff is probably right in seeing the original locus of the variant *sgʷes-, whence Greek *sben-*, in the zero-grade suffixed form *gʷs-ē-, with the intransitive aorist suffix *-ē-, which would automatically be replaced by *kʷs-ē- by voicing assimilation, with subsequent refashioning of the root to restore morphological transparency in relation to forms in which the voiced *gʷ- was preserved. But the details remain elusive.) ASBESTOS, from Greek *asbestos*, unquenchable, inextinguishable, unslaked lime, from compound *n̥-sbes-to-, from earlier *n̥-sgʷes-to-, with root form *sgʷes- seen in Greek *sbennunai*, to extinguish (*n̥-, not, without; see **ne**). [Pokorny gʷes- 479.]

gʷet-¹ Resin (?). Root found only in Germanic and Celtic. Suffixed form *gʷet-u-. **1.** CUD, QUID¹, from Old English *cwudu, cwidu, cudu*, resin, mastic gum, "that which is chewed," from Germanic *kwithu-. **2.** BITUMEN, from Latin *bitumen*, resin (Gaulish loanword), from Celtic *betu-, birch, birch resin. [Pokorny 1. gʷet- 480.]

gʷet-² To say, speak. **1.** Basic form *gʷet-. BEQUEATH, QUOTH, from Old English *cwethan*, to say, speak, from Germanic *kwithan. **2.** Suffixed form *gʷet-ti-. BEQUEST, from Old English *-cwis*, will, from Germanic *kwessiz. [Pokorny 2. gʷet- 480.]

gʷet-³ Intestine. Suffixed o-grade form *gʷot-olo-. BOTULINUM, BOTULISM, BOWEL; BOTULIN, from Latin *botulus*, intestine, sausage (probably a dialect borrowing). [Pokorny gʷet- 481.]

gʷhedh- To ask, pray. **1.** Suffixed form *gʷhedh-yo-. BID, from Old English *biddan*, to ask, pray, from

Germanic *bidjan, to pray, entreat. **2.** BEAD, from Old English bed(u), gebed, prayer (ge-, intensive and collective prefix; see **kom**), from Germanic *bidam, entreaty. **3.** Suffixed form *gʷhedh-to-. INFEST, MANIFEST, from Latin -festus, probably in infestus, hostile (< *n̥-gʷhedh-to-, "inexorable"; *n̥-, not; see **ne**), and perhaps in manifestus, caught in the act, red-handed (manus, hand; see **man-²**). [Pokorny gʷhedh- 488, 2. bhedh- 114.]

gʷhen- To strike, kill. **1.** O-grade form *gʷhon-. **a.** BANE, from Old English bana, slayer, cause of ruin or destruction; **b.** AUTOBAHN, from Middle High Ger- man ban, bane, way, road (< "strike" in a technical sense like "swath"). Both **a** and **b** from Germanic suffixed form *ban-ōn-. **2.** Suffixed zero-grade form *gʷhn̥-tyā-. **a.** GUN, from Old Norse gunnr, war; **b.** GONFALON, from Italian gonfalone, standard, from Germanic compound *gund-fanōn-, "battle flag" (*fanōn-, flag; see **pan-**). Both **a** and **b** from Germanic *gunthjō, war, battle. **3.** Suffixed form *gʷhen-do-. **a.** DEFEND, DEFENSE, FENCE, FEND, from Latin dēfendere, to ward off (dē-, away; see **de-**); **b.** OFFEND, OFFENSE, from Latin offendere, to strike against, be offensive, offend (ob-, against; see **epi**). **4.** Suffixed zero-grade form *gʷhn̥-tro-. BEZOAR, from Persian zahr, poison, from Old Iranian *jathra-. **5.** Full-grade form *gʷhen-. BONZE, KALANCHOE, SANGHA, from Sanskrit hanti, he strikes. **6.** Possibly suffixed zero-grade form in compound *perso-gʷhn̥-t-ya (see **perso-**). [Pokorny 2. gʷhen-(ə)- 491, bhen- 126.]

Language and Culture Note   We are sometimes fortunate to have enough evidence from our ancient texts to recover nuances of usage and meaning of reconstructible Proto-Indo-European words. A case in point is furnished by the root **gʷhen-** (the source of English defense and offense). This root had the basic meaning "to strike, smite, kill," but the evidence of the texts shows it was used specifically of the killing of a monstrous or heroic adversary. It was thus ideally suited to legend and mythology (compare the nuances of English slay). In particular, this verb was the primary verbal vehicle for the central action of the Indo-European dragon-slaying myth, encapsulated in the formula *e-gʷhen-t ogʷhim, "he slew the serpent" (*ogʷhim, from *ogʷhis, serpent; see **angʷhi-**). See also note at **terə-²**.

---

gʷher- To heat, warm. **1.** Zero-grade form *gʷhr̥-. **a.** BURN¹, from Old English beornan, byrnan (intransitive) and bærnan (transitive), to burn; **b.** BRIMSTONE, from late Old English brynstān, "burning mineral," sulfur (stān, stone; see **stāi-**); **c.** BRINDLED, from Old Norse brenna, to burn. **a–c** all from Germanic *brennan (intransitive) and brannjan (transitive), formed from *brenw- with nasal suffix and analogical vocalism. **2a.** BRAND, from Old English brand, piece of burning wood, sword; **b.** BRANDY, from Dutch branden, to burn, distill; **c.** BRANDISH, from Old French brand, sword; **d.** BRANDADE, from Old Provençal brand, sword. **a–d** all from Germanic *brandaz, a burning, a flaming torch, hence also a sword. **3.** Suffixed form *gʷher-m(n)o-. THERM, -THERM, THERMO-, -THERMY; HYPOTHERMIA, LOBSTER THERMIDOR, from Greek thermos, warm, hot, and thermē, heat. **4.** O-grade form *gʷhor-. FORCEPS, FORCIPATE, from Latin forceps, pincers, fire tongs (< "that which holds hot things"; -ceps, agential suffix, "-taker"; see **kap-**). **5.** Suffixed o-grade form *gʷhor-no-. **a.** FORNAX, FURNACE, HORNITO, from Latin furnus, fornus, fornāx, oven; **b.** probably Latin fornix, arch, vault (< "vaulted brick oven"): FORNICATE, FORNIX. **6.** Suffixed zero-grade form *gʷhr̥-to-, heated, likely source of Sanskrit ghr̥tam, ghee, clarified butter: GHEE. [Pokorny gʷher- 493, bh(e)reu- 143.]

gʷhī- Thread, tendon. (Oldest form *gʷhihₓ-, *gʷhyehₓ-, with zero-grade form contracted to *gʷhī-.) **1.** Full-grade form *gʷhyeə-. ZIJ, from Old Iranian *jyā-, bowstring (Avestan jyā-). **2.** Suffixed zero-grade form *gʷhī-slo-. FICELLE, FILAMENT, FILAR, FILARIA, FILE¹, FILLET, FILOSE, FILUM; DEFILE², ENFILADE, FILIFORM, FILIGREE, FILOPLUME, FILOVIRUS, PROFILE, PURFLE, from Latin filum, thread. [Pokorny gʷheia- 489.]

gʷhrē- To smell, breathe. (Contracted from earlier *gʷhreh₁-.) BREATH, BREATHE, from Old English brǣth, odor, exhalation, from Germanic suffixed form *brē-thaz. [Pokorny gʷhrē- 495.]

gʷhren- To think. **1.** FRANTIC, FRENETIC, FRENZY, -PHRENIA, PHRENO-; PHRENITIS, from Greek phrēn, the mind, also heart, midriff, diaphragm. **2.** Extended zero-grade root form *gʷhrn̥-d-. PHRASE; HOLOPHRASTIC, METAPHRASE, PARAPHRASE, PERIPHRASIS, from Greek phrazein, to point out, show. [Pokorny gʷhren- 496.]

gʷō- To feed. (Oldest form *gʷeh₃-, colored to *gʷoh₃-, contracted to *gʷō-.) Suffixed zero-grade form *gʷə-sko-. PROBOSCIS, from Greek boskein, to feed. [In Pokorny gʷou- 482.]

gʷou- Ox, bull, cow. Nominative singular form *gʷōu-s. **1.** COW¹, KINE; COWSLIP, from Old English cū, cȳ, cȳe, cow, from Germanic *kōuz (> *kūz). **2a.** BEEF, BOVINE, BUGLE¹, from Latin bōs (stem bov-), ox, bull, cow; **b.** BUCCINATOR, from Latin būcina, horn, trumpet, from *bou-kanā-, "bellower" (*-kanā-, singer; see **kan-**). **3a.** BOÖTES, BOUSTROPHEDON, BUCOLIC, BUGLOSS, BULIMIA, BUMELIA, BUPRESTID, BUTTER, BUTYRIC, from Greek bous, ox, bull, cow; **b.** BUFFALO, from Greek boubalos, buffalo, perhaps from bous. **4.** GAYAL; GUAR, GURKHA, KOUPREY, NILGAI, from Sanskrit gauh, go-, cow. **5.** Suffixed form *gʷou-no-. GUNNY, from Pali gona, ox. **6.** Suffixed form *gʷōuro-. GAUR, from Sanskrit gauraḥ, wild ox. **7.** Zero-grade suffixed form *gʷw-ā-. HECATOMB, from Greek hekatombē, sacrifice of a hundred oxen (hekaton, hundred; see **dekm̥**). [Pokorny gʷou- 482.]

gʷres- Thick, fat. Perhaps Latin grossus, thick (pre-form uncertain): GROCER, GROSCHEN, GROSS, GROSZ, KURUS; ENGROSS, GROSBEAK, GROSGRAIN. [Pokorny gʷretso- 485.]

gʷrī-wā- Back of the neck. Perhaps a derivative of **gʷerə-⁴**. HRYVNIA, from Russian griva, mane, from Slavic *griva. [In Pokorny 1. gʷer- 474.]

gyeu- Also **geu-**. To chew, eat. (Oldest form *ĝ(y)eu-.) CHEW, from Old English cēowan, to chew, from Germanic *kewwan. [Pokorny ĝ(i)eu- 400.]

[hlaupan To leap. Germanic root. **1a.** LEAP, from Old English hlēapan, to leap; **b.** LAPWING, from Old English hlēapwince, lapwing (-wince, perhaps "move sideways," akin to Old English wincian, to wink; see **weng-**). **2.** LOPE, from Old Norse hlaupa, to leap. **3.** INTERLOPER, ORLOP, from Middle Dutch loopen, to leap, run. **4.** GAUNTLET², from Middle Low German lōp, course, running (> Swedish lopp, course). **5.** LANGLAUF, from Old High German hlouf(f)an, to leap. **6.** GALLOP, WALLOP, from Old French galoper and Old North French waloper, to gallop. **7.** ELOPE, from Middle Dutch lopen, to run.**]**

[hūlē Forest, timber, hence stuff, matter. Greek noun of unknown origin. -YL, YLEM; HYLOZOISM, METHYLENE, PTERYLA.**]**

i- Pronominal stem. **1.** ILK¹, from Old English ilca, same, from Germanic *is-lik- (*lik-, like; see **līk-**). **2.** YON, from Old English geon, that, from Germanic *jaino-, *jeno-. **3a.** YOND, YONDER, from Old English geond, as far as, yonder, from Germanic *jend-; **b.** BEYOND, from Old English geondan, beyond, from Germanic *jendana-. **4.** Extended forms *yām, *yāi. YEA, YES, from Old English gēa, affirmative particle, and gēse, yes (see **es-**), from Germanic *jā, *jai. **5.** YET, from Old English giet, gīeta, still (preform uncertain).

6. Relative stem *yo- plus particle. IF, from Old English *gif*, if, from Germanic *ja-ba. **7.** Basic form *i-, with neuter *id-em. ID, IDEM, IDENTICAL, IDENTITY; IDENTIFY, from Latin *is*, he (neuter *id*, it), and *īdem*, same. **8.** Suffixed form *i-tero-. ITERATE; REITERATE, from Latin *iterum*, again. **9.** Suffixed and extended form *it(ə)-em. ITEM, from Latin *item*, thus, also. **10.** Stem *i- plus locatival particle *-dha-i. IBIDEM, from Latin *ibīdem*, in the same place. **11.** Suffixed variant form *e-tero- in compound *ke-e-tero- (see **ko-**). [Pokorny 3. *e-* 281.]

-(i)ko- Secondary suffix, forming adjectives. **1.** Form *-ko-. -AC, from Greek -*kos* added to nouns in stem -*a*-. **2.** Form *-iko-. **a.** -Y¹, from Old English -*ig*, adjective suffix, from Germanic *-iga-; **b.** -IC, -ICS, from Latin -*icus* and Greek -*ikos*, adjective suffixes; **c.** -AGE, from Latin compound suffix -*āticum* (-*āt*- from -*ātus*, past participle suffix; see **-to-**). **3.** Compound suffix *-enko-, *-ŋko-. **a.** -ING³, from Old English -*ing*, adjective suffix, from Germanic *-inga-, *-unga-; **b.** compound Germanic *suffix* *-linga- (see **-lo-**). **4.** Compound *suffix* *-isko- (first element of uncertain origin). **a.** *(i)* -ISH, from Old English -*isc*, adjective suffix; *(ii)* -ESQUE, from Italian -*esco*, from Vulgar Latin *-iscus*. Both *(i)* and *(ii)* from Germanic *-iska-; **b.** BREWSKY, RUSSKY, from Russian -*skiĭ*, adjective suffix indicating origin, from Slavic *-ĭskŭ*, also found in Slavic family names such as DOSTOYEVSKY, TCHAIKOVSKY, TROTSKY. [Not in Pokorny.]

-is-to- Superlative suffix, formed from the zero-grade of the intensive comparative suffix **-yos-** with the addition of **-to-** marking the accomplishment of the notion of intensity. -EST¹, from Old English -*est*, superlative suffix, from Germanic *-ista-. [Not in Pokorny.]

kā- To like, desire. (Oldest form *keh₂-, colored to *kah₂-, contracted to *kā-.) **1.** Suffixed form *kā-ro-. **a.** *(i)* WHORE, from Old English *hōre*; *(ii)* WHOREDOM, from Old Norse compound *hōrdōmr* (-*dōmr*, "condition"; see **dhē-**). Both *(i)* and *(ii)* from Germanic *hōraz* (feminine *hōrōn-*), "one who desires," adulterer; **b.** CARESS, CHARITY, CHERISH; MOTHER CAREY'S CHICKEN, from Latin *cārus*, dear. **2.** Suffixed form *kā-mo-. KAMA¹; KAMASUTRA, from Sanskrit *kāmaḥ*, love, desire. [Pokorny *kā-* 515.]

kad- To fall. (Oldest form *ḱad-.) CADAVER, CADENCE, CADENT, CADUCOUS, CASCADE, CASE¹; CASUAL, CASUALTY, CASUIST, CHANCE, CHUTE; ACCIDENT, DECAY, DECIDUOUS, ESCHEAT, INCIDENT, OCCASION, OCCIDENT, RECIDIVISM, from Latin *cadere*, to fall, die. [Pokorny 1. *ḱad-* 516.]

kād- Sorrow, hatred. (Oldest form *ḱeh₂d-, colored to *ḱah₂d-, contracted to *ḱād-.) Suffixed zero-grade form *kad-i-. **1.** HATRED, from Old English *hete*, hate, envy, from Germanic *hatiz*. **2.** HATE, from Old English *hatian*, to hate, from Germanic *hatōn*. **3.** HEINOUS, from Old French *hair*, to hate, from Germanic *hatjan*. [Pokorny *ḱād-* 517.]

kādh- To shelter, cover. (Oldest form *keh₂dh-, colored to *kah₂dh-, contracted to *kādh-.) **1.** Suffixed zero-grade form *kədh-u-. HAT, from Old English *hæt(t)*, hat, from Germanic *hattuz*, expressive form of *haduz*. **2.** Basic form *kādh-. **a.** HOOD¹, from Old English *hōd*, hood, from Germanic *hōdaz*; **b.** HEED, from Old English *hēdan*, to heed, care for, protect, from Germanic *hōdjan*. [Pokorny *kadh-* 516.]

kaə-id- To strike. (Oldest form *keh₂-id-, colored to *kah₂-id-.) **1.** CAESURA, CEMENT, CESTUS², CHISEL, -CIDE, SCISSOR; ABSCISE, CIRCUMCISE, CONCISE, DECIDE, EXCISE², INCISE, PRECISE, from Latin *caedere*, to cut, strike. **2.** CAELUM, CEIL, SALLET, from Latin *caelum* (? < *caedum*), sculptor's chisel. [Pokorny *(s) k(h)ai-* 917.]

kagh- To catch, seize; wickerwork, fence. **1a.** HAGGARD, from Old French *hagard*, mature falcon caught in wild and thus difficult to train, from dialectal *hague*,

hedge (where the bird was presumably caught); **b.** HAW²; HAWFINCH, HAWTHORN, from Old English *haga*, hedge, hawthorn, from Germanic *hagōn-*; **c.** HEDGE, from Old English *hecg*, from Germanic *hagjō*. **d.** *(i)* HAG, perhaps short for Old English *hægtesse*, witch; *(ii)* HAG, from Old High German *hagzissa*, witch. Both *(i)* and *(ii)* from Germanic *haga-tusjō*. (The exact form of compound is uncertain. The second member –*tusjō* is perhaps akin to Lithuanian *dvasia*, ghost, and Middle High German *getwās*, specter, phantom, and the compound perhaps originally referred to beings that would haunt the hedges that defined the outskirts of the settlement.) **a–d** all from Germanic *hag-*, hedge, fence. **2.** Suffixed form *kagh-yon-. CAY, KEY², QUAY, from Old French *quai*, quay, from Gaulish *caio*, rampart, retaining wall. **3.** Possible variant *kogh-. **a.** INCHOATE, from Latin *cohum*, strap from yoke to harness; **b.** COLANDER, COULEE, COULOIR, CULLIS; PERCOLATE, from Latin *cōlum*, sieve (< wickerwork), and its derivative *cōlāre*, to filter. [Pokorny *kagh-* 518.]

kaghlo- Pebble, hail. HAIL¹, from Old English *hagol*, *hægl*, hail. [Pokorny *kaghlo-* 518.]

kai- Heat. Extended form *kaid-. **1.** HOT, from Old English *hāt*, hot, from Germanic *haita-*. **2.** HEAT, from Old English *hǣtu*, from Germanic *haiti-*. [Pokorny *kāi-* 519.]

kaiko- One-eyed. CAECILIAN, CAECUM; PICHICIEGO, from Latin *caecus*, blind. [Pokorny *kai-ko-* 519.]

kailo- Whole, uninjured, of good omen. **1a.** HALE¹, WHOLE, from Old English *hāl*, hale, whole; **b.** WHOLESOME, from Old English *hālsum* (> Middle English *holsom*), wholesome; **c.** HAIL²; WASSAIL, from Old Norse *heill*, healthy. **a–c** all from Germanic *haila-*. **2.** HEALTH, from Old English *hǣlth*, health, from Germanic *hailithō*. **3.** HEAL, from Old English *hǣlan*, to heal, from Germanic *hailjan*. **4a.** HOLY; HALIBUT, HALIDOM, HOLIDAY, HOLLYHOCK, from Old English *hālig*, holy, sacred; **b.** HALLOW; ALLHALLOWMAS, HALLOWEEN, from Old English *hālgian*, to consecrate, bless, from Germanic derivative verb *hailagōn*; **c.** HELGA, HELGE, OLEG, OLGA (personal names), from Old Norse *Helge* (feminine *Helga*), "holy" (> Russian *Oleg*, feminine *Ol'ga*). **a–c** all from Germanic *haila-ga-*. [Pokorny *kai-lo-* 520.]

kaito- Forest, uncultivated land. **1.** HEATH, from Old English *hǣth*, heath, untilled land, from Germanic *haithiz*. **2a.** HEATHEN, from Old English *hǣthen*, heathen, "savage" (< "one inhabiting uncultivated land"); **b.** HOYDEN, from Middle Dutch *heiden*, heathen. Both **a** and **b** from Germanic *haithinaz*. [Pokorny *kaito-* 521.]

kak- To enable, help. (Oldest form *ḱak-.) SHAKTI, SIKH, from Sanskrit *śaknoti*, he is able, he is strong. [Pokorny *ḱak-* 522.]

kakka- Also **kaka-.** To defecate. Root imitative of glottal closure during defecation. **1.** CUCKING STOOL, from Middle English *cukken*, to defecate, from a source akin to Old Norse *kūka*, to defecate. **2.** POPPYCOCK, from Latin *cacāre*, to defecate. **3.** CACO-; CAC- ODYL, CACOËTHES, CACOPHONOUS, CACOPHONY, from Greek *kakos*, bad. [Pokorny *kakka-* 521.]

kal-¹ Cup. **1.** Suffixed zero-grade form *kl̥-ik-. CALIX, CHALICE; CALICIVIRUS, from Latin *calix*, cup, goblet; **b.** KYLIX, from Greek *kulix*, cup. **2.** Suffixed zero-grade form *kl̥-uk-. CALYX, from Greek *kalux*, seed-vessel, cup. [Pokorny 7. *kel-* 550.]

kal-² Beautiful. **1.** Suffixed form *kal-wo-. CALLISTO; CALOMEL, KALEIDOSCOPE, from Greek *kalos*, beautiful. **2.** Suffixed form *kal-yo-. CALLIGRAPHY, CALLIOPE, CALLIPYGIAN, HEMEROCALLIS, from Greek *kallos*, beauty. [Pokorny 2. *kal-* 524.]

kal-³ Hard. **1.** CALLOSE, CALLOUS, CALLUS, from Latin *callum*, hard skin. **2.** EXCALIBUR, from Welsh *Caledvwlch* (> Medieval Latin *Caliburnus*), Excalibur, from *caled*, hard, from Celtic **kal-eto-*. [Pokorny 1. *kal-* 523.]

kamp- To bend. **1.** Suffixed form **kamp-ā-*. GAM², GAMBADO¹, GAMBADO², GAMBIT, GAMBOL, GAMBREL, GAMMON³, JAMB, SCAMPI, from Greek *kampē*, a bending, a winding. **2.** Suffixed form **kamp-ulo-*. CAMPYLOBACTER, CAMPYLOTROPOUS, from Greek *kampulos*, bent. [Pokorny *kam-p-* 525.] Compare **kemb-**.

kan- To sing. **1.** HEN, from Old English *hen(n)*, hen, from Germanic **han(e)nī*. **2a.** CANOROUS, CANT², CANTABILE, CANTATA, CANTICLE, CANTILLATE, CANTO, CANTOR, CANZONE, CHANT, CHANTEUSE, CHANTEY, CHANTRY; ACCENT, CHANTICLEER, DESCANT, ENCHANT, INCANTATION, INCENTIVE, PRECENTOR, RECANT, from Latin *canere*, to sing (> *cantāre*, to sing, frequentative of *canere*); **b.** suffixed form **kan-ā-*, "singer," in Latin compound **bou-kanā* (see **g^wou-**). **3.** OSCINE, from Latin *oscen*, a singing bird used in divination (< **obscen*, "one that sings before [the augurs]"; *ob-*, before; see **epi-**). **4.** Suffixed form **kan-men-*. CHARM, from Latin *carmen*, song, poem. [Pokorny *kan-* 525.]

kand- Also **kend-**. To shine. **1.** Suffixed (stative) form **kand-ē-*. CANDELABRUM, CANDELILLA, CANDENT, CANDESCENCE, CANDID, CANDIDA, CANDIDATE, CANDLE, CANDOR; INCANDESCE, from Latin *candēre*, to shine. **2.** INCENDIARY, INCENSE¹, INCENSE²; FRANKINCENSE, from Latin compound *incendere*, to set fire to, kindle (*in-*, in; see **en**), from transitive **candere*, to kindle. [Pokorny *kand-* 526.]

kannabis Hemp. Late Indo-European word borrowed from an unknown source. **1.** HEMP, from Old English *henep*, *hænep*, hemp, from Germanic **hanapaz*. **2.** CANNABIS, CANVAS, from Greek *kannabis*, hemp. [Not in Pokorny.]

kap- To grasp. **I.** Basic form **kap-*. **1.** HEDDLE, from Old English *hefeld*, thread used for weaving, heddle (a device which grasps the thread), from Germanic **haf-*. **2.** HAFT, from Old English *hæft*, handle, from Germanic **haftjam*. **3.** Form **kap-o-*. HAVE; BEHAVE, from Old English *habban*, to have, hold, from Germanic **habai-*, **habēn*. **4.** HEAVY, from Old English *hefig*, heavy, from Germanic **hafiga-*, "containing something," having weight. **5.** HAVEN, from Old English *hæfen*, a haven, from Germanic **hafnō-*, perhaps "place that holds ships." **6.** HAWK¹, from Old English *h(e)afoc*, hawk, from Germanic **habukaz*. **7.** Suffixed form **kap-to-*. ECHT, from Middle Low German *echte*, true, legitimate, akin to Old High German *ēohaft*, according to custom, from *ēohaft*, from *ēwa*, custom, right (see **aiw-**) + *-haft*, characterized by, having, possessing, (< "possessed by, seized by"), from Germanic *haftam*, caught, captured. **8.** Latin combining form *-ceps* (< **kap-s*), "taker" (see **g^wher-, man-², per¹**). **9.** Probably from this root is Germanic **gaf-*, the source of Provençal *gafar*, to seize: GAFF¹. **II.** Suffixed form **kap-yo-*. **1.** HEAVE, HEFT, from Old English *hebban*, to lift, from Germanic **hafjan*. **2.** CABLE, CACCIATORE, CAITIFF, CAPABLE, CAPACIOUS, CAPIAS, CAPSTAN, CAPTION, CAPTIOUS, CAPTIVATE, CAPTIVE, CAPTOR, CAPTURE, CATCH, CATER, CHASE¹, COP², COPPER²; ACCEPT, ANTICIPATE, CATCHPOLE, CONCEIVE, DECEIVE, EXCEPT, INCEPTION, INCIPIENT, INTERCEPT, INTUSSUSCEPTION, MUNICIPAL, NUNCUPATIVE, OCCUPY, PARTICIPATE, PERCEIVE, PRECEPT, RECEIVE, RECIPE, RECOVER, RECUPERATE, SUSCEPTIBLE, from Latin *capere*, to take, seize, catch. **III.** Lengthened-grade variant form **kōp-*. **1a.** BEHOOF, from Old English *behōf*, use, profit, need; **b.** BEHOOVE, from Old English *behōfian*, to have need of. Both **a** and **b** from Germanic compound **bi-hōf*, "that which binds," requirement, obligation (**bi-*, intensive prefix; see **ambhi**), from **hōf-*. **2.** COPEPOD, from Greek *kōpē*, oar, handle. [Pokorny *kap-* 527.] Compare **ghabh-**.

kap-ro- He-goat, buck. Probably derivative of **kap-**, to seize ("the grabby animal"). CABER, CABRILLA, CABRIOLET, CAPELLA, CAPER¹, CAPRINE, CAPRIOLE, CHÈVRE, CHEVRON; CAPREOMYCIN, CAPRIC ACID, CAPRICORN, CAP- RIFIG, CAPROIC ACID, from Latin *caper*, he-goat, and *capra*, she-goat. [Pokorny *kapro-* 529.]

kaput- Head. **1a.** HEAD; BEHEAD, FOREHEAD, from Old English *hēafod*, head; **b.** HETMAN, from Old High German *houbit*, head. Both **a** and **b** from Germanic **haubudam*, **haubidam*. **2.** BACALAO, CADDIE, CADET, CAPE², CAPITAL¹, CAPITAL², CAPITATE, CAPITATION, CAPITELLUM, CAPITULATE, CAPITULUM, CAPO¹, CAPO², CAPRICE, CAPTAIN, CATTLE, CAUDILLO, CHAPITER, CHAPTER, CHEF, CHIEF, CHIEFTAIN, CORPORAL²; ACHIEVE, BICEPS, DECAPITATE, KERCHIEF, MISCHIEF, OCCIPUT, PRECIPITATE, RECAPITULATE, SINCIPUT, TRICEPS, from Latin *caput*, head [Pokorny *kap-ut-* 529.]

kar-¹ Also **ker-**. Hard. **I.** Variant form **ker-*. **1.** Suffixed o-grade form **kor-tu-*. **a.** HARD, HARDLY, from Old English *heard*, hard; **b.** Old High German *hart*, hard, hard, bold, stern, in personal names: (i) LEONARD, from Old High German **Lewenhart* (> Old French *Leonard*), "bold as a lion" (*lewo*, lion); (ii) RICHARD, from Old High German *Rīcohard*, "strong in rule" (*rīhhi*, rule; see **reg-¹**); **c.** -ARD, from Germanic **-hart*, **-hard*, bold, hardy; **d.** STANDARD, from Old French *estandard*, flag marking a rallying place, from Frankish compound **standhard* (probably < "standing firmly, steadfast"), from **hard*, hard (**stand-*, from **standan*, to stand; see **stā-**); **e.** HARDY¹, from Old French *hardir*, to make hard. **a–e** all from Germanic **hardu-*. **2.** Suffixed zero-grade form **kṛt-es-*, from earlier full-grade form **kret-es-*. **a.** -CRACY, from Greek *kratos*, strength, might, power; **b.** combining form *-kratēs* in Greek personal names like SOCRATES, from Greek *Sōkratēs*, "having safe might" (*sōs*, safe; see **teuə-¹**). **II.** Possible basic form **kar-* in derivatives referring to things with hard shells. **1.** Possibly Latin *carīna*, keel of a ship, nutshell: CAREEN, CARINA. **2.** Possibly Greek *karuon*, nut: KARYO-; EUCARYOTE, GILLYFLOWER, SYNKARYON. **3.** Reduplicated form **kar-kr-o-*. CANCER, CANKER, CARANGID, CHANCRE, from dissimilated Latin *cancer*, crab, cancer, constellation Cancer. **4.** Suffixed form **kar-k-ino-*. CARCINO-, CARCINOMA, from Greek *karkinos*, cancer, crab. [Pokorny 3. *kar-* 531.]

kar-² To praise loudly, extol. Hypothetical base form. **1.** Perhaps Germanic **hrōthi-* in Old High German *hrōd-*, fame, in personal names: **a.** ROBERT, from Old High German *Hrōdebert* (> Old North French *Robert*), "bright fame" (*-bert*, bright; see **bherəg-**); **b.** RODERICK, from Old High German *Hrōderīh*, "famous rule" (*rīhhi*, rule; see **reg-¹**); **c.** ROGER, from Old High German *Hrōdgēr* (> Old North French *Roger*), "famous spear" (*gēr*, spear; see **ghaiso-**); **d.** ROLAND, from Old High German *Hrōdland*, "(having a) famous land" (*land*, land; see **lendh-²**); **e.** RUDOLPH, from Old High German *Hrōdulf*, "fame-wolf" (*-ulf*, from *wolf*, wolf; see **wl̥k^wo-**). **2.** Perhaps Germanic **hrōm-*, praise. RUMMER, from Dutch *roemen*, to praise. **3.** Lengthened-grade form **kāru-*. CADUCEUS, KERYGMA, from Greek (Doric) *kārux* (Attic *kērux*), herald. [Pokorny 2. *kar-* 530.]

[karlaz Man. Germanic root of uncertain origin. **1.** CHURL, from Old English *ceorl*, man, churl. **2.** CARL, CAROL, CHARLES, KARL (personal names), from Old High German *kar(a)l*, man, husband, whence Old French *Charles* and Medieval Latin *Carolus*. **3.** CARL, CARLING, from Old Norse *karl*, man, freeman. [In Pokorny *ĝer-* 390.]]

kars- To card. **1.** CARMINATIVE, from Latin *cārere*, *carrere*, to card wool (> *carmen*, a card for wool). **2.** Perhaps Latin *carduus*, thistle, artichoke: CARD², CARDOON, CHARD. [Pokorny *kars-* 532.]

kas- Gray. (Oldest form *k̑as-.) **1a.** HARE, from Old English *hara*, hare, from Germanic *hazōn-*; **b.** HASENPFEFFER, from Old High German *haso*, rabbit, from Germanic *hasōn-*. **2.** Suffixed form *kas-no-*. CANESCENT, from Latin *cānus*, white, gray, grayed hair. [Pokorny k̑as- 533.]

kās- To order, command. Root of uncertain vocalism, *kēs-* or *k̑ōs-* also being possible (oldest form *k̑eh₂-). Suffixed full-grade form *keəs-tro-*. SHASTRA, from Sanskrit *śāstram*, command, teaching, sacred text. [Pokorny k̑ās-, k̑əs- 533.]

kat-¹ Down. **1.** Possibly Greek *kata*, down: CATA-. **2.** Suffixed form *kat-olo-*. CADELLE, from Latin *catulus*, young puppy, young of animals ("dropped"). [Pokorny 2. kat- 534.]

kat-² To fight. (Oldest form *k̑at-.) Suffixed form *kat-u-*. KERN¹, from Old Irish *ceithernn*, band of soldiers, probably akin to *cath*, battle, from Celtic *katu-*. [Pokorny k̑at- 534.]

kau- To hew, strike. (Oldest form *keh₂u-*, colored to *kah₂u-*, with zero-grade *kh₂u-* metathesized to *kuh₂-*, with secondary e-grade *keuh₂-*.) **1a.** HEW, from Old English *hēawan*, to hew; **b.** HAGGIS, HAGGLE; HACKSAW, from Old Norse *höggva*, to cut; **c.** HOE, from Old French *houe*, a hoe. **a–c** all from Germanic *hawwan*. **2.** HAG², from a source akin to Old Norse *högg*, a gap, a cutting blow, from Germanic *hawwō*. **3.** HAY, from Old English *hīeg*, hay, cut grass, from Germanic *haujam*. **4.** Suffixed form *kau-do-*. INCUS, from Latin *cūdere* (< *caudere*), to strike, beat. [Pokorny kāu- 535.]

kāu- To burn. (Oldest form *keh₂u-*, colored to *kah₂u-*, whence *kau-* [before consonants] and *kāw-* [before vowels].) Suffixed zero-grade form *kəw-yo-*. CALM, CAUSTIC, CAUTERY; ENCAUSTIC, HOLOCAUST, HYPOCAUST, INK, from Greek *kaiein*, to burn. [Pokorny 2. k̑ēu- (k̑ misprint for k) 595.]

ked- To go, yield. **1.** Lengthened-grade form *kēd-*. CEASE, CEDE, CESSION; ABSCESS, ACCEDE, ACCESS, ANCESTOR, ANTECEDE, CONCEDE, DECEASE, EXCEED, INCESSANT, INTERCEDE, PRECEDE, PREDECESSOR, PROCEED, RECEDE, RETROCEDE, SECEDE, SUCCEED, from Latin *cēdere*, to go, withdraw, yield. **2.** Prefixed and suffixed form *ne-ked-ti-*, "(there is) no drawing back" (*ne-*, not; see **ne**). NECESSARY, from Latin *necesse*, inevitable, unavoidable. [In Pokorny sed- 884.]

keg- Hook, tooth. **1a.** HAKE, from Old English *haca*, hook, akin to Old Norse *haki*, hook; **b.** HARQUEBUS, from Middle Dutch *hake*, hook. Both **a** and **b** from Germanic *hakan-*. **2a.** HOOK, from Old English *hōc*, hook; **b.** HOOKER¹, from Middle Dutch *hōk*, *hoec*, hook; **c.** HAČEK; HAKENKREUZ, from Old High German *hāko*, hook. **a–c** all from Germanic lengthened form *hōka-*. **3.** HATCHEL, HECKLE, from Middle Dutch *hekel*, hatchel, a flax comb with long metal hooklike teeth, from Germanic *hakila-*. **4.** HACK¹, from Old English *-haccian*, to hack to pieces as with a hooked instrument, from Germanic *hakkōn*. [Pokorny keg- 537.]

kei-¹ To lie; bed, couch; beloved, dear. (Oldest form *k̑ei-.) **I.** Basic form *kei-*. **1.** Suffixed form *kei-wo-*. **a.** HIND³, from Old English *hīwan*, members of a household, from Germanic *hīwa-*; **b.** HIDE³, from Old English *hīgid*, *hīd*, a measure of land (< "household"), from suffixed Germanic form *hīwidō*. **2.** Suffixed form *kei-wi-*. CITY, CIVIC, CIVIL, from Latin *cīvis*, citizen (< "member of a household"). **3.** Suffixed form *kei-liyo-*. CEILIDH, from Old Irish *céle*, companion. **II.** O-grade form *koi-*. **1.** Suffixed form *koi-nā-*. INCUNABULUM, from Latin *cūnae*, a cradle. **2.** Suffixed form *koi-m-ā-*. CEMETERY, from Greek *koimān*, to put to sleep. **III.** Suffixed zero-grade form *ki-wo-*. SHIVA, from Sanskrit *śiva-*, auspicious, dear. [Pokorny 1. k̑ei- 539.]

kei-² Referring to various adjectives of color. (Oldest form *k̑ei-.) **1.** Suffixed o-grade form *koi-ro-*. **a.** *(i)* HOAR; HOREHOUND, from Old English *hār*, gray, hoary; *(ii)* HERR; HERRENVOLK, JUNKER, from Old High German *hēr*, worthy, exalted (comparative *hēr(i)ro*); *(iii)* YOUNKER, from Middle Dutch *here*, master, lord. *(i)-(iii)* all from Germanic *haira-*, "gray-haired," old, venerable, hence master. **b.** SIEROZEM, from Russian *seryī*, gray, from Slavic *sĕrŭ*. **2.** Suffixed zero-grade form *ki-wo-*. HUE¹, from Old English *hiw*, *hēo*, color, appearance, form, from Germanic *hīwam*. [Pokorny 2. k̑ei- 540.]

keit- Bright, shining. **1.** Suffixed zero-grade form *koit-u-*. -HOOD; GODHEAD, MAIDENHEAD, from Old English *-hād*, *-hǣdu*, quality, condition; **b.** GEMÜTLICHKEIT, from Old High German *-heit*, *-haid*, quality, condition. Both **a** and **b** from Germanic *haiduz*, "bright appearance," manner, quality. **2.** Suffixed zero-grade variant form *ki-t-ro-*. CHEETAH, CITRAL, from Sanskrit *citra-*, variegated, many-colored. [Pokorny (s)kāi- 916.]

keiə- To set in motion. (Oldest form *keiə₂-.) **I.** Possibly extended o-grade variant from *koid-* in Germanic *hait-*, to call, summon (but this may be from a separate Indo-European root *kaid-*). **1.** HIGHT, from Old English *hātan*, to call, summon, order, from Germanic *haitan*. **2.** Suffixed form *koid-ti-*. **a.** HEST, from Old English *hǣs*, a command, bidding; **b.** BEHEST, from Old English compound *behǣs*, a vow, promise, command (*be-*, intensive prefix; see **ambhi**). Both **a** and **b** from Germanic *haissiz*, from *hait-ti-*. **II.** Zero-grade form *kiə-*. **1.** Suffixed iterative form *kiə-eyo-*. CITE; EXCITE, INCITE, OSCITANCY, RESUSCITATE, SOLICITOUS, from Latin *ciēre* (past participle *citus*), with its frequentative *citāre*, to set in motion, summon. **2.** Suffixed form *kiə-neu-*. KINEMATICS, KINESICS, -KINESIS, KINETIC; BRADYKININ, CINEMATOGRAPH, HYPERKINESIA, KINESIOLOGY, KINESTHESIA, TELEKINESIS, from Greek *kīnein*, to move. [Pokorny kēi- 538.]

kekʷ- Excrement. (Oldest form *k̑ekʷ-.) Suffixed o-grade form *kokʷ-ro-*. COPRO-, from Greek *kopros*, dung. [Pokorny k̑ekʷ- 544.]

kel-¹ To strike, cut. Hypothetical base of derivatives referring to something broken or cut off; twig, piece of wood. **I.** Suffixed o-grade form *kol-o-*. COLOBOMA; COLOBUS MONKEY, from Greek *kolos*, docked, and *kolobos*, maimed. **II.** Extended form *keld-*. **1.** HILT, from Old English *hilt*, hilt, from Germanic *helt-*. **2.** Zero-grade form *kld-*. **a.** *(i)* HOLT, from Old English *holt*, wood; *(ii)* KRUMMHOLZ, from Old High German *holz*, wood. Both *(i)* and *(ii)* from Germanic *hultam*; **b.** CLADE, CLADOCERAN, CLADODE, CLADOGENESIS, CLADOGRAM, CLADOPHYLL, PHYLLOCLADE, from Greek *klados*, branch, shoot. **3.** Variant Celtic zero-grade form *klad-*. **a.** GLADIATE, GLADIATOR, GLADIOLUS, GLAIVE, from Latin *gladius*, sword, from Celtic *klad-yo-*; **b.** CLAYMORE, from Old Irish *claideb*, sword, from Celtic *klad-ibo-*. **4.** O-grade form *kold-*. **a.** LIMP, from obsolete *limphalt*, lame, probably from Old English *lemphealt*, limping, halting (*lemp-*, hanging loosely), from Germanic *halta-*, "with a broken leg"; **b.** HALT², from Old English *healtian*, to limp, from Germanic derivative verb *haltōn*. **III.** Extended form *kelə-* (oldest form *kelh₂-*). **1.** Zero-grade form *klə-*, becoming *klā-* in Greek. **a.** CLAST, CLASTIC; OSTEOCLAST, PLAGIOCLASE, from Greek *klān*, to break; **b.** CLONE, from Greek *klōn* (< *kla-ōn*), twig; **c.** CLERK, CLEROMANCY, from Greek *klēros*, lot, allotment (< "that which is cut off"); **d.** suffixed form *klə-mn̥*. CLEMATIS, from Greek *klēma*, twig; **e.** suffixed form *klə-mo-*. CALAMITY, from Latin *calamitās*, injury, damage, loss.

2. O-grade form **kolə-*, in suffixed form **kolə-bho-*. COPE¹, COUP, from Greek *kolaphos*, a blow. **IV.** Extended form **keldh-*. **1.** HILDA (personal name), from Old English *Hild*, "battle." **2.** MATILDA, MATILDA, MAUD (personal names), from Medieval Latin *Matilda* (> Old French *Mahhild, Mahault, Maud*), from Germanic **maht-hildiz*, "mighty in battle" (*maht*, might; see **magh-¹**). Both **1** and **2** from Germanic **hildiz*, battle. [Pokorny 3. *ĝel-* 545.] See also extended root **kleg-**.

kel-² To cover, conceal, save. (Oldest form **ĝel-*.)
 I. O-grade form **kol-*. **1a.** HELL, from Old English *hell*; **b.** HEL, from Old Norse *Hel*, the underworld, goddess of death. Both **a** and **b** from Germanic **haljō*, the underworld (< "concealed place"). **2a.** HALL, from Old English *heall*, hall; **b.** VALHALLA, from Old Norse *höll*, hall. Both **a** and **b** from Germanic **hallō*, covered place, hall. **3.** Suffixed form **kol-eyo-*. COLEUS; CO-LEOPTERAN, COLEOPTILE, COLEORHIZA, from Greek *koleon, koleos*, sheath. **II.** Zero-grade form **kḷ-*. **1a.** HOLD², HULL, from Old English *hulu*, husk, pod (< "that which covers"); **b.** HOLE, from Old English *hol*, a hollow; **c.** HOLLOW, from Old English *holh*, hole, hollow; **d.** HAUGH, from Old English *healh*, secret place, small hollow. **a–d** all from Germanic **hul-*. **2a.** HOLSTER, from Old High German *hulft*, covering; **b.** HOUSING², from Medieval Latin *hultia*, protective covering. Both **a** and **b** from suffixed Germanic form **hulftī-*. **3.** Extended form **klā-* becoming **klā-* CLANDESTINE, from Latin *clam*, in secret. **4.** Suffixed variant form **kal-up-yo-*. CA-LYPSO¹, CALYPTRA; APOCALYPSE, EUCALYPTUS, from Greek *kaluptein*, to cover, conceal. **III.** Full-grade form **kel-*. **1a.** HELM², from Old English *helm*, protection, covering; **b.** Old High German *helm*, helmet, in personal names: *(i)* ANSELM, from Old High German *Ansehelm* (> Medieval Latin *Anselmus*), "having a divine helmet, having the gods for a helmet" (*ans-*, god; see **ansu-**); *(ii)* WILLIAM, from Old High German *Willahelm*, "will-helmet" (*willo*, will; see **wel-²**); **c.** HELMET, from Middle English *helmet*, helmet, from a source akin to Frankish **helm*, helmet. **a–c** all from Germanic **helmaz*, "protective covering." **2.** OCCULT, from Latin *occulere* < **ob-kel-* (past participle *occultus*), to cover over (*ob-*, over; see **epi**). **3.** Suffixed form **kel-os-*. COLOR, from Latin *color*, color, hue (< "that which covers"). **4.** Suffixed form **kel-nā-*. CELL, CELLA, CELLAR, CELLARER; RATHSKELLER, from Latin *cella*, storeroom, chamber. **5.** Suffixed form **kel-yo-*. CILIUM, SEEL; SUPERCIL-IOUS, from Latin *cilium*, lower eyelid. **IV.** Lengthened-grade form **kēl-*. CONCEAL, from Latin *cēlāre*, to hide, from suffixed form **kēl-ā-*. [Pokorny 4. *ĝel-* 553.] See also extended root **klep-**.

kel-³ To drive, set in swift motion. Hypothetical base of various loosely connected derivatives. **1.** Extended form **kelt-* or **keldh-*, possibly in Germanic **haldan*, to drive flocks, keep or pasture cattle. **a.** HOLD¹; BE-HOLD, UPHOLSTERER, from Old English *healdan*, to hold, retain; **b.** HALT¹, from Old High German *haltan*, to stop, hold back; **c.** AVAST, from Middle Dutch *houden*, to hold. **2.** Suffixed form **kel-es-*. **a.** CELERITY; AC-CELERATE, from Latin *celer*, swift; **b.** possibly further suffixed form **keles-ri-*. CELEBRATE, CELEBRITY, from Latin *celeber*, (of a place) much frequented, hence famous. **3.** Suffixed zero-grade form **kl-on-*. CLONUS, from Greek *klonos*, turmoil, agitation. [Pokorny 5. *ĝel-* 548.]

kel-⁴ To be prominent; hill. **1.** Zero-grade form **kḷ-*. **a.** HILL, from Old English *hyll*, hill, from suffixed Germanic form **hul-ni-*; **b.** HOLM, from Old Norse *hōlmr*, islet in a bay, meadow, from suffixed Germanic form **hul-maz*. **2.** Suffixed form **kel-d-*. EXCEL, from Latin *excellere*, to raise up, elevate, also to be eminent (*ex-*, up out of; see **eghs**). **3.** O-grade form **kol-*. **a.** COLO-PHON, from Greek *kolophōn*, summit; **b.** suffixed form

*kol(u)men-. CULMINATE, from Latin *culmen*, top, summit; **c.** extended and suffixed form **kol- umnā-*. COLONEL, COLONNADE, COLONNETTE, COLUMN, from Latin *columna*, a projecting object, column. [Pokorny 1. *ĝel-* 544.]

kel-⁵ To prick. HOLLY; HOLM OAK, from Old English *hole(g)n*, holly (from its spiny leaves), from Germanic **hulin-*. [Pokorny 2. *ĝel-* 545.]

kel-⁶ To deceive, trick. Extended form **kelu-*, variant **kalu-*. **1.** CALUMNY, CHALLENGE, from Latin *calvī*, to deceive, trick. **2.** CAVIL, from Latin *cavilla* (< **calvil-la*), a jeering. [Pokorny *ĝēl-* 551.]

kelb- To help. HELP, from Old English *helpan*, to help, from Germanic **helpan*. [Pokorny *ĝelb-* 554.]

kelə-¹ Warm. (Oldest form **ĝelh₁-*, with variant [metathesized] form **ĝleh₁-*, contracted to **ĝlē-*.) **1.** Suffixed variant form **klē-wo-*. **a.** LEE, from Old English *hlēo, hlēow*, covering, protection (as from cold); **b.** LUKEWARM, from Old English *-hlēow*, warm. Both **a** and **b** from Germanic **hlēwaz*. **2.** Suffixed zero-grade form **kḷə-ē-*. **a.** CALENTURE, CHAFE, CHAUFFEUR, CHOLENT; DECALESCENCE, INCALESCENT, NONCHA-LANT, RECALESCENCE, RÉCHAUFFÉ, from Latin *calēre*, to be warm; **b.** CAULDRON, CAUDLE, CHOWDER; SCALD¹, from Latin derivative adjective *calidus*, warm. **3.** Suffixed zero-grade form **kḷə-os-*. CALORIC, CALO-RIE; CALORECEPTOR, CALORIFIC, CALORIMETER, CALO-RIMETRY, from Latin *calor*, heat. [Pokorny 1. *ĝel-* 551.]

kelə-² To shout. (Oldest form **kelh₂-*, with variant [metathesized] form **kleh₂-*, colored to **klah₂-*, contracted to **klā-*.)
 I. Variant form **klā-*. **1.** LOW², from Old English *hlōwan*, to roar, low, from Germanic **hlō-*. **2.** Suffixed form **klā-mā-*. CLAIM, CLAMANT, ACCLAIM, DECLAIM, EXCLAIM, PROCLAIM, RECLAIM, from Latin *clāmāre*, to call, cry out. **II.** O-grade form **kolə-*. **1.** KEELHAUL, from Middle Dutch *halen*, to haul, pull (? < "to call together, summon"). **2.** HALE², HAUL; HALYARD, from Old French *haler*, to haul. Both **1** and **2** from Germanic **halōn*, to call. **III.** Zero-grade form **kḷə-* (> **kal-*). **1.** Suffixed form **kal-yo-*. CONCILIATE, COUNCIL; RECONCILE, from Latin *concilium*, a meeting, gathering (< "a calling together"; *con-*, together; see **kom**). **2.** Suffixed form **kal-end-*. CALENDAR, CALENDS, from Latin *kalendae*, the calends, the first day of the month, when it was publicly announced on which days the nones and ides of that month would fall. **3.** Suffixed form **kal-e-*. EC-CLESIA, PARACLETE, from Greek *kalein* (variant *klē-*), to call. **4.** Suffixed form **kal-ā-*. INTERCALATE, NO-MENCLATOR, from Latin *calāre*, to call, call out. **5.** Suffixed form **kḷə-ro-* or suffixed variant form **klaə-ro-* contracted to **klā-ro-*. CLEAR, GLAIR, GLAIRY; AUFKLÄRUNG, CHIAROSCURO, CLAIRVOYANT, CLARAIN, DECLARE, ÉCLAIR, from Latin *clārus*, bright, clear. **IV.** Possibly extended zero-grade form **kḷ(ə)d-*, becoming **klad-* in suffixed form **klad-ti-*. CLASS, from Latin *classis*, summons, division of citizens for military draft, hence army, fleet, also class in general. [Pokorny 6. *ĝel-* 548.]

kelp- To hold, grasp. O-grade form **kolp-* in Germanic **halb-*. **1.** HELVE, from Old English *hielfe*, handle. **2a.** HELM¹, from Old English *helma*, rudder; **b.** HALBERD, from Middle High German *helm*, handle. Both **a** and **b** from suffixed Germanic form **halb-ma-*. **3.** HAL-TER¹, from Old English *hælftre*, halter, from suffixed Germanic form **half-tra-*. [In Pokorny 1. *(s)kel-* 923.]

kem-¹ Hornless. (Oldest form **ĝem-*.) **1.** SCANT, from Old Norse *skammr*, "hornless," short, from Germanic **skamma-*. **2.** Suffixed form **kem-tyā-*. HIND², from Old English *hind*, doe, from Germanic **hinthjō*. [Pokorny 2. *ĝem-* 556.]

kem-² To compress. HEM¹, from Old English *hem(m)*, a doubling over, a hem, from Germanic **hamjam*, a compressing, hence a doubling. [Pokorny 1. *kem-* 555.]

kemb- To bend, turn, change, exchange. Zero-grade form **kmb-*. **1.** HUMP, from a Low German source akin to Dutch *homp*, hump. **2.** CAMBRIDGE, from Welsh *cam*, crooked, from suffixed Celtic form **kamb-o-*. **3.** CAMBIUM, CHANGE; EXCHANGE, INTERCHANGE, from Latin *cambiāre*, to exchange, from suffixed Celtic form **kamb-i-*. **4.** CANTEEN, CANTON; DECANT, from Latin *cantus*, iron tire, rim, from Celtic suffixed form **kamb-to-* (> **kanto-*). [Pokorny (s)kamb- 918, kantho- 526.] Compare **kamp-**.

kemə- To become tired, tire oneself out (oldest form **kemh₂-*) with suffixed (iterative) o-grade form *komə-eye-*. NOSOCOMIAL, from Greek *komein*, to tend, take care of. [Pokorny 4. *k̑em(ə)-* 557.]

kems- To proclaim, speak solemnly. (Oldest form **k̑ems-*.) **1.** Suffixed form **kems-ē-*. CENSOR, CENSUS; RECENSION, from Latin *cēnsēre*, to judge, assess, estimate, tax. **2.** Suffixed form **kems-ti-* perhaps in the first member of the compound **ke(m)sty-an(d)rā-*, "praise of men" (*-an(d)r-, man, men; see **ner-²**), whence Greek personal name *Kessandrā, Kassandrā* (which is partly from another root **(s)kand-, *(s)kend-*, to shine): CASSANDRA. **2.** Suffixed o-grade form **koms-o-*. COMEDY, ENCOMIUM, from Greek *kōmos*, song of praise, athletic victory ode, victory procession, revelry, carousal. [Pokorny *k̑ens* 566.]

Language and Culture Note In ancient India, the fire-god Agni was sometimes called *naraśaṁsah*, "praise of men," because in his role as messenger of the gods he conveyed the praise-formulae offered by poets (the "men") to the gods. The word *naraśaṁsah* is a compound of *narah*, "man" (from **ner-¹**), and *śaṁsah*, "praise" (*kems-o-*, from **kems-**). The word *śaṁsah* has a close relative, *śastih* (from a form of the reconstructed noun **kems-ti-*), also meaning "praise," which occurs in similar contexts. If we take the Indo-European reconstructions for *nara-* and *śasti-* and make a compound out of them, **kemsti-ən(e)r-*, meaning "praise of men," we have what looks exactly like the ancestor of the Greek name *Kessandrā*, from pre-Greek **ke(m)sti-anr-ā, *kestyanrā*. (The *-ā* is the feminine ending.) This is a variant of *Kassandrā* (Cassandra), the name of the legendary prophetess who was cursed by always being disbelieved. This etymology of Cassandra's name is not universally accepted, but her gift of prophecy has close links to the world of both divine messenger and the Indo-European poet, one of whose functions was as a seer. (Compare the Sanskrit word *kavih*, meaning both "poet" and "seer.")

---

ken-¹ To set oneself in motion, arise, make an effort. **1.** Suffixed o-grade form **kon-o-*. DEACON, from Greek *diākonos*, servant, attendant (*dia-*, thoroughly). **2.** Suffixed lengthened o-grade form **kōn-ā-*. CONATION, from Latin *cōnārī*, to endeavor. **3.** Variant form **sken-*, seen by some in suffixed present **sken-do-* in the forms collected under **skend-**. [Pokorny 4. *ken-* 564.]

ken-² Fresh, new, young. **1.** Suffixed o-grade form **ken-t-*. RECENT, from Latin *recēns*, young, fresh, new (*re-*, again; see **re-**). **2.** Suffixed zero-grade form **kn̥-yo-*. -CENE; CAINOTOPHOBIA, Cenozoic, KAINITE, from Greek *kainos*, new, fresh. [Pokorny 3. *ken-* 563.]

ken-³ Empty. (Oldest form **ken-*.) Suffixed form **ken-wo-*. KENOSIS; CENOTAPH, from Greek *kenos*, empty. [Pokorny *k̑en* 564.]

[ken-⁴ Hypothetical base of two similar Germanic roots. **1.** Root **hnekk-*, neck. **a.** NECK, from Old English *hnecca*, neck; **b.** KNACKER, from Old Norse *hnakkur*, saddle, and *hnakki*, back of the neck. **2.** Root **hnukk-*, sharp projection, tip. **a.** NOCK, from Middle English *nokke*, nock, from a source perhaps akin to

Middle Dutch *nocke*, tip of a bow; **b.** NOOK, from Middle English *nok*, corner, nook, from a Scandinavian source akin to dialectal Norwegian *nok*, projection, hook. [Pokorny 1. *ken-* 558.]**]**

k(e)nəko- Yellow, golden. HONEY, from Old English *hunig*, honey, from Germanic **hunagam*. [Pokorny *k̑nəkó-* 564.]

keni- Dust, ashes. **1.** CINERARIUM, CINEREOUS; INCINERATE, from Latin *cinis*, ashes. **2.** O-grade form **koni-*. CONIDIUM; PNEUMOCONIOSIS, from Greek *konis, koniā*, dust. [In Pokorny 2. *ken-* 559.]

kenk-¹ To gird, bind. Variant form **keng-*. CINCH, CINCTURE, CINGULUM; ENCEINTE², PRECINCT, SHINGLES, SUCCINCT, from Latin *cingere*, to gird. [Pokorny 1. *kenk-* 565.]

kenk-² To suffer from hunger or thirst. Suffixed zero-grade form **kn̥k-ru-*. HUNGER, from Old English *hungor, hungur*, hunger, from Germanic **hungruz*. [Pokorny 2. *kenk-* 565.]

kenk-³ Heel, bend of the knee. **1.** HOCK¹, from Old English *hōh*, heel, from Germanic **hanhaz*. **2.** HEEL¹, from Old English *hēla*, heel, from Germanic **hanhilōn-*. [Pokorny 3. *kenk-* 566.]

kent- To prick, jab. **1.** CENTER; AMNIOCENTESIS, DICENTRA, ECCENTRIC, from Greek *kentein*, to prick. **2.** Suffixed form **kent-to-*. CESTUS¹, from Greek *kestos*, belt, girdle. **2.** Suffixed o-grade form **kont-o-*. HETEROKONT, from Greek *kontos*, goad, punting pole. [Pokorny *k̑ent-* 567.]

ker-¹ Horn, head; with derivatives referring to horned animals, horn-shaped objects, and projecting parts. (Oldest form **k̑er-*.)

   I. Zero-grade form **kr̥-* in suffixed form **kr̥-no-*. **1.** HORN, HORNBEAM, from Old English *horn*, horn; **2.** ALPENHORN, ALTHORN, FLÜGELHORN, HORNBLENDE, from Old High German *horn*, horn. Both **1** and **2** from Germanic **hurnaz*.

   II. Extended o-grade form **koru-*. **1.** CORYMB, from Greek *korumbos*, uppermost point (< "head"). **2.** CORYPHAEUS, from Greek *koruphē*, head. **3.** Suffixed form **koru-do-*. CORYDALIS, from Greek *korudos*, crested lark. **4.** Suffixed form **koru-nā-*. CORYNEBACTERIUM, from Greek *korunē*, club, mace.

   III. Italic and Celtic blend of (**I**) **kr̥-no-* and (**II**) **koru-* yielding **kor-nu-*. CORNEA, CORNEOUS, CORNER, CORNET, CORNICHON, CORNICULATE, CORNU; BICORNUATE, CAPRICORN, CORNIFICATION, LAMELLICORN, LONGICORN, TRICORN, UNICORN, from Latin *cornū*, horn.

   IV. Extended e-grade form **keru-*. **1.** Suffixed form **kerw-o-*, "having horns." **a.** CERVID, CERVINE, SERVAL, from Latin *cervus*, deer; **b.** CERVIX, from Latin *cervīx*, neck. **2.** Suffixed form **keru-do-*. **a.** HART, from Old English *heorot*, hart, stag; **b.** HARTEBEEST, from Middle Dutch *hert*, deer, hart. Both **a** and **b** from Germanic **herutaz*.

   V. Extended zero-grade form **kr̥ə-* (oldest form **kr̥h₂-*). **1.** CHARIVARI; CHEER, from Greek *karē, karā*, head. **2.** CAROTID, from Greek *karoun*, to stupefy, be stupefied (< "to feel heavy-headed"). **3.** CARROT, CAROTENE, from Greek *karōton*, carrot (from its hornlike shape).

   VI. Suffixed further extended form **kr̥ə-no-* (oldest form **kr̥h₂s-no-*). **1.** CRANIUM; MIGRAINE, OLECRANON, from Greek *krānion*, skull, upper part of the head. **2.** HORNET, from Old English *hyrnet*, hornet, from Germanic **hurznuta-*.

   VII. E-grade further extended form **keras-* (oldest form **kerh₂s-*.) **1.** CARAT, CERAMBYCID, CERASTES, KERATO-; CERATOPSIAN, CHELICERA, CLADOCERAN, KERATIN, MONOCEROS, RHINOCEROS, TRICERATOPS, from Greek *keras*, horn. **2.** SIRDAR, from Persian *sar*, head, from Old Iranian **sarah-* (Avestan *sarah-*, head). **3.** Suffixed form **keras-ro-*. CEREBELLUM, CEREBRUM, SAVELOY, from Latin *cerebrum*, brain.

VIII. Extended form **krei-*. **1.** REINDEER, from Old Norse *hreinn*, reindeer, from Germanic **hraina-*. **2.** RINDERPEST, from Old High German *hrind*, ox, from Germanic **hrinda-*. **3.** Possibly extended form **krī-*. CRIOSPHINX, from Greek *krīos*, ram. [Pokorny 1. *k̑er-* 574.]

ker-² Echoic root, base of various derivatives indicating loud noises or birds.

I. Zero-grade form **kr-*, becoming Germanic **hr-*. **1.** RING², from Old English *hringan*, to resound, clink, from Germanic **hringan*. **2.** RETCH, from Old English *hrǣcan*, to clear the throat, from Germanic **hraik-*. **3.** ROOK², from Old English *hrōc*, rook, from Germanic **hrōkaz*, "croaking bird," crow. **4.** RAVEN¹, from Old English *hrǣfn*, raven, from Germanic **hrabnaz*, raven. **5.** Extended form **krep-*. CREPITATE, CREVICE; DECREPIT, DECREPITUDE, QUEBRACHO, from Latin *crepāre*, to crack, burst, creak. **6.** Extended form **kri-*. CRICKET¹, from Old French *criquer*, to creak, click, from Germanic **krik-*.

II. Variant zero-grade form **skr-*. **1.** SHRIKE, from Old English *scrīc*, thrush, from Germanic **skrīk-*. **2.** SCREAK, SCREECH, from Old Norse *skrækja*, to shriek, from Germanic **skrēkjan*. **3.** SCREAM, from Middle English *scremen*, to scream, perhaps from a Scandinavian source akin to Old Norse *scrǣma*, to scream, from Germanic **skrainjan*, to shout, shriek.

III. O-grade form **kor-*. **1.** CORBEL, CORBINA, CORMORANT, CORVID, CORVINE, Corvus, from Latin *corvus*, raven. **2.** CORACOID, from Greek *korax*, raven (> *korakias*, chough). [Pokorny 1. *k̑er-* 567.]

ker-³ To grow. (Oldest form **k̑er-*.) **1.** Suffixed form **ker-es-*. CEREAL, Ceres, from Latin *Cerēs*, goddess of agriculture, especially the growth of grain. **2.** Extended form **krē-* (oldest form **k̑reh₁-*). **a.** Suffixed form **krē-yā-*. CREATE, CREATURE, Creole, CRIA, GRIOT; PROCREATE, from Latin *creāre*, to bring forth, create, produce (< "to cause to grow"); **b.** suffixed form **krē-sko-*. CRESCENDO, CRESCENT, CREW¹; ACCRUE, CONCRESCENCE, CONCRETE, DECREASE, EXCRESCENCE, INCREASE, RECRUIT, from Latin *crēscere*, to grow, increase. **3.** Suffixed o-grade form **kor-wo-*, "growing," adolescent. KORE, KOUROS; DIOSCURI, HYPOCORISM, from Greek *kouros*, *koros*, boy, son, and *korē*, girl. **4.** Compound **sm̥-k̑ēro-*, "of one growth" (**sm̥-*, same, one; see **sem-¹**). SINCERE, from Latin *sincērus*, pure, clean. [Pokorny 2. *k̑er-* 577.]

ker-⁴ Heat, fire. **1.** Suffixed form **ker-tā-*. HEARTH, from Old English *heorth*, hearth, from Germanic **herthō*. **2.** Zero-grade form **kr̥-*. **a.** CARBON, CARBUNCLE, from Latin *carbō*, charcoal, ember; **b.** extended form **krem-*. CREMATE, from Latin *cremāre*, to burn. **3.** Possibly suffixed and extended form **kerə-mo-*. CERAMIC, from Greek *keramos*, potter's clay, earthenware. **4.** Possibly variant extended form **krās-*. CRASH², from Russian *krasit'*, to color. [Pokorny 3. *ker(ə)-* 571.]

ker-⁵ A kind of cherry. **1.** Suffixed zero-grade form **kr̥-no-*. CORNEL, from Latin *cornus*, cornel tree. **2.** Full-grade form **ker-* probably in Greek *kerasos*, cherry: CHERRY. [Pokorny 4. *ker-* 572.]

kerd-¹ Heart. (Oldest form **k̑erd-*.) **1.** Suffixed form **kerd-en-*. HEART, from Old English *heorte*, heart, from Germanic **hertōn-*. **2.** Zero-grade form **kr̥d-*. **a.** CORDATE, CORDIAL, COURAGE, QUARRY¹; ACCORD, CONCORD, CORDIFORM, DISCORD, MISERICORD, RECORD, from Latin *cor* (stem *cord-*), heart; **b.** suffixed form **kr̥d-yā-*. CARDIA, CARDIAC, CARDIO-; ENDOCARDIUM, EPICARDIUM, MEGALOCARDIA, MYOCARDIUM, PERICARDIUM, from Greek *kardiā*, heart, stomach, orifice. **3.** Possibly **kred-dhə-*, "to place trust" (an old religious term; **dhə-*, to do, place; see **dhē-¹**). CREDENCE, CREDIBLE, CREDIT, CREDO, CREDULOUS, CREED, GRANT; MISCREANT, RECREANT, from Latin *crēdere*, to believe. [Pokorny (*k̑ered-*) 579.]

kerd-² Craft. Suffixed form **kerd-ā-*. CAIRD, from Old Irish *cerd*, art, artist. [Pokorny 2. *kerd-* 579.]

kerdh- Row, herd. (Oldest form **kerdh-*.) Suffixed form **kerdh-ā-*. HERD, from Old English *heord*, herd, from Germanic **herdō*. [Pokorny *k̑erdho-* 579.]

kerə-¹ To mix, confuse, cook. (Oldest form **k̑erh₂-*, with variant [metathesized] form **k̑reh₂-*, colored to **k̑rah₂-*, contracted to **k̑rā-*.) **1.** Variant form **krā-*. **a.** UPROAR, from Middle Low German *rōr*, motion, from Germanic **hrōr-*; **b.** RARE², from Old English *hrēr*, lightly boiled, half-cooked, possibly from Germanic **hrōr-* (see **a**). **2.** Zero-grade form **krə-*. **a.** Suffixed form **krə-ti-*. IDIOCRASY, IDIOSYNCRASY; DYSCRASIA, from Greek *krāsis*, a mixing; **b.** suffixed form **krə-ter-*. CRATER, KRATER, from Greek *krātēr*, mixing vessel. [Pokorny *k̑erə-* 582.]

kerə-² To injure, break apart. (Oldest form **k̑erh₂-*.) Suffixed zero-grade form **krə-yē-*. CARIES, from Latin *cariēs*, decay, caries. [Pokorny 4. *k̑er-* 578.]

kerp- To gather, pluck, harvest. Variant **karp-*. **1.** HARVEST, from Old English *hærfest*, harvest, from Germanic **harbistaz*. **2.** CARPET; EXCERPT, SCARCE, from Latin *carpere*, to pluck. **3.** -CARP, CARPEL, CARPO-, -CARPOUS, from Greek *karpos*, fruit. [In Pokorny 4. *sker-* 938.]

kers-¹ Dark, dirty. **1.** Suffixed form **ker(s)-no-*. CHERNOZEM, from Russian *chërnyĭ*, black. **2.** Suffixed zero-grade form **kr̥s-no-*. KRISHNA, from Sanskrit *kr̥ṣṇa-*, black, dark. [Pokorny *kers-* 583.]

kers-² To run. (Oldest form **k̑ers-*.) Zero-grade form **kr̥s-*. **1.** CORRAL, CORRIDA, CORRIDO, CORRIDOR, CORSAIR, COURANTE, COURIER, COURSE, CURRENT, CURSIVE, CURSOR, CURULE; CONCOURSE, CONCUR, DECURRENT, DISCOURSE, EXCURSION, HUSSAR, INCUR, INTERCOURSE, KRAAL, OCCUR, PARKOUR, PERCURRENT, PRECURSOR, RECOURSE, RECUR, SUCCOR, from Latin *currere*, to run. **2.** Suffixed form **kr̥s-o-*. **a.** CAR, CAREER, CARGO, CARICATURE, CARIOLE, CAROCHE, CARRY, CHARGE, CHARIOT, CHARRETTE; DISCHARGE, from Latin *carrus*, a two-wheeled wagon; **b.** CARPENTER, from Latin *carpentum*, a two-wheeled carriage. Both **a** and **b** from Gaulish *carros*, a wagon, cart. [Pokorny 2. *k̑ers-* 583.]

kert- To turn, entwine. **1.** Zero-grade form **kr̥t-*. **a.** Suffixed form **kr̥t-i-*. (*i*) HURDLE, from Old English *hyrdel*, hurdle, frame; (*ii*) HOARDING, from Old French *hourd*, fence, hurdle, scaffold. Both (*i*) and (*ii*) from Germanic **hurdiz*, wickerwork frame, hurdle; **b.** suffixed form **kr̥t-sti-*. HORST, from Old High German *hurst*, thicket, horst, from Germanic **hursti-*. **2.** Perhaps suffixed variant form **kr̥t-i-*. CRATE, GRATE², GRATICULE, GRID, GRIDDLE, GRILL; GRIDIRON, from Latin *crātis*, wickerwork hurdle. [Pokorny *kert-* 584.]

kes-¹ To scratch. **1.** Extended zero-grade form **kseu-*. XYSTER, from Greek *xūein*, to scrape. **2.** Nasalized extended form **ks-n-eu-*. **a.** SNUG¹, perhaps from a source akin to Old Norse *snöggr*, close-cropped, from Germanic **snaww-*; **b.** NOVACULITE, from Latin *novācula*, razor. [Pokorny *kes-* 585.]

kes-² To cut. (Oldest form **k̑es-*.) Variant **kas-*. **1.** Suffixed form **kas-tro-*. **a.** CASTRATE, from Latin *castrāre*, to castrate; **b.** ALCAZAR, CASTELLAN, CASTELLATED, CASTLE, from Latin *castrum*, fortified place, camp (perhaps "separated place"), borrowed into Old English as *ceastre*, in place names: (*i*) -CHESTER (in place names such as WINCHESTER), from Old English *ceaster*; (*ii*) CHESHIRE, after *Cheshire*, English county, from Old English *Cestrescīre*, "shire of the fort" (*scīre*, shire); (*iii*) LANCASTER, from Old English *Loncastre*, "fort on the Lune River" (river in western England). **2.** Suffixed form **kas-to-*. CASTE, CHASTE, CASTIGATE, INCEST, from Latin *castus*, chaste, pure (< "cut off from or free of faults"). **3.** Suffixed (stative) form **kas-ē-*. CARET, from Latin *carēre*, "to be cut off from," lack. **4.** Extended geminated form **kasso-*. CASHIER², QUASH¹,

CASSATION, from Latin *cassus*, empty, void. [Pokorny *kes-* 586.]

keud- Magical glory. Suffixed zero-grade form **kūd-es-* (replacing **keud-es-*). KUDOS, from Greek *kūdos*, magical glory. [In Pokorny 1. *keu-* 587.]

keuə- To swell; vault, hole. (Oldest form **ḱeuhₓ-*.)
I. O-grade form **kouə-*. **1.** Basic form **kouə-* becoming **kaw-*. CAVA, CAVE, CAVERN, CAVETTO, CAVITY; CONCAVE, EXCAVATE, from Latin *cavus*, hollow. **2.** Suffixed form **kow-ilo-*. CELIAC, -COEL, COELOM; COELACANTH, ACOELOMATE, from Greek *koilos*, hollow. **3.** Suffixed lengthened-grade form **kōw-o-*. CODEINE, from Greek *kōos*, hollow place, cavity.
II. Zero-grade form **kū-* (< **kuə-*). **1.** Suffixed shortened form **ku-m-olo.* CUMULATE, CUMULUS; ACCUMULATE, from Latin *cumulus*, heap, mass. **2.** Basic form **kū-*. **a.** Suffixed form **kū-ro-*, "swollen," strong, powerful. *(i)* CHURCH, KIRK, KYRIE; KERMIS, from Greek *kūrios* (vocative *kūrie*), master, lord; *(ii)* CYRIL (personal name), from Late Greek *Kūrillos*, "lordly;" **c.** suffixed form **kuw-eyo-*. CYMA, CYMATIUM, CYME; CYMOPHANE, KYMOGRAPH, PSEUDOCYESIS, from Greek *kuein*, to swell, and derivative *kūma* (< **kū-mn̥*), "a swelling," wave; **c.** suffixed form **en- kū-yo-* (**en*, in; see **en**). ENCEINTE[1]; from Latin *inciēns*, pregnant. [Pokorny 1. *keu-* 592.]

keuk- To be white, be bright, shine. (Oldest form **ḱeuk-*.) Suffixed zero-grade form **kuk-no-*. CYGNET, CYGNUS, from Greek *kuknos*, swan. [Pokorny *ḱeuk-* 597.]

kēw-(e)ro- North, north wind. (Oldest form **ḱeh₁w-(e)ro-*, with zero-grade **ḱuh₁-(e)ro-* becoming **kū-ro-*.) **1.** SHOWER[1], from Old English *scūr*, shower, storm, from West Germanic **skūraz*. **2.** SCOUR[2], from Middle English *scouren*, to range over, probably from a Scandinavian source akin to Old Norse *skūr*, a shower. Both **1** and **2** from Germanic **skūr-*. [Pokorny *ḱēuero-* 597.]

kīgh- Fast, violent. (Oldest form **ḱīgh-*.) HIE, from Old English *hīgian*, to strive, exert oneself, from Germanic **hīg-*. [Pokorny *ḱei-gh-* 542.]

klā- To spread out flat. (Oldest form **kleh₂-*, colored to **klah₂-*, contracted to **klā-*.) Extended shortened form **klat-*. **1.** LADE, from Old English *hladan*, to lade, lay on, load, from Germanic **hlathan*. **2.** Suffixed form **klat-sto-*. **a.** LAST[4], from Old English *hlæst*, burden, load; **b.** BALLAST, from Old Swedish and Old Danish *last*, burden. Both **a** and **b** from Germanic **hlasta-*. [Pokorny *klā-* 599.]

klāu- Possibly hook, peg. (Oldest form **kleh₂u-*, colored to **klah₂u-*, contracted to **klau-* [before consonants] and **klāw-* [before vowels].) **1.** Suffixed form **klau-do-*. CLAUSE, CLAUSTRUM, CLOISONNÉ, CLOISTER, CLOSE, CLOSET, CLOSURE, CLOZE; CONCLUDE, ECLOSION, EXCLUDE, INCLUDE, OCCLUDE, PRECLUDE, RECLUSE, SECLUDE, from Latin *claudere*, to close. **2.** Suffixed form **klāw-i-*. **a.** CLAVE[3], CLAVICLE, CLAVIER, CLEF, KEVEL; CLAVICHORD, CONCLAVE, ENCLAVE, from Latin *clāvis*, key; **b.** further suffixed form **klāw-i-d-*. OPHICLEIDE, STERNOCLEIDOMASTOID, from Greek *kleïs* (stem *kleïd-*), key. **3.** Suffixed form **klāw-o-*. **a.** CLOVE[1], CLOY, CLAFOUTI, from Latin *clāvus*, nail; **b.** CLAVATE, CLAVIFORM, from Latin *clāva*, club. **4.** Suffixed form **klāw-(i)yo-*. **a.** CLATHRATE, from Greek *kleiein*, to close; **b.** CLEISTOGAMOUS, CLEISTOTHECIUM, from Greek verbal adjective *kleistos*, closed. [Pokorny *klēu-* 604.]

kleg- To cry, sound. Extension of **kel-¹**. Variant form **klag-*. **1.** Variant form **klak-*. **a.** LAUGH, from Old English *hlieh(h)an*, to laugh, from Germanic **hlahjan*; **b.** LAUGHTER, from Old English *hleahtor*, laughter, from Germanic **hlahtraz*. **2.** Nasalized form **kla-n-g-*. CLANG, from Latin *clangere*, to sound. [Pokorny *klēg-* 599.]

klei- To lean. (Oldest form **ḱlei-*.)
I. Full-grade form **klei-*. **1.** Suffixed form **klei-n-*. DECLINE, INCLINE, RECLINE, from Latin *-clīnāre*, to lean, bend. **2.** Suffixed form **klei-tro-*. CLITELLUM, from Latin *clītellae*, packsaddle, from diminutive of **clitra*, litter. **3.** Suffixed form **klei-wo-*. ACCLIVITY, DECLIVITY, PROCLIVITY, from Latin *clīvus*, a slope. **4.** Suffixed form **klei-tor-*, "incline, hill." CLITORIS, from Greek diminutive *kleitoris*, clitoris.
II. Zero grade form **kli-*. **1.** LID, from Old English *hlid*, cover, from Germanic **hlid-*, "that which bends over," cover. **2.** Suffixed form **kli-n-*. LEAN¹, from Old English *hlinian* and *hleonian*, to lean, from Germanic **hlinēn*. **3.** Suffixed form **kli-ent-*. CLIENT, from Latin *cliēns*, dependent, follower. **4.** Suffixed form **kli-to-* in compound **aus-klit-ā-* (see **ous-**). **5.** Suffixed form **kli-n-yo-*. -CLINAL, CLINE, -CLINE, -CLINIC, CLINO-, CLISIS, KLISMOS; ACLINIC LINE, ANACLISIS, CLINANDRIUM, ENCLITIC, MATRICLINOUS, PATROCLINOUS, PERICLINE, PROCLITIC, from Greek *klīnein*, to lean. **6.** Suffixed form **kli-mn̥*. CLIMATE, from Greek *klima*, sloping surface of the earth. **7.** Lengthened zero-grade form **klī-*, with lengthening of obscure origin. **a.** Suffixed form **klī-n-ā-*. CLINIC; DICLINOUS, MONOCLINOUS, TRICLINIUM, from Greek *klinē*, bed; **b.** suffixed form **klī-m-*. CLIMAX, from Greek *klīmax*, ladder.
III. Suffixed o-grade form **kloi-tr-*. LADDER, from Old English *hlǣd(d)er*, ladder, from Germanic **hlaidri-*. [Pokorny *ḱlei-* 600.]

kleng- To bend, turn. **1a.** LINKS, from Old English *hlinc*, ridge; **b.** LINK¹, from Middle English *linke*, loop of a chain, from a Scandinavian source akin to Old Norse **hlenkr*, loop of a chain; **c.** FLINCH, from Old French *flenchir*, to turn aside, flinch. **a–c** all from Germanic **hlink-*. **2a.** LANK, from Old English *hlanc*, lean, thin (< "flexible"); **b.** FIANCHETTO, FLANGE, FLANK, FLANKEN, from Old French *flanc*, hip, side (where the body curves). Both **a** and **b** from Germanic **hlanka-*. [Pokorny *kleng-* 603.]

klep- To steal. (Oldest form **ḱlep-*; extension of **kel-²**.) Suffixed form **klep-yo-*. CLEPSYDRA, KLEPTOCRACY, KLEPTOMANIA, from Greek *kleptein*, to steal. [Pokorny *ḱlep-* 604.]

kleu- To hear. (Oldest form **ḱleu-*.)
I. Extended form **kleus-*. LEER, from Old English *hlēor*, cheek (< "side of the face" < "ear"), from Germanic **hleuza-*.
II. Zero-grade form **klu-*. **1.** LIST⁴, from Old English *hlystan*, to listen, from Germanic **hlustjan*. **2.** LISTEN, from Old English *hlysnan*, to listen, from Germanic **hlusinōn*. **3.** Suffixed lengthened form **klū-to-*. **a.** LOUD, from Old English *hlūd*, loud; **b.** ABLAUT, UMLAUT, from Old High German *hlūt*, sound; **c.** Germanic personal name **hlūda-wīgaz*, "famous in battle." *(i)* LOUIS, LUDWIG, from Old High German *Hluod(o)wig* (> Old French *Looïs*); *(ii)* CLOVIS, from Frankish *Chlodovech* (> French *Clovis*). **a–c** all from Germanic **hlūdaz*, "heard," loud.
III. Full-grade form **kleu-*. **1.** Suffixed form **klew-yo-*. CLIO, from Greek *kleiein*, to praise, tell. **2.** Suffixed form **klew-es-*, "fame," in Greek personal names ending in *-klēs* (earlier *-kleēs*). **a.** DAMOCLES, from Greek (Doric) *Dāmoklēs*, "having the people's fame" (*dēmos, dāmos*, people; see **dā-**); **b.** EMPEDOCLES, from Greek *Empedoklēs*, "having lasting fame" (*empedos*, "on the ground," firmly set, lasting, from *en*, in, and *pedon*, ground; see **en** and **ped-**); **c.** HERCULES, from Latin *Herculēs*, from Greek *Hēraklēs, Hērakleēs*, "having Hera's fame" (*Hērā*, Hera); **d.** PERICLES, from Greek *Periklēs*, "far-famed" (*peri-*, all around; see **per¹**); **e.** SOPHOCLES, from Greek *Sophoklēs*, "famed for wisdom" (*sophos*, wise); **f.** THEMISTOCLES, from Greek *Themistoklēs*, "famed in law and right" (*themis*, custom, law, right). **3.** Suffixed form **kleu-to-*. SAROD, from Middle Persian *srōd*, sarod, akin to Avestan *sraota-*, hearing, sound, from Iranian **srauta-*. **4.** Suffixed

form *kleu-ko-. SLOKA, from Sanskrit ślokaḥ, sound, hymn, sloka.
IV. Lengthened o-grade form *klōu-. Slavic *slava, fame, glory, appearing as *-slavŭ in personal names. **1a.** MIROSLAV, from Russian Miroslav, "having peaceful fame" (mir, world, peace; see **mei-⁴**); **b.** MSTISLAV, from Russian Mstislav, "having vengeful fame" (mstit', to have revenge; see **meit-**); **c.** YAROSLAV, from Russian Jaroslav, "famed for fury" (jaryĭ, furious). **2a.** BOHUSLAV, from Czech Bohuslav, "having god's fame" (boh, god; see **bhag-**); **b.** WENCESLAS, from Old Czech *Vęceslavŭ (> Medieval Latin Venceslaus, Modern Czech Václav), "having greater glory" (*vęce-, from Slavic *vętye-, greater). [Pokorny 1. k̂leu- 605.]

Language and Culture Note Occasionally comparative linguists are able not only to reconstruct individual words in Indo-European, but also whole phrases; these are crucial for filling out our picture of the world-view of the Proto-Indo-Europeans, since they allow us to see how particular words and concepts were put together in discourse. Probably the most famous such phrase is *klewos ṇdhgʷhitom, "imperishable fame." The most ancient texts in Indo- European languages, such as the Vedic hymns of ancient India, the Homeric epics, the Germanic sagas, and Old Irish praise-poetry, all demonstrate that the perpetuation of the fame of a warrior or king was of critical importance to early Indo-European society. The preservation of their fame was in the hands of poets, highly skilled and highly paid professionals, who acted both as the repositors and the transmitters of the society's oral culture. The phrase *klewos ṇdhgʷhitom (where *klewos is a noun built to the root **kleu-**, "to hear," and can be thought of literally as "what is heard about someone, reputation") was reconstructed on the basis of the exact equation of Greek kleos aphthiton and Sanskrit śravaḥ akṣitam. (Although these phrases look superficially rather different, they can both be shown to derive, sound for sound, from *klewos ṇdhgʷhitom by regular sound change.) The Greek phrase appears in Homer's Iliad as the fate awaiting that poem's main character, Achilles, if he chooses to die young in battle rather than live a long but obscure peaceful life. • Not surprisingly, "fame" is a recurring element in Indo-European personal names. The name of the Greek poet Sophocles (Sophoklēs) meant "famed for wisdom"; the German name Ludwig (Old High German Hlūd-wīg) means "famed in battle"; and the Czech name Bohuslav means "having the fame (glory) of God."

---

kleuə- To wash, clean. (Oldest form *k̂leuhₓ-.) **1.** CLOACA, from Latin cloāca, sewer, canal. **2.** Zero-grade form *klu(ə)-. CLYSTER; CATACLYSM, from Greek kluzein, to wash out. [Pokorny 2. k̂leu- 607.]

kl̥ə-wo- Bald. (Oldest form *kl̥hₐ-wo-.) **1.** CALVARIUM, from Latin calvāria, skull. **2.** CALVARY¹, from Late Latin Calvāria, translation of Greek Krāniou topos, place of skull(s) (itself a translation of Aramaic gulgultā, skull, Golgotha). Both **1** and **2** from Latin calvus, bald. [Pokorny k̂ₑlə𝑢o- 554.]

kneigʷh- To lean on. **1.** CONNIVE, from Latin cōnīvēre (< *con-nīuēre; com-, together; see **kom**), "to lean together" (said of eyelids), to close the eyes, be indulgent. **2.** Suffixed zero-grade form *knigʷh-to-. NICTITATE, from Latin nictāre, to move the eyelids, wink. **3.** NISUS; RENITENT, from Latin nītī, to lean forward (preform uncertain). [Pokorny knei-gʷh- 608.]

kneu- Nut. **1.** Extended zero-grade form *knud-. NUT, from Old English hnutu, nut, from Germanic *hnut-. **2.** Extended zero-grade form *knuk-. NEWEL, NOISETTE, NOUGAT, NUCELLUS, NUCLEUS, from Latin nux, nut. [In Pokorny 1. ken- 558.]

knid- Egg of a louse. (Oldest form *k̂nid-.) Suffixed form *knid-ā-. NIT¹, from Old English hnitu, egg of

a louse, from Germanic *hnitō. [Pokorny knid-, k̂nid-608.]

ko- Stem of demonstrative pronoun meaning "this." (Oldest form *k̂o-.)
I. Variant form *ki-. **1a.** HE¹, from Old English hē, he; **b.** HIM, from Old English him, him (dative of hē); **c.** HIS, from Old English his, his (genitive of hē); **d.** HER, from Old English hire, her (dative and genitive of heo, she); **e.** IT, from Old English hit, it (neuter of hē); **f.** HERE, from Old English hēr, here; **g.** HENCE, from Old English heonane, heonon, from here; **h.** HARASS, from Old French hare, call used to set dogs on, from Frankish *hara, over here, over there, alteration (perhaps influenced by *dara, thither) of earlier *hera (compare Old High German hera, hither); **a–h** all from Germanic *hi-. **2.** Suffixed form *ki-tro-. HITHER, from Old English hider, hither, from Germanic *hi-thra-. **3.** Suffixed form *ki-s. CIS-, from Latin cis, on this side of.
II. Variant form *ke-. **1.** Preposed in *ke-etero- (*e-tero-, a second time, again; see **i-**). ET CETERA, from Latin cēterus (neuter plural cētera), the other part, that which remains. **2.** Postposed in Latin -ce (see **gho-, nu-**).
III. Attributed by some to this root (but more likely of obscure origin) is Germanic *hind-, behind. **1.** BEHIND, HIND¹, from Old English behindan, in the rear, behind (bi, at; see **ambhi**). **2.** HINTERLAND, from Old High German hintar, behind. **3.** HINDER¹, HINDRANCE, from Old English hindrian, to check, hinder, from Germanic derivative verb *hindrōn, to keep back. [Pokorny 1. ko- 609.]

kō- To sharpen, whet. (Oldest form *k̂eh₃-, colored to *k̂oh₃-, contracted to *k̂ō-.) **1.** Suffixed extended form *koəi-no-. HONE¹, from Old English hān, stone, from Germanic *hainō. **2.** Possibly Greek kōnos, cone, conical object (< "a sharp-pointed object"): CONE, CONIC; CONIFER, CONODONT. [Pokorny k̂ē(i)- 541.]

-ko- See **-(i)ko-**.

kob- To suit, fit, succeed. HAP, HAPPEN, HAPPY; HAPLESS, MISHAP, from Old Norse happ, chance, good luck, from Germanic *hap-. [Pokorny kob- 610.]

koksā- Body part; hip, thigh. COXA, CUISSE, CUSHION, from Latin coxa, hip. [Pokorny koksā 611.]

kolə-mo- Grass, reed. (Oldest form *k̂olh₂-mo-.) **1a.** HAULM, from Old English healm, halm, straw. **b.** MARRAM GRASS, from a Scandinavian source akin to Old Norse marálmr, beach grass, from hálmr, straw (marr, sea; see **mori-**). Both **a** and **b** from Germanic *halmaz. **2.** CULM¹, from Latin culmus, stalk. **3.** Zero-grade form *kl̥ə-mo-. CALAMARI, CALA- MITE, CALAMUS, CALUMET, CARAMEL, SHAWM, from Greek kalamos, a reed, straw. [Pokorny k̂olamo-s 612.]

kom Beside, near, by, with. **1a.** ENOUGH, GEMOT, HANDIWORK, WITENAGEMOT, YCLEPT, YEAN, from Old English ge-, with, also participial, collective, and intensive prefix; **b.** GEBRAUCHSMUSIK, GEMÜTLICH, GEMÜTLICHKEIT, from Old High German gi-, abstract, collective, and intensive prefix. **c.** GIBLETS, from Germanic *ga-baiti- (see **bheid-**). **a–c** from Germanic *ga-, together, with (collective and intensive prefix and marker of the past participle). **2.** CUM¹; COONCAN, from Latin cum, co-, with. **3.** CO-, COM-, from Latin com-, with (collective and intensive prefix). **4.** British Celtic *kom-, collective prefix, in compound *kombrogos (see **merg-**). **5.** Suffixed form *kom-trā-. CON¹, CONTRA-, CONTRARY, COUNTER¹, COUNTER-, COUNTRY; ENCOUNTER, from Latin contrā, against, opposite. **6.** Suffixed form *kom-yo-. COENO-; CENOBITE, EPICENE, KOINE, from Greek koinos, common, shared. **7.** Reduced form *ko- in compounds (see **gher-¹, mei-¹, smei-**). [Pokorny kom 612.]

konə-mo- Shin, leg, bone. (Oldest form *konh₂- mo-.) **1.** HAM, from Old English hamm, ham, thigh, from Germanic *hamma- (assimilated from *hanma-). **2.**

Zero-grade form *kn̥ə-mā-. GASTROCNEMIUS, from Greek knēmē, calf of the leg. [Pokorny konəmo- 613.]

konk- To hang. (Oldest form *k̑onk-.) **1a.** HANG, from Old English hōn, to hang; **b.** HANKER, from Dutch (dialectal) hankeren, to long for; **c.** HINGE, from Middle English henge, hinge, hinge, possibly related (ultimately from the base of Old English hangian, to hang). **a–c** all from Germanic *hanhan (transitive), hangēn (intransitive), hang. **2.** Suffixed form *konk-i-t-ā-. CUNCTATION, from Latin cūnctārī, to delay. [Pokorny k̑enk- 566, k̑onk- 614.]

ko(n)kho- Possible word for mussel, shellfish. **1.** COCKLE[1], CONCH, CONCHA, CONCHO-, from Greek konkhē, konkhos, mussel, conch. **2.** COCHLEA, from Greek kokhlos, land snail. [Pokorny k̑onkho- 614.]

kop- To beat, strike. **1.** Suffixed form *kop-yo-. APOCOPE, SARCOPTIC MANGE, SYNCOPE, from Greek koptein, to strike. **2.** Suffixed form *kop-mn̥. COMMA, from Greek komma, piece cut off, short clause. **3.** Suffixed form *kop-yā-. **a.** PIOLET, from Old Provençal apcha, small ax, from a Germanic source akin to Old High German hāppa, sickle; **b.** HASH[1], HATCHET; NUTHATCH, QUEBRACHO, from Medieval Latin hapia, ax, and Old French hache, small ax. Both **a** and **b** from Germanic *hapjō. **4.** Suffixed lengthened-grade form *kōp-əo-. HOOF, from Old English hōf, hoof, from Germanic *hōfaz. **5.** KOPEK, from Middle Russian kopie, spear from kopat', to hack. [Pokorny kā̆pho- 530.]

kormo- Pain. HARM, from Old English hearm, harm, from Germanic *harmaz. [Pokorny k̑ormo- 615.]

koro- War; also war-band, host, army. **1.** HERIOT, from Old English here, army, also in personal names (see **albho-**). **2.** Old High German heri, army, in personal names (see **bherəg-, man-[1], wal-**). **3.** ARRIÈRE-BAN, from Old French herban, a summoning to military service (ban, proclamation, summons; see **bhā-[2]**). **4a.** HARBOR, from Old English herebeorg, lodging; **b.** HARBINGER, from Old French herberge, lodging. Both **a** and **b** from Germanic compound *harja-bergaz, "army hill," hill-fort, later shelter, lodging, army quarters (*bergaz, hill; see **bhergh-[2]**). **5a.** HERALD, from Anglo-Norman herald, herald; **b.** HAROLD (personal name), from Old Norse Haraldr. Both **a** and **b** from Germanic compound *harja-waldaz, "army commander" (*wald-, rule, power; see **wal-**). **6.** HARNESS, from Old French harneis, from Germanic compound *harja-nestam, "army provisions" (*nestam, food for a journey; see **nes-[1]**). **7.** HARRY, HURRY, from Old English hergian, to ravage, plunder, raid, from Germanic denominative *harjōn. **8.** HARANGUE, from Old Italian aringo, arringa, public square, from Germanic compound *harihring, assembly, "host- ring" (*hringaz, ring; see **(s)ker-[2]**). **1–8** all from Germanic *harjaz, army. [Pokorny koro-s 615.]

koselo- Hazel. HAZEL, from Old English hæsel, hazel, from Germanic *haselaz. [Pokorny kos(e)lo- 616.]

kost- Bone. Probably related to **ost-**. COAST, COSTA, COSTARD, COSTREL, CUESTA, CUTLET; ACCOST, INTERCOSTAL, STERNOCOSTAL, from Latin costa, rib, side. [Pokorny kost- 616.]

kous- To hear. (Oldest form *h₂kous-.) **1a.** HEAR, from Old English hīeran, to hear; **b.** HEARKEN, from Old English he(o)rcnian, to hearken. Both **a** and **b** from Germanic *hauzjan. **2.** Suffixed form *əkous-yo-. ACOUSTIC, from Greek akouein, to hear. [Pokorny 1. keu- 587.]

krāu- To conceal, hide. (Oldest form *kreh₂u- [colored to *krah₂u-], with variant [metathesized] form *kreuh₂-, whence zero-grade *kruh₂- contracted to *krū-.) Suffixed extended variant form *krup-yo-. CRYPT, CRYPTIC, CRYPTO-, GROTESQUE, GROTTO, KRYPTON; APOCRYPHA, PHALLOCRYPT, from Greek kruptein, to hide. [Pokorny krā[u]- 616.]

kred- Framework, timberwork. Possible root. ROOST, from Old English hrōst, roost, from Germanic *hrō(d)st-. [Pokorny kred- 617.]

krei- To sieve, discriminate, distinguish. **1.** Basic form with variant instrumental suffixes. **a.** Suffixed form *krei-tro-. RIDDLE[1], from Old English hridder, hriddel, sieve, from Germanic *hridra-; **b.** suffixed form *kreidhro-. CRIBRIFORM, GARBLE, from Latin crībrum, sieve. **2.** Suffixed form *krei-men-. **a.** CRIME, CRIMINAL; RECRIMINATE, from Latin crīmen, judgment, crime; **b.** DISCRIMINATE, from Latin discrīmen, distinction (dis-, apart). **3.** Suffixed zero-grade form *kri-no-. CERTAIN; ASCERTAIN, CONCERN, CONCERT, DECREE, DISCERN, DISCONCERT, DISCREET, DISCRETE, EXCREMENT, EXCRETE, INCERTITUDE, RECREMENT, SECERN, SECRET, SECRETARY, from Latin cernere (past participle crētus), to sift, separate, decide. **4.** Suffixed zero-grade form *kri-n-yo-. CRISIS, CRITIC, CRITERION; APOCRINE, DIACRITIC, ECCRINE, ENDOCRINE, EPICRITIC, EXOCRINE, HEMATOCRIT, HYPOCRISY, PARACRINE, from Greek krīnein, to separate, decide, judge, and krīnesthai, to explain. [Pokorny 4. sker-, Section II. 945.]

kreiə- To be outstanding, brilliant, masterly, beautiful. Greek and Indo-Iranian root. (Oldest form *k̑reih₃-.) **1.** Suffixed form *kreiə-on(t)- in Greek personal names. CREON; ANACREON, from Greek Kreiōn, Kreōn, ruler, master, and Anakreōn, "up-lord" (ana-, up; see **an**). **2.** Zero-grade form *krī- (< *kriə-). SRI, from Sanskrit śrī-, beauty, also used as honorific prefix in proper names: **a.** CEYLON, SRI LANKA, from Sanskrit Śrī Laṅkā (> Ceylon via Portuguese; Laṅkā, older name for Sri Lanka and its chief city); **b.** SRINAGAR, from Sanskrit Śrīnagaram, splendid city (nagaram, city). [Pokorny k̑rei- 618.]

krek-[1] To weave, beat. **1.** REEL[1], from Old English hrēol, reel, spool for winding cord, from Germanic *hreh-ulaz. **2.** Suffixed o-grade form *krok-u-. CROCIDOLITE, from Greek krokus, nap of cloth. [Pokorny 1. krek- 618.]

krek-[2] Frog spawn, fish eggs. ROE[1], from Middle English row, roe, from Germanic *hrog-. [Pokorny 2. krek- 619.]

krem- Wild garlic, onion. O-grade form *krom-. RAMP[3], RAMPS, RAMSON, from Old English hramsa, onion, garlic, from Germanic *hram-. [Pokorny (krem-) 580.]

kremə- To be suspended. (Oldest form *k̑remh₂-.) Suffixed form *kremə-o-. ASHRAM, from Sanskrit śramati, he is weary. [Not in Pokorny; compare Greek kremān, to hang (semantic connection with the Sanskrit unclear).]

kret-[1] To shake. O-grade form *krot-. RATHE, RATHER; RARERIPE, from Old English hræth(e), nimble, quick, prompt, ready, from Germanic *hratha-, swift, nimble. [Pokorny 1. kret- 620.]

kret-[2] To beat. (Perhaps ultimately identical with **kret-[1]**, to shake.) O-grade form *krot-. CROTAL BELL, CROTALISM, DICROTISM, TRICROTISM, from Greek krotein, to strike, beat. [Pokorny 2. kret- 621.]

kreuə-[1] Raw flesh. (Oldest form *kreuh₂-.) **1.** Suffixed o-grade form *krowə-o-. RAW, from Old English hrēaw, raw, from Germanic *hrawaz. **2.** Suffixed form *krewə-s-. CREATINE, CREODONT, CREOSOTE, PANCREAS, from Greek kreas, flesh. **3.** Suffixed zero-grade form *krū-do- (< *kruə-do-). **a.** CRUDE; ECRU, RECRUDESCE, from Latin crūdus, bloody, raw; **b.** CRUEL, from Latin crūdēlis, cruel. [Pokorny 1. A. kreu- 621.]

kreuə-[2] To push, strike. **1.** RUE[1], RUTH, from Old English hrēowan, to distress, grieve, from Germanic *hrewwan. **2.** Extended o-grade form *krous-. ANACRUSIS, from Greek krouein, to strike. [Pokorny 3. kreu- 622.]

kreus- To begin to freeze, form a crust. **1.** Suffixed zero-grade form *krus-to-. **a.** CROUTON, CRUST, CRUSTACEAN, CRUSTACEOUS, CRUSTOSE; ENCRUST, from Latin *crusta,* crust; **b.** CRYSTAL, CRYSTALLINE, CRYSTALLO-; KRISTALLNACHT, from Greek *krustallos,* ice, crystal. **2.** Suffixed zero-grade form **krus-es-.* CRYO-, from Greek *kruos,* icy cold, frost. **3.** Suffixed zero-grade form **krus-mo-.* CRYMOTHERAPY, from Greek *krūmos,* icy cold, frost. [Pokorny 1. B. *kreu-* 621.]

kreut- Reed. REED, from Old English *hrēod,* reed, from Germanic **hreudam.* [Pokorny *kreu-t-* 623.]

krŏpo- Roof. (Oldest form **krŏpo-.*) ROOF, from Old English *hrōf,* roof, from Germanic **hrōfam.* [Pokorny *krāpo-* 616.]

krut- Musical instrument. **1.** ROTE³, from Old French *rote,* a stringed instrument, from Germanic **hrut-.* **2.** Geminated form **kruttā-.* CROWD², from Welsh *crwth,* an ancient Celtic musical instrument. [Pokorny *krūt-* 624.]

ksero- Dry. (Oldest form **k̑sero-.*) **1.** Lengthened-grade form **ksēro-.* XERO-; ELIXIR, PHYLLOXERA, from Greek *xēros,* dry. **2.** Perhaps suffixed variant form **kseres-no-.* SERENE, from Latin *serēnus,* serene, bright, clear. [Pokorny *k̑sĕ-ro-* 625.]

ksun Preposition and preverb meaning "with." **1.** SYN-, from Greek *sun, xun,* together, with. **2.** Reduced form **su(n)-.* **a.** SOVIET, from Old Russian compound *sŭvĕtŭ,* assembly; **b.** SPUTNIK, from Russian *so-, s-,* with, together. **a** and **b** from Old Russian *sŭ(n)-,* with, together. [In Pokorny 2. *sem-* 902.]

kwas- To kiss. Zero-grade form **kus-.* KISS, from Old English *cyssan,* to kiss, from Germanic **kussjan,* to kiss, denominative from **kussaz,* a kiss (with expressive gemination). [Pokorny *ku-* 626.]

kwat- To ferment, be sour. Possible root. Suffixed variant form **kwāt-so-.* KVASS, from Russian *kvas,* from Slavic **kvasŭ.* [Pokorny *kuat(h)-* 627.]

kʷe And (enclitic). SESQUI-, UBIQUITY, from Latin *-que,* and, generalizing particle. [Pokorny 1. *kʷe* 635.]

kʷed- To sharpen. **1.** WHET, from Old English *hwettan,* to whet, from Germanic **hwatjan.* **2.** TRIQUETRA, TRIQUETROUS, TRIQUETRUM, from Latin *triquetrus,* three-cornered, probably from prefixed and suffixed form **tri- kʷed-ro-,* "having three points" (**tri-,* three; see **trei-**). [Pokorny *kʷĕd-* 636.]

kwei- To hiss, whistle. Imitative root. **1a.** WHINE, from Old English *hwīnan,* to whine, from Germanic suffixed form **hwī-n-;* **b.** WHINGE, from Old English *hwinsian,* to complain, whine, from Germanic **hwinisōn.* **2a.** WHISPER, from Old English *hwisprian,* to whisper; **b.** WHISTLE, from Old English *hwistlian,* to whistle. Both **a** and **b** from Germanic extended form **hwis-.* [Pokorny 2. *kuei-* 628.]

kʷei-¹ To pay, atone, compensate. Suffixed o-grade form **kʷoi-nā-.* PAIN, PENAL, PENALTY, PINE², PUNISH; IMPUNITY, PENOLOGY, PUNITORY, REPINE, SUBPOENA, from Greek *poinē,* fine, penalty. [Pokorny 1. *kʷei-(t-)* 636.]

kʷei-² To pile up, build, make. O-grade form **kʷoi-.* **1.** CHEETAH, from Sanskrit *kāyaḥ,* body. **2.** Suffixed form **kʷoi-wo-,* making, in denominative verb **kʷoiweyo-.* POEM, POESY, POET, POETIC, -POIESIS, -POIETIC; EPOPEE, MYTHOPOEIC, ONOMATOPOEIA, PHARMACOPOEIA, from Greek *poiein,* to make, create. [Pokorny 2. *kʷei-* 637.]

kʷei-³ To perceive, observe, with derivatives referring to the acts of valuing and honoring. **1.** Extended root form **kʷei-ə-* in zero-grade suffixed form **kʷī-mā-* (< **kʷiə-mā-*). TIMOCRACY, from Greek *tīmē,* honor, worth. **2.** Extended root form **kʷei-s-* in zero-grade suffixed form **kʷoi-s-ā-.* CURATE¹, CURATOR, CURE, CURETTE, CURIO, CURIOUS; ACCURATE, ASSURE, ENSURE, INSURE, MANICURE, PEDICURE, POCOCURANTE, PROCTOR, PROCURE, PROCURATE, PROXY, SCOUR¹, SECURE, SINECURE, SURE, from Latin noun *cūra* (Archaic Latin *coisa-*), care, with derived verb *cūrāre,* to care for (for the semantics, compare Avestan *kaēš-,*

ciš-, to assign, determine, and *ṭkaēša-,* doctrine < "that which has been determined"). **3.** Perhaps Hindi and Urdu *ciṭṭhī,* note, letter, bill, probably ultimately from an unattested Indic past participial form **ciṣṭa-* (? "noted, observed, determined") akin to Avestan *kaēš-, ciš-,* to determine, assign (see above); CHIT¹. [In Pokorny 1. *kʷei-(t-)* 636.]

kʷeiə- To rest, be quiet. (Oldest form **kʷeih₁-,* with variant [metathesized] form **kʷyeh₁-,* contracted to **kʷyē-.*)
  I. Suffixed zero-grade form **kʷī-lo-* (< **kʷiə-lo-*). **1a.** WHILE, from Old English *hwīl,* while; **b.** WHILOM, from Old English *hwīlum,* sometimes. Both **a** and **b** from Germanic **hwīlō.* **2.** Possibly Latin *tranquillus,* tranquil (*trāns,* across, beyond; see **terə-²**): TRANQUIL.
  II. Variant form **kʷyē-* (< **kʷyea-*). **1.** Suffixed form **kʷyē-t-.* REQUIEM, from Latin *quiēs,* rest, quiet. **2.** Suffixed form **kʷyē-ske-.* COY, QUIET, QUIT; ACQUIESCE, ACQUIT, QUITCLAIM, QUITE, QUITRENT, REQUIESCAT, from Latin *quiēscere* (past participle *quiētus*), to rest. [Pokorny *kʷeiə-* 638.]

kweit- Also **kweid-.** White; to shine. (Oldest forms **k̑weit-, k̑weid-.*) **1.** Suffixed variant form **kweido-o-.* **a.** WHITE; WHITSUNDAY, from Old English *hwīt,* white; **b.** WITLOOF, from Middle Dutch *wit,* white; **c.** WHITING², from Middle Dutch *wijting,* whiting; **d.** *(i)* EDELWEISS, from Old High German *hwiz, wīz,* white; *(ii)* BISMUTH, from obsolete German *Wismuth, Bismuth* (Modern German *Wismut*), perhaps obscurely related to Old High German *wīz,* white. **a–d** all from Germanic **hwītaz.* **2.** Suffixed o-grade variant form **kwoid-yo-.* WHEAT, from Old English *hwǣte,* wheat (from the fine white flour it yields), from Germanic **hwaitjaz.* [Pokorny 3. *k̑uei-* 628.]

kʷek- To appear, see, show. (Oldest forms **kʷek̑-, *kʷeĝ-.*) Variant form **kʷeg-.* UKASE, from Russian *ukazat',* to order, from Slavic **kaz-.* [Pokorny *kuek̑-* 638.]

kʷel-¹ Also **kʷelə-.**
  I. Basic form **kʷel-.* COLONIA, COLONY, CULT, CULTIVATE, CULTURE, KULTUR; INCULT, INQUILINE, SILVICOLOUS, from Latin *colere,* to till, cultivate, inhabit (< **kʷel-o-*).
  II. Suffixed form **kʷel-es-.* TELIC, TELIUM, TELO-, TELOS; ENTELECHY, TALISMAN, TELEOLOGY, TELEOST, TE- LEUTOSPORE, from Greek *telos,* "completion of a cycle," consummation, perfection, end, result.
  III. Suffixed reduplicated form **kʷ(e)-kʷl-o-,* wheel, circle. **1.** WHEEL, from Old English *hwēol, hweogol,* wheel, from Germanic **hwewlaz.* **2.** CYCLE, CYCLO-, CYCLOID, CYCLONE, CYCLOSIS; BICYCLE, ENCYCLICAL, EPICYCLE, from Greek *kuklos,* circle, wheel. **3.** CHAKRA, CHAKRAM, CHUKKER, from Sanskrit *cakram,* circle, wheel. **4.** Metathesized form **kʷe-lkʷ-o-.* CHARKHA, from Old Persian *carka-,* wheel.
  IV. O-grade form **kʷol-.* **1.** Suffixed form **kʷol-so-,* "that on which the head turns," neck. **a.** *(i)* HAWSE, from Old Norse *hāls,* neck, ship's bow; *(ii)* RINGHALS, from Middle Dutch *hals,* neck; *(iii)* HABERGEON, HAUBERK, from Old French *hauberc,* hauberk, from Germanic compound **h(w)als-berg-,* "neck- protector," gorget (**bergan,* to protect; see **bhergh-¹**). *(i)–(iii)* all from Germanic **h(w)alsaz;* **b.** COL, COLLAR, COLLET, CULLET; ACCOLADE, DECOLLATE¹, DÉCOLLETÉ, MACHICOLATE, TORTICOLLIS, from Latin *collum,* neck. **2.** Suffixed form **kʷol-ā-.* -COLOUS; PRATINCOLE, from Latin *-cola* and *incola,* inhabitant (*in-,* in; see **en**). **3.** Suffixed form **kʷol-o-.* **a.** ANCILLARY, from Latin *anculus,* "he who bustles about," servant (*an-,* short for *ambi-,* around, about; see **ambhi**); **b.** POLE¹, PULLEY, from Greek *polos,* axis of a sphere; **c.** BUCOLIC, from Greek *boukolos,* cowherd, from *-kolos,* herdsman. **4.** Suffixed form **kʷol-es-* (probably a blend of o-grade **kʷol-o-* and expected e-grade **kʷel-es-*). CALASH, KOLACKY, from Slavic **kolo, *koles-,* wheel. **5.** Suffixed

o-grade form *kʷol-eno- in Old Iranian compound *vahā-cārana- (see **wes-¹**).

V. Suffixed zero-grade variant form *kʷ̥l̥ə-i-. PALIMPSEST, PALINDROME, PALINGENESIS, PALINODE, from Greek palin, again (< "revolving"). [Pokorny 1. kʷel- 639.]

kʷel-² Far (in space and time). **1.** Lengthened-grade form *kʷēl-. TELE-, from Greek tēle, far off. **2.** Suffixed zero-grade form *kʷ̥l-ai. PALEO-, from Greek palai, long ago. [Pokorny 2. kʷel- 640.]

kwelp- To arch. **1.** WHELM, from Old English *hwelfan, hwylfan, with parallel form *hwelman (> Middle English whelman), to turn over, from Germanic *hwalbjan. **2.** Suffixed o-grade form *kwolp-o-. GULF; COLPITIS, COLPOSCOPE, COLPOSCOPY, from Greek kolpos, bosom, womb, vagina. [Pokorny 2. ku̯elp- 630.]

kwen- Holy. (Oldest form *k̑wen-.) Suffixed zero-grade form *kwn̥-slo-. HOUSEL, from Old English hūsl, hūsel, sacrifice, Eucharist, from Germanic *hunslam. [Pokorny k̑u̯en- 630.]

kʷent(h)- To suffer. **1.** Suffixed form *kʷenth-es-. NEPENTHE, from Greek penthos, grief. **2.** Zero-grade form *kʷn̥th-. PATHETIC, PATHIC, PATHO-, PATHOS, -PATHY; APATHY, PATHOGNOMONIC, SYMPATHY, from Greek pathos, suffering, passion, emotion, feelings. [Pokorny ku̯enth- 641.]

kwēp- To smoke, cook, move violently, be agitated emotionally. Hypothetical base of possibly related words; root form uncertain. **1.** Suffixed variant form *kup-yo-. COVET, CUPID, CUPIDITY; CONCUPISCENCE, from Latin cupere, to desire. **2.** Zero-grade form *kwap-, becoming *kwap-, possibly in: **a.** VAPOR; EVAPORATE, from Latin vapor, steam, vapor; **b.** VAPID, from Latin vapidus, that has emitted steam or lost its vapor, flat, poor; **c.** ACAPNIA, from Greek kapnos, smoke. [Pokorny (keu̯əp-) 596.]

kʷer- To make. **1.** NAMASKAR, PRAKRIT, PUGGREE, SANSKRIT, from Sanskrit karoti, he makes. **2.** Suffixed form *kʷer-ōr with dissimilated form *kʷel-ōr. PELORIA, from Greek pelōr, monster (perhaps "that which does harm"). **3.** Suffixed form *kʷer-as-. TERA-, TERATO-, from Greek teras, monster. **4.** Suffixed form *kʷer-mn̥. KARMA, from Sanskrit karma, act, deed. **5.** Suffixed form *kʷer-on-. from Middle Persian laškar, army, from Old Iranian *-kara- in compound *raxša-kara- "furnishing protection" (*raxša-, protection; see **lek(s)-**). [Pokorny 1. ku̯er- 641.]

kwes- To pant, wheeze. (Oldest form *k̑wes-.) **1.** WHEEZE, from Old Norse hvæsa, to hiss, from Germanic *hwēsjan. **2.** QUARREL¹, QUERULOUS, from Latin querī, to complain. **3.** Suffixed zero-grade form *kus-ti-. CYST, CYSTO-, from Greek kustis, bladder, bag (< "bellows"). [Pokorny k̑u̯es- 631.]

kwēt- To shake. (Contracted from earlier *kweh₁t-.) Zero-grade form *kwət-, becoming *kwat-. **1.** CASK; CASCARA BUCKTHORN, CASCARA SAGRADA, CONCUSS, DISCUSS, PERCUSS, RESCUE, SCUTCH, SOUKOUS, SQUASH², SUCCUSSION, from Latin quatere (past participle quassus, in composition -cussus), to shake, strike. **2.** PASTA, PASTE¹, PASTEL, PASTICHE, PASTIS, PASTRY, PÂTÉ, PATISSERIE, PATTY, from Greek passein, to sprinkle. [Pokorny ku̯ēt- 632.]

kʷetwer- Four.

I. O-grade form *kʷetwor-. **1.** Probably Germanic *fe(d)wor- (with f- from following numeral *fimf, five; see **penkʷe**). **a.** FOUR, from Old English fēower, four; **b.** FORTY, from Old English fēowertig, forty; **c.** FOURTEEN, FORTNIGHT, from Old English fēowertēne, fourteen (-tēne, ten; see **dekm̥**). **2.** QUATRAIN; CATER-CORNERED, QUATTROCENTO, from Latin quattuor, four. **3.** CZARDAS, from Persian chahār, four, from Old Iranian cathwārō, four.

II. Multiplicatives *kʷeturs, *kʷetrus, and combining forms *kʷetur-, *kʷetru-. **1.** CAHIER, CARILLON, CARNET, CASERN, QUATERNARY, QUATERNION, QUIRE¹,

from Latin quater, four times. **2.** CADRE, QUADRATE, QUADRILLE¹, QUARREL², QUARRY²; ESCADRILLE, SQUAD, SQUARE, TROCAR, from Latin quadrum, square. **3.** QUADRI-; UNUNQUADIUM, from Latin quadri-, four. **4.** QUADRANT, from Latin quadrāns, a fourth part. **5.** QUARANTINE, from Latin quadrāgintā, forty (-gintā, ten times; see **dekm̥**). **6.** QUADRICENTENARY, from Latin quadri(n)gentī, four hundred. **7.** Variant form *kʷet(w)r̥-. **a.** TETRA-, from Greek tetra-, four; **b.** TESSERA; DIATESSARON, from Greek tessares, four; **c.** TETRAD, from Greek tetras, group of four; **d.** zero-grade form *kʷt(w)r̥-. TRAPEZIUM, from Greek tra-, four.

III. Ordinal adjective *kʷetur-to-. **1a.** FOURTH, from Old English fēortha, fēowertha, fourth; **b.** FIRKIN, from Middle Dutch veerde, fourth; **c.** FARTHING, from Old English fēorthing, fēorthung, fourth part of a penny; **a–c** all from Germanic *fe(d)worthōn-. **2.** QUADRILLE², QUADROON, QUART, QUARTAN, QUARTER, QUARTO; ÉCARTÉ, from Latin quārtus, fourth, quarter. [Pokorny ku̯etu̯er- 642.]

kʷezd- A part, piece. PATCH¹, PIECE; APIECE, CODPIECE, PIECEMEAL, from Old French pece, piece, piece, from Gaulish *petssi, from Celtic suffixed form *kʷezd-i-. [Not in Pokorny; compare Russian chast', part (< Slavic *čęstĭ < earlier nasalized form *kʷe-n-zd-).]

kʷo- Also **kʷi-**. Stem of relative and interrogative pronouns. **1a.** WHO, WHOSE, WHOM, from Old English hwā, hwæs, hwǣm, who, whose, whom, from Germanic personal pronouns *hwas, *hwasa, *hwam; **b.** WHAT, from Old English hwæt, what, from Germanic pronoun *hwat; **c.** WHY, from Old English hwȳ, why, from Germanic adverb *hwī; **d.** WHICH, from Old English hwilc, hwelc, which, from Germanic relative pronoun *hwa-līk- (*līk-, body, form; see **līk-**); **e.** HOW, from Old English hū, how, from Germanic adverb *hwō; **f.** (i) WHEN, from Old English hwenne, hwanne, when; (ii) WHENCE, from Old English hwanon, whence. Both (i) and (ii) from Germanic adverb *hwan-; **g.** WHITHER, from Old English hwider, whither, from Germanic adverb *hwithrē; **h.** WHERE, from Old English hwǣr, where, from Germanic adverb *hwar-. **a–h** all from Germanic *hwa-, *hwi-. **2a.** WHETHER; NEITHER, from Old English hwæther, hwether, which of two, whether; **b.** EITHER, from Old English ǣghwæther, æther, either, from Germanic phrase *aiwo gi-hwatharaz, "ever each of two" (*aiwo, *aiwi, ever, and *gi- from *ga-, collective prefix; see **aiw-** and **kom**). Both **a** and **b** from Germanic *hwatharaz. **3.** QUA, QUIBBLE, QUORUM, from Latin quī, who. **4.** HIDALGO, QUIDDITY, QUIDNUNC, QUIP; KICKSHAW, from Latin quid, what, something. **5.** QUASI, from Latin quasi, as if (< quam + sī, if; see **swo-**), from quam, as, than, how. **6.** QUODLIBET, from Latin quod, what. **7.** Suffixed form *kʷo-ti. QUOTE, QUOTIDIAN, QUOTIENT; ALIQUOT, from Latin quot, how many; **b.** further suffixed form *kʷo-ty-o-. POSOLOGY, from Greek posos, how much. **8.** QUONDAM, from Latin quom, when. **9.** COONCAN, from Latin quem, whom. **10.** QUANTITY, from Latin quantus, how great. **11.** QUALITY; KICKSHAW, from Latin quālis, of what kind. **12.** CUE², from Latin quandō, when (from *kʷām + -dō, to, till; see **de-**). **13.** NEUTER, from Latin uter, either of two, ultimately from *kʷo-tero- (becoming -cuter in such compounds as neuter, neither, from which uter was abstracted out by false segmentation). **14.** UBIQUITY, from Latin ubi, where, ultimately from locative case *kʷo-bhi (becoming -cubi in such compounds as ali-cubi, somewhere, from which ubi was abstracted out by false segmentation, perhaps under the influence of ibi, there). **15.** CHEESE³, from Old Persian *ciš-ciy, something (< *kʷid-kʷid). [Pokorny ku̯o- 644.]

kwon- Dog. (Oldest form *k̑won-.) **1.** CYNIC; CYNOSURE, PROCYON, QUINSY, from Greek kuōn, dog. **2.** Suffixed zero-grade form *kwn̥-to-. **a.** HOUND, from Old English hund, dog; **b.** DACHSHUND, from Old

High German *hunt*, dog; **c.** KEESHOND, from Middle Dutch *hond*, dog. **a–c** all from Germanic **hundaz*. **3.** Nominative form **kwō*. CORGI, from Welsh *ci*, dog. **4.** Variant **kan-i-*. CANAILLE, CANARY, CANICULAR, CANINE, CHENILLE, KENNEL¹, from Latin *canis*, dog. [Pokorny k̑uon- 632.]

kʷrep- Body, form, appearance. Probably a verbal root meaning "to appear." **1.** Suffixed form **kʷrep-es-*. MIDRIFF, from Old English *hrif*, belly from Germanic **hrefiz-*. **2.** Suffixed zero-grade form **kʷṛp-es-*. CORPORAL¹, CORPORAL³, CORPORATE, CORPOREAL, CORPOSANT, CORPS, CORPSE, CORPULENCE, CORPUS, CORPUSCLE, CORSAGE, CORSE, CORSET; LEPRECHAUN, from Latin *corpus*, body, substance. [Pokorny 1. *krep-* 620.]

kʷṛmi- Worm. Rhyme word to **wṛmi-*, worm (see **wer-³**). CARMINE, CRIMSON, KERMES, from Arabic *qirmiz*, kermes, borrowed from Sanskrit compound *kṛmi-ja-*, "(red dye) produced by worms" (*-ja-*, produced; see **genə-**), from *kṛmi-*, worm. [Pokorny kʷṛmi- 649.]

lab- Lapping, smacking the lips; to lick. Variant of **leb-²**. **1.** LAP³, from Old English *lapian*, to lap up, from Germanic **lapjan*. **2.** Nasalized form **la-m-b-*. **a.** LAMPOON, from French *lamper*, to gulp down, from Germanic **lamp-*; **b.** LAMBENT, from Latin *lambere*, to lick. [Pokorny *lab-* 651.]

lādh- To be hidden. (Oldest form **leh₂dh-*, colored to **lah₂dh-*, contracted to **lādh-*.) **1.** LETHE; LETHARGY, from Greek *lēthē*, forgetfulness. **2.** Zero-grade form **lədh-* becoming **ladh-*, with nasalized form **landh-*. LANTHANUM; ALASTOR, from Greek *lanthanein* (aorist *lathein*), to escape the notice of, with middle voice *lanthanesthai*, to forget. **3.** Suffixed (*stative*) variant form **lat-ē-*. LATENT, from Latin *latēre*, to lie hidden. [In Pokorny 2. *lā-* 651.]

laiwo- Left. LEVO-; LEVOROTATION, LEVOROTATORY, from Latin *laevus*, left. [Pokorny laiuo- 652.]

Language and Culture Note While the root for "right (hand)," **deks-**, has derivatives in most branches of the Indo-European family, the root **laiwo-**, "left (hand)," only shows up in Greek (*laios*), Latin (*laevus*), and Slavic (Russian *levyĭ*). The reason for this is likely that the left side has traditionally been considered inauspicious, and terms for "left" are subject to taboo replacement. Particularly common are various euphemisms. In Greek, instead of *laios* one often said *aristeros*, "the better one," or *euōnumos*, "(the one) having a good name." Latin *sinister*, "left," may have been a euphemism originally, if (as some suppose) it is related to Sanskrit *saniyān*, "more winning." The Old Irish term for "left" has cognates in Latin and Germanic meaning "good, safe," and in the Scandinavian languages, the words for "left" literally mean "friendlier, more desirable." English *left*, however, is not a euphemistic expression—just the opposite: it comes from an Old English word meaning "useless, weak."

---

laks- Salmon. (Oldest form **laḱs-*.) Suffixed form **lakso-*. **1.** LOX¹, from Old High German *lahs*, salmon. **2.** GRAVLAX, from Swedish *lax*, salmon. Both **1** and **2** from Germanic **lahsaz*. [In Pokorny laḱ- 653.]

laku- Body of water, lake, sea. **1.** LACUNA, LAGOON, LAKE¹, from Latin *lacus*, lake, pond, basin. **2.** LACCOLITH, from Greek *lakkos*, cistern. **3.** O-grade form **loku-*. LOCH, LOUGH, from Old Irish *loch*, lake. [Pokorny laku- 653.]

lap- To light, burn. Nasalized form **la-m-p-*. LAMP, LANTERN; ECLAMPSIA, from Greek *lampein*, to shine. [Pokorny lā[i]p- 652.]

las- To be eager, wanton, or unruly. **1a.** LUST, from Old English *lust*, lust; **b.** WANDERLUST, from Old High German *lust*, desire; **c.** LIST⁵, from Old English *lystan*, to please, satisfy a desire, from Germanic denomi-

native verb **lustjan*. **a–c** all from suffixed Germanic zero-grade form **lustuz*. **2.** Suffixed form **las-ko-*. LASCIVIOUS, from Latin *lascīvus*, wanton, lustful. [Pokorny *las-* 654.]

lat- Wet, moist. LATEX, from Latin *latex*, liquid. [Pokorny *lat-* 654.]

lau- Gain, profit. (Oldest form **leh₂u-*. colored to **lah₂u-*, contracted to **lau-*.) **1.** Suffixed form **launo-*. GUERDON, from Old High German *lōn*, reward from Germanic **launam*. **2.** Suffixed zero-grade form **lu-tlo-*. LUCRATIVE, LUCRE, from Latin *lucrum*, gain, profit. [Pokorny *lāu-* 655.]

lē-¹ To get. (Contracted from earlier **leh₁-*.) Suffixed zero-grade form **lə-tr-*. **1.** -LATRY, from Greek *latreia*, service (for pay), duties, worship. **2.** LARCENY, from Latin *latrō*, robber, from a Greek source akin to Greek *latron*, pay. **3.** IDOLATER, from Greek *-latrēs*, worshiper. [Pokorny 2. *lē(i)-* 665.]

lē-² To let go, slacken. (Contracted from earlier **leh₁-*.)
   I. Extended form **lēd-*. **1a.** LET¹, from Old English *lǣtan*, to allow, leave undone, from Germanic **lētan*; **b.** LIEGE; ALLEGIANCE, from Late Latin *laetus*, semifree colonist, from Germanic derivative **lēthiga-*, freed. **2.** Zero-grade form **lad-*. **a.** LATE, LATTER, LAST¹, from Old English *lǣt*, late, with its comparative *lǣtra*, latter, and its superlative *latost*, last, from Germanic **lata-*; **b.** LET², from Old English *lettan*, to hinder, impede (< "to make late"), from Germanic **latjan*; **c.** suffixed form **lad-to-*. LASSITUDE; ALAS, from Latin *lassus*, tired, weary.
   II. Suffixed basic form **lē-ni-*. LENIENT, LENIS, LENITIVE, LENITY, from Latin *lēnis*, soft, gentle. [Pokorny 3. *lē(i)-* 666.]

leb- To lick; lip. **1.** LIP, from Old English *lippa*, lip, from Germanic **lep-*. **2.** Variant form **lab-*. **a.** Suffixed form **lab-yo-*. LABIAL, LABIUM, from Latin *labium*, lip; **b.** suffixed form **lab-ro-*. LABELLUM, LABRET, LABRUM, from Latin *labrum*, lip. [Pokorny *lēb-* 655.] See also variant root **lab-**.

leg-¹ To collect; with derivatives meaning "to speak." (Oldest form **leĝ-*.) **1.** Perhaps Germanic **lēkjaz*, enchanter, one who speaks magic words. LEECH¹, from Old English *lǣce*, physician. **2.** LECTERN, LECTION, LECTURE, LEGEND, LEGIBLE, LEGION, LESSON; COIL¹, COLLECT¹, DILIGENT, ELECT, FLORILEGIUM, INTELLIGENT, NEGLECT, PRELECT, SACRILEGE, SELECT, SORTILEGE, from Latin *legere*, to gather, choose, pluck, read. **3.** LEXICON, LOGION, -LOGUE, -LOGY; ALEXIA, ANALECTS, ANTHOLOGY, CATALOG, DIALECT, DIALOGUE, DYSLEXIA, ECLECTIC, ECLOGITE, ECLOGUE, HOROLOGE, LECTOTYPE, PROLEGOMENON, from Greek *legein*, to gather, speak, with o-grade derivative *logos*, a gathering, speech (see also **6** below for derivatives independently built to *logos*). **4.** Suffixed form **leg-no-*. LIGNEOUS, LIGNI-, from Latin *lignum*, wood, firewood (< "that which is gathered"). **5.** Possibly lengthened-grade form **lēg-*. **a.** LEGAL, LEGIST, LEGITIMATE, LEX, LOYAL; LEGISLATOR, PRIVILEGE, from Latin *lēx*, law (? < "collection of rules"); **b.** LEGACY, LEGATE; COLLEAGUE, COLLEGIAL, DELEGATE, RELEGATE, from Latin denominative *lēgāre*, to depute, commission, charge (< "to engage by contract"). (It is also possible, but uncertain, that Latin *lēx* comes, like English *law*, from a form meaning "that which is set or laid down," from **legh-**.) **6.** Suffixed o-grade form **log-o-*. LOGIC, LOGISTIC, LOGO-, LOGOS, -LOGY; ANALOGOUS, APOLOGUE, APOLOGY, DECALOGUE, EPILOGUE, HOMOLOGOUS, LOGARITHM, PARALOGISM, PROLOGUE, SYLLOGISM, from Greek *logos*, speech, word, reason. [Pokorny leĝ- 658.]

leg-² To dribble, trickle. **1.** LEAK; LITMUS, from Middle English *leke*, a leak. **2.** LACK, from Middle English *lack*, deficiency. Both **1** and **2** from Germanic **lek-*. [Pokorny 1. *leg-* 657.]

legh- To lie, lay. **1.** Suffixed form *legh-yo-. **a.** LIE[1], from Old English licgan, to lie, from Germanic *ligjan; **b.** (i) LAY[1], LEDGE, LEDGER, from Old English lecg- an, to lay; (ii) BELAY, from Old English belecgan, to cover, surround (be-, over; see **ambhi**). Both (i) and (ii) from Germanic *lagjan. **2.** Suffixed form *legh-ro-. **a.** LAIR, from Old English leger, lair; **b.** LEAGUER[1]; BELEAGUER, from Middle Dutch leger, lair, camp; **c.** LAAGER, LAGER; LAGERSTÄTTE, STALAG, from Old High German legar, bed, lair. **a–c** all from Germanic *legraz. **3.** LEES, from Medieval Latin lia, sediment, from Celtic *leg-yā-. **4.** Lengthened-grade form *lēgh-. LOW[1], from Old Norse lāgr, low, from Germanic *lēga-, "lying flat," low. **5.** Suffixed form *legh-to-. COVERLET, LITTER; WAGON-LIT, from Latin lectus, bed. **6.** Suffixed o-grade form *logh-o-. **a.** LAW; BYLAW, DANELAW, from Old Norse *lagu, lag-, law, "that which is set down"; **b.** FELLOW, from Old Norse lag, a laying down; **c.** OUTLAW, from Old Norse lög, law; **d.** ANLAGE, VORLAGE, from Old High German lāga, act of laying. **a–c** all from Germanic *lagam. **7.** LAGAN, from Old Norse lögn, drag-net (< "that which is laid down"), from Germanic *lag-īnō-. **8.** Suffixed o-grade form *logh-o-. LOCHIA, from Greek lokhos, childbirth, place for lying in wait. [Pokorny legh- 658, 2. lēĝh- 660.]

legʷh- Light, having little weight. **1.** Suffixed form *legʷh-t-. **a.** LIGHT[2], from Old English līht, lēoht, light; **b.** LIGHTER[2], from Old English līhtan, to lighten. Both **a** and **b** from Germanic *līht(j)az. **2.** Suffixed form *legʷh-wi-. LEAVEN, LEVER, LEVITY; ALEVIN, ALLE-VIATE, CARNIVAL, ELEVATE, LEGERDEMAIN, MEZZO-RELIEVO, RELEVANT, RELIEVE, from Latin levis, light, with its derivative levāre, to lighten, raise. **3.** Variant form *lagʷh-. LEPRECHAUN, from Old Irish lū-, small. **4.** Nasalized form *l(e)ngʷh-. LUNG, from Old English lungen, lungs (from their lightness), from Germanic *lung-. **5.** Latin oblīvīscī, to forget, attributed by some to this root, is more likely from **(s)lei-**. [Pokorny legʷh- 660.]

lei- To flow. **1.** Extended form *leib-. LIBATION; PRELI-BATION, from Latin lībāre, to pour out, taste. **2.** Possibly suffixed extended form *leit-es-. LITTORAL, from Latin lītus, shore. [Pokorny 4. lĕi- 664.]

leid- To play, jest. Suffixed o-grade form *loid-o-. LU-DIC, LUDICROUS; ALLUDE, COLLUDE, DELUDE, ELUDE, ILLUSION, INTERLUDE, PRELUDE, PROLUSION, from Latin lūdus, game, play, and lūdere, to play (but both words may possibly be from Etruscan). [Pokorny leid- 666.]

leiə- To waste away. Zero-grade form *lī- (< *liə-). BU-LIMIA, from Greek līmos, hunger, famine. [In Pokorny 2. lei- 661.]

leig-¹ To bind. (Oldest form *leiĝ-.) **1.** LEECH[2], from Middle Low German līk, leech line, from Germanic *līk-. **2.** Suffixed agent noun *l(e)ig-tor-. LICTOR, from Latin lictor, lictor. **3.** Zero-grade form *lig-ā-. LEAGUE[1]; LEGATO, LIABLE, LIAISON, LIANA, LIEN, LIGA-MENT, LIGASE, LIGATE, LIGATURE; ALLOY, ALLY, COL-LIGATE, FURL, OBLIGE, RALLY[1], RELIGION, RELY, from Latin ligāre, to bind. [Pokorny 4. leig- 668.]

leig-² Poor. (Oldest form *h₃leiĝ-.) Perhaps zero-grade *əlig- in Greek oligos, few, little: OLIGO-. [Pokorny 1. leig- 667.]

leig-³ To leap, tremble. (Oldest form leiĝ-.) O-grade form *loig-. WEDLOCK, from Old English -lāc, suffix denoting activity. **2.** LARK[2], LEK; FARTLEK, from Old Norse leika, to play. [Pokorny 3. leig- 667.]

leigh- To lick. (Oldest form *leiĝh-.) **1.** ELECTUARY, LEKVAR, LICHEN, from Greek leikhein, to lick. **2.** Zero-grade form *ligh-. **a.** LICK, from Old English liccian, to lick; **b.** LECHER, from Old French lechier, to live in debauchery. Both **a** and **b** from Germanic *likkōn. **3.** Nasalized zero-grade form *li-n-gh-. ANILINGUS, CUN-NILINGUS, from Latin lingere, to lick. [Pokorny leiĝh- 668.]

leikʷ- To leave. **1.** Basic form *leikʷ-. ECLIPSE, EL-LIPSIS, from Greek leipein, to leave. **2.** O-grade form *loikʷ-. **a.** Suffixed form *loikʷ-nes-. LOAN, from Old Norse lān, loan, from Germanic *laihwniz; **b.** LEND, from Old English lǣnan, to lend, loan from Germanic denominative *laihwnjan. **3.** Zero-grade form *likʷ-. **a.** LIPOGRAM, from Greek lipo-, lacking; **b.** (i) Germanic compound *ain-lif- (see **oi-no-**); (ii) Germanic compound *twa-lif- (see **dwo-**). Both (i) and (ii) from Germanic *-lif-, left. **4.** Nasalized zero-grade form *li-n-kʷ-. DELINQUENT, DERELICT, RELIC, RELINQUISH, from Latin linquere, to leave. [Pokorny leikᵘ- 669.]

leip- To stick, adhere; fat. **1.** LIFE, LIVELY, from Old English līf, life (< "continuance") from Germanic *lībam. **2a.** LIVE[1], from Old English lifian, libban, to live; **b.** LEBENSRAUM, from Old High German lebēn, to live. Both **a** and **b** from Germanic *lībēn. **3a.** LEAVE[1], from Old English lǣfan, to leave, have remaining; **b.** DELAY, RELAY, from Old French laier, to leave, from Frankish *laibjan. Both **a** and **b** from Germanic causative *-laibjan. **4.** LIVER[1], from Old English lifer, liver (formerly believed to be the blood-producing organ), from Germanic *librō. **5.** Zero-grade form *lip-. LIPO-, from Greek lipos, fat. **6.** Variant form *əleibh- (earliest form *h₂leibh-). ALIPHATIC; SYNALEPHA, from Greek aleiphein, to anoint with oil. [Pokorny 1. leip- 670.]

leis-¹ Track, furrow. **1.** O-grade form *lois-. **a.** LAST[3], from Old English lāst, lǣst, sole, footprint, from Germanic *laist-; **b.** LAST[2], from Old English lǣstan, to continue, from Germanic *laistjan, "to follow a track"; **c.** suffixed form *lois-ā-. LORE[1], from Old English lār, learning, from Germanic *laizō. **2.** LEARN, from Old English leornian, to learn, from Germanic zero-grade form *liznōn, "to follow a course (of study)." **3.** Suffixed full-grade form *leis-ā-. DELIRIUM, from Latin līra, a furrow. [Pokorny leis- 671.]

leis-² Small. LEAST, LESS, from Old English compara-tive lǣs, lǣssa and superlative lǣst, lǣrest, from Ger-manic comparative *lais-izō and superlative *lais-ista-. [In Pokorny 2. lei- 661.]

leit-¹ To detest. **1.** LOATH, from Old English lāth, loath-some, from Germanic *laitha-; **2.** LOATHE, from Old English lāthian, to loathe, from Germanic denomina-tive verb *laithōn. [Pokorny 1. leit- 672.]

leit-² To go forth, die. **1.** Suffixed o-grade form *loit-eyo-. **a.** LEAD[1], from Old English lǣdan, to lead; **b.** LEITMOTIF, from Old High German leitan, to lead. Both **a** and **b** from Germanic *laidjan. **2.** Suffixed variant o-grade form *loit-ā-. LOAD, LODE; LIVELI-HOOD, from Old English lād, course, way, from Ger-manic *laidō. [Pokorny leit(h)- 672.]

leizd- Border, band. **1.** LIST[2], from Old English līste, border, edge, strip. **2.** LIST[1], from Old Italian lista, bor-der, strip of paper, list. Both **1** and **2** from Germanic *līstōn-. [Pokorny leizd- 672.]

lek- To ward off, protect. (Oldest form *h₂lek-, becom-ing *alek- in Greek.) **1.** Suffixed zero-grade form *əlk-ā-. ANALCIME, from Greek alkē, strength. **2.** Ex-tended form *aleks-. **a.** ALEXIN, from Greek alexein, to protect; **b.** Greek combining form alex- in personal name Alexandros (see **ner-²**); **c.** GURKHA, from San-skrit rakṣati, he protects. **d.** LASCAR, from Middle Per-sian lashkar, army (see **kʷer-**). [Pokorny aleq- 32.]

lēk- To tear. (Contracted from earlier *leh₁k-.) Zero-grade form *lək- becoming *lak-. **1.** LACINIA, LACINI-ATE, from Latin lacinia, flap of a garment. **2.** Suffixed form *lak-ero-. LACERATE, from Latin lacer, torn. **3.** Nasalized form *la-n-k-. LANCINATING, from Latin lancināre, to pierce, stab. [Pokorny 2. lēk- 674.]

lem- To break in pieces; broken, soft, with deriva-tives meaning "crippled." **1.** LAME[1], from Old English lama, lame, from Germanic *lamōn-. **2.** LAM[1], from a Scandinavian source akin to Old Norse lemja, to flog, cripple by beating, from Germanic *lamjan. **3.** Perhaps Swedish dialectal *loma,* to move heavily, akin to the Scandinavian source of Middle English *lomeren,* to lumber: LUMBER². [Pokorny 1. *lem-* 674.]

lendh-¹ Loin. Suffixed o-grade form **londh-wo-.* LAMBADA, LOIN, LUMBAGO, LUMBAR; HUMBLE PIE, SIRLOIN, from Latin *lumbus,* loin. [Pokorny 2. *lendh-* 675.]

lendh-² Open land. **1a.** LAND; ISLAND, from Old English *land,* land; **b.** BILANDER, LANDSCAPE, UITLANDER, from Middle Dutch *land,* land; **c.** AUSLANDER, GELÄNDESPRUNG, HINTERLAND, LANDSLEIT, LANDSMAN², from Old High German *lant,* land; **d.** LANDGRAVE, LANDGRAVINE, from Middle Low German *lant,* country; **e.** LANDSMÅL, from Old Norse *land,* land. **a–e** all from Germanic **landam.* **2.** LAWN¹, from Old French *launde,* heath, pasture, from Germanic, or from Celtic **landā-.* [Pokorny 3. *lendh-* 675.]

lent-o- Flexible. **1.** Suffixed form **lent-yo-.* **a.** LITHE, from Old English *līthe,* flexible, mild, from Germanic **linthja-;* **b.** LINDEN, from Old English *lind(e),* linden tree (from its pliant bast), from Germanic **lindjō.* **2.** Suffixed form **lent-o-.* LENTAMENTE, LANTANA, LENTANDO, LENTISSIMO, LENTO; RALLENTANDO, RELENT, from Latin *lentus,* flexible, tenacious, sluggish, slow. [Pokorny *lento-* 677.]

lep-¹ To peel. **1.** LEMMA², LEPTO-, LEPTON¹; OOLEMMA, PLASMALEMMA, SARCOLEMMA, from Greek *lepein,* to peel, and derivative *lemma* (< **lep-mṇ*), husk. **2.** Suffixed form **lep-i-.* LEPER, LEPIDO-, LEPIDOTE, from Greek *lepis, lepos,* a scale. **3.** Suffixed variant form **lap-aro-.* LAPAROTOMY, LAPAROSCOPE, from Greek *laparos,* soft. **4.** O-grade form **lop-.* ELAPID, from Greek *elops, ellops,* a fish (< **en-lopos,* having scales; *en-,* in; see **en**). [Pokorny 2. *lep-* 678.]

lep-² To be flat; palm, sole, shoulder blade. Lengthened o-grade form **lōp-.* **1.** GLOVE, from Old English *glōf,* glove, from Germanic **galōfō,* "covering for the hand" (*ga-,* collective prefix; see **kom**). **2.** LUFF, from Old French *lof,* spar, probably from a Germanic source akin to Middle Dutch **loef,* windward side of a ship. Both **1** and **2** from Germanic **lōfō.* [Pokorny 2. *lēp-* 679.]

letro- Leather. **1.** LEATHER, from Old English *lether-,* leather. **2.** LEDERHOSEN, from Old High German *ledar,* leather. Both **1** and **2** from Germanic **lethram.* [Pokorny *letro-* 681.]

leu-¹ To loosen, divide, cut apart.
I. Extended Germanic root **leus-.* **1a.** LORN, LOSEL, from Old English *-lēosan* (< **leu-*), to lose; **b.** (i) FORLORN, from Old English *forlēosan,* to forfeit, lose; (ii) FORLORN HOPE, from Dutch *verliezen* (past participle *verloren*), to lose. Both (i) and (ii) from Germanic **fer-leusan* (**fer-, *far-,* prefix denoting rejection or exclusion; see **per¹**). Both **a** and **b** from Germanic **leusan* (with Old English and Dutch past participle *loren* from Germanic **luzana-,* from Indo-European suffixed zero-grade form **lus-ono-*). **2a.** LEASING, -LESS, from Old English *lēas,* "loose," free from, without, untrue, lacking; **b.** LOSE, LOSS, from Old English *los,* loss; **c.** LOOSE, from Old Norse *lauss, louss,* loose; **d.** LOESS, from German dialectal *lösch,* loose. **a–d** all from Germanic **lausa-.* **3.** LEISTER, from Old Norse *ljōsta,* to strike, perhaps from Germanic **leustan.*
II. Basic form **leu-.* **1.** LAG², probably from a source akin to Swedish *lagg,* barrel stave (< "split piece of wood"), from Germanic **lawwō.* **2.** Zero-grade form **lu-.* **a.** LYO-, LYSIS, LYSO-, -LYTE, LYTIC, -LYTIC; ANALYSIS, CATALYSIS, DIALYSIS, LYASE, PALSY, PARALYSIS, TACHYLYTE, from Greek *lūein,* to loosen, release, untie; **b.** LUES, from Latin *luēs,* plague, pestilence (< "dissolution, putrefaction"); **c.** prefixed form **se-lu-* (**se-,* apart; see **s(w)e-**). SOLUBLE, SOLUTE, SOLVE; ABSOLUTE, ABSOLVE, ASSOIL, CONSOLUTE, DISSOLVE, RESOLUTE, RESOLVE, from Latin *solvere,* to loosen, untie. [Pokorny 2. *leu-* 681.]

leu-² Dirt; to make dirty. **1.** POLLUTE, from Latin *polluere,* to pollute (< **por-leuere; por-* for **prō-,* forth, forward; see **per¹**). **2.** Suffixed zero-grade form **lu-to-.* LUTE², from Latin *lutum,* mud, mire, clay. [Pokorny 1. *leu-* 681.]

lēu-¹ Stone. CROMLECH, from Welsh *llech,* flat stone (preform uncertain). [Pokorny 2. *lēu-* 683.]

lēu-² Echoic root. **1.** Extended shortened form **leut-.* LIED; VOLKSLIED, from Old High German *liod,* song, from Germanic **leutham.* **2.** Extended variant form **laud-.* LAUD, from Latin *laus* (stem *laud-*), praise, glory, fame. [Pokorny 3. *lēu-* 683.]

leubh- To care, desire; love.
I. Suffixed form **leubh-o-.* LIEF; LEMAN, LIVELONG, from Old English *lēof,* dear, beloved, from Germanic **leubaz.*
II. O-grade form **loubh-.* **1a.** LEAVE², from Old English *lēaf,* permission (< "pleasure, approval"); **b.** FURLOUGH, from Middle Dutch *verlof,* leave, permission (*ver-,* intensive prefix, from Germanic **fer-;* see **per¹**); **c.** BELIEF, from Old English *gelēafa,* belief, faith, from Germanic **galaubō* (**ga-,* intensive prefix; see **kom**). **a–c** all from Germanic **laubō.* **2.** BELIEVE, from Old English *gelēfan, belēfan,* to believe, trust (*be-,* about; see **ambhi**), from Germanic **galaubjan,* "to hold dear," esteem, trust (**ga-,* intensive prefix; see **kom**).
III. Zero-grade form **lubh-.* **1.** Suffixed form **lubh-ā-.* LOVE, from Old English *lufu,* love, from Germanic **lubō.* **2.** Suffixed (stative) form **lubh-ē-.* QUODLIBET, from Latin *libēre,* to be dear, be pleasing. **3.** LIBIDO, from Latin *libīdō,* pleasure, desire. [Pokorny *leubh-* 683.]

leud- Small. **1a.** LITTLE, from Old English *lȳtel,* little, from West Germanic **luttila-;* **b.** LOUT², from Old English *lūtan,* to bend down (< "to make small"); **c.** LOUT¹, from Old Norse *lūta,* to bend down. **a–c** all from Germanic **lūt-.* **2.** LOITER, from Middle English *loitren,* to idle away time, perhaps akin to Middle Dutch *loteren,* to shake, totter (< "to make smaller"), perhaps from Germanic **lūt-.* [Pokorny *leud-* 684.]

leudh-¹ To go. (Oldest form **h₁leudh-.*) Zero-grade form **əludh-,* in suffixed zero-grade extended form **elu-to-.* PROSELYTE, from Greek *prosēlutos,* "one who comes to a place," stranger (*pros-,* to; see **per¹**). [In Pokorny 6. *el-* 306.]

leudh-² To mount up, grow. (Oldest form **h₁leudh-.*) **1.** Basic form **leudh-.* LANDSLEIT, from Old High German *liut,* person, people (also in personal names; see **bhel-²**); **2.** Suffixed form **leudh-i-.* **2.** Suffixed form **leudh-ero-.* LIBERAL, LIBERATE, LIBERO, LIBERTINE, LIBERTY, LIVERY; DELIVER, from Latin *līber,* free (the precise semantic development is obscure). [Pokorny 1. *leudh-* 684.]

leu(ə)- To wash. (Oldest form **leu(h₃)-.*) **1.** Suffixed form **lou-kā-.* LYE, from Old English *lēag,* lye, from Germanic **laugō.* **2.** Suffixed form **lou-tro-.* **a.** LATHER, from Old English *lēthran, līthran,* to lather; **b.** LUTEFISK, from Old Norse *laudhr,* soap, foam. **3.** Variant form **law-.* **a.** LOMENT, LOTION; ABLUTION, ALLUVION, COLLUVIUM, DELUGE, DILUTE, ELUENT, ELUTE, ELUVIUM, from Latin *lavere,* to wash (in compounds, *-luere*); **b.** suffixed form **law-ā-.* LAUNDER, LAVABO, LAVAGE, LAVATORY, LAVE, LAVISH, from Latin *lavāre,* to wash; **c.** LATRINE, from Latin *lavātrīna, lātrīna,* a bath, privy. **4.** O-grade form **lou-.* PYROLUSITE, from Greek *louein,* to wash. [Pokorny *lou-* 692.]

leug- To break. Suffixed (stative) form **leug-ē-.* LUGUBRIOUS, from Latin *lūgēre,* to mourn (< "to be broken"). [Pokorny *leuĝ-* 686.]

leugh- To tell a lie. **1a.** WARLOCK, from Old English *lēogan,* to lie; **b.** BELIE, from Old English *belēogan,* to deceive (*be-,* about; see **ambhi**). Both **a** and **b** from Germanic **leugan.* **2.** LIE², from Old English *lyge,* a lie, falsehood, from Germanic *lugiz. [Pokorny 1. leugh- 686.]

leuk- Light, brightness.
I. Basic form *leuk-. **1.** Suffixed form *leuk-to-. **a.** LIGHT¹, from Old English lēoht, līht, light; **b.** LIGHTNING, from Old English līhtan, to shine, from Germanic *leuhtjan, to make light. Both **a** and **b** from Germanic *leuhtam. **2.** Basic form *leuk-. LUCULENT, LUX; LUCIFER, LUCIFERIN, from Latin lūx, light. **3.** Suffixed form *leuk-smen-. LIMBERS, LIMN, LUMEN, LUMINARY, LUMINOUS; ILLUMINATE, PHILLUMENIST, from Latin lūmen, light, opening. **4.** Suffixed form *leuksnā-. LUNA, LUNAR, LUNATE, LUNATIC, LUNE, LUNULA; MEZZALUNA, SUBLUNARY, from Latin lūna, moon. **5.** Suffixed form *leuk-stro-. **a.** LUSTER, LUSTRUM, from Latin lūstrum, purification; **b.** ILLUSTRATE, from Latin lūstrāre, to purify, illuminate. **6.** Suffixed form *leuko-dhro-. LUCUBRATE, ELUCUBRATION, from Latin lūcubrāre, to work by lamplight. **7.** Suffixed form *leuk-o-. LEUKO-; MELALEUCA, from Greek leukos, clear, white. **8.** Suffixed form *leuk-os, *leuk-es-. RISK, perhaps from Arabic rizq, what God provides (for the day), daily bread, from Syriac ruziqā, daily bread, from Middle Iranian rōzig, from rōz, day, from Old Iranian *raocah- (Old Persian raocah-).
II. O-grade form *louk-. **1.** Suffixed form *louk-o-. **a.** LEA, from Old English lēah, meadow (< "place where light shines"), from Germanic *lauhaz; **b.** LEVIN, from Middle English levin, lightning, from Germanic *lauhubni-. **2.** Suffixed (iterative) form *louk-eyo-. LUCENT, LUCID; ELUCIDATE, NOCTILUCA, PELLUCID, RELUCENT, TRANSLUCENT, from Latin lūcēre, to shine.
III. Zero-grade form *luk-. **1.** Suffixed form *luksno-. LINK², LYCHNIS, from Greek lukhnos, lamp. **2.** Attributed by some to this root (but more likely of obscure origin) is Greek lunx, lynx (as if from its shining eyes): LYNX, OUNCE². [Pokorny leuk- 687.]

leup- To peel off, break off. **1.** LEAF, from Old English lēaf, leaf, from Germanic *laubaz. **2a.** LODGE, LOGE, from Old French loge, lodge; **b.** LOBBY, from Medieval Latin lobium, lobia, laubia, monastic cloister. Both **a** and **b** from Germanic *laubja-, "roof made from bark," shelter. **3.** Attributed by some to this root, but probably a separate Germanic root, is Germanic *luftuz, sky (traditionally explained as < "roof of the world"). **a.** LOFT; ALOFT, from Old Norse lopt, air, attic, sky; **b.** LIFT, from Old Norse lypta, to lift, from Germanic *luftjan, to hold up in the air. [Pokorny leup- 690.]

[līk- Body, form; like, same. Germanic root. **1.** LYCHGATE, from Old English līc, form, body. **2.** -LY¹, -LY², from Old English -līc, having the form of. **3a.** ALIKE, LIKE², LIKELY, from Old English gelīc, similar, and Old Norse (g)līkr, like, both from Germanic *galīka- (*ga-, with, intensive prefix; see **kom**); **b.** EACH, EVERY, from Old English ǣlc, each, from Germanic phrase *aiwo galika-, "ever alike" (*aiwo, *aiwi, ever; see **aiw-**). **4.** Germanic compound *is-līk- (see **i-**). **5.** ALIKE, from Old English onlīc, from Germanic *ana-likaz. **6.** FROLIC, from Middle Dutch -lijc, -like. **7.** LIKE¹, from Old English līcian, to please, from Germanic *līkjan. **8.** Germanic compound *hwa-līk- (see **kʷo-**). [Pokorny 2. lēig- 667.]]**

līno- Flax. **1.** Form *lino-. LINOLEIC ACID, from Greek linon, flax. **2.** Form *līno-. LENO, LINE¹, LINE², LINEAGE, LINEN, LINGERIE, LINNET, LINT; ALIGN, CRINOLINE, LINEA ASPERA, LINSEED, from Latin līnum, flax, linen, thread. [Pokorny līˊ-no- 691.]

[līthrā A scale. Mediterranean word, probably the source of Latin lībra, a pound, balance, and Greek litra, unit of weight, pound. **1.** LEVEL, LIBRA, LIRA, LIVRE; DELIBERATE, EQUILIBRIUM, from Latin lībra, a pound, balance. **2.** LITER, from Greek litra, unit of weight, pound.]**

-lo- Secondary suffix, forming diminutives. **1.** -ULAR, -ULE, from Latin -ulus, diminutive suffix, from *-(o)

lo-. **2.** -LET, from Latin -ellus, diminutive suffix, from double diminutive suffix *-olo-lo-. **2.** -LING¹, from Old English -ling, diminutive suffix and nominal suffix, from Germanic *-linga- (< *-l-inga-; see **-(i)ko-**). **3.** Italic i-stem form *-li-, appearing in various Latin adjective suffixes. **a.** -AL¹, -AL², -AR, from Latin -ālis (originally suffix *-li- attached to stems in -ā-), adjective suffix, and dissimilated form -āris (after bases containing l); **b.** -ILE¹, from Latin -ilis, -īlis, adjective suffixes. [Not in Pokorny.]

lobho- Top or back of the head. LOPHOPHORE, from Greek lophos, top of the head, crest. [Not in Pokorny; compare Tocharian A lap, head.]

lūs- Louse. LOUSE, from Old English lūs, louse, from Germanic *lūs-. [Pokorny lūˊs- 692.]

mā-¹ Good; with derivatives meaning "occurring at a good moment, timely, seasonable, early." (Oldest form *meh₂-, colored to *mah₂-, contracted to *mā-.) **1.** Suffixed form *mā-tu-. **a.** Further suffixed form *mā-tu-ro-. MATURE; IMMATURE, PREMATURE, from Latin mātūrus, seasonable, ripe, mature; **b.** further suffixed form *mā-tu-to-. MATINEE, MATINS, MATUTINAL, from Latin Mātūta, name of the goddess of dawn. **2.** Suffixed form *mā-ni-. **a.** MAÑANA, from Latin māne, (in) the morning; **b.** MANES, from Latin mānis, mānus, good. [Pokorny 2. mā- 693.]

mā-² Mother. A linguistic near-universal found in many of the world's languages, often in reduplicated form. **1.** MAMMA², MAMMAL, MAMMILLA, MAMONCILLO, from Latin mamma, breast. **2.** Probably from this root is Greek Maia, "good mother" (respectful form of address to old women), also nurse: MAIA, MAIEUTIC; MAIASAUR. **3.** MAMA, more recently formed in the same way. [Pokorny 3. mā 694.]

mā-³ Damp. (Oldest form *meh₂-, colored to *mah₂-, contracted to *mā-.) **1.** Suffixed form *mā-ro-. MOOR², from Old English mōr, marsh, wilderness, from Germanic *mōra-. **2.** Suffixed form *mā-no-. EMANATE, from Latin mānāre, to flow, trickle. [Pokorny mā-no-699.]

mad- Moist, wet; also refers to various qualities of food. **1.** Suffixed (stative) form *mad-ē-. MATTE²; CASEMATE, from Latin madēre, to be sodden, be drunk, with past participle mattus, stupefied (< *mad-to-; see **3** below). **2.** MYNA, from Sanskrit madati, it bubbles, gladdens, and derivative madana-, delightful, joyful. **3.** Suffixed form *mad-to-. MUSTH, from Middle Persian mast, drunk, from Iranian *masta-. **4.** Suffixed form *mad-i-. **a.** MEAT, from Old English mete, food; **b.** MATE¹, from Middle Low German (ge)mate, "he with whom one shares one's food," companion (ge-, together, from Germanic *ga-; see **kom**). **5.** Suffixed form *mad-stā-, becoming *mazda-. MAST², from Old English mæst, fodder, from Germanic *mastō. **6.** MUESLI, from Old High German muos, meal, mushlike food, from Germanic suffixed lengthened-grade form *mōd-sa-. [Pokorny mad- 694.]

mag- Also **mak-**. To knead, fashion, fit. (Oldest forms *maǵ-, *mak-.) **1a.** (i) MAKE, from Old English macian, to make; (ii) MASON, from Old French masson, mason; (iii) MAQUILLAGE, from Middle Dutch maken, to make. (i)–(iii) all from Germanic verb *makōn, to fashion, fit; **b.** MATCH¹, from Old English gemæcca, mate, spouse, from Germanic compound noun *gamak-(j)ōn-, "one who is fitted with (another)" (*ga-, with, together; see **kom**). Both **a** and **b** from Germanic *mak-. **2a.** MINGLE, from Old English mengan, to mix; **b.** AMONG, MONGREL, from Old English gemang, mixture, crowd (ge-, together; see **kom**). Both **a** and **b** from Germanic nasalized form *mangjan, to knead together. **3.** Suffixed form *mak-yo-. MAGMA, from Greek magma, unguent, from massein (aorist stem mag-), to knead. **4.** Suffixed lengthened-grade form *māg-ya-. MASS; AMASS, from Greek māza, maza, a (kneaded) lump, barley cake. **5.** Suffixed lengthened-grade form *māk-ero-. MACERATE, from Latin *mācerāre*, to tenderize, to soften (food) by steeping. [Pokorny *maĝ-* 696, 2. *māk-* 698, *men(ə)k-* 730.]

magh-¹ To be able, have power. **1a.** MAY¹, from Old English *magan*, to be able; **b.** DISMAY, from Old French *esmaier*, to frighten. Both **a** and **b** from Germanic *magan*, to be able. **2.** MIGHT¹, from Old English *miht*, power, from Germanic suffixed form *mah-ti-*, power (also in personal names; see **kel-²**). **3.** MAIN, from Old English *mægen*, power, from Germanic suffixed form *mag-inam*, power. **4.** Suffixed lengthened-grade form *māgh-anā-*, "that which enables." MACHINE, MECHANIC, MECHANISM, MECHANO-; DEUS EX MACHINA, from Greek (Attic) *mēkhanē*, (Doric) *mākhanā*, device. **5.** Possibly suffixed form *magh-u-*. MAGIC, MAGUS, from Old Persian *maguš*, member of a priestly caste (< "mighty one"). [Pokorny *magh-* 695.]

magh-² To fight. (Oldest form *maĝh-*.) **1.** TITANOMACHY, from Greek *makhesthai*, to fight. **2.** AMAZON, from Greek *Amazōn*, Amazon, possibly borrowed from a hypothetical Iranian compound *ha-mazan-*, "(one) fighting together," warrior (*ha-*, with; see **sem-¹**). [Pokorny *maĝh-* 697.]

maghu- Young person of either sex. Suffixed form *magho-ti-*. **1.** MAID, MAIDEN, from Old English *mægden*, virgin. **2.** MATJES HERRING, from Dutch *maagd*, maid. Both **1** and **2** from Germanic *magadi-*, with diminutive *magadin-*. [Pokorny *maghos* 696.]

mai-¹ To cut. (Oldest form *meh₂i-*, colored to *mah₂i-*, contracted to *mai-*.) **1.** Suffixed form *mai-d-*. **a.** ANT, EMMET, from Old English *æmette*, ant, from Germanic *ē-mait-jōn-*, "the biter" (prefix *ē-*, meaning uncertain; see **ē**); **b.** (i) MITE¹, from Old English *mīte*, mite; (ii) MITE², from Middle Dutch *mīte*, insect, small object, small coin. Both (i) and (ii) from Germanic *mītōn-*, "the biter"; **c.** MAIM, MANGLE¹, MAYHEM, from Old French *mahaignier*, to maim (> Anglo-Norman *mangler*, to hack). **a–c** all from Germanic *mait-*. **2.** Suffixed form *mai-lo-*. **a.** MALCOLM (personal name), from Old Irish *Máel Coluim*, "servant of Saint Columba," from *máel*, hornless, bald, shorn, servant; **b.** MULEY, from a source akin to Old Irish *máel* (see above). [Pokorny 1. *mai-* 697.]

mai-² To soil, defile. Possible root. **1.** Suffixed form *mai-lo-*. MOLE¹, from Old English *māl*, spot, blemish, from Germanic *mail-*. **2.** Suffixed variant form *mian-yo-*. MIASMA; AMIANTHUS, from Greek *miainein*, to pollute. [Pokorny 2. *mai-* 697.]

mak- (Leather) bag. **1.** MAW, from Old English *maga*, stomach, from Germanic *magōn-*, bag, stomach. **2.** Suffixed form *mak-no-*, altered in British Celtic to *mēk-no-* (possibly due to a crossing with the unrelated noun *mēn-o-*, face, cheek). MINAUDIÈRE, from Breton *min*, muzzle. [Pokorny *mak-* 698.]

māk- Long, thin. (Oldest form *meh₂k̑-*, colored to *mah₂k̑-*, contracted to *māk̑-*.) **1.** Zero-grade form *mək-* becoming *mak-*. **a.** (i) MEAGER, from Latin *macer*, thin; (ii) MACRO-, MACRON; AMPHIMACER, from Greek *makros*, long, large. Both (i) and (ii) from suffixed form *mak-ro-*; **b.** EMACIATE, from Latin *maciāre*, to make thin, from suffixed form *mak-ye-*. **2.** Suffixed full-grade form *māk-es-*. MECOPTERAN, PARAMECIUM, from Greek *mēkos*, length. [Pokorny *māk̑-* 699.]

man-¹ Also **mon-**. Man. **1.** Extended forms *manu-*, *manw-*. **a.** MAN; LEMAN, NORMAN¹, from Old English *man(n)* (plural *menn*), man; **b.** FUGLEMAN, LANDS-, MAN², from Old High German *man*, man, also in personal name HERMAN, from Old High German *Hariman*, *Heriman*, "army man" (*heri*, army; see **koro-**); **c.** MANIKIN, MANNEQUIN, from Middle Dutch *man*, man; **d.** YEOMAN, from Old Frisian *man*, man; **e.** NORMAN¹, OMBUDSMAN, from Old Norse *mathr*, *mannr*, man; **f.** ALEMANNI, possibly from Germanic

Ala-manniz, tribal name (< "all men": *ala-*, all; see **al-⁵**). **a–f** all from Germanic *manna-* (plural *manniz*); **g.** MANU, from Sanskrit *manuḥ*, man, from Indo-Iranian *manu-*. **2.** MENSCH, from Old High German *mennisco*, human, from Germanic adjective *manniska-*, human, from *manna-* (see **1**). **3.** MUZHIK, from Russian *muzh*, man, male, from Slavic suffixed form *mon-gyo-*. [Pokorny *manu-s* 700.]

man-² Hand. **1a.** MANACLE, MANAGE, MANÈGE, MANNER, MANUAL, MANUBRIUM, MANUS; AMANUENSIS, MAINTAIN, MANEUVER, MANICOTTI, MANICURE, MANIFEST, MANSUETUDE, MANUFACTURE, MANUMIT, MANURE, MANUSCRIPT, MASTIFF, MORTMAIN, QUADRUMANOUS, from Latin *manus*, hand; **b.** MANIPLE, MANIPULATION, from Latin *manipulus*, handful (-*pulus*, perhaps -ful; see **pelə-¹**). **2.** Suffixed form *man-ko-*, maimed in the hand. MANQUÉ, from Latin *mancus*, maimed, defective. **3.** EMANCIPATE, from Latin compound *manceps*, "he who takes by the hand," purchaser (-*ceps*, agential suffix, "taker"; see **kap-**). **4.** MANDAMUS, MANDATE, MAUNDY THURSDAY; COMMAND, COMMANDO, COMMEND, COUNTERMAND, DEMAND, RECOMMEND, REMAND, from Latin compound *mandāre*, "to put into someone's hand," entrust, order (-*dere*, to put; see **dhē-**). **5.** Suffixed zero-grade form *mn̥-to-*. **a.** Old English *mund*, protection, in personal names: (i) EDMUND, from Old English *Ēadmund*, "protector of riches" (*ēad*, happiness, riches); (ii) OSMUND, from Old English *Ōsmund*, "having divine protection" (*ōs*, god; see **ansu-**); **b.** Old High German *mund*, protection, in *Sigismund*, "victorious protection" (see **segh-**); **c.** RAYMOND (personal name), from Frankish *Raginmund* (> Old French *Raimund*), "counsel protection" (*ragin*, counsel), from *mund*, protection. **a–c** all from Germanic *mundō-*, "guarding hand," protection. [Pokorny *mə-r* 740.]

mari- Young woman. Suffixed form *mari-to-*, "provided with a bride." MARIACHI, MARITAL, MARRIAGE, MARRY¹, from Latin *marītus*, married, a husband. [Pokorny *merjo-* 738.]

marko- Horse. **1.** MARSHAL, from Old French *mareschal*, from Germanic *marha-skalkaz*, "horse-servant, servant who cares for his lord's horses" from *marhaz*, horse (*skalkaz*, servant, of obscure origin). **2.** MARE¹, from Old English *mere*, *miere*, mare, from Germanic feminine *marhjōn-*. [Pokorny *marko-* 700.]

māter- Mother. Based ultimately on the baby-talk form **mā-²**, with the kinship term suffix *-ter-*. **1a.** MOTHER¹, from Old English *mōdor*, mother; **b.** MOTHER², from Middle Dutch *moeder*, mother. Both **a** and **b** from Germanic *mōdar-*. **2.** ALMA MATER, MATER, MATERNAL, MATERNITY, MATRICULATE, MATRIX, MATRON, MATRYOSHKA; MADREPORE, MATRIMONY, from Latin *māter*, mother. **3.** METRO-; METROPOLIS, from Greek *mētēr*, mother. **4.** MATERIAL, MATTER, from Latin *māteriēs*, *māteria*, tree trunk (< "matrix," the tree's source of growth), hence hard timber used in carpentry, hence (by a calque on Greek *hūlē*, wood, matter) substance, stuff, matter. **5.** DEMETER, from Greek compound *Dēmētēr*, name of the goddess of produce, especially cereal crops (*dē-*, possibly meaning "earth"). [Pokorny *mātér-* 700.]

math- Various insect names. (Apparent oldest form *math₂-*.) **1.** MOTH, from Old English *moththe*, moth, from uncertain (perhaps expressive) preform. **2.** Either the same or a homophonous root is *math₂-*, to steal, in Sanskrit *mathnāti*, he steals, as in myths relating to the theft of fire, and possibly Greek *māth-*, base of the name *Promētheus*: EPIMETHEUS, PROMETHEUS. (The name *Promētheus* was later interpreted by the Greeks as meaning "forethought," leading to the creation of the name *Epimētheus*, "afterthought," for his brother.) [Pokorny 1. *math-* 700.]

[Māwort- Name of an Italic deity who became the god of war at Rome (and also had agricultural attributes), hence also the name of the planet Mars (doubtless from its red color, the color of blood). **1.** MARCH, MARS, MARTIAL, MARTIAN, from Latin *Mārs* (stem *Mārt-*), Mars. **2.** Suffixed (adjectival) form **mārt-iko-*. MARCIA, MARCUS, MARK (personal names), from Latin *Mārcus*, a Roman praenomen.]

mazdo- Pole, rod, mast. MAST[1], from Old English *mæst*, mast, from Germanic **mastaz*. [Pokorny *mazdo-s* 701.]

me-¹ Oblique form of the personal pronoun of the first person singular. For the nominative see **eg. 1.** ME, MYSELF, from Old English *mě* (dative and accusative), from Germanic **mě-*. **2.** Possessive adjective **mei-no-*. **a.** MINE[2], MY, from Old English *mīn*, my; **b.** MYNHEER, from Middle Dutch *mijn*, my. Both **a** and **b** from Germanic **mīn-*. **3.** Possessive adjective **me-yo-*. MADAME, MADONNA, MONSIEUR, from Latin *meus*, mine. **4.** Genitive form **me-wo.* MAVOURNEEN, from Old Irish *mo*, my. [Pokorny 1. *me-* 702.]

me-² In the middle of. **1.** Suffixed form **me-dhi.* MIDWIFE, from Old English *mid*, among, with, from Germanic **mid-*. **2.** Suffixed form **me-ta.* META-, from Greek *meta*, between, with, beside, after. [Pokorny 2. *me-* 702.] See also **medhyo-**.

mē-¹ Expressing certain qualities of mind. (Contracted from earlier **meh₁-*.) **1.** Suffixed o-grade form **mō-to-*. **a.** MOOD[1], from Old English *mōd*, mind, disposition; **b.** GEMÜTLICH, GEMÜTLICHKEIT, from Old High German *gimuoti*, spirits, feelings, from *muot*, mind (*gi-*, collective prefix; see **kom**). Both **a** and **b** from Germanic **mōthaz*. **2.** Perhaps suffixed o-grade form **mō-s-*. MORAL, MORALE, MORES, MOROSE, from Latin *mōs*, wont, humor, manner, custom. [Pokorny 5. *mē-* 704.]

mē-² To measure. (Contracted from earlier **meh₁-*.)
I. Basic form *mē-*. **1.** Suffixed form **mē-lo-*. MEAL[2]; PIECEMEAL, from Old English *mǣl*, "measure, mark, appointed time, time for eating, meal," from Germanic **mēlaz*. **2.** Suffixed form **mē-ti-*. **a.** MEASURE, MENSURAL; COMMENSURATE, DIMENSION, IMMENSE, from Latin *mētīrī*, to measure; **b.** METIS, from Greek *mētis*, wisdom, skill. **3.** Possibly Greek *metron*, measure, rule, length, proportion, poetic meter (but referred by some to **med-**): METER¹, METER², METER³, -METER, METRICAL, -METRY; DIAMETER, GEMATRIA, GEOMETRY, ISOMETRIC, METROLOGY, METRONOME, SYMMETRY. **4.** Reduplicated zero-grade form **mi-mə-.* MAHOUT, MAUND, from Sanskrit *mimīte*, he measures.
II. Extended and suffixed forms **mēn-*, **mēn-en-*, **mēn-ōt-*, **mēn-s-*, moon, month (an ancient and universal unit of time measured by the moon). **1.** MOON; MONDAY, from Old English *mōna*, moon, from Germanic **mēnōn-*. **2.** MONTH, from Old English *mōnath*, month, from Germanic **mēnōth-*. **3.** MENO-; AMENORRHEA, CATAMENIA, DYSMENORRHEA, EMMENAGOGUE, MENARCHE, MENISCUS, MENOPAUSE, from Greek *mēn*, *mēnē*, month. **4.** MENSES, MENSTRUAL, MENSTRUATE; BIMESTRIAL, SEMESTER, TRIMESTER, from Latin *mēnsis*, month. [Pokorny 3. *mē-* 703, *mēnōt* 731.]

mē-³ Big. (Contracted from earlier **meh₁-*.) **1.** Suffixed (comparative) form **mē-is-*. MORE, from Old English *māra*, greater, and *māre* (adverb), more, from Germanic **maizōn-*. **2.** Suffixed (superlative) form **mē-isto-*. MOST, from Old English *mǣst*, most, from Germanic **maista-*. **3.** Suffixed form **mē-ro-*, **mē-ri-*. MÄRCHEN, from Old High German *māri*, news, narration. **4.** Suffixed o-grade form **mō-ro-*. CLAYMORE, from Gaelic *mōr*, big, great. [Pokorny 4. *mē-* 704.]

mē-⁴ To cut down grass or grain with a sickle or scythe. (Oldest form **h₂meh₁-*, contracted to **h₂mē-*.) **1.** MOW², from Old English *māwan*, to mow, from Germanic **mē-*. **2.** Suffixed form **mē-ti-*. AFTERMATH, from Old English *mǣth*, a mowing, a mown crop, from Germanic **mēthaz*. **3.** Suffixed form **mē-twā-*, a mown field. MEAD², MEADOW, from Old English

mǣd, meadow, from Germanic **mēdwō*. [Pokorny 2. *mē-* 703.]

med- To take appropriate measures. **1a.** METE¹, from Old English *metan*, to measure (out), from Germanic **metan*; **b.** MEET², from Old English *gemǣte*, "commensurate," fit (*ge-*, with; see **kom**), from Germanic derivative **mētō*, measure. **2a.** MEDICAL, MEDICATE, MEDICINE, MEDICO; METHEGLIN, REMEDY, from Latin *medērī*, to look after, heal, cure; **b.** MEDITATE, from Latin *meditārī*, to think about, consider, reflect. **3.** Suffixed form **med-es-*. **a.** MODEST, IMMODEST, from Latin *modestus*, "keeping to the appropriate measure," moderate; **b.** MODERATE; IMMODERATE, from Latin *moderārī*, "to keep within measure," to moderate, control. Both **a** and **b** from Latin **modes-*, replacing **medes-* by influence of *modus* (see **6** below). **4.** MEDUSA, from Greek *medein*, to rule (feminine participle *medousa* < **med-ont-ya*). **5.** Suffixed lengthened e- grade form **mēd-es-*. DIOMEDES (personal name), from Greek *Diomēdēs*, "having Zeus's counsel" (*Dio-*, Zeus; see **dyeu-**), from *mēdos*, counsel, plan. **6.** Suffixed o-grade form **mod-o-*. MODAL, MODE, MODEL, MODERN, MODICUM, MODIFY, MODULATE, MODULE, MODULUS, MOLD¹, MOOD²; MOULAGE; ACCOMMODATE, COMMODE, COMMODIOUS, COMMODITY, from Latin *modus*, measure, size, limit, manner, harmony, melody. **7.** Suffixed o-grade form **mod-yo-*. MODIOLUS, MUTCHKIN, from Latin *modius*, a measure of grain. **8.** Possibly lengthened o-grade form **mōd-*. **a.** MOTE², MUST¹, from Old English *mōtan*, to have occasion, to be permitted or obliged; **b.** EMPTY, from Old English *ǣmetta*, rest, leisure, from Germanic compound **ē-mōt-ja-* (prefix **ē-*, meaning uncertain; see **ē**). Both **a** and **b** from Germanic **mōt-*, ability, leisure. [Pokorny 1. *med-* 705.]

medhu- Honey; also mead. **1.** MEAD¹, from Old English *meodu*, mead, from Germanic **medu*. **2.** AMETHYST, METHYLENE, from Greek *methu*, wine. [Pokorny *médhu-* 707.]

medhyo- Middle. **1a.** MID¹, MIDST; AMID, from Old English *midd(e)*, middle; **b.** MIDDLE, from Old English *middel*, middle, from West Germanic diminutive form **middila-*; **c.** MIDGARD, from Old Norse *Midhgardhr*, Midgard, from Germanic compound **midjagardaz*, "middle zone," name of the earth conceived as an intermediate zone lying between heaven and hell (**gardaz*, enclosure, yard; see **gher-¹**). a–c all from Germanic **midja-*. **2.** MEAN³, MEDAL, MEDIAL, MEDIAN, MEDIASTINUM, MEDIATE, MEDIUM, MEZZALUNA, MEZZANINE, MEZZOTINT, MIZZEN, MOIETY, MULLION; INTERMEDIATE, MEDIEVAL, MEDIOCRE, MEDITERRANEAN, MERIDIAN, MILIEU, from Latin *medius*, middle, half. **3.** MESO-, from Greek *mesos*, middle. **4.** Celtic **medio-* in Gaulish *medio-*. MILAN, from Italian *Milano*, from Gallo-Roman *Mediolānum*, "in the middle of the plain" (*-lānum*, plain; see **pelə-²**). [Pokorny *medhi-* 706.] See also **me-²**.

meg- Great. (Oldest form **meǵ-*.) **1a.** MICKLE, MUCH, from Old English *micel*, *mycel*, great; **b.** MICKLE, from Old Norse *mikill*. Both **a** and **b** from Germanic suffixed form **mik-ila-*. **2.** Suffixed form **mag-no-*. MAGNATE, MAGNITUDE, MAGNUM; MAGNANIMOUS, MAGNIFIC, MAGNIFICENT, MAGNIFICO, MAGNIFY, MAGNILOQUENT, from Latin *magnus*, great. **3.** Suffixed (comparative) form **mag-yos-*. **a.** MAJOR, MAJOR-DOMO, MAJORITY, MAJUSCULE, MAYOR, from Latin *māior*, greater; **b.** MAESTOSO, MAJESTY, from Latin *māiestās*, greatness, authority; **c.** MAESTRO, MAGISTERIAL, MAGISTRAL, MAGISTRATE, MASTER, MISTER, MISTRAL, MINIATURE, from Latin *magister*, master, high official (< "he who is greater"). **4.** Suffixed (superlative) form **mag-samo-*. MAXIM, MAXIMUM, from Latin *maximus*, greatest. **5.** Suffixed (feminine) form **mag-ya-*, "she who is great." MAY², May, from Latin *Maia*, name of a goddess. **6.** Suffixed root form **meg-ə-* (< oldest form **meǵ-h₂-*). **a.** Basic form **meg-ə-* with suppletive further suffixed form *meg-ə-(l-). MEGA-, MEGALO-; ACROMEGALY, OMEGA, from Greek *megas* (stem *megal-*), great. **b.** Suffixed (superlative) form *meg-(ə)-isto-.* ALMAGEST, HERMES TRISMEGISTUS, from Greek *megistos*, greatest. **7.** Zero-grade *m̥g-ə-* (< oldest form *meĝ-h₂-*) in Greek combining form *aga-*, great (an intensifier found in such Greek forms as the names as *Agamemnōn*, Agamemnon, the adjective *agathos*, good, and the adverb *agān*, too much, as in the famous proverb *mēden agān*, "nothing to excess") in compound *m̥g-ə-pā-*, "(one) offering great protection." AGAPE², from Greek *agapē*, non-sexual love, agape, back-formation from *agapā*, to greet with affection (< "to offer the protection due to a guest from a host"), contracted from *aga-pā-ye-*, from earlier *m̥g-ə-pā-ye-*, to offer the protection due to a guest from a host, verbal stem derived from *m̥g-ə-pā-*, "(one) offering great protection" (-pā-, protector; see **pā-**). **8.** Variant (satem language) form *meĝh-* (< earlier *meĝ-h₂-*). MAHABHARATA, MAHARAJA, MAHA-RANI, MA- HARISHI, MAHATMA, MAHAYANA, MAHOUT, from Sanskrit *mahā-*, *mahat-*, great. [Pokorny *meĝ(h)-* 708.]

mei-¹ To change, go, move; with derivatives referring to the exchange of goods and services within a society as regulated by custom or law. **1.** MEATUS; CONGÉ, IRREMEABLE, PERMEATE, from Latin *meāre*, to go, pass. **2.** Suffixed o-grade form *moi-to-.* **a.** MAD, from Old English *gemǣdan*, to make insane or foolish, from Germanic *ga-maid-jan*, denominative from *ga-maid-az*, "changed (for the worse)," abnormal (*ga-*, intensive prefix; see **kom**); **b.** MEW¹, MOLT, MUTATE; COMMUTE, PERMUTE, REMUDA, TRANSMUTE, from Latin *mūtāre*, to change; **c.** MUTUAL, from Latin *mūtuus*, "done in exchange," borrowed, reciprocal, mutual. **3.** Suffixed zero-grade form *mi-tā-.* AZIMUTH, ZENITH, from Latin *sēmita*, sidetrack, side path (< "thing going off to the side"; *sē-*, apart; see **s(w)e-**). **4.** Suffixed extended zero-grade form *mit-to-.* **a.** MIS-¹, from Old English *mis-*, mis-, and Old French *mes-* (from Frankish *miss-*); **b.** AMISS, MISTAKE, from Old Norse *mis(s)*, *mis(s)-*, miss, mis-; **c.** MISS¹, from Old English *missan*, to miss, from Germanic *missjan*, to go wrong. **a–c** all from Germanic *missa-*, "in a changed manner," abnormally, wrongly. **5.** Suffixed o-grade form *moi-n-* in compound adjective *ko-moin-i-*, "held in common" (*ko-*, together; see **kom**). **a.** MEAN², DEMEAN², from Old English *gemǣne*, common, public, general, from Germanic *gamaini-*; **b.** COMMON, COMMUNE¹, COMMUNE², COMMUNICATE, COMMUNISM; EXCOMMUNICATE, INCOMMUNICADO, from Latin *commūnis*, common, public, general. **6.** Suffixed o-grade form *moi-n-es-.* **a.** MUNICIPAL, MUNIFICENT, REMUNERATE, from Latin *mūnus*, "service performed for the community," duty, work, "public spectacle paid for by a magistrate," gift; **b.** IMMUNE, from Latin *immūnis*, exempt from public service (*in-*, negative prefix; see **ne**). **7.** Suffixed extended zero-grade form *mit-ti-.* Slavic *mĭstĭ*, revenge, and *mĭstiti*, to take revenge, in Russian *mstit'*, to take revenge, in personal name *Mstislav* (see **kleu-**). **8.** Perhaps extended form *(ə)meigʷ-* (oldest form *h₂meigʷ-*) but more likely a separate root. **a.** AMOEBA, from Greek *ameibein*, to change; **b.** MIGRATE; EMIGRATE, from Latin *migrāre*, to change one's place of living. [Pokorny 2. *mei-*, 3. *mei-* 710, *mei-gʷ-* 713, 2. *mei-t(h)-* 715.]

mei-² Small. **1.** MEIOSIS; MEIOFAUNA, MIOCENE, from Greek *meiōn*, less, lesser, from extended variant *meiu-.* **2.** Zero-grade compounded suffixed form *ne-mi-s* (see **ne**). **3.** Suffixed zero-grade form *mi-nu-.* **a.** MENU, MINCE, MINUEND, MINUET, MINUTE²; MINUTIAE, COMMINUTE, DIMINISH, from Latin *minuere*, to reduce, diminish; **b.** MINOR, MINUS; MINUSCULE, from Latin *minor* (influenced by the comparative suffix *-or*), less, lesser, smaller; **c.** further suffixed (superlative) form *minu-mo-.* MINIM, MINIMUM, from Latin *minimus*, least; **d.** MINESTRONE, MINISTER,

MINISTRY, MYSTERY², from Latin *minister*, an inferior, servant (formed after *magister*, master; see **meg-**); **e.** MENSHEVIK, from Russian *men'she*, less. [Pokorny 5. *mei-* 711.]

mei-³ To fix; to build fences or fortifications. **1.** Suffixed o-grade form *moi-ro-.* **a.** MERE³, from Old English *mǣre*, boundary, border, landmark, from Germanic *mair-ja-*; **b.** MURAL, MURE; IMMURE, MURAMIC ACID, from Latin *mūrus*, wall. **2.** Suffixed o-grade form *moi-ni-.* MUNIMENT, MUNITION; AMMUNITION, PRAEMUNIRE, PREMUNITION, from Latin *mūnīre*, to fortify, protect, strengthen. **3.** Possibly suffixed lengthened-grade form *mēi-t-.* METE², from Latin *mēta*, boundary stone, limit. [Pokorny 1. *mei-* 709.]

mei-⁴ To tie. **1.** Suffixed zero-grade form *mi-tro-*, "that which binds." **a.** MITER, from Greek *mitrā*, headband, earlier a piece of armor worn around the waist; **b.** MITRA, from Sanskrit *Mitraḥ*, Mitra; **c.** MITHRAS, MITHRAEUM, from Avestan and Old Persian *Mithra-*, Mithras. Both **b** and **c** from Indo-Iranian *mitram*, contract, whence *mitras*, contractual partner, friend, divinized as a god *Mitras*; **d.** (i) MIR, from Russian *mir*, world, peace; (ii) Old Church Slavonic *mirŭ*, peace, in personal name *Vladimirŭ* (see **wal-**). Both (i) and (ii) from Slavic *mirŭ*, commune, joy, peace (possibly borrowed from Iranian). **2.** Possibly suffixed zero-grade *mi-to-.* MITOSIS; DIMITY, MITOCHONDRION, SAMITE, from Greek *mitos*, a warp thread. [Pokorny 4. *mei-* 710.]

Language and Culture Note The contract was an important type of reciprocal exchange relationship in ancient Indo-European societies. In fact, the first documentarily attested word in any Indo-European language is the Hittite word for "contract," appearing as a loanword in Akkadian (see note at **sai-²**). In Indo-Iranian, the word for "contractual partner," *mitra-*, was divinized as the god Mitra, one of the preeminent deities in the pantheon. His name is also one of the earliest Indic words we possess, being found in clay tablets from Anatolia dating to about 1500 BC.

---

mēi- Mild. (Oldest form *meh₁i-*, with variant [metathesized] form *meih₁-*, whence zero-grade *mih₁-*, contracted to *mī-*.) Suffixed zero-grade form *mī-ti-.* MITIGATE, from Latin *mītis*, soft. [Pokorny 7. *mēi-* 711.]

meigh- To urinate. (Oldest form *h₃meiĝh-*.) **1a.** MIST, from Old English *mist*, mist; **b.** MIZZLE¹, from Middle English *misellen*, to drizzle, from a source perhaps akin to Dutch dialectal *mieselen*, to drizzle; **c.** MISSEL THRUSH, MISTLETOE, from Old English *mistel*, mistletoe, from Germanic diminutive form *mihst-ila-*, mistletoe (which is propagated through the droppings of the missel thrush). **a–c** all from Germanic suffixed form *mih-stu-*, urine, hence mist, fine rain. **2.** Suffixed form *migh-tu-.* MICTURATE, from Latin *micturīre*, to want to urinate (desiderative of *meiere*, to urinate). [Pokorny *meigh-* 713.]

meik- Also **meig-**. To mix. (Oldest forms *meiḱ-*, *meiĝ-*.) **1.** Zero-grade variant form *mig-.* AMPHIMIXIS, APOMIXIS, MIGMATITE, PANMIXIA, from Greek *mignunai*, to mix, and noun *mixis* (< *mig-ti-*), a mingling. **2.** Suffixed zero-grade form *mik-sk-.* MEDDLE, MEDLEY, MÉLANGE, MELEE, MESCLUN, MESTIZO, MISCELLANEOUS, MISCIBLE, MIX, MIXTURE, MUSTANG; ADMIX, COMMIX, IMMIX, MISCEGENATION, PELL-MELL, PROMISCUOUS, from Latin *miscēre* (past participle *mixtus*), to mix. **3.** Possibly Germanic *maisk-* (phonological details unclear). MASH, from Old English *māsc-*, *mācs-*, *māx-*, mashed malt. [Pokorny *mei-ḱ-* 714.]

mei-no- Opinion, intention. **1.** MOAN, from Old English *mān*, opinion, complaint, from Germanic *main-*. **2.** MEAN¹; BEMOAN, from Old English *mǣnan*, to signify, tell, complain of, moan, from Germanic *$main$-jan. [Pokorny mei-no- 714.]

mel-¹ Soft; with derivatives referring to soft or softened materials of various kinds.
I. Extended form *$meld$-. **1.** MELT, from Old English $meltan$, to melt, from Germanic *$meltan$. **2.** Possibly Germanic *$miltjam$. MILT, from Old English $milte$, spleen, and Middle Dutch $milte$, milt. **3.** Possibly Germanic *$maltam$. MALT, from Old English $mealt$, malt. **4.** Suffixed variant form *$mled$-sno-. BLENNY, from Greek $blennos$, slime, also a name for the blenny. **5.** Suffixed zero-grade form *$ml̥d$-wi-. MOIL, MOJITO, MOLLIFY, MOLLUSK, MOUILLÉ; EMOLLIENT, from Latin $mollis$, soft. **6.** Possibly nasalized variant form *$mlad$-. BLAND, BLANDISH, from Latin $blandus$, smooth, caressing, flattering, soft-spoken.
II. Variant form *$smeld$-. **1.** Germanic *$smelt$-. **a.** SMELT¹, from Middle Dutch or Middle Low German $smelten$, to smelt; **b.** SCHMALTZ, from Old High German $smalz$, animal fat; **c.** SMALT, from Italian $smalto$, enamel, glaze; **d.** ENAMEL, from Old French $esmail$, enamel. **2.** SMELT², from Old English $smelt$, $smylt$, a marine fish, smelt, perhaps from Germanic *$smelt$-.
III. Extended form *$meldh$-. **1a.** MILD, from Old English $milde$, mild; **b.** MILDRED (personal name), from Old English $Mildthrȳth$, "mild strength" ($thrȳth$, strength). Both **a** and **b** from Germanic *$mildja$-. **2.** Zero-grade form *$ml̥dh$-, possibly in Greek $maltha$, a mixture of wax and pitch: MALTHA.
IV. Suffixed form *mel-sko-. MULCH, from Old English $mel(i)sc$, $mylsc$, mild, mellow, from Germanic *mil-sk-.
V. Extended form *$ml̥ək$- (oldest form *$ml̥h₂k$-). BONANZA, CHONDROMALACIA, MALACOLOGY, OSTEOMA- LACIA, from Greek $malakos$, soft.
VI. Possibly Celtic *$molto$-, sheep. MUTTON, from Old French $moton$, sheep.
VII. Suffixed zero-grade form *$(ə)ml$-u- (oldest form *$h₂ml$-u-). AMBLYGONITE, AMBLYOPIA, from Greek $amblus$, blunt, dull, dim. [Pokorny 1. mel- 716.]

mel-² Of a darkish color. **1.** MELANO-, MELENA; MELALEUCA, MELANCHOLY, PSILOMELANE, from Greek $melās$, black. **2.** MULLET, from Greek $mullos$, a marine fish. **3.** MULE², from Latin $mulleus$, reddish purple (used only to designate a ceremonial shoe worn by Roman magistrates). **4.** Perhaps Germanic *mal-. MAULSTICK, from Middle Dutch $malen$, to paint. [Pokorny 6. mel- 720.]

mel-³ A limb. MELISMA; ACROMELIC, MELODRAMA, MELODY, from Greek $melos$, limb, hence a musical member or phrase, hence music, song, melody. [Pokorny 5. mel- 720.]

mel-⁴ Strong, great. **1.** Suffixed (comparative) form *mel-yos-. AMELIORATE, MELIORATE, MELIORISM, from Latin $melior$, better. **2.** Possibly suffixed (comparative) zero-grade form *$ml̥$-yes- and derived adjective *$ml̥$-yes-ri-. MULIEBRITY, from Latin $muliebris$, womanly (< *$ml̥$-yes-ri-), akin to $mulier$ (< *$ml̥$-yes-), woman, wife (perhaps < "senior wife," designating the primary spouse of a man at a prehistoric stage of Italic society in which polygyny was practiced). **3.** Suffixed zero-grade form *$ml̥$-to-. MOLTO, MUCHO, MULTI-, MULTITUDE, from Latin $multus$, much, many. [Pokorny 4. mel- 720.]

mel-⁵ False, bad, wrong. **1.** MAL-, MALICE, MALIGN; DISMAL, MALADY, MALARIA, MALEDICT, MALEFACTOR, MALEFIC, MALENTENDU, MALEVOLENCE, MALISON, MALVERSATION, from Latin $malus$, bad, and $male$, ill (> $malignus$, harmful). **2.** Perhaps suffixed zero-grade form *$ml̥$-s-. BLAME, BLASPHEME, from Greek $blasphēmos$, blasphemous, perhaps from *$ml̥s$-$bhā$-mo-, "speaking evil" (*$bhā$-, to speak; see bhā-²). **3.** Suffixed form *mel-yo-. MARKHOR, from Avestan $mairiia$-, treacherous. [Pokorny 2. mel- 719, $mēlo$- 724.]

meldh- To pray, speak words to a deity. Suffixed form *$meldh$-$ā$-. MELD¹, from Old High German $meldōn$, to proclaim, reveal, from Germanic *$meldōn$, from *$meldō$, declaration. [Pokorny 1. $meldh$- 722.]

melə- Also **mel-**. To crush, grind; with derivatives referring to various ground or crumbling substances (such as flour) and to instruments for grinding or crushing (such as millstones). (Oldest form *$melh₂$-.) **1.** O-grade form *mol-. MAELSTROM, from Middle Dutch $malen$, to whirl, from Germanic *mal-. **2.** Full-grade form *mel-iyo-. MEAL¹, from Old English $melu$, meal, from Germanic suffixed form *mel-wa-. **3.** Zero-grade form *$ml̥$-. MOLD³, MOLDER, from Old English $molde$, soil, from Germanic suffixed form *mul-$dō$. Full-grade form *mel-. **a.** MEUNIÈRE, MILL¹, MOLA², MOLAR², MOLE⁴, MOULIN; EMOLUMENT, IMMOLATE, ORMOLU, from Latin $molere$, to grind (grain), and its derivative $mola$, a millstone, mill, coarse meal customarily sprinkled on sacrificial animals; **b.** possible suffixed form *mel-iyo-. MEALIE, MILIARY, MILIUM, MILLET; GROMWELL, from Latin $milium$, millet. **5.** Suffixed variant form *mal-ni-. MALLEABLE, MALLEOLUS, MALLET, MALLEUS, MAUL; PALL-MALL, from Latin $malleus$, hammer, mallet. **6.** Zero-grade form *$ml̥$-. AMYLUM, MYLONITE, from Greek $mulē$, $mulos$, millstone, mill. **7.** Possibly extended form *$mlī$-. BLINI, BLINTZ, from Old Russian $blinŭ$, pancake. [Pokorny 1. mel- 716.]

melg- To rub off; also to milk. (Oldest form *$h₂melg̑$-.) **I. 1.** Zero-grade form *$ml̥g$-. EMULSION, from Latin $mulgēre$, to milk. **2.** Full-grade form *$melg$-. **a.** MILK, from Old English $meolc$, $milc$; **b.** MILCH, from Old English -$milce$, milch, from Germanic suffixed form *$meluk$-ja-, giving milk; **c.** MILCHIG, from Old High German $miluh$, milk. **a–c** all from Germanic *$melkan$, to milk, contaminated with an unrelated noun for milk, cognate with the Greek and Latin forms given in **II** below, to form the blend *$meluk$-.
II. Included here to mark the unexplained fact that no common Indo-European noun for milk can be reconstructed is another root *$g(a)lag$-, *$g(a)lakt$-, milk, found only in: **a.** GALACTIC, GALACTO-, GALAXY; AGALACTIA, POLYGALA, from Greek $gala$ (stem $galakt$-), milk; **b.** LACTATE¹, LACTEAL, LACTESCENT, LACTO-, LATTE, LETTUCE; ARROZ CON LECHE, DULCE DE LECHE, from Latin lac, milk; **c.** the blended Germanic form cited in **I. 2.** above. [Pokorny $mēlg̑$- 722, $glag$- 400.]

melit- Honey. **1a.** HYDROMEL, MARMALADE, MELILOT, MEMBRILLO, OENOMEL, from Greek $meli$ (stem $melit$-), honey; **b.** suffixed form *$melit$-ya. MELISSA (personal name), from Greek (Ionic) $melissa$, honeybee. **2a.** MELLIFEROUS, MELLIFLUOUS, MOLASSES, from Latin mel (stem $mell$-), honey, from *$meld$-, syncopated from *$melid$-; **b.** suffixed zero-grade form *$ml̥d$-to-, "honied." MOUSSE, from Latin $mulsus$, honey-sweet. **3.** MILDEW, from Old English $mildēaw$, honeydew, nectar, from Germanic compound *$melith$-$dauwaz$, honeydew (a substance secreted by aphids on leaves; it was formerly imagined to be distilled from the air like dew; *$dauwaz$, dew; see dheu-²), from *$melith$-. [Pokorny $meli$-t 723.]

melkʷ- To harm. Possibly the source of Kurdish $merg$, death, in $pêshmerga$, one who faces death, peshmerga. See **merk-²**. [Pokorny $melkʷ$- 737.]

[mēlon An apple, or any seed- or pit-bearing fruit. Attic Greek noun (Doric $mālon$), possibly borrowed from a Mediterranean language (compare Hittite $maḫla$-, grapevine, branch). MELON; CHAMOMILE, CHRYSOMELID, MALIC ACID, MARMALADE, MEMBRILLO.]

mēms- Flesh, meat. **1.** Suffixed form *$mēms$-ro-. MEMBER, MEMBRANE, from Latin $membrum$, limb, member. **2.** Suffixed form *$mēms$-no-. MENINX, MYRINGITIS, from Greek $mēninx$, membrane. **3.** Thought by some to come from this root is Latin *mēnsa*, table (? < "food (on a table)"): MESA, MENSA, MENSA, MENSAL; COMMENSAL. [Pokorny *mēmso-* 725.]

men-¹ To think; with derivatives referring to various qualities and states of mind and thought.
I. Zero-grade form **mn̥-*. **1.** Suffixed form **mn̥-ti-*. **a.** MIND, from Old English *gemynd*, memory, mind, from Germanic **ga-mundi-* (**ga-*, collective prefix; see **kom**); **b.** MENTAL¹; AMENTIA, DEMENT, from Latin *mēns* (stem *ment-*), mind; **c.** MENTION, from Latin *mentiō*, remembrance, mention. **2.** Suffixed form **mn̥-to-*. AUTOMATIC, from Greek *-matos*, "willing." **3.** Suffixed form **mn̥-yo-*. **a.** MAENAD, from Greek *mainesthai*, to be mad; **b.** AHRIMAN, from Avestan *mainiiuš*, spirit. **4a.** MANIA, MANIAC, MANIC, from Greek *maniā*, madness; **b.** BALLETOMANE, from Greek *-manēs*, ardent admirer.
II. Full-grade form **men-*. **1.** Suffixed form **men-ti-*. **a.** MINNESINGER, from Old High German *minna*, love; **b.** MINIKIN, from Middle Dutch *minne*, love. Both **a** and **b** from Germanic **minthjō*. **2a.** MEMENTO, from Latin reduplicated form *meminisse*, to remember; **b.** COMMENT, from Latin *comminīscī*, to contrive by thought (*com-*, intensive prefix; see **kom**); **c.** REMINISCENT, from Latin *reminīscī*, to recall, recollect (*re-*, again, back; see **re-**); **d.** possibly Latin *Minerva*, name of the goddess of wisdom: MINERVA. **3a.** MENTOR, from Greek *Mentōr*, Mentor, man's name (probably meaning "adviser"); **b.** -MANCY, MANTIC, MANTIS, from Greek *mantis*, seer (vocalism obscure). **4.** MANDARIN, MANTRA, from Sanskrit *mantraḥ*, counsel, prayer, hymn. **5.** Suffixed form *men-es-*. EUMENIDES, from Greek *menos*, spirit.
III. O-grade form **mon-*. **1.** Suffixed (causative) form **mon-eyo-*. MONISH, MONITION, MONITOR, MONSTER, MONUMENT, MUSTER; ADMONISH, DEMONSTRATE, PREMONITION, SUMMON, from Latin *monēre*, to remind, warn, advise. **2.** Suffixed o-grade form **mon-twa*. MOSAIC, MUSE, MUSEUM, MUSIC, from Greek *Mousa*, a Muse.
IV. Extended form **mnā-* (contracted from **mnah₂-*, colored from oldest form **mneh₂-*). **1.** AMNESIA, AMNESTY, ANAMNESIS, from Greek reduplicated form *mimnēskein*, to remember. **2.** MNEMONIC, from Greek *mnēmōn*, mindful. **3.** MNEMOSYNE, from Greek *mnēmē*, memory.
V. Suffixed form **men-s* (zero-grade **mn̥-s*), mind, in Indo-European verb phrase **mens dhē-*, "to set mind" (**dhē-*, to put; see **dhē-**), underlying compound noun **mn̥s-dhē-*. AHURA MAZDA, MAZDAISM, ORMAZD, from Avestan *mazdā-*, wise. [Pokorny 3. *men-* 726, *mendh-* 730.]

men-² To project. **1.** Suffixed zero-grade form **mn̥-to-* in a western Indo-European word for a projecting body part, variously "chin, jaw, mouth." **a.** MOUTH, from Old English *mūth*, mouth, from Germanic **munthaz*; **b.** MENTAL², from Latin *mentum*, chin. **2.** MENACE, MINACIOUS; AMENABLE, DEMEAN¹, PROMENADE, from Latin *minae*, projecting points, threats. **3.** EMINENT, IMMINENT, PROMINENT, PROMONTORY, from Latin *-minēre*, to project, jut, threaten. **4.** Suffixed o-grade form **mon-ti-*. MONS, MONTAGNARD, MONTANE, MONTE, MONTICULE, MOUNT¹, MOUNT²; MOUNTAIN; AMOUNT, ULTRAMONTANE, from Latin *mōns* (stem *mont-*), mountain. [Pokorny 1. *men-* 726, 2. *menth-* 732.]

men-³ To remain. Variant suffixed (stative) form **man-ē-*. MANOR, MANSE, MANSION, MÉNAGE; IMMANENT, PERMANENT, REMAIN, from Latin *manēre*, to remain. [Pokorny 5. *men-* 729.]

men-⁴ Small, isolated. **1.** MANOMETER, from Greek *manos*, rare, sparse. **2.** Suffixed o-grade form **monwo-*. MONAD, MONASTERY, MONK, MONO-; PSEUDOMONAD, from Greek *monos*, alone, single, sole. **3.** Possibly also suffixed form **men-i-*, a small fish. MINNOW, from Middle English *meneu*, a small fish, from

a source akin to Old English *myne*, *mynwe*, minnow. [Pokorny 4. *men-* 728, *mₑni-* 731.]

-men- Ablaut variants **-mon-*, **-mn̥-*. Suffix forming nouns and adjectives, as in **krei-men-*, a judging (see **krei-**). [Not in Pokorny.]

mend- Physical defect, fault. **1.** MENDICANT; AMEND, EMEND, MEND, from Latin *mendum*, *menda*, defect, fault. **2.** MENDACIOUS, from Latin *mendāx*, lying, liar. [Pokorny *mend(ā)* 729.]

mendh-¹ To learn. Zero-grade form **mn̥dh-*. MATHEMATICAL, MATHEMATICS; CHRESTOMATHY, POLYMATH, from Greek *manthanein* (aorist stem *math-*), to learn. [Pokorny *mendh-* 730.]

mendh-² To chew. **1.** MANDIBLE, MANGE, MANGER; BLANCMANGE, from Latin *mandere*, to chew. **2.** Zero-grade form **mn̥dh-*. **a.** MASSETER, from Greek *masāsthai*, to chew (< **math-ya-*); **b.** MOSTACCIOLI, MUSTACHE, from Greek (Doric) *mustax*, upper lip, mustache, expressive word modeled on *mastax*, mouth; **c.** MASTICATE, from Greek *mastikhān*, to grind the teeth. [Pokorny 2. *menth-* 732.]

menegh- Copious. MANY, from Old English *manig*, *mænig*, many, from Germanic **managa-*. [Pokorny *men(e)gh-* 730.]

mer-¹ To flicker; with derivatives referring to dim states of illumination. **1.** Suffixed form **mer-o-*. MERE¹, from Latin *merus*, pure, unadulterated (< "unmixed wine"). **2.** Extended form **merk-*. **a.** MORN, MORNING, MORROW, from Old English *morgen*, morning; **b.** MORGEN, from Middle Dutch *morghen*, morning; **c.** MORGANATIC, from Old High German *morgan*, morning. **a–c** all from Germanic **murgana-*. **3.** Possibly extended root **mergʷ-*. **a.** Suffixed form **mergʷ-o-*. MURK, from Old English *mirce*, darkness, from Germanic **merkwia-*, twilight. **b.** Suffixed o-grade form **morgʷo-iyo-*. MOLYBDENUM, from Greek *molubdos*, lead, probably from Lydian *mariwda*, dark, black (lead being "the dark metal"). [Pokorny 2. *mer-* 733.]

mer-² To rub away, harm.
I. 1. NIGHTMARE, from Old English *mare*, *mære*, goblin, incubus, from Germanic **marōn-*, goblin. **2.** MARASMUS; AMARANTH, from Greek *marainein*, to waste away, wither. **3.** Probably suffixed zero-grade form **mr̥-to-*, "ground down." MORTAR, from Latin *mortārium*, mortar. **4.** Possibly extended root **merd-*. MORDACIOUS, MORDANT, MORDENT, MORSEL; PREMORSE, REMORSE, from Latin *mordēre*, to bite. **5.** Possibly suffixed form **mor-bho-*. MORBID, from Latin *morbus*, disease (but this is more likely of unknown origin).
II. Possibly the same root is **mer-*, "to die," with derivatives referring to death and to human beings as subject to death. **1.** Zero-grade form **mr̥-*. **a.** Suffixed form **mr̥-tro-*. MURDER, from Old English *morthor*, murder, from Germanic suffixed form **mur-thra-*; **b.** suffixed form **mr̥-ti-*. MORT¹, MORTAL; AMORTIZE, MORTIFY, POSTMORTEM, from Latin *mors* (stem *mort-*), death; **c.** suffixed form **mr̥-yo-*. MORIBUND, MORTGAGE, MORTMAIN, MORTUARY, MURRAIN, from Latin *morī*, to die, with irregular past participle *mortuus* (< **mr̥-two-*), replacing older **mr̥-to-* (for which see **d**); **d.** prefixed and suffixed form **n̥-mr̥-to-*, "undying, immortal." (**n̥-*, negative prefix; see **ne**). (i) IMMORTAL, from Latin *immortālis*, immortal; (ii) AMBROSIA, from Greek *ambrotos*, immortal, divine (*a-* + *-mbrotos*, brotos, mortal); (iii) AMRITA, from Sanskrit *amr̥tam*, immortality (*a-* + *mr̥ta-*, dead). **2.** Suffixed o-grade form **mor-t-yo-*. MANTICORE, from Greek *mantikhōras* (corrupted from *marti(o)khōras*), manticore, probably from Iranian compound **martiya-khvāra-*, "man-eater" (**khvāra-*, eating; see **swel-¹**), from Old Persian *martiya-*, a mortal man. [Pokorny 4. *mer-*, 5. *mer-* 735.] See also extended root **smerd-**.

merə- To hinder, delay. (Oldest form *merh₂-.) MORA, MORATORIUM, MORATORY; DEMUR, REMORA, from Latin *mora*, a delay. [In Pokorny (s)mer- 969.]

merg- Boundary, border. (Oldest form *merǵ-.) **1a.** MARK¹, from Old English *mearc*, boundary, landmark, sign, trace; **b.** MARGRAVE, from Middle Dutch *marc*, border; **c.** MARCH², MARQUEE, MARQUIS, MARQUISE, from Old French *marc*, *marche*, border country; **d.** MARCHESE, MARCHIONESS, from Medieval Latin *marca*, boundary, border; **e.** DEMARCATION, from Old Italian *marcare*, to mark out; **f.** MARK², from Old English *marc*, a mark of weight or money; **g.** MARKKA, from Swedish *mark*, a mark of money; **h.** MARKA, from Middle High German *marke*, mark of money. **a–h** all from Germanic *mark-, boundary, border territory; also to mark out a boundary by walking around it (ceremonially "beating the bounds"); also a landmark, boundary marker, and a mark in general (and in particular a mark on a metal currency bar, hence a unit of currency); these various meanings are widely represented in Germanic descendants and in Romance borrowings. **2.** LETTERS OF MARQUE, MARQUETRY; REMARK, from Old Norse *merki*, a mark, from Germanic *markja-, mark, border. **3.** MARC, MARCH¹, from Frankish *markōn*, to mark out, from Germanic denominative verb *markōn. **4.** MARGIN; EMARGINATE, from Latin *margō*, border, edge. **5.** Celtic variant form *mrog-, territory, land. CYMRY, from Welsh *Cymro*, Wales, from British Celtic *kom-brogos*, fellow countryman (*kom-, collective prefix; see **kom**), from *brogos, district. [Pokorny mereǵ- 738.]

mergh- To wet, sprinkle, rain. Variant form *mregh-. EMBROCATE, from Greek *brekhein*, to wet. [Pokorny meregh- 738.]

merk-¹ To decay. MARCESCENT, from Latin *marcēre*, to decay, wither. [Pokorny 1. merk- 739.]

merk-² To cut up, injure (?). Possibly the source from Kurdish *pêšmerge*, one who faces death, peshmerga, from *merg*, death (*pêš*, in front of, before; see **poti**), from Old Iranian *mṛka-, death (Avestan *mahrka-*): PESHMERGA. Others have seen the source of Old Iranian *mṛka- in a root *melkʷ-, also seen in Greek *blaptein* (< *mlkʷ-ye-), to harm, injure; since the roots *merk- amd *melkʷ- would fall together as *mark- in Indo-Iranian, the attested Indo-Iranian forms may present a blending of the two roots. [Not in Pokorny; compare Hittite *mark-, to cut up.]

[merk-³ Italic root, possibly from Etruscan, referring to aspects of commerce. **1.** MARKET, MART, MERCER, MERCHANT; COMMERCE, from Latin *merx*, merchandise, and derivative *mercārī*, to trade. **2.** MERCENARY, MERCY, from Latin *mercēs*, pay, reward, price. **3.** Probably Latin *Mercurius*, the god of (inter alia) commerce: MERCURY. [In Pokorny merk- 739.]]

[merph- Form. Greek root of unknown origin. **1.** Suffixed o-grade form *morph-. -MORPH, MORPHEME, MORPHO-, MORPHOSIS, from Greek *morphē*, form, beauty, outward appearance. **2.** FORM, -FORM, FORMAL, FORMANT, FORMAT, FORMULA; CONFORM, DEFORM, FIRMER CHISEL, INFORM, PLATFORM, REFORM, TRANSFORM, UNIFORM, from Latin *fōrma*, form, shape, contour, apearance, beauty, possibly borrowed from Greek *morphē* via Etruscan. [In Pokorny 2. mer- 733.]]

mers- To trouble, confuse. Suffixed o-grade form *mors-eyo-. MAR, from Old English *merran*, *mierran*, to impede, from Germanic *marzjan. [In Pokorny 6. mer- 737.]

meuə-¹ To push away. MOB, MOBILE, MOMENT, MOMENTOUS, MOMENTUM, MOSSO, MOTIF, MOTION, MOTIVE, MOTOR, MOVE, MOVEMENT; COMMOTION, EMOTION, PROMOTE, REMOTE, REMOVE, from Latin *movēre*, to move. [Pokorny 2. meu- 743.]

meuə-² Abundant, reproductively powerful. A root found in Anatolian, Greek, Latin, and Irish. (Oldest form *meuh₁- or *meuh₃-.) Suffixed zero-grade form *mū-ri- (< *muə-ri-), abundance, in possessive derivative form *mūri-o-, "having abundance," abundant. MYRIAD, from Greek *mūrios*, countless. [Not in Pokorny; compare Hittite *mūri-, cluster of grapes, Hittite (from Luvian) *mūwa-, power (< "that comes from or results in abundance"), Latin *mūtō, penis, and Middle Irish *moth*, penis.]

meuə-³ To be silent. (Oldest form *meuh₂-.) **1.** Zero-grade form *mū- (< *muə-). MUTE, from Latin *mūtus*, silent, dumb. **2.** MIOSIS, MYSTERY¹, MYSTIC, MYOPIA, from Greek *mūein*, to close the eyes (< "to close the lips"). **3.** MUM, independent creation imitative of the vocal gesture of closing the lips. [Pokorny 1. mū- 751.]

meug- Slimy, slippery; with derivatives referring to various wet or slimy substances and conditions. Related to **meus-**. **1.** Nasalized zero-grade form *mu-n-g-. EMUNCTORY, from Latin *mungere*, to blow the nose. **2.** Possibly Germanic *(s)muk-, referring to wetness and also to figurative slipperiness. **a.** SMOCK, from Old English *smoc*, shirt; **b.** SMUG, from Middle Low German *smucken*, to adorn (< "to make sleek"); **c.** SCHMUCK, from Middle High German *smuck*, "clothing," adornment, jewels; **d.** MUGGY, from Middle English *muggen*, to drizzle, from a source akin to Old Norse *mugga*, drizzle; **e.** SMUGGLE, from Low German *smukkelen, smuggeln*, to smuggle (< "to slip contraband through"); **f.** MOLD², from Middle English *molde*, mold, from a source akin to Old Norse *mygla*, mold, mildew. **3.** MEEK, from Old Norse *mjūkr*, soft, from Germanic *meuk-. **4.** Variant form *meuk-. MOIST, MUCILAGE, MUCO-, MUCUS, MUSTY, from Latin *mūcus*, mucus. **5.** Zero-grade form *muk-. **a.** -MYCETE, MYCO-; SACCHAROMYCES, STREPTOMYCES, STREPTOMYCIN, from Greek *mukēs*, fungus, mushroom; **b.** suffixed form *muk-so-. MATCH², MYXO-, from Greek *muxa*, mucus, lamp wick (< "nozzle of a lamp" < "nostril"). [Pokorny 2. meug- 744.]

meus- Damp; with derivatives referring to swampy ground and vegetation and to figurative qualities of wetness. Related to **meug-**. **1a.** MOSS, from Old English *mos*, bog; **b.** LITMUS, from Middle Dutch *mos*, moss, and from a Scandinavian source akin to Old Norse *mosi*, bog, moss. Both **a** and **b** from Germanic *meus-, *mus-. **2.** MIRE; QUAGMIRE, from Old Norse *mȳrr*, bog, from Germanic suffixed form *meuz-i-. **3.** Suffixed zero-grade form *mus-to-. MUST³, MUSTARD, from Latin *mustus*, new, newborn (< "wet"). **4.** Possibly suffixed zero-grade form *mus-so-. MYSOPHOBIA, from Greek *musos*, uncleanness. [Pokorny 1. meu- 741.]

mezg-¹ To dip, plunge. MERGE; DEMERSAL, EMERGE, IMMERSE, SUBMERGE, from Latin *mergere*, to dip, dive. **2.** MERGANSER, from Latin *mergus*, diver (water bird). [Pokorny 1. mezg- 745.]

mezg-² To knit. MESH, from Middle Dutch *masche*, *maesche*, knitted fabric, from Germanic *mēsk-. [Pokorny 2. mezg- 746.]

[mittere To let go, send off, throw. Latin verb of unclear origin and formation; oldest form probably *smittere (in archaic spelling *cosmittere* of Classical Latin compound *committere*, to bring together). MASS, MESS, MESSAGE, MISSILE, MISSION, MISSIVE; ADMIT, CHRISTMAS, COMMIT, COMPROMISE, DEMIT, DISMISS, EMIT, INTERMIT, INTROMIT, LAMMAS, MARTINMAS, MICHAELMAS, OMIT, PERMIT, PREMISE, PRETERMIT, PROMISE, REMIT, SUBMIT, SURMISE, TRANSMIT. [In Pokorny *smeit- 968.]]

mizdho- Reward. MEED, from Old English *mēd*, reward, compensation, meed, from West Germanic *mēdō-, from Germanic *mizdō. [Pokorny mizdhó- 746.]

-mno- Suffix forming passive participles to verbs, such as *al-o-mno-*, being nourished (see **al-³**). [Not in Pokorny.]

mō- To exert oneself. (Oldest form *meh₃-*, colored to *moh₃-*, contracted to *mō-*.) Suffixed form *mō-l-*. MOLE³, MOLECULE, MOLEST; DEMOLISH, from Latin *mōlēs*, heavy bulk, mass, massive structure, and irregular derivative *molestus*, labored, difficult, troublesome. [Pokorny *mō-* 746.]

-mo- Adjective and noun suffix, appearing ultimately in English -ISM, from Greek *-ismos*, abstract noun suffix to verbs in stem *-id-*. [Not in Pokorny.]

mōd- To meet, assemble. (Oldest form *meh₃d-*, colored to *moh₃d-*, contracted to *mōd-*.) **1.** MEET¹, from Old English *mētan*, to meet, from Germanic *mōtjan*. **2.** MOOT; FOLKMOOT, GEMOT, WITENAGEMOT, from Old English *mōt*, *gemōt*, meeting, moot, assembly, council (*ge-*, together; see **kom**), from Germanic *mōta-*. **3.** Perhaps suffixed zero-grade form *mədtlo-*. **a.** MELVIN (personal name), from Old English *Mǣlwine*, "friend of the council" (*wine*, friend; see **wen-¹**), from *mǣl*, council; **b.** MAIL³; BLACKMAIL, BOKMÅL, RIKSMÅL, from Old Norse *māl*, speech, agreement. Both **a** and **b** from Germanic *mathla-*. [Pokorny *mōd-* 746.]

modhro- A color. MADDER¹, from Old English *mædere*, madder, from Germanic *madraz*. [Pokorny *modhro-* 747.]

molko- Skin bag. MAIL¹, from Old French *male*, bag, from a Germanic source akin to Old High German *malha*, pouch, bag, from Germanic *malhō*. [Pokorny *molko-* 747.]

mon- Neck, nape of the neck. **1.** MANE, from Old English *manu*, mane, from Germanic *manō*. **2a.** MONILIFORM, from Latin *monīle*, necklace. **b.** Possibly the Latin divine epithet *Monēta* in the name Jūnō *Monēta* (the form of Juno in whose temple in Rome coins were struck), if originally meaning "wearing a necklace"; compare the Norse goddess *Menglödh*, literally "rejoicing in her necklace," and the Norse myth in which Freya, the goddess of love, obtains a beautiful necklace after agreeing to lie with the dwarfs who have fashioned it: MINT¹, MONEY. [Pokorny *mono-* 747.]

mori- Body of water; lake (?), sea (?). **1a.** MERE²; MERMAID, from Old English *mere*, sea, lake, pond; **b.** MARRAM GRASS, from a Scandinavian source akin to Old Norse *marálmr*, beach grass, from *marr*, sea (*hálmr*, straw; see **kolə-mo-**); **c.** MEERSCHAUM, from Old High German *mari*, sea; **d.** MEERKAT, from Middle Dutch *meer*, sea. **a–d** all from Germanic *mari-*. **2a.** MARSH, from Old English *mersc*, *merisc*, marsh; **b.** MORASS, from Old French *maresc*, *mareis*, marsh. Both **a** and **b** from Germanic *mariska-*, water-logged land. **3.** MAAR, MARE²; MARINARA, MARINE, MARITIME; BÊCHE-DE-MER, CORMORANT, MARICULTURE, ORMER, ULTRAMARINE, from Latin *mare*, sea. **4.** MURIEL (personal name), from a Celtic source akin to Gaelic *Muirgheal*, "sea-bright," from Old Irish *muir*, sea (*gheal*, bright, from Old Irish *gel*; see **gel-¹**). [Pokorny *mori* 748.]

moro- Blackberry, mulberry. **1.** SYCAMORE, from Greek *sūkomoros*, an African fig tree, probably borrowed from Semitic but folk-etymologized under the influence of Greek *moron*, mulberry. **2.** MORULA, MURREY; MULBERRY, from Latin *mōrum*, mulberry (probably from Greek *moron*). [Pokorny *moro-* 749.]

morwi- Ant. **1.** PISMIRE, from Middle English *mire*, ant, from a Scandinavian source akin to Danish *myre*, ant, from Germanic variant form *meur-*. **2.** Variant form *morm-*. **a.** MYRMECO-, from Greek *murmēx*, ant; **b.** FORMIC, FORMICARY; FORMICIVOROUS, from Latin *formīca*, ant (with dissimilation). [Pokorny *moru̯ī-* 749.]

mozgho- Marrow. MARROW, from Old English *mærg*, *mærh*, marrow, from Germanic *mazgō*. [Pokorny *moz-g-o-* 750.]

mregh-m(n)o- Brain. **1.** BRAIN, from Old English *brægen*, brain, from Germanic *brag-na-*. **2.** BREGMA, from Greek *bregma*, the front part of the head. [Pokorny *mregh-m(n)o-* 750.]

mregh-u- Short. (Oldest form *mreĝh-u-*.) **I.** Suffixed form *mregh-wi-*. BRIEF, BRUMAL; ABBREVIATE, ABRIDGE, from Latin *brevis*, short. **II.** Zero-grade form *mr̥ghu-*. **1a.** MERRY, from Old English *myrge*, *mirige*, pleasant; **b.** MIRTH, from Old English *myrgth*, pleasure, joy, from Germanic *murgithō*, pleasantness. Both **a** and **b** from Germanic *murgja-*, short, also pleasant, joyful. **2.** BRACHY-; AMPHIBRACH, TRIBRACH, from Greek *brakhus*, short. **3.** BRACE, BRACERO, BRACHIUM, BRASSARD, BRASSIERE, PRETZEL; ABRACHIA, EMBRACE, from Greek comparative *brakhiōn*, shorter, hence also "upper arm" (as opposed to the longer forearm). [Pokorny *mreĝhu-* 750.]

mu- Gnat, fly. Imitative root. **1.** MIDGE, from Old English *mycg*, midge, from Germanic *mugjō*. **2.** Suffixed extended form *mus-kā-*. MOSQUITO, MUSCA, MUSCID, MUSCARINE, MUSH², MUSKET, from Latin *musca*, a fly. **3.** Suffixed extended form *mus-ya*. MYIASIS, from Greek *muia*, *mūa*, a fly. [Pokorny 2. *mū-* 752.]

mūs- A mouse; also a muscle (from the resemblance of a flexing muscle to the movements of a mouse). **1.** MOUSE, from Old English *mūs* (plural *mȳs*), mouse, from Germanic *mūs-* (plural *mūsiz*). **2.** MURINE, MUSCLE, MUSSEL, MUSTELID, MUSTELINE, from Latin *mūs*, mouse. **3.** MYELO-, MYO-; EPIMYSIUM, MYOSOTIS, MYSTICETE, PERIMYSIUM, SYRINGOMYELIA, from Greek *mūs*, mouse, muscle. **4.** Perhaps suffixed shortened form *mus-ko-*. MUSCADET, MUSCATEL, MUSK, MUST⁵; NUTMEG, from Sanskrit *muṣkaḥ*, testicle, scrotum (? < "little mouse"). [Pokorny *mūs* 752.]

-n- Verbal infix to form transitive presents. Infixed to verbal root in the zero grade, as in *yu-n-g-*, to yoke (see **yeug-**). Reflected in English in such pairs as *tangible* : *tactile*, where the first word comes from a Latin nasal present and the second from a Latin past participle without the nasal (see **tag-**). [Not in Pokorny.]

nā- To help. (Oldest form *h₃neh₂-*, colored to *h₃nah₂-*, contracted to *h₃nā-*.) JUGGERNAUT, from Sanskrit *nāthate*, he helps, protects (exact preform obscure). [Pokorny 1. *nā-* 754.]

nana Child's word for a nurse or female adult other than its mother. **1.** NANISM, NANO-, from Greek *nanna*, aunt, whence *nannās*, uncle, whence *nannos*, *nānos* "little old man," dwarf. **2.** NUN¹, from Late and Medieval Latin *nonna*, aunt, old woman, nun. **3.** NANA, NANNY, from English baby-talk. [Pokorny *nana* 754.]

nas- Nose. **1.** NOSE, NUZZLE; NOSTRIL, from Old English *nosu*, nose, from Germanic zero-grade form *nusō*. **2.** NESS, from Old English *næss*, headland, from Germanic *nasjaz*. **3.** Lengthened-grade form *nās-*. **a.** NARIS, from Latin *nāris*, nostril; **b.** *expressive* form *nāss-*. NASAL, NASO-; NASTURTIUM, PINCE-NEZ, from Latin *nāsus*, nose. **4.** NARK², from Romany *nāk*, nose, from expressive Indo-Aryan form *nakka-*. [Pokorny *nas-* 755, *neu-ks-* 768.]

nāu-¹ Death; to be exhausted. (Oldest form *neh₂u-*, colored to *nah₂u-*, contracted to *nau-* [before consonants] and *nāw-* [before vowels].) **1.** Suffixed form *nau-ti-*. NEED, from Old English *nēod*, *nēd*, distress, necessity, from Germanic *naudi-*. **2.** Suffixed form *nāw-i-*, corpse. NARWHAL, from Old Norse *nār*, corpse, from Germanic *nāwi-*. **3a.** NUDNIK, from Polish *nuda*, boredom; **b.** NUDGE², from Russian *nudnyī*, tedious. Both **a** and **b** from Slavic suffixed extended form *naud-ā-*. [Pokorny 2. *nāu-* 756.]

nāu-² Boat. (Oldest form *neh₂u-*, colored to *nah₂u-*, contracted to *nau-* [before consonants] and *nāw-* [before vowels].) **1.** NACELLE, NAVAL, NAVE¹, NAVIC-

ULAR, NAVIGATE, NAVY, from Latin *nāvis*, ship. **2.** NAUSEA, NAUTICAL, NAUTILUS, NOISE; AERONAUT, AQUANAUT, ARGONAUT, ASTRONAUT, COSMONAUT, CYBERNAUT, from Greek *naus*, ship, and *nautēs*, sailor. [Pokorny 1. *nāus-* 755.]

ṇdher- Under. **1a.** UNDER, UNDER-, from Old English *under*, under; **b.** U-BOAT, from Old High German *untar*, under. Both **a** and **b** from Germanic *under-*. **2.** INFERIOR, from Latin *īnferus*, lower. **3.** INFERNAL, INFERNO, from Latin *īnfernus*, lower. **4.** INFRA-, from Latin *īnfrā*, below. [Pokorny *ṇdhos* 771.]

ne Not. **1a.** NAUGHT, NAUGHTY, NEITHER, NEVER, NILL, NO[1], NO[2], NONE, NOR[1], NOT, NOTHING, from Old English *ne*, not, and *nā*, no; **b.** NAY, from Old Norse *ne*, not; **c.** NIX[2], from Old High German *ne, ni*, not. **a–c** all from Germanic *ne-, *na-*. **2.** ANNUL, NEFARIOUS, NESCIENCE, NEUTER, NICE, NULL, NULLIFY, NULLIPARA, from Latin *ne-*, not, and *nūllus*, none (*ne- + ūllus*, any; see **oi-no-**). **3.** NIMIETY, from Latin *nimis*, too much, excessively, very (< *ne-mi-s*, "not little"; *mi-*, little; see **mei-²**). **4.** NIHILISM, NIHILITY, NIL; ANNIHILATE, from Latin *nihil, nīl*, nothing, contracted from *nihilum*, nothing (< *ne-hīlum*, "not a whit, nothing at all"; *hīlum*, a thing, trifle; *origin unknown*). **5.** NON-; NONPLUS, NONSUIT, from Latin *nōn*, not (< *ne-oinom*, not one thing"; *oino-*, one; see **oi-no-**). **6.** NISI, from Latin *nisi*, unless, from Archaic Latin *nesei* (*sei*, if; see **swo-**). **7a.** NEGLECT, NEGLIGEE, NEGOTIATE, from Latin prefix *neg-*, not; **b.** NEGATE; ABNEGATE, DENY, RENEGADE, RENEGE, from Latin *negāre*, to deny. Both **a** and **b** from Italic *nek*, not. **8.** NEPENTHE, from Greek *nē-*, not. **9.** Zero-grade combining form *ṇ-*. **a.** (*i*) UN-¹, from Old English *un-*, not; (*ii*) ZUG- UNRUHE, from Old High German *un-*, not. Both (*i*) and (*ii*) from Germanic *un-*; **b.** IN-¹, from Latin *in-*, not; **c.** A-¹, AN-, from Greek *a-, an-*, not; **d.** AHIMSA, from Sanskrit *a-, an-*, not; **e.** compound *ṇ-mṛ-to-* (see **mer-²**). [Pokorny 1. *nē* 756.]

nebh- Cloud. **1.** Suffixed form *nebh-(e)lo-*. **a.** NIFLHEIM, from Old Norse *nifl-*, "mist" or "dark," probably from Germanic *nibilaz*; **b.** NIBELUNG, from Old High German *Nibulunc, Nibilung*, from Germanic suffixed patronymic form *nibul-unga-*, beside Old High German *nebul*, mist, fog, from Germanic *neb- laz.* **2.** Suffixed form *nebh-elā-*. **a.** NEBULA, NEBULOUS, from Latin *nebula*, cloud; **b.** NEPHELINE, NEPHELOMETER, from Greek *nephelē*, cloud. **3.** Suffixed form *nebh-es-*. NEPHOLOGY, from Greek *nephos*, cloud. **4.** Nasalized form *ne-m-bh-*. NIMBUS, from Latin *nimbus*, rain, cloud, aura. [Pokorny 2. (*enebh-*) 315.]

ned- To bind, tie. **1.** O-grade form *nod-*. **a.** NET¹, from Old English *net(t)*, a net, from Germanic *nati-*; **b.** NETTLE, from Old English *netel(e), netle*, nettle, from Germanic *nat-ilōn-*, a nettle (nettles or plants of closely related genera such as hemp were used as a source of fiber); **c.** OUCH², from Anglo-Norman *nouch*, brooch, from Germanic *nat-sk-*. **2.** Lengthened o-grade form *nōdo-*. NODE, NODULE, NODUS, NOIL, NOOSE; DENOUEMENT, from Latin *nōdus*, a knot. **3.** With re-formation of the root. NEXUS; ADIPONECTIN, ADNEXA, ANNEX, CONNECT, FIBRONECTIN, from Latin *nectere* (past participle *nexus*), to tie, bind, connect. [Pokorny 1. *ned-* 758.]

negʷh-ro- Kidney. NEPHRO-, NEPHRON; MESONEPHROS, METANEPHROS, PERINEPHRIUM, PRONEPHROS, from Greek *nephros*, kidney. [In Pokorny *engʷ-* 319.]

nei- To be excited, shine. **1.** Suffixed zero-grade form *ni-to-*. NATTY, NEAT¹, NET², NIT², from Latin *nitēre*, to shine. **2.** Possibly suffixed form *nei-t-slo-*. NEIL (personal name), from Old Irish *níall*, brave. **3.** Possibly Sanskrit *nīla-*, dark blue: LILAC; ANIL, NILGAI. [Pokorny 2. *nei-* 760.]

neiə- To lead. NAINSOOK, from Sanskrit *nayati*, he leads. [Pokorny 1. *nei-* 760.]

neigʷ- To wash. NIX¹, from Old High German *nihhus*, river monster, water spirit, from Germanic *nikwiz*, *nikuz*. [Pokorny *neigʷ-* 761.]

nek-¹ Death. (Oldest form *neḱ-.) **1.** INTERNECINE, PERNICIOUS, from Latin *nex* (stem *nec-*), death. **2.** Suffixed (causative) o-grade form *nok-eyo-*. NOCENT, NOCUOUS, NUISANCE; INNOCENT, INNOCUOUS, from Latin *nocēre*, to injure, harm. **3.** Suffixed o-grade form *nok-s-*. NOXIOUS; OBNOXIOUS, from Latin *noxa*, injury, hurt, damage entailing liability. **4.** Suffixed full-grade form *nek-ro-*. NECRO-, NECROSIS; NECROMANCY, from Greek *nekros*, corpse. **5.** NECTAR, NECTARINE, from Greek *nektar*, the drink of the gods, "overcoming death" (*tar-*, overcoming; see **terə-²**). [Pokorny *nek-* 762.]

nek-² To reach, attain. (Oldest form *h₂neḱ-.) O-grade form *nok-*. ENOUGH, from Old English *genōg*, enough, from Germanic *ganōga-*, sufficient, from *ga-nah*, "suffices" (*ga-*, intensive prefix; see **kom**). [Pokorny *eneḱ-* 316.]

nek-³ To bring. (Oldest form *h₁neḱ-.) Variant form *enk-*. **1.** ONCOGENESIS, ONCOLITE, ONCOLOGY, from Greek reduplicated *enenkein*, to carry (suppletive aorist of *pherein*, to carry; see **bher-¹**), with derived noun *onkos*, a burden, mass, hence a tumor (from suffixed o-grade form *onk-o-*; see **2** below). **2.** Suffixed o-grade form *onk-o-*, perhaps in Sanskrit *aṁśaḥ*, part, portion: PAISA, PICE. **3.** Compound root *bhrenk-* (see **bher-¹**). [Pokorny *enek-* 316.]

nekʷ-t- Night. Probably from a verbal root *negʷ-*, to be dark, be night. O-grade form *nokʷ-t-*. **1a.** NIGHT, FORTNIGHT, from Old English *niht, neaht*, night; **b.** KRISTALLNACHT, from Old High German *naht*, night. Both **a** and **b** from Germanic *naht-*. **2.** NOCTI-, NOCTURN, NOCTURNAL, EQUINOX, from Latin *nox* (stem *noct-*), night. **3.** NOCTUID, NOCTULE, from Latin *noctua*, night owl. **4.** NIX; NYCTALOPIA, NYCTINASTY, from Greek *nux* (stem *nukt-*), night. **5.** Perhaps zero-grade form *ṇkʷ-t-*. ACTINIUM, ACTINO-, from Greek *aktīs* (stem *aktīn-*), ray, traditionally taken as from *ṇkʷ-t-*. This derivation is supported by the Sanskrit cognate *aktúḥ*, meaning both "ray" and "night," but has recently contested in favor of a derivation from **ak-**, "sharp," the rays of the sun originally having been conceived of as a pointed weapon. If the oldest meaning of *nekʷ-t-* is "twilight," however, the traditional derivation of Greek *aktīs*, from *ṇkʷ-t-* can be upheld if the Greek word is considered to have originally referred to the rays of the sun seen in the morning and evening twilight. The night itself would then have originally been designated in Proto-Indo-European by *kʷsep-*, seen for example in Hittite (*i*)*špant-* (< *kʷsp-ent-*, with simplification of the initial cluster) and in Sanskrit *kṣap*, both meaning "night." **6.** Suffixed plain verbal root *negʷ-ro-*, dark. NEGRO, NIELLO, NIGELLA, NIGRESCENCE, NIGROSINE, NOIR; DENIGRATE, PINOT NOIR, from Latin *niger*, black. [Pokorny *nekʷ-(t-)* 762.]

nem- To assign, allot; also to take. **1a.** NUMB; BENUMB, from Old English *niman*, to take, seize; **b.** NIMBLE, from Old English *nǣmel*, quick to seize, and *numol*, quick at learning, seizing; **c.** NIM², from Old High German *nëman*, to take. **a–c** all from Germanic *neman*, to take. **2.** NEMESIS; ECONOMY, from Greek *nemein*, to allot. **3.** Suffix form *nem-os*. NAMASKAR, NAMASTE, from Sanskrit *namaḥ* (stem *namas-*), obeisance (< "due portion, due reverence"). **4.** O-grade form *nom-*. **a.** NOME, -NOMY; ANOMIE, ANTINOMIAN, ANTINOMY, ASTRONOMER, ASTRONOMY, AUTONOMOUS, CHIRONOMID, DEUTERONOMY, METRONOME, NOMOGRAPH, NOMOLOGY, NOMOTHETIC, NUMISMATIC, from Greek *nomos*, portion, usage, custom, law, division, district; **b.** NOMA, from Greek *nomē*, pasturage, grazing, hence a spreading, a spreading ulcer; **c.** NOMAD, from Greek *nomas*, wandering in search of pasture; **d.** NUMMULAR, NUMMULITE, from Greek *nomimos*, legal.

5. Perhaps suffixed o-grade form *nom-eso-. NUMBER, NUMERAL; ENUMERATE, INNUMERABLE, SUPERNUMERARY, from Latin *numerus*, number, division. [Pokorny 1. *nem-* 763.]

nepōt- Grandson, nephew. Feminine *neptī-. NEPHEW, NEPOTISM, NIECE, from Latin *nepōs*, grandson, nephew, and *neptis*, granddaughter, niece. [Pokorny *nepōt-* 764.]

ner-¹ Under, also on the left; hence, with an eastward orientation, north. Suffixed zero-grade form *nr̥-t(r)o-. **1.** NORDIC, NORTH, NORTEÑO, from Old English *north*, north. **2.** NORTHERN, from Old English *northerne*, northern. **3.** NORSE, from Middle Dutch *nort*, north. **4.** NORMAN¹, NORWEGIAN, from Old Norse *nordhr*, north. **1–4** all from Germanic *northa-*. [Pokorny 2. *ner-* 765.] Compare **deks-**.

ner-² Man; basic sense "vigorous, vital, strong." (Oldest form *h₂ner-*.) **1a.** ANDRO-, -ANDROUS, -ANDRY; PHILANDER, from Greek *anēr* (stem *andr-*, from zerograde form *anr̥-*), man; **b.** Greek combining form *andro-*, *-andros*, man, hero, in personal names: (*i*) ANDROMEDA, from Greek *Andromedā*, feminine of *Andromedos*, probably "ruling over men" (*-medos*, from *medein*, to rule over; see **med-**); (*ii*) ALEXANDER, ALEXANDRINE, ALEXANDRITE, from Greek *Alexandros*, "defender of men" (*alex-*, from *alexein*, to defend; see **lek-**); (*iii*) LYSANDER, from Greek *Lūsandros*, "releasing men" (*lūs-*, from *lūein*, to release; see **leu-¹**). **2.** Italic *ner-*, magistrate, "strongman," base of the Latin name *Nerō: NERO. [Pokorny 1. *ner-(t-)* 765.]

nes-¹ To return safely home. **1.** HARNESS, from Old French *harneis*, harness, possibly from a Germanic source akin to Old English, Old High German (in composition), and Old Norse *nest*, food for a journey, from Germanic *nes-tam*. **2.** Suffixed o-grade form *nos-to-*. NOSTALGIA, from Greek *nostos*, a return home. [Pokorny *nes-* 766.]

nes-² Oblique cases of the personal pronoun of the first person plural. For the nominative see **we-**. **1.** Zerograde form *n̥s-*. US, from Old English *ūs*, us (accusative), from Germanic *uns*. **2.** Suffixed (*possessive*) zero-grade form *n̥s-ero-*. OUR, OURS, from Old English *ūser*, *ūre*, our, from Germanic *unsara-*. **3.** O-grade form *nos-*, with suffixed (*possessive*) form *nos-t(e)ro-*. NOSTRATIC, NOSTRUM; PATERNOSTER, from Latin *nōs*, we, and *noster*, our. [Pokorny 3. *ne-* 758.]

nē-tr- Snake. (Contracted from earlier *neh₁-tr-*.) ADDER, from Old English *nǣdre*, snake, from Germanic *nēthrō*. [Pokorny *nē-tr* 767.]

neu-¹ To shout. Suffixed (participial) o-grade form *now-ent-(yo-)*, "shouting." NUNCIO; ANNOUNCE, DENOUNCE, ENUNCIATE, INTERNUNCIO, PRONOUNCE, RENOUNCE, from Latin *nūntius*, "announcing," hence a messenger, also a message, and *nūntium*, message. [Pokorny 1. *neu-* 767.]

neu-² To nod. **1.** NUTATION; INNUENDO, from Latin *nuere*, to nod (attested only in compounds), and frequentative *nutāre*, to nod. **2.** Suffixed form *neu-men-*. NUMEN, from Latin *nūmen*, "a nod," hence "command," divine power, deity. [Pokorny 2. *neu-* 767.]

neud- To make use of, enjoy. **1.** NEAT², from Old English *nēat*, bovine animal. **2a.** MATELOTE, from Middle Dutch *ghenōt*, *noot*, fellow; **b.** HUGUENOT, from Old High German *ginōz*, companion. Both **a** and **b** from Germanic compound *ga-nautaz*, *ga-nautō-*, "he with whom one shares possessions," companion, fellow (*ga-*, with; see **kom**). Both **1** and **2** from Germanic *nautam*, "thing of value, possession." [Pokorny *neu-d-* 768.]

newn̥ Nine. **1.** NINE, NINETEEN, NINETY, NINTH, from Old English *nigon*, nine, with derivatives *nigontig*, ninety, and *nigontēne*, nineteen (*-tēne*, ten; see **dekm̥**), from Germanic *nigun* and derivatives of *niwun*. **2.** NOVEMBER, NOVENA; NONAGENARIAN, from Latin *novem*, nine (< *noven*, with *m* for *n* by analogy with the *m* of

septem, seven, and *decem*, ten). **3.** Ordinal form *neweno-*. NONA, NONES, NOON; NONAGON, NONANOIC ACID, from Latin *nōnus*, ninth. **4.** Prothetic or prefixed oldest forms *h₁newn̥*, *h₁nwn̥*. ENNEAD, ENNEAGRAM, from Greek *ennea*, nine (< *ennewa*, *enwa-*). [Pokorny *e-neuen* 318.]

newo- New. Related to **nu-**. **1.** Suffixed form *newyo-*. **a.** NEW, from Old English *nēowe*, *nīwe*, new; **b.** NYNORSK, SPAN-NEW, from Old Norse *nȳr*, new. Both **a** and **b** from Germanic *neuja-*. **2.** Basic form *newo-*. NEO-, NEON, NEOTERIC; MISONEISM, from Greek *neos*, new. **3.** Suffixed form *new-aro-*. ANEROID, from Greek *nēron*, water, from *nēros*, fresh (used of fish and of water), contracted from *nearos*, young, fresh. **4.** Basic form *newo-*. NOVA, NOVATION, NOVEL¹, NOVEL², NOVELTY, NOVICE, NOVILLADA, NOVILLERO; ERGONOVINE, INNOVATE, RENOVATE, from Latin *novus*, new. **5.** Suffixed form *new-er-ko-*. NOVERCAL, from Latin *noverca*, stepmother (< "she who is new"). **6.** Slavic *novŭ*. Russian *novyj*, new, in compound *Novgorod* (see **gher-¹**). [Pokorny *neu̯os* 769.]

ni Down. **1.** Suffixed form *ni-t-*. BENEATH, UNDERNEATH, from Old English *nithan*, *neothan*, below, from Germanic *nith-*. **2.** Suffixed (comparative) form *nitero-*, lower. NETHER, from Old English *nither*, lower, from Germanic *nithra-*. **3.** Perhaps suffixed form *ni-mno-*, "lowland, marshland," perhaps dissimilated in Greek *limnē*, lake, pool: LIMNETIC; HYPOLIMNION, LIMNOLOGY. **4.** Basic form *ni*. SANNYASI, UPANISHAD, from Sanskrit *ni-*, down. **5.** Compound *ni-zdo-* (see **sed-¹**). [In Pokorny 1. *en* 311.]

-no- Also *-eno-*, *-ono-*. Suffix forming adjectives. When the base is verbal, they are participial (*tak-en*); when the base is nominal, they are adjectival (*brazen*). Found ultimately in the following English suffixes: **a.** -EN³, from Old English *-en*, past participle suffix, from Germanic *-ana-*, from Indo-European variant form *-ono-*; **b.** -EN², from Old English *-en*, suffix forming adjectives of material, from Germanic *-īna-*; **c.** -AN¹, -ANA, -IAN, -IANA, from Latin *-ānus*, adjective suffix (originally from *-no-* suffixed to nouns with stem vowel *-ā-*); **d.** -INE², from Latin *-īnus* and Greek *-inos*, adjective suffixes. [Not in Pokorny.] Compare **-to-**.

nobh- Also **ombh-**. Navel; later also "central knob," boss of a shield, hub of a wheel. (Oldest form *h₃nobh-*, with variant [metathesized] form *h₃onbh-* becoming *h₃ombh-*.) **1a.** NAVE², from Old English *nafu*, *nafa*, hub of a wheel; **b.** AUGER, from Old English *nafogār*, auger, from Germanic compound *nabō-gaizaz*, tool for piercing wheel hubs (*gaizaz*, spear, piercing tool; see **ghaiso-**). Both **a** and **b** from Germanic *nabō*. **2.** Variant form *ombh-*. UMBO, from Latin *umbō*, boss of a shield. **3.** Suffixed form *nobh-alo-*. NAVEL, from Old English *nafela*, navel, from Germanic *nabalō*. Suffixed variant form *ombh-alo-*. **a.** UMBILICUS; NOMBRIL, from Latin *umbilīcus*, navel; **b.** OMPHALOS, from Greek *omphalos*, navel. [Pokorny 1. (*enebh-*) 314.]

nogh- Nail, claw. (Oldest form *h₃nogh-*, with variant [metathesized] form *h₃ongh-*.) **1.** Suffixed (diminutive) form *nogh-elo-*. NAIL, from Old English *nægl*, nail, from Germanic *naglaz*. **2.** Form *nogh-*. ONYX; DEINONYCHUS, PARONYCHIA, PERIONYCHIUM, SARDONYX, from Greek *onux* (stem *onukh-*), nail. **3.** Variant form *ongh-*. UNGUICULATE, UNGUIS, UNGULATE, from Latin *unguis*, nail, claw, hoof, with diminutive *ungula*, hoof, claw, talon (< *ongh-elā-*). [Pokorny *onogh-* 780.]

nogʷ- Naked. **1.** Suffixed forms *nogʷ-eto-*, *nogʷ-oto-*. NAKED, from Old English *nacod*, naked, from Germanic *nakweda-*, *nakwada-*. **2.** Suffixed form *nogʷ-edo-*. NUDE, NUDI-; DENUDE, from Latin *nūdus*, naked. **3.** Suffixed form *nogʷ-mo-*. GYMNASIUM, GYMNAST; GYMNOSOPHIST, GYMNOSPERM, from Greek *gumnos*, naked (with metathesis due to taboo deformation). **4.** Suffixed form *nog^w-no-. NAAN, from Old Persian *nagna-, bare, naked. [Pokorny nog^u- 769.]

nŏ-mṇ Name. (Oldest form *h₁no(h₃)-mṇ; zero-grade form *h₁ṇ(h₃)-men-.) **1.** NAME, from Old English nama, name, from Germanic *namōn-. **2.** NOMINAL, NOMINATE, NOUN; AGNOMEN, ANOMIA, BINOMIAL, COGNOMEN, DENOMINATE, IGNOMINY, MISNOMER, NOMENCLATOR, NUNCUPATIVE, PRAENOMEN, PRONOUN, RENOWN, from Latin nōmen, name, reputation. **3.** ONOMASTIC, -ONYM, -ONYMY; ALLONYM, ANONYMOUS, ANTONOMASIA, EPONYM, EPONYMOUS, EUONYMUS, HETERONYMOUS, HOMONYMOUS, MATRONYMIC, METONYMY, ONOMATOPOEIA, PARONOMASIA, PARONYMOUS, PATRONYMIC, PSEU- DONYM, SYNONYMOUS, from Greek onoma, onuma, name (assimilated from enuma, preserved in proper names in Laconian). **4.** MONIKER, from Old Irish ainm, name. [Pokorny en(o)mṇ- 321.]

nōt- Buttock, back. (Oldest form *neh₃t-, colored to *noh₃t-, contracted to *nōt-.) **1.** NOTOCHORD, from Greek nōton, nōtos, back. **2.** Zero-grade *nat-. NATES; AITCHBONE, from Latin natis, buttock. [Pokorny nōt- 770.]

ṇsi- Sword. ENSIFORM, from Latin ēnsis, sword. [Pokorny ṇsi-s 771.]

-nt- Also **-ent-, -ont-.** Suffix forming active participles to verbs. Appears ultimately in the following English suffixes: **a.** -ING¹, from Old English -ende, present participial suffix; **b.** -ANCE, -ANCY, -ANT, -ENCE, -ENCY, -ENT, from Latin -āns, -ēns (stems -ant-, -ent-), present participial suffixes to verbs in -ā- and -ē-; **c.** -ONT, from Greek ōn (stem ont-), present participle of einai, to be (see **es-**); **d.** -ON¹, from Greek ion (stem iont-), neuter present participle of ienai, to go (see **ei-**). [Not in Pokorny.]

nu- Now. Related to **newo-**. **1.** NOW, from Old English nū, now. **2.** QUIDNUNC, from Latin nunc, now (< *nun-ce; -ce, a particle meaning "this," "here"; see **ko-**). [Pokorny nu- 770.]

-nu- Verbal suffix marking present tense, usually transitive, as in *mi-nu-, to reduce (see **mei-²**). Derives from what was originally a nasal infix -n- (see **-n-**) to roots ending in -u-. [Not in Pokorny.]

ō- To believe, hold as true. (Oldest form *(h₂)eh₃-, colored to *(h₂)oh₃-, contracted to *(h₂)ō-.) Suffixed form *ō-men-. OMEN, from Latin ōmen, a prognostic sign, omen. [Not in Pokorny; compare Hittite ḫā-, to consider true.]

-o- The "thematic" suffix, forming nouns, adjectives, and verbs. Ultimately appears in the English combining vowel -o-, from Latin and Greek combining vowel -o- (used to join the members of a compound). [Not in Pokorny.]

obhel- To avail. (Oldest form *h₃(e)bhel-.) ANOPHELES, from Greek ophelos, advantage. [Pokorny obhel- 772.]

od-¹ To smell. **1.** Suffixed form *od-os-. ODOR, from Latin odor, smell. **2.** Suffixed form *od-es-. CACODYL, COLLODION, GEODE, PHYLLODE, from Greek -ōdēs, adjective suffix, originally "having the smell of," hence characterized by (with secondary lengthening). **3.** Suffixed form *od-ē-. OLFACTORY, REDOLENT, from Latin olēre, to smell (with l for d representing a Sabine borrowing). **4.** Suffixed form *od-yo-. OZONE; OZOSTOMIA, from Greek ozein, to smell. **5.** Suffixed form *od-mā-. OSMATIC, OSMIUM; ANOSMIA, OSMETERIUM, PAROSMIA, from Greek osmē (earlier odmē), smell. [Pokorny 1. od- 772.]

od-² To hate. ANNOY, ENNUI, NOISOME, ODIUM, from Latin ōdī, I hate, and odium, hatred. [Pokorny 2. od- 773.]

ōg- Fruit, berry. (Oldest form *eh₃g-, colored to *oh₃g-, contracted to *ōg-.) **1.** Zero-grade form *ag-. ACORN, from Old English æcern, acorn, from Germanic *ak-

ran-. **2.** UVEA, UVULA; PYRUVIC ACID, from Latin ūva (preform uncertain), grape. [Pokorny ōg- 773.]

og^whi- Snake, eel. OPHIDIAN, OPHIOLITE, OPHITE; OPHICLEIDE, Ophiuchus, OPHIUROID, from Greek ophis, snake, serpent. To **og^whi-** should be compared the phonetically and semantically similar **ang-^whi-** and **eghi-**, all three of which have influenced each other through the millennia, both in the daughter languages of Proto-Indo-European (as in Greek enkhelos, eel, probably deriving primarily from **eghi-** but showing the nasal of **ang^whi-**) and also already in the parent language as well.

oid- To swell. (Oldest form *h₃eid-, colored to *h₃oid-.) **1.** OAT, from Old English āte, oat, possibly ultimately from this root, but the cultivation of oats is no earlier than the Iron Age. **2.** EDEMA; OEDIPUS, from Greek oidein, to swell. **3a.** Possibly suffixed nasalized zero-grade form *i-n-d-ro-. INDRA, from Sanskrit Indraḥ, Indra (divine name); **b.** Suffixed nasalized zero-grade form *i-n-d-u-. BINDI, from Sanskrit binduḥ, drop, probably akin to induḥ, drop (with initial b- of obscure origin). [Pokorny oid- 774.]

oi-no- One, unique.
  I. Basic form *oi-no-. **1a.** A¹, AN¹, ONCE, ONE; ALONE, ANON, ATONE, LONELY, NONCE, NONE, from Old English ān, one; **b.** ELEVEN, from English endleofan, eleven, from Germanic compound *ain-lif-, "one left (beyond ten)," eleven (*lif-, left over; see **leik^w-**); **c.** EINKORN, TURNVEREIN, from Old High German ein, one. **a–c** all from Germanic *aina-. **2.** UNI-, UNION, UNITE, UNITY; COADUNATE, TRIUNE, UNANIMOUS, UNICORN, UNIVERSE, UNUNHEXIUM, UNUNOCTIUM, UNUNPENTIUM, UNUNQUADIUM, UNUNSEPTIUM, UNUNTRIUM, from Latin ūnus, one. **3.** Celtic *oino-. Old Irish oen, one, in personal name Oengus (see **geus-**). **4.** INDRICOTHERE, from Old Russian inŭ, one. **5.** Latin compound *ne-oinom (see **ne**).
  II. Suffixed form *oino-ko-. **1.** ANY, from Old English ænig, one, anyone, from Germanic *ainiga-. **2.** UNIQUE, from Latin ūnicus, sole, single. **3.** INCH¹, OUNCE¹, UNCIAL; QUINCUNX, from Latin ūncia, one twelfth of a unit.
  III. Suffixed form *oino-lo-. Latin ūllus, any, in compound *ne-ūllus, nūllus (see **ne**). [Pokorny 3. D. e- 281.]

oit- To take along, fetch. (Oldest form *h₃eit-, colored to *h₃oit-.) **1a.** USAGE, USE, USUAL, USURY, UTENSIL, UTILIZE, UTILITY; ABUSE, PERUSE, from Latin ūtī, to use; **b.** USURP, from Latin ūsūrpāre, to usurp (see **reup-**). **2.** Suffixed form *oit-to-. ESOPHAGUS, from Greek ois-, nominal stem and future tense stem corresponding to pherein, to carry, abstracted from earlier *oistos, able to be borne, endurable, from earlier *oit-to-s, carried, by regular phonological change. [Not in Pokorny; compare Cuneiform Luwian ḫizza(i)-, to fetch.]

oito- An oath. Probably a suffixed o-grade form *oi-to- (*h₃oi-to-) derived from **ei-**. **1.** OATH, from Old English āth, oath. **2.** HUGUENOT, from Old High German eid, oath. Both **1** and **2** from Germanic *ai-thaz. [In Pokorny 1. ei- 293.]

oktō(u) Eight. (Oldest form *oḱtō(u).) **1a.** EIGHT, EIGHTEEN, EIGHTY, from Old English eahta, eight, with derivatives eahtatig, eighty, and eahtatēne, eighteen (-tēne, ten; see **dekm̥**); **b.** ATTO-, from Old Norse āttjān, eighteen (tjān, ten; see **dekm̥**). Both **a** and **b** from Germanic *ahtō. **2.** OCTANS, OCTANT, OCTAVE, OCTAVO, OCTET, OCTO-, October, OCTONARY; OCTODECIMO, OCTOGENARIAN, from Latin octō, eight. **3.** OCTAD, OCTO-; OCTOPUS, from Greek oktō, eight. **4.** UNUNOCTIUM, partly from Greek oktō, eight, and partly from Latin octō, eight. [Pokorny oktō(u) 775.]

ōku- Swift. (Oldest form *ōḱu-.) **1.** OXYTOCIC, from Greek ōkus, swift. **2.** Possibly altered zero-grade form *aku- in compound *aku-petro-, "swift-flying" (*pet-

ro-, flying; see **pet-**). ACCIPITER, from Latin *accipiter*, hawk. [Pokorny *ōkú-s* 775.] See also **ekwo-.**

okʷ- To see. (Oldest form *h_3ek^w-, colored to *h_3ok^w-; zero-grade *h_3k^w-.) **1a.** EYE; DAISY, from Old English *ēage*, eye; **b.** WALLEYED, WINDOW, from Old Norse *auga*, eye; **c.** OGLE, from Low German *oog, oge*, eye. **d.** AUGEN, from German *Augen*, plural of *Auge*, eye, ultimately from Old High German *ouga*, eye. **a–d** all from Germanic *augōn-* (perhaps with taboo deformation). **2.** Suffixed form *ok^w-olo-. **a.** EYELET, OCELLUS, OCULAR, OCULIST, OCULUS, ULLAGE; ANTLER, INOCULATE, MONOCLE, OCULOMOTOR, PINOCHLE, from Latin *oculus*, eye; **b.** INVEIGLE, from French *aveugle*, blind, from Gallo-Latin compound *ab-oculus*, blind, calqued on Gaulish *exs-ops*, blind ("with eyes out": *exs-*, out + *ops*, eye). **3.** Form *ok^w-s. CERATOPSIAN, METOPIC, MYOPIA, NYCTALOPIA, PELOPS, PHLOGOPITE, PROSOPOGRAPHY, PROSOPOPEIA, PYROPE, TRICERATOPS, from Greek *ōps*, eye (and stem *op-*, to see). **4.** Suffixed form *ok^w-ti-. OPSIN, -OPSIS, -OPSY; AUTOPSY, DROPSY, IODOPSIN, RHODOPSIN, SYNOPSIS, from Greek *opsis*, sight, appearance. **5.** Suffixed form *ok^w-to-. OPTIC; DIOPTER, OPTOELECTRONICS, OPTOMETRY, PANOPTIC, PANOPTICON, from Greek *optos*, seen, visible. **6.** Suffixed form *ok^w-ā-. METOPE, from Greek *opē*, opening. **7.** Suffixed form *ok^w-mn̥. OMMATIDIUM, OMMATOPHORE, from Greek *omma* (< *opma*), eye. **8.** Suffixed form *ok^w-tro-. CATOPTRIC, from Greek *katoptron*, "backlooker," mirror (*kata-*, down, back; see **kat-**). **9.** OPHTHALMO-; EXOPHTHALMOS, from Greek *ophthalmos*, eye (with taboo deformation). **10.** Zero-grade form *$ə k^w$-, in compounds (see **ant-, āter-, ghwer-**). **11.** Perhaps full-grade *ok^w-s- (suffix uncertain). CUSHY, from Persian *xuš* (Modern Iranian Persian *xoš*), good, perhaps from an Old Iranian compound *x^w-axša-* (< *su-ok^w-s-o-), "having good eyes, a good aspect" (< *su-*, good; see **esu-**). [Pokorny *okʷ-* 775.]

olə- To destroy. (Oldest form *h_3elh_1-, colored to *h_3olh_1-, with variant [metathesized] form *h_3leh_1-, contracted to *$h_3lē$-.) Possibly suffixed variant form *lē-to-. LETHAL, from Latin *lētum, lēthum*, death. [Pokorny *ol-(e)-* 777.]

om- Raw; sharp-tasting. **1.** Possibly Latin *amārus*, bitter-tasting (though doubtful in form): AMARELLE, AMARETTO, MARASCA, MARASCHINO, MORELLO. **2.** Suffixed form *om-ro-. AMBARELLA, from Sanskrit *amla-*, tart. [Pokorny *om-* 777.]

ombh-ro- Rain. **1.** Zero-grade form *m̥bh-ro-. IMBRICATE; IGNIMBRITE, from Latin *imber*, rain. **2.** Possibly suffixed zero-grade form *m̥bh-u-. IMBUE, from Latin *imbuere*, to moisten, stain. [In Pokorny 2. *(en-ebh-)* 315.]

om(e)so- Shoulder. **1.** Form *omso-. OS³, from Old Norse *āss*, a (mountain) ridge, from Germanic *amsa-*. **2.** Form *omeso-. HUMERUS, from Latin *humerus*, shoulder. **3.** Lengthened-grade form *ōmso-. ACROMION, from Greek *ōmos*, shoulder. [Pokorny *om(e)so-s* 778.]

oner- Dream. Suffixed form *oner-yo-. ONEIROMANCY, from Greek *oneiros*, dream. [Pokorny *oner-* 779.]

ongʷ- To salve, anoint. OINTMENT, UNCTION, UNCTUOUS, UNGUENT; ANOINT, INUNCTION, PREEN, from Latin *unguere*, to smear, anoint. [Pokorny *ongʷ-* 779.]

-ono- See **-no-.**

-ont- See **-nt-.**

op-¹ To work, produce in abundance. (Oldest form *h_3ep-, colored to *h_3op-.) **1.** Suffixed form *op-es-. OPERA¹, OPERATE, OPEROSE, OPUS; COOPERATE, INURE, MANEUVER, MANURE, OFFICINAL, STOVER, from Latin *opus* (stem *oper-*), work, with its denominative verb *operārī*, to work, and secondary noun *opera*, work. **2.** Italic compound *opi-fici-om* (see **dhē-**). **3.** Suffixed form *op-en-ent-. OPULENT, from Latin dissimilated *opulentus*, rich, wealthy. **4.** Suffixed form *op-ni-. OMNI-; OMNIBUS; OMNIUM-GATHERUM, from

Latin *omnis*, all (< "abundant"). **5.** Suffixed (superlative) form *op-tamo-. OPTIMUM, from Latin *optimus*, best (< "wealthiest"). **6.** COPIOUS, COPY; CORNUCOPIA, from Latin *cōpia*, profusion, plenty, from prefixed form *co-op-* (*co-*, collective and intensive prefix; see **kom**). [Pokorny 1. *op-* 780.]

op-² To choose. **1.** OPTION, from Latin *optiō*, choice (from *opere*, to choose). **2.** OPT, OPTATIVE; ADOPT, CO-OPT, from Latin *optāre*, to choose (frequentative of *opere*, to choose). **3.** Possibly suffixed form *op- ein-o-, whence Italic denominative verb *op-ein-ā-. OPINE, OPINION, from Latin *opīnārī*, to be of an opinion. [Pokorny 2. *op-* 781.]

or- Large bird. (Oldest form *h_3er-, colored to *h_3or-.) **1.** Suffixed form *or-n-. **a.** ERNE, from Old English *earn*, eagle; **b.** ARNOLD (personal name), from Old High German *Arenwald*, "eagle power," from *aro, arn*, eagle (*-walt*, power; see **wal-**). Both **a** and **b** from Germanic *arōn-* (extended to *arnuz*), eagle. **2.** Suffixed form *or-n-īth-. ORNITHO-; AEPYORNIS, NOTORNIS, from Greek *ornīs* (stem *ornīth-*), bird. [Pokorny 1. *er-* 325.]

ōr- To pronounce a ritual formula. ORACLE, ORATION, ORATOR, ORATORY¹, ORATORY²; ADORE, INEXORABLE, PERORATE, from Latin *ōrāre*, to speak, plead, pray. [Pokorny *ōr-* 781.]

orbh- To turn, with derivatives referring to change of allegiance and the passage from one status to another. (Oldest form *h_3erbh-, colored *h_3orbh-.) **1.** Suffixed form *orbh-o-. **a.** In words referring to the act of turning: GASTARBEITER, from Old High German *arabeit(i)*, labor, from Germanic *arb-aithi-* (source of suffix uncertain), perhaps from *orbo-iti-*, "a going of a turn," in reference to the repetitive nature of agricultural labor, such as the repeated turning of an ox while plowing a field (*iti-*, a going; see **ei-**); **b.** In words referring to orphans and persons of reduced and changed status: *(i)* ORPHAN, from Greek *orphanos*, orphaned; *(ii)* ROBOT, from Czech *robota*, compulsory labor, drudgery, from Old Church Slavonic *rabota*, servitude, from *rabŭ*, slave, from Old Slavic *orbŭ*, slave. **2.** Suffixed form *orbh-i-. **a.** ORB, ORBICULAR, ORBICULATE, from Latin *orbis*, disc, sphere (< "that which turns"); **a.** Further suffixed form *orbh-i-t-. ORBIT, from Latin *orbita*, rut, track made by a wheel. **3.** Perhaps from this root is the Greek mythological name *Orpheus* (? < "he who goes to the other side" or "he who turns": ORPHEUS, ORPHIC, ORPHISM. [Pokorny *orbho-* 781.]

Language and Culture Note Reconstructing the form of roots and words in a dead language like Proto-Indo-European is often easy; the phonetic shape of the reconstructed word may be easy to deduce on the basis of its descendant cognates and a knowledge of sound laws. But the meanings of these reconstructed roots and words are often much harder to determine. A case in point is the root **orbh-**, some of whose descendants mean "orphan" or "orphaned" (Greek *orphanos*, Latin *orbus*, Armenian *orb*), some "inheritance" (Old Irish *orbe*, German *Erbe*), and some "slave" (Russian *rab*). Formally, all these words must go together, but the meaning of the putative root from which they are all derived was not clear until a Hittite cognate was discovered in the 20th century. Hittite has a verb *ḫarb-*, with the basic meaning "change allegiance": in the Hittite Laws it is used of a cow that wanders out of its owner's fold into another's. With this new piece of information, the American scholar Craig Melchert proposed that the disparate senses "orphan," "inheritance," and "slave" could now all be understood as stemming from an original concept "to go from one sphere of belonging to another" or "to change status or allegiance." Orphans were no longer in the tutelage of their kin-group; inherited property passed from one holder to another; and slaves were persons whose social status had changed from being free to being unfree. More recently, the American scholar Michael Weiss has proposed that the basic meaning of the root was "to turn," and that the Latin words *orbis*, "disc, sphere," and *orbita*, "track made by a wheel, rut," are also derivatives of this root. The notion of changing status or allegiance found in the derivatives of **orbh-** would be natural development from the central meaning "turn."

[**ōrd-** To arrange; arrangement. Italic root of uncertain origin; oldest form *ōrh$_x$d(h)-*. **1a.** ORDAIN, ORDER, ORDINAL, ORDINANCE, COORDINATE, ORDO; COORDINATION, INORDINATE, SUBORDINATE, from Latin *ōrdō*, order (originally a row of threads in a loom); **b.** ORNAMENT, ORNATE; ADORN, SUBORN, from Latin *ōrnāre* (< *ōrd(i)nā*) to adorn. **2.** EXORDIUM, PRIMORDIAL, from Latin *ōrdīrī*, to begin to weave. [In Pokorny 1. *ar-* 55.]]

ors- Buttocks, backside. **1.** Suffixed form *ors-o-*. **a.** ARSE, ASS[2], from Old English *ærs*, ears, backside; **b.** DODO, from Middle Dutch *ærs*, backside, tail. Both **a** and **b** from Germanic *arsaz*. **2.** Suffixed form *ors-ā-*. **a.** URO-[2], -UROUS; ANTHURIUM, ANURAN, COENURUS, CYNOSURE, DASYURID, EREMURUS, OPHIUROID, OXYURIASIS, SCIURID, SQUIRREL, TRICHURIASIS, from Greek *ourā*, tail; **b.** SILURID, from Greek *silouros*, sheatfish, probably from *ourā*, tail (with an obscure first element). [Pokorny *ers-* 340.]

os- Ash tree. ASH[2], from Old English *æsc*, ash, from Germanic *askiz*. [Pokorny *ōs-* 782.]

ōs- Mouth. (Oldest form perhaps *h$_3$ōs-*, but precise preform uncertain.) **1.** ORAL, OS[1]; OSCILLATE, OSCULATE, OSCULUM, OSTIARY, OSTIUM, USHER; INOSCULATE, ORIFICE, ORONASAL, OROTUND, OSCITANCY, PERORAL, from Latin *ōs* (stem *ōr-*), mouth, face, orifice, and derivative *ōstium* (< suffixed form *ōs-to-*), door. **2.** Possibly Latin *aurīga*, charioteer (< *ōr-īg-*, "he who manages the (horse's) bit"; *-īg-*, lengthened from *-ig-*, driving, from *ag-*; see **ag-**[1]: AURIGA. [Pokorny 1. *ōus-* 784.]

-os- See **-es-**.

ost- Bone. (Oldest forms *h$_2$ost-*, *h$_2$est-*, the latter colored to *h$_2$ast-*.) **1.** OS[2], OSSEOUS, OSSICLE, OSSUARY; OSSIFRAGE, OSSIFY, from Latin *os* (stem *oss-*), bone. **2.** OSTEO-, OSTEON; ENDOSTEUM, EXOSTOSIS, PERIOSTEUM, SYNOSTOSIS, TELEOST, from Greek *osteon*, bone. **3.** Suffixed form *ost-r-*. **a.** OSTRACIZE, OSTRACOD, OSTRACON; OSTRACODERM, PERIOSTRACUM, from Greek *ostrakon*, shell, potsherd; **b.** form *ast-*. OYSTER, from Greek *ostreon*, oyster; **c.** ASTRAGAL, ASTRAGALUS, from Greek *astragalos*, vertebra, ball of the ankle joint, knucklebone, Ionic molding. **4.** Suffixed basic form *ost-ṇ-ko-*. ASTAXANTHIN, from Greek *ostakos*, *astakos*, lobster (< "creature with a bony shell"). [Pokorny *ost(h)-* 783.]

-oto- See **-to-**.

owi- Sheep. (Oldest form *h$_2$owi-*.) **1.** EWE, from Old English *ēwe*, *eōwu*, ewe, from Germanic *awiz*. **2.** OVINE, OVUM, from Latin *ovis*, sheep. [Pokorny *óu̯i-s* 784.]

pā- To protect, feed. (Oldest form *peh$_2$-*, colored to *pah$_2$-*, contracted to *pā-*.) **1.** Suffixed form *pā-trom*. **a.** FODDER, from Old English *fōdor*, fodder; **b.** FORAGE, FORAY, FOURRAGÈRE, from Old French *feurre*, fodder; **c.** FUR, FURRIER, from Old French *forre*, *fuerre*, trimming made from animal skin, fur (< "sheath, case, lining"). **a–c** all from Germanic *fōdram*. **2.** Suffixed form *pā-dhlom* (doublet of *pā-trom*). PABULUM, from Latin *pābulum*, food, fodder. **3.** Extended form *pāt-*. **a.** FOOD, from Old English *fōda*, food, from Germanic *fōd-*, food; **b.** FEED, from Old English *fēdan*, to feed, from Germanic denominative *fōdjan*, to give food to; **c.** suffixed form *pāt-tro-*. FOSTER, from Old English *fōstor*, food, nourishment, from Germanic *fōstra-*. **4.** Extended form *pās-*. **a.** Suffixed form *pās-sko-*. PASTURE; ANTIPASTO, REPAST, from Latin *pāscere*, to feed; **b.** suffixed form *pās-tor-*. PASTERN, PASTOR, PESTER,

from Latin *pāstor*, shepherd; **c.** suffixed form *pāst-t-ni-*. PANADA, PANATELA, PANIC GRASS, PANNIER, PANOCHA, PANTRY, PASTILLE, PENUCHE; APPANAGE, COMPANION[1], COMPANY, PANFORTE, PANKO, from Latin *pānis*, bread. **5.** Suffixed form *pā-tor-*. BEZOAR, from Persian *pād*, protecting against, from Iranian *pātar-* (Avestan *pātar-*). **6.** Suffixed form *pā-won-*, protector. SATRAP, from Old Persian *khshathra-pāvā*, protector of the province. **6.** Compound form *ṃg-ə-pā-* in Greek *agapān*, to greet with affection (see **meg-**). [Pokorny *pā-* 787, 1. *pō(i)-* 839.]

paəwṛ Fire. (Oldest form *peh$_2$wṛ*, colored to *pah$_2$wṛ*, with zero-grade *ph$_2$ur-* metathesized to *puh$_2$r-*, contracted to *pūr-*.) Zero-grade form *pūr-*. **1.** FIRE, from Old English *fȳr*, fire, from Germanic suffixed form *fūr-i-*. **2.** PYRE, PYRETIC, PYRITES, PYRO-, PYROSIS, PYRRHOTITE; EKPYROTIC, EMPYREAL, from Greek *pūr*, fire. [Pokorny *peu̯ōr* 828.]

pag- Also **pak-**. To fasten. (Oldest forms *pag̑-*, *pak̑-*.) **1.** Lengthened-grade form *pāk-*. FAY[1], from Old English *fēgan*, to fit closely, from Germanic *fōgjan*, to join, fit. **2.** Nasalized form *pa-n-g-*, also *pa-n-k-*. **a.** *(i)* FANG, from Old English *fang*, *feng*, plunder, booty, from Germanic *fangam*, *fangiz*; *(ii)* VANG, from Dutch *vangen*, to catch, from remade Germanic verb *fangan*; *(iii)* NEWFANGLED, from Middle English *-fangel*, taken, akin to Old High German *-fangolon*, to close, from Germanic *fanglōn*, to grasp. *(i)–(iii)* all derivatives of Germanic *fanhan*, to seize; **b.** COMPACT[1], IMPACT, IMPINGE, SPINTO, from Latin *pangere*, to fasten. **3.** Root form *pǎk-*. **a.** PACE[2], PAX, PAY[1]; PEACE; APPEASE, PACIFIC, PACIFY, from Latin *pāx*, peace (< "a binding together by treaty or agreement"); **b.** PACT, PATIO, from Latin *pacīscī*, to agree. **4.** Suffixed form *pak-slo-*. **a.** PALE[1], PALISADE, PAWL, PEEL[3], POLE[2]; IMPALE, TRAVAIL, TRAVEL, from Latin *pālus*, stake (fixed in the ground); **b.** probably Latin *pāla*, spade: PALETTE, PEEL[2]. **5.** Lengthened-grade form *pāg-*. **a.** PAGAN, PEASANT, from Latin *pāgus*, "boundary staked out on the ground," district, village, country; **b.** PAGE[1], PAGEANT, from Latin *pāgina*, "trellis to which a row of vines is fixed," hence (by metaphor) column of writing, page; **c.** PROPAGATE, from Latin *prōpāgāre*, to propagate (< "to fix before"; *prō-*, before, in front; see **per**[1]); **d.** PECTIN, PEGMATITE; AREOPAGUS, MASTOPEXY, PAGOPHAGIA, from Greek *pēgnunai*, to fasten, coagulate, with derivative *pagos* (< *pag-o-*), stiff mass, hill, frost. [Pokorny *pǎk-* 787.]

pāl- To touch, feel, shake. (Oldest form *peh$_2$l-*, colored to *pah$_2$l-*, contracted to *pāl-*.) **1a.** FEEL, from Old English *fēlan*, to examine by touch, feel; **b.** SPRACHGEFÜHL, from Old High German *vuolen*, to feel. Both **a** and **b** from Germanic *fōljan*, to feel. **2.** Reduplicated zero-grade form *pal-p-* (from *pal- p(ə)-*. **a.** PALP, from Latin *palpus*, a touching; **b.** PALPABLE, PALPATE[1], PALPITATE, from Latin *palpāri*, *palpāre*, to stroke gently, touch; **c.** PALPEBRA, from Latin *palpebra*, eyelid (< "that which shakes or moves quickly"). **3.** Perhaps *expressive* reduplicated form *pal-pal-*. PAPILIONACEOUS, PAPILLON, PAPILLOTE, PAVILION, from Latin *pāpiliō*, butterfly. **4.** Perhaps suffixed zero-grade form *pal-yo-*. CATAPULT, from Greek *pallein*, to sway, brandish. **5.** Perhaps suffixed form *psal-yo-*. PSALM, PSALTERY, from Greek *psallein*, to pluck, play the harp (but more likely of imitative origin). [Pokorny 1. G. *pel-* 801, *polo-* 841.]

pan- Fabric. **1a.** VANE, from Old English *fana*, flag, banner, weathercock; **b.** Germanic compound *gund-fanōn-* (see **g^when-**). Both **a** and **b** from Germanic *fanōn*. **2.** Extended form *panno-*. PANE, PANEL; PANNA COTTA from Latin *pannus*, piece of cloth, rag. [Pokorny *pǎn-* 788.]

pant- All. Root found only in Tocharian and Greek. PAN-; DIAPASON, PANCRATIUM, PANCREAS, from Greek *pās* (neuter *pan*, stem *pant-*), all. [In Pokorny 1. *k̂eu-* 592.]

papa A child's word for "father," a linguistic near-universal found in many languages. **1.** PAPA, from French *papa*, father. **2.** PAPPUS, POPE, from Greek *pappās*, father, and *pappos*, grandfather. [Pokorny *pap(p)a* 789.]

pāso- Kinsman. PARRICIDE, from Latin *parricīda* (oldest form *paricidas*), murderer of a near relative, with *parri-* perhaps for *pāri-* (but *parri-* is more likely from **parso-*, related to Sanskrit *pŭruṣaḥ*, man). [Pokorny *pāsó-s* 789.]

past- Solid, firm. **1a.** FAST[1]; SHAMEFACED, STEADFAST, from Old English *fæst*, fixed, firm; **b.** AVAST, from Middle Dutch *vast*, firm, fast. Both **a** and **b** from Germanic **fastu-*, firm, fast. **2.** FASTEN, from Old English *fæstnian*, to fasten, establish, from Germanic **fastinōn*, to make firm or fast. **3.** HANDFAST, from Old Norse *festa*, to fix, affirm, from Germanic causative **fastjan*, to make firm. **4a.** FAST[2], from Old English *fæstan*, to abstain from food; **b.** BREAKFAST, from Old Norse *fasta*, to abstain from food. Both **a** and **b** from Germanic **fastēn*, to hold fast, observe abstinence. [Pokorny *pasto-* 789.]

pau-1 Few, little. (Oldest form **peh₂u-*, colored to **pah₂u-*, contracted to **pau-*.)
   I. Adjectival form **pau-*, few, little. **1.** FEW, from Old English *fēawe*, few, from Germanic **fawa-*. **2.** Suffixed form **pau-ko-*. PAUCITY, POCO, from Latin *paucus*, little, few. **3.** Suffixed form **pau-ro-*. **a.** Metathetical form **par-wo-*. PARAFFIN, PARVORDER, PARVOVIRUS, from Latin *parvus*, little, small, neuter *parvum*, becoming *parum*, little, rarely; **b.** further suffixed form **pau-ro-lo-*. PAUL (personal name), from Latin *paullus, paulus*, small. **4.** Compound **pau-paros-*, producing little, poor (**-paros*, producing; see **perǝ-1**), PAUPER, POOR, POVERTY; DEPAUPERATE, IMPOVERISH, from Latin *pauper*, poor.
   II. Suffixed zero-grade form **pu-lo-*, young of an animal. **1.** FOAL, from Old English *fola*, young horse, colt, from Germanic **fulōn-*. **2.** FILLY, from Old Norse *fylja*, young female horse, from Germanic derivative **fuljō*.
   III. Basic form **pau-* and zero-grade form **pŭ-*, boy, child. **1.** Suffixed form **pu-ero-*. PUERILE, PUERPERAL, from Latin *puer*, child. **2.** Extended form **put-*. **a.** POLTROON, PONY, POOL[2], POULARD, POULTRY, PULLET, PUNCHINELLO; CATCHPOLE, POULTER'S MEASURE, from Latin *pullus* (< **putslo-*), young of an animal, chicken; **b.** PUSILLANIMOUS, from Latin *pusillus* (< **putslo-lo-*), old diminutive of *pullus*; **c.** further suffixed form **put-o-*. PUTTO, from Latin *putus*, boy. **3.** Suffixed form **paw-id-*. PEDO-2; ENCYCLOPEDIA, ORTHOPEDICS, from Greek *pais* (stem *paid-*), child (> *paideia*, education). [Pokorny *pōu-* 842.]

pau-2 To cut, strike, stamp. (Oldest form **peh₂u-*, colored to **pah₂u-*.) **1.** Suffixed (participial) zero-grade form **pu-to-*, cut, struck. **a.** PUTAMEN, PUTATIVE; ACCOUNT, AMPUTATE, COMPUTE, COUNT[1], DEPUTE, DISPUTE, IMPUTE, REPUTE, from Latin *putāre*, to prune, clean, settle an account, think over, reflect; **b.** possibly Latin *puteus*, well: PIT[1]. **2.** Basic form **pau-*. **a.** Suffixed form **pau-yo*. PAVE, PAVÉ, from Latin *pavīre*, to beat; **b.** suffixed (stative) form **paw-ē-*. PAVID, from Latin *pavēre*, to fear (< "to be struck"); **c.** perhaps Greek *paiein*, to beat: ANAPEST. [Pokorny 3. *pēu-* 827.]

paus- To leave, desert, cease, stop. PAUSE, PESADE, POSADA, POSE[1]; COMPOSE, DIAPAUSE, MARIPOSA LILY, REPOSE[1], from Greek *pauein*, to stop (> Latin *pausa*, a stopping). [Pokorny *paus-* 790.]

ped-1 Foot.
   I. Nominal root. **1.** Lengthened o-grade form **pōd-*. **a.** FOOT, from Old English *fōt*, foot, from Germanic **fōt-*. **a.** FOOSBALL, from Old High German *fuoz*, foot. Both **a** and **b** from Germanic **fōt-*. **2.** Suffixed form **ped-ero-*. FETTER, from Old English *fetor*,

feter, leg iron, fetter, from Germanic **feterō*. **3.** Suffixed form **ped-el-*. FETLOCK, from Middle English *fitlock*, *fetlock*, fetlock, from a Germanic source akin to Old High German *vizzelach*, fetlock, from Germanic **fetel-*. **4.** Basic form **ped-*. PAWN[2], -PED, PEDAL, PEDATE, PEDESTRIAN, PEDI-, PEDI- CEL, PEDUNCLE, PEON, PES, PIONEER; MILLIPEDE, SESQUIPEDAL, TRIPEDAL, TRIVET, VAMP[1], from Latin *pēs* (stem *ped-*), foot. **5.** Suffixed form **ped-yo-*. **a.** EXPEDITE, from Latin *expedīre*, to free from a snare (*ex-*, out of; see **eghs**); **b.** IMPEDE, from Latin *impedīre*, "to put in fetters, hobble, shackle," entangle, hinder (*in-*, in; see **en**). **6.** Suffixed form **ped-ikā-*. IMPEACH, from Latin *pedica*, fetter, snare. **7.** O-grade form **pod-*. **a.** PEW, -POD, PODIUM; ANTIPODES, APODAL, APPOGGIATURA, APUS, CHENOPOD, LYCOPODIUM, MACROPOD, MONOPODIUM, OCTOPUS, OEDIPUS, PELECYPOD, PHALAROPE, PLATYPUS, PODAGRA, PODIATRY, PODOPHYLLIN, POLYP, POLYPOD, RHIZOPUS, SYMPODIUM, XENOPUS, from Greek *pous* (stem *pod-*), foot; **b.** PODZOL, from Russian *pod*, under. **8.** Suffixed form **ped-ya*. TRAPEZIUM, from Greek *peza*, foot. **9.** Suffixed form **ped-o-*. **a.** PEDO-[1]; PARALLELEPIPED, from Greek *pedon*, ground, soil; **b.** PADA, PAISA, PICE, PIE[3], PUG[3], from Sanskrit *padam*, footstep, foot, and *pāt*, foot; **c.** CHARPOY, PAJAMA, TEAPOY, from Middle Persian *pāy*, foot; **d.** lengthened-grade form **pēd-o-*. (i) PILOT, from Greek *pēdon*, rudder, steering oar; (ii) DIAPEDESIS, from Greek *pēdān*, to leap. **10.** Suffixed form **ped-ī-*. CYPRIPEDIUM, from Greek *pedilon*, sandal.
   II. Verbal root **ped-*, to walk, stumble, fall. **1.** FETCH[1], from Old English *fetian, feccean*, to bring back, from Germanic **fetēn*. **2a.** Suffixed (comparative) form **ped-yos-*. PEJORATION; IMPAIR, from Latin *pēior*, worse (< "stumbling"); **b.** suffixed (superlative) form **ped-samo-*. PESSIMISM, from Latin *pessimus*, worst; **c.** suffixed form **ped-ko-*. PECCADILLO, PECCANT, PECCAVI; IMPECCABLE, from Latin *peccāre*, to stumble, sin. **a-c** all from Latin **ped-*. [Pokorny 2. *pĕd-* 790.]

ped-2 Container. **1.** Suffixed o-grade form **pod-om*. VAT, from Old English *fæt*, cask, from Germanic **fatam*. **2.** Suffixed o-grade form **pod-ilo-*. FETTLE, from Old English *fetel*, girdle, from Germanic **fatilaz*. **3.** Probably full-grade form **ped-*. FRITTER[1], from obsolete English *fritter*, fragment, probably from a source akin to Middle High German *vetze*, "clothes," rags, from Germanic **fet-*. [Pokorny 1. *pĕd-* 790.]

peg- Breast. **1.** Suffixed variant form **pek-tos-*. PECTORAL; EXPECTORATE, PARAPET, from Latin *pectus*, breast. **2.** Possibly suffixed variant form **pek-so-*. PUNKA, from Sanskrit *pakṣaḥ*, wing. [Pokorny (peg-) 792.]

pē(i)- To hurt. (Oldest form **peh₁(i)-*, zero-grade **ph₁(i)-*, with variant [metathesized] full-grade form **peih₁-*, whence zero-grade **pih₁-*, contracted to **pī-*.) **1.** Suffixed (participial) form **pī-ont-* (< **piǝ-ont-*). FIEND, from Old English *fēond, fiond*, enemy, devil, from Germanic **fijand-*, hating, hostile. **2.** Possibly **pē-* in suffixed zero-grade form **pǝ-to-*. PASSIBLE, PASSION, PASSIVE, PATIENT; COMPASSION, from Latin *patī*, to suffer. [Pokorny *pē(i)-* 792.]

peiǝ- To be fat, swell.
   I. Zero-grade form **pī-* (< **piǝ-*). **1.** Possibly suffixed form **pī-tu-*. PIP[5], PITUITARY, from Latin *pītuīta*, moisture exuded from trees, gum, phlegm. **2.** Possibly suffixed form **pī-nu-*. PINE[1], PINEAL, PINNACE, PIÑON, PINOT; PIÑA CLOTH, from Latin *pīnus*, pine tree (yielding a resin). **3.** Suffixed form **pī-won-*. PROPIONIC ACID, from Greek *pīōn*, fat. **4.** Suffixed form **pī-wer-*, "fat, fertile." **a.** EIRE, ERIN, ERSE, HIBERNIA, IRISH; IRELAND, from **Īwer-iū*, the prehistoric Celtic name for Ireland, whence Latin *Hibernia*, Ireland, Old Irish *Ériu*, Ireland, dative *Érinn* (> Irish Gaelic *Éire*), and Old English *Īras*, the Irish; **b.** PIERIAN SPRING, from Greek *Pieriā*, a region of Macedonia, from **Pīwer-iā-*.

II. Extended o-grade form *poid-. FAT, from Old English fǣt(t), fat, from Germanic past participle *faitida-, fattened, from derivative verb *faitjan, to fatten, from *faita-, plump, fat. [Pokorny pei(ǝ)- 793.]

peig-¹ Also **peik-** (oldest forms *peik̑-, *peik-). To cut, mark (by incision). **1.** Alternate form *peik-. FILE², from Old English fīl, fēol, file, from Germanic *fīhalō, cutting tool. **2.** Nasalized zero-grade form *pi-n-g-. PAINT, PICTOR, PICTURE, PICTURESQUE, PIGMENT, PIMENTO, PINT, PINTO; DEPICT, PICTOGRAPH, from Latin pingere, to embroider, tattoo, paint, picture. **3.** Suffixed zero-grade form *pik-ro-. PICRO-, from Greek pikros, sharp, bitter. **4.** O-grade form *poik-. POIKILOTHERM, from Greek poikilos, spotted, pied, various. [Pokorny 1. peig- 794.]

peig-² Also **peik-**. Evil-minded, hostile. **1.** Suffixed zero-grade form *pig-olo-. FICKLE, from Old English ficol, treacherous, false, from Germanic *fikala-. **2.** Suffixed o-grade form *poik-o-. FOE, from Old English gefāh, enemy, from Germanic *gafaihaz (*ga-, collective prefix; see **kom**). **3.** Suffixed o-grade form *poik-yo-. FEY, from Old English fǣge, fated to die, from Germanic *faigja-. **4.** Suffixed o-grade form *poik-itā-. FEUD¹, from Old French faida, hostility, feud, from Germanic *faihithō. [Pokorny 2. peig̑- 795.]

peis-¹ To crush. **1.** Suffixed zero-grade form *pis-to-. PESTO, PESTLE, PISTE, PISTIL, PISTOU, from Latin pistillum, pestle. **2.** Nasalized zero-grade form *pi-n-s-. PISTON, from Latin pīnsāre, to pound. **3.** Possibly suffixed zero-grade form *pis-lo-. PILE², from Latin pīlum, javelin, pestle. **4.** Perhaps Greek ptissein (pt- for p-), to crush, peel: PTISAN, TISANE. [Pokorny 1. (peis-?) 796.]

peis-² To blow. FIZZLE, from Middle English fise, fart, from a Scandinavian source akin to Old Norse físa, to fart. [Pokorny 2. peis- 796.]

peisk- Fish. Zero-grade form *pisk-. **1a.** FISH, from Old English fisc, fish; **b.** WEAKFISH, from Middle Dutch vische, vis, fish; **c.** LUTEFISK, from Old Norse fiskr, fish. **a–c** all from Germanic *fiskaz, fish. **2.** Suffixed form *pisk-i-. PISCARY, PISCATORIAL, PISCES, PISCI-, PISCINA, PISCINE; GRAMPUS, PESCO-VEGETARIAN, PORPOISE, REPECHAGE, from Latin piscis, fish. [Pokorny peisk- 796.]

pek̑-¹ To make pretty. (Oldest form *pek̑-.) **1.** Possibly Germanic *fagra-. FAIR¹, from Old English fæger, beautiful. **2.** Possibly Germanic *fagin-, *fagan-, to enjoy. FAIN, FAWN¹, from Old English fægen, joyful, glad, and derivative fagnian, to rejoice. [Pokorny 1. pek̑- 796.]

pek̑-² To pluck the hair, fleece, comb. (Oldest form *pek̑-.) **1.** Extended form *pekt-. FIGHT, from Old English feohtan, to fight, from Germanic *fehtan, to fight. **2.** Suffixed extended form *pekt-en-. **a.** PECTEN, from Latin pecten, a comb; **b.** zero-grade form *pkt-en-. CTENIDIUM; CTENOID, CTENOPHORE, from Greek kteis (stem kten- < *pkten-), a comb. **3.** Suffixed extended form *pek-smen-. PASHMINA, from Persian pašm, wool. [Pokorny 2. pek̑- 797.]

peku- Wealth, movable property, livestock. (Oldest form *pek̑u-.) **1a.** FELLOW, from Old Norse fē, property, cattle; **b.** FEE, FIEF; ENFEOFF, FEOFFMENT, from Old French fie, fief, and Old English feoh, cattle, goods, money; **c.** FEUD², from Medieval Latin feudum, feudal estate. **a–c** all from Germanic *fehu-. **2.** PECORINO, from Latin pecus, cattle. **3.** Suffixed form *peku-n-. PECUNIARY; IMPECUNIOUS, from Latin pecūnia, property, wealth. **4.** Suffixed form *peku-l-. PECULATE, PECULIAR, from Latin pecūlium, riches in cattle, private property. [In Pokorny 2. pek̑- 797.]

Language and Culture Note The Indo-Europeans typically differentiated between movable and immovable wealth, and in the case of the former, between two- and four-footed wealth. Slaves constituted two-footed chattels, typically expressed by the root

wī̆-ro-, "man." Four-footed chattels, or livestock, were designated **peku-,** also a general term for "wealth" and the source of English fee. Both these roots are frequently combined in phrases referring to the totality of one's movable wealth: compare San- skrit vīrapśa- (< earlier *vīra-psva- < *wīro-pkw-o-), "abundance of men and livestock," Avestan pasu vīra "men (and) livestock," Latin pecudēsque virōsque "both men and livestock," and Umbrian uiro pequo "men (and) livestock." These phrases continue an Indo-European phrase, *wīro- peku-, *peku- wī̆ro-, for the same concept. Another way in which the Indo-Europeans expressed this partitioning was to use words that literally translate as "two-footed" and "four-footed," as in Sanskrit dvipade catuṣpade and Umbrian dupursus peturpursus, both meaning "two-footed (and) four-footed (chattels)." • In an inherited verb phrase found in Sanskrit and Avestan, and Latin and Umbrian, "man (and) livestock" is the object of a verb meaning "protect, keep safe," **pā-,** the root of Latin pāstor, "shepherd." (See also note at **sol-.**)

---

pekʷ- To cook, ripen. **1.** Assimilated form (in Italic and Celtic) *kʷekʷ-. **a.** COOK, CUISINE, KITCHEN, QUITTOR; APRICOT, BISCOTTO, BISCUIT, CHARCUTERIE, CONCOCT, DECOCT, PRECOCIOUS, RICOTTA, SANCOCHO, STERRA COTTA, from Latin coquere, to cook; **b.** CULINARY, KILN, from Latin culīna, kitchen, deformed from coquina. **2.** PEPO; PUMPKIN, from Greek pepōn, ripe. **3.** PEPTIC, PEPTIZE; DRUPE, EUPEPTIC, PEPSIN, PEPTONE, from Greek peptein, to cook, ripen, digest (> peptos, cooked). **4.** DYSPEPSIA, from Greek -pepsiā, digestion. **5.** PUKKA; PAKORA, from Sanskrit pakva-, cooked, roasted, ripe. **6.** CEVICHE, ESCABECHE, from Middle Persian *sikbāg, dish made of meat, wheat flour, and vinegar (sik, vinegar), from -bāg, food, broth, from Old Iranian *-pāka-, cooked. [Pokorny pekʷ- 798.]

pel-¹ Dust, flour. **1.** POLENTA, POLLEN, from Latin pollen, fine flour, dust, and polenta (? < *pollen-tā), crushed grain. **2.** POWDER, PULVERIZE, from Latin pulvis, dust. **3.** PAILLASSE, PALEA, from Latin palea, chaff. **4.** PALYNOLOGY, from Greek palunein, to sprinkle flour. **5.** POULTICE, PULSE², from Latin puls, pottage, probably borrowed (via Etruscan) from Greek poltos, porridge (made from flour). **5.** Probably Latin pulpa, fruit pulp: PAUPIETTE, PULP. [Pokorny 2b. pel- 802.]

pel-² Pale. **1.** Suffixed variant form *pal-wo-. **a.** (i) FALLOW DEER, from Old English fealu, fealo, reddish yellow; (ii) FAUVISM, from Frankish *falw-, reddish-yellow. Both (i) and (ii) from Germanic *falwa-; **b.** PALE², PALLID, PALLIDUM, PALLOR; APPALL, from Latin pallēre, to be pale; **c.** PALOMINO, from Latin palumbēs (influenced in form by Latin columbus, dove), ring-dove, "gray-bird." **2.** Probably suffixed form *pel-ko-. FALCON; GYRFALCON, from Late Latin falcō, falcon, from Germanic *falkōn-, falcon (< "gray bird"; but this is also possibly from the Late Latin). **3.** Suffixed extended form *peli-wo-. **a.** PELOPS, from Greek pelios, dark; **b.** o-grade form *poli-wo-. POLIOMYELITIS, from Greek polios, gray. **4.** Perhaps Greek pelargos, stork (< *pelawo-argos, "black-white bird"; argos, white; see **arg-**): PELARGONIUM. **5.** Suffixed extended form *plei-to-. FLOYD, LLOYD (personal names), from Welsh llwyd, gray. [Pokorny 6. pel- 804.]

pel-³ To fold. **1.** Extended o-grade form *polt-. **a.** FOLD¹, from Old English fealdan, faldan, to fold; **b.** FALTBOAT, from Old High German faldan, to fold; **c.** FURBELOW, from Italian falda, fold, flap, pleat; **d.** (i) FALDSTOOL, from Medieval Latin compound faldistolium, folding chair; (ii) FAUTEUIL, from Old French faldestoel, faldstool. Both (i) and (ii) from Germanic compound *faldistōlaz, "folding stool" (*stōlaz, stool; see **stā-**); **e.** -FOLD, from Old English -feald, -fald, -fold, from Germanic combining form *-falthaz, *-faldaz. **a–e** all from Germanic *falthan, *faldan.

2. Combining form *-plo-*. **a.** DECUPLE, MULTIPLE, OCTUPLE, QUADRUPLE, QUINTUPLE, SEPTUPLE, SEXTUPLE, TRIPLE, from Latin *-plus*, *-fold* (as in *triplus*, threefold); **b.** -PLOID; TRIPLOBLASTIC, from Greek *-plos*, *-ploos*, *-fold* (as in *haploos*, *haplous*, single, and *triploos*, triple). [Pokorny 3a. *pel-* 802.]

pel-⁴ Skin, hide. **1.** Suffixed form *pel-no-*. FELL³, from Old English *fell*, skin, hide, from Germanic *felnam*. **2.** FILM, from Old English *filmen*, membrane, from Germanic suffixed form *fel-man-ja-*. **3.** Suffixed form *pel-ni-*. PELISSE, PELLICLE, PELT¹, PELTRY, PILLION; PELLAGRA, SURPLICE, from Latin *pellis*, skin. **4.** ERYSIP-ELAS, from Greek *-pelas*, skin. **5.** Suffixed form *pel-to-*. PELTATE, from Greek *peltē*, a shield (made of hide). [Pokorny 3b. *pel-* 803.]

pel-⁵ To sell. Lengthened o-grade form *pōl-*. BIBLIOPOLE, MONOPOLY, from Greek *pōlein*, to sell. [Pokorny 5. *pel-* 804.]

pel-⁶ To thrust, strike, drive.

I. Suffixed form *pel-de-*. **1a.** ANVIL, from Old English *anfilt(e)*, *anfealt*, anvil ("something beaten on"); **b.** *(i)* FELT¹, from Old English *felt*, felt; *(ii)* FILTER, FILTRATE, from Medieval Latin *filtrum*, filter, piece of felt. Both *(i)* and *(ii)* from Germanic *feltaz*, *filtiz*, compressed wool. Both **a** and **b** from Germanic *felt-*, *falt-*, to beat. **2.** PELT², POUSSETTE, PULSATE, PULSE¹, PUSH; COMPEL, DISPEL, EXPEL, IMPEL, IMPULSE, PROPEL, REPEL, from Latin *pellere* (past participle *pulsus*), to push, drive, strike. **3a.** Suffixed o-grade form *pol-o-*, fuller of cloth. POLISH, from Latin *polīre*, to make smooth, polish (< "to full cloth"); **b.** suffixed o-grade form *pol-o-* (with different accentuation from the preceding), fulled (of cloth). INTERPOLATE, from Latin compound adjective *interpolis* (also *interpolus*), refurbished (*inter-*, between; see **en**). **II.** Extended form *pelh₂-*. **1.** Present stem *pelnă-*. **a.** APPEAL, PEAL, RAPPEL, REPEAL, from Latin *appellāre*, "to drive to," address, entreat, appeal, call (*ad-*, to; see **ad-**); **b.** COMPELLATION, from Latin *compellāre*, to accost, address (*com-*, intensive prefix; see **kom**). **2.** Possible suffixed zero-grade extended adverbial form *pḷə-ti-*, or locative plural *pḷə-si*. PLESIOMORPHY, PLESIOSAUR, from Greek *plēsios*, near (< "pushed toward"), from pre-Greek *plāti* or *plāsi*. [Pokorny 2a. *pel-* 801.]

pelə-¹ To fill; with derivatives referring to abundance and multitude. (Oldest form *pelh₁-*, with variant [metathesized] form *pleh₁-*, contracted to *plē-*.)

I. Zero-grade form *pḷə-*. **1.** Suffixed form *pḷə-no-*. FULL¹, from Old English *full*, full, from Germanic *fulla-* (< *fulna-*), full. **2.** FILL, from Old English *fyllan*, to fill (from Germanic derivative verb *fulljan*, to fill), and *fyllu*, full amount (from Germanic abstract noun *full-īnō-*, fullness). **3.** PLENARY, PLENITUDE, PLENTY, PLENUM; PLENIPOTENTIARY, REPLENISH, TERREPLEIN, from Latin *plēnus*, full, from Latin stem *plēno-*, replacing *plāno-* (influenced by Latin verb *plēre*, to fill; see **IV. 1.** below). **4.** Suffixed form *pḷə-go-*. **a.** FOLK, from Old English *folc*, people; **b.** HERRENVOLK, VOLKSLIED, from Old High German *folc*, people. Both **a** and **b** from Germanic *folkam*. **II.** Suffixed form *p(e)lə-u-*. **1.** Obscure comparative form. PIÙ, PLURAL, PLUS; NONPLUS, PLUPERFECT, PLURIPOTENT, SURPLUS, from Latin *plūs*, more (Archaic Latin *plous*). See also **IV. 5.** below. **2.** O-grade form *pol(ə)-u-*. POLY-; HOI POLLOI, from Greek *polus*, much, many. **3.** Possibly from this root (but more likely from **pel-¹**) is Latin *palūs*, marsh (? < "inundated"): PALUDAL, PALUSTRINE. **III.** Suffixed form *p(e)lə-o-*. Latin compound *manipulus* (see **man-²**). **IV.** Variant form *plē-*. **1.** ACCOMPLISH, COMPLEMENT, COMPLETE, COMPLIMENT, COMPLY, DEPLETE, EXPLETIVE, IMPLEMENT, REPLETE, SUPPLETION, SUPPLY, from Latin *plēre*, to fill. **2.** Possibly suffixed form *plē-dhw-*. PLEBE, PLEBEIAN, PLEBS; PLEBISCITE, from

Latin *plēbs*, *plēbēs*, the people, multitude. **3.** Suffixed form *plē-dhwo-*. PLETHORA; PLETHYSMOGRAPH, from Greek derivative verb *plēthein*, to be full. **4.** Suffixed adjective (positive) form *plē-ro-*. PLEROCERCOID, from Greek *plērēs*, full. **5.** Suffixed (comparative) form *plē-i(s)on-*. PLEO-, PLEONASM; PLEIOTAXY, PLEIOTROPISM, PLIOCENE, from Greek *pleōn*, *pleiōn*, more. **6.** Suffixed (superlative) form *plē-isto-*. PLEISTOCENE, from Greek *pleistos*, most. **V.** Possibly Sanskrit *pūraḥ*, cake (< "that which fills or satisfies"): POORI. [Pokorny 1. *pel-* 798.]

pelə-² Flat; to spread. (Oldest form *pelh₂-*, with variant [metathesized] form *pleh₂-*, colored to *plah₂-*, contracted to *plā-*.) **1.** Suffixed form *pel(ə)-tu-*. FIELD, from Old English *feld*, open field, from Germanic *felthuz*, flat land. **2.** Suffixed form *pel(ə)-t-es-* (by-form of *pel(ə)-tu-*). **a.** FELDSPAR, from Old High German *feld*, field; **b.** VELDT, from Middle Dutch *veld*, *velt*, field. Both **a** and **b** from Germanic *feltha-*, flat land. **3.** Variant form *plā-*. **a.** Suffixed form *plā-ru-*. FLOOR, from Old English *flōr*, floor, from Germanic *flōruz*, floor; **b.** suffixed form *plā-no-*. *(i)* LLANO, PIANO², PLAIN, PLANARIAN, PLANE¹, PLANE², PLANE³, PLANISH, PLANO-, PLANULA; ESPLANADE, EXPLAIN, PIANOFORTE, from Latin *plānus*, flat, level, even, plain, clear; *(ii)* Celtic *lānon*, plain. Gaulish *-lānon* in Gallo-Roman place name *Mediolānum* (see **medhyo-**). **4.** Suffixed zero-grade form *pḷə-mā-*. PALM¹, PALM², PALMARY, PALMIER, from Latin *palma* (< *palama*), palm of the hand. **5.** Possibly extended variant form *plan-*. **a.** PLANET; APLANATIC, from Greek *planāsthai*, to wander (< "to spread out"); **b.** perhaps Germanic *flan-*. FLÂNEUR, from French *flâner*, to walk the streets idly, from a source akin to Old Norse *flana*, to wander aimlessly. **6.** Suffixed zero-grade form *pḷə-dh-*. -PLASIA, PLASMA, -PLAST, PLASTER, PLASTIC, PLASTID, -PLASTY; DYSPLASIA, METAPLASM¹, TOXOPLASMA, from Greek *plassein* (< *plath-yein*), to mold, "spread out." **7.** O-grade form *pola-*. **a.** POLYNYA, from Russian *polyǐ*, open; **b.** POLACK, POLKA, from Slavic *polje*, broad flat land, field. [Pokorny *pelə-* 805.] See also extended roots **plāk-¹** and **plat-**.

pelə-³ Citadel, fortified high place. (Oldest form perhaps *pelh₃-*, but exact laryngeal uncertain.) Zero-grade form *pḷə-*. **1.** POLICE, POLICY¹, POLIS, POLITIC, POLITY; ACROPOLIS, COSMOPOLIS, COSMOPOLITE, MEGALOPOLIS, METROPOLIS, NECROPOLIS, POLICLINIC, PROPOLIS, from Greek *polis*, city (phonological development unclear). **2.** Sanskrit *pūr*, *puram*, fortress, city. **a.** GOPURAM, from Sanskrit *puram*. **b.** compounded in numerous place names such as SINGAPORE, from Sanskrit *siṃhapuram*, "lion city" (*siṃhaḥ*, lion). [In Pokorny 1. *pel-* 798.]

pel(i)s- Rock, cliff. **1.** HORNFELS, from Old High German *felis*, rock, from Germanic *felesaz*, rock. **2.** FELL⁴, FIELD, from Old Norse *fjall*, *fell*, rock, mountain, barren plateau, from Germanic *felzam*, rock. [Pokorny *peli-s-* 807.]

pen- Swamp. Suffixed o-grade form *pon-yo-*. FEN, from Old English *fenn*, marsh, from Germanic *fanjam*, swamp, marsh. [Pokorny 2. *pen-* 807.]

penkʷe Five.

I. Basic form *penkʷe*. **1.** Assimilated form *pempe*. **a.** *(i)* FIVE; FIFTY, from Old English *fīf*, five, with derivative *fīftig*, fifty (*-tēne*, ten; see **dekṃ**); *(ii)* FIN², from Old High German *finf*, *funf*, five. Both *(i)* and *(ii)* from Germanic *fimf*; **b.** *(i)* FIFTEEN, from Old English *fīftēne*, fifteen; *(ii)* FEMTO-, from Old Norse *fimmtān*, fifteen. Both *(i)* and *(ii)* from Germanic compound *fimftehun*, fifteen (*tehun*, ten; see **dekṃ**). **2.** Assimilated form (in Italic and Celtic) *kʷenkʷe*. **a.** CINQUAIN, CINQUE, QUINQUE-; CINQUECENTO, CINQUEFOIL, QUINCUNX, from Latin *quīnque*, five; **b.** KENO, QUINATE, from Latin distributive *quīnī*, five each; **c.** QUINCEAÑERA, DECENNIAL, QUINDECENNIAL,

from Latin compound *quīndecim*, fifteen (*decem*, ten; see **dekm̥**); **d.** QUINCENTENARY, from Latin *quingentī*, five hundred. **3.** PENTA-, PENTAD; PENSTEMON, PENTAGON, PENTAMETER, PENTATHLON, UNUNPENTIUM, from Greek *pente*, five. **4a.** PUNCH³; PACHISI, from Sanskrit *pañca*, five; **b.** Persian *panj*, five, in place name *panjāb* (see **ap-²**). Both **a** and **b** from Indo-Iranian *panca*.
    II. Compound *penkʷe-(d)konta*, "five tens," fifty (*-(d)konta*, group of ten; see **dekm̥**). **1.** QUINQUAGENARIAN, QUINQUAGESIMA, from Latin *quīnquāgintā*, fifty. **2.** PENTECOST, PINKSTER FLOWER, from Greek *pentēkonta*, fifty.
    III. Ordinal adjective *penkʷ-to-*. **1.** FIFTH, from Old English *fīfta*, fifth, from Germanic *fimftōn-*. **2.** QUINT¹, QUINTAIN, QUINTET, QUINTILE; QUINTESSENCE, QUINTILLION, QUINTUPLE, from Latin *quīntus* (< *quinc-tos*), feminine *quīnta*, fifth.
    IV. Suffixed form *penkʷ-ro-*. FINGER, from Old English *finger*, finger, from Germanic *fingwraz*, finger (< "one of five").
    V. Suffixed reduced zero-grade form *pn̥k-sti-*. **1.** FIST, from Old English *fȳst*, fist. **2.** FOIST, from Dutch *vuist*, fist. Both **1** and **2** from Germanic *funhstiz*. [Pokorny penkᵘe 808, pn̥ksti- 839.]

pent- To tread, go. **1.** FIND, from Old English *findan*, to find, from Germanic *finthan*, to come upon, discover. **2.** Suffixed o-grade form *pont-i-*. **a.** PONS, PONTIFEX, PONTIFF, PONTINE, PONTOON, PUNT¹; OSTEOPONTIN, TRANSPONTINE, from Latin *pōns* (stem *pont-*), bridge (earliest meaning, "way, passage," preserved in the priestly title *pontifex*, "he who prepares the way"; *-fex*, maker; see **dhē-**); **b.** SPUTNIK, from Russian *sputnik*, fellow traveler, sputnik, from *put'*, path, way, from Slavic *pǫtĭ*. **3.** Zero-grade form *pn̥t-*. PERIPATETIC, from Greek *patein*, to tread, walk. **4.** Suffixed zero-grade form *pn̥t-ə-*. **a.** PATH, from Old English *pæth*, path; **b.** PAD²; FOOTPAD¹, from Middle Dutch *pad*, way, path. Both **a** and **b** from Germanic *patha-*, way, path, probably borrowed (? via Scythian) from Iranian *path-* (compare Old Persian *pathĭ*, path). [Pokorny pent- 808.]

per¹ Base of prepositions and preverbs with the basic meanings of "forward," "through," and a wide range of extended senses such as "in front of," "before," "early," "first," "chief," "toward," "against," "near," "at," "around."
    I. Basic form *per* and extended form *peri*. **1a.** (i) TURNVEREIN, from Middle High German *vereinen*, to unite; (ii) FARKLEMPT, from Middle High German *verklemmen*, to grip, clamp, choke up. Both (i) and (ii) from Old High German *far-*; **b.** VEER², from Middle Dutch *vieren*, to let out, slacken; **c.** Germanic compound *fergetan* (see **ghend-**); **d.** FRUMP, from Middle Dutch *verrompelen*, to wrinkle. **a–d** all from Germanic *fer-*, *far-*, used chiefly as an intensive prefix denoting destruction, reversal, or completion. **2.** Suffixed (comparative) form *per-ero-*, farther away. FAR, from Old English *feor(r)*, far, from Germanic *fer(e)ra*. **3.** PER, PER-; PARAMOUNT, PARAMOUR, PARGET, PARTERRE, PARVENU, from Latin *per*, through, for, by. **4.** PERI-; PERISSODACTYL, from Greek *peri*, around, near, beyond. **5a.** PANTOUM, from Sanskrit *pari-*, around; **b.** PARADISE, from Avestan *pairi-*, around; **c.** BARD²; PURDAH, from Old Persian *pari*, around, over; **d.** Old Iranian compound *pari-vāraka-* (see **wer-⁵**). **a–d** all from Indo-Iranian *pari-*, around. **6.** PERESTROIKA, from Old Russian *pere-*, around, again, from Slavic *per-*.
    II. Zero-grade form *pr̥-*. **1a.** FOR, from Old English *for*, before, instead of, on account of; **b.** FOR-, from Old English *for-*, prefix denoting destruction, pejoration, exclusion, or completion. Both **a** and **b** from Germanic *fur*, before, in. **2.** Extended form *pr̥t-*. FORTH; AFFORD, from Old English *forth*, from Germanic *furth-*, forward. **3.** Suffixed (comparative) form *pr̥-tero-*. FURTHER, from Old English *furthra*,

furthor, farther away, from Germanic *furthera-*. **4a.** Compound *pr̥-st-i-* or *por-st-i-*, with o-grade form *por-* (see **stā-**); **b.** PORRECT, from Latin *por-*, forth, forward. Both **a** and **b** from Latin *por-* from *pr̥-*. **5.** Suffixed form *pr̥-sōd*. PARGET, from Latin *porrō*, forward.
    III. Extended zero-grade form *pr̥ə-* (earlier *pr̥h₃-*). **1.** Suffixed (superlative) form *pr̥ə-mo-*. **a.** FORMER², from Old English *forma*, first, from Germanic *fruma-*, *furma-*; **b.** FOREMOST, from Old English *formest*, first, from Germanic *frumista-*, *furmista-*; **c.** Latin compound *prandium*, "first meal," late breakfast, lunch (probably < *prām-d-ium* < *pr̥əm-(e)d-yo-*; second element *-(e)d-*, to eat; see **ed-**). **2.** Suffixed (superlative) form *pr̥ə-isto-*. FIRST, from Old English *fyrst*, *fyrest*, first, from Germanic *furista-*, foremost. **3.** Suffixed form *pr̥ə-wo-*. **a.** PROW, from Greek *prōira*, forward part of a ship, from analogically suffixed form *prōw-arya*; **b.** PROTEIN, PROTIST, PROTO-, PROTON, from Greek *prōtos*, first, foremost, from suffixed (superlative) form *prōw- ato-*. Both **a** and **b** from Greek *prōwo-*, first, foremost. **4.** Suffixed form *pr̥ə-i*. ARPENT, from Latin *arepennis*, half-acre (second element obscure), from Gaulish *ari* (combining form *are-*), before, from Celtic *(p)ari*, *are*.
    IV. Extended form *pr̥ā*. **1a.** FORE, FORE-; FOREFATHER, from Old English *fore*, for, before; **b.** VORLAGE, from Old High German *fora*, before; **c.** BEFORE, from Old English *beforan*, before, from Germanic prefixed and suffixed form *bi-fora-na*, in the front (*bi-*, at, by; see **ambhi**). **a–c** all from Germanic *fura*, before. **2.** PARA-¹; PALFREY, from Greek *para*, beside, alongside of, beyond. **3.** PURANA, from Sanskrit *purā*, before.
    V. Extended form *prō*. **1a.** FRAE, FRO; FROWARD, from Old Norse *frā*, from, from Germanic *fra*, forward, away from; **b.** Germanic *fra-*, completely, in compounds (see **ed-**, **aik-¹**). **2.** Suffixed form *prō-mo-*. **a.** FRAME, FROM, from Old English *fram*, forward, from, from Germanic *fram*, from; **b.** FURNISH, FURNITURE, VENEER, from Old French *f(o)urnir*, to supply, provide, from Germanic derivative verb *frumjan*, to further, from Germanic *frum*, forward; **b.** PRAM², from Czech *prám*, raft. **3.** Suffixed form *prō-wo-*. **a.** (i) FRAU, FRÄULEIN, from Old High German *frouwa*, lady; (ii) FREYA, from Old Norse *freyja*, lady. Both (i) and (ii) from Germanic *frōwō*, lady, lengthened-grade feminine of *frawan-*; **b.** FREY, from Old Norse *Freyr*, from Germanic *frawaz*, alteration of *frawan-*. lord; **c.** form *prō-wo-*, independently created in Slavic. NAPRAPATHY, from Old Church Slavonic *pravŭ*, true. **4.** PRIDE, PRO¹, PRO-¹, PRODIGALITY, PROUD, PROWESS; IMPROVE, PURCHASE, from Latin *prō*, *prŏ-*, before, for, instead of. **5.** Suffixed form *prō-no-*. PRONE, from Latin *prōnus*, leaning forward. **6.** Possible suffixed form *pro-ko-*. RECIPROCAL, from Latin compound *reciprocus*, alternating, "backward and forward" (*re-ko-*, backward; see **re-**). **7.** Suffixed adverb *pro-kʷe*. **a.** APPROACH, RAPPROCHEMENT, REPROACH, from Latin *prope*, near; **b.** suffixed form *prokʷ-inkʷo-*. PROPINQUITY, from Latin *propinquus*, near; **c.** suffixed (superlative) form *prokʷ-isamo-*. PROXIMATE; APPROXIMATE, from Latin *proximus*, nearest. **8.** Compound *pro-bhw-o-*, growing well or straightforward (*bhw-o-*, to grow; see **bheuə-**). PROBABLE, PROBE, PROBITY, PROOF, PROVE; APPROVE, IMPROBITY, REPROVE, from Latin *probus*, upright, good, virtuous. **9.** PRO-², from Greek *pro*, before, in front, forward. **10.** Suffixed (comparative) form *pro-tero-*. HYSTERON PROTERON, PROTEROZOIC, from Greek *pro- teros*, before, former. **11.** PRAKRIT, from Sanskrit *pra-*, before, forth. **12.** Celtic *ro-*, intensive prefix. GALORE, from Old Irish *roar*, enough, from Celtic compound *ro-wero-*, sufficiency (*-wero-*, from root *wer-* also found in Old Irish *feraid*, he provides, supplies).

VI. Extended forms *prai-*, *prei-*. **1a.** PRE-; PRETERISM, PRETERITE, from Latin *prae*, before; **b.** compound *prai-ghes-to-* (see **ghes-**). **2.** Suffixed (comparative) form *prei-yos-*. PRIOR², from Latin *prior*, former, higher, superior. **3.** Suffixed form *prei-wo-*. **a.** PRIVATE, PRIVILEGE, PRIVITY, PRIVY; DEPRIVE, from Latin *prīvus*, single, alone (< "standing in front," "isolated from others"); **b.** PROPER, PROPERTY; AP-PROPRIATE, EXPROPRIATE, PROPRIOCEPTION, PROPRI-OCEPTOR, PROPRIUM, from Latin *proprius*, one's own, particular (< *prō prīvō*, in particular, from the ablative of *prīvus*, single; *prō*, for; see **V. 4.**). **4.** Extended form *preis-*. **a.** Suffixed (superlative) form *preis-mo-*. *(i)* PREMIER, PRIMAL, PRIMARY, PRIMATE, PRIME, PRIMI-TIVE, PRIMO, PRIMUS; IMPRIMIS, PRIMAVERA¹, PRIME-VAL, PRIMIPARA, PRIMOGENITOR, PRIMOGENITURE, PRIMORDIAL, from Latin *prīmus* (< *prīsmus*), first, foremost; *(ii)* PRINCE, PRINCIPAL, PRINCIPLE, from Latin compound *princeps*, "he who takes first place," leader, chief, emperor (*-ceps*, "-taker"; see **kap-**); **b.** suffixed form *preis-tano-*. PRISTINE, from Latin *prīstinus*, former, earlier, original; **c.** suffixed form *preis-ko-*. PRISCILLA (personal name), from Latin *Prīscilla*, feminine diminutive of *priscus*, ancient.

VII. Extended form *pres-* in compound *pres-gʷu-*, "going before" (*gʷ-u-*, going; see **gʷā-**). PRES-BYTER, PRESTER JOHN, PRIEST; PRESBYOPIA, from Greek *presbus*, old, old man, elder.

VIII. Extended form *proti*. PROS-, from Greek *pros*, against, toward, near, at. [Pokorny 2. A. *per* 810.] Other possibly related forms are grouped under **per-²**, **per-³**, **per-⁴**, and **per-⁵**.

per-² To lead, pass over. A verbal root belonging to the group of **per¹**.

I. Full-grade form *per-*. **1.** Suffixed form *per-tu-*. FIRTH, FJORD, from Old Norse *fjördhr*, an inlet, estuary, from Germanic *ferthuz*, place for crossing over, ford. **2.** Suffixed form *per-onā-*. PERONEAL, from Greek *peronē*, pin of a brooch, buckle (< "that which pierces through"). **3.** Suffixed form *per-yo-*. DIAPIR, from Greek *peirein*, to pierce. **4.** Suffixed form *per-trā-*. PETRO-, PETROUS, PIER, PARSLEY, PETRIFY, PE-TROLEUM, SALTPETER, from Greek *petrā*, cliff, rock (dissimilated from *pertrā-*), with possible earlier meaning "bedrock" (< "what one comes through to"). **5.** Suffixed form *per-wṛ*, *per-wṇ-*, bedrock, "a coming through, what one comes through to," and derived adjective *per-wṇ-to-*, rocky. PARVATI, from Sanskrit *Pārvatī*, from *parvatah*, mountain (since Parvati is associated with the Himalayas).

II. O-grade form *por-*. **1a.** *(i)* FARE; WARFARE, WAYFARER, WAYFARING, WELFARE, from Old English *faran*, to go on a journey, get along; *(ii)* FIELDFARE, from Old English *feldeware*, possibly altered by folk etymology in Old English from an earlier *feldefare*, from *fare*, a goer, from *faran* (see *(i)* above); **b.** GAB-ERDINE, from Old High German *faran*, to go, travel; **c.** FARTLEK, from Old Norse *fara*, to go, move. **a–c** all from Germanic *faran*, to go. **2.** Suffixed form *por-o-*, passage, journey. PORE²; APORIA, EMPORIUM, PO-ROMERIC, from Greek *poros*, journey, passage. **3.** Suffixed (causative) form *por-eyo-*, to cause to go, lead, conduct. **a.** FERRY, from Old English *ferian*, to transport, from Germanic *farjan*, to ferry; **b.** GUAR, WAL-LAH, from Sanskrit *pārayati*, *pālayati*, he leads across, brings to safety. **4.** Suffixed form *por-ti-* in Germanic *fardiz*, journey. FERDINAND (personal name), from Germanic *fardi-nanth-*, "adventurer" (> French *Ferdinand*; *nanthiz*, risk). **5.** Lengthened-grade form *pōr-*. **a.** FERE, from Old English *(ge)fēra*, "fellow-traveler," companion (*ge-*, together, with; see **kom-**), from Germanic suffixed form *fōr-ja-*; **b.** FÜHRER, from Old High German *fuoren*, to lead, from Germanic suffixed (causative) form *fōr-jan*. **6.** Possibly suffixed form *por-no-*, feather, wing (< "that which carries a bird in flight"). **a.** FERN, from Old English *fearn*, fern (having

feathery fronds), from Germanic *farnō*, feather, leaf; **b.** PAAN, from Sanskrit *parṇam*, leaf, feather.

III. Zero-grade form *pṛ-*. **1.** Suffixed form *pṛ-tu-*, passage. **a.** FORD, from Old English *ford*, shallow place where one may cross a river, from Germanic *furduz*; **b.** PORT¹; IMPORTUNE, OPPORTUNE, PASSPORT, from Latin *portus*, harbor (< "passage"); **c.** EUPHRATES, from Avestan *huparathuua-*, "good to cross over" (> Greek *Euphrātēs*), from *parətu-*, ford (*hu-*, good; see **(e)su-**). **2.** Suffixed form *pṛ-tā-*. PORCH, PORT³, POR-TAL, PORTCULLIS, PORTER², PORTICO, PORTIÈRE, POR-TULACA, PURSLANE, from Latin *porta*, gate. **3.** Suffixed (denominative) form *pṛ-to-*. PORT⁵, PORTABLE, POR-TAGE, PORTAMENTO, PORTATIVE, PORTER¹; COMPORT, DEPORT, EXPORT, IMPORT, IMPORTANT, PORTFOLIO, PURPORT, RAPPORT, REPORT, SPORT, SUPPORT, TRANS-PORT, from Latin *portāre*, to carry. [Pokorny 2. B. *per* 816.]

per-³ To try, risk (< "to lead over," "press forward"). A verbal root belonging to the group of **per¹**. **1.** Lengthened grade *pēr-*. FEAR, from Old English *fǣr*, danger, sudden calamity, from Germanic *fēraz*, danger. **2.** Suffixed form *perī-tlo-*. PARLOUS, PERIL, from Latin *perīclum*, *perīculum*, trial, danger. **3.** Suffixed form *per-yo-*. EXPERIENCE, EXPERIMENT, EXPERT, from Lat-in *experīrī*, to try, learn by trying (*ex-*, from; see **eghs-**). **4.** Suffixed form *per-ya*. PIRATE; EMPIRIC, from Greek *peira*, trial, attempt. [Pokorny 2. E. *per* 818.]

per-⁴ To strike. A verbal root possibly belonging to the group of **per¹**. Extended forms *prem-*, *pres-*. PREG-NANT², PRESS¹, PRESSURE, PRINT; APPRESSED, APRÈS, COMPRESS, DEPRESS, ESPRESSO, EXPRESS, IMPRESS¹, IMPRIMATUR, IMPRINT, OPPRESS, REPRESS, REPRI-MAND, SUPPRESS, from Latin *premere* (past participle *pressus*), to press. [Pokorny 3. *per-* 818.]

per-⁵ To traffic in, sell (< "to hand over," "distribute"). A verbal root belonging to the group of **per¹**. Base of two distinct extended roots.

I. Root form *pret-*. **1.** INTERPRET, from Latin com-pound *inter-pres* (stem *inter-pret-*), go-between, nego-tiator (*inter-*, between; see **en**). **2.** Suffixed form *pret-yo-*. PRAISE, PRECIOUS, PRICE; APPRAISE, APPRECIATE, DEPRECIATE, from Latin *pretium*, price.

II. Variant root form *perə-* (oldest form *perh₂-*). Suffixed form *p(e)r-n-ə-*, with o-grade *por(ə)-nā-*. PORNOGRAPHY, from Greek *pornē*, prostitute, from *pernanai*, to sell. [In Pokorny 2. **C.** *per* 817.]

perd- To fart. **1a.** FART, from Old English *feortan*, to fart, from Germanic *fertan*, *fartōn*; **b.** FUTZ, perhaps from Yiddish *arumfartsn zich*, to fart around, from Middle High German *varzen*, to fart. Both **a** and **b** from Germanic *fertan*, *fartōn*. **2.** PARTRIDGE, from Greek *perdix*, partridge (which makes a sharp whir-ring sound when suddenly flushed). [Pokorny *perd-* 819.] Compare **pezd-**.

perə-¹ To produce, procure. (Oldest form *perh₃-*; pos-sibly related to **perə-²**. See also **per-⁵ II.**) **1.** Zero-grade form *prə-* (becoming *par-* in Latin). **a.** Suf-fixed form *par-ā-*. PARADE, PARE, PARLAY, PARRY, PARURE; APPARATUS, APPARAL, COMPRADOR, DISPA-RATE, EMPEROR, IMPERATIVE, IMPERATOR, IMPERIAL, PARACHUTE, PARASOL, PREPARE, RAMPART, REPAIR¹, SEPARATE, SEVER, SEVERAL, from Latin *parāre*, to try to get, prepare, equip; **b.** suffixed form *par-yo-*. -PARA, PARITY², -PAROUS, PARTURIENT; POSTPARTUM, REPERTORY, VIPER, from Latin *parere*, *parire*, to get, beget, give birth; **c.** parallel suffixed (participial) form *par-ent-*. PARENT, from Latin *parēns*, parent; **d.** suf-fixed form *par-o-*, producing: *(i)* JUNIPER, from Latin *iūniperus*, juniper, perhaps from compound *yoini-paros*, "producing juniper berries" (*yoini-*, juniper berry); *(ii)* compound *pau-paros* (see **pau-**); *(iii)* Ital-ic compound *wīwo-paros* (see **gʷeiə-¹**), suffixed form *par-ikā-*. PARCAE, from Latin *Parcae*, the Fates (who assign one's destiny). **2.** Suffixed o-grade form *por(ǝ)-sī-. HEIFER, from Old English *hēahfore*, calf, a compound (with obscure first element) of *fearr*, calf, from Germanic *farzī-. [Pokorny 2. D. *per* 818.]

perǝ-² To grant, allot (reciprocally, to get in return). (Oldest form *perh₃-; possibly related to **perǝ-¹**. See also **per-⁵ II.**) Zero-grade form *pṛǝ- (becoming *par- in Latin). **1.** Suffixed form *par-ti-. **a.** PARCEL, PARCENER, PARSE, PART, PARTICLE, PARTISAN¹, PARTISAN², PARTITA, PARTY; BIPARTITE, COMPART, IMPART, PARTICIPATE, REPARTEE, from Latin *pars* (stem *part-*), a share, part; **b.** possibly suffixed form *par-tiōn-. PORTION, PROPORTION, from Latin *portiō*, a part (first attested in the phrase *prō portiōne*, in proportion, according to each part, perhaps assimilated from *prō partiōne*). **2.** Perhaps Latin *pār*, equal: PAIR, PAR, PARITY¹, PEER²; COMPARE, IMPARITY, NONPAREIL, PAREVE, PARI-MUTUEL. **3.** Perhaps nasalized suffixed zero-grade *pṛ-n-k-. PUJA, from Sanskrit *pūjā*, puja, perhaps a reborrowing into Sanskrit of a Prakrit form from Sanskrit *pṛñcā*, a mixing, a filling up, satisfaction, from *pṛnakti*, he mixes, fills, sates. [Pokorny 2. C. *per* 817.]

perk-¹ Speckled. Often used in names of spotted or pied animals. (Oldest form *perk̑-.) PERCH², from Greek *perkē*, the perch. [Pokorny 2. *perk̑-* 820.]

perk-² To dig out, tear out. (Oldest form *perk̑-.) Zero-grade form *pṛk̑-. FURROW; FURLONG, from Old English *furh*, trench, from Germanic *furh-. [Pokorny 3. *perk̑-* 821.]

perkʷu- Oak. **1.** Zero-grade form *pṛkʷ-. FIR, probably from a Scandinavian source akin to Old Icelandic *fýri*, fir, from Germanic *furh-jōn-. **2.** Assimilated form *kʷerkʷu-. QUERCETIN; QUERCITRON, from Latin *quercus*, oak. [Pokorny *perkʷu-s* 822.]

perso- Sheaf (of ears of grain). **1.** Possibly Greek *Persephónē*, Persephone, whose name is also recorded in such early variants as *Persóphata*, *Perrophatta*, from *perso-gʷhṇtya*, probably "she who beats the sheaves, she of the sheaf-beating (*-gʷhṇ-t-ya*, suffixed zero-grade of *gʷhen-*, to strike; see **gʷhen-**); compare the formerly widespread European folk custom of making the last sheaf of grain of the harvest into a female figurine playing in a role in harvest celebrations. **2.** Possibly (although uncertain) Greek *prason*, leek (from its sheaflike shape; alternatively, the Greek word along with its Latin cognate *porrum* may be independent borrowings from an unknown Mediterranean source): PRASE; CHRYSOPRASE, PRASEODYMIUM. [Not in Pokorny; compare Sanskrit *parṣa*, Avestan *parša-*, sheaf.]

persnā- Heel. PEARL¹, from Latin *perna*, ham, leg, sea mussel. [Pokorny *persnā* 823.]

pes- To rub. This root is found as a verb only in Hittite *pešš-*, to rub, but it is continued by a number of nominal derivatives formed with varying suffixes and meaning "penis," such as Greek *peos* and Sanskrit *pasas*, both < *pes-os. Suffixed form *pes-ni-. PENCIL, PENICILLIN, PENICILLIUM, PENIS, from Latin *pēnis* (< *pesnis), penis, tail. [Pokorny 3. *pes-* 824.]

pet- To rush, fly. Also **petǝ-** (oldest form *peth₁-, with variant [metathesized] form *pteh₁-, contracted to *ptē-.) **1.** Suffixed form *pet-rā-. FEATHER, from Old English *fether*, feather, from Germanic *fethrō*, feather. **2.** -PETAL, PETITION, PETULANT; APPETITE, COMPETE, IMPETIGO, IMPETUOUS, IMPETUS, PERPETUAL, REPEAT, from Latin *petere*, to go toward, seek. **3.** Suffixed form *pet-nā-. PANACHE, PEN¹, PENNA, PENNATE, PENNON, PIN, PINNA, PINNACLE, PINNATE, PINNATI-, PINNULE; EMPENNAGE, from Latin *penna*, *pinna*, feather, wing. **4.** Suffixed form *pet-ro- in compound *aku-petro- (see **ōku-**). **5.** Suffixed form *pet-yo-. PROPITIOUS, from Latin *propitius*, favorable, gracious, originally a religious term meaning "falling or rushing forward," hence "eager," "well-disposed" (said of the gods; *prō-*, forward; see **per¹**). **6.** Suffixed zero-grade form *pt-ero-. -PTER; AMINOPTERIN, APTERYX, ARCHAE-

OPTERYX, COLEOPTERAN, DIPTERAL, MECOPTERAN, MONOPTEROS, ORTHOPTERAN, PERIPTERAL, PLECOPTERAN, PTERIDOLOGY, PTEROYLGLATAMIC ACID, PTERYGOID, SAUROPTERYGIAN, from Greek *pteron*, feather, wing, and *pterux*, wing. **7.** Suffixed zero-grade form *pt-ilo-. COLEOPTILE, from Greek *ptilon*, soft feathers, down, plume. **8.** Reduplicated form *pi-pt-. PTOMAINE, PTOSIS; ASYMPTOTE, PERIPETEIA, PROPTOSIS, SYMPTOM, from Greek *piptein*, to fall, with verbal adjective *ptōtos* (< *ptō-to-), falling, fallen, and nominal derivatives *ptōsis* (< *ptō-ti-), a fall, and *ptōma* (< *ptō-mṇ), a fall, fallen body, corpse. **9.** O-grade form *pot-. HIPPOPOTAMUS, POTAMOLOGY, from Greek *potamos* "rushing water," river (*-amo-*, Greek suffix). **10.** Suffixed form *pet-tro-. TALIPOT, from Sanskrit *pattram*, feather, leaf. [Pokorny 2. *pet-* 825.]

petǝ- To spread. (Oldest form *peth₂-.) **1.** Suffixed o-grade form *pot(ǝ)-mo-. FATHOM, from Old English *fæthm*, fathom, from Germanic *fathmaz*, "length of two arms stretched out." **2.** Suffixed (stative) variant zero-grade form *pat-ē-. PATENT, PATULOUS, from Latin *patēre*, to be open. **3.** Probably variant zero-grade form in remade nasalized form *pat-no-. PACE¹, PANDY, PAS, PASEO, PASS, PASSÉ, PASSIM; COMPAS, COMPASS, EXPAND, PASO FINO, PASQUEFLOWER, PASSACAGLIA, PASSAGE¹, PASSAGE², PASSPORT, REPAND, SPAWN, from Latin *pandere* (past participle *passus* < *pat-to-), to spread out. **4.** Suffixed form *pet-alo-. PETAL, from Greek *petalon*, leaf. **5.** Suffixed form *pet-ano-. PAELLA, PAN¹, PATEN, PATINA¹, PATINA², from Greek *patanē* (? < *petanā-), platter, "thing spread out." **6.** PETASOS, from Greek *petasos*, broad-brimmed hat, from Greek suffixed form *peta-so-. [Pokorny 1. *pet-* 824.]

peuǝ- To purify, cleanse. (Oldest form *peuh₂-.) **1.** Suffixed zero-grade form *pū-ro (< *puǝ-ro-). POUR, PURE, PURÉE, PURGE, PURITAN; COMPURGATION, DEPURATE, EXPURGATE, PURBLIND, SPURGE, from Latin *pūrus*, pure, and *pūrgāre*, to purify (< *pūr-igāre < *pūr-agāre; *ag-*, to drive; see **ag-¹**). **2.** Suffixed zero-grade form *pū-yo- (< *puǝ-yo). PIACULUM, PIETY, PIOUS, PITY; EXPIATE, IMPIOUS, from Latin *pius*, devout, dutiful in religious matters (< *"in a state of purity", from earlier *pīos, assimilated from *pūyos), with associated verb *piāre*, to purify, expiate. [Pokorny 1. *peu-* 827.]

peuk- Also **peug-.** To prick. (Oldest forms *peuk̑-, *peug̑-.) Zero-grade form *pug-. **1.** Suffixed form *pug-no-. PONIARD, PUGILISM, PUGIL STICK, PUGNACIOUS; IMPUGN, OPPUGN, REPUGN, from Latin *pugil*, pugilist, and *pugnus*, fist, with denominative *pugnāre*, to fight with the fist. **2.** Nasalized zero-grade form *pu-n-g-. BUNG, PINK², POIGNANT, POINT, POINTILLISM, PONTIL, POUNCE¹, POUNCE³, PUNCHEON¹, PUNCTILIO, PUNCTUAL, PUNCTUATE, PUNCTURE, PUNGENT; BONTEBOK, COMPUNCTION, EXPUNGE, SPONTOON, TRAPUNTO, from Latin *pungere*, to prick. **3.** PYGMAEAN, PYGMY, from Greek *pugmē*, fist. **3.** Seen by some as the base of Germanic *fuk(k)-, in words relating to sexual intercourse: FUCK. [Pokorny *peuk̑-* 828.]

pezd- To fart. **1.** Suffixed form *pezd-i-. FEIST, from Old English *fisting*, a breaking wind, and Middle English *fisten*, to fart, from Germanic *fistiz*, a fart. **2.** PETARD, from Latin *pēdere*, to fart. **3.** Perhaps Latin *pēdis*, louse (? < "foul-smelling insect"): PEDICULAR¹. [Pokorny *pezd-* 829, 2. *peis-* 796.] Compare **perd-.**

pǝter- Father. (Oldest form *ph₂ter-.) **1.** FATHER; FOREFATHER, from Old English *fæder*, father, from Germanic *fadar*. **2.** PADRE, PATER, PATERNAL, PATRI-, PATRICIAN, PATRIMONY, PATRON, PÈRE; COMPADRE, EX- PATRIATE, GOOMBAH, PERPETRATE, from Latin *pater*, father. **3.** PATRI-, PATRIOT; ALLOPATRIC, EUPATRID, PATRIARCH, SYMPATRIC, from Greek *patēr*, father. [Pokorny *patḗr* 829.]

pik- Pitch. **1.** PAY², PICEOUS, PITCH¹; PICOLINE, PITCHBLENDE, from Latin *pix* (stem *pic-*), pitch. **2.** Suffixed form *pik-ya. PITTOSPORUM, from Greek pissa, pitta, pitch. [In Pokorny pei(ə)- 793.]

pilo- Hair. Possible root. **1.** PELAGE, PILAR, PILE³, PILOSE, PILUS, PLUCK, PLUSH, POILU; CATERPILLAR, DEPILATE, PILIFEROUS, STRAMENOPILE, from Latin pilus, hair. **2.** Possibly suffixed reduced form *pil-so-. **a.** PILEUS, PILLAGE, from Latin pileus, felt cap; **b.** PILOCARPINE, from Greek pîlos, felt. [Pokorny pi-lo- 830.]

pīp(p)- To peep. Imitative root. **1.** FIFE, PIPE; PIBROCH, from Latin pīpāre, to chirp. **2.** PIGEON, from Latin pīpīre, to chirp. [Pokorny pīp(p)- 830.]

plāk-¹ Also **plak-.** To be flat. (Oldest form *pleh₂k-, colored to *plah₂k-, contracted to *plāk-; extension of **pelə-².**) **1.** FLOE, from Old Norse flō, layer, coating, from Germanic *flōhō. **2.** Variant form *plāg-. **a.** FLUKE¹, from Old English flōc, flatfish, from Germanic *flōk-; **b.** FLAKE¹, from Middle English flake, flake, from a Scandinavian source probably akin to Norwegian flak, flat piece, flake, from Germanic *flakaz; **c.** FLAKE², from Old Norse flaki, fleki, hurdle, from Germanic *flak-. **3.** Extended form *plakā-. FLAG⁴, FLAW¹, from Old Norse flaga, layer of stone, from Germanic *flagō. **4.** Possibly suffixed (stative) form *plak-ē-, to be calm (as of the flat sea). PLACEBO, PLACID, PLEA, PLEAD, PLEASANT, PLEASE; COMPLACENT, from Latin placēre, to please, be agreeable. **5.** Root noun *plak-. SUPPLE, SUPPLICATE, from Latin supplex, suppliant (whence denominative supplicāre, to beg humbly, first attested in Archaic Latin as sub vōs placō, I entreat you; sub, under; see **upo.**) **6.** Lengthened suffixed form *plāk-ā-. PLACABLE, PLACATE, from Latin plācāre, to calm (causative of placēre). **7.** Nasalized form *plan-k-. PLANCHET, PLANK, from Latin plancus, flat, flat-footed. **8.** Variant form *plag-. **a.** Perhaps Latin plaga, net (? < "something extended"): PLAGIARY; **b.** PLAGAL, PLAGIO-, PLAYA, from Greek plagos, side. **9.** Root form *plak-. PLACENTA, PLACOID; LEUKOPLAKIA, PLACODERM, from Greek plax, flat, flat land, surface, plate. **10.** Possible variant form *pelag-. PELAGIC; ARCHIPELAGO, from Greek pelagos, sea. [Pokorny 1. plā-k- 831.]

plāk-² To strike. (Oldest form *pleh₂k-, colored to *plah₂k-, contracted to *plāk-.) **1.** Nasalized variant forms *pla-n-k-, *pla-n-g-. **a.** FLING, from Middle English flingen, to fling, from a Scandinavian source akin to Old Norse flengja, to flog, whip, from Germanic *flang-; **b.** PLAINT, PLANGENT; COMPLAIN, from Latin plangere, to strike (one's own breast), lament; **c.** suffixed form *plang-yo-. PLANKTON, from Greek plazein, to drive away, turn aside. **2.** Variant form *plāg-. PLAGUE, from Latin plāga, a blow, stroke. **3.** Suffixed form *plāk-yo-. PLECTRUM, -PLEGIA, PLEXOR; APOPLEXY, CATAPLEXY, PARAPLEGIA, from Greek plēssein, to beat, strike. [Pokorny 2. plāk- 832.]

plat- To spread. Also **pletə-** (oldest form *pleth₂-). Extension of **pelə-².** **1.** Variant form *plad-. **a.** FLAT¹, from Old Norse flatr, flat; **b.** FLATTER¹, from Old French flater, to flatter. Both **a** and **b** from Germanic *flata-, flat. **2.** Suffixed variant form *plad-yo-. FLAT², from Old English flet(t), floor, dwelling, from Germanic *flatjam. **3.** Basic form *plat-. FLAN, from Late Latin fladō, flat cake, pancake, from Germanic *flathō(n), flat cake. **4.** FLOUNDER², from Anglo-Norman floundre, flounder, from a Scandinavian source probably akin to Old Swedish flundra, flatfish, flounder, from Germanic suffixed nasalized form *flu-n-th-r-jō. **5.** Nasalized form *pla-n-t-. CLAN, PLAN, PLANT, PLANTAIN¹, PLANTAR; PLANTIGRADE, SUPPLANT, TRANSPLANT, from Latin planta, sole of the foot, and denominative plantāre, to drive in with the sole of the foot, plant, whence planta, a plant. **6.** Suffixed zero-grade form *pl̥t(ə)-u-. PIAZZA, PLACE, PLAICE, PLANE⁴, PLANE TREE, PLATE, PLATEAU, PLATERESQUE, PLATINA, PLATINUM, PLATITUDE, PLATY², PLATY-, PLAZA; PLATEOSUARUS, from Greek platus, flat, broad. [Pokorny plăt- 833.]

plē-(i)k- Also **pleik-.** To tear. (Oldest form *pleh₁-(i)k-.) **1.** Zero-grade form *plək-. FLAY, from Old English flēan, to strip the skin from, from Germanic *flahan. **2.** Perhaps suffixed o-grade form *ploik-sk-. FLESH, from Old English flǣsc, piece of flesh torn off, from Germanic *flaiskjan, piece of meat torn off. **3.** Zero-grade form *plik-. **a.** FLITCH, from Old English flicce, side of a hog; **b.** FLECK, from Old Norse flekkr, piece of skin or flesh, spot, stain, from Germanic ablaut form *flekkja. [Pokorny plēk- 835.]

plek- To plait. (Oldest form *plek̑-; extension of **pel-².**) **1.** Suffixed o-grade form *plok-so-. FLAX, from Old English fleax, flax, from Germanic *flahsam, flax. **2.** Full-grade form *plek-. MULTIPLEX, from Latin -plex, -fold (in compounds such as duplex, twofold; see **dwo-**). **3.** PLAIT, PLEAT, PLIANT, PLICA, PLICATE, PLIGHT¹, PLISSÉ, PLY¹; APPLY, COMPLICATE, COMPLICE, DEPLOY, DISPLAY, EMPLOY, EXPLICATE, EXPLICIT, EXPLOIT, IMPLICATE, IMPLICIT, REPLICATE, REPLY, SPLAY, from Latin plicāre, to fold (also in compounds used as denominatives of words in -plex, genitive -plicis). **4.** Suffixed forms *plek-to- and *plek-t-to-. PLEACH, PLEXUS; AMPLEXICAUL, AMPLEXUS, COMPLECT, COMPLEX, PERPLEXED, from Latin plectere (past participle plexus), to weave, plait, entwine. **5.** PLECOPTERAN, from Greek plekein, to plait, twine, and plektos, twisted. [Pokorny plek̑- 834.]

pleu- To flow.

I. Basic form *pleu-. **1.** PLOVER, PLUVIAL, PLUVIOUS, from Latin pluere, to rain. **2.** PLEOPOD, from Greek plein (< *plewein), to swim. **3.** PLEUSTON, from Greek pleusis, sailing. **4.** Suffixed zero-grade form *plu-elos. PYELITIS, from Greek dissimilated puelos, trough, basin. **5.** Suffixed form *pl(e)u-mon-, "floater," lung(s). **a.** PULMONARY, PULMONOLOGY, from Latin pulmō (< *plumonēs), lung(s); **b.** PNEUMO-, PNEUMONIA, PNEUMONIC, from Greek pleumōn, pneumōn (influenced by pneuma, breath; see **pneu-**), lung. **6.** Suffixed o-grade form *plou-to-. PLUTO; PLUTOCRACY, from Greek ploutos, wealth, riches (< "overflowing"). **7.** Lengthened o-grade form *plō(u)-. **a.** (i) FLOW, from Old English flōwan, to flow; (ii) perhaps Middle Dutch vluwe, fishnet: FLUE². Both (i) and (ii) from Germanic *flōwan, to flow; **b.** suffixed form *plō-tu-. FLOOD, from Old English flōd, flood, from Germanic *flōduz, flowing water, deluge.

II. Extended form *pleuk-. **1.** FLY¹, from Old English flēogan, to fly, from Germanic *fleugan, to fly. **2.** FLY², from Old English flēoge, a fly, from Germanic *fleugōn-, flying insect, fly. **3.** Probably Germanic *fleuhan, to run away. FLEE, from Old English flēon, to flee. **4.** FLEY, from Old English flȳgan, flēgan, to put to flight, from Germanic causative *flaugjan. **5.** FLÈCHE, FLETCHER, from Old French fleche, arrow, from Germanic suffixed form *fleug-ika-. **6.** Zero-grade form *pluk-. **a.** FLEDGE, from Old English *flycge, with feathers (only in unfligge, featherless), from Germanic *flugja-, ready to fly; **b.** FLIGHT¹, FLIGHT², from Old English flyht, act of flying, and *flyht, act of fleeing, escape, from Germanic suffixed form *flug-ti-; **c.** FOWL, from Old English fugol, bird, from Germanic *fuglaz, bird, dissimilated from possible (but unlikely) suffixed form *flug-laz; **d.** FLUGELHORN, FUGLEMAN, from Middle High German vlügel, wing, from Germanic suffixed form *flug-ilaz.

III. Extended form *pleud-. **1.** FLEET¹, FLEET², from Old English flēotan, to float, swim (from Germanic *fleutan), and Old Norse fljōtr, fleet, swift (from Germanic *fleuta-). **2.** Zero-grade form *plud-. **a.** (i) FLOAT, from Old English flotian, to float; (ii) FLOTSAM, from Old French floter, to float. Both (i) and (ii) from Germanic derivative *flotōn, to float; **b.** FLOTILLA, from Old Norse floti, raft, fleet; **c.** FLUTTER, from Old English floterian, flotorian, to float back and forth (-erian, iterative and frequentative suffix); **d.** FLIT, from Old Norse flytja, to further, convey, from Germanic *flutjan, to float. **a–d** all from Germanic *flut-, *flot-. **3.** FLUSTER, probably from a Scandinavian source akin to Icelandic flaustr, hurry, and flaustra, to bustle, from Germanic *flausta-, contracted from suffixed form *flaut-stā-, probably from *pleud-, o-grade *ploud-. [Pokorny pleu- 835, pl(e)u- mon- 837.]

pleus- To pluck; a feather, fleece. **1.** FLEECE, from Old English flēos, from Germanic *fleusaz. **2.** Suffixed zero-grade form *plus-mā-. PLUMATE, PLUME, PLUMOSE, PLUMULE; DEPLUME, from Latin plūma, a feather. [Pokorny pleus- 838.]

plou- Flea. **1.** Extended form *plouk-. FLEA, from Old English flēa(h), flea, from Germanic *flauhaz. **2.** Extended zero-grade form *plus-, metathesized to *pusl-. **a.** PUCE, from Latin pūlex, flea; **b.** PSYLLID, PSYLLIUM, from Greek psulla, flea. [Pokorny blou- 102.]

pneu- To breathe. Imitative root. **1.** SNEEZE, from Old English fnēosan, to sneeze, from Germanic *fneu-s-. **2.** SNORE, SNORT, from Old English fnora, sneezing, from Germanic *fnu-s-. **3.** APNEA, DIPNOAN, DYSPNEA, EUPNEA, HYPERPNEA, HYPOPNEA, POLYPNEA, TACHYPNEA, from Greek pnein, to breathe, with o-grade nouns pnoiā, -pnoia, breathing, and pnoē, breath. **4.** Suffixed form *pneu-mn̥. PNEUMA, PNEUMATIC, PNEUMATO-, PNEUMO-; AMPHIUMA, from Greek pneuma, breath, wind, spirit. **5.** Germanic variant root *fnes-. SNEER, possibly from Old English fnǣran, to snort, gnash one's teeth. [Pokorny pneu- 838.]

pō(i)- To drink. (Oldest form *peh₃(i)-, colored to *poh₃(i)-, contracted to *pō(i)-.)
  I. Unextended form *pō-. **1.** Suffixed form *pō-to-. POTABLE, POTATION, POTATORY, from Latin pōtus, drunk, a drink (whence pōtāre, to drink). **2.** Suffixed form *pō-ti-. POISON, POTION, from Latin pōtiō, a drink. **3.** Suffixed form *pō-tlo-, drinking vessel. HIBACHI, from Sanskrit pātram, cup, bowl. **4.** Suffixed reduplicated zero-grade form *pi-pə-o-, whence *pi-bo-, assimilated to *bi-bo-. BEER, BEVERAGE, BIB, BIBULOUS; IMBIBE, IMBRUE, from Latin bibere, to drink. **5.** Suffixed zero-grade form *pə-ti-, *po-ti-. SYMPOSIUM, from Greek posis, drink, drinking.
  II. Zero-grade form *pī- (< *piə-). **1.** Suffixed form *pī-ro-. PIEROGI, PIROZHKI, from Slavic *pirŭ, feast (Old Church Slavonic pirŭ). **2.** Suffixed (nasal present) form *pī-no-. PINOCYTOSIS, from Greek pīnein, to drink. [Pokorny 2. pō(i)- 839.]

pōl- To fall. Suffixed form *phol-no-. **1a.** FALL, from Old English feallan, to fall; **b.** BEFALL, from Old English befeallan, to fall, from Germanic *bi-fallan, to fall, happen (*bi-, by, at; see **ambhi**). Both **a** and **b** from Germanic *fallan. **2.** FELL¹, from Old English fellan, fyllan, to cut down, from Germanic *falljan, "to cause to fall," strike down. [Pokorny phōl- 851.]

porko- Young pig. (Oldest form *porko-.) **1a.** FARROW¹, from Old English fearh, little pig; **b.** AARDVARK, from Middle Dutch diminutive form varken, small pig. Both **a** and **b** from Germanic *farhaz. **2.** PORCELAIN, PORCINE, PORK; PORCUPINE, PORPOISE, from Latin porcus, pig. [Pokorny porko- 841.]

poti Against, towards. PESHMERGA, from Kurdish pêşmerge, one who faces death, peshmerga, from pêş, in front of, before, from Old Iranian *patiš, against (Kurdish merg, death; see **merk-**). [Pokorny po-ti 842.]

poti- Powerful; lord. **1.** PODESTA, POSSESS, POWER, from Latin potis, powerful, able, and compound possidēre (pos- < *pots), to hold in one's control, possess. **2.** POSSIBLE, POTENT; IMPOTENT, OMNIPOTENT, PREPOTENT, from Latin compound posse, to be able (contracted from potis, able + esse, to be; see **es-**). **3a.** VANASPATI, from Sanskrit patiḥ, lord; **b.** BASHAW, PADISHAH, PASHA, from Old Persian pati-, master. Both **a** and **b** from Indo-Iranian *pati-, lord, master. **4.** Form *pot-. **a.** Compound *ghos-pot- (see **ghos-**

ti-); **b.** compound *dems-pot- (see **dem-**). [Pokorny poti-s 842.]

prek- To ask, entreat. (Oldest form *prek̑-.) **1.** Basic form *prek-. PRAY, PRAYER¹, PRECARIOUS; DEPRECATE, IMPRECATE, PRIE-DIEU, from *prex, prayer (attested only in the plural precēs), with Latin denominative precārī, to entreat, pray. **2.** Suffixed zero-grade form *pr̥(k)-sk- becoming *por(k)-sk- in Italic, contracted to *posk- in suffixed form *posk-to-, contracted to *posto-. POSTULATE; EXPOSTULATE, from Latin postulāre, to ask, request. [Pokorny 4. perk̑- 821.]

prep- To appear. Probably the same root as **kʷrep-**, body, appearance. Suffixed zero-grade form *pr̥p-yo-. FURBISH, from Old French fo(u)rbir, to polish, burnish, from Germanic *furbjan, to cause to have a (good) appearance, polish. [Pokorny prep- 845.]

preu- To hop. **1.** Zero-grade form *pru-. FROG, from Old English frogga (with obscure expressive suffix -gga), frog, from Germanic *fru-. **2.** Suffixed o-grade form *prow-o-. **a.** FROLIC, from Middle Dutch vro, "leaping with joy," happy; **b.** SCHADENFREUDE, from Old High German frō, happy, and derivative frewida, joy. Both **a** and **b** from Germanic *frawa-. [Pokorny preu- 845.]

preus- To freeze, burn. **1.** FREEZE, FRORE, from Old English frēosan, to freeze (past participle froren), from Germanic *freusan, to freeze (with Old English past participle froren from Germanic *fruzana-, from Indo-European suffixed zero-grade form *prus-ono-). **2.** Suffixed zero-grade form *prus-to-. FROST, from Old English forst, frost, from Germanic *frustaz, frost. **3.** Suffixed form *preus-i-. PRURIENT, PRURIGO, PRURITUS, from Latin denominative prūrīre, to burn, itch, yearn for, from *preusis, *preuris, act of burning. **4.** Suffixed zero-grade form *prus-wīnā-. PRUINOSE, from Latin pruīna, hoarfrost. [Pokorny preus- 846.]

prī- To love. (Oldest form *priH̯-, contracted to *prī- [before consonants] and *priy- [before vowels].) **1.** Suffixed form *priy-o-. **a.** FREE, from Old English frēo, free, and frēon, freogan, to love, set free; **b.** FILIBUSTER, FREEBOOTER, from Dutch vrij, free. Both **a** and **b** from Germanic *frija-, beloved, belonging to the loved ones, not in bondage, free, and *frijōn, to love. **2.** Suffixed (participial) form *priy-ont-, loving. FRIEND, from Old English frīond, frēond, friend, from Germanic *frijand-, lover, friend. **3.** Suffixed shortened form *pri-tu-. **a.** Old High German fridu, peace, in personal names: (i) SIEGFRIED, from Old High German Sigifrith, "victorious peace" (sigu, victory; see **segh-**); (ii) GODFREY, from Old High German Godafrid, "peace of god" (got, god; see **gheu(ə)-**); **b.** AFFRAY, AFRAID, from Old French esfreer, to disturb, from Vulgar Latin *exfredāre, to break the peace, from ex-, out, away (see **eghs**) + *fridāre, to make peace, from Germanic *frithu-, peace; **c.** Germanic compound name *Frithu-rik, "peaceful ruler" (*rīk, ruler; see **reg-¹**). FREDERICK, FRIEDRICH (personal names), from Old High German Fridurih (> French Frédéric); **d.** Germanic compound name *Gawja-frithu-, "(having a) peaceful region" (*gawjam, region). GEOFFREY (personal name), from Medieval Latin Galfridus, Gaufridus (> Old French Geoffroi); **e.** Germanic compound *berg-frithu- (see **bhergh-²**). **a–e** all from Germanic *frithuz, peace. **4.** Suffixed feminine form *priy-ā-, beloved. **a.** FRIGG, from Old Norse Frigg, goddess of the heavens, wife of Odin; **b.** FRIDAY, from Old English Frīgedæg, Friday, from Germanic compound *frijedagaz, "day of Frigg" (translation of Latin Veneris diēs, "Venus's day"). Both **a** and **b** from Germanic *frijjō, beloved, wife. [Pokorny prāi- 844.]

prōkto- Anus. (Oldest form *prōkto-.) PROCTITIS, PROCTODEUM, PROCTOLOGY, PROCTOSCOPE, from Greek prōktos, anus. [Pokorny prōkto- 846.]

pster- Also **ster-**. To sneeze. Imitative root. **1.** Suffixed form *ster-nu-. STERNUTATION, from Latin ster-

nuere, to sneeze. **2.** Suffixed form **ster-t-*. STERTOR, from Latin *stertere*, to snore. [Pokorny *pster-* 846.]

pŭ-¹ Also **phŭ-**. To blow, swell. Imitative root. **1.** Extended form **pus-*. PUSTULE, from Latin *pustula*, a bubble, blister. **2.** Perhaps extended form **pūt-*, penis. PREPUCE, from Latin *praepūtium*, foreskin (*prae-*, before, in front; see **per¹**). **3.** Variant form **phū-*. EMPHYSEMA, from Greek *phūsa*, bellows, bladder. [Pokorny 1. *pū-* 847.]

pŭ-² To rot, decay. (Oldest form probably **puh_x-*, becoming **puw-* before vowels.) **1.** Suffixed form **pū-lo-*. **a.** FOUL, from Old English *fūl*, unclean, rotten; **b.** FULMAR, from Old Norse *fūll*, foul; **c.** FILTH, from Old English *fȳlth*, foulness, from Germanic abstract noun **fūlithō*; **d.** FILE¹, FOIL¹; DEFILE¹, from Old English *fȳlan*, to sully, from Germanic denominative **fūljan*, to soil, dirty. **a–d** all from Germanic **fūla-*, rotten, filthy. **2.** Extended form **pug-*. FOG², from Middle English *fog, fogge*, aftermath grass, from a Scandinavian source probably akin to Icelandic *fūki*, rotten sea grass, and Norwegian *fogg*, rank grass, from Germanic **fuk-*. **3.** Extended variant form **pous-*. FUZZY, from Low German *fussig*, spongy, from Germanic **fausa-*. **4.** Suffixed form **pu-tri-*. POONTANG, PUTRESCENT, PUTRID, PUTTANESCA; OLLA PODRIDA, POTPOURRI, PUTREFY, from Latin *puter* (stem *putri-*), rotten. **5.** Suffixed form **puw-os-*. **a.** PURULENT, PUS; SUPPURATE, from Latin *pūs*, pus; **b.** PYO-, from Greek *puon, puos*, pus. **6.** EMPYEMA, from Greek compound *empuein*, to suppurate (*en-*, in; see **en**). [Pokorny 2. *pū-* 848.]

puk- Bushy-haired. In part a taboo deformation of **w|kʷo-** and **w|p-ē-**. Suffixed form **puk-so-*. **1.** FOX, from Old English *fox*, fox, from Germanic **fuhsaz*, fox. **2.** VIXEN, from Old English *fyxe*, she-fox, from Germanic feminine **fuhsīn-*. [Pokorny *pŭk-* 849.]

pūro- A kind of grain. **1.** Possibly suffixed form **pūr-iso-*, suggested by some (but unlikely for semantic reasons) as the source of Old English *fyrs*, furze: FURZE. **2.** Suffixed form **pūr-ēn-*. PYRENE, from Greek *pūrēn*, stone of fruit. [Pokorny *pū-ro-* 850.]

p(y)el- Tree name. Possible root. Possibly broken reduplicated form **pō-pel-*. POPLAR, POPPLE², from Latin *pōpulus*, poplar. [Pokorny *ptel(e)jā* 847.]

[re- Also **red-**. Backward. Latin combining form conceivably from Indo-European **wret-*, metathetical variant of **wert-*, to turn (< "turned back"), an extended form of **wer-³**. **1.** RE-, from Latin *re-, red-*, backward, again. **2.** Suffixed form **re(d)-tro-*. RETRAL, RETRO-; ARREARS, REAR GUARD, REARWARD², REREDOS, from Latin *retrō*, backward, back, behind. **3.** Suffixed form **re-ko-* in Latin *reciprocus* (see **per¹**).]

rē-¹ To bestow, endow. (Contracted from earlier **reh₁-*.) Suffixed form **reə-i-*, goods, wealth, property. RE², REAL¹, REBUS; REIFY, REPUBLIC, from Latin *rēs*, thing. [Pokorny 4. *rei-* 860.]

rē-² Dark-colored, possible root (oldest form **reh₁-*) with suffixed form *rē-mo-*. **1.** RAMA, from Sanskrit *Rāmaḥ*, Rama, from *rāma-*, dark (traditionally said to be in reference to his dark skin). **2.** WOLFRAM, from Middle High German *rām*, dirt, grime (attested earlier in Old High German in the adjective *rāmach*, dirty). [Pokorny 5. *rē-* 853.]

rebh-¹ Violent, impetuous. Suffixed zero-grade form **rabh-yo-*. RABID, RABIES, RAGE; ARRABBIATA, from Latin *rabere*, to rave, be mad. [Pokorny *rabh-* 852.]

rebh-² To roof over. **1.** RIB, from Old English *ribb*, rib. **2.** REEF¹, REEF², from Old Norse *rif*, rib, ridge. **3.** SPARERIBS, from Middle Low German *ribbe*, rib. **1–3** all from Germanic **rebja-*, **rebjō*, "covering of the chest cavity." [Pokorny 2. *rebh-* 853.]

rēd- To scrape, scratch, gnaw. (Contracted from earlier **reh₁d-*.) **1.** O-grade form **rōd-*. **a.** RODENT; CORRODE, ERODE, from Latin *rōdere*, to gnaw; **b.** suffixed (*instrumental*) form **rōd-tro-*. ROSTRUM, from Latin *rōstrum*, beak, ship's bow. **2.** Possibly extended zero-grade form

*rəd-d-, becoming **razd-*, whence **rād-* in Latin. **a.** RADULA, RASCAL, RASH², RASORIAL, RATTEEN, RAZE, RAZOR; ABRADE, CORRADE, ERASE, from Latin *rādere*, to scrape; **b.** suffixed (*instrumental*) form **rād-tro-*. RACLETTE, RASTER, from Latin *rāstrum*, rake. **3.** Zero-grade form **rəd-*. RAT, from Old English *ræt*, rat, from Germanic **rattōn-*. [Pokorny 2. *rēd-* 854.]

reg-¹ To move in a straight line, with derivatives meaning "to direct in a straight line, lead, rule." (Oldest form **h₃reĝ-*.)

I. Basic form **reg-*. **1.** Suffixed form **reg-to-*. RIGHT, from Old English *riht*, right, just, correct, straight, from Germanic **rehta-*. **2.** REALM, RECTITUDE, RECTO, RECTOR, RECTUM, RECTUS, REGENT, REGIME, REGIMEN, REGIMENT, REGION; ADDRESS, ADROIT, ALERT, DERECHO, CORRECT, DIRECT, ERECT, INCORRIGIBLE, PORRECT, RECTANGLE, RECTIFY, RECTILINEAR, RESURGE, RISORGIMENTO, SORD, SOURCE, SURGE, from Latin *regere*, to lead straight, guide, rule (past participle *rēctus*, whence adjective *rēctus*, right, straight). **3.** ANORECTIC, ANOREXIA, from Greek *oregein*, to stretch out, reach out for (with *o-* from oldest root form **h₃reĝ-*).

II. Lengthened-grade form **rēg-*, Indo-European word for a tribal king. **1a.** Old High German *-rih*, king, ruler, in personal names (see **albho-, tkei-**); **b.** Gothic *reiks*, king, in personal names (see **teutā-**). Both **a** and **b** from Germanic **rīks*, king, from Celtic **rīg-*, king. **2a.** BISHOPRIC, ELDRITCH, from Old English *rīce*, realm; **b.** RIKSMÅL, from Old Norse *rīki*, realm; **c.** REICH; REICHSMARK, from Old High German *richi*, realm, also in personal name *Rīcohard* (see **kar-¹**); **d.** RICH, from Old English *rīce*, strong, powerful, and Old French *riche*, wealthy; **e.** Germanic compound **aiza-rikjaz*, "honored ruler" (**aizō*, honor). ERIC (personal name), from Old Norse *Eirīkr*. **a–e** all from Germanic **rīkja-*, from Celtic suffixed form **rīg-yo-*. **3.** REAL², REGAL, REGULUS, REIGN, REX, RIAL¹, RIYAL, ROYAL; REGICIDE, REGIUS PROFESSOR, VICEREINE, VICEROY, from Latin *rēx*, king (royal and priestly title). **4.** Suffixed form **rēg-en-*. RAJ, RAJA, RANI, RYE²; MAHARAJA, MAHARANI, from Sanskrit *rājā*, *rājan-*, king, rajah (feminine *rājñī*, queen, rani); and *rājati*, he rules.

III. Suffixed lengthened-grade form **rēg-olā-*. RAIL¹, REGLET, REGULAR, REGULATE, RILLETTES, RULE, from Latin *rēgula*, straight piece of wood, rod.

IV. O-grade form **rog-*. **1.** RAKE¹, from Old English *raca, racu*, rake (implement with straight pieces of wood), from Germanic **rakō*. **2.** RACK¹, from Middle Dutch *rec*, framework, from Germanic **rak-*. **3.** Possibly Germanic **ranka-* (with nasal infix). RANK² from Old English *ranc*, straight, strong, hence haughty, overbearing. **4.** RECKON, from Old English *gerecenian*, to arrange in order, recount (*ge-*, collective prefix; see **kom**), from Germanic **rakina-*, ready, straightforward. **5.** Suffixed form **rog-ā-*. ROGATION, ROGATORY; ABROGATE, ARROGATE, CORVÉE, DEROGATE, INTERROGATE, PREROGATIVE, PROROGUE, SUBROGATE, SUPEREROGATE, from Latin *rogāre*, to ask (< "stretch out the hand"). **6.** Suffixed form **rog-o-*. ERGO, from Latin *ergō*, therefore, in consequence of, perhaps contracted from a Latin phrase **ē rogō*, "from the direction of" (*ē* < *ex*, out of; see **eghs**), from a possible Latin noun **rogus*, "extension, direction."

V. Lengthened o-grade form **rōg-*. **1.** RECK, from Old English *rec(c)an*, to pay attention to, take care (formally influenced by Old English *reccan*, to extend, stretch out, from Germanic **rakjan*), from Germanic **rōkjan*. **2.** RECKLESS, from Old English *rēcelēas*, careless (*-lēas*, lacking; see **leu-¹**), from Germanic **rōkja-*.

VI. Suffixed zero-grade form **ṛg-yo-*. RAITA, from Sanskrit *ṛjyati*, he stretches out. [Pokorny 1. *reĝ-* 854.]

reg-² Moist. (Oldest form **reĝ-*.) **1.** Suffixed variant form **rek-no-*. RAIN; RAINBOW, from Old English *reg(e)n*, *rēn*, rain, from Germanic **regnaz*, rain. **2.** Possibly

Latin *rigāre*, to wet, water: IRRIGATE. [Pokorny 2. *reĝ*-857.]

reg-³ To dye. Lengthened-grade form **rēg*-. **1.** Suffixed form **rēg-ēs*-. REGOLITH, from Greek *rhēgos*, blanket, rug. **2.** RAGA, from Sanskrit *rāgaḥ*, color, red. **3.** Possibly Sanskrit *rākṣā* (earlier form of *lākṣā*), red dye: LAC¹, LAKE². [Pokorny 1. *reg*- 854.]

regʷ-es- Darkness. (Oldest form **h₁regʷ*-.) EREBUS, from Greek *Erebos*, a place of darkness under the earth. [Pokorny *regʷos*- 857.]

rei-¹ To scratch, tear, cut. Hypothetical base of various extended forms.
   I. Extended form **reik*-. **1.** RIGATONI, from Italian *riga*, line (< "something cut out"), from Germanic **rīgōn*-. **2.** Suffixed form **rei-mā*- or **reig-smā*-. RIMOSE, from Latin *rīma*, crack, cleft, fissure. **3.** Suffixed o-grade form **roik-wo*-. ROW¹, from Old English *rāw*, *rǣw*, a line, row, from Germanic **rai(h)-wa*-.
   II. Possibly extended Germanic form **raip*-. **1.** ROPE, from Old English *rāp*, rope, from Germanic **raipaz*, rope. **2.** Germanic compound **stīg-raipaz* (see **steigh-**).
   III. Extended form **reip*-. **1.** RIVE, from Old Norse *rīfa*, to tear, from Germanic **rīfan*. **2.** Zero-grade form **rip*-. **a.** RIFT¹, from Middle English *rift*, rift, from a Scandinavian source akin to Danish *rift*, breach, from Germanic **rifti*-; **b.** RIFE, from Old English *rȳfe*, abundant, from Germanic **rīf*-. **3.** Suffixed form **reip-ā*-. RIPARIAN, RIVAGE, RIVER; ARRIVE, from Latin *rīpa*, bank (< "that which is cut out by a river").
   IV. Extended form **reib*-. **1.** RIPE, from Old English *rīpe*, ripe, ready for reaping, from Germanic **rīpja*-. **2.** REAP, from Old English *rīpan*, to reap, from Germanic **rīpan*. **3.** RIPPLE², from Middle English *ripelen*, to remove seeds, from a source akin to Middle Low German *repelen*, to remove seeds. **1–3** all from Germanic **rīp*-. [Pokorny 1. *rei*- 857.]

rei-² Striped in various colors, flecked. Suffixed o-grade form **roi-ko*-. ROE², from Old English *rā*, deer, from Germanic **raihaz*. [Pokorny 2. *rei*- 859.]

rē(i)- To reason, count. (Oldest form **h₂reh₁(i)-*, contracted to **h₂rē(i)-*, with zero-grade extended form **h₂rh₁i*- and metathesized zero-grade **h₂rih₁*-, the latter contracted to **h₂rī*-.)
   I. Basic form **(ə)rē*-. **1.** RATE¹, RATIO, RATION, REASON; ARRAIGN, from Latin *rērī*, to consider, confirm, ratify. **2.** Suffixed form **rē-dh*-. **a.** (i) READ, REDE; DREAD, from Old English *rǣdan*, to advise; (ii) HATRED, KINDRED, from Old English *rǣden*, *-rǣden*, condition. Both (i) and (ii) from Germanic **rǣdan*; **b.** (i) Old English *rǣd*, advice, counsel, in personal names (see **al-³, albho-, at-al-**); (ii) RATHSKELLER, from Old High German *rāt*, counsel; (iii) CONRAD (personal name), from Old High German *Kuonrāt*, "bold counsel" (*kuon*, bold); (iv) RALPH (personal name), from Old Norse *Rādhulfr*, "counsel wolf," from Old Norse *rādh*, counsel (*ulfr*, wolf; see **wḷkʷo-**); (v) RIDDLE², from Old English *rǣdels(e)*, opinion, riddle. (i)–(v) all from Germanic **rēdaz*. **3.** Suffixed zero-grade form **rə-t*-. Germanic **radam*, number, in dialectal North and West Germanic compound **hund(a)-rada*- (see **dekṃ**).
   II. Zero-grade extended form **ər(ə)i*- and (metathesized) **əri*-. **1.** Suffixed form **rī-tu*-. RITE, from Latin *rītus*, rite, custom, usage. **2.** Suffixed form **əraidhmo*-. ARITHMETIC, LOGARITHM, from Greek *arithmos*, number, amount. **3.** RHYME, from a Germanic source akin to Old High German *rīm*, number, series. [In Pokorny 1. *ar*- 55.]

reidh- To ride.
   I. Basic form **reidh*-. **1.** RIDE, from Old English *rīdan*, to ride, from Germanic **rīdan*. **2.** PALFREY, from Latin *verēdus*, post horse, from Celtic **wo-rēd*- (**wo*-, under; see **upo**).

II. O-grade form **roidh*-. **1.** Germanic **raidō*. **a.** RAID, ROAD, from Old English *rād*, a riding, road; **b.** possibly in Middle High German *reidel*, rod between upright stakes (< "wooden horse"): RADDLE¹. **2.** Probably Germanic **raid-ja*-. READY; ALREADY, from Old English *rǣde*, *gerǣde*, ready (< "prepared for a journey"). **3.** Probably Germanic **raidjan*. RAIMENT; ARRAY, CURRY¹, from Vulgar Latin **-rēdāre*, to arrange. [Pokorny *reidh*- 861.]

reiə- To flow, run. (Oldest form **h₃reih₂*-.) **1.** Nasalized zero-grade form **ri-ne-ə*-, remade as **ri-nu*-. **a.** RUN, RUNNEL, from Old English *rinnan*, to run, and Old Norse *rinna*, to run (from Germanic **rinnan*, to run, from **ri-nw-an*), and from Old English causative *ærnan*, *eornan*, to run (from secondary Germanic causative **rannjan*); **b.** EMBER DAY, from Old English *ryne*, a running, from secondary Germanic derivative **runiz*; **c.** RENNET, from Old English **rynet*, from secondary Germanic derivative **runita*-. **2.** Suffixed zero-grade form **ri-l*-. RILL, from Dutch *ril* or Low German *rille*, running stream, from Germanic **ril*-. **3.** Suffixed form **rei-wo*-. RIVAL, RIVULET; DERIVE, from Latin *rīvus*, stream. **4.** Suffixed form **rei-no*-. RHINE, from Gaulish *Rēnos* (ultimately > German *Rhein*), "river." [Pokorny 3. *er*- 326.]

reig-¹ To bind. **1.** RIG, from Middle English *riggen*, to rig, from a Scandinavian source akin to Norwegian *rigga*, to bind, from Germanic **rigg*- (the *-gg-* is anomalous). **2.** Zero-grade form **rig*-. SCOURGE, from Latin *corrigia* (probably borrowed from Gaulish), thong, shoelace (*cor*-, from *com*-, together; see **kom**). [Pokorny *reig*- 861.]

reig-² To reach, stretch out. (Oldest form **reiĝ*-.) **1.** O-grade form **roig*-. REACH, from Old English *rǣcan*, to stretch out, reach, from Germanic **raikjan*. **2.** Possibly suffixed (stative) zero-grade form **rig-ē*-. RIGID, RIGOR, from Latin *rigēre*, to be stiff (? < "be stretched out"). [Pokorny *(reiĝ*- 862.]

rem- To come to rest, rest. (Oldest form **h₁rem*-.) **1.** KALANCHOE, from Sanskrit *ārāmaḥ*, pleasure, pleasure garden, from *āramati*, he rests, takes pleasure, from Germanic *ramate*, he rests, takes pleasure (*ā*-, to; see **ē**). [Pokorny *rem*- 864.]

rendh- To tear up. **1.** REND, from Old English *rendan*, to tear, from Germanic **randjan*. **2.** RIND, from Old English *rind(e)*, rind (< "thing torn off"), from Germanic **rind*-. [Pokorny *rendh*- 865.]

rep- To snatch. Suffixed zero-grade form **rap-yo*-. RAPACIOUS, RAPE¹, RAPID, RAPINE, RAPT, RAVAGE, RAVEN², RAVIN, RAVISH; EREPSIN, SUBREPTION, SURREPTITIOUS, from Latin *rapere*, to seize. [Pokorny *rep*- 865.]

rēp-¹ To creep, slink. REPENT², REPTILE, from Latin *rēpere*, to creep. [Pokorny 1. *rēp*- 865.]

rēp-² Stake, beam. Suffixed variant form **rap-tro*-. **1.** RAFTER, from Old English *rǣfter*, rafter. **2.** RAFT¹, from Old Norse *raptr*, beam. Both **1** and **2** from Germanic **raf-tra*-. [Pokorny 2. *rēp*- 866.]

ret- To run, roll. **1.** Prefixed Celtic form **to-wo-ret*-, "a running up to" (**to*-, to; see **to-**; **wo*-, under, up, up from under; see **upo**). TORY, from Old Irish *tóir*, pursuit. **2.** Suffixed o-grade form **rot-ā*-. RODEO, ROLL, ROTA, ROTARY, ROTATE, ROULETTE, ROWEL; BAROUCHE, CONTROL, PRUNE², ROTAVIRUS, ROTAXANE, ROTIFORM, ROTOGRAVURE, from Latin *rota*, wheel. **3.** Suffixed form **rot-ə-o*- (oldest form**rot-h₂-o*-, probably derived from **rot-eh₂*, wheel, oldest form of **rot-ā*, wheel; see **2** above). ROOK², from Persian *rukh*, rook (probably influenced by Arabic *ruḫḫ*, roc, the medieval chesspiece sometimes having the form of a roc), from Prakrit *raha*-, chariot, rook (the original form of the chesspiece being a chariot), from Sanskrit *rathaḥ*, chariot. **4.** Suffixed (participial) form **ret-ondo*-. ROTUND, ROTUNDA, ROUND¹, from Latin *rotundus*, round, probably from earlier *retundus, "rolling." [Pokorny ret(h)- 866.]

rēt- Post. (Contracted from earlier *reh₁t-.) O-grade form *rōt- (< *roət-). ROOD, from Old English rōd, cross, from Germanic *rōd-. [Pokorny rēt- 866.]

reu- To bellow. **1.** Extended form *reud-. **a.** ROUT³, from Old Norse rauta, to roar; **b.** ROTE², from a Scandinavian source akin to Old Norse rauta. Both **a** and **b** from Germanic *rautōn. **2.** Suffixed extended form *reum-os-. RUMOR, from Latin rūmor, rumor, "common talk." **3.** Extended form *reug-. RIOT, RUT², from Latin rūgīre, to roar. **4.** Variant *rau-ko-. RAUCOUS, from Latin raucus, hoarse. [Pokorny 1. reu- 867.]

reudh-¹ Red, ruddy. (Oldest form *h₁reudh-.)
I. O-grade form *roudh-. **1a.** RED, from Old English rēad, red; **b.** RORQUAL, from Old Norse raudhr, red. **c.** ROOIBOS, from Middle Dutch rood, red. **a-c** all from Germanic *raudaz. **2.** Perhaps ultimately also from Germanic *raudaz, red, is Old Spanish roan, roano, roan, possibly from Gothic rauda-, red, or a kindred Germanic source: ROAN. **2.** ROWAN, from a source akin to Old Norse reynir, mountain ash, rowan (from its red berries), from Germanic *raudnia-. **3.** RUFESCENT, RUFOUS, from Latin rūfus (of dialectal Italic origin), reddish. **4.** ROUILLE, RUBIGINOUS, from Latin rōbus, red. **5.** ROBLE ROBORANT, ROBUST; CORROBORATE, RAMBUNCTIOUS, from Latin rōbur, rōbus, red oak, hardness, and rōbustus, strong. **5.** LOLLIPOP, perhaps from Romani lolo, red, from Middle Indic lohita-, red, from Sanskrit rohita-, lohita-.
II. Zero-grade form *rudh-. **1.** Suffixed form *rudh-ā-. **a.** RUDDLE, from Old English rudu, red color; **b.** RUDDOCK, from Old English rudduc, robin; **c.** RUDDY, from Old English rudig, ruddy. **a-c** all from Germanic *rudō. **2.** Suffixed form *rudh-sto-. RUST, from Old English rūst (and perhaps also *rust), rust, from Germanic *rustaz. **3.** ROUGE, RUBEOLA, RUBY; RUBEFACIENT, from Latin rubeus, red. **4.** RUBICUND, from Latin rubicundus, red, ruddy. **5.** RUBIDIUM, from Latin rūbidus, red. **6.** Suffixed (stative) form *rudh-ē-. RUBESCENT, from Latin rubēre, to be red. **7.** Suffixed form *(ə)rudh-ro-. **a.** RUBELLA, RUBRIC; BILIRUBIN, from Latin ruber, red; **b.** RUTILANT, RUTILE, from Latin rutilus, reddish; **c.** ERYTHEMA, ERYTHRO-, from Greek eruthros, red; **d.** ERYSIPELAS, from possibly remade Greek erusi-, red, reddening. **8.** Suffixed form *rudh-to-. RISSOLE, ROUX, RUSSET, from Latin russus, red. [Pokorny reudh- 872.]

reudh-² To clear land. **1.** Suffixed zero-grade form *rudh-yo-. RID, from Old Norse rydhja, to clear land, from Germanic *rudjan. **2.** Zero-grade form *rudh-. ROD, from Old English rodd, stick, from Germanic *rudd-, stick, club, possibly expressive variant of *rud-. [In Pokorny 2. reu- 868.]

reuə-¹ To open; space. **1.** Suffixed zero-grade form *rū-mo- (< *ruə-mo-). **a.** ROOM, from Old English rūm, space; **b.** LEBENSRAUM, from Old High German rūm, space; **c.** RUMMAGE, from Old Provençal run, ship's hold, space. **a-c** all from Germanic *rūmaz; **d.** REAM², from Old English rȳman, to widen, open up, from Germanic denominative *rūmjan. **2.** Suffixed form *reu(ə)-es-. RURAL, RUSTIC, from Latin rūs, "open land," the country. [Pokorny reuə- 874.]

reuə-² To smash, knock down, tear out, dig up, uproot. **1.** Suffixed o-grade form *rouə-lo-. **a.** RAG¹, from Old Norse rögg, röggr, woven tuft of wool; **b.** RUG, from a Scandinavian source akin to Norwegian rugga, rogga, coarse coverlet. Both **a** and **b** from Germanic *rawwa-. **2.** Basic form *reuə-. RABBLE², RUIN, from Latin ruere, to collapse, cause to collapse. **3.** Extended zero-grade form *rūk- (< *ruə-k-). ROUGH, from Old English rūh, rough, coarse, from Germanic *rūhwa-. **4.** Extended zero-grade variant form *rūg- (< *ruə-g-). RUANA, RUGA, RUGOSE; CORRUGATE, from Latin rūga, wrinkle. [Pokorny 2. reu- 868.]

reug- To vomit, belch; smoke, cloud. **1.** REEK, from Old English rēocan, to smoke, reek, and rēcan, to fumigate, from Germanic *reukan. **2.** Suffixed zero-grade form *rug-to-. ERUCT, from Latin rūctāre, to belch. [In Pokorny reu-b- 871.]

reugh-men- Cream. O-grade form *rough-men-. RAMEKIN, from Middle Low German rōm(e), cream, from Germanic *rau(g)ma-. [Pokorny reugh-m(e)n- 873.]

reup- Also **reub-**. To snatch.
I. Basic form *reub-. RIP¹, from Flemish rippen, to rip, from Germanic *rupjan.
II. O-grade form *roup-. **1a.** REAVE¹, from Old English rēafian, to plunder; **b.** BEREAVE, from Old English berēafian, to take away (be-, bi-, intensive prefix; see **ambhi**); **c.** ROVER², from Middle Dutch and Middle Low German roven, to rob. **a-c** all from Germanic *(bi-)raubōn. **2a.** ROB, from Old French rober, to rob; **b.** RUBATO, from Italian rubare, to rob. Both **a** and **b** from a Romance borrowing from Germanic *raubōn, to rob. **3.** ROBE; GARDEROBE, from Old French robe, robe (< "clothes taken as booty"), from Germanic *raubō, booty. **4.** Suffixed form *roup-tro-. LOOT, from Sanskrit loptram, booty. **5.** RUBLE, from Old Russian rubiti, to chop, hew, from Slavic *rub-.
III. Zero-grade form *rup-. **1.** USURP, from Latin ūsūrpāre (< *ūsu-rup-; ūsus, use, usage, from ūtī, to use; see **oit-**), originally "to interrupt the orderly acquisition of something by the act of using," whence to take into use, usurp. **2.** Nasalized zero-grade form *ru-m-p-. ROUT¹, RUPTURE; ABRUPT, BANKRUPT, CORRUPT, DISRUPT, ERUPT, INTERRUPT, IRRUPT, RUPICOLOUS, from Latin rumpere, to break. [In Pokorny 2. reu- 868.]

rezg- To plait, weave, wind. **1.** RUSH², from Old English risc, rysc, rush, from Germanic *ruski-. **2.** Suffixed form *rezg-ti-. RISTRA; RESTIFORM, from Latin restis, cord, rope. [Pokorny rezg- 874.]

-r/-n- An ancient noun category usually of neuter gender with nominative and accusative case in *-r, and the remaining case endings added to *-n-, as in *yĕkʷr̥, *yĕkʷn-, liver (see **yĕkʷr̥**). [Not in Pokorny.]

-ro- Adjectival suffix, as in *ərudh-ro-, red (see **reudh-¹**). [Not in Pokorny.]

r̥tko- Bear. (Oldest form *h₂r̥tko-.) **1.** URSINE, from Latin ursus, bear (< *orcsos). **2.** ARCTIC, ARCTURUS, from Greek arktos, bear. **3.** ARTHUR (personal name), from Welsh (> Medieval Latin Arthurus, Artorius), from Celtic *arto-wiros, "bear-man," from Celtic *artos, bear (*wiros, man; see **wī-ro-**). [Pokorny r̥k̑þo-s 875.]

Language and Culture Note The Proto-Indo-European word for "bear," r̥tko-, was inherited in Hittite hartaggaš, Sanskrit r̥kṣaḥ, Greek arktos, Latin ursus (with ur- the regular Latin continuation of *r̥ and s the regular continuation of *tk), and Old Irish art. But in the northern branches, the word has undergone taboo replacement. The names of wild animals are often taboo to hunters; that is, uttering them is forbidden. The actual name can be distorted in what is called taboo deformation (compare English Judas Priest, Jiminy Cricket for Jesus Christ) or entirely replaced with a descriptive moniker in taboo replacement (compare English rack for antlers among deer hunters). The Old Irish word art, in fact, was no longer the ordinary word for bear, but was instead used as a personal name (surviving today as the masculine name Art). Among the new expressions for "bear" were "the good calf" in Irish, "honey pig" in Welsh, "honey eater" in Russian, and "the licker" in Lithuanian. English bear and its other Germanic cognates are also the result of taboo-replacement, as etymologically they mean "the brown one" (see **bher-³**).

ruk- Fabric, spun yarn. Celtic and Germanic root (compare Old Irish *rucht*, tunic). **1a.** ROCKET¹, from Italian *rocca*, distaff; **b.** RATCHET, from Old French *rocquet*, head of a lance. Both **a** and **b** from Germanic **rukkōn-*. **2.** ROCHET, from Old French *rochet*, rochet, from Germanic **rukka-*. [Pokorny *ruk(k)-* 874.]

rū-no- Mystery, secret. Germanic and Celtic technical term of magic. (Oldest form **ruhₓ-no-*; probably derived from the zero-grade of a root **reuhₓ-*, to intone or mumble.) In **1.** ROUND², from Old English *rūnian*, to whisper. **2.** RUNNYMEDE, from Middle English *Runimede*, "meadow on the council island," from Old English *Rūnīeg*, "council island," with *Runi-* from Old English *Rūnīeg*, from *rūn*, council (*īeg*, island; see **akʷ-ā-**). **3.** RUNE¹, RUNE², from Old Norse *rūn*, secret writing, akin to the Germanic source of Finnish *runo*, song, poem. **1–3** all from Germanic **rūnaz*. [In Pokorny 1. *reu-* 867.]

sā- To satisfy. (Oldest form **seh₂-*, colored to **sah₂-*, contracted to **sā-*.) **1.** Suffixed zero-grade form **sə-to-*. **a.** SAD, from Old English *sæd*, sated, weary, from Germanic **sada-*, sated; **b.** SATE¹, from Old English *sadian*, to sate, from derivative Germanic verb **sadōn*, to satisfy, sate. **2.** Suffixed zero-grade form **sə-ti-*. SATIATE, SATIETY; ASSAI², ASSET, SATISFY, from Latin *satis*, enough, sufficient. **3.** Suffixed zero-grade form **sə-tu-ro-*. SATIRE, SATURATE, from Latin *satur*, full (of food), sated. **4.** Suffixed zero-grade form **sə-d-ro-*. HADRON, from Greek *hadros*, thick. [Pokorny *sā-* 876.]

sab- Juice, fluid. **1a.** SAP¹, from Old English *sæp*, sap; **b.** ZAFTIG, from Old High German *saf*, juice. Both **a** and **b** from Germanic **sapam*, juice of a plant. **2.** ZABAGLIONE, from Italian *zabaglione, zabaione*, a frothy dessert, probably from a source akin to Illyrian *sabaium*, beer. [In Pokorny *sap-* 880.]

saəwel- The sun. (Oldest form **seh₂wel-*, colored to **sah₂wel-*, contracted to **sāwel-*; zero-grade **s(u)wel-*. The element **-el-* was originally suffixal, and alternated with **-en-*, yielding the variant zero-grades **s(u)wen-* and [reduced] **sun-*.) **1.** Variant forms **swen-*, **sun-*. **a.** *(i)* SUN, from Old English *sunne*, sun; *(ii)* SUNDEW, from Middle Dutch *sonne*, sun. Both *(i)* and *(ii)* from Germanic **sunnōn-*; **b.** SUNDAY, from Old English *sunnandæg*, Sunday, from Germanic compound **sunnōn-dagaz*, "day of the sun" (translation of Latin *diēs sōlis*); **c.** SOUTH, SOUTHERN, from Old English *sūth*, south, and *sūtherne*, southern, from Germanic derivative **sunthaz*, "sun-side," south. **2.** Variant form **s(ə)wōl-*. SOL³, SOL, SOLAR, SOLARIUM; GIRASOL, INSOLATE, PARASOL, SOLANACEOUS, SOLANINE, SOLSTICE, TURNSOLE, from Latin *sōl*, the sun. **3.** Suffixed form **sāwel-yo-*. HELIACAL, HELIO-, HELIUM; ANTHELION, APHELION, HELIOTROPE, ISOHEL, PARHELION, PERIHELION, from Greek *hēlios*, sun. [Pokorny *sáu̯el* 881.]

sāg- To seek out. (Oldest form **seh₂g-*, colored to **sah₂g-*, contracted to **sāg-*.) **1.** Suffixed form **sāg-yo-*. SEEK, from Old English *sēcan, sēcan*, to seek, from Germanic **sōkjan*. **2.** Suffixed form **sāg-ni-*. SOKE, from Old English *sōcn*, attack, inquiry, right of local jurisdiction, from Germanic **sōkniz*. **3.** Zero-grade form **səg-*. **a.** SAKE¹, from Old English *sacu*, lawsuit, case, from Germanic derivative noun **sakō*, "a seeking," accusation, strife; **b.** *(i)* FORSAKE, from Old English *forsacan*, to renounce, refuse (*for-*, prefix denoting exclusion or rejection; see **per¹**); *(ii)* RAMSHACKLE, RANSACK, from Old Norse **saka*, to seek. Both *(i)* and *(ii)* from Germanic **sakan*, to seek, accuse, quarrel. Both **a** and **b** from Germanic **sak-*. **4.** Independent suffixed form **sāg-yo-*. PRESAGE, from Latin *sāgīre*, to perceive, "seek to know." **5.** Zero-grade form **səg-*. SAGACIOUS, from Latin *sagāx*, of keen perception. **6.** Suffixed form **sāg-eyo-*. DIEGESIS, EXEGE-

SIS, HEGEMONY, from Greek *hēgeisthai*, to lead (< "to track down"). **7.** Suffixed variant form **seg-no-* (from earlier **seh₂g-no-*, with regular loss of laryngeal before a cluster consisting of a plain voiced stop and a resonant). SCARLET, SCARLATINA, SEAL¹, SEGNO, SIGIL, SIGN; ASSIGN, CONSIGN, DESIGNATE, INSIGNIA, RESIGN, from Latin *signum*, identifying mark, sign. [Pokorny *sāg-* 876.]

sai-¹ Suffering. (Oldest form **seh₂i-*, colored to **sah₂i-*, contracted to **sāi-*.) **1.** SORE, from Old English *sār*, painful, from Germanic **saira-*, suffering, sick, ill. **2.** SORRY, from Old English *sārig*, suffering mentally, sad, from Germanic **sairiga-*, painful (derivative of **saira-* in **1** above). [Pokorny *sāi-* 877.]

sai-² To bind, tie. (Oldest form probably **sh₂eh₁i-*, colored to **sh₂ah₁i-*; laryngeal *h₂* preserved in Hittite *išḫai, išḫiya*, to bind.) **1.** Suffixed form **sai-tlo-*. SECULAR, from Latin *saeculum*, lifetime, age, century. **2.** Suffixed form **sai-tā-*. SETA; EQUISETUM, PADUASOY, from Latin *saeta*, animal hair, bristle. **3.** Zero-grade form **si-*. SINEW, from Old English *sinu, seonu*, tendon, from Germanic **sinwō*. [Pokorny 3. *sē(i)-* 891.]

Language and Culture Note The root **sai-²** furnishes the first attested Indo-European word. In the 19th century BC, Assyrian merchants had set up trading colonies in central Anatolia among the Hittites, from whom they borrowed the word *išḫiul*, "contract," a derivative of the Hittite verb *išḫai, išḫiya*, "to bind," from the Indo-European zero-grade form **sai-*. Contractual obligations and ritualized reciprocal relationships were a particular hallmark of ancient Indo-European societies (see also the note at **ghos-ti-**), so it is fitting that this is the first word in an Indo-European language to appear in a written document. The basic meaning of **sai-²**, "to bind," was extended metaphorically to refer to successive human generations as the links that "bind" the chain of human life. This is seen clearly in the derivatives of the suffixed form **sai-tlo-* (< earlier **seh₂i-tlo-*). This form literally means "that which binds" (*-tlo-* is an "instrumental" suffix; see **-tlo-**), but also "generation, life-span," as in its Latin descendant *saeculum*, "lifetime, age" (whence English *secular*), and its Welsh descendant *hoedl*, "lifespan."

---

sai-³ Thick liquid. Possible root. (Oldest form **seh₂i-*, colored to **sah₂i-*, contracted to **sāi-*.) Suffixed form **sai-mn̥*. -EMIA, HEMATIC, HEMATITE, HEMATO-, HEMO-; ANEMIA, HEMORRHAGE, HEMORRHOID, ISCHEMIA, from Greek *haima* (stem *haimat-*), blood. [Pokorny *sei-* 889.]

sak- To sanctify. **1.** Suffixed form **sak-ro-*. **a.** SACRED, SACRISTAN, SEXTON; CONSECRATE, EXECRATE, from Latin *sacer*, holy, sacred, dedicated; **b.** compound **sakro-dōt-*, "he who gives out the sacralized offering (to the other participants in the sacrifice)" (**-dōt-*, giver; see **dō-**. For the semantics, compare Messapic *tabarnas*, priest, and Old Irish *do-beir, tabir*, Old Irish: both are compounds of a preposition **to*, derived from **to-**, and **bher-**, to bear, carry.): SACERDOTAL, from Latin *sacerdōs*, priest. **2.** Nasalized form **sa-n-k-*. SAINT, SANCTUM; CORPOSANT, SACROSANCT, SANCTIFY, from Latin *sancīre* (past participle *sānctus*), to make sacred, consecrate. [Pokorny *sak-* 878.]

sal-¹ Salt. **1.** Extended form **sald-*. **a.** Suffixed form **sald-o-*. SALT, from Old English *sealt*, salt, from Germanic **saltam*; **b.** *(i)* SOUSE¹, from Old French *sous*, pickled meat; *(ii)* SILT, from Middle English *cylte*, fine sand, from a source probably akin to Danish and Norwegian *sylt*, salt marsh. Both *(i)* and *(ii)* from Germanic zero-grade suffixed extended form **sult-jō*; **c.** SALSA, SAUCE, SAUSAGE, from Latin *sallere* (past participle *salsus* < **sald-to-*), to salt. **2.** SAL, SALAD, SALAMI, SALARY, SALI-, SALINE; SALMAGUNDI, SALTCELLAR, SALTPETER, from Latin *sāl* (genitive *salis*), salt. **3.** HALO-, from Greek *hals* (stem *hal-*), salt, sea. . **3.** SOLONCHAK, from Russian *solonets*, salty soil, akin to Old Church Slavonic *slanŭ*, salt. [Pokorny 1. *sal-* 878.]

sal-² Dirty, gray. Suffixed form **sal-wo-*. SALLOW¹, from Old English *salu*, *salo*, dusky, dark, from Germanic **salwa-*. [Pokorny 2. *sal-* 879.] See also derivative **sal(i)k-**.

sal(i)k- Willow. A derivative of **sal-²**. **1.** Variant form **salk-*. SALLOW², from Old English *sealh*, willow, from Germanic suffixed form **salh-jōn-*. **2.** SALICIN, from Latin *salix*, willow. [In Pokorny 2. *sal-* 879.]

sam- To sing. (Oldest form **sh₂em-*, colored to **sh₂am-*.) Suffixed o-grade form **sₔom-n-*. HYMN; HYMNODY, HYMNOLOGY, from Greek *humnos*, song. [Not in Pokorny; compare Hittite *išḫamai*, "he sings," and Sanskrit *sāman-*, hymn, song.]

[sāno- Healthy. Italic root. SANE, SANITARY, SAINFOIN, from Latin *sānus*, healthy. [Pokorny *sāno-s* 880.]]

saus- Dry. **1.** Suffixed (thematic) form **saus-o-*. **a.** SEAR¹, SERE¹, from Old English *sēar*, withered; **b.** SORREL², from Old French *saur*, *sor*, red-brown, from Frankish **saur*, dry. Both **a** and **b** from Germanic **sauza-*. **2.** Suffixed form **saus-t-*. AUSTERE, from Greek *austēros*, harsh. [Pokorny *saus-* 880.]

sē-¹ To sow. (Contracted from earlier **seh₁-*.) **1.** SOW¹, from Old English *sāwan*, to sow, from Germanic **sēan*. **2.** Suffixed form **sē-ti-*, sowing. **a.** SEED, from Old English *sǣd*, seed; **b.** COLZA, from Middle Dutch *saet* and Middle Low German *sāt*, seed. Both **a** and **b** from Germanic **sēdiz*, seed. **3.** Reduplicated zero-grade form **si-s(ə)-*. SEASON, from Latin *serere*, to sow, and derived noun *satiō* (< **sə-tiō*), sowing. **4.** Suffixed form **sē-men-*, seed. SEMÉ, SEMEN, SEMINARY; DISSEMINATE, INSEMINATE, SINSEMILLA, from Latin *sēmen*, seed. [In Pokorny 2. *sē(i)-* 889.]

sē-² Long, late. (Contracted from earlier **seh₁-*, with extended form **seh₁i-*, metathesized to **seih₁-*, with zero-grade **sih₁-*, contracted to **sī-*.) **1.** Suffixed form **sē-ro-*. **a.** SEROTINOUS, SOIREE, from Latin *sērus*, late; **b.** MENHIR, from Middle Breton *hir*, long. **2.** Germanic **sī-*, perhaps from zero-grade variant form **sī-* (< **siə-*). **a.** SIDE, from Old English *sīde*, side, from Germanic **sīdō*, "long surface or part"; **b.** SINCE, SITH, SYNE, from Old English *siththon*, *siththan*, after, after that, since, from Germanic **sīth*, "later," after. [In Pokorny 2. *sē(i)-* 889.]

sē-³ To sift. (Contracted from earlier **seh₁-*.) Suffixed form **sē-dho-*. ETHMOID, from Greek *ēthein*, to sift. [Pokorny 1. *sē(i)-* 889.]

sed-¹ To sit.
I. Basic form **sed-*. **1.** Suffixed form **sed-yo-*. **a.** SIT, from Old English *sittan*, to sit; **b.** SITZ BATH, SITZMARK, from Old High German *sizzen*, to sit. Both **a** and **b** from Germanic **sitjan*. **2.** Suffixed form **sed-lo-*, seat. SETTLE, from Old English *setl*, seat, from Germanic **setlaz*. **3.** Suffixed (stative) form **sed-ē-*. SÉANCE, SEDENTARY, SEDERUNT, SEDILE, SEDIMENT, SESSILE, SESSION, SEWER²; SIEGE; ASSESS, ASSIDUOUS, ASSIZE, DISSIDENT, INSIDIOUS, OBSESS, POSSESS, PRESIDE, RESIDE, SUBSIDY, SUPERSEDE, SURCEASE, from Latin *sedēre*, to sit. **4.** Suffixed form **sed-rā-*. -HEDRON; CATHEDRA, CATHEDRAL, CHAIR, EPHEDRINE, EXEDRA, SANHEDRIN, from Greek *hedrā*, seat, chair, face of a geometric solid. **5.** Prefixed and suffixed form **pi-sed-yo-*, to sit upon (**pi*, on; see **epi**). PIEZO-; ISOPIESTIC, from Greek *piezein*, to press tight. **6.** Basic form **sed-*. **a.** EDAPHIC, from Greek *edaphos*, ground, foundation (with Greek suffix *-aphos*); **b.** UPANISHAD, from Sanskrit *upaniṣad*, Upanishad, from *-sad*, sitting; **c.** TANIST, from Old Irish *tánaise*, designated successor, from Celtic **tānihessio-*, "one who is waited for," from **to-ad-ni-sed-tio-*, from **to-ad-ni-sed-*, to wait for (**to-*, to; **ad-*, to; **ni-*, down; see **ad-** and **ni**). **7.** Suffixed form **sed-o-*, sitting. EISTEDDFOD, from

Welsh *eistedd*, sitting, from Celtic **eks-dī-sedo-* (**eks-*, out, and **dī-*, out, from; see **eghs** and **de-**).
II. O-grade form **sod-*. **1.** Perhaps suffixed form **sod-dhlo-*. SADDLE, from Old English *sadol*, saddle, from Germanic **sadulaz*, seat, saddle. **2.** Suffixed (causative) form **sod-eyo-*. **a.** SET¹, from Old English *settan*, to place; **b.** BESET, from Old English *besettan*, to set near; **c.** ERSATZ, from Old High German *irsezzan*, to replace, from *sezzan*, to set. **a–c** all from Germanic **(bi-)satjan*, to cause to sit, set. **3.** Suffixed form **sod-yo-*. SOIL¹, from Latin *solium*, throne, seat.
III. Zero-grade form **-sd-* (in compounds), assimilated to **-zd-*. **1.** Reduplicated form **si-sd-* becoming **si-zd-*. **a.** SUBSIDE, from Latin *sīdere*, to sit down, settle; **b.** SYNIZESIS, from Greek *hizein*, to sit down, settle down. **2.** Compound suffixed form **ni-zd-o-*, nest, literally "(bird's place of) sitting down" (**ni-*, down). **a.** NEST, from Old English *nest*, from Germanic **nistaz*; **b.** NICHE, NICK, NIDE, NIDUS; EYAS, NIDICOLOUS, NIDIFUGOUS, NIDIFY, from Latin *nīdus*. nest. **3.** Compound suffixed form **kuzdho-zd-* (see **(s)keu-**).
IV. Lengthened-grade form **sēd-*. **1.** SEE², from Latin *sēdēs*, seat, residence. **2.** Suffixed form **sēd-i-*, settler. **a.** COSSET, possibly from Old English *-sǣta*, *-sǣte*, inhabitant(s), also in place names in (Modern English) *-set*, such as SOMERSET, from Old English *Sumorsǣtan*, "inhabitants of *Sumortūn*, summer-dwelling"; **b.** Old High German *sāzzo*, settler, inhabitant, in compound *Eli-sāzzo* (see **al-¹**). Both **a** and **b** from Germanic **sētōn-*, **sāti-*. **3.** Suffixed form **sēd-yo-*. SEAT, from Old Norse *sæti*, seat, from Germanic **(ge)sētjam*, seat (**ge-*, **ga-*, collective prefix; see **kom-**). **4.** Suffixed form **sēd-ā-*. SEDATE¹, from Latin *sēdāre*, to settle, calm down. **5.** Suffixed form **sēd-es-*, seat. BANSHEE, from Old Irish *síd*, fairy mound.
V. Lengthened o-grade form **sōd-*. SOOT, from Old English *sōt*, soot (< "that which settles"), from Germanic **sōtam*, from suffixed form **sōd-o-*. [Pokorny *sed-* 884.]

sed-² To go. Suffixed o-grade form **sod-o-*. -ODE; ANODE, CATHODE, EPISODE, EXODUS, HYATHODE, METHOD, ODOGRAPH, ODOMETER, PERIOD, PROCTODEUM, STOMODEUM, SYNOD, from Greek *hodos*, way, journey. [Pokorny *sed-* B. 887.]

segh- To hold. (Oldest form **seǵh-*.) **1.** Suffixed form **segh-es-* in Germanic **sigiz-*, victory (< "a holding or conquest in battle") in Old High German *sigu*, *sigo*, victory, in personal names: **a.** SIEGFRIED, from Old High German *Sigifrith*, "having victorious peace" (*fridu*, *-frith*, peace; see **prī-**); **b.** SIGISMUND, SIGMUND, from Old High German *Sigismund*, "protector of peace" (*mund*, protector; see **man-²**). **2a.** HECTIC; CACHEXIA, CATHEXIS, ENTELECHY, EUNUCH, OPHIUCHUS, from Greek *ekhein*, to hold, possess, be in a certain condition, and *hexis*, habit, condition; **b.** suffixed (agent noun) form **segh-tor*, "holder, guarder, defender." HECTOR, HECTOR (personal name), from Greek *Hektōr*. **3.** Possible suffixed (abstract) noun form **segh-wēr*, toughness, steadfastness, with derivative **segh-wēr-o-*, tough, stern. SEVERE; ASSEVERATE, PERSEVERE, from Latin *sevērus*, stern; **b.** STHENIA; ASTHENIA, CALISTHENICS, HYPERSTHENE, HYPOSTHENIA, MYASTHENIA, THROMBOSTHENIN, from Greek *sthenos*, physical strength, from a possible related abstract noun form **sgh-wen-es-* (with zero-grade of the root). **4.** O-grade form **sogh-*. EPOCH, from Greek *epokhē*, "a holding back," pause, cessation, position in time (*epi-*, on, at; see **epi**). **5.** Zero-grade form **sgh-*. **a.** SCHEME, from Greek *skhēma*, "a holding," form, figure; **b.** SCHOLAR, SCHOLASTIC, SCHOLIUM, SCHOOL¹, from Greek *skholē*, "a holding back," stop, rest, leisure, employment of leisure in disputation, school. **6.** Reduplicated form **si-sgh-*. ISCHEMIA, from Greek *iskhein*, to keep back. [Pokorny *seǵh-* 888.]

seib- To pour out, sieve, drip, trickle. **1.** Basic form **seib-*. SEEP, from Old English *sīpian*, *sypian*, to drip, seep, from Germanic *sīpōn. **2.** Suffixed o-grade form *soib-on-. **a.** SOAP, from Old English sāpe, soap (originally a reddish hair dye used by Germanic warriors to give a frightening appearance); **b.** SAPONACEOUS, SAPONATE, SAPONIFY, SAPONIN, SAPONITE, from Latin sāpō, soap. Both **a** and **b** from Germanic *saipōn-, "dripping thing," resin. **3a.** SIEVE, from Old English sife, a filter, sieve; **b.** SIFT, from Old English siftan, to sieve, drain. Both **a** and **b** from variant Germanic form *sib-. [Pokorny seip- 894.]

seikʷ- To flow out. Extended expressive zero-grade form *sikko-. SACK³, SECCO, SICCATIVE; DESICCATE, EX- SICCATE, from Latin siccus, dry. [Pokorny seikʷ- 893.]

sek- To cut. **1.** SCYTHE, from Old English sīthe, sigthe, sickle, from Germanic *segithō, sickle. **2.** Suffixed o-grade form *sok-ā-. SAW¹; HACKSAW, from Old English sagu, sage, saw, from Germanic *sagō, a cutting tool, saw. **3.** Suffixed o-grade form *sok-yo-. SEDGE, from Old English secg, sedge, from Germanic *sagjaz, "sword," plant with a cutting edge. **4.** Suffixed o-grade form *sok-so- in Germanic *sahsam, knife. **a.** ZAX, from Old English seax, knife; **b.** traditionally (but doubtfully) regarded as from Germanic *sahsam is the West Germanic tribal name *Saxon-, Saxon (as if "warrior with knives"). (i) SAXON, from Late Latin Saxō (plural Saxonēs), a Saxon; (ii) ESSEX, MIDDLESEX, SUSSEX, WESSEX, from Old English Ēast-Seaxe, "East Saxons," Middel-Seaxe, "Middle Saxons," Sūth-Seaxe, "South Saxons," and West-Seaxe, "West Saxons," from Seax, a Saxon. **5.** Extended root *skend-, to peel off, flay. SKIN, from Old Norse skinn, skin, from Germanic *skinth-. **6.** Basic form *sek-. **a.** SECANT, -SECT, SECTILE, SECTION, SECTOR, SEGMENT; DISSECT, INSECT, INTERSECT, RESECT, TRANSECT, from Latin secāre, to cut; **a.** EXTISPICY, from Latin extispex, diviner who observes entrails, from exta, perhaps contracted from exsecta, things cut out, neuter plural past participle of exsecāre, to cut out, from secāre, to cut (-spex, he who sees; see **spek-**). **c.** SEECATCH, from Russian sech', to cut. **7.** Lengthened-grade form *sēk-. SICKLE, from Latin sēcula, sickle. **8.** Possible suffixed variant form *sak-so-. SASSAFRAS; SAXICOLOUS, SAXIFRAGE, from Latin saxum, stone (< "broken-off piece"?). [Pokorny 2. sĕk- 895, sken-(d-) 929.] See also extended roots **sked-, skei-,** and **(s)ker-¹.**

sekʷ-¹ To follow. **1.** SECT, SEGUE, SEGUIDILLA, SEQUACIOUS, SEQUEL, SEQUENCE, SUE, SUIT, SUITE, SUITOR; CONSEQUENT, ENSUE, EXECUTE, OBSEQUIOUS, PERSECUTE, PROSECUTE, PURSUE, SUBSEQUENT, from Latin sequī, to follow. **2.** SEQUESTER, SEQUESTRUM, from Latin sequester, "follower," mediator, depositary. **3.** Suffixed (participial) form *sekʷ-ondo-. SECOND², SECONDO, SECUND, SECUNDINES, from Latin secundus, following, coming next, second. **4.** Suffixed form *sekʷ-os, following. EXTRINSIC, INTRINSIC, from Latin secus, along, alongside of. **5.** Suffixed o-grade form *sokʷ-yo-. SOCIABLE, SOCIAL, SOCIETY, SOCIO-; ASSOCIATE, CONSOCIATE, DISSOCIATE, from Latin socius, ally, companion (< "follower"). [Pokorny 1. sekʷ- 896.]

sekʷ-² To perceive, see. **1.** SEE¹, from Old English sēon, to see, from Germanic *sehwan, to see. **2.** SIGHT, from Old English sihth, gesiht, vision, spectacle, from Germanic abstract noun *sih-tiz. [Pokorny 2. sekʷ- 897.]

sekʷ-³ To say, utter. **1.** O-grade form *sokʷ-. **a.** Suffixed form *sokʷ-yo-. SAY; GAINSAY, from Old English secgan, to say, from Germanic *sagjan; **b.** suffixed form *sokʷ-ā-. (i) SAW², from Old English sagu, a saying, speech; (ii) SAGA, from Old Norse saga, a saying, narrative. Both (i) and (ii) from Germanic *sagō, a saying. **2.** Perhaps suffixed zero-grade form *skʷ-e- tlo-, narration. **a.** SKALD, from Old Norse skáld, poet, "satirist"; **b.** SCOLD, from Middle English scolde, an abusive person, from a Scandinavian source akin to Old Norse

skáld (see above). Both **a** and **b** from North Germanic *skathla. [In Pokorny 2. sekʷ- 897.]

sel-¹ Human settlement. **1.** O-grade form *sol-. SALON, SALOON, from Italian sala, hall, room, from Germanic *sal-, room. **2.** Suffixed e-grade form *sel-o-. SOLE¹, SOLUM; ENTRESOL, LATOSOL, SOLIFLUCTION, from Latin solum, bottom, foundation, hence sole of the foot. [Pokorny 1. sel- 898, 3. (sṷel-) 1046.]

sel-² Also **selə-** (oldest form *selh₂-.) Of good mood; to favor. **1.** SILLY, from Old English gesǣlig, happy (ge-, completely; see **kom**), from Germanic lengthened-grade form *sēl-. **2.** Suffixed lengthened o-grade form *sōl-ā-. SOLACE; CONSOLE, from Latin sōlārī, to comfort, console. **3.** Possibly suffixed variant form *selə-ro-. HILARITY; EXHILARATE, from Greek hilaros (< *helaros), gay. [Pokorny 3. sel- 899.]

sel-³ To take, grasp. **1.** Suffixed o-grade (causative) form *sol-eyo-. SELL, from Old English sellan, to sell, betray, from Germanic saljan, to offer up, deliver (whence West and North Germanic, "to sell"). **2a.** SALE, from Old Norse sala, sale; **b.** HANDSEL, from Old Norse compound handsal, giving of the hand (in closing a bargain). Both **a** and **b** from Germanic *sal-, giving, sale. [Pokorny 3. sel- 899.]

sel-⁴ To jump. **1.** Suffixed zero-grade form *sal-yo-. **a.** SALACIOUS, SALIENT, SALLY, SALTO, SAUTÉ; ASSAIL, ASSAULT, DESULTORY, DISSILIENT, EXULT, INSULT, RESILE, RESULT, SOMERSAULT, from Latin salīre, to leap; **b.** HALTER², from Greek hallesthai, to leap, jump. **2.** Probably Latin salmō (borrowed from Gaulish), salmon (< "the leaping fish"): SALMON. [Pokorny 4. sel- 899.]

sel-es- Swamp, marsh, sea. **1.** ELODEA, from Greek helos, marsh. **2a.** SARUS CRANE, from Sanskrit sarah (stem saras-), lake; **b.** SARASVATI, from Sanskrit Sarasvatī, name of a sacred river, Sarasvati, from Indo-Iranian *sarasvatī, "of waters" (*-vatī, feminine of *-vat, containing). Both **a** and **b** from Indo-Iranian *saras-, body of water. [Pokorny selos- 901.]

selk- To pull, draw. **1.** Perhaps Germanic *selhaz, seal (the animal), "that which drags its body along with difficulty" (but more likely an early Germanic borrowing from Finnic). SEAL², from Old English seolh, seal. **2.** Suffixed o-grade form *solk-o-. SULCATE, SULCUS, from Latin sulcus, furrow, groove (< "result of drawing or plowing"). **3.** Full-grade form *selk-. HULK, FELUCCA, from Greek helkein, to pull, with o-grade derivative holkos, machine for pulling ships. [Pokorny selk- 901.]

selp- Fat, butter. **1.** SALVE¹, from Old English sealf, healing ointment, from Germanic *salb-. **2.** QUACKSALVER, from Middle Dutch salven, to anoint, from Germanic denominative verb *salbōn. [Pokorny selp- 901.]

sem-¹ One; also adverbially "as one," together with. **I.** Full-grade form *sem-. **1a.** HENDECASYLLABIC, HENDIADYS, HENOTHEISM, HYPHEN, from Greek heis (< nominative singular masculine *hen-s < *hem-s), one; **b.** Greek he- in hekaton, one hundred (* dissimilated from *hem-katon; see **dekm̥**). Both **a** and **b** from Greek *hem-. **2.** Suffixed form *sem-el-. SIMULTANEOUS; ASSEMBLE, ENSEMBLE, from Latin simul, at the same time. **3.** Suffixed form *sem-golo-. SINGLE, from Latin singulus, alone, single. **4.** Compound *sem-per- (*per, during, for; see **per¹**). SEMPRE; SEMPERVIVUM, SEMPITERNAL, from Latin semper, always, ever (< "once for all").

II. O-grade form *som-. **1.** BONZE, KALANCHOE, SAMBAL, SAMHITA, SAMSARA, SANDHI, SANGHA, SANKHYA, SANNYASI, SANSKRIT, from Sanskrit sam, together. **2.** Suffixed form *som-o-. **a.** SAME, from Old Norse samr, same, from Germanic *sama-, same; **b.** HOMEO-, HOMO-; ANOMALOUS, from Greek homos, same; **c.** HOMILY, from Greek homīlos, crowd. **3.** Suffixed form *som-alo-. HOMOLOGRAPHIC, from Greek homalos, like, even, level.

III. Lengthened o-grade form *sōm-*. **1.** Suffixed form *sōm-i-*. SEEM, SEEMLY, from Old Norse *sǣmr*, fitting, agreeable (< "making one," "reconciling"), from Germanic *sōmi-*. **2.** Suffixed lengthened o-grade form *sōm-o-*. SAMIZDAT, SAMOVAR, from Russian *sam(o)-*, self.

IV. Zero-grade form *sm̥-*. **1.** ACOLYTE, ANACOLUTHON, from Greek compound *akolouthos*, accompanying (-*kolouthos*, from o-grade of *keleuthos*, way, path), from *ha-*, *a-*, together. **2.** Compound form *sm̥-plo-* (*-plo-*, -fold; see **pel-³**). **a.** SIMPLE, from Latin *simplus*, simple; **b.** HAPLOID, HAPLORRHINE, from Greek *haploos*, *haplous*, single, simple. **3.** Suffixed form *sm̥m-o-*. **a.** SOME, from Old English *sum*, one, a certain one; **b.** -SOME¹, from Old English -*sum*, -like. Both **a** and **b** from Germanic *suma-*. **4.** Suffixed form *sm̥m-alo-*. SIMILAR; ASSIMILATE, RESEMBLE, from Latin *similis*, of the same kind, like. **5.** Compound *sm̥-kēro-*, of one growing (see **ker-³**). **6.** Suffixed form *sm̥-tero-*. HETERO-, from Greek *heteros* (earlier *hateros*), one of two, other. **7.** Compound *sm̥-plek-*, "one-fold," simple (*-plek-*, -fold; see **plek-**). SEMPLICE, SIMPLEX, SIMPLICITY, from Latin *simplex*, simple. **8.** Suffixed compound form *sm̥-gʷelbh-(e)yo-* (see **gʷelbh-**). **9.** Extended form *sm̥ma*. HAMADRYAD, from Greek *hama*, together with, at the same time. [Pokorny 2. *sem-* 902.]

sem-² Summer. Also **semə-** (oldest form *semh₂-*). **1.** Suffixed zero-grade form *sm̥a-aro-*. SUMMER¹, from Old English *sumor*, summer, from Germanic *sumaraz*. **2.** Suffixed zero-grade form *sm̥a-oni-*. SAMHAIN, from Old Irish *samain*, Samhain (for the discrepancy in time of occurrence, Samhain taking place in the autumn, compare English *Indian summer*. [Pokorny 3. *sem-* 905.]

sēmi- Half-, as first member of a compound. **1.** SANDBLIND, from Old English *sām-*, half, from Germanic *sēmi-*. **2.** SEMI-, from Latin *sēmi-*, half. **3.** SESQUI-, SESTERCE, from Latin *sēmis*, half. **4.** HEMI-, from Greek *hēmi-*, half. [Pokorny *sēmi-* 905.]

sen- Old. **1.** SEIGNIOR, SENATE, SENECTITUDE, SENESCENT, SENILE, SENIOR, SEÑOR, SIGNORE, SIGNORY, SIR, SIRE, SURLY; SENOPIA, from Latin *senex*, old, an elder. **2.** SHANACHIE, from Old Irish *sen*, old. **3.** SENESCHAL, from Old French *senechal*, from Frankish *siniska-lkaz*, literally "old servant," or a kindred Germanic source (attested in Medieval Latin as *siniscalcus*), from *sin(i)-*, old (compare Gothic *sineigs*, old; Germanic *skalkaz*, servant). [Pokorny *sen(o)-* 907.]

sendhro- Crystalline deposit. **1.** CINDER, from Old English *sinder*, iron slag, dross. **2.** SINTER, from Old High German *sintar*, slag. Both **1** and **2** from Germanic *sendra-*, slag. [Pokorny *sendhro-* 906.]

senə-¹ Also **sen-**. Apart, separated. **1.** Suffixed variant form *sn̥-ter-*. **a.** ASUNDER, from Old English *sundor*, *sunder*, apart, from Germanic *sundrō*; **b.** SUNDER, from Old English *syndrian*, *sundrian*, to put apart, from Germanic denominative verb *sundrōn*; **c.** SUNDRY, from Old English *syndrig*, apart, separated, from Germanic derivative adjective *sundriga-*. **2.** Zero-grade form *sn̥a-i* (with a locative case ending). SANS; SINECURE, SINSEMILLA, from Latin *sine*, without. [Pokorny *seni-* 907.]

senə-² To accomplish, achieve. (Oldest form *senh₂-*.) AUTHENTIC, EFFENDI, from Greek *authentēs*, author (< *aut-hen-tē*; *aut-*, *auto-*, self). [Pokorny *sen-* 906.]

sengʷ- To sink. **1.** SINK, from Old English *sincan*, to sink. **2.** SAG, from Middle English *saggen*, to subside, from a Scandinavian source akin to Swedish *sacka*, to sink, from Scandinavian intensive form *sakk-*. Both **1** and **2** from Germanic *sinkwan*. [Pokorny *sengʷ-* 906.]

sengʷh- To sing, make an incantation. **1a.** SING, from Old English *singan*, to sing; **b.** MEISTERSINGER, MINNESINGER, SINGSPIEL, from Old High German *singan*,

to sing. Both **a** and **b** from Germanic *singan*. **2.** Suffixed o-grade form *songʷh-o-*, singing, song. SONG, from Old English *sang*, *song*, song, from Germanic *sangwaz*. [Pokorny *sengʷh-* 906.]

senk- To burn. Suffixed (causative) o-grade form *sonk-eyo-*. SINGE, from Old English *sengan*, to singe, from Germanic *sangjan*, to cause to burn. [Pokorny *senk-* 907.]

sent- To head for, go. **1.** WIDDERSHINS, from Old High German *sin(d)*, direction, from Germanic form *sinthaz*. **2.** Suffixed (causative) o-grade form *sont-eyo-*. SEND¹, from Old English *sendan*, to send, from Germanic *sandjan*, to cause to go. **3.** Suffixed o-grade form *sont-o-*. GODSEND, from Old English *sand*, message, messenger, from Germanic *sandaz*, that which is sent. **4.** Perhaps suffixed form *sent-yo-*. SCENT, SENSE, SENSILLUM, SENTENCE, SENTIENT, SENTIMENT, SENTINEL; ASSENT, CONSENT, DISSENT, PRESENTIMENT, RESENT, SENSU LATO, SENSU STRICTO, from Latin *sentīre*, to feel (< "to go mentally"). [Pokorny *sent-* 908.]

sep-¹ To taste, perceive. Suffixed zero-grade form *sap-yo-*. SAGE¹, SAPID, SAPIENT, SAPOR, SAVANT, SAVOR, SAVVY; INSIPID, from Latin *sapere*, to taste, have taste, be wise. [Pokorny *sap-* 880.]

sep-² To handle (skillfully), hold (reverently). Suffixed form *sep-el-yo-*. SEPULCHER, SEPULTURE, from Latin *sepelīre*, to embalm, bury (originally, "to perform ritual manual operations on a corpse"). [Pokorny *sep-* 909.]

septm̥ Seven. **1.** SEVEN; SEVENTEEN, SEVENTY, from Old English *seofon*, seven, with derivatives (*hund*) *seofontig*, seventy, and *seofontīne*, seventeen (-*tīne*, ten; see **dekm̥**), from Germanic *sebun*. **2.** SEPTEMBER, SEPTENNIAL, SEPTET, SEPTUAGINT, SEPTUPLE; SEPTENTRION, UNUNSEPTIUM, from Latin *septem*, seven. **3.** HEBDOMAD, HEPTA-, HEPTAD, from Greek *hepta*, seven. [Pokorny *septm̥* 909.]

ser-¹ To protect. **1.** Extended form *serw-*. CONSERVE, OBSERVE, PRESERVE, RESERVE, RESERVOIR, from Latin *servāre*, to keep, preserve. **2.** Perhaps suffixed lengthened-grade form *sēr-ōs-*. HERO, from Greek *hērōs*, "protector," hero. [Pokorny 2. *ser-* 910.]

ser-² To flow. **1.** Suffixed form *ser-o-*. SERAC, SERUM, from Latin *serum*, whey. **2.** Basic form *ser-*. SAMSARA, from Sanskrit *sarati*, *sasarti*, it flows, runs. **3.** Extended root forms *sr-edh-*, *sr-et-*, to whirl, bubble. STRUDEL, from Middle High German *strudel*, whirlpool, from (by ablaut) Old High German *stredan*, to whirl, swirl. [Pokorny 1. *ser-* 909, *sr-edh-* 1001.]

ser-³ To line up. **1.** SERIES, SERTULARIAN; ASSERT, DESERT³, DISSERTATE, EXERT, EXSERT, INSERT, from Latin *serere*, to arrange, attach, join (in speech), discuss. **2.** Suffixed form *ser-mon-*. SERMON, from Latin *sermō* (stem *sermōn-*), speech, discourse. **3.** Perhaps suffixed form *ser-ā-*. SEAR², SERRIED, from Latin *sera*, a lock, bolt, bar (? < "that which aligns"). **4.** Suffixed zero-grade form *sr̥-ti-*. SORCERER, SORT; ASSORT, CONSORT, ENSORCEL, SORTILEGE, from Latin *sors* (stem *sort-*), lot, fortune (perhaps from the lining up of lots before drawing). [Pokorny 4. *ser-* 911.]

ser-⁴ Base of prepositions and preverbs with the basic meaning "above, over, up, upper." Possibly zero-grade variant form *sro-*. FRONS, FRONT, FRONTAL¹, FRONTAL², FRONTIER, FRONTLET, FRONTON; AFFRONT, CONFRONT, EFFRONTERY, FRONTISPIECE, FRONTENIS, from Latin *frōns*, forehead, front. [Not in Pokorny; compare Hittite *šarā*, up (< *sro*), and Greek *rhion*, peak, foreland (< *sri-*).]

ser-⁵ To seize. Zero-grade form *sr̥-*. HERESY; APHAERESIS, DIERESIS, SYNERESIS, from Greek *hairein*, to seize, from *sr̥-yo-* (details of formation unclear). [Not in Pokorny; compare Hittite *šaru*, booty, Welsh *herw*, booty (both from suffixed o-grade form *sor-u-*).]

serk- To make whole. SARTORIUS, from Latin *sarcīre*, to mend, repair. [Pokorny *serk-* 912.]

Language and Culture Note   In Roman customary law, if a son or a slave committed an offense that demanded restitution (such as theft or murder), the restitution could be met by the father or the master paying the damages or surrendering his son or slave to the offended party. The Latin phrase meaning "pay for the damages" in this particular context was *noxiam sarcīre*, where *sarcīre*, basically meaning "to mend, repair," has here the technical meaning "to pay or make amends for (damages done by one's son or slave)." The Latin verb comes from the Indo-European verbal root **serk-**, "to make whole." The root also appears with nasal infix (see **-n-**) in the Hittite verb *šarnik-*, which has the same legal usage as the Latin verb. The precise equivalence of both legal expression and legal content in these two branches of Indo-European suggests that the Indo-European root **serk-** had the same legal meaning, and that the Indo-Europeans employed the same procedure.

serp-¹   Sickle, hook. **1.** SARMENTOSE, from Latin *sarpere*, to cut off, prune (> *sarmentum*, twigs). **2.** HARPOON, from Greek *harpē*, sickle. [In Pokorny 5. *ser-* 911.]

serp-²   To crawl, creep. **1.** SERPENT, SERPIGINOUS, from Latin *serpere*, to crawl. **2.** HERPES; HERPETOLOGY, Greek *herpein*, to crawl, creep. [Pokorny *serp-* 912.]

seuə-¹   To give birth. Suffixed zero-grade form in derivative noun **su(ə)-nu-*, son. SON, from Old English *sunu*, son, from Germanic **sunuz*. [Pokorny 2. *seu-* 913.] See also **sū-**.

seuə-²   To take liquid.

   I. Suffixed zero-grade form **suə-yo-*, contracted to **sū-yo-*. HYETAL; ISOHYET, from Greek *hüetos*, rain, from *hüein*, to rain.

   II. Possible extended zero-grade form **sūb-*. **1a.** SUP¹, from Old English *sūpan, sūpian*, to drink, sip; **b.** SOUP, SUP², from Old French *soup(e)*, soup; **c.** SOPAIPILLA, from Old Spanish *sopa*, food soaked in liquid. **a–c** all from Germanic **sūp-*. **2a.** SOP, from Old English *sopp-* in *soppcuppe*, cup for dipping bread in, from Germanic **supp-*; **b.** SIP, from Middle English *sippen*, to sip, from a source probably akin to Low German *sippen*, to sip, possibly from Germanic **supp-*.

   III. Possible extended zero-grade form **sūg-*. **1.** SUCK, from Old English *sūcan*, to suck, from Germanic **sūk-*. **2.** SOAK, from Old English *socian*, to steep, from Germanic shortened form **sukōn*. **3.** SUCTION, SUCTORIAL; PROSCIUTTO, from Latin *sūgere*, to suck. **4.** Variant form **sūk-*. SUCCULENT, from Latin *sūcus, succus*, juice. [Pokorny 1. *seu-* 912.]

seut-   To seethe, boil. **1.** SEETHE, SODDEN, from Old English *sēothan*, to boil, from Germanic **seuthan*, with Old English past participle *soden*, boiled, from Germanic **sudana-* (from Indo-European suffixed zero-grade **sut-ono-*). **2a.** SUDS, from Middle English *sudde, sudse*, marsh, swamp; **b.** SUTLER, from Middle Dutch *soetler*, sutler, akin to Middle High German *sudelen*, to soil, do sloppy work, from Germanic suffixed form **suth-l-*. Both **a** and **b** from Germanic **suth-*. [Pokorny 4. *seu-* 914.]

[servus   Slave. Latin noun of uncertain origin (perhaps < *"protector of cattle and sheep, shepherd," and thus a derivative of **serw-*, extended form of **ser-¹**). SERF, SERGEANT, SERVE, SERVANT, SERVILE, SERVITUDE, SIRVENTE; CONCIERGE, SERVOMECHANISM, SERVOMOTOR.**]**

si-lo-   Silent. Suffixed (stative) form **sil-ē-*. SILENT, from Latin *silēre*, to be silent. [In Pokorny 2. *sē(i)-* 889.]

skabh-   To prop up, support. Suffixed form **skabh-no-*. SHAMBLES, from Latin *scamnum*, a bench (< Old English *sceamel*, table, stool). [Pokorny *skabh-* 916.]

skai-   To gleam. (Oldest form **sḱeh₂i-*, colored to **sḱah₂i-*, contracted to **sḱai-*, with zero-grade **sḱ(h₂)i-*

and variant [metathesized] zero-grade **sḱih₂-*, contracted to **sḱī-*.) **1.** Suffixed zero-grade form **skī-no-*. **a.** SHINE, from Old English *scīnan*, to shine; **b.** GEGENSCHEIN, from Old High German *scīnan*, to shine. Both **a** and **b** from Germanic **skīnan*, to gleam, shine. **2.** SHIMMER, from Old English *scimerian, scymrian*, to shine brightly, from Germanic extended form **ski-m-*. **3.** Possibly suffixed form **ski-nto-*, shining. SCINTILLA, SCINTILLATE, STENCIL, TINSEL, from Latin *scintilla*, a spark. **4.** Suffixed zero-grade form **skiə-ā-* becoming **skiyā-*. SCIAENOID, SCIURID, SKIAGRAM, SKIASCOPE, SQUIRREL, from Greek *skiā*, shadow. [Pokorny *sḱāi-* 917.]

skand-   Also **skend-**. To leap, climb. Seen by some as an extended variant form of **ken-¹**. **1.** SCAN, SCANDENT, SCANSION, SCANSORIAL, SCANTLING; ASCEND, CONDESCEND, DESCEND, TRANSCEND, from Latin *scandere*, to climb. **2.** Suffixed form **skand-alo-*. SCANDAL, SLANDER, from Greek *skandalon*, a snare, trap, stumbling block. **3.** Suffixed form **skand-slā-*. ECHELON, ESCALADE, SCALE², from Latin *scālae*, steps, ladder. [Not in Pokorny; compare Sanskrit *skandati*, he jumps, and Old Irish *scendim*, I jump.]

sked-   To split, scatter. Extension of **sek-**. **1.** O-grade form **skod-*. SCATTER, SHATTER, from Old English **sc(e)aterian*, to scatter, from Germanic **skat-*. **2.** Variant nasalized form **ska-n-d-*. SHINGLE¹, from Latin *scandula*, a shingle for roofing (< "split piece"). [Pokorny *(s)k(h)ed-* 918.]

skei-   To cut, split. Extension of **sek-**. **1a.** SHIN¹, from Old English *scinu*, shin, shinbone (< "piece cut off"); **b.** CHINE, from Old French *eschine*, backbone, piece of meat with part of the backbone. Both **a** and **b** from Germanic suffixed form **ski-nō-*. **2.** SCIENCE, SCILICET, SCIOLISM; ADSCITITIOUS, CONSCIENCE, CONSCIOUS, NESCIENCE, NICE, OMNISCIENT, PLEBISCITE, PRESCIENT, from Latin *scīre*, to know (< "to separate one thing from another," "discern.") **3.** Suffixed zero-grade form **skiy-enā-*. SKEAN, from Old Irish *scían*, knife. **4.** Extended root **skeid-*. **a.** (i) SHIT, SHITE; GOBSHITE, from Old English *scītan*, to defecate; (ii) SKATE³; BLATHERSKITE, from Old Norse *skīta*, to defecate; (iii) SHYSTER, from Old High German *skīzzan*, to defecate. (i)–(iii) all from Germanic **skītan*, to separate, defecate; **b.** suffixed zero-grade form **sk(h)id-yo-*. SCHISM, SCHIST, SCHIZO-, from Greek *skhizein*, to split; **c.** nasalized zero-grade form **ski-n-d-*. SCISSION; ABSCISSA, ABSCISSION, EXSCIND, PRESCIND, RESCIND, from Latin *scindere*, to split. **5.** Extended root **skeit-*. **a.** (i) SHED¹, SHODDY, from Old English *scēadan*, to separate, from Germanic **skaith-, **skaidan*; (ii) SHEATH, from Old English *scēath*, sheath (< "split stick"), perhaps from Germanic **skaith-s*; **b.** SKI, from Old Norse *skīdh*, log, stick, snowshoe, from Germanic **skīdam*; **c.** o-grade form **skoit-*. ÉCU, ESCUDO, ESCUTCHEON, ESQUIRE, SCUDO, SCUTUM, SQUIRE, from Latin *scūtum*, shield (< "board"). **6.** Extended root **skeip-*. **a.** SHEAVE², from Middle English *sheve*, pulley (< "piece of wood with grooves"); **b.** SKIVE, from a Scandinavian source akin to Old Norse *skīfa*, to slice, split; **c.** SHIVER², from Middle English *shivere, scivre*, splinter, possibly from a Low German source akin to Middle Low German *schever*, splinter. **a–c** all from Germanic **skif-*. [Pokorny *skĕi-* 919.]

(s)kel-¹   To cut. **1a.** SHELL, from Old English *scell, sciel*, shell; **b.** SCAGLIOLA, from Italian *scaglia*, chip. Both **a** and **b** from Germanic **skaljō*, piece cut off, shell, scale. **2a.** SHALE, from Old English *sc(e)alu*, husk, shell; **b.** SCALE¹, from Old French *escale*, husk, shell. Both **a** and **b** from Germanic **skalō*. **3a.** SCALL, from Old Norse *skalli*, bald head (< "closely shaved skull"); **b.** SCALP, from Middle English *scalp*, top of the head, from a source akin to Old Norse *skalpr*, sheath, shell. Both **a** and **b** from Germanic **skal-*. **4.** SCALE³, SKOAL, from Old Norse *skāl*, bowl, drinking vessel (made from a shell), from Germanic **skēlō*. **5.**

SHIELD, from Old English *scield*, shield (< "board"), from Germanic **skelduz*. **6a.** SKILL, from Old Norse *skil*, reason, discernment, knowledge (< "incisiveness"); **b.** SHEL- DRAKE, from Middle English *scheld*, variegated, from a Low German source akin to Middle Dutch *schillen*, to diversify, with past participle *schillede*, separated, variegated. Both **a** and **b** from Germanic **skeli-*. **7.** SCHOOL², SHOAL², from Middle Low German *schôle*, troop, or Middle Dutch *scôle*, both from Germanic **skulô*, a division. **8.** Suffixed variant form **kel-tro-*. COULTER, CULTRATE, CUTLASS, from Latin *culter*, knife. **9.** Suffixed zero-grade form **skl̥-yo-*. SCALENE, from Greek *skallein*, to stir up, hoe (> *skalenos*, uneven). **10.** Extended root **skelp-*. **a.** SHELF, from Middle Low German *schelf*, shelf (< "split piece of wood"), from Germanic **skelf-*; **b.** possibly Germanic **halbaz* (< variant root **kelp-*), divided. HALF, HALVE, from Old English *healf*, half; **c.** perhaps variant **skalp-*. SCALPEL, SCULPTURE, from Latin *scalpere*, to cut, scrape, with derivative *sculpere* (originally as the combining form of *scalpere*), to carve. [Pokorny 1. *(s)kel-* 923.]

skel-² To be under an obligation. O-grade (perfect) form **skol-*. SHALL, from Old English *sceal* (used with the first and third person singular pronouns), shall, from Germanic **skal*, I owe, hence I ought. [Pokorny 2. *(s)kel-* 927.]

(s)kel-³ Crooked. With derivatives referring to a bent or curved part of the body, such as a leg, heel, knee, or hip. **1.** Suffixed form **skel-o-*. SALWAR, from Old Iranian compound **šara-vāra-*, "thigh covering," from **šara-*, thigh (**vāra-*, covering; see **wer-⁵**). **2.** Suffixed form **skel-ko-*. SCHILLER, from Old High German *scilihen*, to wink, blink. **3.** Suffixed form **skel-es-*. ISOSCELES, TRISKELION, from Greek *skelos*, leg. **4.** Suffixed o-grade form **skol-yo-*. SCOLIOSIS, from Greek *skolios*, crooked. **5.** Lengthened o-grade form **skōl-*. SCOLEX, from Greek *skōlēx*, earthworm, grub (< "that which twists and turns"). **6.** Suffixed lengthened o-grade variant form **kōl-o-*. COLON¹, from Greek *kōlon*, limb, member. **7.** Attributed (doubtfully) by some to this root is Greek *kulindein*, to roll: CYLINDER. [Pokorny 4. *(s)kel-* 928.]

skelə- To parch, wither. (Oldest form **skelh₁-*, with variant [metathesized] form **skleh₁-*, contracted to **sklē-*.) **1.** SKELETON, from Greek *skellesthai*, to dry, whence *skeletos* (< suffixed form **skelə-to-*), dried up (body), mummy. **2.** Suffixed variant form **sklē-ro-*. SCLERA, SCLERO-, SCLEROMA, SCLEROSIS, SCLEROTIC, SCLEROTIUM, SCLEROTIZATION, SCLEROUS, from Greek *sklēros*, hard. [Pokorny 3. *(s)kel-* 927.]

skeng- Crooked. SHANK, from Old English *sc(e)anca*, shinbone, from Germanic **skankōn-*, "that which bends," leg. [Pokorny *(s)keng-* 930.]

(s)kep- Base of words with various technical meanings such as "to cut," "to scrape," "to hack." **1a.** SHAPE, from Old English *gesceap*, form, creation (< "cutting"; *ge-*, collective prefix; see **kom**), and verb *sceppan*, to form (from Germanic **skapjan*); **b.** -SHIP, from Old English *-scipe*, state, condition (collective suffix); **c.** LANDSCAPE, from Dutch *-schap*, -ship, condition (collective suffix). **a–c** all from Germanic **skap-*. **2.** SCOOP, SCUPPER¹, from Middle Dutch and Middle Low German *schôpe*, bucket for bailing water, from Germanic ablaut variant **skōpō*, "thing cut out," container. **3.** SHAFT¹, from Old English *sceaft*, rod of a spear, from Germanic **skaftaz*. **4a.** SHABBY, from Old English *sceabb*, a scab, scratch; **b.** SCAB, from Old Norse *skabb*, a scab. Both **a** and **b** from Germanic expressive form **skabb-*. **5.** Variant form **skabh-*. **a.** *(i)* SHAVE, from Old English *sceafan*, to scrape, pare away; *(ii)* SAPSAGO, from Old High German *skaban*, to scrape. Both *(i)* and *(ii)* from Germanic **skaban*; **b.** SCABIES, from Latin *scabere*, to scrape; **c.** suffixed form **skabh-ro-*. SCABROUS, from Latin *scaber*, rough (< "scratched"); **d.** SCAPHOID;

BATHYSCAPHE, SCAPHOCEPHALIC, SCAPHOPOD, from Greek *skaphē*, boat (< "thing cut out"). **6.** Variant form **skap-*. SCAPULA, from Latin *scapula*, shoulder blade (used as a tool for scraping). **7.** Variant form **kap-*. **a.** CAPON, from Latin *capō*, castrated cock; **b.** SCABBLE, from Late Latin *capulāre*, to cut. [Pokorny 2. *(s)kep-* 931.]

(s)ker-¹ To cut.
I. Basic form **sker-*, **ker-*. **1a.** SHEAR, from Old English *scieran*, *sceran*, to cut; **b.** SHEER¹, from Low German *scheren*, to move to and fro, and Dutch *scheren*, to withdraw, depart. Both **a** and **b** from Germanic **skeran*. **2a.** SHARE², from Old English *scēar*, plowshare; **b.** SHARE¹, from Old English *scearu*, *scaru*, portion, division (but recorded only in the sense of "fork of the body," "tonsure"). Both **a** and **b** from Germanic **skeraz*. **3a.** SHEAR, from Old English *scēar*, scissors, from Germanic **skēr-ō* and **sker-iz-*; **b.** compound **skērberg-*, "sword protector," scabbard (**berg-*, protector; see **bhergh-¹**). SCABBARD, from Old French *escauberc*, scabbard, possibly from a Germanic source akin to Old High German *scarberc*, scabbard. Both **a** and **b** from Germanic **skēr-*. **4.** SCORE, from Old Norse *skor*, notch, tally, twenty, from Germanic **skur-*. **5.** SCAR², SKERRY, from Old Norse *sker*, low reef (< "something cut off"), from Germanic suffixed form **skar-jam*. **6.** Suffixed o-grade extended form **skorp-o-*. SCARF², from Old Norse *skarfr*, diagonally-cut end of a board, from Germanic **skarfaz*. **7.** Suffixed o-grade extended form **skord-o-*. SHARD, from Old English *sceard*, a cut, notch, from Germanic **skardaz*. **8.** Extended form **skerd-* in suffixed zero-grade form **skr̥d-o-*. **a.** SHORT, from Old English *scort*, *sceort*, "cut," short; **b.** SHIRT, from Old English *scyrte*, skirt (< "cut piece"); **c.** SKIRT, from Old Norse *skyrta*, shirt. **a–c** all from Germanic **skurtaz*. **9a.** SCARAMOUCH, SCRIMMAGE, SKIRMISH, from Old French *eskermir*, to fight with a sword, fence, and Old Italian *scaramuccia*, skirmish, from a source akin to Old High German *skirmen*, to protect; **b.** SCREEN, from Middle Dutch *scherm*, shield. Both **a** and **b** from Germanic extended form **skerm-*. **10.** Variant form **kar-*. CARNAGE, CARNAL, CARNASSIAL, CARNATION, CARNIVAL, CARRION, CARUNCLE, CHARNEL, CRONE; CARNE ASADA, CARNIVOROUS, CHARCUTERIE, INCARNATE, from Latin *carō* (stem *carn-*), flesh. **11.** Suffixed o-grade form **koryo-*. CORIACEOUS, CORIUM, CUIRASS, CURRIER; EXCORIATE, from Latin *corium*, leather (originally "piece of hide"). **12.** Suffixed zero-grade form **kr̥-to-*. CURT, CURTAL, KIRTLE, from Latin *curtus*, short. **13.** Suffixed o-grade form **kor-mo-*. CORM, from Greek *kormos*, a trimmed tree trunk. **14.** Suffixed o-grade form **kor-i-*. COREOPSIS, from Greek *koris*, bedbug (< "cutter"). **15.** Suffixed zero-grade form **skr̥-ā-*. SHORE¹, from Old English *scora*, shore, from Germanic **skur-ō*.
II. Extended roots **skert-*, **kert-*. **1.** Zero-grade form **kr̥t-* or o-grade form **kort-*. CORTEX; DECORTICATE, from Latin *cortex*, bark (< "that which can be cut off"). **2.** Suffixed form **kert-snā-*. CENACLE, from Latin *cēna*, meal (< "portion of food").
III. Extended root **skerp-*. SCURF, probably from a Scandinavian source akin to Old English *sceorf*, scab, scurf, from Germanic **skerf-*.
IV. Extended root **skerb(h)-*, **skreb(h)-*. **1a.** SHARP, from Old English *scearp*, sharp; **b.** SCARP, from Italian *scarpa*, embankment, possibly from a Germanic source akin to Gothic *skarpō*, pointed object. Both **a** and **b** from Germanic **skarpa-*, cutting, sharp. **2a.** SCRAP¹, from Old Norse *skrap*, "pieces," remains; **b.** SCRAPE, from Old Norse *skrapa*, to scratch. Both **a** and **b** from Germanic **skrap-*. **3a.** SCRABBLE, from Middle Dutch *schrabben*, to scrape; **b.** SCRUB¹, from Middle Dutch *schrobben*, to scrape. Both **a** and **b** from Germanic **skrab-*. **4.** SHRUB¹, from Old English *scrybb*, shrub (< "rough plant"), from Germanic **skrub-*. **5.** SCROBICULATE, from Latin *scrobis*, trench,

ditch. **6.** SCREW, SCROFULA, from Latin *scrōfa*, a sow (< "rooter, digger").
V. Extended root **(s)kers-*. BIAS, from Greek *epikarsios*, at an angle (*epi-*, at; see **epi**), from suffixed zero-grade form **kr̥s-yo-*. [Pokorny 4. *(s)ker-*, Section I. 938.] See also extended roots **skreu-** and **skrībh-**.

(s)ker-² To leap, jump about. Perhaps same root as **(s)ker-³**. **1.** Extended form **skerd-*. SCHERZO, from Middle High German *scherzen*, to leap with joy, from Germanic **skert-*. **2.** O-grade variant form **kor-*. CORUSCATE, from Latin *coruscāre*, to vibrate, glisten, glitter. [Pokorny 2. *(s)ker-* 933.]

(s)ker-³ To turn, bend. Presumed base of a number of distantly related derivatives. **1.** Extended form **(s)kreg-* in nasalized form **(s)kre-n-g-*. **a.** SHRINK, from Old English *scrincan*, to wither, shrivel up, from Germanic **skrink-*; **b.** variant **kre-n-g-*. (i) RUCK², from Old Norse *hrukka*, a crease, fold; (ii) FLOUNCE¹, from Old French *fronce*, pleat, from Frankish *hrunkjan, to wrinkle. Both (i) and (ii) from Germanic **hrunk-*. **2.** Extended form **(s)kregh-* in nasalized form **skre-n-gh-*. **a.** RING¹, from Old English *hring*, a ring; **b.** RANCH, RANGE, RANK¹, RINK; ARRANGE, DERANGE, from Old French *renc*, *reng*, line, row; **c.** RING- HALS, from Middle Dutch *rinc* (combining form *ring-*), a ring. **a–c** all from Germanic *hringaz, something curved, circle. **3.** Extended form **kreuk-*. **a.** RIDGE, from Old English *hrycg*, spine, ridge; **b.** RUCKSACK, from Old High German *hrukki*, back. Both **a** and **b** from Germanic *hrugjaz. **4.** Suffixed variant form **kur-wo-*. CURB, CURVATURE, CURVE, CURVET, from Latin *curvus*, bent, curved. **5.** Suffixed extended form **kris-ni-*. CRINOLINE, from Latin *crīnis* (< *crisnis), hair. **6.** Suffixed extended form **kris-tā-*. CREST, CRISTA, CRISTATE, from Latin *crista*, tuft, crest. **7.** Suffixed extended form **krip-so-*. CREPE, CRISP, CRISPATE, from Latin *crispus* (metathesized from *cripsus), curly. **8.** Extended expressive form **kriss-*. CRISSUM, from Latin *crīsāre*, (of women) to wiggle the hips during copulation. **9.** Perhaps reduplicated form **ki-kr-o-*. CERCLAGE, CIRCA, CIRCADIAN, CIRCINATE, CIRCINUS, CIRCLE, CIRCUM-, CIRCUS, CIRQUE; CRICOID, RECHERCHÉ, RESEARCH, from Greek *kirkos*, *krikos*, a ring. **10.** Suffixed o-grade form **kor-ōno-*. CORONA, CROWN, KORUNA, KRONA¹, KRONA², KRONE¹, KRONE², from Greek *korōnos*, curved. **11.** Suffixed variant form **kur-to-*. KURTOSIS, from Greek *kurtos*, convex. [Pokorny 3. *(s)ker-* 935.] See also extended root **(s)kerb-**.

sker-⁴ Excrement, dung. (Oldest form **sk̑er-*; derived from the noun for "excrement," **sk̑-ōr*, stem **sk̑-n-*.) **1.** Noun form *sk-ōr, **sk-n-*. **a.** SCATO-, SCORIA, SKATOLE, from Greek *skōr* (stem *skat-* < **sk-n̥-t-*), dung. **b.** SKARN, from Old Norse *skarn*, dung, from Germanic *skar, alternating with a stem derived from **sk-n̥-*. **2.** Form **sker-*. Extended form **skert-* in taboo metathesis **sterk-os-*. **a.** STERCORACEOUS, from Latin *stercus*, dung; **b.** variant forms **(s)terg-*, **(s)treg-*. DRECK, from Middle High German *drëc*, dung, from Germanic **threkka-*. [Pokorny *sk̑er-(d-)* 947, 8. *(s)ter-* 1031.]

(s)kerb- To turn, bend. Extension of **(s)ker-³**. **1.** SCORCH, from Middle English *scorchen*, to scorch, probably from a Scandinavian source akin to Old Norse *skreppa*, to shrink, be shriveled, and derivative *skorpna*, to shrink, be shriveled. **2.** Nasalized variant form **(s)kre-m-b-*. **a.** (i) RIMPLE, from Old English *hrympel*, wrinkle, fold; (ii) RUMPLE, from Middle Dutch *rompelen*, to wrinkle; (iii) RAMP², from Old French *ramper*, to climb, rear up. (i)–(iii) all from Germanic **hramp-*; **b.** (i) SHRIMP, from Middle English *shrimp*, pygmy, shrimp, possibly from a Low German source perhaps akin to Middle Low German *schrempen*, to shrink, wrinkle; (ii) SCRIMP, possibly from a Scandinavian source perhaps akin to Swedish *skrympa*, to shrink. Both (i) and (ii) from Germanic **skrimp-*. **3.** Variant form **kramb-*. CRAMBO, from

Greek *krambē*, cabbage (having wrinkled, shrunken leaves). **4.** Perhaps Celtic suffixed nasalized variant form **krumb-i-*. CROMLECH, from Welsh *crwm*, crooked, arched. [Pokorny *(s)kerb(h)-* 948.]

skēt- To injure. (Contracted from earlier **skeh₁t-*.) Suffixed zero-grade form **skət-on-*. **1a.** SCATHE, from Old Norse *skadha*, to harm; **b.** SCHADENFREUDE, from Old High German *scado*, harm, injury. Both **a** and **b** from Germanic **skathōn-*. **2.** Perhaps Germanic **scathi-* in *Skathinaujō, Scandinavia (see **akʷ-ā-**). [Pokorny *skēth-* 950.]

(s)keu- To cover, conceal. Zero-grade form **(s)ku-*. Variant **(s)keuə-*, zero-grade form **(s)kuə-*, contracted to **(s)kū-*. **1.** Suffixed basic form. **a.** SKY, from Old Norse *skȳ*, cloud; **b.** SKEWBALD, from a Scandinavian source akin to Old Norse *skȳ*, cloud. Both **a** and **b** from Germanic *skeu-jam, cloud ("cloud cover"). **2.** Zero-grade form **skū-*. **a.** Suffixed form **skū-mo-*. (i) SKIM, from Old French *escume*, scum; (ii) MEERSCHAUM, from Old High German *scūm*, scum; (iii) SCUM, from Middle Dutch *schūm*, scum. (i)–(iii) all from Germanic *skūmaz, foam, scum (< "that which covers the water"); **b.** suffixed form **skū-ro-*. OBSCURE; CHIAROSCURO, from Latin *obscūrus*, "covered," dark (*ob-*, away from; see **epi**). **3.** Zero-grade form **kū-*. **a.** Suffixed form **kū-ti-*. HIDE², from Old English *hȳd*, skin, hide, from Germanic *hūdiz; **b.** suffixed form **ku-ti-*. CUTANEOUS, CUTICLE, CUTIS; CUTIN, from Latin *cutis* skin; **c.** possibly suffixed form **kū-lo-*. CULET, CULOTTE; BASCULE, RECOIL, from Latin *cūlus*, the rump, backside; **d.** suffixed form **ku-to-*. -CYTE, CYTO-, from Greek *kutos*, a hollow, vessel. **4.** Extended zero-grade form **kus-*. **a.** (i) HOSE, HOSEL, from Old English *hosa*, hose, covering for the leg; (ii) LEDERHOSEN, from Old High German *hosa*, leg covering. Both (i) and (ii) from Germanic **husōn-*; **b.** suffixed form **kuz-dho-* (or suffixed extended form **kudh-to-*). (i) HOARD, from Old English *hord*, stock, store, treasure (< "thing hidden away"), from Germanic *huzdam; (ii) compound **kuzdho-zd-*, "sitting (over) a treasure" (**-zd-*, sitting; see **sed-¹**). CUSTODY, from Latin *custōs*, guard; **c.** KISHKE, from Russian *kishka*, gut (< "sheath"). **5.** Suffixed extended zero-grade form **kut-no-*. CUNNILINGUS, from Latin *cunnus*, vulva (< "sheath"). **6.** Extended root **keudh-*. **a.** HIDE¹, from Old English *hȳdan*, to hide, cover up, from Germanic suffixed lengthened zero-grade form *hūd-jan; **b.** HUT, from French *hutte*, hut, from Germanic suffixed zero-grade form **hūd-jōn-*; **c.** HUDDLE, from Low German *hudeln*, to crowd together, probably from Germanic **hūd-*. **7.** SHIELING, from a Scandinavian source akin to Old Norse *skāli*, hut, from Germanic zero-grade form **skaw-ala-*. [Pokorny 2. *(s)keu-* 951.]

skeubh- To shove. **1a.** SHOVE, from Old English *scūfan*, to shove; **b.** SCUFF, SCUFFLE, probably from a Scandinavian source akin to Old Norse *skūfa*, to push. Both **a** and **b** from Germanic *skeuban and derivative lengthened zero-grade form *skūban. **2a.** SHOVEL, from Old English *scofl*, a shovel; **b.** SCUFFLE², from Middle Dutch *schoffel*, *schuffel*, a shovel, hoe. Both **a** and **b** from Germanic suffixed form *skub-ilō. **3a.** SCOFF¹, from Middle English *scof*, mocking, from a Scandinavian source probably akin to Danish *skof*, jest, teasing; **b.** SHUFFLE, probably from a source akin to Low German *schüffeln*, to wask clumsily, shuffle cards. Both **a** and **b** from Germanic **skub-*, **skuf-*. **4.** Germanic **skup-*, perhaps (but quite doubtfully) in Old English *scop*, poet ("jester"): SCOP. [Pokorny *skeub-* 955.]

skeud- To shoot, chase, throw. **1.** SHOOT, from Old English *scēotan*, to shoot, from Germanic *skeutan, to shoot. **2a.** SHOT¹, from Old English *sceot*, *scot*, shooting, a shot; **b.** SCHUSS, from Old High German *scuz*, shooting, a shot; **c.** SCOT, SCOT AND LOT, from Old Norse *skot* and Old French *escot*, contribution, tax (< "money thrown down"); **d.** WAINSCOT, from Middle

Dutch *sc(h)ot*, crossbar, wooden partition. **a–d** all from Germanic **skutaz*, shooting, shot. **3.** SHUT, from Old English *scyttan*, to shut (by pushing a crossbar), probably from Germanic **skutjan*. **4.** SHUTTLE, from Old English *scytel*, a dart, missile, from Germanic **skutilaz*. **5a.** SHEET[2], from Old English *scēata*, corner of a sail; **b.** SHEET[1], from Old English *scēte*, piece of cloth. Both **a** and **b** from Germanic **skautjōn-*. **6a.** SCOUT[2], from a Scandinavian source akin to Old Norse *skūta*, mockery (< "shooting of words"); **b.** SHOUT, from Old Norse *skūta*, a taunt. Both **a** and **b** from Germanic **skut-*. [Pokorny 2. *(s)keud-* 955.]

(s)keuə- To pay attention, perceive. **1.** Suffixed (stative) variant form **kouə-ē-*, becoming **kaw-ē-* in Latin. CAUTION, CAVEAT; PRECAUTION, from Latin *cavēre*, to beware, watch, guard against. **2.** Variant o-grade form **skou-*. **a.** (*i*) SHOW, from Old English *scēawian*, to look at; (*ii*) WELTANSCHAUUNG, from Old High German *scouwōn*, to look at; (*iii*) SCAVENGER, from Flemish *scauwen*, to look at. (*i*)-(*iii*) all from Germanic **skauwōn*; **b.** SCONE, from Middle Dutch *schoon*, beautiful, bright (< "conspicuous, attractive"), from Germanic **skaunjaz*; **c.** SHEEN, from Old English *scīene*, bright, sheen, from Germanic **skauniz*. **3.** Suffixed o-grade form **kouə-ēi-*, **kouə-i-*. KAVYA, from Sanskrit *kāvyam*, power of a seer, poet's magical power, poetry, from *kaviḥ*, seer, poet. [Pokorny 1. *keu-* 587.]

(s)keup- Cluster, tuft, hair of the head. **1.** O-grade form **skoup-*. SHEAF, from Old English *scēaf*, bundle, sheaf, from Germanic **skauf-*. **2.** Possibly Germanic **hupp-*. HOP[2], from Middle Dutch *hoppe*, the hop plant (having tuftlike inflorescence). [Pokorny *(s)keup-* 956.]

[skipam Ship. Germanic noun of obscure origin. **1.** SHIP, from Old English *scip*, ship. **2.** SHIPPERKE, SKIPPER[1], from Middle Dutch *schip*, ship. **3.** SKIFF, from Italian *schifo*, ship, skiff. **4.** EQUIP, from Old French *esquiper*, to embark, prepare for embarcation, equip, probably from a Scandinavian source akin to Old Norse *skipa*, to man a vessel, from *skip*, ship. [In Pokorny *skēi-* 919.]]

-sko- (Oldest form **-sk̑o-*.) Verbal suffix marking iterative or imperfective aspect in the present tense, as **gn̥ə-sko-* (< earlier **ĝn̥ə₁-sk̑o-*), to be born (see **genə-**). Appears ultimately in the English suffixes -ESCENCE, -ESCENT, from Latin verbs in **-ēscere*, inchoative suffix (< **-ē-sko-*). [Not in Pokorny.]

skot- Dark, shade. **1.** Suffixed form **skot-wo-*. SHADE, SHADOW, SHED[2], from Old English *sceadu*, shade, from Germanic **skadwaz*. **2.** Suffixed form **skot-o-*. SCOTIA, SCOTOMA, SCOTOPHOBIA, from Greek *skotos*, darkness. [Pokorny *skot-* 957.]

skreu- To cut; cutting tool. Extension of **(s)ker-[1]**. **1.** Basic form **skreu-*. SHREW, SHREWD, from Old English *scrēawa*, shrew (having a pointed snout), from Germanic **skraw-*; **b.** SCREED, SHRED, from Old English *scrēade*, piece, fragment, from Germanic **skraud-*; **c.** (*i*) SHROUD, from Old English **scrūd*, garment (< "piece of garment"); (*ii*) SCROLL, from Old French *escro(u)e*, scroll. Both (*i*) and (*ii*) from Germanic **skrūd-*. **2.** Extended form **skreut-*. SCRUTINY; INSCRUTABLE, from Latin *scrūta*, trash, frippery. **3.** Extended variant form **skraut-*. SCROTUM, from Latin *scrōtum*, scrotum (probably identified with *scrautum*, leather quiver for arrows). [In Pokorny 4. *(s)ker-*, Section III, 947.]

skrībh- To cut, separate, sift. Extension of **(s)ker-[1]**. **1.** SCRIBBLE, SCRIBE, SCRIPT, SCRIPTORIUM, SCRIPTURE, SERIF, SHRIVE; ASCRIBE, CIRCUMSCRIBE, CONSCRIPT, DESCRIBE, FESTSCHRIFT, INSCRIBE, MANUSCRIPT, POSTSCRIPT, PRESCRIBE, PROSCRIBE, RESCRIPT, SUBSCRIBE, SUPERSCRIBE, TRANSCRIBE, from Latin *scribere*, to scratch, incise, write. **2.** SCARIFY[1], from

Greek *skariphos*, scratching, sketch, pencil. [Pokorny 4. *(s)ker-*, Section II. 945.]

(s)kʷal-o- Big fish. **1a.** WHALE[1], from Old English *hwæl*, whale; **b.** NARWHAL, RORQUAL, from Old Norse *hvalr*, whale. Both **a** and **b** from Germanic **hwalaz*. **2.** SQUALENE, from Latin *squalus*, a sea fish. **3.** Variant form **kʷal-i-* or **kʷal-es-* WELS CATFISH, from German *Wels*, sheatfish. [Pokorny *(s)kʷalo-s* 958.]

(s)lagʷ- To seize. **1.** Suffixed variant form **lagʷ-yo-*. LATCH, from Old English *læccan*, to seize, grasp, from Germanic **lakjan*. **2.** Variant form **slagʷ-* becoming **lab-* in Greek, nasalized to **la-m-b-*. LEMMA[1], -LEPSY; ANALEPTIC, ASTROLABE, CATALEPSY, EPILEPSY, NYMPHOLEPT, ORGANOLEPTIC, PROLEPSIS, SYLLABLE, SYLLEPSIS, from Greek *lambanein*, to take, seize (verbal adjective *lēptos*). [Pokorny *(s)lăgʷ-* 958.]

slak- To strike. **1.** SLAY, from Old English *slēan*, to strike, from Germanic **slahan*. **2.** SLEDGEHAMMER, from Old English *slecg*, hammer, from Germanic suffixed form **slag-jō*. **3.** SLAUGHTER, from Middle English *slaughter*, killing, probably from a Scandinavian source akin to Old Norse *slātr*, butchery, "striking," from Germanic suffixed form **slah-tram*. **4a.** SCHLOCK, from Old High German *slag*, a blow; **b.** ONSLAUGHT, from Middle Dutch *slag*, a blow. Both **a** and **b** from Germanic **slag-*; **c.** SLAG, from Middle Dutch *slagge*, metal dross (< "that which falls off in the process of striking"), probably from Germanic **slag-*. **5.** SLEIGHT, SLY, from Old Norse *slœgr*, clever, cunning (< "able to strike"), from Germanic suffixed lengthened-grade form **slōgi-*. [Pokorny *slak-* 959.]

slēb- To be weak, sleep. Possibly related to **slēg-** through a hypothetical base **slē-* (contracted from earlier **sleh₁-*.) SLEEP, from Old English *slǣpan*, to sleep, and *slēp*, sleep, from Germanic **slēpan*, **slēpaz*. [In Pokorny *lēb-* 655.]

(s)lēg- To be slack, be languid. Possibly related to **slēb-** through a hypothetical base **slē-* (contracted from earlier **sleh₁-*.) Zero-grade form **slag-*, becoming **slag-*. **1.** SLACK[1], from Old English *slæc*, "loose," indolent, careless, from Germanic **slak-*. **2.** Suffixed form **lag-so-*. LAX, LEASE, LESSOR; RELAX, RELEASE, RELISH, from Latin *laxus*, loose, slack. **3.** Suffixed nasalized form **la-n-g-u-*. LACHES, LANGUID, LANGUISH, LUSH[1], from Latin *languēre*, to be languid. **4.** Compound **lag-ō-o-*, "with drooping ears" (derived from **ous-*, ear; see **ous-**). LAGOMORPH, from Greek *lagōs*, *lagos*, hare. **5.** Suffixed form **lag-no-*. ALGOLAGNIA, from Greek *lag- nos*, lustful, lascivious. **6.** Basic form **slēg-*. CATALECTIC, from Greek *lēgein*, to leave off. [Pokorny *(s)lēg-* 959.]

(s)lei- Slimy. **1a.** SLIME, from Old English *slīm*, slime; **b.** SLIPPERY, from Old English *slipor*, slippery; **c.** SLICK, from Old English **slice*, smooth, and -SLICIAR, to make smooth; **d.** LIME[3], from Old English *līm*, cement, birdlime; **e.** LOAM, from Old English *lām*, loam; **f.** SLIGHT, from Middle English *slight*, slender, probably from a Scandinavian source akin to Old Norse *slēttr*, smooth, sleek; **g.** SLIP[1], from Middle English *slippen*, to slip, probably from a source akin to Middle Dutch and Middle Low German *slippen*, to slip, slip away; **h.** SCHLEP, from Middle Low German *slēpen*, to drag. **a–h** all from Germanic **slī-* with various extensions. **2.** Suffixed form **lei-mo-*. LIMACINE, LIMICOLINE, from Latin *līmus*, slime. **3.** Suffixed form **lei-w-*. OBLIVION, OBLIVIOUS, from Latin *oblīvīscī*, to forget (< "to wipe, let slip from the mind"; *ob-*, away; see **epi**). **4.** Suffixed form **lei-wo-*. LEIOMYOMA, from Greek *leios*, smooth. **5.** Suffixed form **(s)leiə-*, with metathesis **(s)leə(i)-*. **a.** Zero-grade form with nasal infix **li-n-ə-*. LINIMENT, from Latin *linere* (perfect *lēvī*), to anoint; **b.** suffixed zero-grade form **lī-* (< **liə-*). LITOTES, from Greek *lītos*, plain, simple; **c.** suffixed metathesized form **leə-wo-*, whence **lē-wo-*. LEVIGATE, from Latin *lēvis*, smooth; **d.** Sanskrit *lināti*, *layate*, sticks, stays, in compound derivative *ālayaḥ*, abode (*ā-*, to; see **ē**), in compound *Himālayaḥ* (see **ghei-²**). [Pokorny 3. *lei-* 662.]

sleidh- To slip, slide. **1.** SLIDE, from Old English *slīdan*, to slide, from Germanic **slīdan*, to slip, slide. **2a.** SLED, from Middle Low German *sledde*, a sled, sledge; **b.** SLEIGH, from Middle Dutch *slēde*, a sled; **c.** SLEDGE, from Middle Dutch *sleedse*, sleigh. **a–c** all from Germanic **slid-*. [Pokorny (s)*leidh-* 960.]

sleiə- Bluish. **1.** O-grade form **sloi(ə)-*. SLOE, from Old English *slāh*, *slā*, sloe (< "bluish fruit"), from Germanic **slaihwōn*. **2.** Zero-grade form **slī-*. **a.** Suffixed form **slī-wo-*. LAVENDER, LIVID, from Latin *līvēre*, to be bluish; **b.** suffixed form **slī-wā-*. SLIVOVITZ, from Serbo-Croatian *šljiva*, plum. [Pokorny (s)*li-* 965.]

slengʷh- To slide, make slide, sling, throw. **1.** SLING¹; SLINGSHOT, from Middle English *sling*, sling, possibly from a source akin to Old Frisian *slinge*, sling, from Germanic verb **slingwan* and suffixed form **slingw-ō*. **2.** SLINK, from Old English *slincan*, to creep, from Germanic variant verb **slinkan*. **3.** Possible suffixed o-grade form **slongʷh-rī-ko-*. LUMBRICOID, from Latin *lumbrīcus*, intestinal worm, earthworm. [In Pokorny (s)*leidh-* 960, *slenk-* 961.]

sleubh- To slide, slip.
I. Basic form **sleubh-*. **1.** SLEEVE, from Old English *slēf*, *slif*, *slief*, sleeve (into which the arm slips), from Germanic **sleub-*. **2.** SLOVEN, from Middle Low German *slōven*, to put on clothes carelessly, from Germanic **slaubjan*. **3.** Suffixed form **sleubh-ro-*. LUBRICATE, LUBRICIOUS, LUBRICITY, from Latin *lūbricus*, slippery.
II. Variant Germanic root form **sleup-*. **1a.** SLIP³; COWSLIP, OXLIP, from Old English *slypa*, *slyppe*, *slipa*, slime, slimy substance; **b.** SLOP¹, from Old English **sloppe*, dung; **c.** SLOP², from Old English (*ofer*)*slop*, surplice. **a–c** all from Germanic **slup-*. **2.** SLOOP, from Middle Dutch *slūpen*, to glide. [Pokorny *sleub(h)-* 963.]

sloug- Help, service. Celtic and Balto-Slavic root. Suffixed form **sloug-o-*. SLEW¹, SLOGAN, from Old Irish *slúag*, *slóg*, army, host. [Pokorny *slougo-* 965.]

smē- To smear. (Contracted from earlier **smeh₁-*.) **1.** Zero-grade form **sma-*. Suffixed zero-grade form **smə-tlā-* perhaps in Latin *macula*, spot, blemish, also a hole in a net, mesh: MACKLE, MACLE, MACULA, MACULATE, MACULE, MAIL², MAILLOT, MAQUETTE, MA- QUIS; IMMACULATE, TRAMMEL. **2.** Extended root **smeid-* (< **smeə-id-*). SMITE, from Old English *smītan*, to daub, smear, pollute, from Germanic **smītan* (the semantic channel may have been slapping mud on walls in wattle and daub construction). [Pokorny *smē-* 966.]

smeg- To taste. Germanic and Baltic root. **1.** SMACK², from Old English *smæc*, flavor, taste. **2.** SMACK¹, from a source akin to Middle Dutch and Middle Low German *smacken*, to taste, make a sound with the lips while tasting food. Both **1** and **2** from Germanic **smak-*. [Pokorny *smeg(h)-* 967.]

smei- To laugh, smile. **1.** SMIRK, from Old English *smercian*, to smile (with -*k*- formative), from Germanic reshaped forms **smer-*, **smar-*. **2.** SMILE, from Middle English *smilen*, to smile, from a Scandinavian source probably akin to Swedish *smila*, to smile, from Germanic **smīl-*. **3.** Suffixed form **smei-ro-*. MARVEL, MIRACLE, MIRAGE, MIRROR; AD- MIRE, from Latin *mīrus*, wonderful. **4.** Prefixed zero-grade form **ko(m)-smi-*, smiling with (**ko-*, **kom-*, together; see **kom**). COMITY, from Latin *cōmis* (Archaic Latin *cosmis*), courteous. [Pokorny 1. (s)*mei-* 967.]

(s)mēlo- Small animal. (Contracted from earlier **smeh₁lo-*.) Zero-grade form **sməlo-*. SMALL, from Old English *smel*, small, from Germanic **smal-*, small animal, hence also small. [Pokorny *mēlo-* 724.]

(s)mer-¹ To remember. **1.** Suffixed zero-grade form **mr̥-no-*. MOURN, from Old English *murnan*, to mourn,

from Germanic **murnan*, to remember sorrowfully. **2.** Reduplicated form **me-mor-*. MEMORABLE, MEMO- RANDUM, MEMORY; COMMEMORATE, REMEMBER, from Latin *memor*, mindful. [Pokorny (s)*mer-* 969.]

(s)mer-² To get a share of something. **1.** Suffixed (stative) form **mer-ē-*. MERETRICIOUS, MERIT; DEMERIT, EMERITUS, TURMERIC, from Latin *merēre*, *merērī*, to receive a share, deserve, serve. **2.** Suffixed form **mer-o-*. -MER, -MERE, MERISTEM, MERO-, -MEROUS; ALLOM- ERISM, DIMER, ISOMER, MONOMER, POLYMER, TRIMER, from Greek *meros* (feminine *meris*), a part, division. [In Pokorny (s)*mer-* 969.]

(s)mer-³ Grease, fat. **1.** Suffixed form **smer-wo-*. **a.** SCHMEER, from Old High German *smero*, fat; **b.** SMORGASBORD, from Old Norse *smjör*, grease, butter. Both **a** and **b** from Germanic **smerwa-*, grease, fat. **2a.** SMEAR, from Old English *smierwan*, *smerian*, to smear; **b.** SMEARCASE, from Old High German *smir- wen*, *smerian*, to apply salve, smear. Both **a** and **b** from Germanic denominative verb **smerwjan*, to spread grease on. **3.** Variant form **mer-*. MEDULLA, from Latin *medulla*, marrow (perhaps < **merulla*, influenced by *medius*, middle). [Pokorny *smeru-* 970.]

smerd- Pain. Extension of **mer-²**. SMART, from Old English *smeart*, causing pain, painful, from Germanic **smarta-*. [Pokorny *smerd-* 970.]

smeug- To smoke; smoke. SMOKE, from Old English *smoca*, smoke, from Germanic **smuk-*. [Pokorny (s)*meukh-* 971.]

smī- To cut, work with a sharp instrument. (Contracted from earlier **smih₁-*.) **1.** SMITH, from Old English *smith*, smith, from Germanic **smithaz*. **2.** SMITHY, from Old Norse *smidhja*, smithy, from Germanic **smith-ja-*. **3.** Suffixed form **smī-lā-*. KERATOMILEU- SIS, from Greek *smílē*, knife. [Pokorny 2. *smēi-* 968.]

smīk- Small. **1.** MICA, from Latin *mīca*, crumb, small piece, grain. **2.** MICRO-, MICRON; CHYLOMICRON, OMICRON, from Greek (s)*mīkros*, small. [In Pokorny *smē-* 966.]

snā- To swim. (Oldest form **sneh₂-*, colored to **snah₂-*, contracted to **snā-*.) **1.** Extended form **snāgh-*. NEK- TON, from Greek *nēkhein*, to swim. **2.** Suffixed zero-grade form **(s)nə-to-*. NATANT, NATATION, NATATO- RIAL, NATATORIUM; SUPERNATANT, from Latin *nāre*, to swim, and frequentative *natāre*, to swim. **3.** Attributed by some to this root (but more likely obscure) is Greek *nēsos*, island: CHERSONESE, MELANESIA, MICRO- NE- SIA, POLYNESIA (the last three being geographical names meaning "black islands," "small islands," and "many islands"). [Pokorny *snā-* 971.] See also extended root **(s)nāu-**.

(s)nāu- To swim, flow, let flow, whence suckle. (Oldest form **sneh₂u-*, colored to **snah₂u-*, contracted to **(s)nau-* [before consonants] and **(s)nāw-* [before vowels]. Extension of **snā-**.) **1.** Suffixed basic form **nāw-yo-*. NAIAD, from Greek *Naias*, fountain nymph, probably from *nān*, to flow. **2.** Variant (metathesized) root form **(s)neu(ə)-*. NEUSTON, from Greek *nein*, to swim. **3.** Zero-grade form **(s)nū-* (< **snua-*) in suffixed form **nū-trī* (with feminine agent suffix). NOURISH, NURSE, NURTURE, NUTRIENT, NUTRIMENT, NUTRITION, NUTRI- TIOUS, NUTRITIVE; NUTRIFY from Latin *nūtrīx*, nurse, and *nūtrīre*, to suckle, nourish. [In Pokorny *snā-* 971.]

(s)nē- To spin, sew. (Contracted from earlier **sneh₁-*.) **1.** Suffixed form **nē-tlā-*. NEEDLE, from Old English *nǣdl*, needle, from Germanic **nēthlō*. **2.** Suffixed form **snē-mn̥*. NEMATO-; AGLAONEMA, AXONEME, CHROMONEMA, PROTONEMA, SYNAPTINEMAL COM- PLEX, TREPONEMA, from Greek *nēma*, thread. **3.** Suffixed o-grade form **snō-tā-*. SNOOD, from Old English *snōd*, headband, from Germanic **snōdō*. [Pokorny (s) *nē-* 973.] See also extended root **(s)nēu-**.

sneg- To creep; creeping thing. **1.** Suffixed o-grade form **snog-on-*. SNAKE, from Old English *snaca*, snake, from Germanic **snak-ōn-*. **2.** Variant (Germanic) root *sneg-. **a.** O-grade form *snog-. SNAIL, from Old English *snæg(e)l, sneg(e)l, snail, from Germanic suffixed form *snag-ila-. **b.** Variant geminated form *snegg-. SNICKERDOODLE, from Middle High German *snecke, snegge*, from Old High German *sneggo*. [Pokorny ? *sneig-* 974.]

sneig^wh- Snow; to snow. **1.** Suffixed o-grade form *snoig^wh-o-. SNOW, from Old English *snāw*, snow, from Germanic *snaiwaz*. **2.** Zero-grade form *snig-^wh-. NÉVÉ, NIVAL, NIVEOUS, from Latin *nix* (stem *niv-*), snow. [Pokorny *sneig^wh-* 974.]

sneit- To cut. **1.** SNICKERSNEE, from Dutch *snijden*, to cut, from Germanic *snīthan*. **2.** SCHNITZEL, from Middle High German *sniz*, slice, from Germanic expressive form *snitt-ja-. [Pokorny *sneit-* 974.]

sner- Expressive root of various verbs for making noises. **1.** SNEER, perhaps from a source possibly akin to North Frisian *sneere*, scornful remark, from Germanic *sner-. **2.** O-grade form *snor- **a.** SCHNORRER, from Middle High German *snurren*, to hum, whirr; **b.** SNORKEL, from German *schnarchen*, to snore; **c.** SNARL[1], from Middle Low German *snarren*, to snarl; **d.** possibly Old Norse *Norn*, goddess of fate (< "the whisperer"): NORN. [Pokorny 1. *(s)ner-* 975.] Compare **snu-**.

(s)nēu- Tendon, sinew. (Contracted from earlier *sneh₁u-; extension of *sneh₁-, to sew; see **(s)nē-**.) Suffixed form *(s)nēw-r̥-, with further suffixes. **1.** *neu-r-o-. NEURO-, NEURON, NEURULA; APONEUROSIS, from Greek *neuron*, sinew. **2.** Metathesized form *nerwo-. NERVE; ENERVATE, from Latin *nervus*, sinew. [Pokorny *snēu-* 977.]

sneubh- To marry. **1.** NUBILE, NUPTIAL; CONNUBIAL, from Latin *nūbere*, to marry, take a husband. **2.** Possibly nasalized zero-grade form *nu-m-bh-. NYMPH, from Greek *numphē*, nymph, bride. [Pokorny *sneubh-* 977.]

sneudh- Mist, cloud. NUANCE; NUÉE ARDENTE, OBNUBILATE, from Latin *nūbēs*, cloud. [Pokorny 2. *sneudh-* 978.]

sneud(h)- To be sleepy. Expressive root. Zero-grade form *snud-to-. NYSTAGMUS, from Greek *nustazein*, to be sleepy (with *nust-* < *nud-t-). [Pokorny 1. *sneud(h)-* 978.] Compare **snu-**.

[snu- Imitative beginning of Germanic words connected with the nose. **1a.** SNOT, from Old English *gesnot(t)*, nasal mucus (*ge-*, collective prefix; see **kom**); **b.** SNOUT, from Middle English *snute*, snout, probably from a source akin to Middle Dutch *snut(e)*, snout; **c.** SCHNAUZER, SCHNOZ, from German *Schnauze*, snout. **a–c** all from Germanic *snūt-, *snut-. **2a.** SNUFFLE, from Low German *or* Dutch *snuffelen*, to sniff at; **b.** SNUFF[1], from Middle Dutch *snuffen*, to snuffle; **c.** SNIVEL, from Old English *snyflan* (> Middle English *snyvelen*), to run at the nose; **d.** SNIFF, from Middle English *sniffen*, to sniff. **a–d** all from Germanic *snuf-. **3.** SNOOP, from Dutch *snoepen*, to eat on the sly, pry, from Germanic *snup-. **4.** SNIP, from Low German and *Dutch snippen*, to snap at, from Germanic *snip-. **5.** SNAP, from Middle Low German and Middle Dutch *snappen*, to snap at, from Germanic *snap-. **6.** SNUB, from Old Norse *snubba*, "to snub, turn one's nose at," scold, from Germanic *snub-. **7.** SNATCH, from Middle English *snacchen*, to snatch, from a Low German source akin to Middle Dutch *snakken*, to snap at. [In Pokorny *snā-* 971.] Compare **sner-** and **sneud(h)-**.]

so- This, that (nominative). For other cases see **to-**. **1.** THE[1], from Late Old English *the*, masculine demonstrative pronoun, replacing *se* (with *th-* from oblique forms; see **to-**). **2.** HOI POLLOI, from Greek *ho*, the. **3.** Feminine form *syā-. SHE, from Old English *sēo*, *sīe*, she, from Germanic *sjō*. **4.** Compound variant form *sei-ke (*-ke, "this"; see **ko-**). SIC[1], from Latin *sīc*, thus, so, in that manner. [Pokorny *so(s)* 978.]

sol- Whole. Also **solǝ-** (oldest form *solh₂-).

I. Basic form *sol-. **1.** Suffixed form *sol-ido-. SOLDER, SOLDIER, SOLID, SOU; CONSOLIDATE, from Latin *solidus*, solid. **2.** Suffixed form *sol-wo-. HOLO-; CATHOLIC, from Greek *holos*, whole. **3.** Dialectal geminated form *soll-o-. **a.** SOLICIT, SOLICITOUS; INSOUCIANT, from Latin *sollus*, whole, entire, unbroken; **b.** SOLEMN, from Latin *sollemnis* (second element obscure), celebrated at fixed dates (said of religious rites), established, religious, solemn.

II. Variant form *solǝ-. **1.** Suffixed zero-grade form *sl̥ǝ-u- giving *sal-u-. SALUBRIOUS, SALUTARY, SALUTE, from Latin *salūs* (stem *salūt-*), health, a whole or sound condition, from earlier *salū-t-s, from *saluǝ-t-, metathesized from *sl̥ǝ-u-t-. **2.** Suffixed zero-grade form *sl̥ǝ-wo- giving *sala-wo-. SAFE, SAGE[2], SALVAGE, SALVO[1], SALVO[2], SAVE[1], SAVE[2], from Latin *salvus*, whole, safe, healthy, uninjured. [Pokorny *solo-* 979.]

Language and Culture Note The Latin word *salvus*, "safe, whole" (the source of such English words as *safe* and *save*), appears in an ancient prayer to the god Mars in the phrase *pāstōrēs pecuaque salva servāssīs*, "(I pray that) you keep (*servāssīs*) shepherds (*pāstōrēs*) and livestock (*pecuaque*) safe." The same sentiment, using three of the four same words, appears in a prayer in another ancient Italic language, Umbrian: *uiro pequo salua seritu*, "may he keep (*seritu*) men (*uiro*) (and) livestock (*pequo*) safe (*salua*)." The phrase meaning "keep safe" (Latin *salva servāssīs*, Umbrian *salua seritu*) continues two Indo-European forms, *sl̥ǝ-wo-, "safe," and *serw-, "to protect" (see **ser-[1]**), and both Latin and Umbrian have cognate words for "livestock" (Latin *pecua*, Umbrian *pequo*), which is likewise an Indo-European inheritance (see **peku-**). The phrasal association of these roots with one another in the formulaic language of prayer in fact goes back to Proto-Indo-European itself, because the combination of *sl̥ǝ-wo- and *serw- with *peku- is found also in Iranian.

---

spē-[1] To thrive, prosper. (Contracted from earlier *speh₁-.) **1.** Suffixed o-grade form *spō-ti-. SPEED; GODSPEED, from Old English *spēd*, success, from Germanic *spōdiz*. **2.** Suffixed form *spē-s-. DESPAIR, ESPERANCE, from Latin *spērāre*, to hope, denominative of *spēs* (plural *spērēs*), hope. **3.** Suffixed zero-grade form *spǝ-ro-. PROSPER, from Latin *prosperus*, favorable, prosperous (traditionally regarded as from *prō spērē*, according to one's hope; *prō*, according to; see **per[1]**). [Pokorny 3. *sp(h)ē(i)-* 983.]

spē-[2] Long, flat piece of wood. (Contracted from earlier *speh₁-.)

I. Basic form *spē-. **1a.** SPOON, from Old English *spōn*, chip of wood, splinter; **b.** SPAN-NEW, from Old Norse *spānn*, shingle, chip. Both **a** and **b** from Germanic *spē-nu-. **2.** Possibly Greek *sphēn*, wedge (formation unclear; earliest Greek form *sphān*): SPHENE, SPHENO-.

II. Suffixed zero-grade form *spǝ-dh-. **1a.** SPADE[1], from Old English *spadu*, digging tool; **b.** SPATHIC, from Middle High German *spat*, spar. Both **a** and **b** from Germanic *spadan*. **2.** ÉPAULEMENT, EPAULET, ESPALIER, SPADE[2], SPATHE, SPATULA, SPAY, from Greek *spathē*, broad blade. [Pokorny *sp(h)ē-* 980.]

spei- Sharp point.

I. Basic form *spei-. **1.** Zero-grade form *spi-. **a.** SPIT[2], from Old English *spitu*, stake on which meat is roasted, from Germanic *spituz*; **b.** SPITZ, from German *spitz*, pointed, from Germanic *spitja-. **2.** Germanic *spī-ra-. **a.** SPIRE[1], from Old English *spīr*, slender stalk; **b.** possibly Middle Dutch *spierlinc*, a small, slender fish, smelt, akin to the source of Old French *esperlinge*, smelt: SPARLING. **3.** SPIKE[1], from Middle English *spyk*, spike, perhaps from a source possibly akin to Old Norse *spīk*, nail, from Germanic *spīk-. **4.** SPILE, SPILL[2], from Middle Low German *spīle*, wooden peg, from Germanic *spīl-. **5.** Suffixed form *spei-nā-. SPINE, SPINEL, SPINNEY; PORCUPINE, from Latin spīna, thorn, prickle, spine. **6.** Suffixed form *spei-kā-. SPICA, Spica, SPICULUM, SPIKE[2], from Latin spīca, point, ear of grain.

II. Extended o-grade form *spoig-. SPOKE[1], from Old English spāca, spoke, from Germanic *spaikōn-. [Pokorny 1. (s)p(h)ēi- 981.]

(s)peik- Bird's name, woodpecker, magpie. **1.** Suffixed form *peik-o-. PICARO, PICKET, PIKE[1], PIQUE, from Latin pīcus, woodpecker. **2.** Suffixed form *peik-ā-. PICA[2], PIE[2], from Latin pīca, magpie. [Pokorny (s) pī́ko- 999.]

spek- To observe. (Oldest form *spek̂-.)
I. Basic form *spek-. **1a.** ESPY, SPY, from Old French espier, to watch; **b.** ESPIONAGE, from Old Italian spione, spy, from Germanic derivative *speh-ōn-, watcher. Both **a** and **b** from Germanic *spehōn. **2.** Suffixed form *spek-yo-. SPECIMEN, SPECTACLE, SPECTRUM, SPECULATE, SPECULUM, SPICE; ASPECT, CIRCUMSPECT, CONSPICUOUS, DESPISE, EXPECT, FRONTISPIECE, INSPECT, INTROSPECT, PERSPECTIVE, PERSPICACIOUS, PROSPECT, RE- SPECT, RESPITE, RETROSPECT, SPIEGELEISEN, SUSPECT, TRANSPICUOUS, from Latin specere, to look at. **3.** SPECIES, SPECIOUS; ESPECIAL, from Latin speciēs, a seeing, sight, form. **4.** Suffixed form *spek-s, "he who sees," in Latin compounds extispex (see **sek-**), haruspex (see **ghera-**), and auspex (see **awi-**). **5.** Suffixed form *spek-ā-. DESPICABLE, from Latin (denominative) dēspicārī, to despise, look down on (dē-, down; see **de-**). **6.** Suffixed metathetical form *skep-yo-. SKEPTIC, from Greek skeptesthai, to examine, consider.

II. Extended o-grade form *spoko-. SCOPE, -SCOPE, -SCOPY; BISHOP, EPISCOPAL, HOROSCOPE, TELESCOPE, from metathesized Greek skopos, one who watches, also object of attention, goal, and its denominative skopein (< *skop-eyo-), to see. [Pokorny spek̂- 984.]

spel-¹ To split, break off. **1.** Extended form *speld-. SPELT[1], from Late Latin spelta, spelt, from a Germanic source akin to Middle Dutch spelte, wheat (probably from the splitting of its husks at threshing), from Germanic *spilt-. **2.** Extended form *spelt-. SPILL[1], from Old English spillan, to spill, destroy, from Germanic *spilthjan. **3.** Suffixed o-grade form *spol-yo- perhaps in Latin spolium, hide torn from an animal, armor stripped from an enemy, booty: SPOIL; DESPOIL. [Pokorny 1. (s)p(h)el- 985.] See also extended root **(s)plei-**.

spel-² To say aloud, recite. Suffixed form *spel-no-. **1a.** SPELL[2], from Old English spell, discourse, story; **b.** GOSPEL, from Old English spel, news. Both **a** and **b** from Germanic *spellam. **2.** SPELL[1], from Old French espeller, espelir, to read out, from Germanic denominative verb *spellōn. [Pokorny (s)pel- 985.]

spelgh- Spleen, milt. **1.** SPLEEN, from Greek splēn, spleen (preform uncertain). **2.** SPLANCHNIC; SPLANCHNOLOGY, SPLANCHNOPLEURE, from Greek splankhna, inward parts (exact preform uncertain). [Pokorny sp(h)elĝh(en) 987.]

(s)pen- To draw, stretch, spin.
I. Basic form *spen-. **1.** Suffixed form *spen-wo-. **a.** SPIDER, SPIN, from Old English spinnan, to spin, and spīthra, spider, contracted from Germanic derivative *spin-thrōn-, "the spinner"); **b.** SPINDLE, from Old English spinel, spindle, from Germanic derivative *spin-ilōn-. Both **a** and **b** from Germanic *spinnan, to spin. **2.** Extended form *pend-. PAINTER[2], PANSY, PENCHANT, PENDANT[1], PENDENTIVE, PENDULOUS, PENDULUM, PENSILE, PENSION[1], PENSIVE, PESO, POISE[1]; ANTEPENDIUM, APPEND, APPENDIX, AVOIRDUPOIS, COMPENDIUM, COMPENSATE, COUNTERPOISE, DEPEND, DISPENSE, EXPEND, IMPEND, PENTHOUSE, PERPEND, PERPENDICULAR, PREPENSE, PROPEND, RECOMPENSE, STIPEND, SUSPEND, VILIPEND, from Latin pendēre, to

hang (intransitive), and pendere, to cause to hang, weigh, with its frequentative pēnsāre, to weigh, consider. **3.** Perhaps suffixed form *pen-yā-. -PENIA, from Greek peniā, lack, poverty (< "a strain, exhaustion"). **4.** GEOPONIC, LITH- OPONE, from Greek ponos, toil, and ponein, to toil, o-grade derivatives of penesthai, to toil.

II. O-grade forms *spon-, *pon-. **1a.** SPAN[2], SPANCEL, from Middle Dutch spannen, to bind; **b.** SPANNER, from Old High German spannan, to stretch. Both **a** and **b** from Germanic *spannan. **2.** SPAN[1], from Old English span(n), distance, from Germanic *spanno-. **3.** Perhaps Germanic *spangō. SPANGLE, from Middle Dutch spange, clasp. **4.** Suffixed and extended form *pond-o-. POUND[1], from Latin pondō, by weight. **5.** Suffixed and extended form *pond-es-. PONDER, PONDEROUS; EQUIPONDERATE, PREPONDERATE, from Latin pondus (stem ponder-), weight, and its denominative ponderāre, to weigh, ponder. **6.** Suffixed o-grade form *spon-t-. SPONTANEOUS, from Latin sponte, of one's own accord, spontaneously (but this is more likely related to the Germanic verb *spanan, to entice, from a homophonous root). [Pokorny (s)pen-(d-) 988.]

spend- To make an offering, perform a rite, hence to engage oneself by a ritual act. O-grade from *spond-. **1.** Suffixed form *spond-eyo-. SPONSOR, SPOUSE; DESPOND, ESPOUSE, RESPOND, from Latin spondēre, to make a solemn promise, pledge, betroth. **2.** Suffixed form *spond-ā-. SPONDEE, from Greek spondē, libation, offering. [Pokorny spend- 989.]

sper-¹ Spear, pole. **1a.** SPEAR[1], from Old English spere, spear; **b.** SPARERIBS, from Middle Low German spēr, spit. Both **a** and **b** from Germanic *speru. **2.** SPAR[1], from Old Norse sperra, rafter, beam, from Germanic *sparjōn-. [Pokorny 1. (s)per- 990.]

sper-² To turn, twist. **1.** Suffixed form *sper-ya. SPIRE[2]; BUSPIRONE, from Greek speira, a winding, coil, spire. **2.** Suffixed zero-grade form *spr-to-. ESPARTO, SPARTEINE, from Greek sparton, rope, cable. [Pokorny 3. sper- 991.]

sper-³ Bird's name, sparrow. Suffixed o-grade form *spor-wo-. SPARROW, from Old English spearwa, spearwe, from Germanic *sparwan-. [Pokorny sper-(g-) 991.]

sper-⁴ To strew.
I. Zero-grade form *spr-. **1.** SPRAWL, from Old English sprēawlian, to sprawl, from Germanic *spr-. **2.** Extended form *spreud-. **a.** SPROUT, from Old English -sprūtan, to sprout (only in ā-sprūtan, to sprout forth); **b.** SPRITZ, SPRITZER, from Middle High German sprützen, to spurt, spray; **c.** SPRIT, from Old English sprēot, pole (< "sprout, stem"); **d.** BOWSPRIT, from Middle Low German bōchsprēt, bowsprit. **a–d** all from Germanic *sprūt-. **3.** Extended form *spreit-. SPREAD, from Old English -sprēdan, to spread, from Germanic *spraidjan.

II. Basic form *sper-. **1.** Suffixed form *sper-yo-. DIASPORA, from Greek speirein, to scatter, with derivative sporā, a scattering, sowing (see **III. 1.**). **2.** Suffixed form *sper-mn. SPERM[1], from Greek sperma, sperm, seed (< "that which is scattered").

III. O-grade form *spor-. **1.** Suffixed form *spor-ā-. SPORE, SPORO-, from Greek sporā, a sowing, seed. **2.** Suffixed form *spor-nd. SPORADIC, from Greek sporas (stem sporad-), scattered, dispersed.

IV. Extended Germanic root *sprē(w)-. SPRAY[1], from Middle Dutch spraeien, sprayen, to sprinkle, from Germanic *sprēwjan. [Pokorny 2. (s)p(h)er- 993.]

sperə- Ankle. (Oldest form *sperh₂-.) Zero-grade form *spr(ə)-. **1.** SPUR, from Old English spura, spora, spur, from Germanic suffixed form *spur-ōn-. **2.** Nasalized zero-grade form *spr-n-ə-. SPURN, from Old English spurnan, spornan, to kick, strike against, from Germanic *spurnōn. **3.** SPOOR, from Middle Dutch *spor, spoor*, track of an animal, from Germanic suffixed form **spur-am.* [Pokorny 1. *sp(h)er-* 992.]

spergh- To move, hasten, spring. Nasalized European root form **sprengh-.* **1a.** SPRING, from Old English *springan*, to spring; **b.** KLIPSPRINGER, SPRINGBOK, from Middle Dutch *springen*, to leap; **c.** GELÄNDESPRUNG, SPRINGERLE, from Old High German *springan*, to jump. **a–c** all from Germanic **springan.* **2a.** BESPRENT, from Old English *besprengan*, to sprinkle, scatter; **b.** SPRINGE, from Old English **sprencg*, snare used to catch game. Both **a** and **b** from Germanic causative **sprangjan*, "to cause to spring." [Pokorny *spergh̑-* 998.]

(s)peud- To push, repulse. Zero-grade form **(s) pud-.* **1.** PUDENCY, PUDENDUM; IMPUDENT, from Latin *pudēre*, to feel shame. **2.** REPUDIATE, from Latin *repudium*, a casting off, divorce (*re-*, off; see **re-**). [In Pokorny *pēu-* 827.]

(s)ping- Bird's name, sparrow, finch. **1.** FINCH, from Old English *finc*, finch. **2.** FINK; DISTELFINK, from Old High German *finco*, finch. Both **1** and **2** from Germanic **finkiz*, **fink(j)ōn-*, finch. [Pokorny *(s)pingo-* 999.]

(s)plei- To splice, split. European root form, perhaps an extension of **spel-¹**. **1.** Variant form **plei-* in Germanic **flī-.* **a.** FLINT, from Old English *flint*, flint; **b.** FLINDERS, from Middle English *flendris*, bits, splinters, from a Scandinavian source akin to Norwegian *flindra*, splinter; **c.** perhaps Norwegian *flense*, flense: FLENSE. **2a.** SPLINTER, from Middle Dutch *splinter*, splinter; **b.** SPLIT, from Middle Dutch *splitten*, to split; **c.** SPLICE, from Middle Dutch *splissen*, to splice; **d.** SPLINT, from Middle Low German and Middle Dutch *splente*, *splinte*, splint. **a–d** all from Germanic **splī-.* [Pokorny *(s)plei-* 1000.]

splend- To shine, glow. European root form. SPLENDID, RESPLENDENT, from Latin *splendēre*, to shine. [In Pokorny 2. *(s)p(h)el-* 987.]

(s)poi-mo- Foam. **1.** Variant form **poi-mo-.* FOAM, from Old English *fām*, foam, from Germanic **faimaz.* **2.** Variant form **spoi-mā-.* SPUME, from Latin *spūma*, foam. **3.** Suffixed *reduced* form **poim-ik-.* POUNCE², PUMICE, from Latin *pūmex*, pumice (from its spongelike appearance). [Pokorny *(s)poimno-* 1001.]

spreg-¹ To speak. European root form in Germanic **sprek-*, **spek-* (with Germanic loss of *r*), to speak. **1.** SPEAK, from Old English *specan*, to speak. **2.** SPRECHSTIMME, from Old High German *sprehhan*, to speak. **3.** BESPEAK, from Old English *bisprecan*, *besprecan*, to speak about, from Germanic **bisprekan* (**bi-*, about; see **ambhi**). **4.** SPEECH, from Old English *sprǣc*, *spēc*, speech. [In Pokorny **(s)p(h)ereg-* 996.]

(s)preg-² To jerk, scatter. European root form. **1a.** SPRINKLE, from Middle English *sprenklen*, to sprinkle, possibly from a source akin to Middle Dutch *sprenkelen*, to sprinkle; **b.** FRECKLE, from Old Norse *freknur*, freckles (< "that which is scattered on the skin"); **c.** SPRAG, from a Scandinavian source akin to Swedish dialectal *spragg*, twig (< "that which is jerked off a branch"); **d.** SPRY, from a Scandinavian source akin to Swedish dialectal *sprygg*, brisk, active. **a–d** all from Germanic **sprek-*, **frek-* (the latter from variant Indo-European form **preg-*). **2.** Zero-grade form **sprg-* in variant **sparg-.* SPARGE, SPARSE, SPURRY; ASPERSE, DISPERSE, INTERSPERSE, from Latin *spargere*, to strew, scatter. [Pokorny **(s)p(h)ereg-* 996.]

sp(y)eu- To spew, spit. Expressive root. **1.** SPIT¹, from Old English *spittan*, to spit, from Germanic **spitjan.* **2.** SPEW, from Old English *spīwan*, *spīowan*, to spew, from Germanic **speiw-.* **3.** SPITTLE, from Old English *spātl*, spittle, from Germanic **spait-.* **4a.** SPOUT, from Middle English *spouten*, to spout forth; **b.** SPUTTER, probably from a Low German source akin to Dutch *sputteren*, to sputter. Both **a** and **b** from Germanic **spūt-.* **5.** Zero-grade form **spu-.* SPUTUM; CUSPI-

DOR, from Latin *spuere*, to spit. **6.** Zero-grade form **(s)pyu-.* HEMOPTYSIS, PTYALIN, from Greek *ptuein*, to spit. [Pokorny *(s)p(h)i̯ēu-* 999.]

srebh- To suck, absorb. Zero-grade form **sr̥bh-.* **1.** SLURP, from Dutch *slurpen*, to slurp, altered from Germanic **surp-.* **2.** Suffixed form **sr̥bh-ē-.* ABSORB, ADSORB, RESORB, from Latin *sorbēre*, to suck. [Pokorny *srebh-* 1001.]

srenk- To snore. O-grade form **sronk-.* **1.** RHONCHUS, from Greek *rhonkos*, *rhonkhos*, a snoring. **2.** RHYNCHOCEPHALIAN, from Greek *rhunkhos*, snout, bill, beak. [Pokorny *srenk-* 1002.]

sreu- To flow. **1.** Suffixed o-grade form **srou-mo-.* **a.** STREAM, from Old English *strēam*, stream; **b.** MAELSTROM, from Middle Dutch *stroom*, stream. Both **a** and **b** from Germanic **straumaz*, stream. **2.** Basic form **sreu-.* **a.** RHEO-, -RRHEA; CATARRH, DIARRHEA, HEMORRHOID, RHYOLITE, from Greek *rhein*, to flow, with o-grade *rhoos*, flowing, a flowing; **b.** suffixed form **sreu-mn̥.* RHEUM, from Greek *rheuma*, stream, humor of the body. **3.** Suffixed zero-grade form **srudhmo-.* RHYTHM, from Greek *rhuthmos*, measure, recurring motion, rhythm. **4.** Suffixed zero-grade form **sru-to-.* RHYTON, from Greek *rhutos*, fluid, liquid. **5.** Perhaps zero-grade extended form **srug-.* SASTRUGA, from Russian *struga*, deep place. [Pokorny *sreu-* 1003.]

srīg- Cold. **1.** Suffixed form **srīg-es-.* REFRIGERATE, from Latin *frīgus*, the cold. **2.** Suffixed (stative) form **srīg-ē-.* FRIGID, FRISSON; SEMIFREDDO, from Latin *frīgēre*, to be cold, and adjective *frīgidus*, cold. [Pokorny *srīg-* 1004.]

stā- To stand; with derivatives meaning "place or thing that is standing." (Oldest form **steh₂-*, colored to **stah₂-*, contracted to **stā-*.)

   I. Basic form **stā-.* **1.** Extended form **stādh-.* **a.** STEED, from Old English *stēda*, stallion, studhorse (< "place for breeding horses"), from Germanic **stōdjōn-*; **b.** STUD², from Old English *stōd*, establishment for breeding horses, from Germanic **stōdō.* **2.** Suffixed form **stā-lo-.* **a.** STOOL, from Old English *stōl*, stool; **b.** Germanic compound **faldistōlaz* (see **pel-³**). Both **a** and **b** from Germanic **stōlaz.* **3.** ESTANCIA, STAGE, STANCE, STANCH¹, STANCHION, STANZA, STATIVE, STATOR, STAY¹, STET; ARREST, CIRCUMSTANCE, CONSTANT, CONTRAST, COST, DISTANT, EXTANT, INSTANT, OBSTACLE, OBSTETRIC, OUST, REST², RESTHARROW, RESTIVE, SUBSTANCE, from Latin *stāre*, to stand. **4.** STIR², from Romani *stiraben*, jail, prison, from *star*, variant of *astar*, to seize, causative of *ast*, to remain, stop, from Middle Indic *atthaï*, from earlier **āsthāti*, from Sanskrit *ātiṣṭhati* (stem *ā-sthā-*), he stands by, remains on (*ā-*, near, all the up way to, at; see **ē**). **4.** Suffixed form **stā-men-.* ETAMINE, STAMEN, STAMMEL, from Latin *stāmen*, thread of the warp (a technical term). **5.** Suffixed form **stā-mon-.* PENSTEMON, from Greek *stēmōn*, thread. **6.** Suffixed form **stā-ro-.* STARETS, from Old Church Slavonic *starŭ*, old ("longstanding"). **7.** Suffixed form **stā-no-* in Indo-Iranian **stānam*, place ("where one stands"), becoming Persian *-stān*, country, the source of names of Asian countries ending in *-stan* like AFGHANISTAN, BALUCHISTAN, HINDUSTAN.

   II. Zero-grade form **stə-* (before consonants). **1.** Nasalized extended form **stə-n-t-.* **a.** STAND, from Old English *standan*, to stand; **b.** UNDERSTAND, from Old English *understandan*, to know, stand under (*under-*, under-; see **n̥dher**); **c.** STANDARD, from Frankish **standan*, to stand; **d.** STOUND, from Old English *stund*, a fixed time, while, from secondary zero-grade form in Germanic **stund-ō.* **a–d** all from Germanic **standan.* **2.** Suffixed form **stə-tyo-.* STITHY, from Old Norse *stedhi*, anvil, from Germanic **stathjōn-.* **3.** Suffixed form **stə-tlo-.* STADDLE, STALL², STARLING²; STALWART, from Old English *stathol*, foundation, from

Germanic *stathlaz. **4.** Suffixed form *stə-mno-. **a.** *(i)* STEM¹, from Old English stefn, stem, tree trunk; *(ii)* STALAG, from Old High German stam, stem. Both *(i)* and *(ii)* from Germanic *stamniz; **b.** ESTAMINET, probably from Walloon stamen, post to which a cow is tied at the feeding-trough, from a source derived from or akin to Germanic *stamniz. **5.** Suffixed form *stə-ti-. **a.** *(i)* STEAD, from Old English stede, place; *(ii)* SHTETL; LAGERSTÄTTE, from Old High German stat, place. Both *(i)* and *(ii)* from Germanic *stadiz; **b.** STAT², from Latin statim, at once; **c.** STATION, from Latin statiō, a standing still; **d.** ARMISTICE, SOLSTICE, from Latin -stitium, a stoppage; **e.** STASIS, from Greek stasis (see **III. 1. b.**), a standing, a standstill. **6.** Suffixed form *stə-to-. **a.** BESTEAD, from Old Norse stadhr, place, from Germanic *stadaz, placed; **b.** -STAT, STAT-IC, STATICE, STATO-; ASTASIA, ASTATINE, from Greek statos, placed, standing. **7.** Suffixed form *stə-no-. **a.** DESTINE, from Latin dēstināre, to make firm, establish (dē-, thoroughly; see **de-**); **b.** OBSTINATE, from Latin obstināre, to set one's mind on, persist (ob-, on; see **epi**). **8.** Suffixed form *stə-tu-. ESTATE, ÉTAGÈRE, STAGE, STATE, STATISTICS, STATUE, STATURE, STATUS, STATUTE; CONSTITUTE, DESTITUTE, INSTITUTE, PROS-TITUTE, RESTITUTE, SUBSTITUTE, SUPERSTITION, from Latin status, manner, position, condition, attitude, with derivatives statūra, height, stature, statuere, to set up, erect, cause to stand, and superstes (< *-stə-t-), witness ("who stands beyond"). **9.** Suffixed form *stə- dhlo-. STABLE²; CONSTABLE, from Latin stabulum, "standing place," stable. **10.** Suffixed form *stə-dhli-. ESTAB-LISH, STABLE¹, from Latin stabilis, standing firm. **11.** Suffixed form *stə-tā. -STAT; ENSTATITE, from Greek -statēs, one that causes to stand, a standing. **12.** Suffixed form *stə-mno-. STAMNOS, from Greek stamnos, stamnos (< "one that stands upright"). **13.** Perhaps in Latin īnstar, counterpart, equal, equivalent, possibly from compound suffixed form *en-stə-r, "that which stands in the place of" (en-, in; see **en**): INSTAR.

III. Zero-grade form *st-, *st(ə)- (before vowels). **1.** Reduplicated form *si-st(ə)-. **a.** ASSIST, CONSIST, DESIST, EXIST, INSIST, INTERSTICE, PERSIST, RESIST, SUBSIST, from Latin sistere, to set, place, stop, stand; **b.** APOSTASY, CATASTASIS, DIASTASE, ECSTASY, EPISTASIS, EPISTEMOLOGY, HYPOSTASIS, ICONOSTASIS, ISOSTASY, METASTASIS, PROSTATE, SYSTEM, from Greek histanai (aorist stanai), to set, place, with stasis (*stə-ti-), a standing (see **II. 5. e.**); **c.** HISTO-; HISTIOCYTE, HIS-TOGRAM, from Greek histos, web, tissue (< "that which is set up"). **2.** Compound form *tri-st-i- (see **trei-**). **3.** Compound form *por-st-i- (see **per¹**). POST¹, from Latin postis, post. **4.** Suffixed form *st-o- in compound *upo-st-o- (see **upo**).

IV. Extended root *stāu- (< *staəu-), becoming *stau- before consonants, *stāw- before vowels; basic meaning "stout-standing, strong." **1.** Suffixed extended form *stāw-ā-. STOW, from Old English stōw, place, from Germanic *stōwō. **2.** Probable o-grade suffixed extended form *stōw-yā-. STOA, STOIC, from Greek stoā (also stoiā, stōiā), porch. **3.** Suffixed extended form *stau-ro-. **a.** *(i)* STORE; INSTAURATION, from Latin īnstaurāre, to restore, set upright again (in-, on; see **en**); *(ii)* RESTORE, from Latin restaurāre, to restore, rebuild (re-, anew, again; see **re-**); **b.** STAUROLITE, from Greek stauros, cross, post, stake. **4.** Variant *tau-ro-, bull (see **tauro-**).

V. Zero-grade extended root *stū- (< *stuə-). **1.** Suffixed form *stū-lo-. STYLITE; AMPHISTYLAR, ASTY-LAR, EPISTYLE, HEXASTYLE, HYPOSTYLE, OCTASTYLE, PERISTYLE, PROSTYLE, STYLOBATE, from Greek stūlos, pillar. **2.** Secondary full-grade form *steuə-. Suffixed form *steuə- ro-. THERAVADA, from Sanskrit sthavira-, thick, stout, old. **3.** Variant zero-grade extended root *stu-. Suffixed form *stu-t-. STUD¹, from Old English stuthu, studu, post, prop.

VI. Secondary full-grade form *steu-. **1.** Suffixed form *steu-rā-. STARBOARD, from Old English stēor-, a steering, from Germanic *steurō, "a steering." **2a.** STEER¹, from Old English stieran, stēran, to steer; **b.** STERN², from Middle English sterne, stern of a boat, possibly from a source akin to Old Norse stjōrn, a rudder, a steering, derivative of stȳra, to steer. Both **a** and **b** from Germanic denominative *steurjan. **3.** Suffixed form *steu-ro-, a larger domestic animal. STEER², from Old English stēor, steer, from Germanic *steuraz, OX. **4.** Probably Germanic diminutive *steur-ika-. STIRK, from Old English stirc, stierc, calf. [Pokorny stā- 1004.] See also extended root **stāk-**.

stag- To seep, drip. Possible root. **1.** STAGNANT, from Latin stagnum, pond, swamp. **2.** Suffixed form *stag-yo-. STACTE; EPISTAXIS, from Greek stazein, to ooze, drip. [Pokorny stag- 1010.]

stāi- Stone. (Oldest form possibly *steh₂i-, colored to *stah₂i-, contracted to *stai- [before consonants] and *stāy- [before vowels].) **1.** Suffixed o-grade form *stoi-no-. **a.** STONE, from Old English stān; **b.** STEENBOK, from Middle Dutch steen, stone; **c.** TUNGSTEN, from Old Norse steinn, stone; **d.** STEIN, from Old High German stein, stone. **a–d** all from Germanic *stainaz. **2.** Possibly suffixed form *stāy-r̥. STEARIC, STEARIN, STE-ATITE, STEATO-; STEAPSIN, from Greek stear, solid fat, suet. [Pokorny (s)tāi- 1010.]

stāk- To stand, place. (Oldest form *steh₂k-, colored to *stah₂k-, contracted to *stāk-; extension of *steh₂-, to stand; see **stā-**.) Zero-grade form *stak-. **1.** Suffixed form *stək-o-. **a.** STAY³, in Old English stæg, rope used to support a mast; **b.** STAY², from Old French staie, a support. Both **a** and **b** from Germanic *stagaz. **2.** Suffixed form *stək-lo-. STEEL, from Old English stēli, stȳle, steel (< "that which stands firm"). [Pokorny stāk-1011.]

stebh- Post, stem; to support, place firmly on, fasten. **I.** Basic form *stebh-. **1.** STAFF¹, from Old English stæf, stick, rod, from Germanic *stab-. **2.** STEMMA, STEPHANOTIS, from Greek stephein, to tie around, encircle, crown, wreathe. **II.** Unaspirated form *steb-. **1a.** STAPLE², from Old English stapol, post, pillar; **b.** STEP, from Old English stæpe, step (< "a treading firmly on, foothold"); **c.** STAPLE¹, from Middle Dutch stapel, pillar, foundation; **d.** STOOP², from Middle Dutch stoep, stoop; **e.** STOPE, from Low German stope, a step. **a–e** all from Germanic *stap-. **2a.** STAMP, from Middle English stampen, to pound, stamp; **b.** STUMP, from Middle Low German stump, stump; **c.** STAMPEDE, from Provençal estampir, to stamp. **a–c** all from Germanic nasalized form *stamp-. **III.** Variant form *stabh-. STAPHYLINID, STAPHY-LO-, from Greek staphulē, grapevine, bunch of grapes. [Pokorny steb(h)- 1011.]

steg-¹ Pole, stick. O-grade form *stog-. **1.** STAKE¹, from Old English staca, stake. **2.** STACK, from Old Norse stakkr, a haystack. **3.** STAGGER, from Old Norse staka, to push, cause to stumble (as with a stick). **4.** ATTACK, from Italian attacare, to attack. **5.** ATTACH, from Old French attachier, to attack. **6.** STOCKADE, from Spanish estaca, stake. **1–6** all from Germanic *stakōn-, a stake. [Pokorny 2. (s)teg- 1014.]

(s)teg-² To cover. **I.** O-grade form *tog-. **1a.** THATCH, from Old English theccan, to cover; **b.** DECK², from Middle Dutch decken, to cover; **c.** DECKLE, from Old High German decchen, to cover. **a–c** all from Germanic *thakjan. **2a.** THATCH, from Old English thæc, thatch; **b.** DECK¹, from Middle Dutch dec, decke, roof, covering. Both **a** and **b** from Germanic *thakam. **3.** Suffixed form *tog-ā-, covering. TOGA, from Latin toga, toga. **4.** Possibly Sanskrit sthagayati, he covers: THUG. **II.** Basic form *steg-. STEGANOGRAPHY, STEGODON, STEGOSAUR, from Greek stegein, to cover.

III. Basic form *teg-. TECTRIX, TECTUM, TEGMEN, TEGMENTUM, TEGULAR, TEGUMENT, TILE, TUILE, TUILLE; DETECT, INTEGUMENT, OBTECT, PROTECT, from Latin *tegere*, to cover, and *tēgula*, tile (with lengthened-grade root). [Pokorny 1. *(s)teg-* 1013.]

stegh- To stick, prick; pointed. **1.** Perhaps nasalized form *stengh-*. STING, from Old English *stingan*, to sting, from Germanic *stingan*. **2.** O-grade form *stogh-*. **a.** STAG, from Old English *stagga*, stag, from Germanic *stag-*; **b.** STOCHASTIC, from Greek *stokhos*, pointed stake or pillar (used as a target for archers), goal. [Pokorny *stegh-* 1014.]

steig- To stick; pointed. Partly blended with **stegh-**.
I. Zero-grade form *stig-*. **1.** STICKLEBACK, from Old English *sticel*, a prick, sting, from Germanic suffixed form *stik-ilaz*. **2.** Suffixed form *stig-i-*. STITCH, from Old English *stice*, a sting, prick, from Germanic *stikiz*. **3.** STICK, from Old English *sticca*, stick, from Germanic expressive form *stikkōn-*. **4.** ETIQUETTE, TICKET, from Old French *estiquier*, to stick, from Germanic stative *stikkēn*, "to be stuck." **5.** SNICKERSNEE, from Middle Dutch *steken*, to stick, stab, from Germanic blended variant *stekan*. **6.** Nasalized zero-grade form *sti-n-g-*. DISTINGUISH, EXTINGUISH, INSTINCT, from Latin *stinguere*, to quench, perhaps originally to prick, and its apparent derivative *distinguere*, to separate (phonological and semantic transitions obscure). **7.** Suffixed form *stig-yo-*. STIGMA; ASTIGMATISM, from Greek *stizein*, to prick, tattoo. **8.** Suffixed reduced form *tig-ro-*. TIGER, from Greek *tigris*, tiger (from its stripes), from the same Iranian source as Old Persian *tigra-*, sharp, pointed, and Avestan *tighri-*, arrow.
II. Basic form *(s)teig-*. **1.** INSTIGATE, from Latin *īnstīgāre*, to urge, from *-stīgāre*, to spur on, prod. **2.** RAITA, from Sanskrit *tejate* (verbal adjective *tikta-* < suffixed zero-grade form *tig-to-*), it is sharp. **3.** Suffixed o-grade form *stoig-ā-*. STEAK, from Old Norse *steik*, roast, steak, and *steikja*, to roast (on a spit), from Germanic *staikō*.
III. Extended variant form *steigs-*. **a.** THISTLE, from Old English *thistel*; **b.** DISTELFINK, from Old High German *distil*, thistle. Both **a** and **b** from Germanic *thistilaz*, perhaps simplified from earlier *thīhstilaz*. [Pokorny *(s)teig-* 1016.]

steigh- To stride, step, rise. **1.** Basic form *steigh-*. STY[2]; STIRRUP, from Old English *stīgan*, to go up, rise, from Germanic *stīgan*. **2.** Zero-grade form *stigh-*. **a.** STILE[1], from Old English *stigel*, series of steps, from Germanic *stigila-*; **b.** suffixed form *stigh-to-*. STICKLE, from Old English *stiht(i)an*, to settle, arrange, from Germanic *stihtan*, "to place on a step or base"; **c.** suffixed form *stigh-o-*. STICH; ACROSTIC, CADASTRE, DISTICH, HEMISTICH, PENTASTICH, STICHOMETRY, STICH- OMYTHIA, from Greek *stikhos*, row, line, line of verse. **3.** O-grade form *stoigh-*. **a.** Suffixed form *stoigh-ri-*. STAIR, from Old English *stæger*, stair, step, from Germanic *staigrī*. **b.** STOICHIOMETRY, from Greek *stoikheion*, shadow line, element. [Pokorny *steigh-* 1017.]

steip- To stick, compress. **1.** STIFF, from Old English *stīf*, rigid, stiff, from Germanic *stīfa-*. **2.** STIPPLE, from Dutch *stip*, tip, point (preform uncertain). **3.** STIPE, STIPES, from Latin *stīpes*, post, tree trunk. **4.** Suffixed form *steip-ā-*. STEEVE[1], STEVEDORE; CONSTIPATE, from Latin *stīpāre*, to compress, stuff, pack. **5.** Suffixed zero-grade form *stip-olā-*. ETIOLATE, STIPULE, STUBBLE, from Latin *stipula*, stalk, straw. [Pokorny *stēib(h)-* 1015.]

stel- To put, stand; with derivatives referring to a standing object or place.
I. Basic form *stel-*. **1.** Suffixed form *stel-ni-*. STILL[1], from Old English *stille*, quiet, fixed, from Germanic *stilli-*. **2.** Suffixed form *stel-yo-*. APOSTLE, DIASTOLE, EPISTLE, PERISTALSIS, SYSTALTIC, from Greek

stellein, to put in order, prepare, send, make compact (with o-grade and zero-grade forms *stol-* and *stal-*).
II. O-grade form *stol-*. **1.** Suffixed form *stol-no-*. **a.** STALL[1]; FORESTALL, from Old English *steall*, standing place, stable; **b.** STALE[1]; INSTALLMENT[1], from Old French *estal*, place; **c.** STALLION, from Anglo-Norman *estaloun*, stallion; **d.** PEDESTAL, from Old Italian *stallo*, stall; **e.** INSTALL, from Medieval Latin *stallum*, stall; **f.** GESTALT, from Old High German *stellen*, to set, place, from Germanic denominative *stalljan*. **a–f** all from Germanic *stalla-*. **2.** Suffixed form *stol-ōn-*, from Latin *stolō*, branch, shoot. **3.** Suffixed form *stol-ido-*. STOLID, from Latin *stolidus*, "firm-standing," stupid. **4.** Suffixed form *stol-ā-*. **a.** STALK[1], from Old English *stalu*, upright piece, stalk, from Germanic *stalō*; **b.** STOLE[1], from Greek *stolē*, garment, array, equipment.
III. Zero-grade form *stḷ-*. **1.** Suffixed form *stḷ-to-*. STULTIFY, from Latin *stultus*, foolish (< "unmovable, uneducated"). **2.** Suffixed zero-grade form *stḷ-no-*. STULL, STOLLEN, from Old High German *stollo*, post, support, from Germanic *stullōn-*. **3.** Suffixed zero-grade form *stal-nā-*. STELE, from Greek *stēlē*, pillar.
IV. Extended form *steld-*. **1.** STILT, from Middle English *stilte*, crutch, stilt, from a source akin to Low German and Flemish *stilte*, stick, from Germanic *stiltjōn-*. **2.** Zero-grade form *stḷd-*. STOUT, from Old French *estout*, stout, from Germanic *stult-*, "walking on stilts," strutting. [Pokorny 3. *stel-* 1019.]

stelə- To extend. (Oldest form *stelh₂-*.) Zero-grade form *stḷə-*. **1.** Suffixed form *stḷə-to-*. LATITUDE; DILATE, SENSU LATO, from Latin *lātus*, broad, wide. Attributed by some to this root (as though suffixed zero-grade form *stḷə-men-*), but more likely of obscure origin, is Latin *lāmina*, plate, layer: LAME[2], LAMÉ, LAMELLA, LAMINA, LAMINARIN, LAMINATE, LAMINITIS, OMELET. [Pokorny 2. *stel-* 1018.]

sten- Narrow. Suffixed form *sten-wo-*. STENO-, STENOSIS, from Greek *stenos*, narrow. [Pokorny 2. *sten-* 1021.]

(s)tenə- To thunder. (Oldest form *stenh₂-*.) **1.** Zero-grade form *stṇa-*. **a.** THUNDER; THURSDAY, from Old English *thunor*, thunder, Thor; **b.** BLUNDERBUSS, DUNDERHEAD, from Middle Dutch *doner*, *donder*, thunder; **c.** THOR, from Old Norse *Thórr* (older form *Thunarr*), "thunder," thunder god. **a–c** all from Germanic *thunaraz*. **2.** O-grade form *tona-*. TORNADO; ASTONISH, DETONATE, STUN, from Latin *tonāre*, to thunder. [Pokorny 1. *(s)ten-* 1021.]

ster-[1] Stiff.
I. O-grade form *stor-*. **1.** Suffixed form *stor-ē-*. STARE, from Old English *starian*, to stare, from Germanic *starēn*. **2.** Extended form *stor-g-*. **a.** STARK, from Old English *stearc*, hard, severe, from Germanic *starka-*; **b.** STARCH, from Old English *stercan*, to stiffen, from Germanic denominative *starkjan*, to make hard.
II. Full-grade form *ster-*. **1.** STERN[1], from Old English *stierne*, *styrne*, firm, from Germanic *sternja-*. **2.** Suffixed form *ster-ewo-*. STERE, STEREO-; CHOLESTEROL, from Greek *stereos*, solid. **3.** Lengthened-grade form *stēr-*. STERIGMA, from Greek *stērizein*, to support.
III. Zero-grade form *stṛ-*. **1.** Extended form *stṛg-*. STORK, from Old English *storc*, stork (probably from the stiff movements of the bird), from Germanic *sturkaz*. **2.** STRUT, from Old English *strūtian*, to stand out stiffly, from Germanic *strūt-*.
IV. Extended form *sterd-*. **1.** REDSTART, STARKNAKED, from Old English *steort*, tail, from Germanic *stertaz*. **2a.** START, from Old English *styrtan*, to leap up (< "move briskly, move stiffly"); **b.** STARTLE, from Old English *steartlian*, to kick, struggle. Both **a** and **b** from Germanic *stert-*.

V. Extended form **sterbh-*. STARVE, from Old English *steorfan*, to die (< "become rigid"), from Germanic **sterban*.

VI. Extended form **(s)terp-* in suffixed (stative) zero-grade form **trp-ē-*. TORPEDO, TORPID, TORPOR, from Latin *torpēre*, to be stiff. [Pokorny 1. *(s)ter-* 1022.] See also extended root **(s)ter-n-**.

ster-² Star. (Oldest form **h₂ster-*.) **1.** Suffixed form **ster-s-*. STAR, from Old English *steorra*, star, from Germanic **sterzōn-*. **2.** Suffixed lengthened-grade form **stēr-lā-*. STELLAR, STELLATE; CONSTELLATION, from Latin *stēlla*, star. **3.** Basic form **əster-*. ASTER, ASTERIATED, ASTERISK, ASTERISM, ASTEROID, ASTRAL, ASTRO-; APASTRON, ASTEROSEISMOLOGY, ASTRAPHOBIA, DISASTER, PERIASTRON, from Greek *astēr*, star, with its derivative *astron*, star, and possible compound *astrapē, asteropē*, lightning, twinkling (< "looking like a star"; *ōps, op-*, eye, appearance; see **okʷ-**). **4.** ESTHER¹, perhaps from Persian *sitareh*, star, from Iranian stem **stār-* (or perhaps of Semitic origin). [Pokorny 2. *stĕr-* 1027.]

ster-³ To rob, steal. Possible variant form **stel-*. **1.** STEAL, from Old English *stelan*, to steal, from Germanic **stelan*. **2.** STEALTH, from Middle English *stelth*, stealth, from Germanic derivative noun **stēl-ithō* (**-ithō*, abstract suffix). **3.** STALK², from Old English **stealcian*, to move stealthily, from extended variant form in Germanic frequentative **stalkōn*. [Pokorny 3. *ster-* 1028.]

ster-⁴ Barren. STERILE, from Latin *sterilis*, unfruitful. [Pokorny 6. *ster-* 1031.]

sterə- Also **ster-**. To spread. (Oldest form **sterh₃-*.)
I. Extended variant form **streu-*. **1.** STRAIN², from Old English *strēon*, something gained, offspring, from Germanic suffixed form **streu-nam*. **2.** STRUCTURE; CONSTRUCT, DESTROY, INSTRUCT, INSTRUMENT, OBSTRUCT, SUBSTRUCTION, from Latin *struere*, to pile up, construct. **3.** Zero-grade form **stru-*. INDUSTRY, from Latin *industrius*, diligent, from Archaic Latin *indostruus* (*endo-*, within; see **en**). **4.** BREMSSTRAHLUNG, from Old High German *strāla*, arrow, lightning bolt, from Germanic **strēlō*.
II. O-grade extended form **strou-*. **1.** Suffixed form **strow-eyo-*. **a.** STREW, from Old English *strē(o)wian*, to strew; **b.** STREUSEL, from Old High German *strouwen, strowwen*, to sprinkle, strew. Both **a** and **b** from Germanic **strawjan*. **2.** Suffixed form **strow-o-*. STRAW, from Old English *strēaw*, straw, from Germanic **strawam*, "that which is scattered."
III. O-grade extended form **stroi-*. PERESTROIKA, from Old Russian *strojĭ*, order.
IV. Basic forms **ster-, *sterə-*. **1.** Nasalized form **ster-n-ə-*. ESTRAY, STRATUS, STRAY, STREET; CONSTERNATE, PROSTRATE, SUBSTRATUM, from Latin *sternere* (past participle *strātus* from suffixed zero-grade form **strə-to-*), to stretch, extend. **2.** Suffixed form **sterno-*. STERNUM; STERNOCLEIDOMASTOID, from Greek *sternon*, breast, breastbone.
V. Zero-grade form **str̥-, *str̥ə-*. **1.** Suffixed form **str̥-to-*. STRATAGEM; STRATOCRACY, from Greek *stratos*, multitude, army, expedition. **2.** Suffixed form **str̥ə- to-*. STRATH, from Old Irish *srath*, a wide river valley, from Celtic **s(t)rato-*. **3.** Suffixed extended form **str̥ə-mn̥*. **a.** STROMA; BIOSTROME, STROMATOLITE, from Greek *strōma*, mattress, bed. **b.** STRAMENOPILEOMA, from Latin *strāmen*, straw strewn as bedding. [Pokorny 5. *ster-* 1029.]

(s)ter-n- Name of thorny plants. Extension of **ster-¹**. Suffixed zero-grade variant form **tr̥-n-u-*. THORN, from Old English *thornu*, thorn, from Germanic **thurnu-*. [Pokorny 7. *ster-n-* 1031.]

(s)teu-¹ To push, stick, knock, beat; with derivatives referring to projecting objects, fragments, and certain related expressive notions and qualities.

I. Extended forms **steup-, *steub-*. **1.** STEEP¹, from Old English *stēap*, lofty, deep, projecting, from Germanic **staup-*. **2.** STEEPLE, from Old English *stȳpel, stēpel*, steeple, from Germanic **staupilaz*. **3.** STEP-, from Old English *stēop-*, step-, from Germanic **steup-*, "bereft" (< "pushed out"). **4.** STOOP¹, from Old English *stūpian*, to stoop, from Germanic **stūp-*. **5.** STUB, from Old English *stubb, stybb*, stump, from Germanic expressive form **stubb-*. **6.** STIVER, from Middle Dutch *stuyver*, stiver, from Germanic **stuf-*, "fragment," small coin.
II. Extended form **steud-*. **1.** Nasalized form **stu-n-d-*. STINT¹, from Old English *styntan*, to dull, from Germanic **stuntjan*. **2a.** STOSS, from Old High German *stōzan*, to push; **b.** STUTTER, from Middle English *stutten*, to stutter, from a source akin to Middle Low German and Middle Dutch *stōten*, to force. Both **a** and **b** from Germanic **staut-*.
III. Extended form **steug-*. **1a.** STOCK, from Old English *stocc*, tree trunk; **b.** ALPENSTOCK, from Old High German *stoc*, staff; **c.** LINSTOCK, from Middle Dutch *stoc*, stick; **d.** TUCK³, from Old French *estoc*, rapier, sword. **a–d** all from Germanic **stukkaz*. **2a.** SHTICK, from Old High German *stukki*, crust, fragment, covering; **b.** STUCCO, from Italian *stucco*, stucco. Both **a** and **b** from Germanic **stukkjam*. **3.** STOKER, from Dutch *stoken*, to poke, from Germanic **stok-*.
IV. Suffixed (stative) zero-grade extended form **stup-ē-*. STUPENDOUS, STUPID; STUPEFY, from Latin *stupēre*, to be stunned.
V. Suffixed (stative) extended zero-grade form **stud-ē-*. ÉTUDE, ÉTUI, STUDENT, STUDY, TWEEZERS, from Latin *studēre*, to be diligent (< "to be pressing forward").
VI. Extended zero-grade form **stug-*. STYX, from Greek *Stux*, the river Styx (< "hatred").
VII. Variant extended zero-grade form **tud-*. **1.** TOIL¹; RATATOUILLE, from Latin *tudēs*, hammer. **2.** Suffixed form **tud-ti-*. TUSSIS; PERTUSSIS, from Latin *tussis*, cough. **3.** Nasalized form **tu-n-d-*. CONTUSE, OBTUND, PERSE, PIERCE, RETUSE, from Latin *tundere*, to beat.
VIII. Variant zero-grade form **tup-*. **1.** Suffixed form **tup-o-*. TYPE; ANTITYPE, ARCHETYPE, from Greek *tupos*, a blow, mold, die. **2.** Nasalized form **tu-m-p-*. TIMPANI, TIMPANO, TYMPANUM, from Greek *tumpanon*, drum. [Pokorny 1. *(s)teu-* 1032.]

steu-² To praise. ZEND-AVESTA, from Avestan *staoiti*, he praises. [Pokorny 2. *steu-* 1035.]

stom-en- Denoting various body parts and orifices. STOMA, STOMACH, STOMATO-, STOMATOUS, -STOME, -STOMY; ANASTOMOSIS, ANCYLOSTOMIASIS, DEUTEROSTOME, GNATHOSTOME, OZOSTOMIA, PROSTOMIUM, PROTOSTOME, SCYPHISTOMA, XEROSTOMIA, from Greek *stoma*, mouth. [Pokorny *stomen-* 1035.]

storo- Starling. STARLING¹, from Old English *stær*, starling, from Germanic **staraz*. [Pokorny *storos* 1036.]

streb(h)- To wind, turn. European root. **1.** STREPTO-, STROP, STROPHE, STROPHOID, STROPHULUS; ANASTROPHE, APOSTROPHE¹, BOUSTROPHEDON, CATASTROPHE, DIASTROPHISM, EPISTROPHE, STREPSIRRHINE, from Greek *strephein*, to wind, turn, twist, with o-grade derivatives *strophē*, a turning, and *strophion*, headband. **2.** Unaspirated o-grade form **strob-*. STROBILUS; STROBOSCOPE, from Greek *strobos*, a whirling, whirlwind. **3.** Unaspirated zero-grade form **strb-*. STRABISMUS, STRABOTOMY, from Greek *strabos*, squinting. [In Pokorny 1. *(s)ter-* 1022.]

(s)trei- To hiss, buzz. Imitative root. **1.** Extended form **strīd-*. STRIDENT, from Latin *strīdēre*, to make a harsh sound. **2.** Extended variant form **trig-*. TRISMUS, from Greek *trismos, trigmos*, a grinding, scream. [Pokorny 3. *(s)treig-* 1036.]

streig- To stroke, rub, press. European root.

I. Basic form *streig-. **1a.** STRIKE, from Old English strīcan, to stroke; **b.** TRICOT, from Old French estriquier, to strike. Both **a** and **b** from Germanic *strīkan. **2.** STRICKLE, from Old English stricel, implement for leveling grain, from Germanic diminutive *strik-ila-. **3.** STREAK, from Old English strica, stroke, line, from Germanic *strikōn-.
II. O-grade form *stroig-. STROKE¹, from Old English *strāc, stroke, from Germanic *straik-.
III. Zero-grade form *strig-. **1.** Suffixed form *strig-ā-. STRIGOSE, from Latin striga, row of grain, furrow drawn lengthwise over the field. **2.** Suffixed form *strig-yā-. STRIA, from Latin stria, furrow, channel. **3.** Nasalized zero-grade form *stri-n-g-. STRAIN¹, STRAIT, STRESS, STRETTO, STRICT, STRINGENDO, STRINGENT; ASTRINGENT, CONSTRAIN, DISTRAIN, DISTRESS, PRESTIGE, RESTRAIN, RESTRICT, SENSU STRICTO, from Latin stringere, to draw tight, press together. **4.** STRIGIL, from Latin strigilis, strigil, possibly akin to stringere. [Pokorny 1. streig-, 2. streig- 1036; 4. ster- 1028.]

strenk- Tight, narrow. Possible European root. **1.** O-grade form *stronk-. **a.** STRING, from Old English streng, string, from Germanic *strangi-; **b.** STRONG, from Old English strang, strong, powerful, strict, from Germanic stranga-; **c.** STRENGTH, from Old English strengthu, strength, strictness, from Germanic *strangithō. **a–c** all from Germanic *strang-. **2.** Variant *strang-. **a.** STRANGLE, STRANGLES, STRANGULATE, from Greek strangalē, halter; **b.** STRANGURY, from Greek stranx, drop (< "that which is squeezed out"). [Pokorny strenk- 1036.]

strep- To make a noise. Imitative European root. OBSTREPEROUS, from Latin strepere, to make noise. [Pokorny (s)trep- 1037.]

(s)twer-¹ To turn, whirl. **1.** Zero-grade form *stur-. **a.** Suffixed form *stur-mo-. STORM, from Old English storm, storm, from Germanic *sturmaz, storm (< "whirlwind"); **b.** STIR¹, from Old English styrian, to move, agitate, from Germanic *sturjan. **2.** Suffixed zero-grade variant form *tur-bā-. TROUBLE, TURBID, TURBINADO, TURBINE; BIOTURBATION, DISTURB, PERTURB, from Greek turbē, tumult, disorder (> Latin turba, disorder, turbō, spinning top, and turbāre, to confuse, disorder). [Pokorny 1. tu̯er- 1100.]

(s)twer-² To grasp, hold; hard. Variant form *twer-. QUARTZ, from Middle High German quartz, quartz, from a source perhaps akin to West Slavic kvardy, quartz, altered from Slavic *tvr̥d-. [Pokorny 2. tu̯er- 1101.]

sū- Pig. (Contracted from earlier *suə-; probably a derivative of **seuə-¹**.) **1.** Suffixed form *suə-ino-. **a.** SWINE, from Old English swīn, swine; **b.** KEELSON, from Old Norse svīn, swine. Both **a** and **b** from Germanic *swīnam. **2.** Suffixed reduced form *su-kā-. **a.** (i) HOG, from Old English hogg, hog, from British Celtic *hukk-, from Celtic expressive form *sukko-, swine, snout of a swine; (ii) SOCKET, from Anglo-Norman soc, plowshare, perhaps from Celtic *sukko-; **b.** sow², from Old English sugu, sow, from Germanic *sugō. **3.** Basic form *sū-. sow², from Germanic *sū-. **4.** SOIL², from Latin sūs, pig. **5.** HYADES, HYENA; HYOSCINE, from Greek hūs, swine. [Pokorny sū-s 1038.]

sūro- Sour, salty, bitter. **1.** SOUR, from Old English sūr, sour. **2.** CHOUCROUTE, SAUERBRATEN, SAUERKRAUT, from Old High German sūr, sour. **3.** SORREL¹, from Old French sur, sour. **1–3** all from Germanic *sūra-, sour. [Pokorny sū-ro- 1039.]

swād- Sweet, pleasant. (Oldest form *sweh₂d-, colored to *swah₂d-, contracted to *swād-.) **1.** SWEET, from Old English swēte, sweet, from Germanic *swōtja-. **2.** Suffixed form *swād-ē-. SUASION; ASSUASIVE, DISSUADE, PERSUADE, from Latin suādēre, to advise, urge (< "recommend as good"). **3.** Suffixed form *swād-wi-. SUAVE; ASSUAGE, from Latin suāvis, delightful.

4. Suffixed form *swād-es-. AEDES, from Greek ēdos, pleasure. **5.** Suffixed form *swād-onā. HEDONIC, HEDONISM, from Greek hēdonē, pleasure. [Pokorny su̯ād- 1039.]

(s)wāgh- To resound. **1.** SOUGH, from Old English swōgan, to resound, from Germanic *swōgan. **2.** Suffixed form *wāgh-ā-. CATECHIZE, from Greek ēkhē, sound. **3.** Suffixed form *wāgh-ōi-. ECHO, from Greek ēkhō, noise, echo. [Pokorny u̯āgh- 1110.]

s(w)e- Pronoun of the third person and reflexive (referring back to the subject of the sentence); further appearing in various forms referring to the social group as an entity, "(we our)selves." **1.** Suffixed extended form *sel-bho-. SELF, from Old English self, sylf, self, same, from Germanic *selbaz, self. **2.** Suffixed form *s(w)e-bh(o)-. SIB; GOSSIP, from Old English sibb, relative, from Germanic *sibja-, "one's own," blood relation, relative. **3.** Suffixed form *se-ge. BUSTLE¹, from Old Norse -sk, reflexive suffix (as in būask, to make oneself ready), from sik, oneself (reflexive pronoun), from Germanic *sik, self. **4.** Suffixed form *swoi-no-. SWAIN; BOATSWAIN, from Old Norse sveinn, herdsman, boy, from Germanic *swai- naz, "one's own (man)," attendant, servant. **5.** Suffixed form *s(u)w-o-, one's own. **a.** SUICIDE, from Latin suī (genitive), of oneself; **b.** SWAMI, from Sanskrit svāmī, "one's own master," owner, prince, from sva- (< *swo-), one's own. **c.** SOBER, from Latin compound sōbrius, not drunk (ēbrius, drunk; see **egʷh-**). **6.** Extended form *sed. SECEDE, SECERN, SECLUDE, SECRET, SECURE, SEDITION, SEDUCTION, SEDULOUS, SEGREGATE, SELECT, SEPARATE, SEVER, SURE, from Latin sēd, sē, sē(d)-, without, apart (< "on one's own"). **7.** Possibly suffixed lengthened o-grade form *sō-lo. SOLE², SOLITARY, SOLITUDE, SOLO, SULLEN; DESOLATE, SOLILOQUY, SOLIPSISM, from Latin sōlus, by oneself alone. **8.** Extended root *swēdh-, "that which is one's own," peculiarity, custom. **a.** SODALITY, from Latin sodālis (Archaic Latin suodāl-), companion (< "one's own," "relative"); **b.** suffixed form *swēdh-sko-. CONSUETUDE, CUSTOM, DESUETUDE, MANSUETUDE, MASTIFF, from Latin suēscere, to accustom, get accustomed; **c.** ETHIC, ETHOS; CACOË- THES, from Greek ēthos, custom, disposition, trait; **d.** suffixed form *swedh-no-. ETHNIC, ETHNO-, from Greek ethnos, band of people living together, nation, people (< "people of one's own kind"). **9.** Suffixed extended form *swet-aro-. HETAERA, from Greek hetairos, comrade, companion, earlier hetaros. **10.** Suffixed extended form *swed-yo-. IDIO-, IDIOM, IDIOT; IDIOPATHY, IDIOSYNCRASY, from Greek idios, personal, private ("particular to oneself"). **11.** Suffixed form *swei-no-. SINN FEIN, from Old Irish féin, self. **12.** Suffixed (ablatival) form *swe-tos, from oneself. KHEDIVE, from Old Iranian khvadāta-, lord, by haplology from compound form *khvatō-dāta-, created from oneself (dāta-, created; see **dhē-**). **13.** Perhaps suffixed form *swe-tono-. KHOTANESE, from Khotanese Hvatana-, perhaps "those holding their own (power), masters." [Pokorny se- 882.] Derivative **swo-.**

swei-¹ To whistle, hiss. Imitative root. SIBILATE; CHUFA, PERSIFLAGE, from Latin sībilāre, to whistle at, hiss down. [Pokorny su̯ei- 1040.]

swei-² To bend, turn. Base of various Germanic forms. **1.** SWOOP, from Old English swāpan, to sweep, drive, swing, from Germanic o-grade form *swaip-. **2.** SWIFT, from Old English swift, swift, quick (< "turning quickly"), from Germanic zero-grade form *swip-. **3.** SWIVEL, from Middle English swyvel, a swivel, from Germanic full-grade form *swīf-. **4.** Possibly Germanic *swīh-. SWITCH, from Middle Dutch swijch, bough, twig. **5.** SWAP, from Middle English swappen, to splash, from a source akin to German schwappen, to flap, splash. [Pokorny su̯ē(i) 1041.]

sweid-¹ To shine. Possible suffixed form *sweid-es-. **1.** SIDEREAL, from Latin sīdus, constellation, star. **2.** CON-

SIDER, DESIRE, from Latin augury terms *cōnsīderāre*, to examine, "observe the stars carefully" (*con-*, intensive prefix; see **kom**), and *dēsīderāre*, to long for, miss ("observe the absence of"; formed on analogy with *cōnsīderāre*; *dē-*, from; see **de-**). **3.** Possible variant form **sweit-*. SWIDDEN, from Old Norse *svidha*, to be singed. [Pokorny 1. *su̯eid-* 1042.]

sweid-² Sweat; to sweat.
　　I. O-grade form **swoid-*. **1.** SWEAT, from Old English *swǣtan*, to sweat, from Germanic **swaitaz*, sweat, with its denominative **swaitjan*, to sweat. **2.** Suffixed form **swoid-os-*. SUDORIFIC; SUDORIFEROUS, from Latin *sūdor*, sweat. **3.** O-grade form **swoid-ā-*. SUDATORIUM, SUINT; EXUDE, TRANSUDE, from Latin *sūdāre*, to sweat.
　　II. Suffixed zero-grade form **swid-r-os-*. HIDROSIS, from Greek *hex*, six. [Pokorny 2. *su̯eid-* 1043.]

s(w)eks Six. (Oldest form **s(w)ek̑s-*.)
　　I. Form **seks*. **1.** SIX; SIXTEEN, SIXTY, from Old English *s(i)ex*, six, with derivatives *sixtig*, sixty, and *sixtȳne*, sixteen (*-tȳne*, ten; see **dekm̥**), from Germanic **seks*. **2.** SENARY, SEX-; SEICENTO, SEMESTER, from Latin *sex*, six. **3.** Suffixed form **seks-to-*. SESTET, SESTINA, SEXT, SEXTANT, SEXTILE; SEXTODECIMO, SIESTA, SISTINE, from Latin *sextus*, sixth.
　　II. Form **sweks*. HEXA-, HEXAD; UNUNHEXIUM, from Greek *hex*, six. [Pokorny *su̯ek̑s* 1044.]

swel-¹ To eat, drink. **1.** Perhaps Germanic **swil-*. SWILL, from Old English *swilian*, to wash out, gargle. **2.** Extended form **swelk-*. SWALLOW¹; GROUNDSEL¹, from Old English *swelgan*, to swallow, from Germanic **swelgan*, **swelhan*. **3.** MANTICORE, MARKHOR, from Iranian **khvāra-*, eating. [Pokorny 1. *su̯el(k-)* 1045.]

swel-² To shine, burn. **1.** Extended form **sweld-*. SULTRY, SWELTER, from Old English *sweltan*, to die, perish (perhaps < "be overcome with heat"), from Germanic **swiltan*. **2.** O-grade form **swol-*. SWALE, from Middle English *swale*, shade, shady place, from a Scandinavian source akin to Old Norse *svalr*, cool (< "lukewarm" < "hot"), from Germanic **swal-*. [Pokorny 2. *su̯el-* 1045.]

swel-³ Post, board. SILL, from Old English *syll(e)*, doorsill, threshold, from Germanic **suljō*. [Pokorny 2. *sel-* 898.]

swelə- To swell up, become swollen. (Oldest form **swelhₓ-*.) **1.** SWELL, from Old English *swellan*, to swell, from Germanic **swellan*. **2.** Suffixed zero-grade form **swl̥ə-ē-*. INSOLENT, from Latin *insolēns*, insolent (< "swollen with pride, puffed up"). [Not in Pokorny; compare Hittite *šulle-*, *šulla-*, to become an upstart, become disrespectful.]

swem- To move, stir, swim. Possibly an Indo-European root, but perhaps Germanic only. **1.** SWIM, from Old English *swimman*, to swim, from Germanic **swimjan*. **2.** Suffixed zero-grade form **swum-to-*. **a.** SOUND³, from Old English *sund*, swimming, sea; **b.** SOUND⁴; RADIOSONDE, ROCKETSONDE, from Old French *sonde*, sounding line. Both **a** and **b** from Germanic **sundam*. [Pokorny *su̯em-* 1046.]

swen- To sound. Also **swenə-** (oldest form **swenə₂-*). **1.** Suffixed o-grade form **swon-o-*. **a.** SWAN¹, from Old English *swan*, swan, from Germanic **swanaz*, **swanōn-*, "singer." **b.** SONE, SONIC, SONNET, SOUND¹; UNISON, from Latin *sonus*, a sound. **2.** Basic variant form **swenə-*. SONANT, SONATA, SONOROUS; ASSONANCE, CONSONANT, DISSONANT, RESOUND, from Latin *sonāre*, to sound. [Pokorny *su̯en-* 1046.]

sweng(w)- To wing, turn, toss. Germanic root. **1.** SWING, from Old English *swingan*, to whip, strike, swing, from Germanic **swingan*. **2.** SWINGLETREE, from Middle Dutch *swinghel*, instrument for beating hemp, from Germanic **swing-*. **3.** O-grade form **swong-*. **a.** Suffixed (causative) form **swong-eyo-*. SWINGE, from Old English *swengan*, to swing, shake, from Germanic **swangjan*; **b.** SWANK, from Middle

High German *swanken*, to turn, swing, from Germanic variant **swank-*. **4.** SWAG, from a Scandinavian source akin to Norwegian *swagga*, to sway (preform uncertain). [Pokorny *su̯eng-* 1047.]

swen-to- Healthy, strong. Germanic root, rhyming with the **kwen-to-* underlying the words for "holy" in Iranian and Balto-Slavic (see **kwen-**). Zero-grade form **sun-to-*. **a.** SOUND², from Old English *gesund*, healthy; **b.** GESUNDHEIT, from Old High German *gisunt(i)*, healthy. Both **a** and **b** from Germanic **gasunda-* (**ga-*, intensive prefix; see **kom**), from **sund-*. [Pokorny *su̯ento-* 1048.]

swep-¹ To sleep. **1.** Suffixed form **swep-os-*. SOPOR; SOPORIFIC, from Latin *sopor*, a deep sleep. **2.** Suffixed form **swep-no-*. SOMNI-, SOMNOLENT; INSOMNIA, from Latin *somnus*, sleep. **3.** Suffixed zero-grade form **sup-no-*. HYPNO-, HYPNOSIS, HYPNOTIC, from Greek *hupnos*, sleep. [Pokorny 1. *su̯ep-* 1048.]

swep-² To throw, sling, cast. **1.** O-grade form **swop-*, possibly in Germanic variant expressive form **swabb-*. SWAB, from Middle Dutch *swabbe*, mop, splash. **2.** Suffixed zero-grade form **sup-ā-*. DISSIPATE, from Latin *dissipāre* (< **dissupāre*), to disperse (**dis-*, apart). [Pokorny 2. *su̯ep-* 1049.]

swer-¹ To speak, talk. O-grade form **swor-*. **1.** SWEAR, from Old English *swerian*, to swear, proclaim, from Germanic **swarjan*. **2.** ANSWER, from Old English *andswaru*, answer, from Germanic **and-swarō*, "a swearing against," "rebuttal" (**andi-*, against; see **ant-**). [Pokorny 1. *su̯er-* 1049.]

swer-² To buzz, whisper. Imitative root. **1.** O-grade form **swor-*. SWIRL, from Middle English *swyrl*, eddy, from a Low German source akin to Dutch *zwirrelen*, to whirl, from Germanic **swar-*. **2.** Suffixed o-grade form **swor-mo-*. SWARM, from Old English *swearm*, swarm, from Germanic **swarmaz*. **3.** Possibly suffixed zero-grade form **sur-do-*. **a.** SORDINO, SOUR- DINE, SURD, from Latin *surdus*, deaf, mute; **b.** ABSURD, from Latin *absurdus*, discordant, away from the right sound, harsh (*ab-*, away; see **apo-**). **4.** In names of small animals. **a.** Suffixed zero-grade form **sur-ak-*. HYRAX; HYRACOTHERE, from Greek *hurax*, hyrax; **b.** suffixed lengthened o-grade form **swōr-ak-*. SORICINE, from Latin *sōrex*, shrew. **5.** Reduplicated *expressive* zero-grade form **su-surr-*. SUSURRATION, from Latin *susurrus*, whisper. [Pokorny 2. *su̯er-* 1049.]

swer-³ To heft, weigh, lift. (Obscurely related to **wer-²**, with oldest form **h₂wer-*, in the same meanings.) **1.** SWORD, from Old English *sweord*, sword, from Germanic **swerdam* (for the semantics, note the image of "hefting" an object by holding in the two hands to guess its weight). **2.** Suffixed lengthened-grade variant form **sēr-yo-*. SERIOUS, from Latin *sērius*, serious, grave (< **"heavy"). [Pokorny 5. *su̯er-* 1050, *u̯er-* 1150.]

swerbh- To turn, wipe off. **1.** SWERVE, from Old English *sweorfan*, to file away, scour, polish, from Germanic **swerb-*. **2.** O-grade form **sworbh-*. SWARF, from a Scandinavian source akin to Old Norse *svarf*, filings. [Pokorny *su̯erbh-* 1050.]

swergh- To worry, be sick. SORROW, from Old English *sorh*, *sorg*, anxiety, sorrow, from Germanic **sorg-*. [Pokorny *su̯ergh-* 1051.]

swesor- Sister. Perhaps originally a compound of **s(w)e-** and **esōr**, woman, so literally "woman of one's own kin group" in an exogamous society. **1.** Zero-grade form **swesr-*. **a.** SISTER, from Old English *sweostor*, sister, and Old Norse *systir*, sister, both from Germanic **swestar* (with *-t-* from stem **swestr-* < **swesr-*); **b.** suffixed form **swesr-īno-*. COUSIN, from Latin *sobrīnus*, maternal cousin. **2.** SORORAL, SORORITY; SORORICIDE, from Latin *soror*, sister. [Pokorny *su̯esor-* 1051.]

swī- To be silent. APOSIOPESIS, from Greek *siōpē*, silence (expressive formation). [Pokorny *su̯ī-* 1052.]

swo- Pronominal stem; so. Derivative of **s(w)e-**. **1a.** so¹, from Old English *swā*, so; **b.** SUCH, from Old English *swylc*, such, from Germanic compound **swa-lik-*, "so like," of the same kind (**līk-*, same; see **līk-**). **2.** Adverbial form **swai*. NISI, QUASI, from Latin *sī* (Archaic Latin *sei*), if, in *nisi*, unless (Archaic Latin *nesei*; *ne*, not; see **ne**), and *quasi*, as if (*quam*, as; see **kʷo-**). [In Pokorny *se-* 882.]

s(w)okʷo- Resin, juice. Variant form **sokʷo-*. OPIUM, from Greek *opos* (< **hopos*), juice. [Pokorny *s(u̯)ekʷo-s* 1044.]

swombho- Spongy; also a word for mushroom. **1.** SUMP, from Middle Low German *sump*, swamp. **2.** SWAMP, from a Low German source akin to Low German *zwamp*, swamp. [Pokorny *s(u̯)omb(h)o-s* 1052.]

swordo- Black, dirty. **1.** SWART, SWARTHY, from Old English *sweart*, swarthy, from Germanic **swarta-*. **2.** Zero-grade suffixed (stative) form **swr̥d-ē-*. SORDID, from Latin *sordēre*, to be dirty. [Pokorny *su̯ordo-s* 1052.]

syū- Also **sū-**. To bind, sew. (Oldest form **syuhₓ-*.)
I. Basic form **syū-*. SEW, from Old English *seowian*, *siowan*, to sew, from Germanic **siwjan*.
II. Variant form **sū-*. **1.** SEAM, from Old English *sēam*, seam, from Germanic **saumaz*. **2.** SUTURE; ACCOUTER, COUTURE, from Latin *suere* (past participle *sūtus*), to sew. **3.** Suffixed form **sū-dhlā-*. SOUVLAKI, SUBULATE, from Latin *sūbula*, awl (< "sewing instrument"). **4.** Suffixed form **sū-tro-*. SUTRA; KAMASUTRA, from Sanskrit *sūtram*, thread, string.
III. Suffixed shortened form **syu-men-*. HYMEN, from Greek *humēn*, thin skin, membrane. [Pokorny *si̯ū-* 915.]

tā- To melt, dissolve. (Oldest form **teh₂-*, colored to **tah₂-*, contracted to **tā-*.) **1.** Extended form **tāw-*. THAW, from Old English *thāwian*, to thaw, from Germanic **thāwōn*. **2.** Extended form **tābh-*. TABES, TABESCENT, from Latin *tābēs*, a melting, wasting away, putrefaction. **3.** Extended form **tāk-*. EUTECTIC, from Greek *tēkein*, to melt. [Pokorny *tā-* 1053.]

tag- To touch, handle. **1.** Nasalized form **ta-n-g-*. TACT, TANGENT, TANGIBLE, TASK, TASTE, TAX; ATACTIC, ATTAIN, CONTACT, INTACT, from Latin *tangere*, to touch, with derivatives *taxāre*, to touch, assess (possibly a frequentative of *tangere*, but probably influenced by Greek *tassein*, *taxai*, to arrange, assess), and *tāctus*, touch. **2.** Compound form **n̥-tag-ro-*, "untouched, intact" (**n̥-*, negative prefix; see **ne**). ENTIRE, INTEGER, INTEGRATE, INTEGRITY, from Latin *integer*, intact, whole, complete, perfect, honest. **3.** Suffixed form **tag-smen-*. CONTAMINATE, from Latin *contāmināre*, to corrupt by mixing or contact (< **con-tāmen-*, "bringing into contact with"; *con-*, *com-*, with; see **kom**). [Pokorny *tag-* 1054.]

tāg- To set in order. (Oldest form probably **teh₂g-*, colored to **tah₂g-*, contracted to **tāg-*.) Suffixed form **tag-yo-* (probably < *tag-yo-*). TACTICS, TAGMA, TAXEME, TAXIS, -TAXIS, TAXO-; ATAXIA, HYPOTAXIS, PARATAXIS, SYNTAX, from Greek *tassein*, *tattein*, to arrange, with derivatives *taxis* (< **tag-ti-*), arrangement, and *tagma* (< **tag-mn̥*), arrangement. [Pokorny *tāg-* 1055.]

tak-¹ To be silent. Suffixed (stative) form **tak-ē-*. TACET, TACIT; PAPPATACI FEVER, RETICENT, from Latin *tacēre*, to be silent. [Pokorny *tak-* 1055.]

[tak-² To take. Germanic root. TAKE; WAPENTAKE, from Old Norse *taka*, to take, from Germanic **takan*.]

tauro- Bull. Derivative of **stā-** (via extended form **(s)tah₂u-*), but an independent word in Indo-European. **1.** TAURINE¹, TAURUS, TOREADOR, TORERO; BIT- TERN¹, from Latin *taurus*, bull. **2.** TAURINE²; TAUROCHOLIC ACID, from Greek *tauros*, bull. [In Pokorny *tēu-* 1080.]

[taw- To make, manufacture. Germanic root. **1.** TOW², from Old English *tow-*, spinning (only in compounds

such as *tow-hūs*, spinning house or room). **2.** TAW¹, from Old English *tawian*, to prepare, from Germanic **tawjan*, **tawōn*. **3.** HERIOT, from Old English *geatwa*, *geatwe*, equipment, from Germanic **gatawja-*, equipment (**ga-*, collective prefix; see **kom**). **4.** TOOL, from Old English or Old Norse *tōl*, implement, from Germanic variant **to(w)lam*, implement. [In Pokorny 2. *(deu-)* 218.]

tegu- Thick. THICK, from Old English *thicce*, thick, from Germanic **thiku-*. [Pokorny *tegu-* 1057.]

tek- To beget, give birth to. **1.** Suffixed form **tek-no-*, child. THANE, from Old English *thegn*, freeman, nobleman, military vassal, warrior, from Germanic **theg-naz*, boy, man, servant, warrior. **2.** Suffixed o-grade form **tek-o-*. OXYTOCIC, TOCOLOGY, TOCOLOGY, from Greek *tokos*, birth. [Pokorny 1. *tek-* 1057.]

teks- To weave; also to fabricate, especially with an ax; also to make wicker or wattle fabric (for mud-covered) house walls. (Oldest form **tek̂s-*.) **1.** TEXT, TISSUE; CONTEXT, PRETEXT, from Latin *texere*, to weave, fabricate. **2.** Suffixed form **teks-lā-*. **a.** TILLER², TOIL², from Latin *tēla*, web, net, warp of a fabric, also weaver's beam (to which the warp threads are tied); **b.** SUBTLE, from Latin *subtīlis*, thin, fine, precise, subtle (< **sub-tēla*, "thread passing under the warp," the finest thread; *sub*, under; see **upo**). **3.** Suffixed form **teks-ōn-*, weaver, maker of wattle for house walls, builder (possibly contaminated with **teks-tōr*, builder). TECTONIC; ARCHITECT, from Greek *tektōn*, carpenter, builder. **4.** Suffixed form **teks-nā-*, craft (of weaving or fabricating). TECHNICAL, POLYTECHNIC, TECHNOLOGY, from Greek *tekhnē*, art, craft, skill. **5a.** DACHSHUND, from Old High German *dahs*, badger; **b.** DASSIE, from Middle Dutch *das*, badger. Both **a** and **b** from Germanic **thahsuz*, badger, possibly from this root ("the animal that builds," referring to its burrowing skill) but more likely borrowed from the same pre-Indo-European source as the Celtic totemic name **Tazgo-* (as in Gaulish *Tazgo-*, Gaelic *Tadhg*), originally "badger." [Pokorny *tek̂p-* 1058.]

tekʷ- To run, flee. Possibly suffixed o-grade form **tokʷ-so-*. TOXIC, from Greek *toxon*, bow, also (in the plural) bow and arrow (< "that which flies"), from Iranian **taxša-*, bow. [Pokorny *tekʷ-* 1059.]

tel- Ground, floor, boar. **1.** DEAL², from Middle Low German and Middle Dutch *dele*, plank, from Germanic **thil-jō*. **2.** Suffixed form **tel-n-*. TELLURIAN, TELLURIC, TELLURION, TELLURIUM, TELLURO-, from Latin *tellūs*, earth, the earth. **3.** Possibly reduplicated form **ti-tel-*. TITLE, from Latin *titulus*, placard, label, superscription. [Pokorny 2. *tel-* 1061.]

telǝ- To lift, support, weigh; with derivatives referring to measured weights and thence to money and payment. (Oldest form **telh₂-*.) **1.** Suffixed form **tela-mon-*. TELAMON, from Greek *telamōn*, supporter, bearer. **2.** Suffixed form **tel(a)-es-*. **a.** TOLL¹; PHILATELY, from Greek *telos*, tax, charge; **b.** TOLERATE, from Latin *tolerāre*, to bear, endure. **3.** Suffixed zero-grade form **tl̥a-i-*. TALION; RETALIATE, from Latin *tāliō*, reciprocal punishment in kind, possibly "something paid out," from **tali-* (influenced by *tālis*, such). **4.** Suffixed variant zero-grade form **tala-nt-*. TALENT, from Greek *talanton*, balance, weight, any of several specific weights of gold or silver, hence the sum of money represented by such a weight. **5.** Perhaps (but unlikely) intensive reduplicated form **tantal-*. TANTALIZE, TANTALUS, from Greek *Tantalos*, name of a legendary king, "the sufferer." **6.** Perhaps (but unlikely) zero-grade form **tl̥a-*. ATLANTIC, ATLAS, from Greek *Atlās* (stem *Atlant-*), name of the Titan supporting the world. **7.** Suffixed zero-grade form **tl̥a-to-*. ABLATION, ABLATIVE¹, ALLATIVE, COLLATE, DILATORY, ELATE, ELATIVE, ILLATION, ILLATIVE, LEGISLATOR, OBLATE¹, PRELATE, PROLATE, RELATE, SUBLATE, SUPERLATIVE, TRANSLATE, from Latin *lātus*, "carried, borne," used as the suppletive past participle of *ferre*, to bear (see **bher-¹**), with its compound*s*. **8.** Suffixed zero-grade form *tḷə-ā-. TOLA, from Sanskrit *tulā*, scales, balance, weight. **9.** Nasalized zero-grade form *tḷ-n-ə-. EXTOL, from Latin *tollere*, to lift. [Pokorny 1. *tel-* 1060.]

temə-¹ To cut. **1.** Nasalized form *t(e)m-n-ə-. **a.** TMESIS, TOME, -TOME, -TOMY; ACROTOMOPHILIA, ANATOMY, APOTEMNOPHILIA, ATOM, DIATOM, DICHOTOMY, ENTOMO-, EPITOME, from Greek *temnein*, to cut, with o-grade forms *tomos*, cutting, a cut, section, volume, and *tomē*, a cutting. **b.** CONTEMN, from Latin *temnere*, to despise (< *"cut down, cut apart, wound, abuse verbally"). **2.** Suffixed form *temə-lo-. TEMPLE¹, TEMPLE³; CONTEMPLATE, from Latin *templum*, temple, shrine, open place for observation (augury term < "place reserved or cut out"), small piece of timber, syncopated from earlier *temalom. **3.** Extended form *tem-d- becoming *tend- in o-grade suffixed (iterative) form *tond-eyo-. TONSORIAL, TONSURE, from Latin *tondēre*, to shear, shave. **4.** Suffixed o-grade form *tomə-o-. **a.** ESTIMATE, from Latin *aestimāre*, perhaps denominative verb from a pre-Latin compound *ais-tomos (see **ayes-**). **b.** CONTUMELY, from Latin *contumēlia*, from an unattested adjective *comtumēlis, degrading, disparaging, probably derived (on the model of the sematically similar *crūdēlis*, cruel; see **kreuə-**) from an earlier *kom-tom(ə)-os, "one who cuts (another's hair, beard, or garments with the intention of degrading him)" (*kom-, intensive prefix, source of Latin *com-; see **kom**). **3.** Perhaps from this root is Latin *autumnus*, autumn, if from earlier *au-tom-ino-s, pertaining to the harvest time, derived from a compound *au-tomos, harvest (< "the cutting off, the cutting away"; *au-, off, away; see **au-**): AUTUMN. [Pokorny 1. *tem-* 1062.]

temə-² Dark. Suffixed form *temə-s-. **1.** TEMERARIOUS, TEMERITY, from Latin *temere*, blindly, rashly, originally ablative of a noun *temus, stem *temer-, "blindness." **2.** GÖTTERDÄMMERUNG, from Old High German *demar*, twilight. **3.** Further suffixed form *temə-s-rā-. TENEBRAE, TENEBRIONID, from Latin *tenebrae* (plural), darkness. [Pokorny *tem(ə)-* 1063.]

temp- To stretch. Extension of **ten-** (assimilated from *tenp-). **1.** TEMPLE², from Latin *tempus*, temple of the head (? where the skin is stretched from behind the eye to the ear), possibly from this root. **2.** Perhaps zero-grade form *tṃp-. **a.** TAFFETA, from Persian *tāftan*, to weave (the warp threads are stretched on the loom), from Iranian *tāp-; **b.** TAPESTRY, TAPIS, from Greek *tapēs*, carpet, from Iranian *tap-, "carpet." [Pokorny *temp-* 1064.]

ten- To stretch.
I. Derivatives with the basic meaning. **1.** Suffixed form *ten-do-. **a.** TEND¹, TENDER², TENDU, TENSE¹, TENT¹; ATTEND, CONTEND, DETENT, DÉTENTE, DISTEND, EXTEND, INTEND, OSTENSIBLE, PRETEND, SUBTEND, from Latin *tendere*, to stretch, extend; **b.** PORTEND, from Latin *portendere*, "to stretch out before" (*por-, variant of *pro-, before; see **per¹**), a technical term in augury, "to indicate, presage, foretell." **2.** Suffixed form *ten-yo-. TENESMUS; ANATASE, BRONCHIECTASIS, CATATONIA, ENTASIS, EPITASIS, HYPOTENUSE, NEOTENY, PARATENIC HOST, PERITONEUM, PROTASIS, SYNTONIC, TELANGIECTASIA, from Greek *teinein*, to stretch, with o-grade form *ton-* and zero-grade noun *tasis (< *tṇ-ti-), a stretching, tension, intensity. **3.** Reduplicated zero-grade form *te-tṇ-o-. TETANUS, from Greek *tetanos*, stiff, rigid. **4.** Suffixed full-grade form *ten-tro-. **a.** TANTRA, from Sanskrit *tantram*, loom; **b.** SITAR, from Persian *tār*, string. **5.** Basic form (with stative suffix) *ten-ē-. TENABLE, TENACIOUS, TENACULUM, TENANT, TENEMENT, TENET, TENON, TENOR, TENURE, TENUTO; ABSTAIN, CONTAIN, CONTINUE, DETAIN, ENTERTAIN, LIEUTENANT, MAINTAIN, OBTAIN, *PERTAIN, PERTINACIOUS, REIN, RETAIN, RETINACULUM, RETINUE, SUSTAIN, from Latin *tenēre*,

to hold, keep, maintain (< "to cause to endure or continue, hold on to").
II. Derivatives meaning "stretched," hence "thin." **1.** Suffixed zero-grade form *tṇ-u-. THIN, from Old English *thynne*, thin, from Germanic *thunni-, from *thunw-. **2.** Suffixed full-grade form *ten-u-. TENUOUS; ATTENUATE, EXTENUATE, from Latin *tenuis*, thin, rare, fine. **3.** Suffixed full-grade form *ten-ero-. TENDER¹, TENDRIL; INTENERATE, from Latin *tener*, tender, delicate.
III. Derivatives meaning "something stretched or capable of being stretched, a string." **1.** Suffixed form *ten-ōn-. TENDON, TENO-, from Greek *tenōn*, tendon. **2.** Suffixed o-grade form *ton-o-. TONE; BARITONE, TONOPLAST, from Greek *tonos*, string, hence sound, pitch. **3.** Suffixed zero-grade form *tṇ-yā-. TAENIA; POLYTENE, from Greek *tainiā*, band, ribbon. [Pokorny 1. *ten-* 1065.] See also extended roots **temp-**, **tenk-¹**, and **tens-**.

teng- To soak. **1.** TAINT¹, TINCT, TINGE, TINT; INTINCTION, STAIN, from Latin *tingere*, to moisten, soak, dye. **2.** Zero-grade form *tṇg-. DUNK, from Old High German *thunkōn*, *dunkōn*, to soak, from Germanic *thunk-. [Pokorny 1. *teng-* 1067.]

tenk-¹ To stretch. Extension of **ten-**. Perhaps Germanic *thingam, assembly (? < "meeting-time for an assembly" < "stretch of time"). **1.** THING, from Old English *thing*, assembly, (legal) case, thing. **2.** ALTHING, HUSTINGS, from Old Norse *thing*, assembly. **3.** DINGUS, from Old High German *thing*, *ding*, thing. [Pokorny 1. *tenk-* 1067.]

tenk-² To become firm, curdle, thicken. **1.** Suffixed form *tenk-to-, thickened. TIGHT, from Middle English *thight*, dense, from a Scandinavian source akin to Old Norse *thēttr*, dense, watertight, from Germanic *thinhta-. **2.** Possibly suffixed o-grade form *tonk-lo-. TANGLE², from a source akin to Old Norse *thöngull*, seaweed (? < "thick mass"), from Germanic *thangul-. [Pokorny 2. *tenk-* 1068.]

tens- To stretch, draw. Extension of **ten-**. Suffixed zero-grade form *tṇs-ero-. TUSSAH, from Sanskrit *tasaram*, shuttle. [Pokorny *tens-* 1068.]

tep- To be hot. **1.** Suffixed (stative) form *tep-ē-. TEPID, from Latin *tepēre*, to be warm. **2.** Probably suffixed form *tep-n-. BELTANE, from Old Irish *tene*, fire (*Bel*, Celtic deity; see **bhel-¹**). **3.** Suffixed form *tep-es-. TAPAS, from Sanskrit *tapas*, heat, austerity. [Pokorny *tep-* 1069.]

ter- Base of derivatives meaning peg, post, boundary marker, goal. **1.** Suffixed form *ter-men-, boundary marker. TERM, TERMINATE, TERMINUS; DETERMINE, EXTERMINATE, from Latin *terminus*, boundary, limit. **2.** Suffixed zero-grade form *tṛ-m-. THRUM², from Old English -thrum, broken-off end (attested only in *tunge-thrum*, the ligament of the tongue), from Germanic *thrum-. [Pokorny 4. *ter-* 1074.]

-ter- Also **-tor-**. Suffix forming agent nouns from verbs. **1.** -ATOR, -ATORY, from Latin -*ātor*, agent noun suffix to verbs with stem vowel *-ā-. **2.** Feminine *-tr-ī (< *-tr-ia). -TRIX, from Latin -*trix*, feminine agent noun suffix, from *-trī-k-. [Not in Pokorny.]

terə-¹ To rub, turn; with some derivatives referring to twisting, boring, drilling, and piercing; and others referring to the rubbing of cereal grain to remove the husks, and thence to the process of threshing either by the trampling of oxen or by flailing with flails. (Oldest form *terh₁-, with variant [metathesized] form *treh₁-, contracted to *trē-.)
I. Full-grade form *ter(ə)-. **1a.** TRITE, TRITURATE; ATTRITION, CONTRITE, DETRIMENT, from Latin *terere* (past participle *trītus*), to rub away, thresh, tread, wear out; **b.** TEREDO, from Greek *terēdōn*, a kind of biting worm. **2.** Suffixed form *ter-et-. TERETE, from Latin *teres* (stem *teret-*), rounded, smooth. **3.** Suffixed form *ter-sko-. **a.** THRASH, THRESH, from Old English

therscan, to thresh; **b.** THRESHOLD, from Old English *therscold*, *threscold*, sill of a door (over which one treads; second element obscure). Both **a** and **b** from Germanic **therskan*, **threskan*, to thresh, tread.
   II. O-grade form **tor(ə)-*. **1.** TOREUTICS, from Greek *toreus*, a boring tool. **2.** Suffixed form **tor(ə)-mo-*, hole. DERMA², from Old High German *darm*, gut, from Germanic **tharma-*. **3.** Suffixed form **tor(ə)-no-*. TURN; ATTORN, ATTORNEY, CONTOUR, DETOUR, RETURN, from Greek *tornos*, tool for drawing a circle, circle, lathe.
   III. Zero-grade form **tr̥-*. DRILL¹, from Middle Dutch *drillen*, to drill, from Germanic **thr-*.
   IV. Variant form **trē-* (< **treə-*). **1.** THROW, from Old English *thrāwan*, to turn, twist, from Germanic **thrēw-*. **2.** Suffixed form **trē-tu-*. THREAD, from Old English *thrǣd*, thread, from Germanic **thrēdu-*, twisted yarn. **3.** Suffixed form **trē-mn̥* (< **treə-* or **tr̥ə-*). DIATREME, MONOTREME, TREMATODE, from Greek *trēma*, perforation. **4.** Suffixed form **trē-ti-* (< **treə-* or **tr̥ə-*). ATRESIA, from Greek *trēsis*, perforation.
   V. Form **trī-* (< **triə-*, metathesized from **trəi-*, zero-grade of extended form **treəi-*). **1.** Probably suffixed form **trī-ōn-*. SEPTENTRION, from Latin *triō*, plow ox. **2.** Suffixed form **trī-dhlo-*. TRIBULATION, from Latin *trībulum*, a threshing sledge.
   VI. Various extended forms **1.** Forms **trō-*, **trau-*. TRAUMA, from Greek *trauma*, hurt, wound. **2.** Form **trīb-*. DIATRIBE, TRIBOELECTRICITY, TRIBOLOGY, TRIBOLUMINESCENCE, TRYPSIN, from Greek *trībein*, to rub, thresh, pound, wear out. **3.** Form **trōg-*, **trag-*. **a.** TROGON, TROUT, from Greek *trōgein*, to gnaw; **b.** DREDGE², from Greek *tragēma*, sweetmeat. **4.** Form **trup-*. TREPAN¹; TRYPANOSOME, from Greek *trupē*, hole. **5.** Possible form **trūg-*. TRUANT, from Old French *truant*, beggar. [Pokorny 3. *ter-* 1071.]
terə-² To cross over, pass through, overcome. (Oldest form **terh₂-*, with variant [metathesized] form **treh₂-*, colored to **trah₂-*, contracted to **trā-*.)
   I. Zero-grade form **tr̥(ə)-*. **1.** THRILL; NOSTRIL, from Old English *thyr(e)l*, *thȳrel*, a hole (< "a boring through"), from Germanic suffixed form **thur-ila-*. **2.** Suffixed form **tr̥ə-kʷe*. THOROUGH, THROUGH, from Old English *thurh*, *thuruh*, through, from Germanic **thurh*. **3.** Combining zero-grade form **-tr̥(ə)* in Greek *nektar* (see **nek-¹**). **4.** Zero-grade form **tr̥ə-* and full-grade form **ter(ə)-*. AVATAR, from Sanskrit *tirati*, *tarati*, he crosses over.
   II. Variant form **trā-*. **1.** TRANS-, TRANSIENT, TRANSOM, from Latin *trāns*, across, over, beyond, through (perhaps originally the present participle of a verb **trāre*, to cross over). **2.** Suffixed form **trā-yo-*. SERAGLIO, SERAI; CARAVANSARY, LAMASERY, from Persian *sarāy*, inn, palace, from Iranian **thrāya-*, to protect.
   III. Possible extended form **tru-*. **1.** Suffixed form **tru-k-*. TRUCULENT, from Latin *trux* (stem *truc-*), savage, fierce, grim (< "overcoming," "powerful," "penetrating"). **2.** Suffixed nasalized zero-grade form **tru-n-k-o-*. TRANCHE, TRENCH, TRUNCATE, TRUNK, from Latin *truncus*, deprived of branches or limbs, mutilated, hence trunk (? < "overcome, maimed"). [Pokorny 5. *ter-* 1075.]

Language and Culture Note The lowly Latin preposition *trāns* "across, beyond" (familiar to us in words like *transfigure* and *transmigrate*) conceals a much more colorful past. It is a fossilized participle from the verbal root **terə-²** meaning "cross over, overcome." In several traditions, this root is used especially of "crossing over" or overcoming death (**nek-¹**). Thus the mythical substance that the Olympian gods drank that bestowed immortality was called *nektar* in Greek, a compound of these two roots meaning literally "overcoming death." In Hittite, the verb *tarḫ-*, "to overcome," is used in combination with the related name

of the storm god, *Tarḫunnaš*, in the Anatolian retelling of the Indo-European dragon-slaying myth (see note at **gʷhen-**) with the initial temporary victory of the monster: "the Serpent (Illuyankas) overcame the Overcomer (Tarhunnas)." The myth is told at the New Year's festival (*purulli*), which has to do with renewal and rebirth; the serpent (in this and other versions of the Indo-European dragon-slaying myth) metaphorically represents death, dissolution, and the forces of chaos.

terkʷ- To twist. **1.** Possible variant (metathesized) form **twerk-*. **a.** QUEER, from Middle Low German *dwer*, oblique; **b.** THWART, from Old Norse *thverr*, transverse. Both **a** and **b** from Germanic **thwerh-*, twisted, oblique. **2.** Suffixed (causative) o-grade form **torkʷ-eyo-*. TORCH, TORMENT, TORQUE¹, TORQUE², TORSADE, TORSION, TORT, TORTUOUS, TORTURE, TRUSS; CONTORT, DISTORT, EXTORT, NASTURTIUM, RETORT¹, TORTICOLLIS, from Latin *torquēre*, to twist. [Pokorny *terk-* 1077.]
-tero- Adjectival suffix of comparative, marking contrast, as in **eks-tero-*, outer (see **eghs**). [Not in Pokorny.] Compare **-yos-**.
terp- To take pleasure. **1.** TERPSICHORE, from Greek *terpein*, to delight, cheer. **2.** EUTERPE, from Greek *Euterpē*, "the well-pleasing one" (*eu-*, well; see **(e)su-**). [Pokorny *terp-* 1077.]
ters- To dry. **1.** Suffixed zero-grade form **tr̥s-*. **a.** THIRST, from Old English *thurst*, dryness, thirst, from Germanic suffixed form **thurs-tu-*; **b.** CUSK, TORSK, TUSK², from Old Norse *thorskr*, cod (< "dried fish"). Both **a** and **b** from Germanic **thurs-*. **2.** Suffixed basic form **ters-ā-*. TERRACE, TERRAIN, Terran, TERRENE, TERRESTRIAL, TERRIER, TERRITORY, TUREEN; FUMITORY, INTER, MEDITERRANEAN, PARTERRE, SUBTERRANEAN, TARTUFO, TERRAQUEOUS, TERREPLEIN, TERREVERTE, TERRICOLOUS, TERRIGENOUS, TERROIR, TURMERIC, VERDITER, from Latin *terra*, "dry land," earth. **3.** Suffixed o-grade form **tors-eyo-*. TOAST¹, TORRENT, TORRID, TOSTONES, from Latin *torrēre*, to dry, parch, burn. **4.** Suffixed zero-grade form **tr̥s-o-*. TARSUS, from Greek *tarsos*, frame of wickerwork (originally for drying cheese), hence a flat surface, sole of the foot, ankle. [Pokorny *ters-* 1078.]

Language and Culture Note Etymologically, *terrain* is simply "dry land." Already in Indo-European times, the root for "dry," **ters-**, was used as a standard epithet for land or ground. A suffixed noun form of this root, **ters-ā-*, became *terra* in Latin, "land," the source of English *terrain*, *territory*, and other such words. In this way, a word that started out as the word for "dry" in the phrase "dry land" became the word for "land" itself—an example of what linguists call a "transferred epithet." • A similar example from a much less familiar language is provided by the Tocharian words for "land," *yapoy* in Tocharian B and *ype* in Tocharian A. These are descended from the Indo-European word **yewos*, "grain," as used in the phrase "grain-giving earth."

teuə-¹ To pay attention to, turn. **1.** O-grade form **tou(ə)-*. THEW, from Old English *thēaw*, usage, custom (< "observance"), later good characteristic, strength. **2.** Suffixed zero-grade form **tuə-ē-*. TUITION, TUTELAGE, TUTELARY, TUTOR; INTUITION, from Latin *tuērī*, to look at, watch, protect. [Pokorny 2. *teu-* 1079.]
teuə-² Also **teu-**. To swell. (Oldest form **teuh₂-*.) **1.** Extended form **teuk-*. THIGH, from Old English *thēoh*, thigh, from Germanic **theuham*, "the swollen or fat part of the leg," thigh. **2.** Extended form **tūs-*. THOUSAND, from Old English *thūsend*, thousand, from Germanic compound **thūs-hundi-*, "swollen hundred," thousand (**hundi-*, hundred; see **dekm̥**). **3.** Prob-

ably suffixed zero-grade form *tu-l-. **a.** THOLE, from Old English thol(l), oar pin, oarlock (< "a swelling"), from Germanic *thul-; **b.** TYLECTOMY, TYLOSIS[1], from Greek tulos, callus, lump. **4.** Extended zero-grade form *tūm-. **a.** THIMBLE, THUMB, from Old English thūma, thumb (< "the thick finger"), from Germanic *thūmōn-; **b.** suffixed (stative) form *tum-ē-. TUMESCENT, TUMID, TUMOR; DETUMESCENCE, INTUMESCE, TUMEFACIENT, TUMEFY, from Latin tumēre, to swell, be swollen, be proud; **c.** suffixed form *tum-olo-. TUMULUS, from Latin tumulus, raised heap of earth, mound. **5.** Extended zero-grade form *tūbh-. TRUFFLE, TUBER; PROTUBERATE, TARTUFO, from Latin tūber, lump, swelling. **6.** Suffixed zero-grade form *tū-ro- (< *tuə-ro-). **a.** BUTTER, TYROSINE, from Greek tūros, cheese (< "a swelling," "coagulating"); **b.** OBTURATE, from Latin -tūrāre, to stop up, possibly from *tūros, swollen, coagulated, stopped up. **7.** Suffixed variant form *twō-ro-. **a.** SORITES, SORUS, from Greek sōros, heap, pile; **b.** QUARK[2], from Old Church Slavonic tvarogŭ, curds, cottage cheese. **8.** Suffixed variant form *twō-mn̥. SOMA[1], SOMATO-, -SOME[3]; PROSOMA, from Greek sōma, body (< "a swelling," "stocky form"). **9.** Suffixed zero-grade form *twə-wo-. CREOSOTE, SOTERIOLOGY, from Greek saos, sōs, safe, healthy (< "swollen," "strong"), with adverbial verb sōzein, to save. **10.** Perhaps nasalized extended form *tu-m-b(h)- (or extended zero-grade form *tum-). TOMB, from Greek tumbos, barrow, tomb. [Pokorny tēu- 1080.]

teutā- Tribe. **1a.** DUTCH, from Middle Dutch duutsch, German, of the Germans or Teutons; **b.** PLATTDEUTSCH, from Old High German diutisc, of the people. Both **a** and **b** from Germanic *theudiskaz, of the people; **c.** Germanic personal name *thiudō-rīk-, "people's king" (*rīk-, king; see **reg-[1]**). (i) THEODORIC, from Gothic *Thiudareiks (> Late Latin Theodōricus); (ii) DIETRICH, from Old High German Diutarīch. **a–c** all from Germanic *theudō, people. **2.** Suffixed form *teut-onōs, "they of the tribe." TEUTON, from Latin Teutōnī, the Teutons, borrowed via Celtic from Germanic tribal name *theudanōz. **3.** Possibly Latin tōtus, all, whole (? < "of the whole tribe"): TOTAL, TUTTI; FACTOTUM, TEETOTUM. [In Pokorny tēu- 1080.]

-ti- Suffix forming abstract nouns to verbal roots. Appears ultimately in the following English suffixes: **a.** -ATION, -IZATION, from Latin -tiō (stem -tiōn-), verbal abstract suffix, from *-ti- plus extension by the nasal suffix *-ōn-; **b.** -IASIS, from Greek -iāsis (< *-iad-ti-), abstract noun suffix to verbs formed with the stem formant *-iad-; **c.** -OSIS, from Greek -ōsis (< *-ō-ti-), abstract noun suffix to verbs with stem vowel -ō-. [Not in Pokorny.]

tit- Also tik-, kit-. To tickle. Expressive root. **1.** KITTLE, from Middle English kytyllen, to tickle, probably from a source akin to Old Norse kitla, to tickle. **2.** TITILLATE, from Latin titillāre, to tickle, titillate. [In Pokorny geid- 356.]

tkē- To gain control of, gain power over. (Oldest form *tk̑eh₁-.) **1.** Zero-grade form *tkə-. **a.** KSHATRIYA, from Sanskrit kṣatram, rule, power; **b.** SATRAP, from Old Persian khshathra-, kingdom, province, in compound khshathra-pāvā, protector of the province (-pāvā, protector; see **pā-**). Both **a** and **b** from Indo-Iranian suffixed form *kṣa-tram (built to verb *kṣayati in **2** below). **2.** Zero-grade suffixed (present) form *tkə-eyo-. **a.** XERXES (personal name), from Old Persian khshayārshan-, "ruling over men" (arshan-, man, hero; see **ers-[2]**), from *khshaya-, to rule over; **b.** CHECK, SHAH; BASHAW, CHECKMATE, EXCHEQUER, PADISHAH, PASHA, from Old Persian khshāyathiya-, king (> Modern Persian shāh, king). Both **a** and **b** from Indo-Iranian *kṣayati, he has power over, rules. [Pokorny k̑þē(i)- 626.]

tkei- To settle, dwell, be home. (Oldest form *tk̑ei-.) **1.** Suffixed o-grade form *(t)koi-mo-. **a.** HOME,

from Old English hām, home; **b.** NIFLHEIM, from Old Norse heimr, home; **c.** HAIMISH, from Old High German heim, home, also in personal name HENRY, from Old High German Heimerich, "ruler of the house" (rich, ruler; see **reg-[1]**); **d.** HAME, from Middle Dutch hame, hame (< "covering"); **e.** HAMLET, from Old French ham, village, home; **f.** HAUNT, from Old French hanter, to frequent, haunt, from Germanic *haimatjan, to go or bring home; **g.** HANGAR, from Old French hangard, shelter, possibly from Germanic *haimgardaz (*gardaz, enclosure; see **gher-[1]**). **a–g** all from Germanic *haimaz, home; **h.** dialectal Germanic *haima-, home, in Latin Boihaemum (see **bheiə-**). **2.** Zero-grade form *tki-. **a.** AMPHICTYONY, PROTOCTIST, from Greek ktizein, to found, settle, from metathesized *kti-; **b.** probably Italic *si-. SITUATE, SITUS, from Latin situs, location, from suffixed form *si-tu-. [Pokorny 1. k̑ei- 539, k̑þei- 626.]

-tlo- See -tro-.

to- Demonstrative pronoun. For the nominative singular see **so-. 1a.** THE[2]; NATHELESS, from Old English thē, thȳ (instrumental case), by the; **b.** DECOY, from Middle Dutch de, the; **c.** LEST, from Old English the, a conjunction. **a–c** from Germanic *thē, from Indo-European instrumental form *tē. **2.** THOUGH, from Middle English though, though, from a Scandinavian source akin to Old Norse thō, though, from Germanic *thauh, "for all that." **3.** THESE, THIS, THOSE, from Old English thes, this, this, from Germanic *thasi-. **4.** THAN, THEN, from Old English thanne, thænne, thenne, than, then, from Germanic *thana-. **5.** THENCE, from Old English thanon, thence, from Germanic *thanana-. **6.** THERE, from Old English thær, thēr, there, from Germanic *thēr. **7.** THITHER, from Old English thæder, thider, thither, from Germanic *thathro. **8a.** THEY, from Old Norse their, they; **b.** BOTH, from Old Norse bādhir, both, from Germanic *bai thaiz, "both the" (*bai, both; see **ambhō**). Both **a** and **b** from Germanic nominative plural *thai. **9.** THEIR, from Old Norse their(r)a, theirs, from Germanic genitive plural *thaira. **10a.** THEM, from Old Norse theim and Old English thām, thæm, them; **b.** NONCE, from Middle English for then anes, for the nonce, for the occasion, from then, dative singular article, from Old English thām, thæm, dative singular article, originally dative plural used as singular. Both **a** and **b** from Germanic dative plural *thaimiz. **11.** Extended neuter form *tod-. THAT, from Old English thæt, that, from Germanic *that. **12.** THUS, from Old English thus, thus, from Germanic *thus-. **13.** Adverbial (originally accusative) form *tam. TANDEM, TANTAMOUNT, from Latin tandem, at last, so much, and tantus, so much. **14.** Suffixed reduced form *t-āli-. TALES, from Latin tālis, such. **15.** TAUTO-, from Greek to, the. **16.** Probably related to this pronoun, although the details are obscure, is the Old Irish preverb to-, do-, to, towards (compare Albanian te, to, and Messapic ta- in tabaras, priest < "he who distributes the sacralized offering to others"; see **sak-**). **a.** TAOISEACH (see **wedh-**). **b.** TORY (see **ret-**). [Pokorny 1. to- 1086.]

-to- Also -eto-, -oto-. Suffix forming adjectives marking the accomplishment of the notion of the base. Where the base is verbal, they are participial (finished); where the base is nominal, they mark possession (beard-ed). It is also found in superlative suffixes and ordinal numeral suffixes (as in Latin sex-tus, sixth, and English six-th; see **-is-to-** for a discussion of the semantics). It appears ultimately in the following English suffixes: **a.** -ED[2], from Old English -ed, -ad, -od, from Germanic *-da- (preceded by stem vowel of verb); **b.** -ED[3], from Old English -ed, -od, from Germanic *-da-; **c.** -TH[3], from Old English -the, ordinal numeral suffix, from Germanic *-tha-; **d.** -ATE[1], -EE[1], from Latin -ātus, past participial suffix to verbs in -āre (< *-ā-to-); **e.** -ETIC, from Greek -etos, verbal adjective suffix. [Not in Pokorny.] See also compound suffix **-is-to-** and compare **-no-**.

tolkʷ- To speak. Metathesized form *tlokʷ-. LOCU-TION, LOQUACIOUS; ALLOCUTION, CIRCUMLOCUTION, COLLOQUIUM, COLLOQUY, ELOCUTION, GRANDILO-QUENCE, INTERLOCUTION, MAGNILOQUENT, OBLOQUY, PROLOCUTOR, SOLILOQUY, VENTRILOQUISM, from Latin *loquī*, to speak. [Pokorny *tolkʷ-* 1088.]

tong- To think, feel. **1.** THANK, from Old English *thanc*, thought, good will, and *thancian*, to thank, from Germanic *thankaz*, thought, gratitude, and *thankōn*, to think of, thank. **2.** THINK; BETHINK, from Old English *(bi)thencan*, to think, from Germanic *(bi-)thankjan*. **3.** THOUGHT, from Old English *(ge)thōht*, thought, from Germanic *(ga)thanht-* (*ga-*, collective prefix; see **kom**). **4.** METHINKS, from Old English *thyncan*, to seem, from Germanic *thunkjan*. [Pokorny 1. *tong-* 1088.]

-tor- See **-ter-**.

tragh- To draw, drag, move. Rhyming variant **dhragh-**. TRACE[1], TRACE[2], TRACEUR, TRACT[1], TRAC-TABLE, TRACTION, TRAIL, TRAIN, TRAIT, TREAT; AB-STRACT, ATTRACT, CONTRACT, DETRACT, DISTRACT, EXTRACT, PORTRAY, PROTRACT, RETRACT, SUBTRACT, from Latin *trahere* (past participle *tractus*), to pull, draw. [Pokorny *trāgh-* 1089.]

treb- Dwelling. **1.** Zero-grade form *tr̥b-. **a.** THORP, from Old English *thorp*, village, hamlet; **b.** DORP, from Middle Dutch *dorp*, village. Both **a** and **b** from Germanic *thurpam*. **2.** TRABEATED, TRABECULA, TRAVE; ARCHITRAVE, from Latin *trabs*, beam, timber. [Pokorny *trĕb-* 1090.]

trei- Three.
   I. Nominative plural form *treyes. **1a.** THREE, THRICE; THIRTEEN, THIRTY, from Old English *thrīe*, *thrēo*, *thri*, three, with its derivatives *thrīga*, *thrīwa*, thrice, *thrītig*, thirty, and *thrēotīne*, thirteen (*-tīne*, ten; see **dekm̥**); **b.** TRILLIUM, from Old Swedish *thrīr*, three. Both **a** and **b** from Germanic *thrijiz*. **2.** TREY; TRAMMEL, TRECENTO, TREPHINE, TRIUMVIR, TROCAR, from Latin *trēs*, three. **3.** TRISKAIDEKAPHOBIA, from Greek *treis*, *tris*, three.
   II. Zero-grade form *tri-. **1.** Suffixed form *tri-tyo-. **a.** *(i)* THIRD, from Old English *thrid(d)a*, *thirdda*, third; *(ii)* RIDING[2], from Old Norse *thridhi*, third. Both *(i)* and *(ii)* from Germanic *thridja-*, third; **b.** TERCEL, TERCET, TERTIAN, TERTIARY, TIERCE; SESTERCE, from Latin *tertius*, third. **2.** Combining form *tri-. **a.** TRI-, TRIBE, TRIO, TRIPLE, from Latin *tri-*, three; **b.** TRI-; TRICLINIUM, TRICROTIC, TRIDACTYL, TRI- GLYPH, TRITONE, from Greek *tri-*, three; **c.** TRIMURTI, from Sanskrit *tri-*, three. **3.** TRIAD, from Greek *trias*, the number three. **4.** TRICHOTOMY, from Greek *trikha*, in three parts. **5.** TRIERARCH, from Greek compound *triērēs*, galley with three banks of oars, trireme (*-ērēs*, oar; see **erə-**[1]). **6.** Suffixed form *tri-to-. TRITIUM, from Greek *tritos*, third. **7.** Compound form *tri-pl-, "threefold" (*-pl- < combining form *-plo-, -fold; see **pel-**[3]). TRIPLOBLASTIC, from Greek *triploos*, triple. **8.** Compound form *tri-plek-, "threefold" (*-plek-, -fold; see **plek-**). TRIPLEX, from Latin *triplex*, triple. **9.** Compound form *tri-st-i-, "third person standing by" (*-st-, standing; see **stā-**). TESTAMENT, TESTIMONY, TESTICLE, TESTIS; ATTEST, CONTEST, DETEST, OBTEST, PROTEST, TESTIFY, from Latin *testis*, a witness. **10.** SI-TAR, TEAPOY, from Persian *si*, three.
   III. Extended zero-grade form *tris, "thrice." **1.** TERN[2]; TERPOLYMER, from Latin *ter*, thrice. **2.** TRI-SOCTAHEDRON, HERMES TRISMEGISTUS, from Greek *tris*, thrice. **3.** Suffixed form *tris-no-. TRINE, TRINITY, from Latin *trīnī*, three each.
   IV. Suffixed o-grade form *troy-o-. TROIKA, from Russian *troje*, group of three. [Pokorny *trei-* 1090.]

trem- To tremble. Possibly related to **trep-**[1] and **tres-** through a hypothetical base *ter-. TREMENDOUS,

TREMOR, TREMULOUS, from Latin *tremere*, to shake, tremble. [Pokorny *trem-* 1092.]

trep-[1] To tremble. Possibly related to **trem-** and **tres-** through a hypothetical base *ter-. TREPID; INTREPID, from Latin *trepidus*, agitated, alarmed. [Pokorny 1. *trep-* 1094.]

trep-[2] To turn. **1.** -TROPOUS; APOTROPAIC, ATROPOS, HELIOTROPE, TREPONEMA, ZOETROPE, from Greek *trepein*, to turn, with o-grade derivative *-tropos*, turning. **2.** O-grade form *trop-. **a.** Suffixed form *trop-o-. TROPE, TROUBADOUR, TROVER; CONTRIVE, RETRIEVE, from Greek *tropos*, a turn, way, manner; **b.** suffixed form *trop-ā-. TROPHY, TROPIC, TROPO-; ENTROPY, from Greek *tropē*, a turning, change. [Pokorny 2. *trep-* 1094.]

tres- To tremble. Possibly related to **trem-** and **trep-**[1] through a hypothetical base *ter-. Metathesized form *ters- in o-grade suffixed (causative) form *tors-eyo-. TERRIBLE, TERROR; DETER, TERRIFIC, from Latin *terrēre*, to frighten (< "cause to tremble"), with *-e-* from *terror*, terror (from suffixed e-grade form *ters-os-). [Pokorny *tres-* 1095.]

treud- To squeeze. **1.** Suffixed o-grade form *troud-o-. THREAT, from Old English *thrēat*, oppression, use of force, from Germanic *thrautam*. **2.** Variant form *trūd-. THRUST, from Old Norse *thrȳsta*, to squeeze, compress, from Germanic *thrūstjan*. **3.** ABSTRUSE, EXTRUDE, INTRUDE, OBTRUDE, PROTRUDE, from Latin *trūdere*, to thrust, push. [Pokorny *tr-eu-d-* 1095.]

-tro- Variant forms **-tlo-, -dhro-, -dhlo-**. Suffix form-ing nouns of instrument, as in *rō-tro-, rudder (see **erə-**[1]), *pō-tlo-, drinking vessel (see **pō(i)-**), *krei-dhro-, sieve (see **krei-**), and *sod-dhlo-, saddle (see **sed-**[1]). Appears ultimately in the English suffixes -ABILITY, -ABLE, -IBLE, -IBILITY, from Latin *-bilis*, ad-jective suffix, and compound suffix *-ābilis* (from verbs with stem vowel *-ā-*), from i-stem form *-dhli-. [Not in Pokorny.]

trozdo- Thrush. **1.** THROSTLE, from Old English *throstle*, thrush, from Germanic *thrust-. **2.** THRUSH[1], from Old English *thrysce*, from Germanic *thruskjōn-. **3.** Zero-grade form *tr̥zdo-. STURDY, from Latin *tur-dus*, thrush. **4.** Perhaps altered in Greek *strouthos*, sparrow, ostrich: STRUTHIOUS; OSTRICH. [Pokorny *trozdos* 1096.]

tu- Second person singular pronoun; you, thou. **1.** Lengthened form *tū (accusative *te, *tege). THEE, THOU[1], from Old English *thū (accusative *thec, *thē), thou, from Germanic *thū (accusative *theke). **2.** Suf-fixed extended form *t(w)ei-no-. THINE, THY, from Old English *thīn, thine, from Germanic *thīna-. [Pokorny *tū* 1097.]

-tu- Suffix forming abstract nouns. Appears ultimately in the following English suffixes: **a.** -NESS, from Old English *-ness*, abstract noun suffix, from Germanic *-in-assu- (*-in-, noun stem + *-assu-, abstract noun suffix, probably from Indo-European *-tu- added to verb stems in final dental); **b.** -TUDE, from Latin *-tūdō (stem *-tūdin-*), abstract noun suffix, from *-tu- ex-tended by a suffix *-din-. [Not in Pokorny.]

twei- To agitate, shake, toss. **1.** Extended form *tweid-. **a.** WHITTLE, from Old English *thwītan, to strike, whittle down; **b.** DOIT, from Middle Dutch *duit, a small coin (? < "piece cut or tossed off"). Both **a** and **b** from Germanic *thwīt-. **2.** Extended form *tweis-. SEISM, SEISMO-, SISTRUM, from Greek *seiein*, to shake. [Pokorny 2. *tu̯ei-* 1099.]

twengh- To press in on. **1.** THONG, from Old English *thwong, thwang, thong, band (< "constraint"), from Germanic *thwang-. **2.** TWINGE, from Old English *twengan*, to pinch, from Germanic suffixed vari-ant form *twangjan. [Pokorny *tuengh-* (misprint for *tu̯engh-*) 1099.]

twerk- To cut. (Oldest form *twerk̑-.) Zero-grade form *twr̥k-. SARCASM, SARCO-, SARCOID, SARCOMA,

SARCOUS; ANASARCA, ECTOSARC, SARCOPHAGUS, SAR-
COPTIC MANGE, SYSSARCOSIS, from Greek *sarx*, flesh
(< "piece of meat"). [Pokorny *tuerk̑-* 1102.]

ud- Also **ūd-**. Up, out. **1a.** OUT; UTMOST, from Old
English *ūt*, out; **b.** CAROUSE; AUSLANDER, from Old
High German *ūz*, out; **c.** OUTLAW, from Old Norse *ūt*,
out; **d.** UITLANDER, from Middle Dutch *ute*, *uut*, out;
e. UTTER[1], from Middle Low German *ūt*, out; **f.** UT-
TER[2], from Old English *ūtera*, outer, from Germanic
suffixed (comparative) form *ūt-era-*; **g.** BUT; ABOUT,
from Old English *būtan*, *būte*, outside (adverb), from
Germanic compound *bi-ūtana*, "at the outside" (*bi-*,
by, at; see **ambhi**). **a–g** all from Germanic *ūt-*, out. **2.**
Extended form *uds*. **a.** ERSATZ, from Old High German *irsezzan*, to replace, from *ir-*, out; **b.** ORT, from
Middle Dutch *oor*, out; **c.** Germanic compound *uz-
dailjam* (see **dail-**); **d.** URSPRACHE, from Old High
German *ur-*, out of, original. **a–d** all from Germanic
uz, *uz-*, out. **3.** Suffixed (comparative) form *ud-
tero-*. HYSTERESIS, HYSTERON PROTERON, from Greek
husteros, later, second, after. **4.** HUBRIS, from Greek
compound *hubris*, violence, outrage, insolence (*bri-*,
perhaps "heavy," "violent"; see **gʷerə-²**), from *hu-*. **5.**
VIGORISH, from Russian *vy-*, out. [Pokorny *ŭd-* 1103.]

udero- Abdomen, womb, stomach; with distantly
similar forms (perhaps taboo deformations) in various languages. **1.** UTERUS, from Latin *uterus*, womb
(reshaped from *udero-*). **2.** Perhaps taboo deformation *wen-tri-*. VENTER; VENTRILOQUISM, from Latin
venter, belly. **3.** Perhaps taboo deformation *wṇd-ti-*.
VESICA, from Latin *vēsīca*, bladder. **4.** Variant form
ud-tero-. HYSTERIC, HYSTERO-, from Greek *husterā*,
womb. [Pokorny *udero-* 1104.]

uks-en- Bull, ox. **1.** OX, from Old English *oxa*, ox.
2. AUROCHS, from Old High German *ohso*, ox. Both
1 and **2** from Germanic *uhsōn-*. [In Pokorny *ŭegʷ-*
1118.]

uper Over. **1.** Extended form *uperi*. **a.** OVER, OVER-,
from Old English *ofer*, over; **b.** ÜBER-, from Old High
German *ubar*, *uber* (preposition) and *ubari* (adverb),
over; **c.** ORLOP, from Middle Low German *over*, over.
a–c all from Germanic *uberi*. **2.** Variant form *(s)
uper*. **a.** SOUBRETTE, SOVEREIGN, SUPER-, SUPERABLE,
SUPERIOR, SUPREME, SUPREMO, SUR-; SIRLOIN, from
Latin *super*, *super-*, above, over; **b.** suffixed form *(s)
uper-no-*. SUPERNAL, from Latin *supernus*, above, upper, top; **c.** suffixed form *super-bhw-o-*, "being above"
(*bhw-o-*, being; see **bheuə-**). SUPERB, from Latin
superbus, superior, excellent, arrogant; **d.** suffixed
(superlative) reduced form *sup-mo-*. SUM[1], SUMMIT,
from Latin *summus*, highest, topmost; **e.** suffixed
form *super-o-*. SO- PRANINO, SOPRANO, SUPRA-; SOM-
ERSAULT, from Latin *suprā* (feminine ablative singular), above, beyond. **3.** Basic form *uper*. HYPER-, from
Greek *huper*, over. [Pokorny *upér* 1105.]

upo Under, up from under, over. **1a.** UP, from Old English *up*, *uppe*, up; **b.** UP-, from Old English *ŭp-*, *upp-*,
up; **c.** UPROAR, from Middle Low German *up*, up; **d.**
AUFKLÄRUNG, from Old High German *ūf*, up. **a–d** all
from Germanic *upp-*, up. **2.** OPEN, from Old English
open, open, from Germanic *upana-*, "put or set up,"
open. **3.** ABOVE, from Old English *būfan*, above, over,
from Germanic compound *bi-ufana*, "on, above"
(*bi-*, by, at; see **ambhi**). **4.** Possibly suffixed form
up-t-. OFT, OFTEN, from Old English *oft*, often, from
Germanic *ufta*, frequently. **5.** Extended form *upes-*.
a. EAVES, from Old English *efes*, eaves; **b.** EAVESDROP,
from Old English *yfesdrype*, water from the eaves,
from Germanic *obisdrup-*, dripping water from the
eaves (*drup-*, to drip; see **dhreu-**). Both **a** and **b**
from Germanic *ubaswō*, *ubizwō*, vestibule, porch,
eaves (< "that which is above or in front"). **6.** Variant
form *(s)up-*. **a.** SOUTANE, SUB-, from Latin *sub*, under; **b.** SUPINE; RESUPINATE, from Latin *supīnus*, lying
on the back (< "thrown backward or under"); **c.** suf-

fixed form *sup-ter*. SUBTERFUGE, from Latin *subter*,
secretly; **d.** Latin compound *supplex* (< *sub-plak-*; see
plāk-¹). **7.** Basic form *upo*. HYPO-, from Greek *hupo*,
under. **8.** Suffixed variant form *ups-o-*. HYPSO-, from
Greek *hupsos*, height, top. **9.** Basic form *upo*. Celtic
wo-, under, in compound *wo-rēd-* (see **reidh-**). **10.**
Probably compound *upo- st-o-*. VALET, VARLET, VAS-
SAL, from Vulgar Latin *vassus*, vassal, from Celtic
wasso-, "one who stands under," servant, young man
(*sto-*, standing; see **stā-**). **11a.** OPAL, UPANISHAD,
from Sanskrit *upa*, near to, under; **b.** ZEND-AVESTA,
from Avestan *upa*, up to, at (in *upastāvaka-*, praise).
Both **a** and **b** from Indo-Iranian *upa*. [Pokorny *upo*
1106.]

u(wa)l- To howl. Imitative root. (Oldest form
h₂u(wa)l-.) **1.** OWL, from Old English *ūle*, owl, from
Germanic *uwwalōn-*. **2.** HOWL, from Middle English
houlen, to howl (like an owl), possibly from Germanic
by-form *uwwilōn-*, owl. **3.** Reduplicated *contracted*
form *ul-ul-*. ULULATE, from Latin *ululāre*, to howl.
[Pokorny 1. *u-* 1103, *ul-* 1105.]

wāb- To cry, scream. Suffixed form *wāb-eyo-*. WEEP,
from Old English *wēpan*, to weep, from Germanic
wōpjan. [Pokorny *u̯āb-* 1109.]

wadh-¹ A pledge; to pledge. **1a.** WEDLOCK, from
Old English *wedd*, a pledge, marriage; **b.** WED, from
Old English *weddian*, to pledge, bind in wedlock; **c.**
GAGE[1]; DÉGAGÉ, ENGAGE, ENGAGÉ, MORTGAGE, from
Old French *gage*, a pledge; **d.** WAGE, WAGER, from Old
North French *wage*, a pledge, payment, and wager; to
pledge. **a–d** all from Germanic *wadi-*. **2.** PRAEDIAL,
from Latin *praes*, *praed-* (< *prai-vad-*), surety, pledge
(< "that which is given before"; *prai-*, before; see
per¹). [Pokorny *u̯adh-* 1109.]

wadh-² To go. **1.** Basic form *wadh-*. **a.** WADE, from
Old English *wadan*, to go, from Germanic *wadan*; **b.**
VADOSE, from Latin *vadum*, ford. **2.** Lengthened-grade
form *wādh-*. VAMOOSE; EVADE, INVADE, PERVADE,
from Latin *vādere*, to go, step. [Pokorny *u̯ādh-* 1109.]

wāg- To break, split, bite. (Oldest form perhaps *we-
h₂g-*, colored to *wah₂g-*, contracted to *wāg-*.) Suffixed
form *wāg-īnā-*. VAGINA, VANILLA; EVAGINATE, IN-
VAGINATE, from Latin *vāgīna*, sheath (probably made
of a split piece of wood). [Pokorny 1. *u̯āg-* 1110.]

wai Alas (interjection). **1.** WOE; WELLAWAY, from Old
English *wā*, *wei*, woe (interjection), alas, from Germanic *wai*. **2.** WAIL, from Middle English *wailen*, to
wail, from a Scandinavian source akin to Old Norse
vēla, *væla*, *veila*, to lament. [Pokorny *u̯ai-* 1110.]

wak- Cow. (Oldest form *wak̑-*.) Expressive form
wakkā-. BUCKAROO, VACCINE, VAQUERO, from Latin
vacca, cow. [Pokorny *u̯āk̑ā* (misprint for *u̯ák̑ā*) 1111.]

wal- To be strong.

   I. 1. Suffixed (stative) form *wal-ē-*. VALE[2], VA-
LENCE, VALETUDINARIAN, VALIANT, VALID, VALOR,
VALUE; AMBIVALENCE, AVAIL, CONVALESCE, COUN-
TERVAIL, E- QUIVALENT, EVALUATE, INVALID[1], INVAL-
ID[2], PREVAIL, VALEDICTION, from Latin *valēre*, to be
strong. **2.** Suffixed form *wal-o-*. Celtic *walos*, "ruler,"
in personal name *dubno-walos* (see **dheub-**).

   II. Extended o-grade form *wold(h)-*. **1.** WIELD,
from Old English *wealdan*, to rule, and *wieldan*, to
govern, from Germanic *waldan*, to rule. **2a.** Old
English *weald*, power, in personal name *Ōsweald* (see
ansu-); **b.** Old High German *-walt*, *-wald*, power,
in personal names: *(i)* WALTER, probably from Old
High German *Walthari*, "army commander" (*hari*,
heri, army; see **koro-**); *(ii)* Old High German *Gērald*
(see **ghaiso-**); *(iii)* Old High German *Arenwald* (see
or-); **c.** RONALD (personal name), from Old Norse
Rögnvaldr, "having the gods' power" (*rögn*, "decreeing
powers," gods, plural of *regin*, decree), from Old Norse
valdr, ruler; **d.** Germanic compound *harja-waldaz*
(see **koro-**). **a–d** all from Germanic *waldaz*, power,
rule. **3.** Old Church Slavonic *vlasti* (stem *vlad(i)-*),

to rule over. VLADIMIR (personal name), from Old Church Slavonic *Vladimirŭ* (> Russian *Vladimir*), "ruling peace," (*mirŭ*, peace; see **mei-⁴**). **4.** Suffixed extended o-grade form *wold-ti-*. OBLAST, from Old Church Slavonic *vlastĭ*, rule. [Pokorny *ual-* 1111.]

walso- A post. **1.** VALLATION, WALL; INTERVAL, from Latin *vallus*, post, stake, whence *vallum*, a palisade, wall. **2.** MYCELIUM, from Greek *hēlos* (< *hālos < *walsos*), stud, nail, wart. [In Pokorny 7. *uel-* 1140.]

wap- Bad, evil. (Oldest form *h₂wap-*.) Suffixed zero-grade form *up-elo-*. EVIL, from Old English *yfel*, evil, from Germanic *ubilaz*, evil. [Not in Pokorny; compare Hittite *ḫuwapp-*, evil.]

we- We. For oblique cases of the pronoun see **nes-²**. Suffixed variant form *wey-es*. WE, from Old English *wē*, *we*, we, from Germanic *wiz*. [Pokorny *uĕ* - 1114.]

wē- To blow. (Oldest form *h₂weh₁-*, contracted to *h₂wē-*.) **1.** Suffixed *shortened* form *we-dhro-*. WEATHER, from Old English *weder*, weather, storm, wind, from Germanic *wedram* wind, weather. **2.** Suffixed (participial) form *wē-nt-o-*, blowing. **a.** *(i)* WIND¹, from Old English *wind*, wind; *(ii)* WINDOW, from Old Norse *vindr*, wind. Both *(i)* and *(ii)* from Germanic *windaz*; **b.** VENT¹, VENTAIL, VENTILATE; ÉVENTAIL, from Latin *ventus*, wind. **3.** WING, from Middle English *wenge*, wing, from a Scandinavian source akin to Old Norse *væ ngr*, wing, from suffixed Germanic form *wē-ingjaz*. **4.** Basic form *wē-*. NIRVANA, from Sanskrit *vāti* (stem *vā-*), it blows. [Pokorny 10. *au(e)-* 81.]

webh- To weave, also to move quickly. **1.** WEAVE, WOOF¹, from Old English *wefan*, to weave, from Germanic *weban*. **2.** WEFT, from Old English *wefta*, weft, cross thread, from Germanic *weftaz*. **3.** Suffixed o-grade form *wobh-yo-*. WEB, WEBSTER, from Old English *web(b)*, web, from Germanic *wabjam*, fabric, web. **4.** WEEVIL, from Old English *wifel*, weevil (< "that which moves briskly"), from suffixed Germanic form *webilaz*. **5a.** *(i)* GAUFRETTE, GOFFER, from Old French *gaufre*, honeycomb, waffle; *(ii)* WAFER, from Old North French *waufre*, wafer. Both *(i)* and *(ii)* from a source akin to Middle Low German *wāfel*, honeycomb; **b.** WAFFLE¹, from Middle Dutch *wāfel*, waffle. Both **a** and **b** from suffixed Germanic form *wabila-*, web, honeycomb. **6.** Possibly Germanic *wab-*, to move back and forth as in weaving. **a.** WAVE, from Old English *wafian*, to move (the hand) up and down; **b.** WAVER, from Middle English *waveren*, to waver; **c.** WOBBLE, from Low German *wabbeln*, to move from side to side, sway. **7.** Suffixed zero-grade form *ubh-ā-*. HYPHA, from Greek *huphē*, web. [Pokorny *uebh-* 1114.]

wed-¹ Water; wet. **1.** Suffixed o-grade form *wod-ōr*. **a.** WATER, from Old English *wæter*, water; **b.** KIRSCHWASSER, from Old High German *wassar*, water. Both **a** and **b** from Germanic *watar*. **2.** Suffixed lengthened-grade form *wēd-o-*. WET, from Old English *wæt*, *wēt*, wet, from Germanic *wēta-*. **3.** O-grade form *wod-*. WASH, from Old English *wæscan*, *wacsan*, to wash, from Germanic suffixed form *wat-skan*, to wash. **4.** Nasalized form *we-n-d-*. WINTER, from Old English *winter*, winter, from Germanic *wintruz*, winter, "wet season." **5.** Suffixed zero-grade form *ud-ōr*. HYDRANT, HYDRIA, HYDRO-, HYDROUS, UTRICLE¹; ANHYDROUS, CLEPSYDRA, DROPSY, HYDATHODE, HYDATID, from Greek *hudōr*, water. **6.** Suffixed nasalized zero-grade form *u-n-d-ā-*. UNDINE, UNDULATE; ABOUND, INUNDATE, REDOUND, REDUNDANT, SURROUND, from Latin *unda*, wave. **7.** Suffixed zero-grade form *ud-ro-*, *ud-rā-*, water animal. **a.** OTTER, from Old English *otor*, otter, from Germanic *otraz*, otter; **b.** NUTRIA, from Latin *lutra*, otter (with obscure *l-*); **c.** HYDRUS, from Greek *hudros*, a water snake; **d.** HYDRA, HYDRILLA, from Greek *hudrā*, a water serpent, Hydra. **8.** Suffixed zero-grade form *ud-skio-*. USQUEBAUGH, WHISKEY,

from Old Irish *uisce*, water. **9.** Suffixed o-grade form *wod-ā-*. VODKA, from Russian *voda*, water. [Pokorny 9. *au(e)-* 78.]

wed-² To speak. (Oldest form *h₂wed-*.) **1.** Possible reduplicated form *awe-ud-* becoming *awe-ud-*, dissimilated to *aweid-*, becoming Greek *a(w)eid-*, to sing (but more likely from a separate root *h₂weid-*). ODE; COMEDY, EPODE, HYMNODY, MELODY, MONODY, PARODY, RHAPSODY, TRAGEDY, from Greek *aeidein* (Attic *āidein*), to sing, and *aoidē* (Attic *ōidē*), song, ode, with *aoidos* (Attic *ōidos*), a singer, singing (the latter two from suffixed o-grade form *awoid-o-*). **2.** Suffixed o-grade form *wod-o-*. THERAVADA, from Sanskrit *vādaḥ*, sound, statement. [Pokorny 6. *au-* 76.]

wedh- To drive, lead. TAOISEACH, from Old Irish *toísech*, first, leader, from Celtic *to-wessākos*, from *to-wessus*, a leading, position in front, from earlier *to-wedh-tu-* (compare Old Irish *do-fed*, he brings, leads, from earlier *to-wedheti*; *to-*, to, towards; see **to-**). [Pokorny 2. *wedh-* 1115.]

wedhǝ- To push, strike. Suffixed lengthened o-grade form *wōdh(ǝ)-eyo-*. OSMOSIS, from Greek *ōthein*, to push. [Pokorny 1. * uedh-* 1115.]

weg-¹ To weave a web. Related to **wokso-**. Suffixed form *weg-slo-*. VEIL, VELA, VELARIUM, VELUM, VEXILLUM, VOILE; REVEAL¹, from Latin *vēlum*, a sail, curtain, veil. [Pokorny *ueg-* 1117.]

weg-² To be strong, be lively. (Oldest form *weĝ-*.) **1.** Suffixed o-grade form *wog-ē-*. WAKE¹, from Old English *wacan*, to wake up, arise, and *wacian*, to be awake, from Germanic *wakēn*. **2.** Suffixed o-grade form *wog-no-*. WAKEN, from Old English *wæcnan*, *wæcnian*, to awake, from Germanic *waknan*. **3.** WATCH, from Old English *wæccan*, to be awake, from Germanic *wakjan*. **4.** Suffixed form *weg-yo-*. WICCA, WICKED, WITCH; BEWITCH, from Old English *wicca*, sorcerer, wizard (feminine *wicce*, witch), from Germanic *wikkjaz*, necromancer (< "one who wakes the dead"). **5.** Suffixed o-grade form *wog-to-*. BIVOUAC, from Old High German *wahta*, watch, vigil, from Germanic *wahtwō*. **6a.** WAIT, from Old North French *waitier*, to watch; **b.** WAFT, from Middle Dutch and Middle Low German *wachten*, to watch, guard. Both **a** and **b** from Germanic *waht-*. **7.** Suffixed (causative) o-grade form *wog-eyo-*. VEGETABLE, from Latin *vegēre*, to be lively. **8.** Suffixed (stative) form *weg-ē-*. VIGOR; RAVIGOTE, from Latin *vigēre*, to be lively. **9.** Suffixed form *weg-(e)li-*. VEDETTE, VIGIL, VIGILANT, VIGILANTE; REVEILLE, SURVEILLANT, from Latin *vigil*, watchful, awake. **10.** Suffixed form *weg-slo-*. VELOCITY, from Latin *vēlōx*, fast, "lively." [Pokorny *ueĝ-* 1117.]

wegh- To go, transport in a vehicle. (Oldest form *weĝh-*.) **1.** WEIGH¹, from Old English *wegan*, to carry, balance in a scale, from Germanic *wegan*. **2.** WEE, from Old English *wǣg(e)*, weight, unit of weight, from Germanic lengthened-grade form *wēgō*. **3.** Suffixed form *wegh-ti-*. WEIGHT, from Old English *wiht*, *gewiht*, weight, from Germanic *wihti-*. **4a.** WAY; ALWAYS, AWAY, from Old English *weg*, way; **b.** NORWEGIAN, from Old Norse *vegr*, way; **c.** THALWEG, from Old High German *weg*, way. **a–c** all from Germanic *wegaz*, course of travel, way. **5.** Suffixed o-grade form *wogh-no-*. **a.** WAIN, from Old English *wæ(g)n*, wagon; **b.** WAGON, from Middle Dutch *wagen*, wagon. Both **a** and **b** from Germanic *wagnaz*. **6.** Suffixed o-grade form *wogh-lo-*. **a.** WALLEYED, from Old Norse *vagl*, chicken roost, perch, beam, eye disease, from Germanic *waglaz*; **b.** OCHLOCRACY, OCHLOPHOBIA, from Greek *okhlos*, populace, mob (< "moving mass"). **7.** Distantly related to this root are: **a.** *(i)* GRAYWACKE, from Old High German *waggo*, *wacko*, boulder rolling on a riverbed, from Germanic *wag-*, "to move about"; *(ii)* WAG¹, from Middle English *waggen*, to wag, possibly from Germanic *wag-*; **b.** VOGUE, from Old French *voguer*, to row, sail, from Old Saxon *wogōn*, to rock, sway, from Germanic *wēga-, water in motion; **c.** *(i)* EARWIG, from Old English *wicga*, insect (< "thing that moves quickly"); *(ii)* WIGGLE, from Middle Dutch and Middle Low German *wiggelen*, to move back and forth, wag. Both *(i)* and *(ii)* from Germanic *wig-. **8.** Basic form *wegh-. VECTOR, VEHEMENT, VEHICLE; ADVECTION, CONVECTION, EVECTION, INVECTIVE, INVEIGH, from Latin *vehere* (past participle *vectus*), to carry. **9.** Suffixed basic form *wegh-yā-. FOY, VIA, VIATICAL, VOYAGE; CONVEY, CONVOY, DEVIATE, DEVIOUS, ENVOI, ENVOY¹, INVOICE, OBVIATE, OBVIOUS, OGEE, OGIVE, PERVIOUS, PREVIOUS, TRIVIAL, TRIVIUM, VIADUCT, from Latin *via*, way, road. **10.** Suffixed form *wegh-s-. VEX, from Latin *vexāre*, to agitate (< "to set in motion"). **11.** Probably suffixed form *wegh-so-. CONVEX, from Latin *convexus*, "carried or drawn together (to a point)," convex (*com-*, together; see **kom**). [Pokorny u̯eĝh- 1118.]

Language and Culture Note The root **wegh-**, "to convey, especially by wheeled vehicle," is found in virtually every branch of Indo-European, including now Anatolian. This root, as well as other widely represented roots such as **aks-** and **nobh-**, attests to the presence of the wheel—and vehicles using it—at the time Proto-Indo-European was spoken. From this root was derived the word for "wagon, wheeled vehicle," variously *wegh-no-, *wogh-no-, or *ugh-no-, continued for example by English *wain* and *wagon* (the latter a borrowing from Old Norse). Wheeled vehicles were apparently an innovation of late Indo-European date; the word for wheel itself, reconstructed as *kʷekʷlo-, is from a reduplicated form of the root **kʷel-¹**, "to turn," and its reduplicated form has the feel of a slangy new term. Archaeologists have dated the invention of the wheel to about 4500 BC, which fits rather well with the date assumed by many linguists for late Proto-Indo-European.

---

wegʷ- Wet. **1.** WAKE², from Old Norse *vök*, a crack in ice (< "wet spot"), from Germanic *wakw-ō. **2.** *Proposed by some, but doubtfully, is* suffixed zero-grade form *ugʷ-sm- as the base of Latin *(h)ūmēre*, to be wet, and *(h)ūmor*, fluid: HUMECTANT, HUMID, HUMOR. **3.** Suffixed zero-grade form *ugʷ-ro-. HYGRO-, from Greek *hugros*, wet, liquid. [Pokorny u̯egʷ- 1118.]

wegʷh- To preach, speak solemnly. (Oldest form probably *h₁wegʷh-, with variant [metathesized] form *h₁eugʷh-.) Suffixed o-grade form *wogʷh-eyo-. VOTARY, VOTE, VOTIVE, VOW; DEVOTE, DEVOUT, from Latin *vovēre*, to plege, vow. [Pokorny eu̯egʷh- 348.]

wei-¹ Also **weiə-** (oldest form *weih₁-). To turn, twist; with derivatives referring to suppleness or binding.

    I. Form *wei-. **1a.** WIRE, from Old English *wīr*, wire; **b.** GARLAND, from Old French *garlande*, wreath, from Frankish *wiara*, *weara*, wire. Both **a** and **b** from Germanic suffixed form *wi-ra-, *wē-ra-. **2.** Probably suffixed Germanic form *wai-ra-. SEAWARE, from Old English *wār*, seaweed. **3.** Suffixed zero-grade form *wi-riā-. FERRULE, from Latin *viriae*, bracelets (of Celtic origin). **4.** Suffixed form *wei-ti-. WITHY, from Old English *wīthig*, willow, withy, from Germanic *with-, willow. **5.** Suffixed zero-grade form *wi-t-. WITHE, from Old English *withthe*, supple twig, from Germanic *withjōn-.

    II. Form *weiə-, zero-grade *wī- (< *wiə-). **1.** Suffixed form *wī-ti-. VISE; VITICULTURE, from Latin *vītis*, vine. **2.** Suffixed form *wī-tā- becoming *wittā-. VITTA, from Latin *vitta*, headband. **3.** Suffixed form *wī-men-. MIMBRES, from Latin *vīmen*, withy, wicker. **4.** Probably suffixed form *wī-ri-. IRIDACEOUS, IRIDO-, IRIS, IRIS; IRIDIUM, IRITIS, from Greek *īris*, rainbow, and *Īris*, rainbow goddess. **5.** Perhaps suffixed form *wī-n-. INION; EXINE, INOSINE, INOSITOL, INOTROPIC, from Greek *īs*, sinew. [Pokorny 1. u̯ei- 1120.]

wei-² To wither. Extended form *weis-. WIZEN, from Old English *wisnian*, to wither, shrivel, shrink, from Germanic suffixed form *wis-n-ōn, from Germanic *wis-. [Pokorny 2. u̯ei- 1123.]

wei-³ Vice, fault, guilt. **1.** Suffixed zero-grade form *wi-tio-. VICE¹, VICIOUS, VITIATE, from Latin *vitium*, fault, vice. **2.** Suffixed form *wi-tu-. **a.** VITILIGO, from Latin *vitilīgō*, tetter (< "blemish"); **b.** VITUPERATE, from Latin *vituperāre*, to abuse (perhaps formed after Latin *recuperāre*, to regain). [Pokorny 1. u̯ī̆ - 1175.]

weid- To see.

    I. Full-grade form *weid-. **1a.** TWIT, from Old English *wītan*, to reproach; **b.** GUIDE, GUIDON, from Old Provençal *guidar*, to guide; **c.** GUY¹, from Old French *guier*, to guide; **d.** WITE, from Old English *wīte*, fine, penalty, from Germanic derivative noun *wīti-. **a–d** all from Germanic *wītan*, to look after, guard, ascribe to, reproach. **2.** Suffixed form *weid-to-. **a.** WISE¹, from Old English *wīs*, wise; **b.** WISDOM, from Old English *wīsdōm*, learning, wisdom (*-dōm*, abstract suffix; see **dhē-**); **c.** WISEACRE, from Old High German *wīzag*, knowledgeable; **d.** *(i)* WISE², from Old English *wise*, *wīs*, manner; *(ii)* GUISE, from Old French *guise*, manner. Both *(i)* and *(ii)* from Germanic *wissōn-, appearance, form, manner. **a–d** all from Germanic *wissaz. **3.** Suffixed form *weid-es-. EIDETIC, EIDOLON, IDOL, IDYLL, -OID; IDOCRASE, KALEIDOSCOPE, from Greek *eidos*, form, shape.

    II. Zero-grade form *wid-. **1a.** WIT¹, from Old English *wit*, *witt*, knowledge, intelligence; **b.** WIT- ENA-GEMOT, from Old English *wita*, wise man, councilor. Both **a** and **b** from Germanic *wit-. **2.** WIT², WOT; UNWITTING, from Old English *witan*, to know, from Germanic *witan* (Old English first and third person singular *wāt*, from Germanic *wait*, from Indo-European o-grade form *woid-). **3.** Suffixed form *wid-to-. IWIS, from Old English *gewis*, *gewiss*, certain, sure, from Germanic *(ga)wissa-, known (*ga-, past participial prefix; see **kom**). **4.** Form *wid-ē- (with the participial form *weid-to-). VIDE, VIEW, VISA, VISAGE, VISION, VISIT, VISOR, VISTA, VOYEUR; ADVICE, ADVISE, BELVEDERE, BLACK-A-VISED, CLAIRVOYANT, DÉJÀ VU, ENVY, EVIDENT, IMPROVISE, INTERVIEW, INVIDIOUS, PREVISE, PROVIDE, PRUDENT, PURVEY, PURVIEW, REVIEW, REVISE, SUPERVISE, SURVEY, from Latin *vidēre*, to see, look. **5.** Suffixed form *wid-es-yā-. IDEA, IDEO-, from Greek *idéā*, appearance, form, idea. **6.** Suffixed form *wid-tor-. HISTORY, STORY¹; POLYHISTOR, from Greek *histōr*, wise, learned, learned man. **7.** HADAL, HADES, from Greek *Haidēs* (also *Aidēs*), the underworld, perhaps "the invisible," and from *wid-. **8.** Suffixed nasalized zero-grade form *wi-n-d-o-. **a.** COLCANNON, from Old Irish *find*, white (< "clearly visible"); **b.** PENGUIN, from Welsh *gwyn*, *gwynn*, white. **9.** Celtic *wid-, seer, in compound *dru-wid- (see **deru-**). **III.** Suffixed o-grade form *woid-o-. VEDA; RIGVEDA, from Sanskrit *vedaḥ*, knowledge. [Pokorny 2. u̯(e)di- (misprint for u̯(e)id-) 1125.]

weidh- To divide, separate. **1.** Suffixed zero-grade form *widh-ewo-, "bereft," feminine *widh-ewā-, "woman separated (from her husband by death)," widow. WIDOW, from Old English *widuwe*, widow, from Germanic *widuwō. **2.** Zero-grade form *widh-. DEVISE, DIVIDE; POINT-DEVICE, from Latin *dīvidere*, to separate (*dis-*, intensive prefix). [Pokorny u̯eidh-1127.]

weiə- To go after someting, pursue with vigor, desire, with noun forms meaning force, power. Related to **wī-ro-**. **1.** Zero-grade form *wī- (< *wiə-). VIM, VIOLATE, VIOLENT, from Latin *vīs*, force, with irregular derivatives *violāre*, to treat with force, and *violentus*, vehement. **2.** Suffixed o-grade form *woi(ə)-tyā-. GAIN¹; ROWEN, from Old French, *gaaignier*, *gaignier*, to obtain, from Germanic *waithanjan*, to hunt, plunder, denominative verb from *wai-thjō, "pursuit," hunting. **3.** Suffixed zero-grade form *wiə-to- becoming *wī-

to-. INVITE, from Latin *invītāre*, to invite (*in*-, in; see **en**). [Pokorny 3. *ṷei*- 1123.]

weik-¹ Clan (social unit above the household). (Oldest form **weik̑*-.) **1.** Suffixed form **weik̑-slā*-. VILLA, VILLAGE, VILLAIN, VILLANELLE, VILLEIN; BIDONVILLE, NASTY, from Latin *vīlla*, country house, farm. **2.** Suffixed o-grade form **woik̑-o*-. **a.** VICINAGE, VICINITY; BAILIWICK, from Latin *vīcus*, quarter or district of a town, neighborhood; **b.** ANDROECIUM, AUTOECIOUS, DIOCESE, DIOECIOUS, ECESIS, ECOLOGY, ECONOMY, ECUMENICAL, HETEROECIOUS, MONOECIOUS, PARISH, PAROCHIAL, from Greek *oikos*, house, and its derivatives *oikiā*, a dwelling, and *oikēsis*, dwelling, ad- ministration. **3.** Zero-grade form **wik̑*-. VAISYA, from Sanskrit *viśáḥ*, dwelling, house. [Pokorny *ṷeik̑*- 1131.]

weik-² Consecrated, holy. In words connected with magic and religious notions in Germanic (German *Weihnacht(en)*, Christmas) and perhaps Latin. **1.** GUILE, from Old French *guile*, cunning, trickery, from a Germanic source akin to Old English *wigle*, divination, sorcery, from Germanic suffixed form *wih-l-. **2.** Possibly suffixed zero-grade form *wik-t-. VICTIM, from Latin *victima*, animal used as sacrifice, victim (although this may belong to another root **(ə)wek*- not otherwise represented in English). [Pokorny 1. *ṷeik*- 1128.]

weik-³ To be like. **1.** Suffixed variant form *weik-on-. ICON, ICONIC, ICONO-; ANISEIKONIA, from Greek *eikōn*, likeness, image. **2.** Prefixed and suffixed zero-grade form *ṇ-wik-ēs, not like (*ṇ-, not; see **ne**). AECIUM, from Greek *aîkēs*, unseemly. [Pokorny 3. *ṷeik*- 1129.]

weik-⁴ Also **weig-**. To bend, wind.
I. Form *weig-. **1a.** WYCH ELM, from Old English *wice*, wych elm (having pliant branches); **b.** WICKER, from Middle English *wiker*, wicker, from a Scandinavian source akin to Swedish *viker*, willow twig, wand; **c.** WICKET, from Old North French *wiket*, wicket (< "door that turns"), from a Scandinavian source probably akin to Old Norse *vikja*, to bend, turn. **a–c** all from Germanic *wik-. **2a.** WEAK, from Old Norse *veikr*, pliant; **b.** WEAKFISH, from Middle Dutch *weec*, weak, soft. Both **a** and **b** from Germanic *waikwa-. **3.** WEEK, from Old English *wicu*, *wice*, week, from Germanic *wikōn-, "a turning," series.
II. Form *weik-. Zero-grade form *wik-. **1.** VICAR, VICARIOUS, VICE-; VICISSITUDE, from Latin *vix (genitive *vicis*), turn, situation, change. **2.** VETCH, from Latin *vicia*, vetch (< "twining plant"). [Pokorny 4. *ṷeik*- 1130.]

weik-⁵ To fight, conquer. **1.** WIGHT², from Old Norse *vīgr*, able in battle, from Germanic *wīk-. **2.** Nasalized zero-grade form *wi-n-k-. VANQUISH, VICTOR, VINCIBLE; CONVICT, CONVINCE, EVICT, EVINCE, from Latin *vincere*, to conquer. **3.** Zero-grade form *wik-. ORDOVICIAN, from Celtic *Ordovices* (*ordo-wik-), "those who fight with hammers" (*ordo-, hammer). [Pokorny 2. *ṷeik*- 1128.]

weip- To turn, vacillate, tremble ecstatically. **1.** O-grade form *woip-. WAIF¹, WAIF²; WAIVE, WAIVER, from Anglo-Norman *waif*, ownerless property, from a Scandinavian source probably akin to Old Norse *veif*, waving thing, flag, from Germanic *waif-. **2.** Variant form *weib-. **a.** WIPE, from Old English *wīpian*, to wipe; **b.** GUIPURE, from Old French *guiper*, to cover with silk; **c.** WHIP, from Middle English *wippen*, to whip. **a–c** all from Germanic *wīpjan-, to move back and forth. **3.** Perhaps suffixed nasalized zero-grade form *wi-m-p-ila-. **a.** WIMPLE, from Old English *wimpel*, covering for the neck (< "something that winds around"); **b.** GIMP¹, GUIMPE, from Old High German *wimpal*, guimpe; **c.** perhaps Middle Dutch *wimmel*, auger (< "that which turns in boring"): WIMBLE. **4.** Suffixed zero-grade variant form *wib-ro-. VIBRATE, from Latin *vibrāre*, to vibrate. [Pokorny *ṷeip*- 1131.]

weis- To flow.
I. 1. OOZE², from Old English *wāse*, mire, mud, from Germanic *wisōn-, *waisōn-. **2.** Taken by many as a derivative of this root, but probably an independent Indo-European word, is the suffixed form *wīs-o- in Latin *vīrus*, slime, poison: VIRUS. **3.** Extended zero-grade form *wisk-. VISCID, VISCOUS, from Latin *viscum*, mistletoe, birdlime, possibly from this root.
II. Attributed by some to this root, but more likely of obscure origin, are some Germanic words for strong-smelling animals. **1.** WEASEL, from Old English *wesle*, *weosule*, weasel, from Germanic *wisulōn-. **2.** Suffixed form *wis-onto-. **a.** WISENT, from Old High German *wisunt*, bison; **b.** BISON, from Latin *bisōn* (stem *bisont*-), bison. Both **a** and **b** from Germanic *wisand-, *wisund-, European bison (which emits a musky smell in the rutting season). [Pokorny 3. *ṷeis*- 1134.]

weit(ə)- To speak, adjudge. Suffixed o-grade form *woit-o-. Old Russian *vĕtŭ*, council, in compound *sŭ-vĕtŭ* (see **ksun**). [Not in Pokorny; compare Avestan *vaēth*-, to judge.]

wekti- Thing, creature. **1.** WHIT, WIGHT¹; AUGHT², NAUGHT, NOT, from Old English *wiht*, person, thing. **2.** NIX², from Old High German *wiht*, thing, being. Both **1** and **2** from Germanic *wihti-. [Pokorny *ṷek-ti*- 1136.]

wekʷ- To speak. **1.** O-grade form *wŏkʷ-. **a.** VOCAL, VOICE, VOWEL, from Latin *vōx*, voice; **b.** CALLIOPE, from Greek *ops*, voice. **2.** Suffixed o-grade form *wokʷ-ā-. VOCABLE, VOCATION, VOUCH; ADVOCATE, AVOCATION, CONVOKE, EQUIVOCAL, EVOKE, INVOKE, PROVOKE, REVOKE, UNIVOCAL, from Latin *vocāre*, to call. **3.** Suffixed form *wekʷ-es-. EPIC, EPOS; EPOPEE, ORTHOEPY, from Greek *epos*, song, word. [Pokorny *ṷekʷ*- 1135.]

wel-¹ To see. **1.** Suffixed zero-grade form *wl-id-. LITMUS, from a source akin to Old Norse *litr*, appearance, color, dye, from Germanic *wlituz, appearance. **2.** Suffixed form *wel-uno- perhaps in Sanskrit *Varuṇaḥ*, "seer, wise one," sovereign god: VARUNA. [Pokorny 1. *ṷel*- 1136.]

wel-² To wish, will. **1.** WELL², from Old English *wel*, well (< "according to one's wish"), from Germanic *welō. **2.** WEAL¹, WEALTH, from Old English *wela*, *weola*, well-being, riches, from Germanic *welōn-. **3a.** WILL¹, from Old English *willa*, desire, will power; **b.** Old High German *willo*, will, in personal name *Willahelm* (see **kel-¹**). Both **a** and **b** from Germanic *wiljōn-. **4.** WILL²; NILL, WILLY-NILLY, from Old English *willan*, to desire, from Germanic **wil(l)jan*. **5.** Germanic compound *wil-kumōn- (see **gʷā-**). **6.** O-grade form *wol-. **a.** GALLOP, from Old French *galoper*, to gallop; **b.** WALLOP, from Old North French *walo-per, to gallop; **c.** GALLANT; GALLIMAUFRY, from Old French *galer*, to rejoice, from Frankish Latin *walāre, to take it easy, from Frankish *wala, good, well. **a–c** all from Germanic *wal-. **7.** Basic form *wel-. VELLEITY, VOLITION, VOLUNTARY; BENEVOLENT, MALEVOLENCE, from Latin *velle* (present stem *vol*-), to wish, will. **8.** Probably suffixed extended form *wel-p-i-. VOLUPTUARY, VOLUPTUOUS, from Latin *voluptās*, pleasure, from an adjective *volupis, pleasing (probably preserved in the adverb *volup*, with pleasure, from neuter *volupe). [Pokorny 2. *ṷel*- 1137.]

wel-³ To turn, roll; with derivatives referring to curved, enclosing objects. **1a.** WALTZ, from Old High German *walzan*, to roll, waltz; **b.** WELTER, from Middle Low German or Middle Dutch *welteren*, to roll. Both **a** and **b** from Germanic *walt-. **2.** WHELK¹, from Old English *weoluc*, *weoloc*, mollusk (having a spiral shell), whelk, from Germanic *weluka-. **3.** Perhaps Germanic *wel-. WILLOW, from Old English *welig*, willow (with flexible twigs). **4.** Perhaps Germanic *welk-. WALK, from Old English *wealcan*, to roll, toss, and *wealcian*, to muffle up. **5.** O-grade form *wol-. **a.** WELL¹, from Old English *wiella, wælla, welle,* a well (< "rolling or bubbling water," "spring"); **b.** GABERDINE, from Old High German *wallōn,* to roam; **c.** WALLET, possibly from Old North French *walet,* roll, knapsack. **a–c** all from Germanic **wall-.* **6.** Perhaps suffixed o-grade form **wol-ā-.* **a.** WALE, from Old English *walu,* streak on the skin, weal, welt; **b.** Old High German **-walu,* a roll, round stem, in compound **wurzwalu* (see **wrād-**). Both **a** and **b** from Germanic **walō.* **7.** Extended form **welw-.* **a.** WALLOW, from Old English *wealwian,* to roll (in mud), from Germanic **walwōn;* **b.** VAULT¹, VAULT², VOLT², VOLUBLE, VOLUME, VOLUTE, VOLUTIN, VOLVOX, VOUSSOIR; ARCHIVOLT, CIRCUMVOLVE, CONVOLVE, DEVOLVE, EVOLVE, INVOLUCRUM, INVOLVE, MULTIVOLTINE, REVOLVE, from Latin *volvere,* to roll; **c.** suffixed o-grade form **wolw-ā-.* VOLVA, VULVA, from Latin *vulva, volva,* covering, womb; **d.** suffixed zero-grade form **wl̥w-ā-.* VALVE, VALVULE, from Latin *valva,* leaf of a door (< "that which turns"); **e.** suffixed form **welu-tro-.* ELYTRON, from Greek *elutron,* sheath, cover. **8.** Suffixed form **wel-n-.* ILEUS; NEURILEMMA, from Greek *eilein* (< **welnein*), to turn, squeeze. **9.** Perhaps variant **wall-.* VAIL¹, VALE¹, VLEI, from Latin *vallēs, vallis,* valley (< "that which is surrounded by hills"). **10.** Possibly suffixed form **wel-enā-.* HELEN; ELECAMPANE, INULIN, from the Greek name *Helenē* (oldest form *Welenā*), Helen. **11.** Suffixed form **welik-.* HELICON, HELIX; HELICOPTER, from Greek *helix,* spiral object. **12.** Suffixed form **wel-mi-nth-.* HELMINTH; ASCHELMINTH, ANTHELMINTIC, PLATYHELMINTH, from Greek *helmis, helmins* (stem *helminth-*), parasitic worm. [Pokorny 7. u̯el- 1140.]

wel-⁴ To pull, tear. **1.** Suffixed form **wel-do-.* AVULSE, CONVULSE, DIVULSE, EVULSION, REVULSION, SVELTE, from Latin *vellere,* to tear, pull. **2.** Suffixed form **wel-no-.* VELOUR, VELVET, VILLUS, from Latin *villus,* shaggy hair, wool. [Pokorny 8. u̯el- 1144.]

welə-¹ Wool. (Oldest form **welh₂-;* probably related to **wel-⁴**.) **1.** Suffixed extended zero-grade form **wl̥ə-nā-.* **a.** WOOL, from Old English *wul(l),* wool, from Germanic **wullō;* **b.** LANATE, LANNER, LANOSE, LANUGO; LANOLIN, from Latin *lāna* (< Italic **wlānā*), wool, and its derivative *lānūgō,* down; **c.** FLANNEL, from Welsh *gwlan,* from Celtic **wlanā.* **2.** Possibly suffixed o-grade form **wol(ə)- no-.* ULOTRICHOUS, from Greek *oulos,* wooly, curly. **3.** Suffixed full-grade form **wel(ə)-nes-.* VELLUS, from Latin *vellus,* wool. [Pokorny 4. u̯el- 1139.]

welə-² To strike, wound. (Oldest form **welh₂-.*) **1.** Suffixed o-grade form **wol(ə)-o-.* **a.** VALHALLA, from Old Norse *Valhöll,* Valhalla; **b.** VALKYRIE, from Old Norse *Valkyrja,* "chooser of the slain," name of one of the twelve war goddesses (*-kyrja,* chooser; see **geus-**). Both **a** and **b** from Old Norse *valr,* the slain in battle, from Germanic **walaz.* **2.** Suffixed basic form **welnes-.* VULNERABLE, from Latin *vulnus* (stem *vulner-*), a wound. **3.** Suffixed zero-grade form **wl̥ə-to-.* BERDACHE, from Old Iranian **varta-* (Avestan *varəta-*), seized, prisoner. [In Pokorny 8. u̯el- 1144.]

welg- Wet. **1.** WELKIN, from Old English *wolc(e)n,* cloud, sky. **2.** WILT¹, from Middle English *welken,* to wilt. Both **1** and **2** from Germanic **welk-.* [Pokorny 2. u̯elk- 1145.]

welt- Woods; wild. **1.** Suffixed o-grade form **wolt-u-.* **a.** WEALD, WOLD¹, from Old English *weald, wald,* a forest; **b.** VOLE¹, from Old Norse *völlr,* field. Both **a** and **b** from Germanic **walthuz.* **2.** WELD², from Middle English *welde,* a plant yielding a yellow dye, weld, from Germanic **walthōn-.* **3a.** WILD, from Old English *wilde,* wild; **b.** WILDERNESS, from Old English *wildēor,* wilddēor, wild beast (*dēor,* animal; see **dheu-¹**); **c.** WILDEBEEST, from Dutch *wild,* wild. **a–c** all from Germanic **wilthja-.* [In Pokorny 4. u̯el- 1139.]

wemə- To vomit. (Oldest form **wemh₁-.*) **1.** WAMBLE, from Middle English *wam(e)len,* to feel nausea, stag-

ger, from a Scandinavian source probably akin to Old Norse *vamla,* qualm, and Danish *vamle,* to become sick, from Germanic **wam-.* **2.** VOMIT; NUX VOMICA, from Latin *vomere,* to vomit. **3.** EMESIS, EMETIC, from Greek *emein,* to vomit. [Pokorny u̯em- 1146.]

wen-¹ To desire, strive for. **1.** Suffixed form **wen-w-.* WIN, from Old English *winnan,* to win, from Germanic **winn(w)an,* to seek to gain. **2.** Suffixed zero-grade form **wn̥-yā-.* WYNN, WINSOME, from Old English *wynn, wen,* pleasure, joy, from Germanic **wunjō.* **3.** Suffixed (stative) zero-grade form **wn̥-ē-,* to be contented. WON¹, WONT, from Old English *wunian,* to become accustomed to, dwell, from Germanic **wunēn.* **4.** Suffixed (causative) o-grade form **won-eyo-.* WEAN, from Old English *wenian,* to accustom, train, wean, from Germanic **wanjan.* **5.** WEEN, from Old English *wēnan,* to expect, imagine, think, from Germanic denominative **wēnjan,* to hope, from **wēniz,* hope. **6.** Germanic **wini-,* "beloved," in Old English *wine,* friend, protector, in personal names: **a.** EDWIN, from Old English *Ēadwine,* "friend of riches" (*ēad,* wealth, joy); **b.** Old English *Mælwine* (see **mōd-**). **7.** Suffixed zero-grade form **wn̥-sko-.* WISH, from Old English *wȳscan,* to desire, wish, from Germanic **wunsk-.* **8.** Perhaps o-grade form **won-.* **a.** VANIR, from Old Norse *Vanir,* the Vanir; **b.** VANADIUM, from Old Norse *Vanadis,* name of the goddess Freya. Both **a** and **b** from Germanic **wana-.* **9.** Suffixed form **wen-es-.* **a.** VENERATE, VENEREAL, VENERY¹, VENUS, from Latin *venus,* love; **b.** suffixed form **wen-es-no-.* VENOM, from Latin *venēnum,* love potion, poison. **10.** Possibly suffixed form **wen-eto-,* "beloved." WEND, from Old High German *Winid,* Wend, from Germanic **Weneda-,* a Slavic people. **11.** Suffixed form **wen-yā-.* VENIAL, from Latin *venia,* favor, forgiveness. **12.** Lengthened-grade form **wēn- ā-.* VENERY², VENISON, from Latin *vēnārī,* to hunt. **13.** Suffixed basic form **wen-o-.* WANDEROO, from Sanskrit *vanam,* forest. **14.** Possibly zero-grade suffixed form **wn̥-ig-.* BANYAN, from Sanskrit *vaṇik, vāṇijaḥ,* merchant (? < "seeking to gain"). [Pokorny 1. u̯en- 1146.]

wen-² To beat, wound. **1.** Suffixed zero-grade form **wn̥-to-.* WOUND¹, from Old English *wund,* a wound, from Germanic **wundaz.* **2.** Suffixed o-grade form **won-yo-.* WEN¹, from Old English *wen(n), wæn(n),* wen, from Germanic **wanja-,* a swelling. [Pokorny u̯en- 1108 (misalphabetized).]

wendh- To turn, wind, weave. **1a.** WIND², from Old English *windan,* to wind; **b.** WINDLASS, from Old Norse *vinda,* to wind. Both **a** and **b** from Germanic **windan,* to wind. **2a.** WEND, WENT, from Old English *wendan,* to turn to; **b.** WENTLETRAP, from Dutch *wenden,* to turn. Both **a** and **b** from Germanic causative form **wandjan.* **3a.** WANDER, from Old English *wandrian,* to wander; **b.** WANDERLUST, from German *wandern,* to wander. Both **a** and **b** from Germanic **wandrōn,* to roam about. **4.** WAND, from Old Norse *vöndr,* a supple twig, from Germanic **wanduz.* **5.** Perhaps Germanic **wandljaz,* "wanderer," Vandal. **a.** VANDAL, from Latin *Vandalus,* a Vandal. [Pokorny 1. u̯endh- 1148.]

weng- To bend, curve. **1a.** WINK, from Old English *wincian,* to close the eyes (< "to bend down the eyelids"); **b.** LAPWING, from Old English *-wince,* one that wavers, from **wincan,* to waver. Both **a** and **b** from Germanic **wink-.* **2.** WINCH, from Old English *wince,* a reel, roller, from Germanic **winkila-.* **3.** PERIWINKLE¹, from Old English *-wincel,* spiral shell, from Germanic **winkil-.* **4a.** WENCH, from Old English *wencel,* youth, maid (< "inconstant one"); **b.** WONKY, from Old English *wancol,* inconstant, unsteady. Both **a** and **b** from Germanic **wankila-, *wankula-.* **5a.** GAUCHE, from Old French *gauchir,* to turn aside; **b.** WINCE, from Anglo-Norman **wencir,* to turn aside, avoid (> Middle English *wincen,* to kick). Both **a** and **b** from Germanic **wankjan.* [Pokorny u̯e-n-g- 1148.]

wer-¹ High raised spot or other bodily infirmity. **1.** Suffixed form *wer-d-. WART, from Old English *wearte*, wart, from Germanic *wartōn-. **2.** O-grade form *wor- possibly in Germanic *war-. WARBLE², from a source akin to obsolete Swedish *varbulde*, "pus swelling" (*bulde*, swelling; see **bhel-²**). **3.** VAIR, VARIEGATE, VARIETY, VARIOLA, VARIORUM, VARIOUS, VARY; MINIVER, from Latin *varius*, spotty, speckled, changeable. **4.** VARIX, from Latin *varix*, varicose vein. **5.** Suffixed and extended zero-grade form *wr̥su-ko-. VERRUCA, from Latin *verrūca*, wart. [Pokorny 2. *er-* 1151, 2. *u̯ā-* 1108.]

wer-² To raise, lift, hold suspended. (Oldest form *h₂wer-.) **1.** Basic form *ǝwer-, becoming *awer- in Greek. AORTA, ARSIS, ARTERIO-, ARTERIOLE, ARTERY; METEOR, from Greek *aeirein*, to raise, and *artēriā*, windpipe, artery. **2.** Possibly from this root is Greek *āēr*, air (from an obscure basic form *āwer-): AERIAL, AERO-, AIR, ARIA; MALARIA. **3.** Zero-grade form *aur-. AURA, from Greek *aurā*, breath, vapor (related to Greek *āēr*, air; see **2** above). [Pokorny 1. *u̯er-* 1150.]

wer-³ Conventional base of various Indo-European roots; to turn, bend.
   I. Root *wert-, to turn, wind. **1.** Germanic *werth-. **a.** (*i*) -WARD, from Old English *-weard*, toward (< "turned toward"); (*ii*) INWARD, from Old English *inweard*, inward, from Germanic *inwarth*, inward (*in, in; see **en**). Both (*i*) and (*ii*) from Germanic variant *warth; **b.** perhaps Germanic derivative *wertha-, "toward, opposite," hence "equivalent, worth." WORTH¹; STALWART, from Old English *weorth*, worth, valuable, and derivative noun *weorth*, *wierth*, value. **2.** WORTH², from Old English *weorthan*, to befall, from Germanic *werthan*, to become (< "to turn into"). **3.** Zero-grade form *wr̥t-. WEIRD, from Old English *wyrd*, fate, destiny (< "that which befalls one"), from Germanic *wurthiz. **4.** VERSATILE, VERSE¹, VERSION, VERSUS, VERTEBRA, VERTEX, VERTIGO, VORTEX; ADVERSE, ANNIVERSARY, AVERT, BOULEVERSEMENT, CONTROVERSY, CONVERSE¹, CONVERT, DEXTRORSE, DIVERT, EVERT, EXTRORSE, EXTROVERSION, EXTROVERT, INTRORSE, INTROVERT, INVERT, MALVERSATION, OBVERT, PEEVISH, PERVERT, PROSE, RETRORSE, REVERT, SINISTRORSE, SUBVERT, TERGIVERSATE, TRANSVERSE, UNIVERSE, from Latin *vertere*, to turn, with its frequentative *versāre*, to turn, and passive *versārī*, to stay, behave (< "to move around a place, frequent"). **5.** VERST, from Russian *versta*, line, from Balto-Slavic *wirstā-, a turn, bend.
   II. Root *wreit-, to turn. **a.** WREATH, from Old English *writha*, band (< "that which is wound around"); **b.** WRITHE, from Old English *writhan*, to twist, torture; **c.** WRATH, WROTH, from Old English *wrāth*, angry (< "tormented, twisted"). **a–c** all from Germanic *writh-, *wraith-.
   III. Root *wergh-, to turn. **1.** WORRY, from Old English *wyrgan*, to strangle, from Germanic *wurgjan. **2.** Nasalized variant *wrengh-. **a.** WRING, from Old English *wringan*, to twist, from Germanic *wreng-; **b.** (*i*) WRONG, from Middle English *wrong*, wrong, from a Scandinavian source akin to Old Norse *vrangr*, *rangr*, curved, crooked, wrong; (*ii*) WRANGLE, from Middle English *wranglen*, to wrangle, from a Low German source akin to *wrangeln*, to wrestle. Both (*i*) and (*ii*) from Germanic *wrang-.
   IV. Root *werg-, to turn. **1.** Nasalized variant form *wreng-. **a.** WRENCH, from Old English *wrencan*, to twist; **b.** WRINKLE, from Old English *gewrinclian*, to wind (*ge-, collective prefix; see **kom**). Both **a** and **b** from Germanic *wrankjan. **2.** VERGE²; CONVERGE, DIVERGE, from Latin *vergere*, to turn, tend toward. **3.** VEDDA, from Sinhalese *vädda*, perhaps from Middle Indic *vajjita-, excluded, from Sanskrit *varjita-, past passive participle of *varjayati*, he avoids, shuns, causative of *vr̥ṇakti* (stem *vr̥j-), he bends, turns.
   V. Root *wreik-, to turn. **1a.** WRY; AWRY, from Old English *wrīgian*, to turn, bend, go; **b.** WRIGGLE,

from Middle Low German *wriggeln*, to wriggle. Both **a** and **b** from Germanic *wrīg-. **2a.** WRIST, from Old English *wrist*, wrist; **b.** GAITER, from Old French *guietre*, gaiter, from Frankish *wrist-. Both **a** and **b** from Germanic *wristiz, *wrihst-. **3.** WREST, WRESTLE, from Old English *wrēstan*, to twist, from secondary Germanic derivative *wraistjan. **4.** Possibly from this root are European words for heather. **a.** HYPERICIN, HYPERICUM, from Greek *ereikē*, tree heath (exact preform uncertain); **b.** Possibly suffixed o-grade form *wroik-o-. BRIAR¹, BRUSQUE, from Late Latin *brūcus*, heather, from Gaulish *brūko-.
   VI. RIBALD, from Old French *riber*, to be wanton, from Germanic root *wrib-.
   VII. Root *werb-, also *werbh-, to turn, bend. **1.** WARP, from Old English *weorpan*, to throw away, from Germanic *werpan, "to fling by turning the arm." **2.** REVERBERATE, from Latin *verber*, whip, rod. **3.** VERBENA, VERVAIN, from Latin *verbēna*, sacred foliage. **4.** Zero-grade form *wr̥b-. RHABDOMANCY, RHABDOVIRUS, from Greek *rhabdos*, rod. **5.** Nasalized variant form *wrembh-. RHOMBUS, from Greek *rhombos*, magic wheel, rhombus.
   VIII. Root *werp-, to turn, wind. **1.** Metathesized form *wrep-. WRAP, from Middle English *wrappen*, to wrap, from a source akin to Danish dialectal *vravle*, to wind, from Germanic *wrap-. **2.** Zero-grade form *wr̥p-. RAPHE, RHAPHIDE; RHAPSODY, STAPHYLORRHAPHY, TENORRHAPHY, from Greek *rhaptein*, to sew.
   IX. Root *wr̥mi-, worm; rhyme word to **kʷr̥mi-**. **1.** WORM, from Old English *wyrm*, worm, from Germanic *wurmiz. **2.** VERMEIL, VERMI-, VERMICELLI, VERMICULAR, VERMIN, from Latin *vermis*, worm. [Pokorny 3. *u̯er-* 1152.]

wer-⁴ To perceive, watch out for.
   I. O-grade form *wor-. **1.** Suffixed form *wor-o-. **a.** WARY, from Old English *wær*, watchful; **b.** AWARE, from Old English *gewær*, aware (*ge-, collective and intensive prefix; see **kom**); **c.** WARE², from Old English *warian*, to beware. **a–c** all from Germanic *waraz. **2.** Suffixed form *wor-to-. **a.** (*i*) WARD; LORD, STEWARD, from Old English *weard*, a watching, keeper; (*ii*) WARDER², from Old English *weardian*, to ward, guard; **b.** WARDEN; AWARD, REWARD, WARDROBE, from Old North French *warder*, to guard; **c.** GUARD; GARDEROBE, REGARD, from Old French *guarder*, to guard; **d.** REARWARD², from Anglo-Norman *warde*, guard. **a–d** all from Germanic *wardaz, guard, and *wardōn, to guard. **3.** WARE¹, from Old English *waru*, goods, protection, guard, from Germanic *warō. **4.** Suffixed form *wor-wo-. ARCTURUS, PYLORUS, from Greek *ouros*, a guard. **5.** Probably variant *(s)wor-, *s(w)or-. EPHOR, PANORAMA, from Greek *horān*, to see.
   II. Suffixed (stative) form *wer-ē-. REVERE¹, from Latin *verērī*, to respect, feel awe for. [Pokorny 8. *u̯er-* 1164.]

wer-⁵ To cover.
   I. Basic form *wer-. **1.** WEIR, from Old English *wer*, dam, fish trap, from Germanic *wer-jōn-. **2.** Compound form *ap-wer-yo- (*ap-, off, away; see **apo-**). APERIENT, APÉRITIF, APERTURE; OVERT, OVERTURE, PERT, from Latin *aperīre*, to open, uncover. **3.** Compound form *op-wer-yo- (*op-, over; see **epi**). OPERCULUM; COVER, KERCHIEF, from Latin *operīre*, to cover. **4.** Suffixed form *wer-tro-. WAT; AMBARELLA, from Sanskrit *vāṭaḥ*, enclosure, from lengthened-grade derivative *vār-t(r)a-.
   II. O-grade form *wor-. **1.** WARN, from Old English *war(e)nian*, to take heed, warn, from Germanic *warnōn. **2a.** (*i*) GUARANTY, from Old French *garant*, warrant, authorization; (*ii*) WARRANT, WARRANTEE, WARRANTY, from Old North French *warant*, warrant, and *warantir*, to guarantee; **b.** GARAGE, from Old French *garer*, to guard, protect; **c.** GARRET, GARRISON, from Old French *g(u)arir*, to defend, protect; **d.** WARREN, from Old North French *warenne*, enclosure, game

preserve; **e.** GARMENT, GARNISH, GARNITURE, from Old French *g(u)arnir*, to equip. **a–e** all from Germanic **war-*. **3.** Suffixed form **wor-o-*. **a.** Germanic **warōn-*, protector, in compound **burg-warōn-* (see **bhergh-²**); **b.** SALWAR, from Old Iranian compound **šara-vāra-*, thigh covering (**šara-*, thigh; see (**s**) **kel-³**). **c.** BARBICAN, from Old Iranian compound **pari-vāraka-*, protective (**pari-*, around; see **per¹**). [Pokorny 5. *u̯er-* 1160.]

wer-⁶ To burn. Suffixed lengthened o-grade (causative) form **wōr-yo-*. SAMOVAR, from Russian *varit'*, to boil. [Pokorny 12. *u̯er-* 1166.]

wer-⁷ Squirrel. Reduplicated expressive form **wī-wer(r)-*. VIVERRID, from Latin *vīverra*, a ferret. [Pokorny 13. *u̯er-* 1166.]

wē-r- Water, liquid, milk. (Contracted from earlier **weh₁-r-*; zero-grade **uh₁-r-*, contracted to **ūr-*. Related to **eua-dh-r̥.**) Suffixed zero-grade form **ūr-īnā-*. URINE, from Latin *ūrīna*, urine. [In Pokorny 9. *au̯(e)-* 78.]

werə-¹ Wide, broad. (Oldest form **werh₁-*.) Zero-grade suffixed form **wrə-u-*, metathesized to **əur-u-*. EURY-; ANEURYSM, EURYDICE, from Greek *eurus*, wide. [Pokorny 8. *u̯er-* 1165.]

werə-² To find. (Oldest form **werh₁-*, with variant [metathesized] form **wreh₁-*, contracted to **wrē-*.) Reduplicated variant form **we-wrē-*. EUREKA, HEURISTIC, from Greek *heuriskein* (perfect tense *heurēka*), to find. [Pokorny 4. *u̯er-* 1160.]

werə-³ To speak. (Oldest form **werh₁-*, with metathesized variant form **wreh₁-*, contracted to **wrē-*.) **1a.** Compound form **werə-dh(ə)-o-* ("a doing of speech"; *dhē-*, *dhə-*, to do; see **dhē-**). VERB, VERVE; ADVERB, PROVERB, from Latin *verbum*, word. **b.** Zero-grade form in compound **wrə-dh(ə)-o-* ("a doing of speech"; *dhē-*, *dhə-*, to do; see **dhē-**). WORD, from Old English *word*, word, from Germanic **wurdam*. In both **a** and **b**, the first member of the compound has undergone the regular loss of a laryngeal occurring when the laryngeal is preceded by a consonant and followed by a two-consonant cluster. **2.** Also ultimately from this root is the Greek verbal present stem *eir-*, with infinitive *eirein*, to say, speak, possibly back-formed from future stem *ere-*, with infinitive *erein*, from **erə-s-*: IRONY. **3.** Variant form **wrē-*. **a.** Suffixed form **wrē-tor-*. RHETOR, from Greek *rhētōr*, public speaker; **b.** suffixed form **wrē-m̥*. RHEME, from Greek *rhēma*, word. [Pokorny 6. *u̯er-* 1162.]

Language and Culture Note There is a famous Greek epitaph attributed to the poet Simonides about the Spartans under Leonidas who died defending the pass at Thermopylae against the invading Persians: "O stranger, tell the Spartans that here we lie, obedient to their words." The phrase "obedient to their words" translates the Greek phrase *rhēmasi peithomenoi*. *Peithomenai* means "obeying" and comes from the root **bheidh-** with derivatives referring to mutual trust and obedience (see the note there). *Rhēmasi* is a plural form of the word *rhēma*, which literally means "word" but refers here to the covenant of the spoken word. A close relative of this word, *rhētra*, is the term for the military and social contract of Sparta. Both *rhēma* (whence English *rheme*) and *rhētra* (related to English *rhetoric*) derive from the root **werə-³** "to speak," a root also appearing in English *verb* and *proverb*.

---

wērə-o- True, trustworthy. (Oldest form **wērh₁-o-*.) **1.** WARLOCK, from Old English *wǣr*, faith, pledge, from Germanic **wēra-*. **2.** VERACIOUS, VERISM, VERITY, VERY; AVER, VERDICT, VERIDICAL, VERIFY, VERISIMILAR, VOIR DIRE, from Latin *vērus*, true. [Pokorny 11. *u̯er-* 1165.]

werg- To do. (Oldest form **werĝ-*.)

I. Suffixed form **werg-o-*. **1a.** WORK; HANDIWORK, from Old English *weorc*, *werc*, work; **b.** BOULEVARD, BULWARK, from Old High German *werc*, work. Both **a** and **b** from Germanic **werkam*, work. **2.** ERG¹, ERGATIVE, -URGY; ADRENERGIC, ALLERGY, ARGON, CHOLINER- GIC, DEMIURGE, DRAMATURGE, ENDERGONIC, ENDOERGIC, ENERGY, ERGOGRAPH, ERGOMETER, ERGONOMICS, EXERGONIC, EXERGUE, EXOERGIC, GEORGIC, HYPERGOLIC, LETHARGY, LITURGY, METALLURGY, SURGERY, SYNERGID, SYNERGISM, THAUMATURGE, from Greek *ergon*, work, action, and o-grade agent noun (in composition) *-orgos* (< **worgos*), doer, worker. **II.** Zero-grade form **wr̥g-*. **1.** Suffixed forms **wr̥g-yo-*, **wr̥g-to-*. **a.** WROUGHT, from Old English *wyrcan*, to work; **b.** IRK, from Old Norse *yrkja*, to work. Both **a** and **b** from Germanic **wurkjan*, to work, participle **wurhta-*. **2.** Suffixed form **wr̥g-t-*. WRIGHT, from Old English *wryhta*, maker, wright, from Germanic **wurhtjō-*. **III.** O-grade form **worg-*. **1.** ORGAN, ORGANON, from Greek *organon* (with suffix *-ano-*), tool. **2.** ORGY, from Greek *orgia*, secret rites, worship (< "service"). [Pokorny 2. *u̯erĝ-* 1168.]

wers-¹ To confuse, mix up. **I.** Suffixed basic form. **1a.** WAR, from Old North French *werre*, war; **b.** GUERRILLA, from Spanish *guerra*, war. Both **a** and **b** from Germanic **werra-*, from **werz-a-*. **2.** WORSE, from Old English *wyrsa*, worse, from Germanic comparative **wers-izōn-*. **3.** WORST, from Old English *wyrsta*, worst, from Germanic superlative **wers-ista-*. **II.** Suffixed zero-grade form **wr̥s-ti-*. WURST; LIVERWURST, from Old High German *wurst*, sausage (< "mixture"), from Germanic **wursti-*. [Pokorny *u̯ers-* 1169.] Compare **ers-¹**.

wers-² To rain, drip. (Oldest form **h₂wers-*.) Suffixed o-grade form **(ə)wors-o-*. URETER, URETHRA, URETIC, -URIA, URO-¹; DIURETIC, ENURESIS, NATRIURESIS, from Greek *ouron*, urine, whence verb *ourein*, to urinate, make water. [In Pokorny 9. *au̯(e)-* 78.] Compare **ers-²**.

-wer/-wen- Suffix of the *-r/-n-* class (see **-r/-n-**), forming verbal abstracts, with nominative and accusative case in **-wer-* (variant **-wr̥*) and the remaining cases added to **-wen-* (variants **-won-*, **-wn̥-*, **-un-*), as in **pī-wer*, **pīwon-*, fat (see **peiə-**). [Not in Pokorny.]

wes-¹ To buy, sell. **1.** Suffixed form **wes-no-*. VENAL, VEND, from Latin *vēnum*, sale. **2.** Suffixed o-grade form **wos-no-*. DUOPSONY, MONOPSONY, from Greek *ōneisthai*, to buy. **3.** Suffixed form **wes-ā-*. BAZAAR, from Persian *bāzār*, from Old Iranian **vahā-cārana-*, "sale-traffic." **4.** Perhaps suffixed form **wes-li-*. VILE; REVILE, VILIFY, VILIPEND, from Latin *vīlis*, cheap, base. [Pokorny 8. *u̯es-* 1173.]

wes-² Wet. OOZE¹, from Old English *wōs*, juice, from Germanic **wōs-*. [Pokorny 3. *u̯es-* 1171.]

wes-³ To live, dwell, pass the night, with derivatives meaning "to be." (Oldest form **h₂wes-*.) **1.** O-grade (perfect tense) form **wos-*. WAS, from Old English *wæs*, was, from Germanic **was-*. **2.** Lengthened-grade form **wēs-*. WERE, from Old English *wǣre* (subjunctive), *wǣron* (plural), were, from Germanic **wēz-*. **3.** WASSAIL, from Old Norse *vesa*, *vera*, to be, from Germanic **wesan*. **4.** Perhaps suffixed form **wes-tā-*. VESTA, from Latin *Vesta*, household goddess. **5.** Possibly suffixed variant form **was-tu-*. ASTUTE, from Latin *astus*, skill, craft (practiced in a town), from Greek *astu*, town (< "place where one dwells"). **6.** Suffixed form **wes-eno-*. DIVAN, from Old Persian *vahanam*, house. [Pokorny 1. *u̯es-* 1170.]

wes-⁴ To clothe. Extension of **eu-**. **1.** Suffixed o-grade (causative) form **wos-eyo-*. WEAR, from Old English *werian*, to wear, carry, from Germanic **wazjan*. **2.** Suffixed form **wes-ti-*. VEST; DEVEST, INVEST, REVET,

TRAVESTY, from Latin *vestis*, garment. **3.** Suffixed form **wes-nu-*. HIMATION, from Greek *hennunai*, to clothe, with nominal derivative *heima, hīma* (< **wes-mn̥*), garment. [Pokorny 5. *u̯es-* 1172.]

wes-⁵ To eat, consume. O-grade form **wos-*. GÂTEAU, from Old French *gastel*, cake, from Frankish **wastil*, cake, from suffixed Germanic form **was-tilaz*. [Pokorny 2. *u̯es-* 1171.]

wes-pero- Evening, night.
  I. Reduced form **wes-*. **1.** Suffixed form **wes-to-*. **a.** WEST, from Old English *west*, west; **b.** WESTERN, from Old English *westerne*, western; **c.** WESTERLY, from Old English *westra*, more westerly. **a–c** all from Germanic **west-*. **2.** Possibly Germanic **wis-*, west, in Late Latin *Visigothī*, "West Goths" (*Gothī*, the Goths): VISIGOTH.
  II. Basic form **wespero-*. **1.** PIPISTRELLE, VESPER, VESPERTILIONID, from Latin *vesper*, evening. **2.** HESPERIAN, HESPERIDES, HESPERUS, from Greek *hesperos*, evening. [Pokorny *u̯esperos* 1173.]

wesr̥ Spring. VERNAL; PRIMAVERA¹, from Latin *vēr*, spring (phonologically irregular). [Pokorny *u̯es-r̥* 1174.]

wesu- Good. Old Persian *va(h)u-*, good, the good, in personal name *Dārayava(h)uš* (see **dher-²**). [Pokorny *u̯ésu-* 1174.]

wet-¹ To blow, inspire, spiritually arouse. (Oldest form **h₂wet-*; related to **h₂weh₁-*, see **wē-**.) **1.** Lengthened-grade form **wōt-*. **a.** WODEN, WEDNESDAY, from Old English *Wōden*, Woden; **b.** ODIN, from Old Norse *Ôdhinn*, Odin; **c.** WOTAN, from Old High German *Wuotan*. **a–c** all from Germanic suffixed form **wōd-eno-, *wōd-ono-*, "raging," "mad," "inspired," hence "spirit," name of the chief Teutonic god **Wōd-enaz*; **d.** WOOD², from Old English *wōd*, mad, insane, from Germanic **wōda-*; **e.** Celtic **wāt-*. VATIC, from Latin *vātēs*, prophet, poet, from a Celtic source akin to Old Irish *fáith*, seer. **2.** O-grade form **wot-*. WEDELN, from Old High German *wedil*, fan, from Germanic suffixed form **wath-ilaz*. **3.** Suffixed variant form **wat-no-*. FAN¹, VAN³, from Latin *vannus*, a winnowing fan. **4.** Oldest basic form **əwet-* becoming Greek **awet-* in suffixed form **awet-mo-*. ATMOS- PHERE, from Greek *atmos* (< **aetmos*), breath, vapor. [Pokorny 1. *u̯āt-* 1113.]

wet-² Year. **1.** Suffixed form **wet-ru-*. WETHER; BELL-WETHER, from Old English *wether*, wether, from Germanic **wethruz*, perhaps "yearling." **2.** Suffixed form **wet-es-*. **a.** VETERAN; INVETERATE, from Latin *vetus*, old (< "having many years"); **b.** VETERINARY, from Latin *veterīnus*, of beasts of burden, of cattle (perhaps chiefly old cattle); **c.** ETESIAN, from Greek *etos*, year. **3.** Suffixed form **wet-olo-*. VEAL, VITELLUS, from Latin *vitulus*, calf, yearling. [Pokorny *u̯et-* 1175.]

wi- Apart, in half. **1.** Suffixed form **wi-ito-*. WIDE, from Old English *wīd*, wide (< "far apart"), from Germanic **wīdaz*. **2.** Suffixed (comparative) form **wi-tero-*. **a.** WITH, WITHERS, from Old English *wither*, against, with its derivative *with*, with, against; **b.** GUERIDON; WIDDERSHINS, from Old High German *widar*, against. Both **a** and **b** from Germanic **withrō*, against. [Pokorny 1. *u̯ī-* 1175.]

widhu- Tree, wood. WOOD¹, from Old English *wudu*, wood, from Germanic **widu-*. [Pokorny *u̯idhu-* 1177.]

wīkm̥tī- Twenty. (Oldest form **wīk̑m̥tī-*; compound of **wi-**, in half, hence two, and **(d)k̑m̥ t-ī* [nominative dual], decade, reduced zero-grade form of **dekm̥**.) **1.** VICENARY, VIGESIMAL, VIGINTILLION, from Latin *vigintī*, twenty. **2.** EICOSANOID, EICOSAPENTAENOIC ACID, ICOSAHEDRON, from Greek *eikosi*, twenty. **3.** PACHISI, from Sanskrit *viṁśatiḥ*, twenty. [Pokorny *u̯ī-k̑m̥t-ī* 1177.]

[wīn-o-] Wine. Italic noun, related to words for wine in Greek, Armenian, Hittite, and non-Indo-European

Georgian and West Semitic. Probably from a Mediterranean word **wīn-, *woin-*, wine. **1.** VINACEOUS, VINE, VINI-, WINE; VINEGAR, VINHO VERDE, from Latin *vīnum*, wine. **2.** ENOPHILE, ENOLOGY, OENOMEL, OINOCHOE, from Greek *oinos* (earlier *woinos*), wine.]

wī-ro- Man. (Oldest form **wih̥-ro-*; derivative of **weiə-**.) **1a.** WEREWOLF, WERGELD, from Old English *wer*, man; **b.** *(i)* WORLD, from Old English *weorold*, world; *(ii)* WELTANSCHAUUNG, WELTSCHMERZ, from Old High German *weralt*, world. Both *(i)* and *(ii)* from Germanic compound **wer-ald-*, "life or age of man" (**-ald-*, age; see **al-³**); **c.** LOUP-GAROU, from Old French *garoul*, werewolf, from Frankish **wer-wulf*, "man-wolf" (**wulf*, wolf; see **wĺkʷo-**). Both **a** and **b** from Germanic **weraz*, from shortened form **wiraz*. **2.** VIRAGO, VIRILE, VIRTUE, VIRTUOSA, VIRTUOSO; DECEMVIR, DECURION, DUUMVIR, TRIUMVIR, from Latin *vir*, man. **3.** CURIA, from Latin *cūria*, curia, court, possibly from **co-vir-ia*, "men together" (**co-*, together; see **kom**). **4.** Celtic **wiros*. **a.** Old Irish *fer*, man, in personal name *Fergus* (see **geus-**); **b.** Gaulish *viro-* in Gallo-Roman place name *Viro-dūnum* (see **dheuə-**). [Pokorny *u̯ī̆ro-s* 1177.]

Language and Culture Note Proto- Indo-European was not limited to just one word for "man, male person": several Indo-European roots have furnished words for this concept in the daughter languages. The root **man-¹**, appearing in English *man* for instance, was apparently a fairly neutral, all-purpose term. The reconstructed word **wī-ro-**, a derivative of the root **weiə-** "be vigorous," was used especially of men in their capacity as warriors or as slaves. (Slaves were often captured warriors.) In Sanskrit, for example, *vīraḥ* means "man, hero," but is also paired with the word *paśu*, "cattle," to refer to two-footed property (slaves), as in the compound *vīrapṣa-*, "(abundance of) men and cattle" (see note at **peku-**). In Italic languages, too, Latin *vir* "man" and its relatives can appear as a type of property, such as the Latin phrase *pecudēsque virōsque* "cattle and men." There is also the word **ner-²**, "man," which embodied the notion of strength. This is the source of Greek *anēr, andr-*, "man," as well as various Italic words meaning "magistrate"; it also underlies the name of the Roman emperor *Nerō*.

---

wleik- To flow, run. Zero-grade form **wlik-*. **1.** Adjective **wlik-u-*, wet. **a.** Suffixed form **wlik-w-ā-*. LIQUATE, from Latin *liquāre*, to dissolve; **b.** suffixed form **wlik-w-ē-*. LIQUESCENT, LIQUID, LIQUOR; DELIQUESCE, LIQUEFY, from Latin *liquēre*, to be liquid. **2.** Suffixed form **wlik-s-*. **a.** LIXIVIATE, from Latin *lixa*, lye; **b.** PROLIX, from Latin *prōlixus*, poured forth, stretched out in front, extended (*prō-*, forth; see **per¹**). [In Pokorny *leik-* 669.]

wĺkʷo- Wolf. **1a.** *(i)* WOLF, from Old English *wulf*, wolf; *(ii)* RANDAL (personal name), from Old English *Randulf*, "shield-wolf" (*rand*, shield); **b.** AARDWOLF, from Middle Dutch *wolf, wulf*, wolf; **c.** WOLFRAM, from Old High German *wolf*, wolf (also in personal names; see **at-al-, kar-²**); **d.** Frankish **wulf*, wolf, in compound **wer-wulf* (see **wī-ro-**); **e.** Old Norse *ulfr*, wolf, in personal name *Rādhulfr* (see **ar-**). **a–e** all from Germanic **wulfaz*. **2.** Taboo variant **lupo-*. LOBO, LUPINE¹, LUPINE², LUPUS, ROBALO; LOUP-GAROU, from Latin *lupus*, wolf. **3.** Taboo variant **lukʷo-*. LYCANTHROPE, LYCOPENE, LYCOPODIUM, from Greek *lukos*, wolf; **b.** suffixed form **lukʷ-ya*. LYTTA; ALYSSUM, from Greek *lussa*, martial rage, madness, rabies ("wolf-ness"). [Pokorny *u̯ĺkʷos* 1178.]

wĺp-ē- Fox. **1.** VULPINE, from Latin *vulpēs*, fox. **2.** Taboo variant **əlōp̑ĕk-*. ALOPECIA, from Greek *alōpēx*, fox. [Pokorny *u̯l̥p-* 1179.]

-wo- Adjective suffix, as in *$g^w\bar{\imath}$-wo-*, alive (see **g^weiə-**). It ultimately appears in English -IVE, from Latin *-īvus*, adjective suffix. [Not in Pokorny.]

wog^wh-ni- Plowshare, wedge. **1.** Probably Germanic **wagjaz.* WEDGE, from Old English *wecg*, wedge. **2.** Probably Latin *vōmer*, plowshare: VOMER. [Pokorny *u̯ogʷhni-s* 1179.]

wokso- Wax. Related to **weg-**^{1}. WAX^1, from Old English *wæx*, *weax*, wax, from Germanic **wahsam.* [Pokorny *u̯okso-* 1180.]

wopsā- Wasp. Metathesized form **wospā-.* **1.** WASP, from Old English *wæsp*, *wæps*, wasp, from Germanic **wasp-.* **2.** VESPIARY, from Latin *vespa*, wasp. [Pokorny *u̯obhsā* 1179.]

wŏs You (plural). RENDEZVOUS, from Latin *vōs*, you. [In Pokorny 1. *i̯u-* 513.]

wrād- Branch, root. (Oldest form **wreh₂d-*, colored to **wrah₂d-*, contracted to **wrād-.*)
I. Basic form **wrād-.* ROOT^1; RUTABAGA, from Old Norse *rōt*, root, from Germanic **wrōt-.*
II. Zero-grade form **wr̥əd-.* **1a.** WORT^1, from Old English *wyrt*, plant, herb; **b.** GEWÜRZTRAMINER, from Old High German *wurz*, plant, root; **c.** MANGEL-WURZEL, from German *Wurzel*, root (< **wurzwala*, rootstock; **-wala*, a roll, round stem; see **wel-**^{3}). **a–c** all from Germanic **wurtiz.* **2.** Suffixed form **wr̥əd-yā-.* WORT^2, from Old English *wyrt*, brewer's wort, from Germanic **wurtjō.* **3.** Suffixed form **wr̥əd-ī-.* RADICAL, RADICLE, RADISH, RADIX; DERACINATE, ERADICATE, IRRADICABLE, from Latin *rādīx*, root. **4.** Suffixed form **wr̥əd-mo-.* RAMOSE, RAMUS; RAMIFY, from Latin *rāmus*, branch. **5.** Perhaps suffixed reduced form **wr̥(ə)d-ya.* RHIZO-, RHIZOME; COLEORHIZA, LICORICE, MYCORRHIZA, from Greek *rhiza*, root. [Pokorny *u̯(e)rād-* 1167.]

wreg- To push, shove, drive, track down. **1.** Basic form **wreg-.* **a.** WREAK, from Old English *wrecan*, to drive, expel; **b.** WRECK, from Anglo-Norman *wrec*, wreck, from a Scandinavian source akin to Old Norse *rek* (older form *vrek*), wreckage. Both **a** and **b** from Germanic **wrekan.* **2.** O-grade form **wrog-.* **a.** (i) WRETCH, from Old English *wrecca*, exile; (ii) GASKET, from French *garce*, girl, perhaps from Frankish **wrakjō*, "one pursued, an exile." Both (i) and (ii) from Germanic **wrakjōn-*, "pursuer, one pursued"; **b.** (i) WRACK^1, from Old English *wræc*, exile, punishment, and Middle Dutch *wrak*, wreckage; (ii) RACK^3, from Middle English *rak*, mass of driven clouds, from a source akin to Swedish *rak*, wreckage. Both (i) and (ii) from Germanic **wrakaz.* **3.** Suffixed zero-grade form **wr̥g-eyo-*, **urg-eyo-.* URGE, from Latin *urgēre*, to urge, drive. [Pokorny *u̯reg-* 1181.]

wrēg- To break. (Oldest form **wreh₁ǵ-*, contracted to **wrēǵ-.*) Suffixed form **wrēǵ-nu-.* -RRHAGIA, from Greek *rhēgnunai*, to burst forth. [Pokorny *u̯rēǵ-* 1181.]

[wrod- Rose. A word (not common Indo-European) of unknown origin. **1.** Suffixed form **wrod-o-.* RHODO-; RHODIUM, from Greek *rhodon*, rose. **2.** Suffixed form **wrod-ya-* (perhaps via Etruscan). ROSE^1, from Latin *rosa*. **3.** Suffixed zero-grade form **wr̥d-o-.* JULEP, from Persian *gul*, rose, from Iranian **vr̥da-.*]

wrōd- To root, gnaw. ROOT^2, from Old English *wrōtan*, to dig up, from Germanic **wrōt-.* [In Pokorny 7. *u̯er-* 1163.]

wrōg- To burgeon, swell with strength. (Oldest form **wreh₃ǵ-*, colored to **wroh₃ǵ-*, contracted to **wrōǵ-.*) Suffixed zero-grade form **wr̥ǵ-ā-.* ORGASM, from Greek *organ*, to swell. [Pokorny 3. *u̯erǵ-* 1169.]

wrughyo- Rye. European root. RYE^1, from Old English *ryge*, rye, from Germanic **rugi-.* [Pokorny *urughi̯o-* 1183.]

yā- To seek, request, desire. (Oldest form **yeh₂-*, colored to **yah₂-*, contracted to **yā-.*) JALOUSIE, JEAL-

OUS, ZEAL, ZEALOT, from Greek *zēlos*, zeal. [Pokorny *i̯ā-* 501.]

yag- To worship; reverence. **1.** Perhaps suffixed form **yag-yo-.* HAGIO-, from Greek *hagios*, holy. **2.** Suffixed form **yag-no-.* AGNES (personal name), from Greek *hagnē* (> Late Latin *Agnēs*), feminine of *hagnos*, holy, pure. **3a.** Perhaps suffixed form **yag-yu-* in Latin *iāiūnus*, *iēiūnus*, fasting (perhaps < "worshiping the household gods reverently," since the Roman paterfamilias would begin the day by offering the Penates a ritual meal, before having his own breakfast; compare Sanskrit *yajyu-*, worshipping readily): JEJUNE. **b.** DINE, DINNER, from Vulgar Latin **disiēiūnāre*, to break one's fast, from Latin *iēiūnus*, fasting (Latin *dis-*, apart, asunder). [Pokorny *i̯ag-* 501.]

yē- To throw, impel. (Oldest form **h₁yeh₁-*, contracted to **h₁yē-.*) **1.** Extended zero-grade form **yak-*, becoming **yak-* in Italic. Suffixed forms **yak-yo-* and **yak-ē-* (stative). GISANT, GIST, GITE, JACTITATION, JESS, JET^2, JETÉ, JETSAM, JETTISON, JETTY^1, JOIST, JUT; ABJECT, ADJACENT, ADJECTIVE, AMICE, CIRCUMJACENT, CONJECTURE, DEJECT, EJACULATE, EJECT, INJECT, INTERJECT, OBJECT, PARGET, PROJECT, REJECT, SUBJACENT, SUBJECT, SUPERJACENT, TRAJECT, from Latin *iacere*, to throw, lay, *iacēre*, to lie down (< "to be thrown") and *iaculum*, dart. **2.** Reduplicated form **(ə)yi-ayē-.* CATHETER, DIESIS, ENEMA, PARESIS, SYNESIS, from Greek *hienai*, to send, throw, and combining noun form *-esis*, "a throwing" (< suffixed zero-grade form **(ə)yə-ti-*). [Pokorny *i̯ē-* 502.]

yeg- Ice. ICICLE, from Old English *gicel*, icicle, ice, from Germanic **jakilaz*, **jekilaz.* [Pokorny *i̯eg-* 503.]

yēg^w-ā- Power, youthful strength. (Probably contracted from earlier **yeh₁g^w-eh₂-* [*-eh₂-*, feminine ending, becoming *-ā-*].) HEBE; EPHEBE, HEBEPHRENIA, from Greek *hēbē*, youth. [Pokorny *i̯ēgʷā* 503.]

yek-^{1} To speak. Suffixed o-grade form **yok-o-.* JEWEL, JOCOSE, JOCULAR, JOKE, JUGGLE, JUGGLER; JEOPARDY, from Latin *iocus*, joke. [Pokorny *i̯ek-* 503.]

yek-^{2} To hunt. Suffixed o-grade form **yok-o-.* JAEGER, YACHT, from Old High German *jagōn*, to hunt. [Not in Pokorny; compare Hittite *ekt-* and Luvian *aggat(i)-* (both < **yek-t-*), hunting net.]

yēk- To heal. (Contracted from earlier **yeh₁k-.*) Possible suffixed zero-grade form **yək-es-.* AUTACOID, PANACEA, from Greek *akos*, cure. [Pokorny *i̯ēk-* 504.]

yĕk^wr̥ Liver. **1.** HEPATIC, HEPATO-; HEPARIN, HEPATITIS, from Greek *hēpar*, liver (stem *hēpat-* < **yĕk^wn̥-t-* < Indo-European oblique stem **yĕk^wn-*). **2.** GIZZARD, from Persian *jigar*, liver. [Pokorny *i̯ek^u-r̥(t-)* 504.]

yem- To pair. Perhaps altered in Latin *geminus*, twin: GEMINATE, GEMINI, GIMMAL; BIGEMINAL, TRIGEMINUS. [Pokorny *i̯em-* 505.]

yēr- Year, season. (Contracted from earlier **yeh₁r-*; probably original meaning "that which makes [a complete cycle]," derivative of a verbal root **yeh₁-* meaning "to do, make.") **1.** Suffixed basic form **yēr-o-.* **a.** YEAR, from Old English *gēar*, year; **b.** YAHRZEIT, from Old High German *jār*, year. Both **a** and **b** from Germanic **jēram*, year. **2.** Suffixed o-grade form **yōr-ā-.* HORARY, HOUR; HOROLOGE, HOROLOGY, HOROSCOPE, from Greek *hōrā*, season. [In Pokorny 1. *ei-* 293.]

yes- To boil, foam, bubble. **1.** YEAST, from Old English *gist*, yeast, from Germanic **jest-.* **2.** KIESELGUHR, from Old High German *jësan*, to ferment, and *jerian*, to cause to ferment, from Germanic **jesan.* **3.** ECZEMA, ZEOLITE, from Greek *zeein*, *zein*, to boil. [Pokorny *i̯es-* 506.]

yeu- Vital force, youthful vigor. (Oldest form **h₂yeu-*. Derivative of **h₂eyu-*, vital force; see **aiw-**.) Suffixed zero-grade form **yuwen-* (< **yu-əen-*), "possessing youthful vigor," young. **1.** Further suffixed form **yuwn̥-ti-.* YOUTH, from Old English *geoguth*, youth, from Germanic **jugunthi-*, **jugunthō.* **2.** Further suffixed form **yuwn̥-ko-.* **a.** (i) YOUNG, from Old English *geong*, young; *(ii)* JUNKER, from Old High German *junc*, young; *(iii)* YOUNKER, from Middle Dutch *jonc*, young. *(i)–(iii)* all from Germanic **junga-*, from **juwunga-*; **b.** *(i)* GALLOWGLASS, from Old Irish *óac*, young; *(ii)* EVAN (personal name), from Welsh *ieuanc*, young. Both *(i)* and *(ii)* from Celtic **yowanko-*. **3a.** JUVENILE; REJUVENATE, from Latin *iuvenis*, young; **b.** zero-grade form **yūn-* (< **yu-ən-*). *(i)* JUNIOR, from Latin comparative *iūnior*, younger; *(ii)* JUNE, JUNO, from Latin *Iūnō*, Juno (probably "the young one," perhaps because she was the goddess of the new moon), and Latin month name *Iūnius*, traditionally derived from *Iūnō*. [Pokorny 3. *i̯eu-* 510.]

yeudh- To move violently, fight. (Oldest form **h₂yeudh-*.) Suffixed o-grade causative form **youdh-eye-*. JUSSIVE, from Latin *iubēre*, to command (< "to set in motion"). The short *u* in *iubēre* was introduced analogically from other forms of the verb, such as the perfect participle *iussus*, from **yudh-to-*. [Pokorny *i̯eu-dh-* 511.]

yeuə- To blend, mix food. Zero-grade form **yū-* (< **yuə-*). **1.** Suffixed form **yū-s-*. JUICE, from Latin *iūs*, juice, broth. **2.** Suffixed form **yū-s-mā-*. -ZYME, ZYMO-; ENZYME, from Greek *zūmē*, leaven. [Pokorny 1. *i̯eu-* 507.]

yeug- To join.
  I. Zero-grade form **yug-*. **1.** Suffixed form **yug-o-*. **a.** YOKE, from Old English *geoc*, yoke, from Germanic **yukam*; **b.** JUGATE, JUGULAR, JUGUM; CONJUGATE, SUBJUGATE, from Latin *iugum*, yoke; **c.** ZYGO-, ZYGOMA, ZYGOTE, -ZYGOUS; AZYGOS, SYZYGY, from Greek *zugon*, yoke, and *zugoun*, to join; **d.** YUGA, from Sanskrit *yugam*, yoke. **2.** Suffixed (superlative) form **yugisto-*. JOSTLE, JOUST; ADJUST, JUXTAPOSE, JUXTAPOSITION, from Latin *iūxtā*, close by, perhaps from **iugistā* (*viā*), "on a nearby (road)." **3.** Nasalized zero-grade form **yu-n-g-*. JOIN, JOINDER, JOINT, JOINTURE, JUNCTION, JUNCTURE, JUNTA; ADJOIN, CONJOIN, CONJUGAL, CONJUNCT, ENJOIN, INJUNCTION, REJOIN¹, REJOINDER, SUBJOIN, from Latin *iungere*, to join.
  II. Suffixed form **yeug-mn̥*. ZEUGMA, from Greek *zeugma*, a bond.
  III. Suffixed o-grade form **youg-o-*. YOGA, from Sanskrit *yogaḥ*, union. [Pokorny 2. *i̯eu-* 508.]

yewes- Law. **1.** JURAL, JURIST, JURY¹; ABJURE, ADJURE, CONJURE, INJURY, JURIDICAL, JURISCONSULT, JURISDICTION, JURISPRUDENCE, NONJUROR, OBJURGATE, PERJURE, from Latin *iūs* (stem *iūr-*), law, and its derivative *iūrāre*, "to pronounce a ritual formula," swear. **2.** Compound form **yewes-dik-* (see **deik-**). **3.** Suffixed from **yewes-to-*. JUST¹, from Latin *iūstus*, just. [Pokorny *i̯eu̯os-* 512.]

yewo- A grain, probably barley. Suffixed form **yew-ya*. ZEIN, from Greek *zeia*, one-seeded wheat. [Pokorny *i̯eu̯o-* 512.]

Language and Culture Note The root **yewo-** is the source of the noun **yewos*, the basic Indo-European term for "grain." Its descendant in Sanskrit, *yavaḥ*, referred to grain in general and barley in particular. Barley was a sacred grain in numerous Indo-European societies, and probably in Proto-Indo-European as well. In Indic mythology, barley was the one plant that sided with the gods in their protean struggle against the demons. In the cognate Iranian (Avestan) tradition, the sowing of *yauua-* is equated with the sowing of religious truth. In ancient Rome, barley (*far*, see **bhars-²**) was described as *pium*, "holy, pious."

-yo-¹ Verbal suffix marking present tense of verbs, as in **sed-yo-*, to sit (see **sed-¹**). [Not in Pokorny.]

-yo-² Verbal suffix used to form verbs from other parts of speech, as in **argu-yo-*, to make clear (see **arg-**). Becomes **-jan* in Germanic. By combining with the final sounds of stems that it is added to, many new verbal suffixes were created, such as the one ultimately appearing as English -IZE, from Greek *-izein*, verbal suffix < **id-yo-*. [Not in Pokorny.]

-yo-³ Relational adjectival suffix, "of or belonging to." Appears ultimately in the following English suffixes: **a.** -ARY, -EER, -ER¹, from Latin *-ārius*, adjective suffix, from Italic **-ās-io-* (first element obscure); **b.** -ATORY, from Latin *-ātōrius*, adjective suffix for agent nouns in *-ātor* (see **-ter-**). [Not in Pokorny.]

yoi-ni- Also **yoi-no-**. Juniper berry. JUNIPER, from Latin *iūniperus*, juniper, probably from **yoini-paros*, "bearing juniper berries" (**-paros*, bearing; see **perə-¹**). [Pokorny *i̯oi-ni-* 513.]

yōs- To gird. (Oldest form **yeh₃s-*, colored to **yoh₃s-*, contracted to **yōs-*.) **1.** Suffixed form **yōs-ter-*. ZOSTER, from Greek *zōstēr*, girdle. **2.** Suffixed form **yōs-nā-*. ZONE; EVZONE, from Greek *zōnē*, girdle. **3.** Suffixed form **yōs-mo-*. PAJAMA, from Persian *jāma*, garment, from Middle Persian *yāmak*, *jāmak*. [Pokorny *i̯ō(u)s-* 513.]

-yos- Adjective suffix of comparative, marking intensity. Zero-grade form **-is-*. -ER², from Old English *-re*, *-ra*, comparative suffix, from Germanic **-iz-on-* (**-on-*, individualizing suffix). [Not in Pokorny.] Compare **-tero-** and see also compound suffix **-is-to-**.

yu- You. Second person (plural) pronoun. YE², YOU, from Old English *gē* and *ēow*, you, from Germanic **jūz* (nominative) and **iwwiz* (oblique). [Pokorny 1. *i̯u-* 513.]

Index

A

O

Indo-European Sound Correspondences

Probably the most basic element of language change is a gradual shift in the way individual speech sounds are pronounced. As the Indo-European speech community expanded over the centuries into new territories, local dialectal variations gave rise to increasingly divergent language families. This table shows the historical development of sounds from Proto-Indo-European to the principal older Indo-European languages. For example, reading down the first column, it can be seen that Proto-Indo-European initial **p** remains **p** in Latin, but it is lost entirely in Old Irish and becomes **f** in Germanic and consequently in Old English; thus Indo-European ***pəter-**, meaning "father," becomes Latin *pater*, Old Irish *athir*,

LANGUAGE	CONSONANTS												CONTINUANT	LARYNGEALS		
	STOPS															
	Unvoiced				Voiced				Voiced Aspirate							
Indo-European	p	t	k	kʷ	b	d	g	gʷ	bh	dh	gh	gʷh	s	h₁	h₂	h₃
Hittite	p	t	k	ku	p	t	k	ku	p	t	k	ku	s	–	ḫ	ḫ
Tocharian	p	t/c/ts	k/ś	k/ś	p	t/c/ts	k/ś	k/ś	p	t/c/ts	k/ś	k/ś	s/ṣ	–	–	–
Sanskrit	p	t	ś	k/c	b	d	j	g/j	bh	dh	h	gh/h	s/ṣ	–	–	–
Avestan	p	t	s	k/c	b	d	z	g/j	b	d	z	g/j	h	–	–	–
Old Persian	p	t	th	k	b	d	d	g/j	b	d	d	g/j	h	–	–	–
Old Church Slavonic	p	t	s	k/č/c	b	d	z	g/ž/z	b	d	z	g/ž/z	s	–	–	–
Lithuanian	p	t	š	k	b	d	ž	g	b	d	ž	g	s	–	–	–
Armenian	h	th	s	kh	p	t	c	k	b	d	j	g	h	–/a	–/a	–/a
Greek	p	t	k	p/t/k	b	d	g	b/d/g	ph	th	kh	ph/th/kh	h	–/e	–/a	–/o
Latin	p	t	c	qu	b	d	g	v	f	f	h	f	s	–	–	–
Old Irish	–	t	c	c	b	d	g	b	b	d	g	g	s	–	–	–
Common Germanic	f	th	h	hw	p	t	k	kw/k	b	d	g	b/g	s	–	–	–
Gothic	f	th	h	hw/w	p	t	k	q	b	d	g	b/g	s	–	–	–
Old Norse†	f	th	h	hv	p	t	k	kv	b	d	g	b/g	s	–	–	–
Old High German†	f	d	h	hw/w	p/pf	z	k	qu	b	t/d	g	b/g	s	–	–	–
Middle Dutch†	v	th/d	h	w	p	t	k	qu	b	d	g	b/g	s	–	–	–
Old English†	f	th	h	hw	p	t	c	cw/c	b	d	g	b/g	s	–	–	–

NOTES:
– means "lacking": p was lost in Old Irish.
w was lost in Greek.
y was lost in Old Irish, Old Norse.
Initial laryngeals are preserved only in Hittite.
A slash (/) differentiates reflexes of the same sound in different environments.
†The effects of umlaut are not considered.
‡Common Greek ā, whence ē in Attic-Ionic dialect, source of most Greek words in English.

and Common Germanic ***fadar**, Old English *fæder*. A more precise way of describing this relationship is to say that initial **p** in Proto-Indo-European corresponds to **p** in Latin, to **f** in Germanic and Old English, and to zero in Old Irish. The correspondences shown in the table are regular. That is, they always occur as stated unless specific factors intervene. This table shows only the initial consonants and vowels in initial syllables, which are generally the simplest elements involved in sound change. All other phonetic elements including stress and environment also show regular correspondences, but often with considerable complexity.

SONORANTS						VOWELS													
Nasals		Liquids		Glides		Short					Long					Syllabic Sonorants			
m	n	r	l	y	w	e	o	a	i	u	ē(eǝ)	ō(oǝ)	ā(aǝ)	ī(iǝ)	ū(uǝ)	m̥	n̥	r̥	l̥
m	n	r	l	y	w	e/i	a	a	i	u	e/i	a	a/ah	i	u/uh	am	an	ar	al
m	n	r	l	y	w	ā	e	ā	ǎ/ī	ǎ/u	e	o/ā	o/ā	i	u	ǎm	ǎn	ǎr	ǎl
m	n	r/l	r/l	y	v	a	a/ā	a	i	u	ǎ	ǎ	ǎ	ī	ū	a	a	r̥	r̥
m	n	r	r	y	v	a	a/ā	a	i	u	ǎ	ǎ	ǎ	ī	ū	a	a	ǝrǝ	ǝrǝ
m	n	r	r	y	v	a	a/ā	a	i	u	ǎ	ǎ	ǎ	ī	ū	a	a	(a)r	(a)r
m	n	r	l	j	v	e	o	o	ī	ū	e	a	a	i	u	ẹ	ẹ	rū	lū
m	n	r	l	j	v	e	a	a	i	u	ē	uo	o	y	u	im	in	ir	il
m	n	r	l	y	g/v	e	o	a	i	u	i	u	a	i	u	am	an	ar	ał
m	n	r	l	h/z	–	e	o	a	i	u	ē	ō	ǎ/ē‡	ī	ū	a	a	ar/ra	al/la
m	n	r	l	i	v	e	o	a	i	u	ē	ō	ǎ	ī	ū	em	en	or	ul
m	n	r	l	–	f	e/i	o/u	a	i/e	u/o	ī	ǎ	ǎ	ī	ū	(*am>)ē	(*an>)ē	ri	li
m	n	r	l	j	w	e	a	a	i	u	ē	ō	ō	ī	ū	um	un	ur	ul
m	n	r	l	j	w	i/ai	a	a	i/e	u	ē	ō	ō	ī	ū	um	un	aur	ul
m	n	r	l	–	v/–	e	a	a	i/e	u/o	ǎ	ō	ō	ī	ū	um	un	ur/or	ul/ol
m	n	r	l	j	w	e	a	a	i/e	u/o	ǎ	uo	uo	ī	ū	um	un	ur/or	ul/ol
m	n	r	l	g	w	e	a	a	i/e	u/o	ē	ō	ō	ī	ū	um	un	ur/or	ul/ol
m	n	r	l	g/y	w	e	æ/a	æ/a	i/e	u/o	ǣ	ō	ō	ī	ū	um	un	ur/or	ul/ol

Indo-European Family of Languages

The Indo-European family of languages, of which English is one member, is descended from the prehistoric Proto-Indo-European language, which was spoken in an as yet unidentified area between eastern Europe and the Aral Sea around the fifth millennium BC. This chart displays the genetic relationships

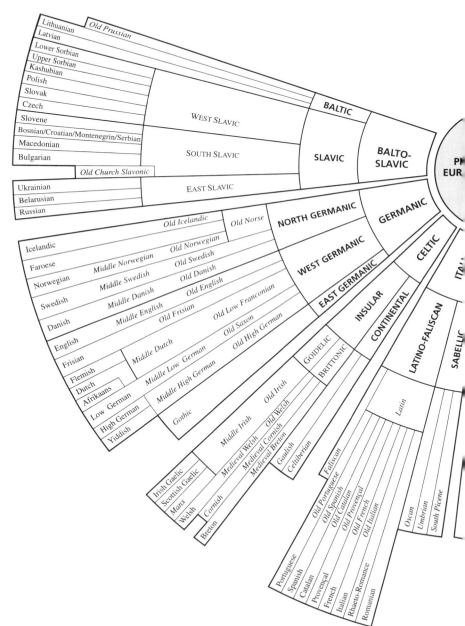

among the principal languages of the Indo-European family and loosely suggests their geographic distribution. The European branches are shown in somewhat fuller detail than the Asian ones, and in the Germanic group, to which English belongs, the intermediate historic phases of the languages are also shown. Extinct languages are in italics. A table of the principal Indo-European sound correspondences appears on pages 148–149.

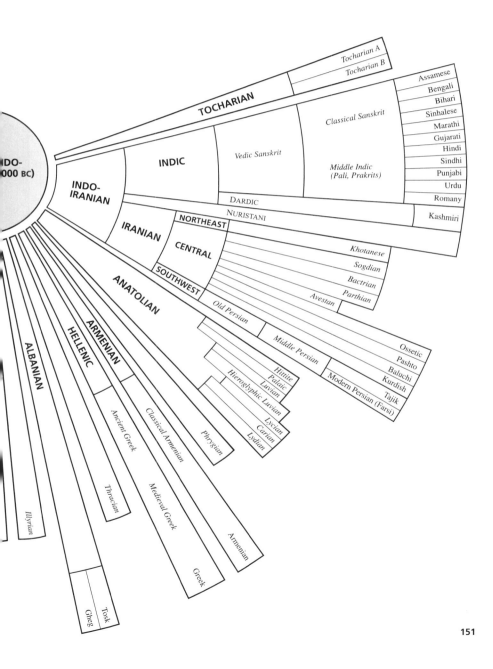